Catalog of
American Car
I D Numbers
1960-69

Compiled by the Staff of Cars & Parts Magazine

Published by Amos Press Inc.
911 Vandemark Road
Sidney, Ohio 45365

Publishers of Cars & Parts
(The Magazine Serving the Car Hobbyist),
the Collector Car Annual,
and the Cars & Parts Legends Series:
Muscle Cars of the '60s/'70s

Distribution by Motorbooks International Publishers and Wholesalers,
P.O. Box 2, Osceola, WI 54020 USA

Printed and bound in the United States of America

Library of Congress Cataloging-In-Publication Data
ISBN 0-87938-449-2

ACKNOWLEDGEMENTS

The staff of *Cars & Parts* Magazine devoted more than a year to the research and development of the Catalog of American Car ID Numbers 1960-69. It has been a labor-intensive project which required assistance from hundreds of car collectors, clubs, researchers, computer programmers and a tremendous amount of interviewing and photography at car shows, swap meets and auctions.

This book wouldn't have been possible without very special help from the following:

William Bailey - Researcher
Motor Vehicle Manufacturers Association
Dan Kirchner - Researcher
Studebaker National Museum
Tom Hinson - Computer Programmer
Chrysler Corporation
Automotive History Collection of the
   Detroit Public Library
Ford Motor Company

In addition, there were others who helped enormously in specific areas, including Tom Deptulski, Greg Donahue, Chuck Kuhn, Jeff Kennedy, Fred Fox, Darryl Salisbury, Jerry Pogue, and others. Thank you for making this book possible.

Catalog of
American Car
ID Numbers
1960-69

Compiled by the Staff of Cars & Parts Magazine

INTRODUCTION

Authentication has become such a critical issue within the old car hobby that the need for a comprehensive, accurate and dependable identification guide has become quite apparent to anyone involved in buying, selling, restoring, judging, owning, researching or appraising a collector car. With this in-depth and detailed ID guide, the staff of *Cars & Parts* magazine has compiled as much data as possible on the years and makes covered to help take the fear out of buying a collector car.

Deciphering trim codes, verifying vehicle identification numbers (VIN), interpreting body codes and authenticating engine numbers will become a much easier process with this guide at your side. Putting this information at your fingertips has not been a simple task, but one worth the tremendous time and expense.

Each car manufacturer used a different system of identification and changed its system almost annually in the '60s. The *Cars & Parts* staff has developed the most consistent information possibly from year to year for each manufacturer. Some data are not presented due to availability, space, time considerations, and inability to verify sources.

Each manufacturer is different in his coding, and changes are often made from model to model and from model year to model year. General Motors, for instance, listed accessory codes on its body plates, but we were unable to verify all of the codes for each year and each division, therefore we deleted all of them from the guide. Chrysler Corporation revealed some option codes in the early to mid-'60s on its body plates. However, body plates from the late '60s carry codes taken from the build sheets and sometimes more than one plate is required to present all of the information. It simply wasn't feasible to verify and publish all of this information.

Each corporation, division, year, model, VIN, body plate and engine number required decisions about what to print. The staff of *Cars & Parts* is justifiably proud of this book and invites your comments. Additional information is especially welcome.

The information contained in The Catalog of American ID Numbers 1960-69 was compiled from a variety of sources including original manufacturers' catalogs (when available) and official published shop manuals. The *Cars & Parts* staff and researchers made every attempt to verify the information contained herein. However, many manufacturers made changes from year-to-year, model-to-model, as well as mid-year. And, in some instances, conflicting information and reports surfaced during the course of our indepth research. As a result, *Cars & Parts* does not guarantee the absolute accuracy of all data presented in this ID Guide.

The Catalog of American ID Numbers 1960-69 reflects a monumental effort, and we're so confident that this reference book will become such an invaluable resource for car collectors that we've begun work on a second edition covering a different era.

Vehicle Identification Number

B-10551

The serial number is stamped on a plate attached to the right wheel-house panel.

THE FIRST DIGIT : Identifies the car line.

Rebel 8 .... A
American 6 .... B
Rambler 6 C
Ambassador 8 .... H

BODY NUMBER PLATE

A unit body number plate is riveted to the left front body hinge pillar above the lower hinge. Included are the body, model, trim, paint code and car code numbers which indicates date of manufacture. The model number identifies the body style. It follows by number 1, 2, 3 0r 4 which denote different optional appointment groups built into the car as original equiptment.

**ALL WELDED
SINGLE UNIT
CONSTRUCTION**

THIS RAMBLER IS BUILT WITH AN ADVANCED METHOD OF BODY CONSTRUCTION IN WHICH THE BODY AND FRAME ARE COMBINED INTO A SINGLE ALL-WELDED STRUCTURAL UNIT.
PIONEERED AND BUILT EXCLUSIVELY BY

AMERICAN MOTORS CORP.
DETROIT MICH.
BODY NO.   3218
MODEL NO.   6018-2
TRIM NO.   42
PAINT NO.   15-72
              E-10911

AMERICAN	Code
2-Dr. Business Coupe-D	6002
2-Dr. Wagon-D	6004
2-Dr. Wagon-S	6004-1
4-Dr. Wagon-C	6304-2
4-Dr. Sedan-D	6005
4-Dr. Sedan-S	6005-1
4-Dr. Sedan-C	6005-2
2-Dr. Club Sedan-D	6006
2-Dr. Club Sedan-S	6006-1
2-Dr. Club Sedan-C	6006-2

RAMBLER	Code
4-Dr. Sedan-D	6015
4-Dr. Sedan-S	6015-1
4-Dr. Sedan-C	6015-2
4-Dr. Wagon-D	6018
2-Dr. Wagon-S	6018-1
4-Dr. Wagon-C	6018-2
4-Dr. 2 Seat Wagon-S	6018-3
4-Dr. 2 Seat Wagon-C	6018-4
4-Dr. Hardtop Sedan-C	6019-2

RAMBLER REBEL	Code
4-Dr. Sedan-D	6025
4-Dr. Sedan-S	6025-1
4-Dr. Sedan-C	6025-2
2-Dr. Wagon-S	6028-1
2-Dr. Wagon-C	6028-2
2-Dr. Wagon-S	6028-3
4-Dr. Wagon-C	6028-4
4-Dr. Hardtop Sedan-C	6029-2

RAMBLER AMBASSADOR	Code
4-Dr. Hardtop Wagon-C	6083-2
4-Dr. Sedan-D	6085
4-Dr. Sedan-S	6085-1
4-Dr. Sedan-C	6085-2

	Code
4-Dr. Wagon-D	6088
4-Dr. Wagon-S	6088-1
4-Dr. Wagon-C	6088-2
4-Dr. Wagon-s	6088-3
4-Dr. Wagon-C	6088-4
4-Dr. Hardtop Sedan-C	6089-2

THE PAINT CODE furnishes the key to the paint colors used on the car. A two number code indicated the color of the car. A two-toned car has two sets of numbers. First number is body color, second is the roof.

COLOR	Code
Classic Black	P1
Autum Yellow	P5
Lt. Chatsworth Green	P8
Lt. Placid Blue	P10
Oriental Red	P13
Med. Westchester Green	P18
Med. Sovereign Blue	P19
Lt. Dartmouth Gray	P20
Med. Harvard Gray	P21
Auburn Red (Metallic)	P24
Festival Rose	P25
Frost White	P72
Lt.Dartmouth Gray	P20-21
Med. Harvard Gray (Mettalic)	
Lt. Dartmouth Gray	P20-72
Frost White	
Med. Harvard Gray	P21-20
(Mettalic) Lt.Dartmouth Gray	
Med. Harvard Gray	P21-72
(Mettalic) Frost White	
Lt. Chatsworth Green	P8-18
Med. Westchester Green (Metallic)	
Lt. Chatsworth Green	P8-72
Frost White	
Med. Westchester Green	P18-8
(Metallic)Lt. Chatsworth Green	
Med. Westchester Green	P18-72
(Metallic) Frost White	
Lt. Placid Blue	P10-19
Med. Sovereign Blue (Mettalic)	
Lt. Placid Blue	P10-72
Frost White	
Oriental Red	P13-21
Med. Harvard Gray(Mettalic)	
Oriental Red	P13-72
Frost White	
Med. Harvard Gray	P21-13
(Metallic) Oriental Red	
Classic Black	P1-72
Frost White	
Autum Yellow	P5-72
Frost White	
Med. Harvard Gray	P21-5
(Metallic)Autum Yellow	
Festival Rose	P25-72
Frost White	
Lt.Dartmouth Gray	P20-24
Auburn Red (Metallic)	
Auburn Red (Metallic)	P24-20
Lt.Dartmouth Gray	

THE TRIM NUMBER furnishes the key to trim color and material for each model series.

AMERICAN

T001 T002 T003 T004 T005
T011* T012* T013 T014* T015*
RAMBLER AND REBEL

T021 T027 T028 T029 T041 T042 T043 T044 T045 T046 T047 T048 T049 T022 T023 T024 T025
T031* T037* T038* T039*T051*T052* T053* T054*T055*T056*T057*T058* T059* T032 T033*T034* T035*

AMBASSADOR

T062 T063 T064 T065
T072* T073*T074*T075*

AMBASSADOR CUSTOM

T067 T068 T069 T081 T082 T083 T084 T085 T086 T087 T088 T089
T077* T078* T079* T091* T092* T093* T094* T095* T096* T097* T098* T099*

* VINYL

ENGINE ID

The engine code number is located on a machined surface of the engine block or stamped on a tag.These engines are marked with a code identifing: year, month, engine letter code, and day of manufacture.
Letter Identification, Size of Bore, Main Bearings and Connecting Rod Bearings
In the machining of cylinder blocks and crankshafts, it is sometimes necessary to machine the cylinder bores to .010" oversize, and the crankshaft main bearing journals or crank pins to .010" undersize.

EXAMPLE	2	2	A	24
	1960	month	code	day

First Letter .... Size of the Bore
Second Letter .... Size of the main Bearings
Third Letter .... Size of the Connecting Rod Bearings

Letter "A" Standard
Letter "B" .010" Undersize
Letter "C" .010" Oversize

ENGINE SPECIFICATIONS

Code	Engine	CID	Comp. Ratio	Carburator	HP
A	6	195.6	8.0:1	Holley 1-BBl .	90
B	6	195.6	8.7:1	Holley 1-BB .l	125
C	6	195.6	8.7:1	Holley 1-BBl .	127
					138*
?	8	250	8.7:1	Holley 2-BBl .	200
				**	215
E	8	327	8.7:1	Holley 2-BBl .	250*
F	8		9.7:1	**	270

*   Optional 138 @ 4500 RPM with 2-barrel carb.
**   Optional Holley 4-barrel.

Vehicle Identification Number

```
B-221001
```

The serial number is stamped on a plate attached to the right wheel-house panel.

THE FIRST DIGIT : Identifies the car line.

Rebel 8	A
American 6	B
Rambler 6	C
Ambassador 8	H

BODY NUMBER PLATE

A unit body number plate is riveted to the left front body hinge pillar above the lower hinge. Included are the body, model, trim, paint code and car code numbers which indicates date of manufacture. The model number identifies the body style. It follows by number 1, 2, 3, 4 or 5 which denote different optional appointment groups built into the car as original equiptment.

```
        ALL WELDED
       SINGLE UNIT
       CONSTRUCTION

THIS RAMBLER IS BUILT
WITH   AN   ADVANCED
METHOD OF BODY CON-
STRUCTION IN WHICH THE
BODY AND FRAME ARE
COMBINED INTO A SINGLE
ALL-WELDED STRUCTURAL
UNIT.
PIONEERED AND BUILT EX-
CLUSIVELY BY

AMERICAN MOTORS CORP.
DETROIT MICH.
BODY NO.      3218
MODEL NO.     6118-2
TRIM NO.      128
PAINT NO.     30-72
        E-000001
```

AMERICAN

	Code
2-Dr. Business Coupe-D	6102
2-Dr. Wagon-D	6104
2-Dr. Wagon-S	6104-1
4-Dr. Wagon-C	6104-2
4-Dr. Sedan-D	6105
4-Dr. Sedan-S	6105-1
4-Dr. Sedan-C	6105-2
2-Dr. Club Sedan-D	6106
2-Dr. Club Sedan-S	6106-1
2-Dr. Club Sedan-C	6106-2

RAMBLER

	Code
4-Dr. Sedan-D	6115
4-Dr. Sedan-S	6115-1
4-Dr. Sedan-C	6115-2
4-Dr. Wagon-D	6118
2-Dr. Wagon-S	6118-1
4-Dr. Wagon-C	6118-2
4-Dr. 2 Seat Wagon-S	6118-3
5-Dr. 2 Seat Wagon-C	6118-4
4-Dr. Hardtop Sedan-C	6119-2

RAMBLER REBEL

	Code
4-Dr. Sedan-D	6125
4-Dr. Sedan-S	6125-1
4-Dr. Sedan-C	6125-2
2-Dr. Wagon-S	6128-1
2-Dr. Wagon-C	6128-2
2-Dr. Wagon-S	6128-3
5-Dr. Wagon-C	6128-4
4-Dr. Hardtop Sedan-C	6129-2

RAMBLER AMBASSADOR

	Code
4-Dr. Sedan-D	6185
4-Dr. Sedan-S	6185-1
4-Dr. Sedan-C	6185-2
4-Dr. Sedan-C	6185-5
4-Dr. Wagon-S	6188-1
4-Dr. Wagon-C	6188-2
5-Dr. Wagon-S	6188-3
5-Dr. Wagon-C	6188-4

THE PAINT CODE furnishes the key to the paint colors used on the car. A two number code indicated the color of the car. A two-toned car has two sets of numbers. First number is body color, second is the roof.

COLOR	Code
Classic Black	P1
Frost White	P72
Inca Silver (Metallic)	P31
Briarcliff Red	P30
Lt. Sonata Blue	P27
Med. Berkeley Blue	P28
Lt. Chatsworth Green	P8
Med. Valley Green	P26
Alamo Beige	P4
Whirlwind Tan (metallic)	P29
Jasmine Rose	P33
Fire Glow Red (Mettalic)	P34
Waikiki Gold	P32
Aqua Mist (Metallic)	P15
Lt. Echo Green (Metallic)	P23
Incz Silver (Metallic	P31-72
Frost White	

Classic Black P1-72
White Frost
Inca Silver (Mettalic) P31-1
Classic Black
Classic Black P1-31
Inca Silver (Mettalic)
Briarcliff Red P30-72
Frost White
Classic Black P1-31
Briarcliff Red
Briarcliff Red P31-1
Classic Black
Lt. Sonata Blue P27-72
White Frost
Med. Berkeley Blue P28-72
(Mettalic) Frost White
Lt. Sonata Blue P27-28
Med. Berkeley Blue (Mettalic)
Med. Berkeley Blue P28-27
(Mettalic) Lt. Sonata Blue
Lt. Chatsworth Green P8-72
Frost White
Med. Valley Green P26-72
(Mettalic) Frost White
Lt. Chatsworth Green P8-26
Med. Valley Green (Metallic)
Med. Valley Green P26-8
(Metallic) Lt. Chatsworth Green
Alamo Beige P4-72
Frost White
Med. Whirlwind Tan P29-72
(Metallic) Frost White
Alamo Beige P4-29
Med. Whirlwind Tan (Metallic)
Med. Whirlwind Tan P29-4
(Metallic) Alamo Beige
Jasmine Rose P33-72
Frost White
Fire Glow Red (Metallic) P34-72
Frost White
Jasmine Rose P33-34
Fire Glow Red (Metallic)
Fire Glow Red (Metallic) P34-33
Jasmine Rose
Waikiki Gold P32-72
Frost White
Aqua Mist (Metallic) P15-72
Frost White
Lt. Echo Green (Metallic) P23-72
Frost White

THE TRIM NUMBER furnishes the key to trim color and material for each model series.

AMERICAN

T101 T102 T103 T104 T105
T111* T112* T113 T114* T115*

CUSTOM

T128 T129 T141 T142 T143 T145 T146 T149
T138* T139* T151* T152* T153* T154* T156* T159*
T127* T137* T140* T147* T148* T150* T157* T158* T160*

RAMBLER CLASSIC

T121 T122 T123 T124 T125 T126
T131* T132* T133* T134* T135* T136*

CUSTOM

T128 T129 T141 T143 T144 T145 T146 T149
T138* T139* T151* T152* T153* T154* T155* T156* T159*

AMBASSADOR

T162 T163 T164 T165 T166
T172* T173* T174* T175* T176*

CUSTOM

T168 T169 T181 T182 T183 T184 T185 T186 T189
T178* T179* T191* T192* T193* T194* T195* T196* T199*

* VINYL

ENGINE ID

The engine code number is located on a machined surface of the engine block or stamped on a tag. These engines are marked with a code identifing: year, month, engine letter code, and day of manufacture.
Letter Identification, Size of Bore, Main Bearings and Connecting Rod Bearings
In the machining of cylinder blocks and crankshafts, it is sometimes necessary to machine the cylinder bores to .010" oversize, and the crankshaft main bearing journals or crank pins to .010" undersize.

EXAMPLE	3	2	A	24
	1961	month	code	day

First Letter .... Size of the Bore
Second Letter .... Size of the main Bearings
Third Letter .... Size of the Connecting Rod Bearings

Letter "A" Standard
Letter "B" .010" Undersize
Letter "C" .010" Oversize

ENGINE SPECIFICATIONS

Code	Engine	CID	Comp. Ratio	Carburator	HP
A	6	195.6	8.0:1	Holley 1-BBI .	90
B	6	195.6	8.7:1	Holley 1-BBI .	125
C	6	195.6	8.7:1	Holley 1-BBI .	127
					138*
?	8	250	8.7:1	Holley 2-BBI .	200
				**	215
E	8	327	8.7:1	Holley 2-BBI .	250*
F	8		9.7:1	**	270

* Optional 138 @ 4500 RPM with 2-barrel carb.
** Optional Holley 4-barrel.

Vehicle Identification Number

B-375001

The serial number is stamped on a plate attached to the right wheel-house panel.

THE FIRST DIGIT : Identifies the car line.

Rebel 8...A
American 6 .... B
Rambler 6 C
Ambassador 8 .... H

BODY NUMBER PLATE

A unit body number plate is riveted to the left front body hinge pillar above the lower hinge. Included are the body, model, trim, paint code and car code numbers which indicates date of manufacture. The model number identifies the body style. It follows by number 1, 2, 3, 4 or 5 which denote different optional appointment groups built into the car as original equiptment.

ALL WELDED SINGLE UNIT CONSTRUCTION

THIS RAMBLER IS BUILT WITH AN ADVANCED METHOD OF BODY CON-STRUCTION IN WHICH THE BODY AND FRAME ARE COMBINED INTO A SINGLE ALL-WELDED STRUCTURAL UNIT.
PIONEERED AND BUILT EX-CLUSIVELY BY

AMERICAN MOTORS CORP.
DETROIT MICH.
BODY NO.   0000001
MODEL NO.   6118-2
TRIM NO.   T284
PAINT NO.   P37
　　　　E-00000

AMERICAN

	Code
2-Dr. Business Coupe-D	6202
2-Dr. Convertible	6207-5
2-Dr. Wagon-D	6204
2-Dr. Wagon-C	6204-2
4-Dr. Wagon-C	6208-2
4-Dr. Wagon-S	6208-5
4-Dr. Sedan-D	6205
4-Dr. Sedan-C	6205-2
4-Dr. Sedan-S	6205-5
2-Dr. Club Sedan-D	6206
2-Dr. Club Sedan-S	6206-2
2-Dr. Club Sedan-C	6206-5

RAMBLER

	Code
4-Dr. Sedan-D	6215
4-Dr. Sedan-C	6215-2
4-Dr. Sedan-S	6215-5
4-Dr. Wagon-D	6218
4-Dr. Wagon-C	6218-2
4-Dr. Wagon-C	6218-4
4-Dr. Wagon-S	6218-5
4-Dr. Club Sedan-D	6216
4-Dr. Club Sedan-C	6216-2
4-Dr. Club Sedan-S	6216-5

AMBASSADOR

	Code
4-Dr. Sedan-D	6285
4-Dr. Sedan-C	6285-2
4-Dr. Sedan-S	6285-5
4-Dr. Wagon-C	6288-2
5-Dr. Wagon-S	6288-5
5-Dr. Wagon-S	6288-6

THE PAINT CODE furnishes the key to the paint colors used on the car. A two number code indicated the color of the car. A two-toned car has two sets of numbers. First number is body color, second is the roof.

COLOR

	Code
Classic Black	P1
Frost White	P72
Inca Silver (Metallic)	P31
Briarcliff Red	P30
Lt. Sonata Blue	P27
Med. Baron Blue (Mettalic)	P35
Dk. Majestic Blue (Metallic)	P40
Lt. Glen Cove Green	P36
Med. Elmhurst Green (Metallic)	P37
Sirocco Beige	P42
Algiers Rose Copper (Metallic)	P38
Jasmine Rose	P33
Villa Red (Metallic)	P39
Aqua Mist (Metallic)	P15
Corsican Gold (Metallic)	P41

Inca Silver (Mettalic) Frost White	P31-72
Classic Black Frost White	P1-72
Inca Silver (Mettalic) Classic Black	P31-1
Briarcliff Red Frost White	P30-72
Classic Black Briarcliff Red	P1-31
Lt. Sonata Blue White Frost	P27-72
Med. Baron Blue (Mettalic) Frost White	P35-72
Lt. Sonata Blue Med. Baron Blue (Metallic)	P27-35
Dk. Majestic Blue (Metallic) Frost White	P40-72
Dk. Majestic Blue (Mettalic) Med. Baron Blue (Metallic)	40-35
Dk. Majestic Blue (Metallic) Lt. Sonata Blue	P40-27
Lt. Glen Cove Green Frost White	P36-72
Med. Elmhurst Green (Mettalic) Frost White	P37-72
Lt. Glen Cove Green Med. Elmhurst Green (Mettalic)	P36-37

Sirocco Beige P42-72
Frost White
Aljiers Rose Copper P38-72
(Metallic) Frost White
Sirocco Beige P42-38
Aljiers Rose Copper (Metallic)
Jasmine Rose P33-72
Frost White
Villa Red (Metallic) P39-72
Frost White
Jasmine Rose P33-39
Villa Red (Metallic)
Aqua Mist (Metallic) P15-72
Frost White
Corsican Gold P41-72
(Metallic) Frost White

THE TRIM NUMBER furnishes the key to trim color and material for each model series.

AMERICAN

T222 T223 T224 T225   T226 T228 T229
T222* T223* T224* T225* T226*
T232 T233 T234 T235   T236 T238 T239
              T245* T246* T248* T249*

CUSTOM

T202 T212 T213 T214 T215 T216
T202* T212* T213* T214* T215* T216*

RAMBLER CLASSIC

T272 T273 T274 T275 T276 T278 T279
T272* T273* T274* T275* T276* T278* T279*

CUSTOM

T252 T262 T263 T264 T265 T266
T252* T262* T263* T264* T265* T266*

AMBASSADOR

T292 T293 T294 T295 T296 T298 T299
T292* T293* T294* T295* T296* T298* T299*
              T245* T246* T248* T249*

CUSTOM

T282 T283 T284 T285 T286
T282* T283* T284* T285* T286*

* VINYL

ENGINE ID

The engine code number is located on a machined surface on of the engine block or stamped on a tag. These engines are marked with a code identifing: year, month, engine letter code, and day of manufacture.
Letter Identification, Size of Bore, Main Bearings and Connecting Rod Bearings
In the machining of cylinder blocks and crankshafts, it is sometimes necessary to machine the cylinder bores to .010" oversize, and the crankshaft main bearing journals or crank pins to .010" undersize.

EXAMPLE	4	2	A	24
	1962	month	code	day

First Letter .... Size of the Bore
Second Letter .... Size of the main Bearings
Third Letter .... Size of the Connecting Rod Bearings

Letter "A" Standard
Letter "B" .010" Undersize
Letter "C" .010" Oversize

ENGINE SPECIFICATIONS

Code	Engine	CID	Comp. Ratio	Carburator	HP
A	6	195.6	8.0:1	Holley 1-BBI .	90
B	6	195.6	8.7:1	Holley 1-BBI .	125
C	6	195.6	8.7:1	Holley 1-BBI .	127
					138*
?	8	250	8.7:1	Holley 2-BBI .	200
				**	215
E	8	327	8.7:1	Holley 2-BBI .	250*
F	8		9.7:1	**	270

*   Optional 138 @ 4500 RPM with 2-barrel carb.
**   Optional Holley 4-barrel.

Vehicle Identification Number

B-100551

The serial number is stamped on a plate attached to the right wheelhouse panel.

THE FIRST DIGIT : Identifies the car line.

Rebel 8 .... A
American 6 .... B
Rambler 6 C
Ambassador 8 .... H

BODY NUMBER PLATE

A unit body number plate is riveted to the left front body hinge pillar above the lower hinge. Included are the body, model, trim, paint code and car code numbers which indicates date of manufacture. The model number identifies the body style. It follows by number 1, 2, 3 0r 4 which denote different optional appointment groups built into the car as original equiptment.

ALL WELDED SINGLE UNIT CONSTRUCTION

THIS RAMBLER IS BUILT WITH AN ADVANCED METHOD OF BODY CONSTRUCTION IN WHICH THE BODY AND FRAME ARE COMBINED INTO A SINGLE ALL-WELDED STRUCTURAL UNIT. PIONEERED AND BUILT EX-CLUSIVELY BY

AMERICAN MOTORS CORP. DETROIT MICH.
BODY NO.   000001
MODEL NO.   6308-2
TRIM NO.   3120
PAINT NO.   72
            E-000001

AMERICAN   Code

2-Dr. Business Coupe-D 6002
2-Dr. Wagon-D 6004
2-Dr. Wagon-S 6004-1
4-Dr. Wagon-C 6304-2
4-Dr. Sedan-D 6005
4-Dr. Sedan-S 6005-1
4-Dr. Sedan-C 6005-2

2-Dr. Club Sedan-D 6006
2-Dr. Club Sedan-S 6006-1
2-Dr. Club Sedan-C 6006-2

RAMBLER   Code

4-Dr. Sedan-D 6015
4-Dr. Sedan-S 6015-1
4-Dr. Sedan-C 6015-2
4-Dr. Wagon-D.....................6018
2-Dr. Wagon-S 6018-1
4-Dr. Wagon-C 6018-2
4-Dr. 2 Seat Wagon-S..... 6018-3
4-Dr. 2 Seat Wagon-C 6018-4
4-Dr. Hardtop Sedan-C ... 6019-2

RAMBLER REBEL   Code

4-Dr. Sedan-D 6025
4-Dr. Sedan-S 6025-1
4-Dr. Sedan-C 6025-2
2-Dr. Wagon-S 6028-1
2-Dr. Wagon-C 6028-2
2-Dr. Wagon-S 6028-3
4-Dr. Wagon-C 6028-4
4-Dr. Hardtop Sedan-C ... 6029-2

AMBASSADOR   Code

4-Dr. Hardtop Wagon-C 6083-2
4-Dr. Sedan-D 6085
4-Dr. Sedan-S 6085-1
4-Dr. Sedan-C 6085-2

THE TRIM NUMBER furnishes the key to trim color and material for each model series.

AMERICAN

	220	330				
Vinyl Bolster Color	Silver	Silver	Blue	Aqua	Red	Ivory
Soft Trim Color	Black	Black	Blue	Aqua	Red	Gold
Fabric (Standard)	T302C	T312C	T313C	T314C	T315C	T316C
Porous Vinyl(E.C.O.)	T302P	T312P	T313P	T314P	T315P	T316P

AMERICAN 440/440-H

	Silver	Blue	Aqua		Gold	Coral
Vinyl Bolster Color	Metallic	Metallic	Metallic	Red	Metallic	Metallic
Soft Trim Color	Black	Blue	Aqua	Red	Gold	Maroon
Fabric(Stand., N.A. Conv. & 440-H, H.T.)	T322C	T323C	T324C	T325C	T326C	T327C
Porous Vinyl(E.C.O., N.A., 440-H, H.T.)	T322P	T323P	T324P	T325P	T326P	T327P
Pleated All-Vinyl(Conv., Stand.)	T332V	T333V	T334V	T335V	T336V	T337V
Bucket Seats, Fabric Insert(E.C.O.)	T342C	T343C	T344C	T345C	T346C	T347C
Bucket Seats, All Vinyl(E.C.O.)	T342V	T343V	T344V	T345V	T346V	T347V

RAMBLER CLASSIC 550

	Silver	Blue	Aqua
Vinyl Bolster Color	Silver	Blue	Aqua
Soft Trim Color	Black	Blue	Aqua
Fabric (Standard)	T352C	T353C	T354C
Porous Vinyl(E.C.O.)	T352P	T353P	T354P

RAMBLER CLASSIC 660

	Silver	Blue	Aqua	Red	Ivory
Vinyl Bolster Color	Silver	Blue	Aqua	Red	Ivory
Soft Trim Color	Black	Blue	Aqua	Red	Gold
Fabric (Standard)	T362C	T363C	T364C	T365C	T366C
Porous Vinyl(E.C.O.)	T362P	T363P	T364P	T365P	T366P

RAMBLER CLASSIC 770

	Silver	Blue	Aqua		Gold	Coral
Vinyl Bolster Color	Metallic	Metallic	Metallic	Red	Metallic	Metallic
Soft Trim Color	Black	Blue	Aqua	Red	Gold	Maroon
Fabric(Stand.)	T372C	T373C	T374C	T375C	T376C	T377C
Porous Vinyl(E.C.O.,)	T372P	T373P	T374P	T375P	T376P	T377P
Bucket Seats, Fabric Insert(E.C.O.)	T342C	T343C	T344C	T345C	T346C	T347C
Bucket Seats, All Vinyl(E.C.O.)	T342V	T343V	T344V	T345V	T346V	T347V

AMBASSADOR 880

	Silver	Blue	Aqua		Gold
Vinyl Bolster Color	Metallic	Metallic	Metallic	Red	Metallic
Soft Trim Color	Black	Blue	Aqua	Red	Gold
Fabric(Stand.)	T382C	T383C	T384C	T385C	T386C
Porous Vinyl(E.C.O.,)	T382P	T383P	T384P	T385P	T386P

AMBASSADOR 990

	Silver	Blue	Aqua		Gold	Coral
Vinyl Bolster Color	Metallic	Metallic	Metallic	Red	Metallic	Metallic
Soft Trim Color	Black	Blue	Aqua	Red	Gold	Maroon
Fabric(Stand.)	T392C	T393C	T394C	T395C	T396C	T397C
Porous Vinyl(E.C.O.,)	T392P	T393P	T394P	T395P	T396P	T397P
Bucket Seats, Fabric Insert(E.C.O.)	T342C	T343C	T344C	T345C	T346C	T347C
Bucket Seats, All Vinyl(E.C.O.)	T342V	T343V	T344V	T345V	T346V	T347V

THE PAINT CODE furnishes the key to the paint colors used on the car. A two number code indicated the color of the car. A two-toned car has two sets of numbers. First number is body color, second is the roof.

ENGINE ID

The engine code number is located on a machined surface of the engine block or stamped on a tag. These engines are marked with a code identifing: year, month, engine letter code, and day of manufacture.
Letter Identification, Size of Bore, Main Bearings and Connecting Rod Bearings
In the machining of cylinder blocks and crankshafts, it is sometimes necessary to machine the cylinder bores to .010" oversize, and the crankshaft main bearing journals or crank pins to .010" undersize.

EXAMPLE	5	2	A	24
	1963	month	code	day

First Letter .... Size of the Bore
Second Letter .... Size of the main Bearings
Third Letter .... Size of the Connecting Rod Bearings

Letter "A" Standard
Letter "B" .010" Undersize
Letter "C" .010" Oversize

COLOR	Code
Classic Black	P1
Frost White	P72
Sceptre Silver (Metallic)	P31
Briarcliff Red	P30
Lt. Bahama Blue	P44
Med. Cape Cod Blue (Mettallic)	P45
Dk. Majestic Blue (Metallic)	P4
Lt. Palisade Green	P46
Med. Aegean Aqua (Metallic)	P47
Valencia Ivory	P49
Corsican Gold (Metallic)	P41
Med. Calais Coral (Metallic)	P48
Concord Maroon (Mettallic)	P50
Classic Black / Frost White	P1-72
Sceptre Silver (Mettallic) / Frost White	P43-72
Briarcliff Red / Frost White	P30-72
Sceptre Silver (Metallic) / Classic Black	P43-1
Briarcliff Red / Classic Black	P1-31
Lt. Bahama Blue / White Frost	P44-72
Med. Cape Cod Blue (Mettallic) / Frost White	P35-72
Dk. Majestic Blue (Metallic) / Frost White	P40-72
Lt. Bahama Blue / Med. Cape Cod Blue (Mettallic)	P44-35
Lt. Bahama Blue / Dk. Majestic Blue (Metallic)	P44-40
Lt. Palisade Green / Frost White	P46-72
Med. Aegean Aqua (Mettallic) / Frost White	P37-72
Lt. Palisade Green / Med. Aegean Aqua (Mettalic)	P46-37
Valencia Ivory / Frost White	P49-72
Corsican Gold (Metallic) / Frost White	P41-72
Corsican Gold (Metallic) / Valencia Ivory	P49-1
Classic Black / Corsican Gold (Metallic)	P49-1
Med. Calais Coral (Metallic) / Frost White	48-72
Med. Calais Coral (Metallic) / Concord Maroon (Metallic)	P48-50
Concord Maroon (Metallic) / Frost White	P50-72

ENGINE SPECIFICATIONS

6 Cyl. - Aluminum Block

Type	Valve-in-Head
No. of Cylinders	6
Displacement	195.6 Cu. In.
Compressions Ratio	8.7:1
Carburetor:	
Standard	Holley 1909-Single Throat
Optional	Carter W.C.D.-Twin Throat

Brake Horsepower
Single Throat Carb. ....125 Code B
Twin Throat Carb. ....138 Code C

6 Cyl. - Cast Iron Block

Type	Valve-in-Head
No. of Cylinders	6
Displacement	195.6 Cu. In.
Compressions Ratio	8.7:1
Carburetor:	
Standard	Holley 1909-Single Throat
Optional	Carter W.C.D.-Twin Throat

Brake Horsepower
Single Throat Carb. ....127 Code C
Twin Throat Carb. ....138 Code C

6 Cyl. - L-Head

Type	L-Head
No. of Cylinders	6
Displacement	195.6 Cu. In.
Compressions Ratio	8.0:1
Brake Horsepower	90 Code A

6 Cyl. - Overhead Valve

Type	Valve-in-Head
No. of Cylinders	6
Displacement	195.6 Cu. In.
Compressions Ratio	8.7:1
Carburetor:	
Standard	Holley 1909-Single Throat
Optional	Carter W.C.D.-Twin Throat

Brake Horsepower
Single Throat Carb. ....127 Code C
Twin Throat Carb. ....138 Code C

8 Cyl.

Type	90^ V-8 O.H.V.
No. of Cylinders	8
Displacement	327 Cu. In.
Compressions Ratio:	
Standard	8.7:1
Optional	9.7:1
Carburetor:	
Standard	Holley Two Barrel
Optional	Holley Four Barrel

Brake Horsepower
Standard ....250 Code E
Optional ....270 Code F

8 Cyl. (287 cu. in.)

Type	90^ V-8 O.H.V.
No. of Cylinders	8
Displacement	287 Cu. In.
Compressions Ratio	8.7:1
Carburator	Holley 2209 - Two Barrel
Brake Horsepower	198 Code G

Vehicle Identification Number

B-155001

The serial number is stamped on a plate attached to the right wheelhouse panel.

THE FIRST DIGIT : Identifies the car line.

American 6 .... B
Rambler 6 C
Ambassador 8 .... H

BODY NUMBER PLATE

A unit body number plate is riveted to the left front body hinge pillar above the lower hinge. Included are the body, model, trim, paint code and car code numbers which indicates date of manufacture. The model number identifies the body style. It follows by number 2, 4, 5 Or 7 which denote different optional appointment groups built into the car as original equiptment.

RANBLER ADVANCED UNIT CONSTRUCTION

THIS RAMBLER IS BUILT WITH AN ADVANCED METHOD OF BODY CONSTRUCTION IN WHICH THE BODY AND FRAME ARE COMBINED INTO A SINGLE ALL-WELDED STRUCTURAL UNIT. PIONEERED AND BUILT EXCLUSIVELY BY

AMERICAN MOTORS CORP.

BODY NO.   R 000001
MODEL NO.   64155-2
TRIM NO.   3120
PAINT NO.   72
                       E-000001

AMERICAN	Code
2-Dr. Convertible-C	6407-5
2-Dr. Wagon-D	6408
4-Dr. Wagon-C	6408-2
4-Dr. Sedan-D	6405
4-Dr. Sedan-S	6405-1
4-Dr. Sedan-C	6405-2
2-Dr. Club Sedan-D	6406
2-Dr. Club Sedan-C	6406-2
2-Dr. Hardtop-D	6409-5
2-Dr. Hardtop-C	6409-7

RAMBLER	Code
4-Dr. Sedan-D	6415
4-Dr. Sedan-S	6415-2
4-Dr. Sedan-C	6415-5
4-Dr. Wagon-D	6418
2-Dr. Wagon-S	6418-2
4-Dr. Wagon-C	6418-5
2-Dr. Club Sedan-D	6416
2-Dr. Club Sedan-S	6416-2
4-Dr. Club Sedan-C	6416-5
2-Dr. Hardtop Sedan-C	6419-5

AMBASSADOR	Code
4-Dr. Wagon-C	6488-5
4-Dr. Sedan-D	6085
2-Dr. Hardtop-S	6489-5
2-Dr. Hardtop-C	6489-7

THE PAINT CODE furnishes the key to the paint colors used on the car. A two number code indicated the color of the car. A two-toned car has two sets of numbers. First number is body color, second is the roof.

COLOR	Code
Classic Black	P1
Frost White	P72
Sceptre Silver (Metallic)	P43
Rampart Red	P51
Lt.Sentry Blue(Metallic)	P52A
Dk. Forum Blue	P53
Lt. Woodside Green (Metallic)	P54A
Dk. Westminster Green	P55
Lt. Aurora Turquoise	P56
Med. Lancelot Turquoise (Metallic)	P57
Bengal Ivory	P58
Emperor Gold(Metallic)	P59
Contessa Rose(Metallic)	P60A
Vintage Maroon(Metallic)	P61
Classic Black Frost White	P1-72
Sceptre Silver (Metallic) Frost White	P43A-72
Sceptre Silver (Metallic) Classic Black	P43A-1
Rampart Red Frost White	P51-72
Rampart Red Classic Black	P51-1
Lt. Sentry Blue(Metallic) Frost White	P52A-72
Dk. Forum Blue Frost White	P53-72

Lt. Sentry Blue (Metallic) Dk. Forum Blue	P52A-53
Lt.Woodside Green (Metallic) Frost White	P54A-72
Dk.Westminster Green Frost White	P55-72
Lt.Woodside Green (Metallic) Dk.Westminster Green	P54A-55
Dk.Westminster Green Bengal Ivory	P55-58
Lt. Aurora Turquoise Frost White	P56-72
Med. Lancelot Turquoise (Metallic) Frost White	P57-72
Lt. Aurora Turquoise Med. Lancelot Turquoise (Metallic)	P56-57
Bengal Ivory Frost White	P58-72
Emperor Gold (Metallic) Frost White	P59-72
Bengal Ivory Emperor Gold (Metallic)	P58-59
Contessa Rose (Metallic) Frost White	P60A-72
Vintage Maroon (Metallic) Frost White	P61-72
Contessa Rose (Metallic) Vintage Maroon (Metallic)	P60A-61

THE TRIM NUMBER furnishes the key to trim color and material for each model series.

AMERICAN

Trim Colors	220 Silver & Black	330 Silver & Black	Blue	Green	Red	Gold	Turq.
Fabric (Standard)	T422C	T432C	T433C	T434C	T435C	T436C	T438C
Porous Vinyl(E.C.O.)	T422P	T432P	T433P	T434P	T435P	T436P	T438P

AMERICAN 440/440-H

Soft Trim Color	Black	Silver Black	Blue	Green	Red	Gold	Maroon	Turq.
Fabric(Stand.440, N.A. 440 Conv.)	T441C	T442C	T443C	T444C	T445C	T446C	T447C	T448C
Porous Vinyl(E.C.O. 440)	T441P	T442P	T443P	T444P	T445P	T446P	T447P	T448P
All-Vinyl(Stand.440 Conv.,E.O.C. 440-H)	T441V	T442V	T443V	T444V	T445V	T446V	T447V	T448V
Fabric Bucket(Stand.440-H, E.C.O.440)Slim	T441D	T442D	T443D	T444D	T445D	T446D	T447D	T448D
Fabric Bucket(E.C.O.440)Wide	T441G	T442G	T443G	T444G	T445G	T446G	T447G	T448G
All Vinyl Bucket(E.C.O.440, N.C.O.440-H)Slim	T441E	T442E	T443E	T444E	T445E	T446E	T447E	T448E
All Vinyl Bucket (E.C.O.440)Wide	T441H	T442H	T443H	T444H	T445H	T446H	T447H	T448H

RAMBLER CLASSIC 550

Trim Colors	Silver & Black	Blue	Green
Fabric (Standard)	T452C	T453C	T454C
Porous Vinyl(E.C.O.)	T452P	T453P	T454P

RAMBLER CLASSIC 660

Trim Colors	Silver & Black	Blue	Green	Red	Gold	Turq.
Fabric (Standard)	T462C	T463C	T464C	T465C	T466C	T468C
Porous Vinyl(E.C.O.)	T462P	T463P	T464P	T465P	T466P	T468P

RAMBLER CLASSIC 770

Trim Colors	Black	Silver Black	Blue	Green	Red	Gold	Maroon	Turq.
Fabric(Stand.)	T471C	T472C	T473C	T474C	T475C	T476C	T477C	T478C
Porous Vinyl(E.C.O.,)	T471P	T472P	T473P	T474P	T475P	T476P	T477P	T478P
Fabric Bucket(E.C.O.)Slim	T471D	T472D	T473D	T474D	T475D	T476D	T477D	T478D
Fabric Bucket(E.C.O.)Wide	T471G	T472G	T473G	T474G	T475G	T476G	T477G	T478G
All Vinyl Bucket(E.C.O.)Slim	T471E	T472E	T473E	T474E	T475E	T476E	T477E	T478E
All Vinyl Bucket(E.C.O.)Wide	T471H	T472H	T473H	T474H	T475H	T476H	T477H	T478H

AMBASSADOR 990/990-H

Trim Colors	Black	Silver Black	Blue	Green	Red	Gold	Maroon	Turq.
Fabric(Stand.990)	T491C	T492C	T493C	T494C	T495C	T496C	T497C	T498C
All Vinyl(E.C.O.990)	T491V	T492V	T493V	T494V	T495V	T496V	T497V	T498V
Fabric Bucket(E.C.O. 990)Slim	T491D	T492D	T493D	T494D	T495D	T496D	T497D	T498D
Fabric Bucket(Stand. 990-H)Slim	T491K	T492K	T493K	T494K	T495K	T496K	T497K	T498K
All Vinyl Bucket(E.C.O. 990)Slim	T491E	T492E	T493E	T494E	T495E	T496E	T497E	T498E
All Vinyl Bucket(N.C.O. 990-H)Slim	T491L	T492L	T493L	T494L	T495L	T496L	T497L	T498L

ENGINE ID

The engine code number is located on a machined surface of the engine block or stamped on a tag. These engines are marked with a code identifing year, month, engine letter code, and day of manufacture.

Letter Identification, Size of Bore, Main Bearings and Connecting Rod Bearings
In the machining of cylinder blocks and crankshafts, it is sometimes necessary to machine the cylinder bores to .010" oversize, and the crankshaft main bearing journals or crank pins to .010" undersize.

EXAMPLE	6	2	A	24
	1964	month	code	day

First Letter .... Size of the Bore
Second Letter .... Size of the main Bearings
Third Letter .... Size of the Connecting Rod Bearings

Letter "A" Standard
Letter "B" .010" Undersize
Letter "C" .010" Oversize

ENGINE SPECIFICATIONS

6 Cyl. - Aluminum Block

Type	Valve-in-Head
No. of Cylinders	6
Displacement	195.6 Cu. In.
Compressions Ratio	8.7:1
Carburator:	
Standard	Holley 1909-Single Throat
Optional	Carter W.C.D.-Twin Throat
Brake Horsepower	
Single Throat Carb.	125 Code B
Twin Throat Carb.	138 Code C

6 Cyl. - Cast Iron Block

Type	Valve-in-Head
No. of Cylinders	6
Displacement	195.6 Cu. In.
Compressions Ratio	8.7:1
Carburator:	
Standard	Holley 1909-Single Throat
Optional	Carter W.C.D.-Twin Throat
Brake Horsepower	
Single Throat Carb.	127 Code C
Twin Throat Carb.	138 Code C

6 Cyl. - L-Head

Type	L-Head
No. of Cylinders	6
Displacement	195.6 Cu. In.
Compressions Ratio	8.0:1
Brake Horsepower	90 Code A

6 Cyl. - Overhead Valve

Type	Valve-in-Head
No. of Cylinders	6
Displacement	232 Cu. In.
Compressions Ratio	8.5:1
Carburator:	
Standard	Holley 1909-Single Throat
Brake Horsepower	
Single Throat Carb.	145 Code L

8 Cyl. (287 cu. in.)

Type	90^ V-8 O.H.V.
No. of Cylinders	8
Displacement	287 Cu. In.
Compressions Ratio	8.7:1
Carburator	Holley 2209 - Two Barrel
Brake Horsepower	198 Code G

8 Cyl. -Overhead Valve

Type	90^ V-8 O.H.V.
No. of Cylinders	8
Displacement	327 Cu. In.
Compressions Ratio:	
Standard	8.7:1
Optional	9.7:1
Carburator:	
Standard	Holley Two Barrel
Optional	Holley Four Barrel
Brake Horsepower	
Standard	250 Code E
Optional	270 Code F

Vehicle Identification Number

B100551

The serial number is stamped on a plate attached to the right wheelhouse panel.

THE FIRST DIGIT : Identifies the car line.

American 6 .... B
Rambler 6 C
Ambassador 8 .... H

BODY NUMBER PLATE

A unit body number plate is riveted to the left front body hinge pillar above the lower hinge. Included are the body, model, trim, paint code and car code numbers which indicates date of manufacture. The model number identifies the body style. It follows by number 1, 2, 3 Or 4 which denote different optional appointment groups built into the car as original equiptment.

RAMBLER ADVANCED UNIT CONSTRUCTION

THIS RAMBLER IS BUILT WITH AN ADVANCED METHOD OF BODY CONSTRUCTION IN WHICH THE BODY AND FRAME ARE COMBINED INTO A SINGLE ALL-WELDED STRUCTURAL UNIT. PIONEERED AND BUILT EXCLUSIVELY BY

AMERICAN MOTORS CORP.

BODY NO.   000005
MODEL NO.   6505-2
TRIM NO.   532C
PAINT NO.   P1-72
      E-000005

AMERICAN	Code
4-Dr. Wagon-D	.6508
4-Dr. Wagon-C	6508-2
4-Dr. Sedan-D	6505
4-Dr. Sedan-S	6505-2
4-Dr. Sedan-C	.6505-5
2-Dr. Club Sedan-D	6506
2-Dr. Club Sedan-S	6506-2
2-Dr. Convertible-C	6507-5
2-Dr. Hardtop-S	6509-5
2-Dr. Hardtop-C	.6509-7

RAMBLER	Code
4-Dr. Sedan-D	6515
4-Dr. Sedan-S	6515-2
4-Dr. Sedan-C	..6515-5
4-Dr. Wagon-D	6518
4-Dr. Wagon-S	6518-2
4-Dr. Wagon-C	.6518-5
2-Dr. Club Sedan-S.............	6516
2-Dr. Club Sedan-C.........	6516-2
4-Dr. Convertible-C	6517-5
2-Dr. Hardtop-S	.6519-5
2-Dr. Hardtop-C	6519-5

AMBASSADOR	Code
4-Dr. Sedan-S	.6585-2
4-Dr. Sedan-C	.6585-5
4-Dr. Wagon-S	.6588-2
4-Dr. Wagon-C	.6588-5
2-Dr. Club Sedan	6586
4-Dr. Convertible-C	6587-5
2-Dr. Hardtop-S	6519-5
2-Dr. Hardtop-C	6519-5

THE PAINT CODE furnishes the key to the paint colors used on the car. A two number code indicated the color of the car. A two-toned car has two sets of numbers. First number is body color, second is the roof.

COLOR	Code
Classic Black	P1A
Frost White	P72A
Antigua Red	P3A
Mystic Gold(Metallic)	P4A
Lt. Legion Blue	P5A
Med.Viscount Blue (Metallic)	P5A
Lt. Woodside Green	P54A
(Metallic)	
Lt. Seaside Aqua	P7A
Med.Marina Aqua(Metallic) ...	P8A
Dk. Atlantis Aqua(Metallic)	P9A
Lt. Montego Rose	P10A
Med. Barcelona Taupe	P11A
(Metallic)	
Dk. Corral Cordovan	P12A
(Metallic)	
Solar Yellow	P13A
Classic Black	P1A-72A
Frost White	
Antigua Red	P3A-72A
Frost White	
Antigua Red	P3A-1A
Classic Black	
Mystic Gold(Metallic)	P4A-72A
Frost White	
Mystic Gold(Metallic)	P4A-1A
Classic Black	
Lt. Legion Blue	P5A-72A
Frost White	
Med. Viscount Blue	P6A-72A
(Metallic) Frost White	

Lt.Legion Blue P5A-6A
Med.Viscount Blue(Metallic)
Lt.Woodside Green P54A-72A
(Metallic) Frost White
Lt. Seaside Aqua P7A-72A
Frost White
Med. Marina Aqua P8A-72A
(Metallic) Frost White
Lt.Seaside Aqua P7A-72A
Frost White
Lt. Seaside Aqua P7A-9A
Dk. Atlantis Aqua (Metallic)
Med. Marina Aqua P8A-9A
(Metallic)Dk.Atlantis Aqua
(Metallic)
Lt. Montego Rose P10A-72A
Frost White
Med. Barcelona Taupe P11A-72A
(Metallic) Frost White
Dk.Corral Cordovan ... P12A-72A
(Metallic) Frost White
Lt. Montego Rose P10A-12A
Dk. Corral Cordovan(Metallic)
Lt. Montego Rose P10A-11A
Med.Barcelona Taupe(Metallic)
Med. Barcelona P11A-12A
Taupe (Metallic) Dk.Corral
Cordovan (Metallic)
Solar Yellow P13A-72A
Frost White

TRIM CODES

AMERICAN

Upholstery Colors	220 Black & Gray	330 Black & White	Blue	Green	Red	Cordo. & Taupe	Aqua
Fabric (Standard)	T522C	T532C	T533C	T534C	T535C	T536C	T537C
Porous Vinyl(E.C.O.)	T522P	T532P	T533P	T534P	T535P	T536P	T537P

AMERICAN 440/440-H

Upholstery Colors	Black	Blue	Green	Red	Cordo. & Taupe	Aqua	Black & White
Fabric(Stand.440, N.A. 440 Conv.)	T541C	T543C	T544C	T545C	T546C	T547C	T548C
Porous Vinyl(E.C.O. 440, N.A. 440 Conv.)	T541P	T543P	T544P	T545P	T546P	T547P	T548P
All-Vinyl(Stand.440 Conv.,E.O.C. 440-H)	T541V	T543V	T544V	T545V*	T546V	T547V	T548V**
Fabric Bucket(E.C.O.440, 440 Conv.)Slim & Console	T541D	T543D	T544D	T545D	T546D	T547D	T548D
Fabric Bucket(E.C.O.440, Stand.440-H)Wide	T541G	T543G	T544G	T545G	T546G	T547G	T548G
All Vinyl Bucket(E.C.O.440, 440-H)Slim & Console	T541E	T543E	T544E	T545E*	T546E	T547E	T548E**
All Vinyl Bucket (E.C.O.440, N.O.C.440-H)Wide	T541H	T543H	T544H	T545H*	T546H	T547H	T548H**

* And Maroon
** All-White

RAMBLER CLASSIC 550

Upholstery Colors	Black & White	Blue	Aqua
Fabric (Standard)	T552C	T553C	T557C
Porous Vinyl(E.C.O.)	T552P	T553P	T557P

RAMBLER CLASSIC 660

Upholstery Colors	Black & White	Blue	Green	Red	Cordo. & Taupe	Aqua
Fabric (Standard)	T562C	T563C	T564C	T565C	T566C	T567C
Porous Vinyl(E.C.O.)	T562P	T563P	T564P	T565P	T566P	T567P

RAMBLER CLASSIC 770/770-H

Upholstery Colors	Black	Blue	Green	Red	Cordo. & Taupe	Aqua	Black & White
Fabric(Stand.770, N.A. 770 Conv.)	T571C	T573C	T574C	T575C	T576C	T577C	T578C
Porous Vinyl(E.C.O. 770, N.A. 770 Conv.)	T571P	T573P	T574P	T575P	T576P	T577P	T578P
All-Vinyl(Stand.770 Conv.,E.O.C. 770-H)	T571V	T573V	T574V	T575V	T576V	T577V	T578V**
Fabric Bucket(E.C.O.770, 770 Conv.)Slim & Console	T571D	T573D	T574D	T575D	T576D	T577D	T578D
Fabric Bucket(E.C.O.770, Stand.770-H)Wide	T571G	T573G	T574G	T575G	T576G	T577G	T578G
All Vinyl Bucket(E.C.O.770, 770-H)Slim & Console	T571E	T573E	T574E	T575E	T576E	T577E	T578E**
All Vinyl Bucket (E.C.O.770, N.O.C.770-H)Wide	T571H	T573H	T574H	T575H	T576H	T577H	T578H**

** All-White

AMBASSADOR 880

Upholstery Colors	Black & White	Blue	Green	Red	Cordo. & Taupe	Aqua
Fabric (Standard)	T582C	T583C	T584C	T585C	T586C	T587C
Porous Vinyl(E.C.O.)	T582P	T583P	T584P	T585P	T586P	T587P

AMBASSADOR 990/990-H

Upholstery Colors	Black	Blue	Green	Red	Cordo. & Taupe	Aqua	Turq.
Fabric(Stand.990, NA 990 Conv.)	T591C	T593C	T594C	T595C	T596C	T597C	T598C
All Vinyl(Stand.990 Conv.,E.C.O.990)	T591V	T593V	T594V	T595V	T596V	T597V	T598V**
Fabric Bucket(E.C.O. 990)Slim	T591D	T593D	T594D	T595D	T596D	T597D	T598D
Fabric Bucket(Stand. 990-H)Slim	T591K	T593K	T594K	T595K	T596K	T597K	T598K
All Vinyl Bucket(E.C.O. 990)Slim	T591E	T593E	T594E	T595E	T596E	T597E	T598E**
All Vinyl Bucket(N.C.O. 990-H)Slim	T591L	T593L	T594L	T595L	T596L	T597L	T598L**

** All-White

ENGINE ID

The engine code number is located on a machined surface of the engine block or stamped on a tag. These engines are marked with a code identifing: year, month, engine letter code, and day of manufacture.
Letter Identification, Size of Bore, Main Bearings and Connecting Rod Bearings
In the machining of cylinder blocks and crankshafts, it is sometimes necessary to machine the cylinder bores to .010" oversize, and the crankshaft main bearing journals or crank pins to .010" undersize.

EXAMPLE	7	2	A	24
	1965	month	code	day

First Letter .... Size of the Bore
Second Letter .... Size of the main Bearings
Third Letter .... Size of the Connecting Rod Bearings

Letter "A" Standard
Letter "B" .010" Undersize
Letter "C" .010" Oversize

ENGINE SPECIFICATIONS

6 Cyl. - Overhead Valve(232 Cu. In)

Type .... Valve-in-Head
No. of Cylinders 6
Displacement .... 232 Cu. In.
Compressions Ratio 8.5:1
Carburetor: ....
Standard .... Holley 1931-Single Throat
Optional .... Carter W.C.D.-Twin Throat
Brake Horsepower
  Single Throat Carb. 145   Code   L
  Twin Throat Carb. 155   Code   L

6 Cyl. - Overhead Valve(199 cu. In.)

Type .... Valve-in-Head
No. of Cylinders 6
Displacement .... 199 Cu. In.
Compressions Ratio 8.5:1
Carburetor .... Carter R.B.S.-Single Throat
Brake Horsepower 128   Code   J

6 Cyl. - L-Head

Type .... L-Head
No. of Cylinders 6
Displacement .... 195.6 Cu. In.
Compressions Ratio 8.0:1
Brake Horsepower 90   Code   A

6 Cyl. - Overhead Valve

Type .... O.H.V.
No. of Cylinders 6
Displacement .... 195.6 Cu. In.
Compressions Ratio 8.7:1
Brake Horsepower
  Standard 125   Code   B
  W/AC 138   Code   C

8 Cyl. (287 cu. In.)

Type .... 90^ V-8 O.H.V.
No. of Cylinders 8
Displacement .... 287 Cu. In.
Compressions Ratio 8.7:1
Carburetor .... Holley 2209 - Two Barrel
Brake Horsepower 198   Code   G

8 Cyl. (327 cu. In.)

Type .... 90^ V-8 O.H.V.
No. of Cylinders 8
Displacement .... 327 Cu. In.
Compressions Ratio 9.7:1
Carburetor .... Holley 4150 - Four Barrel
Brake Horsepower 270   Code   F

1966 AMERICAN MOTORS

Vehicle Identification Number

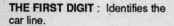

B6KS52B100001

Stamped and embossed on a stainless steel plate welded to the right front fender under the hood. It consists of Manufacturer's symbol, Model year symbol, Transmission type symbol, Body identity symbol, Class of body symbol, Series and Engine identity symbol, and a sequential Production number for each series.

THE FIRST DIGIT : Identifies the car line.

American 6	B
Rambler 6	C
Ambassador 8	H

THE SECOND DIGIT: Year-"6"- for 1966.

THE THIRD DIGIT : Plant of Manufacture "K" for Kenosha.

THE FOURTH DIGIT: Transmission Type.

Standard Collumn Shift (3 speed)	S
Overdrive Column Shift (3 speed)	O
Automatic Collumn Shift (3 speed)	A
Floor Shift Automatic (3 speed)	C
Four Speed Floor Shift	F

THE FIFTH DIGIT : Body Type.

2-Dr. Wagon	4
4-Dr. Sedan	5
2-Dr. Sedan	6
2-Dr. Convertible	7
4-Dr. Wagon	8
2-Dr. Hardtop	9

THE SIXTH DIGIT : Model.

550/220	0
880	2
440/770/990	5
Rebel, Marlin, DPL, Rogue	7

THE SEVENTH DIGIT : Series and Engine.

AMERICAN

199 CID, OHV 6, 1-BC	A
232 CID, OHV 6, 2-BC	B
290 CID, V-8, 2-BC	C
287 CID, V-8, 2-BC	H
327 CID, V-8, 2-BC (L.C.)	J
327 CID, V-8, 4-BC (H.C.)	K

AMBASSADOR

232 CID, OHV 6, 2-BC	M
287 CID, V-8, 2-BC	N
327 CID, V-8, 2-BC (L. Cp.)	P
327 CID, V-8, 4-BC (H.C.)	Q

MARLIN

232 CID, OHV 6, 2-BC	S
287 CID, V8, 2-BC	T
327 CID, V8, 4-BC (H.C.)	U
232 CID, OHV 6, 1-BC	V
327 CID, V-8, 2-BC (L.C.)	W

LAST SIX DIGITS: Sequential production nomber.

BODY NUMBER PLATE

A unit body number plate rivited to the left front door below the door lock and is visible when door is open. This body plate includes the model, body, trim, paint code, and car built sequence numbers. The model number identifies the body style. This number when followed by numbers 2, 5, or 7 denotes different groups of optional appointments built into the car as origional equiptment.

RAMBLER ADVANCED UNIT CONSTRUCTION

THIS RAMBLER IS BUILT WITH AN ADVANCED METHOD OF COMBINING BODY AND FRAME INTO A SINGLE ALL-WELDED STRUCTURAL UNIT. FEATURING ONE-PEICE UNISIDE PANELS. GALVINIZED STEEL PLUS DEEP -DIP PRIMER PAND AND BAKED ENAMEL ASSURE BODY RUST PROTECTION. PIONEERED AND BUILT EXCLUSIVELY BY

AMERICAN MOTORS CORP.	
BODY NO.	A000036
MODEL NO.	6669-7
TRIM NO.	697K
PAINT NO.	29A-20A
W0000145	

AMERICAN   Code

-Dr. Wagon-D	6608
-Dr. Wagon-C	6608-5
-Dr. Sedan-D	6605
-Dr. Sedan-C	6605-5
-Dr. Sedan-D	6606
-Dr. Sedan-C	6606-5
-Dr. Convertible-C	6607-5
-Dr. Hardtop-S	6609-5
-Dr. Hardtop-C	6609-7

AMBLER   Code

-Dr. Sedan-D	6615
-Dr. Sedan-C	6615-5
-Dr. Wagon-D	6618
-Dr. Wagon-C	6618-5
-Dr. Club Sedan-C	6616
-Dr. Convertible-C	6617-5
-Dr. Hardtop-S	6619-5
-Dr. Hardtop-C	6619-7

AMBASSADOR   Code

-Dr. Wagon-S	6688-2
-Dr. Wagon-C	6688-5
-Dr. Sedan-S	6685-2
-Dr. Sedan-C	6685-5
-Dr. Club Sedan-S	6686-2
-Dr. Convertible-C	6687-5
-Dr. Hardtop-S	6689-5
-Dr. Hardtop-C	6689-7

THE PAINT CODE furnishes the key to the paint colors used on the car. A two number code indicated the color of the car. A two-toned car has two sets of numbers. First number is body color, second is the roof.

COLOR   Code

Classic Black	1
Frost White	72
Antigua Red	3
Lt. Brisbane Blue (Metallic)	15
Lt. Britannia Blue (Metallic)	16
Lt. Cresent Green	17
Med. Granada Green (Metallic)	18
Lt. Balboa Aqua	19
Med. Cortez Aqua (Metallic)	20
Samoa Gold (Metallic)	23
Med. Caballero Tan (Metallic)	24
Apollo Yellow	25
Classic Black Frost White	1-72
Antigua Red Frost White	3-72
Lt. Brisbane Blue (Metallic) Lt. Britannia Blue (Metallic)	15-16

Lt. Cresent Green	17-18
Med. Granada Green (Metallic)	
Lt. Balboa Aqua	19-20
Med. Cortez Aqua (Metallic)	
Samoa Gold (Metallic)	23-24
Med. Caballero Tan (Metallic)	
Antigua Red	3-1
Classic Black	
Lt. Brisbane Blue (Metallic) Frost White	15-72
Lt. Britannia Blue (Metallic) Frost White	16-72
Lt. Cresent Green Frost White	17-72
Med. Granada Green (Metallic) Frost White	18-72
Lt. Balboa Aqua Frost White	19-72
Med. Cortez Aqua (Metallic) Frost White	20-72
Samoa Gold (Metallic) Frost White	23-72
Med. Caballero Tan Frost White	24-72

THE TRIM NUMBER furnishes the key to trim color and material for each model SERIES.

MARLIN

2-Dr. Fastback Hardtop

	Black	Red	Aqua	White	Saddle
Fabric (Standard)	T691Q(1,3)	T695Q(1,3)	T697Q(1,3)	T699Q(1,3)	
4 Fabric Bucket(E.C.O.)	T691M(4)	T695M(4)	T697M(4)	T699M(4)	
5 Vinylair(E.C.O.)	T691N(4)	T695N(4)	T697N(4)	T698N(4)	T699N(4)

AMERICAN

2 & 4 Dr. Sedan

	Blue	Black &White	Tan
Fabric (Standard)	T623C(1,2)	T628C(1,2)	T629C(1,2)

4 Dr. Station Wagon

	Blue	Black &White	Tan
Fabric (Standard)	T623C(1,2)	T628C(1,2)	T629C(1,2)
Porous Vinyl(E.C.O.)	T623P(2)	T628P(2)	T629P(2)

AMERICAN 440

2 & 4 Dr. Sedan/2-Dr. Hardtop

	Black	Blue	Green	Red	Aqua	Saddle
Fabric (Standard)	T641C(1,2,3)	T643C(1,2,3)	T644C(1,2,3)	T645C(1,2,3)	T647C(1,2,3)	T649C(1,2,3)

4 Dr. Station Wagon

	Black	Blue	Green	Red	Aqua	Saddle
Fabric (Standard)	T641C(1,2,3)	T643C(1,2,3)	T644C(1,2,3)	T645C(1,2,3)	T647C(1,2,3)	T649C(1,2,3)
Porous vinyl(E.C.O.)	T641P(2,3)	T643P(2,3)	T644P(2,3)	T645P(2,3)	T647P(2,3)	T649P(2,3)

2-Dr. Convertible

	Black	Blue	Green	Red	Aqua	White	Saddle
All-Vinyl(Standard)	T641V(1,2,3)	T643V(1,2,3)	T644V(1,2,3)	T645V(1,2,3)	T647V(1,2,3)	T648V(1,2,3)	T649V(1,2,3)

AMERICAN 440/ROGUE

2-Dr. Hardtop

	Black	Blue	Green	Red	Aqua	White	Saddle
Fabric	T641D(5)	T643D(5)	T644D(5)	T645D(5)	T647D(5)	T649D(5)	
All-Vinyl	T641E(5)	T643E(5)	T644E(5)	T645E(5)	T647E(5)	T648E(5)	T649E(5)

2-Dr. Convertible

	Black	Blue	Green	Red	Aqua	White	Saddle
All-Vinyl	T641E(4)	T643E(4)	T644E(4)	T645E(4)	T647E(4)	T648E(4)	T649E(4)

RAMBLER CLASSIC 550

2 & 4 Dr. Sedan

	Blue	Black &White	Tan
Fabric (Standard)	T653C(1,2)	T658C(1,2)	T659C(1,2)

4 Dr. Station Wagon

	Blue	Black &White	Tan
Fabric (Standard)	T653C(1,2)	T658C(1,2)	T659C(1,2)
Porous Vinyl(E.C.O.)	T653P(2)	T658P(2)	T659P(2)

RAMBLER CLASSIC 770

4-Dr. Sedan/2-Dr. Hardtop

	Black	Blue	Green	Red	Black &Mauve	Aqua	Saddle
Fabric (Standard)	T671C(1,2,3)	T673C(1,2,3)	T674C(1,2,3)	T675C(1,2,3)	T676C(1,2,3)	T677C(1,2,3)	T679C(1,2,3)

4-Dr. Station Wagon

	Black	Blue	Green	Red	Black &Mauve	Aqua	Saddle
Fabric (Standard)	T671C(1,2,3)	T673C(1,2,3)	T674C(1,2,3)	T675C(1,2,3)	T676C(1,2,3)	T677C(1,2,3)	T679C(1,2,3)
Porous Vinyl(E.C.O.)	T671B(2,3)	T673B(2,3)	T674B(2,3)	T675B(2,3)	T676B(2,3)	T677B(2,3)	T679B(2,3)

2-Dr. Convertible

	Black	Blue	Green	Red	Black &Mauve	Aqua	White	Saddle
Fabric (Standard)	T671V(1,2,3)	T673V(1,2,3)	T674V(1,2,3)	T675V(1,2,3)	T676V(1,2,3)	T677V(1,2,3)	T678V(1,2,3)	T679V(1,2,

4-Dr. Sedan

	Black	Blue	Green	Red	Black &Mauve	Aqua		Saddle
Fabric (Standard)	T671D(4)	T673D(4)	T674D(4)	T675D(4)	T676D(4)	T677D(4)		T679D(4)

2-Dr. Convertible/4-Dr. Station Wagon

	Black	Blue	Green	Red	Black &Mauve	Aqua	White	Saddle
All-Vinyl	T671E(4)	T673E(4)	T674E(4)	T675E(4)	T676E(4)	T677E(4)	T678E(4)	T679E(4)

RAMBLER CLASSIC 770/REBEL

2-Dr. Hardtop

	Black	Blue	Green	Red	Black &Mauve	Aqua	White	Saddle
Fabric	T671D(6)	T673D(6)	T674D(6)	T675E(6)	T676D(6)	T677D(6)	T678D(6)	T679D(6)
All-Vinyl	T671E(6)	T673E(6)	T674E(6)	T675E(6)	T676E(6)	T677E(6)	T678E(6)	T679E(6)
Rebel*	T671W(6)	T673W(6)		T675W(6)		T677W(6)		T679W(6)

*Rebel Custom Trim Package, (Vinyl-Covered Roof Standard) "Hialeah Plaid" Fabric Extra-Cost option includes two pillows

AMBASSADOR 880

4-Dr. Station Wagon

	Blue	Green	Red	Aqua	Saddle
Fabric	T683D(1,2,3)	T684D(1,2,3)	T685D(1,2,3)	T687D(1,2,3)	T689D(1,2,3)
All-Vinyl	T683E(2,3)	T684E(2,3)	T685E(2,3)	T687E(2,3)	T689E(2,3)

2 & 4-Dr. Sedan

	Blue	Green	Red	Aqua	Saddle
All-Vinyl	T683E(1,2,3)	T684E(1,2,3)	T685E(1,2,3)	T687E(1,2,3)	T689E(1,2,3)

AMBASSADOR 990

4-Dr. Sedan/2-Dr. Hardtop

	Black	Blue	Green	Red	Black &Mauve	Aqua		Saddle
Fabric (Standard)	T691C(1,2,3)	T693C(1,2,3)	T694C(1,2,3)	T695C(1,2,3)	T696C(1,2,3)	T697C(1,2,3)		T699C(1,2,3)

4-Dr. Station Wagon

	Black	Blue	Green	Red	Black &Mauve	Aqua	White	Saddle
Fabric(Standard)	T691C(1,2,3)	T693C(1,2,3)	T694C(1,2,3)	T695C(1,2,3)	T696C(1,2,3)	T697C(1,2,3)		T699C(1,2,3)
Vinylair(Stand. Conv.)	T691B(2,3)	T693B(2,3)	T694B(2,3)	T695B(2,3)	T696B(2,3)	T697B(2,3)	T698B(2,3)	T699B(2,3)

2-Dr. Convertible

	Black	Blue	Green	Red	Black &Mauve	Aqua	White	Saddle
Vinylair(Stand. Conv.)	T691B(1,2,3)	T693B(1,2,3)	T694B(1,2,3)	T695B(1,2,3)	T696B(1,2,3)	T697B(1,2,3)	T698B(1,2,3)	T699B(1,2,3)

AMBASSADOR 990/DPL

4-Dr. Sedan

	Black	Blue	Green	Red	Black &Mauve	Aqua		Saddle
Fabric (Standard)	T691D(4)	T693D(4)	T694D(4)	T695D(4)	T696D(4)	T697D(4)		T699D(4)

2-Dr. Convertible/4-Dr. Station Wagon

	Black	Blue	Green	Red	Black &Mauve	Aqua	White	Saddle
All-Vinyl	T691H(4)	T693H(4)	T694H(4)	T695H(4)	T696H(4)	T697H(4)	T698H(4)	T699H(4)

2-Dr. Hardtop

	Black	Blue	Green	Red	Black &Mauve	Aqua	White	Saddle
Fabric	T691(7,8)	T693(7,8)	T694(7,8)	T695(7,8)	T696(7,8)	T697(7,8)		T699(7,8)
Vinylair	T691(7,8)	T693(7,8)	T694(7,8)	T695(7,8)	T696(7,8)	T697(7,8)	T698(7,8)	T699(7,8)
DPL*	T691(8)	T693(8)		T695(8)		T697(8)		T699(8)

DPL "Custom Trim Package" (Vinyl ccovered roof Standard) "Houndstooth Check" Fabric Extra-Cost Option Includes Two Pillows

SEAT CODES

1) Bench Cushion - Non-Reclining - Standard
2) Bench Cushion - Reclining - Extra-Cost Option
3) Individual Cushion - Reclining - Extra-Cost Option
4) Bucket Seats - Reclining - Extra-Cost Option
5) Bucket Seats - Reclining - Extra-Cost Option on 440 - Standard on ROGUE
6) Bucket Seats - Reclining - Extra-Cost Option on 770 - Standard on REBEL
7) Bucket Seats - Reclining - Extra-Cost Option on 990(Suffix "D" on Fabric, "H" on Vinylair)
8) Bucket Seats - Reclining - Standard on DPL(Suffix "K" on Fabric, "L" on Vinylair, & "Y" on Custom)

ENGINE ID

The engine code number is located on a machined surface of the engine block or stamped on a tag. These engines are marked with a code identifing: year, month, engine letter code, and day of manufacture.
Letter Identification, Size of Bore, Main Bearings and Connecting Rod Bearings
In the machining of cylinder blocks and crankshafts, it is sometimes necessary to machine the cylinder bores to .010" oversize, and the crankshaft main bearing journals or crank pins to .010" undersize.

EXAMPLE	8	2	A	24
	1966	month	code	day

First Letter .... Size of the Bore
Second Letter .... Size of the main Bearings
Third Letter .... Size of the Connecting Rod Bearings

Letter "A" Standard
Letter "B" .010" Undersize
Letter "C" .010" Oversize

ENGINE SPECIFICATIONS

6 Cyl. - Overhead Valve (232 cu. in.)

Type ....Valve-in-Head
No. of Cylinders 6
Displacement ....232 Cu. In.
Compressions Ratio 8.5:1
Carburetor:
..........................Holley 1931-Single Throat
..........................Carter R.B.S.-Single Throat
..........................Carter W.C.D.-Twin Throat

Brake Horsepower
..........................145   Code   L
..........................155   Code   L

6 Cyl. - Overhead Valve(199 cu. in.)

Type ....Valve-in-Head
No. of Cylinders 6
Displacement ....199 Cu. In.
Compressions Ratio 8.5:1
Carburetor ....Holley 1931-Single Throat
Brake Horsepower ....128 Code   J

8 Cyl. (287 cu. in.)

Type ....90^ V-8 O.H.V.
No. of Cylinders 8
Displacement ....287 Cu. In.
Compressions Ratio 8.7:1
Carburetor ....Holley 2209 - Two Barrel
Brake Horsepower ....198 Code   G

8 Cyl. (327 cu. in.)

Type ....90^ V-8 O.H.V.
No. of Cylinders 8
Displacement ....327 Cu. In.
Compressions Ratio....................8.7:1
Carburetor ....Holley 2209 - Four Barrel
Brake Horsepower 250   Code   E

8 Cyl. (327 cu. in.)

Type ....90^ V-8 O.H.V.
No. of Cylinders 8
Displacement ....327 Cu. In.
Compressions Ratio 9.7:1
Carburetor ....Holley 4160 - Four Barre
Brake Horsepower 270   Code   F

8 Cyl. (290 cu. In.)

Type ....90^ V-8 O.H.V.
No. of Cylinders 8
Displacement ....290 Cu. In.
Compressions Ratio 2BC-9.7:1
..........................4BC-10.0:1
Brake Horsepower ....2BC-200   Code   H
..........................4BC-225   Code   H

Vehicle Identification Number

B7KS52B100551

Stamped and embossed on a stainless steel plate welded to the right front fender under the hood. It consists of Manufacturer's symbol, Model year symbol, Transmission type symbol, Body identity symbol, Class of body symbol, Series and Engine identity symbol, and a sequential Production number for each series.

THE FIRST DIGIT : Identifies the car line.

American 6 .... B
Rambler 6 C
Ambassador 8 .... H

THE SECOND DIGIT:Year-"7" for 1967.

THE THIRD DIGIT : Plant of Manufacture "K" for Kenosha, "B" for Brampton Ontario.

THE FOURTH DIGIT : Transmission Type.

Standard Collumn Shift .... S
(3 speed)
Overdrive Column Shift .... O
(3 speed)
Automatic Collumn Shift .... A
(3 speed)
Floor Shift Automatic C
(3 speed)
Four Speed Floor Shift .... F
Four Speed Floor Shif .... M
Floor Mounted

THE FIFTH DIGIT : Body Type.
4-Dr. Sedan 5
2-Dr. Sedan 6
2-Dr. Convertible 7
4-Dr. Wagon 8
2-Dr. Hardtop 9

THE SIXTH DIGIT : Model.

550/220 0
880 2
440/770/990 5
Rebel,Marlin, DPL, Rogue 7

THE SEVENTH DIGIT : Series and Engine.

AMERICAN

199 CID, OHV 6, 1-BC .... A
232 CID, OHV 6, 2-BC .... B
290 CID, V-8, 2-BC C
290 CID, V-8,4-BC .... D
232 CID, OHV 6, 1-BC .... E
343 CID, V-8, 4-BC X

AMBASSADOR

232 CID, OHV 6, 2-BC .... M
287 CID, V-8, 2-BC .... N
327 CID, V-8, 2-BC (L. Cp.) ..... P
327 CID, V-8, 4-BC (H.C.) .... Q

REBEL

232 CID, OHV 6, 1-BC .... F
232 CID, OHV 6, 2-BC .... G
290 CID, V-8, 2-BC .... H
343 CID, V-8, 2-BC .... J
343 CID, V-8, 2-BC .... K

MARLIN

232 CID, OHV 6, 2-BC .... S
287 CID, V8, 2-BC .... T
327 CID, V8, 4-BC (H.C.) .... U
232 CID, OHV 6, 1-BC V
327 CID, V-8, 2-BC (L.C.) .... W

LAST SIX DIGITS: Production sequence number.

BODY NUMBER PLATE

A unit body number plate rivited to the left front door below the door lock and is visible when the door is open.

This body plate includes the model, body, trim, paint code, and car built sequence numbers.

The model number identifies the body style. This number when followed by numbers 2, 5, or 7 denotes different groups of optional appointments built into the car as origional equiptment.

RAMBLER ADVANCED UNIT CONSTRUCTION

THIS RAMBLER IS BUILT WITH AN ADVANCED METHOD OF COMBINING BODY AND FRAME INTO A SINGLE ALL-WELDED STRUCTURAL UNIT. FEATURING ONE-PEICE UNISIDE PANELS. GALVINIZED STEEL PLUS DEEP -DIP PRIMER PAND AND BAKED ENAMEL ASSURE BODY RUST PROTECTION. PIONEERED AND BUILT EXCLUSIVELY BY

AMERICAN MOTORS CORP.
BODY NO.   000024
MODEL NO.   6788-5
TRIM NO.   799C
PAINT NO.   36A
      W000032

AMERICAN

-Dr. Sedan-D	6705
-Dr. Sedan-C	6705-5
-Dr. Sport Sedan-D	6706
-Dr. Sport Sedan-C	6706-5
-Dr. Convertible-C	6707-7
-Dr. Station Wagon-D	6708
-Dr. Station Wagon-C	6708-5
-Dr. Hardtop-S	6709-5
-Dr. Hardtop-C	6709-7

RAMBLER REBEL

-Dr. Sedan-D	6715
-Dr. Sedan-C	6715-5
-Dr. Sport Sedan-D	6716
-Dr. Convertible-C	6717-7
-Dr. Station Wagon-D	6718
-Dr. Station Wagon-C	6718-5
-Dr. Hardtop-S	6719-5
-Dr. Hardtop-C	6719-7

RAMBLER AMBASSADOR

-Dr. Sedan-S	6785-2
-Dr. Sedan-C	6785-5
-Dr. Sport Sedan-S	6786-2
-Dr. Convertible-C	6787-7
-Dr. Station Wagon-S	6788-2
-Dr. Station Wagon-C	6788-5
-Dr. Hardtop-S	6789-5
-Dr. Hardtop-C	6789-7

MARLIN

-Dr. Hardtop-C	6759-7

THE PAINT CODE furnishes the key to the paint colors used on the car. A two number code indicated the color of the car. A two-toned car has two sets of numbers. First number is body color, second is the roof.

COLOR	Code
Classic Black	1
Frost White	72
Apollo Yellow	25
Lt. Strato Blue(Metallic)	31
Med.Barbados Blue (Metallic)	32
Dk.Royale Blue(Metallic)	33
Med. Granada Green (Metallic)	18
Lt. Alameda Aqua	34
Med. Marina Aqua(Metallic)	8
Lt. Yuma Tan(Metallic)	36
Med. Sungold(Metallic)	37
Med. Stallion Brown (Metallic)	38
Matador Red	39
Lt. Strato Blue(Metallic)	31-33
Dk. Royale Blue(Metallic)	33-31
Lt. Alameda Aqua	34-8
Med. Marina Aqua (Metallic)	8-34
Lt. Yuma Tan(Metallic)	36-38

Dk. Stallion Brown (Metallic)	38-36
Classic Black	1-72
Frost White	
Apollo Yellow	25-1
Classic Black	
Lt. Strato Blue(Metallic)	31-72
Frost White	
Med. Barbados Blue (Metallic) Frost White	32-72
Med. Barbados Blue (Metallic) Dk. Royale Blue (Metallic)	32-33
Med. Granada Green (Metallic) Frost White	18-72
Med. Marina Aqua (Metallic) Frost White	8-72
Lt. Yuma Tan (Metallic) Frost White	36-72
Med. Sungold (Metallic) Frost White	37-72
Med. Sungold (Metallic) Classic Black	37-1
Matador Red Frost White	39-72

ENGINE ID

V8 - The engine number is located on a tag which is attached to the alternator mounting bracket.

Letter	Bore	Comp.Rat.
H	290 Cu. In.	V8 (L/C)
N	290 Cu. In.	V8
S	343 Cu. In.	V8 (L/C)
Z	343 Cu. In.	V8

6 Cyl. - Code number located on boss adjacent to distributor.

Letter	Bore	Comp. Rat.
J	199 Cu. In.	Six
P	199 Cu. In.	Six (L/C)
L	232 Cu. In.	Six
M	232 Cu. In.	Six (L/C)

The engines are marked with a code identifing: year, month, engine letter code, and day of manufacture.

EXAMPLE	9	2	A	24
	1967	month	code	day

These engines are marked with a three letter code, stamped below the engine code number. The letters are decoded as follows:

First Letter	Size of the Bore
Letter "A"	Standard
Second Letter	Size of the main Bearings
Letter "B"	.010" Undersize
Third Letter	Size of the Connecting Rod Bearings
Letter "C"	.010" Oversize

ENGINE SPECIFICATIONS

6 Cyl. - Overhead Valve (232 cu. in.)

Type	Valve-in-Head
No. of Cylinders	6
Displacement	232 Cu. In.
Compressions Ratio	8.5:1
Brake Horsepower	
	145
	155

6 Cyl. - Overhead Valve(199 cu. in.)

Type	Valve-in-Head
No. of Cylinders	6
Displacement	199 Cu. In.
Compressions Ratio	8.5:1
Brake Horsepower	128

8 Cyl. (290 cu. in.)

Type	90^ V-8 O.H.V.
No. of Cylinders	8
Displacement	290 Cu. In.
Compressions Ratio	2 BC - 9.0:1
	4 BC - 10.0:1
Brake Horsepower	
	2 BC - 200
	4 BC - 235

8 Cyl. (343 cu. in.)

Type	90^ V-8 O.H.V.
No. of Cylinders	8
Displacement	343 Cu. In.
Compressions Ratio	4 BC - 10.2:1
Brake Horsepower	280

THE TRIM NUMBER furnishes the key to trim color and material for each model SERIES.

MODEL	SEAT UPHOLSTERY	FLOOR COVERING	INSTRUMENT PANEL	HEADLINING
220	T723.......C & B	Black	Dk. Blue	White
	T728.......C & B	Black	Black	White
	T729.......C & B	Black	Dk. Tan	White
440 or ROGUE	T741.......B,D & E	Black	Black	White
	T743.......B,C,D & E	Dk. Blue	Dk. Blue	White
	T744.......C	Dk. Green	Dk. Green	White
	T745.......B,C,D & E	Red	Red	White
	T747.......C	Med. Aqua	Dk. Aqua	White
	T748.......B & E	Black	Black	White
	T749.......B,C,D & E	Med. Tan	Dk. Tan	White
550	T753.......B & C	Black	Dk. Blue	Lt. Blue
	T753.......B & C	Black	Black	White
	T753.......B & C	Black	Dk. Tan	Lt. Tan
770, SST or SST Custom	T771.......B,C,D,E & W	Black	Black	White(A)
	T773.......B,C,D,E & W	Dk. Blue	Dk. Blue	Lt. Blue
	T774.......C	Dk. Green	Dk. Green	Lt. Green
	T775.......B,D,E & W	Red	Red	White(B)
	T776.......B,C,D,E & W	Dk. Burgandy	Dk. Burgandy	Lt. Burgandy
	T777.......C	Aqua	Dk. Aqua	Lt. Aqua
	T778.......B & E	Black	Black	White
	T779.......B,C,D,E & W	Dk. Tan	Dk. Tan	Lt. Tan
880	T781.......B & C	Black	Black	White
	T783.......B & C	Dk. Blue	Dk. Blue	Lt. Blue
	T787.......C	Dk. Aqua	Dk. Aqua	Lt. Aqua
	T789.......B & C	Dk. Tan	Dk. Tan	Lt. Tan
990, DPL or DPL Custom	T791.......B,C,E,K,L & W	Black	Black	White(A)
	T793.......B,C,E,K,L & W	Dk. Blue	Dk. Blue	Lt. Blue
	T794.......C	Dk. Green	Dk. Green	Lt. Green
	T795.......B,E,K,L & W	Red	Red	White(B)
	T796.......B,C,E,K,L & W	Dk. Burgandy	Dk. Burgandy	Lt. Burgandy
	T797.......C	Dk. Aqua	Dk. Aqua	Lt. Aqua
	T798.......B,L & E	Black	Black	White
	T799.......B,C,E,K,L & W	Dk. Tan	Dk. Tan	Lt. Tan
Marlin	T791.......B,C,K & L	Black	Black	Black
	T793.......B,C,K & L	Dk. Blue	Dk. Blue	Blue
	T795.......C,K & L	Red	Red	Red
	T799.......B,C,K & L	Dk. Tan	Dk. Tan	Tan

NOTES: (A)   Black Headlining on SST Hardtop with T771 Trims
              Black Headlining on DPL Hardtop with T791 Trims
      (B)   Red Headlining on SST Hardtop with T775 Trims
              Red Headlining on DPL Hardtop with T795 Trims

B.............Opt. All Vinyl
C.............Std. Fabric
D.............Fabric for Buckets
E.............Vinyl for Buckets
W............Fabric for Buckets
K.............Fabric for Buckets (LaScala pattern)
L.............Vinyl for Buckets (Tahiti pattern)

Vehicle Identification Number

A8SO50A100551

Stamped and embossed on a stainless steel plate welded to the right front fender under the hood. It consists of Manufacturer's symbol, Model year symbol, Transmission type symbol, Body identity symbol, Class of body symbol, Series and Engine identity symbol, and a sequential Production number for each series.

THE FIRST DIGIT : MAKE: "A" For American Motors Corp.

THE SECOND DIGIT: Year-"8" for 1968.

THE THIRD DIGIT : Transmission Type.

Standard Collumn Shift .... S (3 speed)
Overdrive Column Shift .... O (3 speed)
Automatic Collumn Shift .... A (3 speed)
Floor Shift Automatic .... C (3 speed)
Four Speed Floor Shift .... F
Four Speed Floor Shif .... M
Floor Mounted

THE FOURTH DIGIT : Series.

American .... 'O'
Rebel .... '1'
AMX .... '3'
Javelin .... '7'
Ambassador .... '8'

THE FIFTH DIGIT : Body Type.

4-Dr. Sedan 5
2-Dr. Sedan 6
2-Dr. Convertible 7
4-Dr. Wagon 8
2-Dr. Hardtop 9

THE SIXTH DIGIT : Body Class.

550/220 0
880 2
440/770/990 5
Rebel, Marlin, DPL, Rogue 7

THE SEVENTH DIGIT : Engine.

199 CID, OHV SIX, 1-BC .... A
232 CID, OHV SIX, 1-BC .... B
232 CID, OHV SIX, 2-BC C
290 CID, V-8, 2-BC .... M
290 CID, V-8, 4-BC .... N
343 CID, V-8, 2-BC .... S
343 CID, V-8, 4-BC .... T
390 CID, V-8, 2-BC .... W
390 CID, V-8, 4-BC X

LAST SIX DIGITS: Production sequence number.

BODY NUMBER PLATE

A unit body number plate rivited to the left front door below the door lock and is visible when door is open. This body plate includes the model, body, trim, paint code, and car built sequence numbers. The model number identifies the body style. This number when followed by numbers 2, 5, or 7 denotes different groups of optional appointments built into the car as origional equiptment.

```
RAMBLER ADVANCED UNIT
      CONSTRUCTION

THIS RAMBLER IS BUILT
WITH AN ADVANCED METHOD
OF COMBINING BODY AND
FRAME INTO A SINGLE ALL-
WELDED STRUCTURAL UNIT.
FEATURING ONE-PEICE
UNISIDE PANELS. GALVINIZED
STEEL PLUS DEEP -DIP
PRIMER PAND AND BAKED
ENAMEL ASSURE BODY RUST
PROTECTION. PIONEERED
AND BUILT EXCLUSIVELY BY

AMERICAN MOTORS CORP.
BODY NO.      W000019
MODEL NO.     6885-5
TRIM NO.      894C
PAINT NO.     46A-72A
      W0000192
```

MERICAN

Dr. Sedan-D	6805
Dr. Sedan-C....................	6805-5
Dr. Sport Sedan-D..........	6806
Dr. Station Wagon-S	6808-5
Dr. Hardtop-C	6809-7

AMBLER REBEL

Dr. Sedan-D	6815
Dr. Sedan-C	6815-5
Dr. Convertible-D	6817
Dr. Convertible-C	6817-7
Dr. Station Wagon-D	6818
Dr. Station Wagon-C	6818-5
Dr. Hardtop-D	6819
Dr. Hardtop-S	6819-5
Dr. Hardtop-C	6819-7

AMBLER AMBASSADOR

Dr. Sedan-S	6885-2
Dr. Sedan-C	6885-5
Dr. Sedan-C	6885-5
Dr. Station Wagon-C	6888-5
Dr. Hardtop-S	6889-2
Dr. Hardtop-C	6889-5
Dr. Hardtop-C	6889-7

AVELIN

Dr. Hardtop-S	6859-5
Dr. Hardtop-C	6859-7

MX

Dr. Sport Coupe.............	6839-7

HE PAINT CODE furnishes the
y to the paint colors used on the
r. A two number code indicated
e color of the car. A two-toned car
s two sets of numbers. First
mber is body color, second is the
f.

OLOR	Code
assic Black	P1A
atador Red	P39A
Saturn Blue (Metallic)	P43A
ed. Caravelle Blue	P44A
etallic)	
azer Blue (Metallic)	P45A
Laurel Green	P46A
etallic)	
Rally Green	P47A
etallic)	
ed. Tahiti Turquoise	P48A
etallic)	
Lanedo Tan	P49A
etallic)	
Calcutta Russet	P50A
etallic)	
arrab Gold (Metallic)	P52A
Turbo Silver	P54A
etallic)	
leah Yellow	P58A
st White	P72A

ENGINE ID

V8 - The engine number is located on a tag which is attached to the alternator mounting bracket.

The letter contained in the code number denotes the size of the cylinder bore and also the compression rate.

Letter	Bore	Comp. Rat.
H	290 Cu. In.	V8 (L/C)
N	290 Cu. In.	V8
S	343 Cu. In.	V8 (L/C)
Z	343 Cu. In.	V8
W	390 Cu. In.	V8

6 Cyl. - Code number located on panel adjacent to distributor.

Letter	Bore	Comp. Rat.
J	199 Cu. In.	Six
P	199 Cu. In.	Six (L/C)
L	232 Cu. In.	Six
M	232 Cu. In.	Six (L/C)

The engines are marked with a code identifing: year, month, engine letter code, and day of manufacture.

EXAMPLE	10	2	A	24
	1968	month	code	day

These engines are marked with a three letter code, stamped below the engine code number. The letters are decoded as follows:

First Letter .... Size of the Bore
.... Letter "A" Standard
Second Letter .... Size of the main Bearings
.... Letter "B" .010" Undersize
Third Letter .... Size of the Connecting Rod Bearings
.... Letter "C" .010" Oversize

ENGINE SPECIFICATIONS

6 Cyl. - Overhead Valve (232 cu. in.)

Type	Valve-in-Head
No. of Cylinders	6
Displacement	232 Cu. In.
Compressions Ratio	8.5:1
Brake Horsepower	145
....	155

6 Cyl. - Overhead Valve (199 cu. in.)

Type	Valve-in-Head
No. of Cylinders	6
Displacement	199 Cu. In.
Compressions Ratio	8.5:1
Brake Horsepower	128

8 Cyl. (290 cu. in.)

Type	90^ V-8 O.H.V.
No. of Cylinders	8
Displacement	290 Cu. In.
Compressions Ratio	2 BC - 9.0:1
....	4 BC - 10.0:1
Brake Horsepower	2 BC - 200
....	4 BC - 225

8 Cyl. (343 cu. in.)

Type	90^ V-8 O.H.V.
No. of Cylinders	8
Displacement	343 Cu. In.
Compressions Ratio	2 BC - 9.0:1
....	4 BC - 10.2:1
Brake Horsepower	2 BC - 235
....	4 BC - 280

8 Cyl. (390 cu. in.)

Type	90^ V-8 O.H.V.
No. of Cylinders	8
Displacement	390 Cu. In.
Compressions Ratio	4V, 10.2:1
Brake Horsepower	315 @ 4600 RPM
....	425 @ 3200 RPM

THE TRIM NUMBER furnishes the key to trim color and material for each model SERIES.

MODEL	CODE	COLOR
American	T828C	Gray / White
	T828B	Black / White
440	T843C&B	Blue
Rogue	T844C&B	Green
	T845C&B	Red
	T848C&B	Black / White
AMX	T831A	Black
	T832A	Tan
	T835A	Red
Javelin	T831J	Black
	T838J	Black / White
Javelin SST	T831D&E	Black
	T832D&E	Tan
	T835D&E	Red
Rebel 550	T851C&V	Black
	T853C&V	Blue
	T855C&V	Red
Rebel 770	T871C&V	Black
	T873C&V	Blue
	T874C&V	Green
	T876C&V	Gold
	T879C	Rosset
Rebel SST	T871W,K&E	Black
	T873W,K&E	Blue
	T874W,K&E	Green
	T876W,K&E	Gold
	T879W,K&E	Russet
Ambassador	T881C&V	Black
	T883C&V	Blue
	T885C&V	Red
Ambassador DPL	T891C&V	Black
	T893C&V	Blue
	T894C&V	Green
	T896C&V	Gold
	T899C&V	Russet
Ambassador SST	T891W,K&E	Black
	T893W,K&E	Blue
	T894W,K&E	Green
	T896W,K&E	Gold
	T899W,K&E	Russet

A- Vinyl (ventilair)
B- Option (all vinyl)
C- Standard Fabric
D- Fabric (strata-stripe)
E- Vinyl (ventilair)
J- Vinyl
K- Vinyl
W- Fabric

Vehicle Identification Number

A9S050A100551

Stamped and embossed on a stainless steel plate welded to the right front fender under the hood. It consists of Manufacturer's symbol, Model year symbol, Transmission type symbol, Body identity symbol, Class of body symbol, Series and Engine identity symbol, and a sequential Production number for each series.

THE FIRST DIGIT : MAKE "A" For American Motors Corp.

THE SECOND DIGIT : Year "9" for 1969.

THE THIRD DIGIT : Transmission Type.

Standard Column Shift .... S
(3 speed)
Overdrive Column Shift .... O
(3 speed)
Automatic Column Shift .... A
(3 speed)
Floor Shift Automatic C
(3 speed)
Four Speed Floor Shif .... M
Floor Mounted

THE FOURTH DIGIT: SERIES.

American .... 'O'
Rebel .... '1'
AMX .... '3'
Javelin .... '7'
Ambassador .... '8'

THE FIFTH DIGIT : Body Type.

4-Dr. Sedan 5
2-Dr. Sedan 6
4-Dr. Wagon 8
2-Dr. Hardtop 9

THE SIXTH DIGIT : Body Class.

550/220 0
880 2
440/770/990 5
Rebel, Marlin, DPL, Rogue 7

THE SEVENTH DIGIT : Engine.

199 CID, OHV SIX, 1-BC .... A
232 CID, OHV SIX, 1-BC .... B
232 CID, OHV SIX, 2-BC C
290 CID, V-8, 2-BC .... M
290 CID, V-8, 4-BC .... N
343 CID, V-8, 2-BC .... S
343 CID, V-8, 4-BC .... T
390 CID, V-8, 2-BC .... W
390 CID, V-8, 4-BC X

LAST SIX DIGITS: Production sequence number.

BODY NUMBER PLATE

A unit body number plate rivited to the left front door below the door lock and is visible when door is open. This body plate includes the model, body, trim, paint code, and car built sequence numbers. The model number identifies the body style. This number when followed by numbers 2, 5, or 7 denotes different groups of optional appointments built into the car as origional equiptment.

RAMBLER ADVANCED UNIT CONSTRUCTION

THIS RAMBLER IS BUILT WITH AN ADVANCED METHOD OF COMBINING BODY AND FRAME INTO A SINGLE ALL-WELDED STRUCTURAL UNIT. FEATURING ONE-PEICE UNISIDE PANELS. GALVINIZED STEEL PLUS DEEP -DIP PRIMER PAND AND BAKED ENAMEL ASSURE BODY RUST PROTECTION. PIONEERED AND BUILT EXCLUSIVELY BY

AMERICAN MOTORS CORP.
BODY NO.   000006
MODEL NO.   6906
TRIM NO.   928-A
PAINT NO.   77A-72A
      E000009

MERICAN

Dr. Sedan-D	6905
Dr. Sedan-C	6905-5
Dr. Sport Sedan-D	6906
Dr. Station Wagon-C	6908-5
Dr. Hardtop-C	6909-7

AMBLER REBEL

Dr. Sedan-D	6915
Dr. Sedan-C	6915-7
Dr. Station Wagon-D	6918
Dr. Station Wagon-C	6918-7
Dr. Hardtop-D	6919
Dr. Hardtop-C	6919-7

AMBLER AMBASSADOR

Dr. Sedan-D	6985-2
Dr. Sedan-S	6985-5
Dr. Sedan-C	6985-7
Dr. Station Wagon-S	6988-5
Dr. Station Wagon-C	6988-7
Dr. Hardtop-D	6989-2
Dr. Hardtop-S	6989-5
Dr. Hardtop-C	6989-7

VELIN

Dr. Hardtop-D	6979-5
Dr. Hardtop-C	6979-7

MX

Dr. Sports Coupe-C	6939-7

E PAINT CODE furnishes the
to the paint colors used on the
. A two number code indicated
color of the car. A two-toned car
two sets of numbers. First
nber is body color, second is the
f.

LOR	Code
ssic Black	P1A
d. Marina Aqua	P8A
tallic)	
d. Granada Green	P18A
tallic)	
llo Yellow	P25A
Strato Blue	P31A
tallic)	
d. Barbados Blue	P32A
tallic)	
Royal Blue	P33A
tallic)	
Alameda Aqua	P334A
Yuma Tan	P36A
tallic)	
d. Sungold (Metallic)	P37A
Stallion Brown	P38A
ador Red	P39A
Flamingo Burgandy	P40A
tallic)	
Rajah Burgandy	P41A
tallic)	
eah Yellow	P58A
Green (Metallic)	P59A
st White	P72A

ENGINE ID

V8 - The engine number is located on a tag which is attached to the alternator mounting bracket.

The letter contained in the code number denotes the size of the cylinder bore and also the compression rate.

Letter	Bore	Comp. Rat.
H	290 Cu. In.	V8 (L/C)
N	290 Cu. In.	V8
S	343 Cu. In.	V8 (L/C)
Z	343 Cu. In.	V8
W	390 Cu. In.	V8

6 Cyl. - Code number located on panel adjacent to distributor.

Letter	Bore	Comp. Rat.
J	199 Cu. In.	Six
P	199 Cu. In.	Six (L/C)
L	232 Cu. In.	Six
M	232 Cu. In.	Six (L/C)

The engines are marked with a code identifing: year, month, engine letter code, and day of manufacture.

EXAMPLE	11	2	A	24
	1969	month	code	day

These engines are marked with a three letter code, stamped below the engine code number. The letters are decoded as follows:

First Letter	Size of the Bore
....	Letter "A" Standard
Second Letter	Size of the main Bearings
....	Letter "B" .010" Undersize
Third Letter	Size of the Connecting Rod Bearings
....	Letter "C" .010" Oversize

ENGINE SPECIFICATIONS

6 Cyl. - Overhead Valve (232 cu. in.)

Type	Valve-in-Head
No. of Cylinders	6
Displacement	232 Cu. In.
Compressions Ratio	8.5:1
Brake Horsepower	145
	155 (w/2BC)

6 Cyl. - Overhead Valve (199 cu. in.)

Type	Valve-in-Head
No. of Cylinders	6
Displacement	199 Cu. In.
Compressions Ratio	8.5:1
Brake Horsepower	128

8 Cyl. (290 cu. in.)

Type	90^ V-8 O.H.V.
No. of Cylinders	8
Displacement	290 Cu. In.
Compressions Ratio	2 BC - 9.0:1
	4 BC - 10.0:1
Brake Horsepower	2 BC - 200
	4 BC - 225

8 Cyl. (343 cu. in.)

Type	90^ V-8 O.H.V.
No. of Cylinders	8
Displacement	343 Cu. In.
Compressions Ratio	2 BC - 9.0:1
	4 BC - 10.2:1
Brake Horsepower	2 BC - 235
	4 BC - 280

8 Cyl. (390 cu. in.)

Type	90^ V-8 O.H.V.
No. of Cylinders	8
Displacement	390 Cu. In.
Compressions Ratio	4V, 10.2:1
Brake Horsepower	315 @ 4600 RPM
	425 @ 3200 RPM

THE TRIM NUMBER furnishes the key to trim color and material for each model SERIES.

Model	Code	Seat Upholstery	Door Panels	Instrument Panel	Floor	Headlining
AMX	931	Charcoal	Charcoal	Charcoal Metallic	Black	Charcoal
	932	Platinum	Platinum	Charcoal Metallic	Black	Charcoal
	935	Red	Red	Red	Red	Red
	936	Saddle	Saddle	Brown Metallic	Brown	Saddle
Javelin	961	Charcoal	Charcoal	Charcoal Metallic	Black	Charcoal
	968	Parchment	Parchment	Charcoal Metallic	Black	Charcoal
Javelin SST	961	Charcoal	Charcol	Charcoal Metallic	Black	Charcoal
	962	Platinum	Platinum	Charcoal Metallic	Black	Charcoal
	963	Blue	Blue	Med. Blue Metallic	Med. Blue	Blue
	965	Red	Red	Red	Red	Red
	966	Beige	Beige	Brown Metallic	Brown	Saddle
Rambler	923	Blue	Blue	Med. Blue Metallic	Black	Parchment
	928	Parchment	Parchment	Charcoal Metallic	Black	Parchment
Rambler 440	941	Charcoal	Charcoal	Charcoal Metallic	Black	Parchment
	943	Blue	Blue	Med. Blue Metallic	Med. Blue	Parchment
	944	Green	Green	Med. Green Metallic	Med. Green	Parchment
	945	Red	Red	Red	Red	Parchment
Rambler Rogue	941	Charcoal	Charcoal	Charcoal Metallic	Black	Parchment
	943	Blue	Blue	Med. Blue Metallic	Med. Blue	Parchment
	944	Green	Green	Med. Green Metallic	Med. Green	Parchment
	945	Red	Red	Red	Red	Parchment
Rebel	951	Charcoal	Charcoal	Charcoal Metallic	Black	Platinum
	953	Blue	Blue	Med. Blue Metallic	Blue	Med. Blue
	956	Beige or Brown	Beige	Brown Metallic	Brown	Beige
	957	Avocado	Avocado	Med. Avocado Metallic	Med. Avocado	Med. Avocado
Rebel SST	972	Platinum	Platinum	Charcoal Metallic	Black	Platinum
	973	Blue	Blue	Med. Blue Metallic	Med. Blue	Med. Blue
	975	Red	Red	Red	Red	Red
	976	Brown or Beige	Brown or Beige	Brown Metallic	Brown	Beige
	977	Avocado	Avocado	Med. Avocado Metallic	Med. Avocado	Med. Avocado
	979	Yellow	Yellow	Med. Avocado Metallic	Med. Avocado	Med. Avocado
Ambassador	981	Charcoal	Charcoal	Charcoal Metallic	Black	Platinum
	983	Blue	Blue	Med. Blue Metallic	Med. Blue	Med. Blue
	986	Beige or Brown	Brown	Brown Metallic	Brown	Beige
	987	Avocado	Avocado	Med. Avocado Metallic	Med. Avocado	Med. Avocado
Ambassador DPL	991	Charcoal	Charcoal	Charcoal Metallic	Charcoal	Platinum
	993	Blue	Med. Blue	Med. Blue Metallic	Med. Blue	Med. Blue
	995	Red	Red	Red	Red	Red
	996	Beige or Brown	Beige or Brown	Brown Metallic	Brown	Beige
	997	Avocado	Avocado	Med. Avocado Metallic	Med. Avocado	Med. Avocado
Ambassador SST	991	Charcoal	Charcoal Met.	Charcoal Metallic	Black	Platinum
	992	Platinum	Platinum Met.	Charcoal Metallic	Black	Platinum
	993	Blue	Blue	Med. Blue Metallic	Med. Blue	Med. Blue
	995	Red	Red	Red	Red	Red
	996	Beige or Brown	Beige	Brown Metallic	Brown	Beige
	997	Avocado	Avocado	Med. Avocado Metallic	Med. Avocado	Med. Avocado
	999	Yellow	Yellow	Med. Avocado Metallic	Med. Avocado	Med. Avocado

VEHICLE IDENTIFICATION NUMBER

```
BUICK
4G1101555
```

Commonly referred to as the VIN NUMBER, this series of numbers and letters is stamped on a plate attached to left front door hinge pillar. Also on the top surface of engine block forward of valve cover on left side.

EXAMPLE

4	G	1	101555
Series	Year	Assy Plant	Production Number

FIRST DIGIT: Identifies the SERIES: 4 for 4400 (leSabre), 6 for 4600 (Invicta), 7 fof 4700 (Electra), and 8 for 4800 (Electra 225).

SECOND DIGIT: Identifies the YEAR, G for 1960.

THIRD DIGIT: Identifies the Assembly Plant.

ASSEMBLY PLANT	CODE
Flint	1
South Gate	2
Linden	3
Kansas City, Kansas	4
Wilmington, De	5
Atlanta, Ga	6
Framingham	7
Arlington	8

LAST 6 DIGITS: Represent the Basic Production Numbers.

FISHER BODY NUMBER PLATE

Complete identification of each body is provided by a plate riveted to the cowl at the left of center under the hood.

THE STYLE NUMBER is a combination of the year, division, series, and body style. In the number plate illustrated, 60 represents the model year 1960; the first digit 4 indicates Buick Motor Division. The second digit "7" indicates Series 4700; 19 indicates the 4-Door Sedan body style. An "X" following the body style indicates that the body is equipped with electric power assists.

LESABRE 4400	CODE
2-Door Sedan	4411
4-Door 2-Seat Estate Wagon	4435
2-Door Hardtop	4437
4-Door Hardtop	4439
4-Door 3-Seat Estate Wagon	4445
2-Door Convertible	4467
4-Door Sedan	4419

INVICTA 4600	CODE
4-Door, 6 Window Thin Pillar	4619
4-Door (6 Passenger) Estate Wagon	4635
2-Door Hardtop Coupe	4637
4-Door, 4 Window Hardtop Sedan	4639
4-Door (3 Seats) Estate Wagon	4645
2-Door Convertible Coupe	4667

ELECTRA 4700	CODE
4-Door Sedan	4719
2-Door Hardtop Coupe	4737
4-Door Hardtop Sedan	4739

ELECTRA "225" 4800	CODE
4-Door Riviera Sedan	4829
4-Door Hardtop Sedan	4839
2-Door Convertible Coupe	4867

THE BODY NUMBER is the production serial number of the body. The prefix letter denotes the plant in which the body was built. FB indicates the Flint plant.

```
STYLE 60 4719
BODY FB 3321

BUICK DIV. GENERAL MOTORS FLINT MICH.

TRIM 001      PAINT A      ACC. BFGIU

BODY BY FISHER
```

ASSEMBLY PLANT	CODE
Flint, Mich	FB
South Gate, Calif	BC
Linden	BL
Kansas City, Kan	BK
Wilmington, Del	BW
Atlanta, Ga	BA
Framingham	BF
Arlington	BT

The digits following the plant code reveal the production sequence number within the plant.

THE PAINT CODE furnishes the key to the paint colors used on the car. A two letter code indicates the bottom and top colors respectively.

COLOR	CODE
Sable Black	A
Gull Gray	B
Arctic White	C
Silver Mist	D
Chalet Blue	H
Lucerne Green	K
Titian Red	L
Casino Cream	M
Cordaveen	N
Pearl Fawn	P
Tahiti Beige	R
Turquoise	T
Tampico Red	V
Midnight Blue	W
Verde Green	X

THE TRIM NUMBER furnishes the key to trim color and material for each model SERIES.

Green Cordaveen	40
Green & Black Pattern Cloth	40
Green Cordaveen	40
Blue Cordaveen	41
Blue & Black Pattern Cloth	41
Blue Cordaveen	41
Grey Cordaveen	42
Grey & Black Pattern Cloth	42
Grey Cordaveen	42
Fawn Cordaveen	43
Fawn & Black Pattern Cloth	43
Fawn Cordaveen	43
Maroon Cordaveen	44
Red Cordaveen	46
Red & Black Pattern Cloth	47
Green Cordaveen	60
Green & Black Pattern Cloth	60
Green Pattern Cloth	60
Green & Black Pattern Cloth	60
Blue Cordaveen	61
Blue & Black Pattern Cloth	61
Blue Pattern Cloth	61
Blue & Black Pattern Cloth	61
Blue Leather	61
Blue Leather	61
Grey Cordaveen	62
Grey & Black Pattern Cloth	62
Grey Pattern Cloth	62
Grey Cordaveen	62
Gray & Black Pattern Cloth	62
Fawn Cordaveen	63
Fawn & Black Pattern Cloth	63
Fawn Pattern Cloth	63
Fawn & Black Pattern Cloth	63

ENGINE NUMBER

Along with the VIN number the engine block is stamped with an engine production code. The code is a series of letters that identify the engine and a numeric production date code. The production code is stamped on the right side of the engine block. The production prefix code for 1960 is:

A 8.5:1 and 10.25:1 comp. ratio 364 cid.

G 9.0:1 comp. ratio 364 cid.

K: 401 cid.

A-inch dash "-" following code indicates .010" oversize cylinder bore.

ENGINES

Series	Trans.	CID	Use	Comp.	Carb.	HP
4400	(1)	364	Premium	10.25:1	2-bbl	250
4400	(1)	364	Regular	9.0:1	2-bbl	235
4400	(1)	364	Premium	10.25:1	4-bbl	300
4400	(2)	364	Regular	8.5:1	2-bbl	210
**	(1)	401	Premium	10.25:1	4-bbl	325

**   4600, 4700, 4800 Series
(1)   Twin Turbine Transmission
(2)   Synchromesh Transmission

VEHICLE IDENTIFICATION NUMBER

```
BUICK
4H1001555
```

Commonly referred to as the VIN NUMBER, this series of numbers and letters is stamped on a plate attached to left front door hinge pillar. 4000, 4100, 4300 SERIES is stamped on left dash to frame brace . Also stamped on the top surface of the engine block forward of valve cover on left side.

EXAMPLE

4	H	1	001555
Series	Year	Assy	Production
		Plant Number	

FIRST DIGIT: Identifies the SE-RIES, 0 for 4000 (Special), 1 for 4100 (Special Deluxe), 3 for 4300 (Skylark), 4 for 4400 (leSabre), 6 for 4600 (Invicta), 7 for 4700 (Electra), and 8 for 4800 (Electra 225).

SECOND DIGIT: Identifies the YEAR, H for 1961.

THIRD DIGIT: Identifies the PLANT.

ASSEMBLY PLANT	CODE
Flint, Mich	1
South Gate, Calif.	2
Linden	3
Kansas City, Kan	4
Wilmington, De.	5
Atlanta, Ga	6
Arlington	8

LAST 6 DIGITS: Represent the BASIC PRODUCTION NUMBERS. Exception: SERIES 4000, 4100, 4300.

* EXCEPTION: 4000, 45100, and 4300 Series Fourth Digit is a number 5. The remaining 5 digits represent the basic production numbers. The 4000, 4100, and 4300 were assembled only in the Flint & South Gate Plants.

FISHER BODY NUMBER PLATE

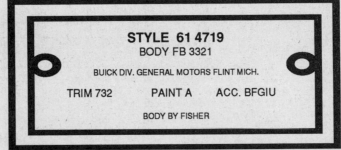

```
STYLE 61 4719
BODY FB 3321

BUICK DIV. GENERAL MOTORS FLINT MICH.

TRIM 732      PAINT A     ACC. BFGIU

BODY BY FISHER
```

Complete identification of each body is provided by a plate riveted to the cowl at the left of center under the hood.

THE STYLE NUMBER is a combination of the year, division, series, and body style. In the number plate illustrated, 61 represents the model year 1961; the first digit 4 indicates Buick Motor Division; the second digit 7 indicates Series 4700; 19 indicates the 4-Door Sedan body style. An X following the body style indicates that the body is equipped with electric power assists.

SPECIAL 4000	CODE
4-Door Sedan	4019
2-Door Sedan	*4027
4-Door 2-Seat Wagon	4035
4-Door 3-Seat Wagon	4045

SPECIAL DELUXE 4100	CODE
4-Door Sedan	4119
4-Door 2-Seat Wagon	4135

SKYLARK 4300	CODE
2-Door Coupe	*4317

LESABRE 4400	CODE
2-Door Sedan	4411
4-Door 2-Seat Estate Wagon	4435
2-Door Hardtop	4437
4-Door Hardtop	4439
4-Door 3-Seat Estate Wagon	4445
2-Door Convertible	4467
4-Door Sedan	4469

INVICTA 4600	CODE
2-Door Hardtop Coupe	4637
4-Door Hardtop Sedan	4639
2-Door Convertible Coupe	4667

ELECTRA 4700	COD□
4-Door Sedan	471
2-Door Hardtop Coupe	473
4-Door Hardtop Sedan	473

ELECTRA "225" 4800	COD□
4-Door Riviera Sedan	483
2-Door Convertible Coupe	48□

* Introduced May 15, 1961

THE BODY NUMBER is the pr□ duction serial number of the bo□ The prefix letter denotes the pla□ in which the body was built. FB □ dicates the Flint plant.

ASSEMBLY PLANT	COD□
Flint, Mich	□
South Gate, Calif	□
Linden	□
Kansas City, Kan	□
Wilmington, Del	□
Atlanta, Ga	□
Arlington	□

The digits following the plant co□ reveal the production sequen□ number within the plant.

THE TRIM NUMBER furnishes the key to trim color and material for each model SERIES. * Denotes Bucket-Type Front Seats.

MODELS	MATERIAL	GREEN	BLUE	GRAY	FAWN	LIGHT SADDLE	TURQUOISE	RED	MAROON	BLACK & RED	BLACK	CREAM
4019	CLOTH & VINYL	001	011	021	031							
4027	CLOTH & VINYL	001	011	021	031							
4035	VINYL	005	015	025	035			065				
4045	VINYL	005	015	025	035			065				
4119	CLOTH & VINYL	101	111	121	131		151				181	
4135	VINYL	105	115	125	135		155	165				
4317	CLOTH & VINYL		113	123	133							
* 4317	CLOTH & VINYL		117	127	137							
4411	CLOTH & VINYL	401	411	421	431						481	
4435	VINYL	405	415		435		455	465				
4435	CLOTH & VINYL	406	416		436		456	466				
* 4435	LEATHER & VINYL					443						
4437	CLOTH & VINYL	401	411	421	431						481	
4439	CLOTH & VINYL	401	411	421	431						481	
4445	VINYL	405	415		435		455	465				
4467	VINYL	400	410		430			460				490
4469	CLOTH & VINYL	401	411	421	431						481	
4637	CLOTH & VINYL	601	611	621	631		651		661			
* 4637	VINYL		617		637				667			
4639	CLOTH & VINYL	601	611	621	631		651		661			
4639	LEATHER & VINYL					643			663		683	
4667	VINYL	600	610		630		650	660				690
4719	CLOTH & VINYL	702	712	722	732		752		762			
4737	CLOTH & VINYL	702	712	722	732		752		762			
4739	CLOTH & VINYL	702	712	722	732		752		762			
4829	CLOTH & VINYL	801	811	821	831		851					
4867	LEATHER & VINYL		810	820	830		850	860				
4867	LEATHER & VINYL		819	829	839			869				

THE PAINT CODE furnishes the key to the paint colors used on the car. A two letter code indicates the bottom and top colors respectively.

PAINT	CODE
Granada Black	A
Artic white	C
Newport Silver	D
Venice Blue	E
Laguna Blue	F
Bimini blue	H
Dublin Blue	J
Kerry Green	K
Rio Red	L
Sun Valley Cream	M
Cordovan	N
Turquoise	P
Phoenix Beige	R
Desert Fawn	T
Tampico Red	V

ENGINE NUMBER

Along with the VIN number the engine block is stamped with an engine production code. The code as a prefix series of letters and numbers that identify the engine and year, then a four digit numeric production sequence code. The production code is stamped on the right front of the engine block opposite the VIN number. When viewed from the front of the engine the number is upside down. The production prefix code for 1961 is:

3H: 10.25:1 comp. ratio 364 cid.
L3H: 9.0:1 comp. ratio 364 cid.
4H: 401 cid.
H: 8.8:1 standard comp. ratio 215 cid.
LH: 8.8:1 low comp. 215 cid.
?: 10.25:1 comp. ratio 215 cid
1/4-inch dash "-" following code indicates .010" oversize cylinder bore.

ENGINES

Series	CID	Comp.	Carb/trans	HP
				155
4000	215	8.8:1 (1)(2)	2-bbl.	
4000	215	8.8:1 (1)	4-bbl.	
4100	215	8.8:1 (1)(2)	2-bbl.	
4100	215	8.8:1 (1)	4-bbl.	185
4300	215	10.25:1 (1)	4-bbl.	235
4400	364	9.0:1(2)	2-bbl./A-T	250
4400	364	10.25:1 (3)	2-bbl./A-T	300
4400	364	10.25:1 (4)	4-bbl./A-T	325
*	401	10.25:1	4-bbl./A-T	325

* 4600, 4700, 4800
S-M .... Synchro-mesh
A-T - Auto Trans .... (1)
Regular Gas Option .... (2)
Std .... (3)
Power Pack .... (4)

VEHICLE IDENTIFICATION NUMBER

BUICK
4I1001555

Commonly referred to as the VIN NUMBER, this series of numbers and letters is stamped on a plate attached to left front door hinge pillar, and stamped on the top surface of the engine block forward of valve cover on left side.

EXAMPLE

4	I	1	001555
Series	Year	Assy Production Plant	Number

FIRST DIGIT: Identifies the SERIES, 0 for 4000 (Special), A for 4000 with V-6, 1 for 4100 (Special Deluxe), 3 for 4300 (Skylark), 4 for 4400 (leSabre), 6 for 4600 (Invicta), and 8 for 4800 (Electra 225).

SECOND DIGIT: Identifies the YEAR, I for 1962.

THIRD DIGIT: Identifies the PLANT.

ASSEMBLY PLANT	CODE
Flint, Mich	1
South Gate, Calif.	2
Linden	3
Kansas City, Kan	4
Wilmington, De.	5
Atlanta, Ga	6
Arlington	8

LAST 6 DIGITS: Represent the basic production numbers.

* EXCEPTION: 4000, 4100, and 4300 Series Fourth Digit is a number 5. The remaining 5 digits represent the basic production numbers. The 4000, 4100, and 4300 were assembled only in the Flint, South Gate, and Kansas City Plants.

FISHER BODY NUMBER PLATE

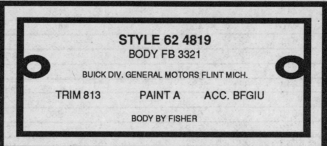

STYLE 62 4819
BODY FB 3321
BUICK DIV. GENERAL MOTORS FLINT MICH.
TRIM 813   PAINT A   ACC. BFGIU
BODY BY FISHER

Complete identification of each body is provided by a plate riveted to the cowl at the left of center under the hood.

THE STYLE NUMBER is a combination of the year, division, series, and body style. In the number plate illustrated, 62 represents the model year 1962; the first digit 4 indicates Buick Motor Division; the second digit 8 indicates Series 4800; 19 indicates the 4-Door Sedan body style. An X following the body style indicates that the body is equipped with electric power assists.

SPECIAL 4000	CODE
4-Door Sedan	4019
2-Door Sedan	4027
4-Door 2-Seat Wagon	4035
4-Door 3-Seat Wagon	4045
2-Door Convertible Coupe	4067

SPECIAL DELUXE 4100	CODE
4-Door Sedan	4119
4-Door 2-Seat Wagon	4135
2-Door Convertible Coupe	4167

SKYLARK 4300	CODE
2-Door Coupe	4347

2-Door Convertible Coupe	4367

LESABRE 4400	CODE
2-Door Sedan	4411
4-Door Hardtop	4439
2-Door Coupe	4447
4-Door Sedan	4469

INVICTA 4600	CODE
4-Door 2-Seat Estate Wagon	4635
4-Door Hardtop Sedan	4639
4-Door 3-Seat Estate Wagon	4645
2-Door Coupe	4647
2-Door Convertible Coupe	4667

ELECTRA "225" 4800	CODE
4-Door Sedan	4819
4-Door Riviera Sedan	4829
4-Door Sedan	4839
2-Door Coupe	4847
2-Door Convertible Coupe	4867

THE BODY NUMBER is the production serial number of the body. The prefix letter denotes the plant in which the body was built. FB indicates the Flint plant.

ASSEMBLY PLANT	CODE
Flint, Mich	FB
South Gate, Calif	BC
Wilmington, Del	BV
Linden	B
Kansas City, Kan	BH
Atlanta, Ga	BA
Arlington	BT

The digits following the plant code reveal the production sequence number within the plant.

THE PAINT CODE furnishes the key to the paint colors used on the car. A two letter code indicates the bottom and top colors respectively.

COLOR	CODE
Regal Black	A
Artic White	C
Silver Cloud	D
Cadet Blue	E
Marlin Blue	F
Glacier Blue	H
Willow Mist	J
Cameo Cream	M
Burgandy	N
Teal Mist	P
Aquamarine	Q
Desert Sand	R
Fawn Mist	T
Cardinal Red	V
Camelot Rose	X

ENGINE NUMBER

Along with the VIN number the engine block is stamped with an engine production code. The code has a prefix series of letters and numbers that identify the engine and year, the a four digit numberic production sequence code on the V-8 engines. The production code is stamped on the right front of the engine block opposite the VIN number. When viewed from the front of the engine the number is upside down. On the V-6 engine the number is on the front of the

THE TRIM NUMBER furnishes the key to trim color and material for each model SERIES. * Denotes Bucket-Type Front Seats.

MODELS	MATERIAL	GREEN	BLUE	SILVER	WHITE	FAWN	GOLD	AQUA	ROSE	RED	BLACK	SADDLE
4019	CLOTH & VINYL	001	011	021	031	031						
4019	VINYL			024								
4027	CLOTH & VINYL	001	011	021		031						
4035	VINYL		015	025		035				075		
4045	VINYL		015	025		035				075		
4067	VINYL		010			030				070		
4067	VINYL									**		
4119	CLOTH & VINYL	101	111	121		131			161			
4135	VINYL	105	115	125		135				175		
4347	CLOTH & VINYL		113	123		133-138	143		163			
4347	VINYL		118		126					178	188	
4367	VINYL		117		127					177	187	197
4411	CLOTH & VINYL		411	421		431						
4411	VINYL										484	
4439	CLOTH & VINYL		411	421		431		451	461			
4447	CLOTH & VINYL		411	421		431		451	461			
4469	CLOTH & VINYL		411	421		431		451	461			
4469	VINYL										484	
4635	VINYL	605	615			635		655		675		
4635	CLOTH & VINYL		616			636				676		
4635	VINYL	603	613			633		653		673		
4639	CLOTH & VINYL		611			631		651	661			
4639	CLOTH & VINYL	602	612	622		632						
4639	LEATHER & VINYL									677	687	697
4645	VINYL	605	615			635		655		675		
4645	VINYL	603	613			633		653		673		
4647	VINYL		618		628	638				678		
4667	VINYL		614			634	644	654	664	674		
4667	VINYL				624	639				679		
4819	CLOTH & VINYL	803	813	823		833						
4829	CLOTH & VINYL	801	811	821		831						
4839	CLOTH & VINYL	802	812	822		832	842		862			
4847	CLOTH & VINYL	803	813	823		833						
4847	LEATHER & VINYL				826					878		898
Code U7 - Power Windows - Required with these Trims												
4867	LEATHER & VINYL		810				840		860	870	880	890
4867	LEATHER & VINYL		819	827						879		899

lock below the left cylinder head
asket. The production prefix code
or 1962 is:

000 Series
8.8:1 comp 198 cid V-6

000, 4100, 4300 Series
9.0:1 std comp 215 cid V-8
7.6:1 Export 215 cid V-8
11.0:1 high comp 215 cid V-8

400 Series
10.25:1 comp 401 cid V-8
9.0:1 comp 401 cid V-8

400, 4600, 4800 Series
10.25:1 comp 401 cid V-8
8.75:1 Export 401 cid V-8

/4-inch dash "-" following code
ndicates .010" oversize cylinder
ore.

Series	CID	Comp.
Carb./Trans.		
4000	198	8.8:1 (1)(2)(5)
2-bbl.		
**	215	8.8:1 (1)(2)
2-bbl.		
**	215	10.25:1 (1)(4) 4-bbl.
4400	401	9.0:1 (2) 2-bbl./A-T
4400	401	10.25:1 (3) 2-bbl./A-T
*	401	10.25:1 4-bbl./A-T

* 4400, 4600, 4800
** 4000, 4100, 4300

BASIC ENGINE IN SERIES

The 135 HP, 198 CID V-6 engine was standard in the 4000 series for 1962. A 215 CID engine was optional in the 4000 series and standard in the 4100 and 4300 series.

S-M ....Synchro-mesh
A-T - Auto Trans ....(1)
Regular Gas Option ....(2)
Std..(3)
Power Pack ....(4)
V-6 ....(5)

The 215 V-8 came with a "Power Pack" option, 11.0:1 comp ratio pistons, 4-barrel carb and produced 185 HP. 9.0:1 comp. version was standard with 2-barrel carb and produced 155 HP.

The 280 HP 401 CID was standard in the 4400 series. It was also available in a 265 HP 2-barrel regular gas option or the 325 HP 4-

VEHICLE IDENTIFICATION NUMBER

```
BUICK
4J1001555
```

Commonly referred to as the VIN NUMBER, this series of numbers and letters is stamped on a plate attached to left front door hinge pillar, and stamped on the top surface of the engine block forward of valve cover on left side.

Exception: 4700 Series, the number is on the right cowl under the hood.

EXAMPLE

4	J	1	001555
Series	Year	Assy Plant	Production Number

FIRST DIGIT: Identifies the SERIES, 0 for 4000 (Special V-8), A for 4000 (Special V-6), 1 for 4100 (Special Deluxe V-8), B for 4100 (Special Deluxe V-8), 3 for 4300 (Skylark), 4 for 4400 (leSabre), 6 for 4600 (Wildcat), 7 for 4700 (Riviera), and 8 for 4800 (Electra 225).

SECOND DIGIT: Identifies the YEAR, J for 1963.

THIRD DIGIT: Identifies the PLANT.

ASSEMBLY PLANT	CODE
Flint, Mich	1
South Gate, Calif.	2
Linden	3
Kansas City, Kan	4
Wilmington, De.	5
Atlanta, Ga	6
Arlington	8

LAST 6 DIGITS: Represent the BASIC PRODUCTION NUMBERS.

* Exception: 4000, 4100, and 4300 Series Fourth digit is a number 5. The remaining 5 digits represent the basic production numbers. The 4000, 4100, and 4300 were assembled only in the Flint, South Gate, and Kansas City Plants.

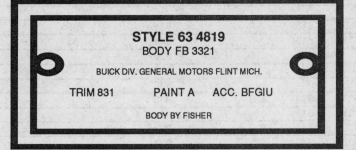

```
STYLE 63 4819
BODY FB 3321

BUICK DIV. GENERAL MOTORS FLINT MICH.

TRIM 831      PAINT A    ACC. BFGIU

BODY BY FISHER
```

FISHER BODY NUMBER PLATE

Complete identification of each body is provided by a plate riveted to the cowl at the left of center under the hood.

THE STYLE NUMBER is a combination of the year, division, series, and body style. In the number plate illustrated, 63 represents the model year 1963; the first digit 4 indicates Buick Motor Division; the second digit 8 indicates Series 4800; 19 indicates the 4-Door Sedan body style. An X following the body style indicates that the body is equipped with electric power assists.

SPECIAL 4000	CODE
4-Door Sedan	4019
2-Door Sedan	4027
4-Door 2-Seat Wagon	4035
4-Door 3-Seat Wagon	4045
2-Door Convertible	4067

SPECIAL DELUXE 4100	CODE
4-Door Sedan	4119
4-Door 2-Seat Wagon	4135

SKYLARK 4300	CODE
2-Door Coupe	4347
2-Door Convertible	4367

LESABRE 4400	CODE
2-Door Sedan	4411
4-Door 2-Seat Estate Wagon	4435
4-Door Hardtop	4439
4-Door 3-Seat Estate Wagon	4445
2-Door Coupe	4447
2-Door Convertible	4467
4-Door Sedan	4469

INVICTA 4600	CODE
4-Door 2-Seat Estate Wagon	4635

WILDCAT 4600	COD
4-Door Hardtop Sedan	463
2-Door Coupe	464
2-Door Convertible Coupe	466

RIVIERA 4700	COD
2-Door Sports Coupe	474

ELECTRA "225" 4800	COD
2-Door Sedan	481
4-Door Riviera Sedan	482
4-Door Hardtop	483
2-Door Coupe	484
2-Door Convertible Coupe	486

THE BODY NUMBER is the production serial number of the body. The prefix letter denotes the plant in which the body was built. FB indicates the Flint plant.

ASSEMBLY PLANT	CODE
Flint, Mich	F
South Gate, Calif	B
Linden	B
Kansas City, Kan	B
Wilmington, Del	BW
Atlanta, Ga	BA
Arlington	B

The digits following the plant code reveal the production sequence number within the plant.

THE TRIM NUMBER: P - Police Option   B - Bucket Seates   W - Power Windows   * - Bucket Seats & Power Windows

MODELS	MATERIAL	AQUA	BLACK	BLUE	RED	RED & BLACK	ROSE	SANDLE-WOOD	SADDLE	SILVER	WHITE
4019-4019	CLOTH & VINYL	051		011		071		031			
4019	VINYL	P085	016	076			036				
4027	CLOTH & VINYL	051		011		071		031			
4027	VINYL				B079			B039			
4035	VINYL	055	085	015	B075-079			B035-079			
4045	VINYL	055	085	015	075			035			
4067	VINYL		080	010	B070-079			B030-039			
4119	CLOTH & VINYL	151		111		171	161	131			
4135	VINYL	155	185	115	175			135		195	
4347	CLOTH & VINYL	B157		B117			B167	B137			
4347	VINYL		B188		B178				B198		B148
4367	VINYL		B189	B119	B179			B139	B199		B149
4411	CLOTH & VINYL	451		411	471			431			
4435-4445	VINYL	455	485	415	475			435	495		
4439-4447	CLOTH & VINYL	452		412		472	462	432			
4439-4447	VINYL			416	476			436			
4467	VINYL			410	B470-479		460	B430-439	490		
4469	CLOTH & VINYL	451		411		471	461	431			
4469	VINYLBlack & Silver Trim 484										
4635	CLOTH & VINYL			615			665	635			
4635	VINYL		B687		B677			B637	B697		
4639	VINYL		B681-688		B671-678			B631-638	B691-698		
4647-4667	VINYL		B689	B619	B679				B699		B649
4747	CLOTH & VINYL		B787	B717				B737			
4747	LEATHER & VINYL		B788	B718	B778				B798	B728	B748
4747	VINYL			B716				B736		B726	
4819	CLOTH & VINYL	851		811				831		821	
4829	CLOTH & VINYL	W851-856		W811-816				W831-836		W821-826	
4839	CLOTH & VINYL	W851-856		W811-816				W831-836		W821-826	
4839	LEATHER & VINYL		*888		*878				*898		
4847	CLOTH & VINYL	851		811				831		821	
4847	LEATHER & VINYL		*888		*878				*898		
4867	LEATHER & VINYL		B880-889	810	B870-879			830		B899	B849

THE PAINT CODE furnishes the key to the paint colors used on the car. A two letter code indicates the bottom and top colors respectively.

COLOR	CODE
Regal Black	A
Arctic White	C
Silver Cloud	D
Spruce Green	E
Marlin Blue	F
Willow Mist	J
Burgundy	N
Teal Mist	P
Twilight Aqua	Q
Desert Sand	R
Bronze Mist	S
Fawn Mist	T
Granada Red	V
Diplomat Blue	W
Rose Mist	X

ENGINE NUMBER

Along with the VIN number the engine block is stamped with an engine production code. The code has a prefix series of letters and numbers that identify the engine and year, then a four digit numeric production sequence code. On the V-8 engines the production code is stamped on the right front of the engine block opposite the VIN number. When viewed from the front of the engine the number is upside down. On the V-6 engine the number is on the front of the block below the left cylinder head gasket. The production prefix code for 1963 is:

4000, 4100, 4300 Series
JL 8.8:1 comp. 198 cid V-6
JZ low comp. 198 cid V-6 (export)
JM 9.0:1 std. comp. 215 cid V-8
JN 11.0:1 comp. 215 cid V-8
JP 7.6:1 comp. 215 cid (export)
4400 Series
JS 9.0:1 comp. 401 cid V-8.
4400, 4600, 4700, 4800 Series
JR 10.25:1 std. comp. 401 cid V-8
JT 10.25:1 comp. 4- bbl. 401 cid

V-8
JU 8.75:1 comp. Export 401 cid.
JW 10.25:1 comp. 425 cid V-8.

Series	CID	Comp.	Carb./Trans.
4000	198	8.8:1 (1)(2)(5)	2-bbl.
**	215	9.0:1 (1)(2)	2-bbl.
4100	198	8.8:1 (1)(2)(5)	2-bbl.
**	215	11.0:1 (1)	4-bbl.
4400	401	9.0:1 (1)(2)	2-bbl.
4400	401	10.25:1 (1)(3)	2-bbl.
4600	401	10.25:1 (1)	4-bbl.
*	401	10.25:1	4-bbl./A-T

* 4000, 4100, 4300
** 4400, 4600, 4700, 4800
S-M .... Synchro-mesh
A-T - Auto Trans ....(1)
Regular Gas Option ....(2)
Std ....(3)
Power Pack ....(4)
V-6 ....(5)

BASIC ENGINE IN SERIES

The 135 HP 198 cid V-6 engine was standard in the 4000 series and optional on 4100 series this year. A 9.0:1 compression 155 HP 2-barrel 215 cid engine was standard on 4100 series and optional on 4000 series. The 11.0:1 compression 200 HP 4-barrel 215 cid was standard on the 4300 series and optional on the 4000 and 4100 series. The 401 cid 280 HP 2-barrel V-8 was standard in the 4400 series. Also available was a 265 HP 2-barrel regular gas option. The 325 HP 4-barrel 401 cid was standard in the 4600, 4700, and 4800 series and optional in the 4400 series. An optional 340 HP 425 cid was available for the Rivera in 1963.

VEHICLE IDENTIFICATION NUMBER

```
BUICK
4K1001555
```

Commonly referred to as the VIN NUMBER, this series of numbers and letters is stamped on a plate attached to left front door hinge pillar, and stamped on the top surface of the engine block forward of valve cover on left side.

Exception: 4700 Series, the number is on the left cowl under the hood.

EXAMPLE

4	K	1	001555
Series	Year	Assy Plant	Production Number

FIRST DIGIT: Identifies the SERIES, 0 for 4000 (Special V-8), A for 4000 (Special V-6), 1 for 4100 (Special Deluxe V-8), B for 4100 (Special Deluxe V-6), 3 for 4300 (Skylark V-8), C for (Skylark V-6), 4 for 4400 (leSabre), 6 for 4600 (Wildcat), 7 for 4700 (Riviera), and 8 for 4800 (Electra 225).

SECOND DIGIT: Identifies the YEAR, K for 1964.

THIRD DIGIT: Identifies the PLANT.

ASSEMBLY PLANT	CODE
Flint, Mich	1
South Gate, Calif.	2
Fremont	3
Kansas City, Kan	4
Wilmington, De.	5
Atlanta, Ga	6
Baltimore, Md	7
Kansas City, Mo	8

LAST 6 DIGITS: Represent the BASIC PRODUCTION NUMBERS.

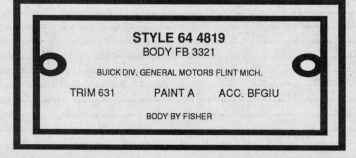

```
STYLE 64 4819
BODY FB 3321

BUICK DIV. GENERAL MOTORS FLINT MICH.

TRIM 631        PAINT A      ACC. BFGIU

BODY BY FISHER
```

FISHER BODY NUMBER PLATE

Complete identification of each body is provided by a plate riveted to the cowl at the left of center under the hood.

THE STYLE NUMBER is a combination of the year, division, series, and body style. In the number plate illustrated, 64 represents the model year 1964; the first digit 4 indicates Buick Motor Division; the second digit 8 indicates Series 4800; 19 indicates the 4-Door Sedan body style. An X following the body style indicates that the body is equipped with electric power assists.

SPECIAL 4000	Code
2-Door Sedan	4027
4-Door 2-Seat Wagon	4035
2-Door Convertible	4067
4-Door Sedan	4069

SPECIAL DELUXE 4100	CODE
2-Door Sedan	4127
4-Door 2-Seat Wagon	4135
4-Door Sedan	4169

SKYLARK 4300	CODE
2-Door Coupe	4337
2-Door Convertible	4367
4-Door Sedan	4369

SKYLARK CUSTOM	CODE
4-Door 2-Seat wagon	4355
4-Door 3-Seat Wagon	4365

SKYLARK STANDARD	CODE
4-Door 2-Seat Wagon	4255
4-Door 3-Seat Wagon	4265

LESABRE 4400	CODE
4-Door 2-Seat Estate Wag.	4435
4-Door Hardtop	4439
4-Door 3-Seat Estate Wag.	4445
2-Door Coupe	4447
2-Door Convertible	4467
4-Door Sedan	4469

WILDCAT 4600	CODE
4-Door Hardtop Sedan	4639
2-Door Coupe	4647
2-Door Convertible Coupe	4667
4-Door Sedan	4669

RIVIERA 4700	CODE
2-Door Sports Coupe	4747

ELECTRA "225" 4800	CODE
2-Door Sedan	4819
4-Door Sedan	4829
4-Door Hardtop	4839
2-Door Coupe	4847
2-Door Convertible Coupe	4867

THE BODY NUMBER is the production serial number of the body. The prefix letter denotes the plant in which the body was built. FB indicates the Flint plant.

ASSEMBLY PLANT	CODE
Flint, Mich	FB
South Gate, Calif	BC
Fremont	
Kansas City, Kan	BK
Wilmington, Del.	BW
Atlanta, Ga	BA
Baltimore	
Kansas City, Mo	

The digits following the plant code reveal the production sequence number within the plant.

THE TRIM NUMBER: P - Police Option   B - Bucket Seates   W - Power Windows   * - Bucket Seats & Power Windows

Models	Materials	Black	Blue	Fawn	Green	Maroon	Red	Saddle	Silver	White
4027	CLOTH & VINYL		001	003					002	
4035	VINYL	028	021				027	029		
0467	VINYL	028	021	023			027-087B			084B
4069	CLOTH & VINYL	092P	001	003					002	
4069	VINYL		011	013						
4127	CLOTH & VINYL		101	103	100				102	
4127	VINYL						197B			194B
4135	VINYL	128	131				127	129		
4169	CLOTH & VINYL		101	103	100				102	
4169	VINYL		111	113		117				
4255-4265	VINYL	028	021				027	029		
4337	CLOTH & VINYL		131	133						
4337	VINYL	B158	B151		B150		B157	B159		B154
4355	VINYL		171		170	177		179		174-184
4365	VINYL		171		170	177		179		174
4367	VINYL	B168	141		B160		B147-167	B169		B164
4369	CLOTH & VINYL		131	133	130	137				
4369	VINYL	148						149		
4439	CLOTH & VINYL		401-411	403-413	400	417			402	
4439	VINYL		421	423		427				
4447	CLOTH & VINYL		401	403	400					
4447	VINYL		B421-471	B423-473		B427-477				
4467	VINYL	448	441	443			B447-487	B489		B484
4469	CLOTH & VINYL		401-411	403-413	400	417			402	
4635-4645	CLOTH & VINYL		461	463		467				
4635-4645	VINYL	438	431	433		437		439		
4639	CLOTH & VINYL		401-411	403-413	400	417			402	
4639	VINYL	B688-658	421	423		427	687	B689-659		
4647	CLOTH & VINYL		401	403	400					
4647	VINYL	B698	421	B423-473		B274-477	B697	B699		B694
4647	VINYL		B471-691							
4667	VINYL	B448-698	B441-691	443			447	B489-699		B484-694
4667	VINYL						B487-697			
4669	CLOTH & VINYL		401-411	403-413	400	417			402	
4747	CLOTH & VINYL		B611	B613	B610					
4747	VINYL	B608-628	B601-621	B603			B607	B629	B602	B624
4819	CLOTH & VINYL		631	633	630				632	
4829-4839	CLOTH & VINYL		631-641	633-643	630-640				632-642	
4847	CLOTH & VINYL		631	633					632	
4847	LEATHER & VINYL	678					677	679		
4867	LEATHER & VINYL	B668-678	661				B667-677	B669-679		B674

THE PAINT CODE furnishes the key to the paint colors used on the car. A one letter code indicates the bottom and top colors respectively.

COLOR	CODE
Regal Black	A
Arctic White	C
Silver Cloud	D
Marlin Blue	F
Wedgewood Blue	H
Surf Green	J
Sunburst Yellow	K
Claret Mist	L
Coral Mist	N
Teal Mist	P
Desert Beige	R
Bronze Mist	S

Color	Code
Tawny Mist	S
Granada Red	V
Diplomat Blue	W

ENGINE NUMBER

Along with the VIN number the engine block is stamped with an engine production code. The code has a prefix series of letters and numbers that identify the engine and year, then a four digit numeric production sequence code. The production code is stamped on the right front of the engine block opposite the VIN number. The production prefix code for 1964 is:

KH	225 cid. V-6 Standard	
KJ	225 cid. V-6 Low Comp.	
KL	300 cid. V-8 Standard	
KM	300 cid. V-8 Stan. (export)	
KR	300 cid. V-8 export	
KP	300 cid. V-8 High Perf.	
KT	401 cid. V-8 Standard	
KV	401 cid. V-8 export	
KW	425 cid. V-8	
KX	425 cid. V-8 2 / 4-bbl.	

Series	CID	Comp.	Carb./Trans.
*	225	9.0:1 (1)(2)(5)	1-bbl.
*	300	9.0:1 (1)(2)	2-bbl.
*	300	11.0:1 (1)	4-bbl.
**	300	9.0:1 (1)(2)	2-bbl.
**	401	10.25:1 (1)	4-bbl.
**	425	10.25:1 (1)	4-bbl.
**	300	11.0:1 (1)	4-bbl.
**	425	10.25:1 (1)	4-bbl.
**	425	10.25:1 (1)	2 / 4-bb

*	4000, 4100, 4300
**	4400, 4600, 4700, 4800

S-M .... Synchro-mesh
A-T - Auto Trans .... (1)
Regular Gas Option .... (2)
Std .... (3)
Power Pack .... (4)
V-6 .... (5)

BASIC ENGINE IN SERIES

THE 135 HP 198 cid V-6 engine was standard in the 4000 series and optional on 4100 series this year. A 9.0:1 compression 155 HP 2-barrel 215 cid engine was standard on 4100 series and optional on 4000 series. The 11.0:1 compression 200 HP 4-barrel 215 cid was standard on the 4300 series and optional on the 4000 and 4100 series. The 401 cid 280 HP 2-barrel V-8 was standard in the 4400 series. Also available was a 265 HP 2-barrel regular gas option. The 325 HP 4-barrel 401 cid was standard in the 4600, 4700, and 4800 series and optional in the 4400 series. The 425 cid engine was used for the Rivera, 340 HP with a 4-bbl carb. and a 360 HP with 2 / 4-bbl. for 1964.

VEHICLE IDENTIFICATION NUMBER

```
BUICK
444275H001555
```

Commonly referred to as the VIN NUMBER, this series of numbers and letters is stamped on a plate attached to left front door hinge pillar, and stamped on the engine block.

EXAMPLE

4	44	27	5	H	001555
BUICK DIV.	SERIES	BODY STYLE	YEAR	ASSY PLANT	PRODUCTION CODE

FIRST DIGIT: Identifies Buick Motor Division.

SECOND AND THIRD DIGITS: Identify the Series:

SERIES	CODE
LeSabre	52
LeSabre	54
Wildcat	62
Wildcat Deluxe	64
Wildcat Custom	66
Electra	82
Electra Custom	84
Riviera	94

SERIES	V-6	V-8
Special	33	34
Special Deluxe	35	36
Sportwagon	41	42
Skylark	43	44
Custom Wagon		

FOURTH AND FIFTH DIGITS: Identify the Body Style:

2-Door Coupe	27
4-Door 2-Seat Station Wagon	35
2-Door Hardtop Coupe	37
4-Door Hardtop	39
2-Door Hardtop Coupe	47
4-Door 2-Seat Sportwagon	55
4-Door 3-Seat Sportwagon	65
2-Door Convertible	67
4-Door Sedan	69

SIXTH DIGIT, a number 5 is for Production Year 1965.

SEVENTH DIGIT, is a letter code used to identify the Assembly Plant.

ASSEMBLY PLANT	CODE
Flint	H
South Gate	C
Fremont	Z
Kansas City, Kansas	X
Wilmington	Y
Atlanta	D
Baltimore	B
Kansas City, Mo	K
Bloomfield	V

LAST 6 DIGITS: Represent the Basic Production Numbers.

FISHER BODY NUMBER PLATE

Complete identification of each body is provided by a plate riveted to the cowl at the left of center under the hood.

THE STYLE NUMBER is a combination of the year, division, series, and body style. In the number plate illustrated, 65 represents the model year 1965; the first digit 4 indicates Buick Motor Division. The second and third digits 44, represent the body series V-8 Skylark. The fourth and fifth digits 27, identify the body style 2-Door Coupe. An X following the body style indicates that the body is equipped with electric power assists.

SPECIAL V-6	CODE
2-Door Coupe Thin Pillar	43327
4-Door 2-Seat Station Wagon	43335
2-Door Convertible	43367
4-Door Sedan Thin Pillar	43369

SPECIAL V-8	CODE
2-Door Coupe Thin Pillar	43427
4-Door 2-Seat Station Wagon	43435

	CODE
2-Door Convertible	43467
4-Door Sedan Thin Pillar	43469

SPECIAL DELUXE V-6	CODE
4-Door 2-Seat Station Wagon	43535
4-Door Sedan Thin Pillar	43569

SPECIAL DELUXE V-8	CODE
4-Door 2-Seat Station Wagon	43635
4-Door Sedan Thin Pillar	43669

SPORTWAGON V-8	CODE
4-Door 2-Seat Station Wagon	44255
4-Door 3-Seat Station Wagon	44265

SKYLARK V-6	CODE
2-Door Coupe Thin Pillar	44327
2-Door Coupe Hardtop	44337
2-Door Convertible	44367
4-Door Sedan Thin Pillar	44369

SKYLARK V-8	CODE
2-Door Coupe Thin Pillar	44427
2-Door Coupe Hardtop	44437
2-Door Convertible	44467

GENERAL MOTORS CORPORATION

ST 65-44427   H 001555 **BODY**
TR 108   **AC PAINT**

BODY BY FISHER

THE TRIM NUMBER: B - Bucket Seates

Models	Materials	Auqua	Black	Blue	Fawn	Gray	Green	Ivory	Red	Saddle	Silver
33-3427	CLOTH & VINYL			001	003						002
33-3467	VINYL		B028-088	021				024	B027-087	029	
33-3469	CLOTH & VINYL			001	003						002
33-3469	VINYL		118	111						119	
35-3635	VINYL			121			120		127	129	
35-3669	CLOTH & VINYL	106		101	103		100				
35-3669	VINYL		118	111						119	
4200	VINYL			021			020		027	029	
43-4427	CLOTH & VINYL		108	101	103						
43-4427	VINYL		B198	B191					B197	B199	
43-4437	CLOTH & VINYL		138-188	131	133						
43-4437	VINYL			B151				B154	B157	B159	
43-4467	VINYL		B148-158	141				B154	B147-157	B159	
43-4469	CLOTH & VINYL	136	138	131	133		130				
43-4469	VINYL		148							149	
4455-65	VINYL			171			140		147	149	
5237-39-69	CLOTH & VINYL			401	403		400				402
5437	VINYL		B428-478	421					427	429	
5439	CLOTH & VINYL	416	418	411	413						
5439	VINYL			421						429	
5467	VINYL		B448-488	441					B447-487	449	
5469	CLOTH & VINYL		418	411	413						
5469	VINYL			421						429	
6237-39-69	CLOTH & VINYL			401	403		400				402
6437	VINYL		B428-478	421					427	429	
6439	CLOTH & VINYL	416	418	411	413						
6439	VINYL			421						429	
6467	VINYL		B448-488	441					B447-487	449	
6469	CLOTH & VINYL	416	418	411	413						
6469	VINYL			421						429	
6637	VINYL		B658-678	B671				B674		B679	
6639	VINYL		658	651			B654-674		657	659	
6667	VINYL		B658-678	B671				B674	B677	B679	
8237-39-69	CLOTH & VINYL	636		631	633		B654-674				632
8437	VINYL		698				690			699	
8439	CLOTH & VINYL			641	643	642	640				
8439	VINYL		698							699	
8467	VINYL		B698-688	691				694	697	B699-689	
8469	CLOTH & VINYL			641	643	642	640				
9447	CLOTH & VINYL		B618	B611	B613		B610				
9447	VINYL		B608-628	B601			B620	B624		B609-629	

4-Door Sedan Thin Pillar....44469

SPORTWAGON CUSTOM
V-8   **CODE**

4-Door 2-Seat Station Wagon.....
.... 44455
4 -Door 3-Seat Station Wagon....
....44465

LESABRE   **CODE**

2-Door Coupe Hardtop......45237
4-Door Hardtop.................45239
4-Door Sedan Thin Pillar....45269

LESABRE (CUSTOM)   CODE

2-Door Coupe Hardtop.......45437
4-Door Hardtop.................45439
2-Door Convertible.............45467
4-Door Sedan Thin Pillar....45469

WILDCAT   **CODE**

2-Door Coupe Hartop.........46237
4-Door Hardtop.................46239
4-Door Sedan Thin Pillar....46269

WILDCAT (DELUXE)   CODE

2-Door Coupe Hardtop.......46437
4-Door Hardtop.................46439
2-Door Convertible.............46467
4-Door Sedan Thin Pillar....46469

WILDCAT (CUSTOM)   CODE

2-Door Coupe Hardtop.......46637
4-Door Hardtop.................46639
2-Door Convertible.............46667

ELECTRA   **CODE**

2-Door Coupe Hardtop.......48237
4-Door Hardtop.................48239
4-Door Sedan   Semi Thin Pillar...
....48269

ELECTRA (CUSTOM)   CODE

2-Door Coupe Hardtop.......48437
4-Door Hardtop.................48439
2-Door Convertible.............48467

4-Door Sedan Thin Pillar.....48469

RIVIERA   **CODE**

2-Door Coupe Hardtop.......49447

THE PAINT CODE furnishes the key to the paint colors used on the car. A two letter code indicates the bottom and top colors respectively.

COLOR

COLOR	Code
Regal Black	A
Arctic White	C
Astro Blue	D
Midnight Blue	E
Sea Foam Green	H
Verde Green	J
Turquoise Mist	K
Midnight Aqua	L
Burgundy Mist	N
Bamboo Cream	Y
Flame Red	R
Sahara Mist	S
Champagne Mist	T
Shell Beige	V
Silver Cloud	Z

*Note: Code letter can be found on the Fisher Body Number Plate.

ENGINE NUMBER

Along with the VIN number the engine block is stamped with an engine production code. The code has a series of letters that identify the engine and a numeric production date code. The production code is stamped on the right side of the engine block. The production prefix code for 1965 is:

THE BODY NUMBER is the production serial number of the body. The prefix letter denotes the plant in which the body was built.

ASSEMBLY PLANT	Code
Flint, Mich	H
South Gate, Calif	C
Fremont	Z
Kansas City, Kan	X
Wilmington, Del	Y
Atlanta, Ga	D
Baltimore	B
Kansas City, Mo	K
Bloomfield	V

Transmissions

	Standard	Optional
Special	(1)	(2)(3)
Skylark	(1)	(2)(3)
LeSabre	(1)	(3)(4)
Wildcat	(1)	(2)(4)
Electra "225"	(4)	
Riviera	(4)	

(1) .... Manual 3 Speed
(2) .... Manual 4 Speed
(3) .... Super Turbine "300"
(4) .... Super Turbine "400"

Series	Engine Code# Prefix	CID	Use	Comp.	Carb.	HP
45000	LL	300	Standard	9.0:1	2-bbl	210
	LP	300	Optional	11.0:1	4-bbl	250
	LM	300	Export	7.6:1	4-bbl	—
46000	LT	401	Standard	10.25:1	4-bbl	325
48000	LV	401	Export	8.75:1	4-bbl	315
	LX	425	Optional	10.25:1	2-4-bbl	360
49000	LW	401	Standard	10.25:1	4-bbl	325
	LX	425	Optional	10.25:1	2-4-bbl	360
*	LH	225-V6	Standard	9.0:1	2-bbl	155
**	LL	300	Standard	9.0:1	2-bbl	210
	LP	300	Optional	10.25:1	2-bbl	250
***	LR	400	Standard	10.25:1	4-bbl	325
****	LX	425	Optional	10.25:1	4-bbl	340

*	43300, 43500, 44100, 44300
**	43400, 43600, 44200, 44400
***	44427, 44437, 44467 (Skylark Gran Sport)

VEHICLE IDENTIFICATION NUMBER

BUICK
444076H101555

Commonly referred to as the VIN NUMBER, this series of numbers and letters is stamped on a plate attached to left front door hinge pillar, and stamped on the engine block.

EXAMPLE

4	44	07		H	101555
BUICK DIV.	SERIES	BODY STYLE	YEAR	ASSY PLANT	PRODUCTION CODE

FIRST DIGIT: Identifies Buick Motor Division.

SECOND AND THIRD DIGITS: Identify the Series:

SERIES	CODE
Sport Wagon	42
Skylark Gran Sport	46
LeSabre	52
LeSabre Custom	54

	Wildcat	64
	Wildcat Custom	66
	Electra	82
	Electra Custom	84
	Riviera	94

SERIES	V-6	V-8
Special	33	34
Special Deluxe	35	36
Skylark Custom Wagon	43	44

FOURTH AND FIFTH DIGITS: Identify the Body Style:

2-Door Sport Coupe -Pillar Post	07
2-Door Sport Coupe -Hard Top	17
4-Door 2-Seat Station Wagon	35
2-Door Hardtop Coupe	37
4-Door Sedan Hardtop	39
4-Door 2-Seat Sportwagon	55
2-Door Sport Coupe Hardtop	57
4-Door 3-Seat Sportwagon	65
2-Door Convertible Coupe	67
4-Door Sedan -Pillar Post	69
2-Door Sport Coupe Hardtop	87

SIXTH DIGIT, a number 6 is for Production Year 1966.

SEVENTH DIGIT, is a letter code used to identify the Assembly Plant.

ASSEMBLY PLANT	CODE
Flint	H
South Gate	C
Fremont	Z
Kansas City, Kansas	X
Wilmington	Y
Atlanta	D
Baltimore	B
Kansas City, Mo	K
Bloomfield	V

Oshawa, Ontario, Canada I

LAST 6 DIGITS: Represent the Basic Production Numbers.

FISHER BODY NUMBER PLATE

Complete identification of each body is provided by a plate riveted to the cowl at the left of center under the hood.

THE STYLE NUMBER is a combination of the year, division, series, and body style. In the number plate illustrated, 66 represents the model year 1966; the first digit 4 indicates Buick Motor Division. The second and third digits 44, represent the body series V-8 Skylark. The fourth and fifth digits 07, identify the body style 2-Door Sport Coupe. An X following the body style indicates that the body is equipped with electric power assists.

SPECIAL V-6	CODE
2-Door Coupe Thin Pillar ...43307	
4-Door 2-Seat Station	
Wagon 43335	
2-Door Convertible 43367	
4-Door Sedan Thin Pillar .. 43369	

SPECIAL V-8	CODE
2-Door Coupe Thin Pillar ...43407	
4-Door 2-Seat Station	
Wagon........................... 43435	
2-Door Convertible............43467	
4-Door Sedan Thin Pillar ...43469	

SPECIAL DELUXE V-6	CODE
2-Door Coupe Thin Pillar ...43507	
2-Door Coupe Hardtop.......43517	
4-Door 2-Seat Station	
Wagon........................... 43535	
4-Door Sedan Thin Pillar ...43569	

SPECIAL DELUXE V-8	CODE
2-Door Coupe Thin Pillar ...43607	
2-Door Coupe Hardtop.......43617	
4-Door 2-Seat Station	
Wagon........................... 43635	
4-Door Sedan Thin Pillar ...43669	

SPORTWAGON V-8	CODE
4-Door 2-Seat Station	
Wagon 44255	
4-Door 3-Seat Station	
Wagon 44265	
4-Door 2-Seat Station	
Wagon 44455	
4-Door 3-Seat Station	
Wagon 44465	

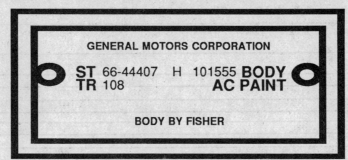

GENERAL MOTORS CORPORATION
ST 66-44407 H 101555 **BODY**
TR 108   **AC PAINT**

BODY BY FISHER

SKYLARK V-6	CODE
2-Door Coupe Thin Pillar ...44307	
2-Door Coupe Hardtop 44317	
4-Door Hardtop 44339	
2-Door Convertible 44367	

SKYLARK V-8	CODE
2-Door Coupe Thin Pillar ...44407	
2-Door Coupe Hardtop 44417	
4-Door Hardtop 44439	
2-Door Convertible 44467	

SKYLARK Gran Sport	CODE
2-Door Coupe Thin Pillar ...44607	
2-Door Coupe Hardtop 44617	
2-Door Convertible 44667	

LESABRE	CODE
2-Door Coupe Hardtop 45237	
4-Door Hardtop 45239	
4-Door Sedan Thin Pillar ...45269	

LESABRE (CUSTOM)	CODE
2-Door Coupe Hardtop 45437	
4-Door Hardtop 45439	
2-Door Convertible 45467	
4-Door Sedan Thin Pillar ...45469	

WILDCAT	CODE
2-Door Coupe Hardtop 46437	
4-Door Hardtop 46439	
2-Door Convertible 46467	
4-Door Sedan Thin Pillar ...46469	

WILDCAT (CUSTOM)	CODE
2-Door Coupe Hardtop 46637	
4-Door Hardtop 46639	
2-Door Convertible 46667	

ELECTRA	CODE
2-Door Coupe Hardtop 48237	
4-Door Hardtop 48239	
4-Door Sedan	
Semi Thin Pillar 48269	

ELECTRA (CUSTOM)	CODE
2-Door Coupe Hardtop 48437	
4-Door Hardtop 48439	
2-Door Convertible 48467	
4-Door Sedan	
Semi Thin Pillar 48469	

RIVIERA	CODE
2-Door Coupe Hardtop 49487	

THE BODY NUMBER is the production serial number of the body. The prefix letter denotes the plant in which the body was built (refer to the assembly plant codes on the VIN plate).

THE PAINT CODE furnishes the key to the paint colors used on the car. A two letter code indicates the bottom and top colors respectively.

COLOR	CODE
Regal Black .... A	
Gunmetal .... B	
Arctic White C	
Astro Blue .... D	
Midnight Blue .... E	
Blue Mist .... F	
Gold .... G	
Seafoam Green .... H	
Verde Green .... J	
Turquoise Mist .... K	
Shadow Turquoise L	
Riviera Red .... M	
Burgundy Mist .... N	
Flame Red.................................. R	
Champagne .... S	
Saddle Mist .... T	
Plum .... U	
Shell Beige V	
Silver Mist .... W	
Riviera White X	
Cream .... Y	
Riviera Silver Green .... Z	

ENGINE NUMBER

Along with the VIN number the engine block is stamped with an engine production code. The code has a series of letters that identify the engine and a numeric production date code. The production code is stamped on the right side of the engine block. The production prefix code for 1966 is:

Transmissions		
	Standard	Optional
Special ....(1) .... (2)(3)		
Skylark ....(1) .... (2)(3)		
LeSabre ....(1) .... (3)(4)		
Wildcat ....(1) .... (2)(4)		
Electra ....(4)		
"225"		
Riviera ....(4)		

(1) .... Manual 3 Speed
(2) .... Manual 4 Speed
(3) .... Super Turbine "300"
(4) .... Super Turbine "400"

1966 BUICK

THE TRIM NUMBERS: N=Notch Seats B=Bucket Seats CT=Custom Trim ST=Standard Trim

MODELS	MATERIAL	AQUA	BLACK	BLUE	LIGHT FAWN	FAWN	GREEN	PLUM	RED	SADDLE	SLATE	WHITE	BRONZE
33-3407	CLOTH & VINYL		108										
	VINYL		448	111	113								
33-3435	VINYL			111	113				117				
33-3467	VINYL		448	111	113				117				
33-3469	CLOTH & VINYL		408	101		103							
	VINYL	126	128	121									
35-3607	VINYL	166N	138-168N	131-161N	133-163N				167N				
35-3617	VINYL	166N	138-168N	131-161N	133-163N				167N				
35-3635	VINYL		138	131					137	139			
35-3669	CLOTH & VINYL	146		141		143							
	VINYL	126	128	121									
43-4407	CLOTH & VINYL		188	181		183							
	VINYL	166N	168N-198B	161N-191B	163N-193B				167N				
43-4417	CLOTH & VINYL		188	181		183							
	VINYL	166N	168N-198B	161N-191B	163N-193B				167N				
43-4467	VINYL		168N-198B	161N-191B	193B				167N-197B				
	VINYL		185		182								
43-4439	CLOTH & VINYL	156N		151N		153N	150N						
	VINYL		168N	161N	163N								
4255-65	VINYL			161	133				137				
4455-65	VINYL		178	171			170		177	179			
4607-17	VINYL	166N	168N-198B	161N-191B	163N-193B				167N				
4667	VINYL		168N-198B	161N-191B	193B				167N-197B				
5200	CLOTH & VINYL		408	401		403	400						
5437	VINYL	426	428-478B	421					427	429			
5439	CLOTH & VINYL	416		411		413			417				
	VINYL		428	421									
5467	VINYL		428-478B	421	423				427				
5469	CLOTH & VINYL	416		411		413			417				
	VINYL		428	421									
6437	VINYL	426	428-478B	421					427	429			
6439	CLOTH & VINYL	416		411		413			417				
	VINYL		428	421									
6467	VINYL		428-478B	421	423				427				
6469	CLOTH & VINYL	416		411		413			417				
	VINYL		428	421									
6637	VINYL		458N-498B	451N	453N-493B								
6639	VINYL	456N	458N	451N	453N								
6667	VINYL		458N-498B	451N	493B				457N				
8200	CLOTH & VINYL	636	678	631		633	630				632		
8437	VINYL		698N		693N				697N				
8439	CLOTH & VINYL			641		643	640				642		
	VINYL		698N		693N				697N				
8467	VINYL		698N-688B	691N	693N-683B				697N				
8469	CLOTH & VINYL		698N	641		643	640				642		
9487	VINYL BENCH		608ST	6015	6035								
	VINYL BUCKET	656BCT	658BCT-668BST	651BCT	653B-663BST								
	CLOTH & VINYL STRATO BENCH		628CT	621CT				627CT					
	VINYL STRATO BENCH		618CT	611CT			610CT					614CT	617CT

Series	Engine Code# Prefix	CID	Use	Comp.	Carb.	HP
43400	ML	300	Standard	9.0:1	2-bbl	210
43600	MB	340	Optional	10.25:1	4-bbl	260
44400	MM	300	Export	7.6:1	2-bbl	210
*	MC	340	Optional Export	7.6:1	2-bbl	220
44255						
44265	MA	340	Standard	9.0:1	2-bbl	220
44455	MB	340	Optional	10.25:1	4-bbl	260
44465	MC	340	Export	7.6:1	2-bbl	220
45000						
**	MH	225-V6	Standard	9.0:1	2-bbl	160

Series	Engine Code# Prefix	CID	Use	Comp.	Carb.	HP
44600	MR	400	Standard	10.25:1	4-bbl	325
***	MT	401	Standard	10.25:1	4-bbl	325
***	MV	401	Export	8.75:1	4-bbl	325
***	MW	425	Optional	10.25:1	4-bbl	340
49000	MW	425	Standard	10.25:1	4-bbl	340
	MW	425	Optional	10.25:1	2/4-bbl	360
	MT	401	Optional	10.25:1	4-bbl	325

*   Except 55 & 56
** 43300, 43500, 44300 Models
*** 46000 & 48000

VEHICLE IDENTIFICATION NUMBER

```
BUICK
444 077 H101555
```

Commonly referred to as the VIN NUMBER, this series of numbers and letters is stamped on a plate attached to left front door hinge pillar, and stamped on the engine block.

FIRST DIGIT: Identifies Buick Motor Division.

SECOND AND THIRD DIGITS: Identify the Series:

SERIES	CODE
Special	33
Special Deluxe	35
Special Deluxe Wagon	36
Skylark	43 & 44
Sport Wagon	44
Sport Wagon-Wood Grain	48
GS400	46
LeSabre	52
LeSabre Custom	54
Wildcat	64
Wildcat Custom	66
Electra	82
Electra Custom	84
Riviera	94

FOURTH AND FIFTH DIGITS: Identify the Body Style:

2-Door Sport Coupe Pillar Post	07
2-Door Sport Coupe -Hard Top	17
4-Door 2-Seat Station Wagon	35
2-Door Hardtop Coupe	37
4-Door Sedan Hardtop	39
4-Door 2-Seat Sportwagon	55
2-Door Sport Coupe Hardtop	57
4-Door 3-Seat Sportwagon	65
2-Door Convertible Coupe	67
4-Door Sedan Pillar Post	69
2-Door Sport Coupe Hardtop	87

SIXTH DIGIT, a number 7 is for Production Year 1967.

EXAMPLE

4	44	07	7	H	101555
BUICK DIV.	SERIES	BODY STYLE	YEAR	ASSY PLANT	PRODUCTION CODE

SEVENTH DIGIT, is a letter code used to identify the Assembly Plant.

ASSEMBLY PLANT	CODE
Flint	H
South Gate	C
Fremont	
Kansas City, Kansas	
Wilmington	
Atlanta	
Baltimore	
Kansas City, Mo	

Bloomfield V
Oshawa, Ontario, Canada I

LAST 6 DIGITS: Represent the Basic Production Numbers.

FISHER BODY NUMBER PLATE

Complete identification of each body is provided by a plate riveted to the cowl at the left of center under the hood.

THE STYLE NUMBER is a combination of the year, division, series, and body style. In the number plate illustrated, 67 represents the model year 1967; the first digit 4 indicates Buick Motor Division. The second and third digits 44, represent the body series Skylark. The fourth and fifth digits 07, identify the body style 2-Door Sport Coupe. An X following the body style indicates that the body is equipped with electric power assists.

SPECIAL	CODE
2-Door Coupe Thin Pillar ...43307	
4-Door 2-Seat Station	
-Wagon 43335	
4-Door Sedan Thin Pillar ...43369	

SPECIAL DELUXE	CODE
2-Door Coupe....................43517	
4-Door (2 Seats)...................	
Station Wagon 43635	
4-Door Sedan Thin Pillar ...43569	

SKYLARK	CODE
2-Door Coupe Thin Pillar ...44307	
2-Door Coupe Hardtop.......44417	
4-Door Hardtop 44439	
2-Door Convertible 44467	
4-Door Sedan Thin Pillar ...44469	

SPORTWAGON	CODE
4-Door (2 Seates)................	
-Station Wagon 44455	
4-Door (3 Seats).................	
-Station Wagon 44465	

G.S.400	CODE
2-Door Coupe Thin Pillar ...44607	
2-Door Coupe Hardtop.......44617	
2-Door Convertible 44667	

LESABRE	CODE
4-Door Hardtop 45239	
4-Door Sedan Thin Pillar ...45269	
2-Door Coupe Hardtop.......45287	

GENERAL MOTORS CORPORATION

ST 67-44407 FBD 101555 BODY
TR 108   AC PAINT

BODY BY FISHER

LESABRE (CUSTOM)	CODE
4-Door Hardtop 45439	
2-Door Convertible 45467	
4-Door Sedan Thin Pillar ...45469	
2-Door Coupe Hardtop 45487	

WILDCAT	CODE
4-Door Hardtop 46439	
2-Door Convertible 46467	
4-Door Sedan Thin Pillar ...46469	
2-Door Coupe Hardtop 46487	

WILDCAT (CUSTOM)	CODE
4-Door Hardtop 46639	
2-Door Convertible 46667	
2-Door Coupe Hardtop 46687	

ELECTRA	CODE
4-Door Hardtop 48239	
2-Door Coupe Hardtop 48257	
4-Door Sedan	
Semi Thin Pillar 48269	

ELECTRA (CUSTOM)	CODE
4-Door Hardtop 48439	
2-Door Coupe Hardtop 48457	
2-Door Convertible 48467	
4-Door Sedan	
Semi Thin Pillar 48469	

RIVIERA	CODE
2-Door Coupe Hardtop 49487	

G.S. 340	CODE
2-Door Coupe....................34017	

THE BODY NUMBER is the production serial number of the body. The prefix letter denotes the plant in which the body was built (refer to the assembly plant codes on the VIN plate).

THE PAINT CODE furnishes the key to the paint colors used on the car. A two letter code indicates the bottom and top colors respectively.

COLOR	CODE
Regal Black ....A
Riviera Turquoise ....B
Arctic White C
Sapphire Blue...........................D
Midnight Blue ....E
Blue Mist ....F
Gold Mist ....G
Green Mist ....H
Verde Green ....J
Aquamarine ....K
Shadow Turquoise L
Burgundy Mist ....N
Platinum Mist ....P
Apple Red ....R
Champagne Mist ....S
Ivory ....T
Riviera Plum ....U
Riviera Charcoal V
Riviera Fawn ....W
Riviera Red................................X
Riviera Gold ....Z

ENGINE NUMBER

Along with the VIN number the engine block is stamped with an engine production code. The code has a series of letters that identify the engine and a numeric production date code. The production code is stamped on the right side of the engine block. The production prefix code for 1967 is:

Transmissions		
	Standard	Optional
Special ....(1)...............(3)		
Skylark ....(1)...............(3)		
LeSabre ....(1)...............(3)(4)		
Wildcat ....(4)		
Electra ....(4)		
"225"		
Riviera ....(4)		
G.S.400 ....(1)............(2)(4)		

(1)	Manual 3 Speed
(2)	Manual 4 Speed
(3)	Super Turbine "300"
(4)	Super Turbine "400"

THE TRIM NUMBERS: N=Notch Seats B=Bucket Seats CT=Custom Trim ST=Standard Trim

Models	Material	Aqua	Black	Blue	Lt.Fawn	Green	Saddle	Maroon	Plum	Red	Ivory
33-3407	Cloth & Vinyl		108								
	Vinyl		118-138CT	111-131CT	114-134CT						
33-3438	Vinyl			111	114					117	
33-3469	Cloth & Vinyl		108	101			103				
	Vinyl		138	131	134						
35-3617	Cloth & Vinyl		188	181			183				
	Vinyl	166N	138-168N	131-161N	134-164N						
35-3635	Vinyl		138	131			133				
35-3669	Cloth & Vinyl	146	148	141			143				
	Vinyl		138	131	134						
43-4407	Cloth & Vinyl		188	181			183				
	Vinyl	166N	168N-198B	161N-191B	164N-194B						
43-4417	Cloth & Vinyl		188	181			183				
	Vinyl	166N	168N-198B	161N-191B	164N-194B						
43-4439	Cloth & Vinyl		158N	151N			153N	157N			
	Vinyl		168N	161N	164N						
43-4467	Cloth & Vinyl		185		184						
	Vinyl		168N-198B	161N-191B			163N			167N-197B	
4455-65	Vinyl		178	171		170	173			177	
4855-65	Vinyl		178	171		170	173			177	
4607-17	Vinyl	196B	185N-198B	191B	184N-194B		193B				
4667	Vinyl		185N-198B	191B	184N		193B			197B	
5200	Cloth & Vinyl		408	401		400	403				
5487	Cloth & Vinyl			411			413				
	Vinyl	426	428-478B	421			423				
5439	Cloth & Vinyl	416		411			413	417			
	Vinyl		428	421			423				
5467	Vinyl		428	421			423			427	
5469	Cloth & Vinyl	416		411			413	417			
	Vinyl		428	421			423				
6487	Cloth & Vinyl			411			413				
	Vinyl	426	428-478B	421			423				
6439	Cloth & Vinyl	416		411			413	417			
	Vinyl		428	421			423				
6467	Vinyl		428	421			423			427	
6469	Cloth & Vinyl	416		411			413	417			
	Vinyl		428	421			423				
6687	Vinyl	456N	458N-498B	451N	454N						
6639	Vinyl	456N	458N	451N	454N						
6667	Vinyl		458N-498B	451N	454N					457N	
8200	Cloth & Vinyl	636	638	631			633				
	Vinyl		678		674						
8457-67	Vinyl		698N-688B	691N	694N		693N			697N	
8439-69	Cloth & Vinyl		648	641	644	640		647			
	Vinyl		698N-695CT	691N	694N		693N				
9487	Vinyl Bench		608s		604s						
	Vinyl Bucket	656BCT	668Ns-658BCT	651BCT	664Ns		653BCT				
	Cloth & Vinyl Strato Bench		628CT		624CT						
	Vinyl Strato Bench		618N			610CT			619NCT		612NCT

Series	Engine Code# Prefix	CID	Use	Comp.	Carb.	HP
43400	NL	300	Standard	9.0:1	2-bbl	210
43600	NB	340	Optional	10.25:1	4-bbl	260
(1)	NH	225	Standard	9.0:1	2-bbl	160
(2)	NA	340	Standard	9.0:1	2-bbl	220
(2)	NB	340	Optional	10.25:1	4-bbl	260
44600	NR	400	Standard	10.25:1	4-bbl	340
(3)	MD/ND	430	Standard	10.25:1	4-bbl	360
Export	NM	300		7.6:1	2-bbl	210
Export	NX	340		8.1:1	2-bbl	220
Export	NE	430	Export	8.75:1	4-bbl	360

(1) 43300, 43500, 44300, 44400
(2) 44855, 44865, 44439, 44455, 44465, 44467, 44469, 45000
(3) 46000, 48000, 49000

VEHICLE IDENTIFICATION NUMBER

```
BUICK
444378H101555
```

Commonly referred to as the VIN NUMBER, this series of numbers and letters is stamped on a plate attached to left front door hinge pillar, and stamped on the engine block.

FIRST DIGIT: Identifies Buick Motor Division.

SECOND AND THIRD DIGITS: Identify the Series:

SERIES	CODE
G.S. 350	34
Special Deluxe	34
Skylark	35
Skylark Custom	44
G.S. 400	46
Sportwagon	44
Sportwagon Wood Grain	48
LeSabre	52
LeSabre Custom	54
Wildcat	64
Wildcat Custom	66
Electra 225	82
Electra 225 Custom	84
Riviera	94

FOURTH AND FIFTH DIGITS: Identify the Body Style:

2-Door Coupe	27
4-Door 2-Seat Station Wagon	35
2-Door Hardtop Coupe	37
4-Door Hardtop	39
2-Door Hardtop Coupe	47
4-Door 2-Seat Sportwagon	55
2-Door Hardtop Coupe	57
4-Door 3-Seat Sportwagon	65
Convertible	67
4-Door Sedan	69
2-Door Hardtop Coupe	87

SIXTH DIGIT, a number 8 is for Production Year 1968.

SEVENTH DIGIT, is a letter code used to identify the Assembly Plant.

EXAMPLE

4	44	37	8	H	101555
BUICK DIV.	SERIES	BODY STYLE	YEAR	ASSY PLANT	PRODUCTION CODE

ASSEMBLY PLANT	CODE
Flint	H
South Gate	C
Fremont	Z
Kansas City, Kansas	X
Wilmington	Y

Atlanta	D
Baltimore	E
Kansas City, Mo	K
Bloomfield	V
Oshawa, Ontario, Canada	

LAST 6 DIGITS: Represent the

THE TRIM NUMBERS: N=Notch Seats B=Bucket Seats

Models	Material	Black	Teal Blue	Green (PLATINUM)	Buckskin	Gold (Champagne)	Maroon	Parchment	Red	White (Ivory)
3327	CLOTH & VINYL	108				103				
	VINYL	198	191					194		
3369	CLOTH & VINYL	108	101			103				
3435	VINYL		111		113			114		
3437	VINYL	118-178*	111-171*	170*	173*			114		172*
3537	VINYL	118-168#	111-161#	160#				114		162#
3569	CLOTH & VINYL	128	121	120		123				
	VINYL	118	111					114		
4437	CLOTH & VINYL	138	131							
	VINYL	168#-178*	161#-171*	160#-170*	173*	133				162#-172*
4467	VINYL	158-178*	161#-171*	160#	163#				167#	152-172*
4439	CLOTH & VINYL		141#	140#		143#	147#			
	VINYL	168#								162#
4469	CLOTH & VINYL	138	131			133	137			
	VINYL	158								
4455-65	VINYL	188	181	180	183				187	
4855-65	VINYL	188	181	180	183				187	
4637	VINYL	158-178*	171*	170*	173*					152-172*
4667	VINYL	158-178*	171*							152-172*
5239-69-87	CLOTH & VINYL	408	401	400		403	407			
5487-6487	CLOTH & VINYL		411			413				
	VINYL	428-478*	421	420	423					
5439-6439	CLOTH & VINYL		411	410		413	417			
	VINYL	428	421		423					
5467	VINYL	428	421		423				427	
5469-6469	CLOTH & VINYL		411	410		413	417			
	VINYL	428	421		423					
6687	VINYL	458#-498*	451#	450#						452#
6639	CLOTH & VINYL	468#	461#							
	VINYL	498*	451#	450#						452#
6667	VINYL	458#-498*	451#						457#	452#
8239-57	CLOTH & VINYL	608	601			603				
	VINYL	618						614		
8269	CLOTH & VINYL	608	601			603				
8439	CLOTH & VINYL	628-658	621-651	620		654	627			
	VINYL	638#-668	631#		633#					
8457	VINYL	638#	631#		633#				637#	
8467	VINYL	638#	631#		633#				637#	
8469	CLOTH & VINYL	628	621	620			627			
	VINYL	638#	631#		633#					
9487	VINYL BENCH	675						672		
	VINYL BUCKET	698-678	691	690	693			674		
	CLOTH & VINYL -STRATO BENCH	685				684				
	VINYL -STRATO BENCH	688		680	683					682

Basic Production Numbers.

FISHER BODY NUMBER PLATE

Complete identification of each body is provided by a plate riveted to the cowl at the left of center under the hood.

THE STYLE NUMBER is a combination of the year, division, series, and body style. In the number plate illustrated, 68 represents the model year 1968; the first digit 4 indicates Buick Motor Division. The second and third digits 44, represent the body series Skylark Custom. The fourth and fifth digits 37, identify the body style 2-Door Hardtop Coupe. An X following the body style indicates that the body is equipped with electric power assists.

```
┌─────────────────────────────────────┐
│ ┌─────────────────────────────────┐ │
│ │  GENERAL MOTORS CORPORATION     │ │
│ │                                 │ │
│ ○ │ ST 68-44437  H  101555 BODY  │ ○ │
│ │   TR 138              AC PAINT  │ │
│ │                                 │ │
│ │        BODY BY FISHER           │ │
│ └─────────────────────────────────┘ │
└─────────────────────────────────────┘
```

SPECIAL DELUXE	CODE
2-Door Coupe Thin Pillar	43327
4-Door Sedan Thin Pillar	43369
4-Door 2-Seat Wagon	43435

G.S. 350	CODE
2-Door Coupe Hardtop	43437

SKYLARK	CODE
2-Door Coupe Hardtop	43537
4-Door Sedan Thin Pillar	43569

SKYLARK CUSTOM	CODE
2-Door Hardtop Coupe	44437
4-Door Hardtop Sedan	44439
Convertible	44467
4-Door Sedan	44469

SPORTWAGON	CODE
4-Door (2 Seats)	

1968 BUICK

Station Wagon 44455
4-Door (3 Seats) ....
Station Wagon 44465

G.S.400	CODE

2-Door Hardtop Coupe 44637
Convertible 44667

SPORTWAGON WOOD GRAIN	CODE

4-Door 2-Seat Wagon 44855
4-Door 3-Seat Wagon 44865

LESABRE	CODE

4-Door Hardtop 45239
4-Door Sedan Thin Pillar ...45269
2-Door Coupe Hardtop 45287

LESABRE (CUSTOM)	CODE

4-Door Hardtop 45439
2-Door Convertible 45467
4-Door Sedan Thin Pillar ...45469
2-Door Coupe Hardtop 45487

WILDCAT	CODE

4-Door Hardtop 46439
4-Door Sedan Thin Pillar....46469
2-Door Coupe Hardtop 46487

WILDCAT (CUSTOM)	CODE

4-Door Hardtop 46639
2-Door Convertible 46667
2-Door Coupe Hardtop 46687

ELECTRA 225	CODE

4-Door Hardtop 48239
2-Door Coupe Hardtop 48257
4-Door Sedan ....
  -Semi Thin Pillar..............48269

ELECTRA 225 (CUSTOM)	CODE

4-Door Hardtop 48439
2-Door Coupe Hardtop 48457
2-Door Convertible 48467
4-Door Sedan ....
  Semi Thin Pillar 48469

RIVIERA	CODE

2-Door Coupe Hardtop 49487

THE BODY NUMBER is the production serial number of the body. The prefix letter denotes the plant in which the body was built (refer to the assembly plant codes on the VIN plate.

THE PAINT CODE furnishes the key to the paint colors used on the car. A one letter code indicates the bottom and top colors respectively.

COLOR	CODE
Regal Black C/O ....A
Midnight Teal ....B
Arctic White C/O C
Blue Mist ....D
Deep Blue Metallic ....E
Teal Blue Mist ....F
Ivory Gold Mist ....G
Aqua Mist ....K
Med. Teal Blue Mist L
Burnished Saddle ....M
Maroon Metallic ....N
Tarpon Green Mist ....P
Scarlet Red ....R
Olive Gold Metallic ....S
Desert Beige ....T
Riviera Plum ....U
Charcoal Metallic V
Silver Beige Mist ....W
Buckskin X
Cameo Cream ....Y
Inca Silver Mist ....Z

ENGINE NUMBER

Along with the VIN number the engine block is stamped with an engine production code. The code has a series of letters that identify the engine and a numeric production date code. The production code is stamped on the right side of the engine block. The production prefix code for 1968 is:

Transmissions		
	Standard	Optional
Spec. Deluxe .(1) ....(3)
Skylark ....(1) ....(3)
Special Deluxe Station		
Wagon ....(1) ....(3)
LeSabre ....(1) ....(3)(4)
Wildcat.........(1) ....(4)
Electra 225 ....(4)
Riviera ....(4)
G.S. 350 ....(1) ....(3)
G.S.400 ....(1) ....(2)(4)
Stortwagon ....(1) ....(3)

(1) ....Manual 3 Speed
(2) ....Manual 4 Speed
(3) ....Super Turbine "300"
(4) ....Super Turbine "400"

Series	Engine Code# Prefix	CID	Use	Comp.	Carb.	HP
43300	?	250	Standard	8.5:1	2-bbl	155
43500	?	250	Standard	8.5:1	2-bbl	155
43435	PO	350	Standard	9.0:1	2-bbl	230
44400	PO	350	Standard	9.0:1	2-bbl	230
44800	PO	350	Standard	9.0:1	2-bbl	230
43300	PO	350	Optional	9.0:1	2-bbl	230
43500	PO	350	Optional	9.0:1	2-bbl	230
45000	PO	350	Standard	9.0:1	2-bbl	230
43000	PP	350	Optional	10.25:1	4-bbl	280
44000	PP	350	Optional	10.25:1	4-bbl	280
45000	PP	350	Optional	10.25:1	4-bbl	280
43437	PP	350	Standard	10.25:1	4-bbl	280
45000	PW	350	Optional	7.6:1	2-bbl	230
44600	PR	400	Standard	10.25:1	4-bbl	340
46000	PD	430	Standard	10.25:1	4-bbl	360
48000	PD	430	Standard	10.25:1	4-bbl	360
49000	PD	430	Standard	10.25:1	4-bbl	360
49000	PE	430	Export	8.75:1	4-bbl	?

VEHICLE IDENTIFICATION NUMBER

> BUICK
> 444 379 H101555

Commonly referred to as the VIN NUMBER, this series of numbers and letters is stamped on a plate attached to the top of the dash on the drivers side to be viewed through the windshield outside the car.

FIRST DIGIT: Identifies Buick Motor Division.

SECOND AND THIRD DIGITS: Identify the Series:

SERIES	CODE
Special Deluxe	33
Special Deluxe Wagon	34
G.S. 350	34
Skylark	35
Skylark Custom	44
Sportwagon	44
G.S. 400	46
LeSabre	52
LeSabre Custom	54
Wildcat	64
Wildcat Custom	66
Electra 225	82
Electra 225 Custom	84
Riviera	94

FOURTH AND FIFTH DIGITS: Identify the Body Style:

2-Door Coupe	27
4-Door 2-Seat Station Wagon	35
4-Door 2-Seat Wagon	36
2-Door Hardtop Coupe	37
4-Door Hardtop	39
4-Door 2-Seat Sportwagon	56
2-Door Hardtop Coupe	57
4-Door 3-Seat Sportwagon	66
Convertible	67
4-Door Sedan	69
2-Door Hardtop Coupe	87

SIXTH DIGIT, a number 9 is for Production Year 1969.

SEVENTH DIGIT, is a letter code used to identify the Assembly Plant.

EXAMPLE

4	44	37	9	H	101555
BUICK DIV.	SERIES	BODY STYLE	YEAR	ASSY PLANT	PRODUCTION CODE

ASSEMBLY PLANT	CODE
Flint	H
South Gate	C
Fremont	Z
Kansas City, Kansas	X
Wilmington	Y
Atlanta	D
Baltimore	B
Kansas City, Mo	K
Bloomfield	V
Oshawa, Ontario, Canada	I

LAST 6 DIGITS: Represent the Basic Production Numbers.

FISHER BODY NUMBER PLATE

Complete identification of each body is provided by a plate riveted to the cowl at the left of center under the hood.

THE BODY NUMBER PLATE identifies the model year, car division, series, style, body assembly plant, body number, trim combination, paint code and date build code.

THE STYLE NUMBER is a combination of the year, division, series, and body style. In the number plate illustrated, 69 is the model year 1969, digits 444 represent (4) Buick, (44) represents Skylark Custom. Digits (37) represents 2-door hardtop coupe.

SPECIAL DELUXE	CODE
2-Door Coupe Thin Pillar	43327
4-Door Sedan Thin Pillar	43369
4-Door 2-Seat Wagon	43435
4-Door 2-Seat Wagon	43436

G.S. 350	CODE
2-Door Coupe Hardtop	43437

SKYLARK	CODE
2-Door Coupe Hardtop	43537
4-Door Sedan Thin Pillar	43569

SKYLARK CUSTOM	CODE
2-Door Coupe Hardtop	44437
2-Door Convertible	44467
4-Door Hardtop	44439
4-Door Sedan Thin Pillar	44469

SPORTWAGON	CODE
4-Door 2-Seat Wagon	44456
4-Door 3-Seat Wagon	44466

GENERAL MOTORS CORPORATION

ST 69-44437 H 101555 **BODY**
TR 000 **AC PAINT**

BODY BY FISHER

G.S. 400	CODE
2-Door Coupe Hardtop	44637
2-Door Convertible	44667

LESABRE	CODE
2-Door Coupe Hardtop	45237
4-Door Hardtop	45239
4-Door Sedan Thin Pillar	45269

LESABRE CUSTOM	CODE
2-Door Coupe Hardtop	45437
4-Door Hardtop	45439
2-Door Convertible	45467
4-Door Sedan Thin Pillar	45469

WILDCAT	CODE
2-Door Coupe Hardtop	46437
4-Door Hardtop	46439
4-Door Sedan Thin Pillar	46469

WILDCAT CUSTOM	CODE
2-Door Coupe Hardtop	46637
4-Door Hardtop	46639
2-Door Convertible	46667

ELECTRA 225	CODE
2-Door Coupe Hardtop	48257
4-Door Hardtop	48239
4-Door Sedan Thin Pillar	48269

ELECTRA 225 CUSTOM	CODE
2-Door Coupe Hardtop	48457
4-Door Hardtop	48439
2-Door Convertible	48467
4-Door Sedan Thin Pillar	48469

RIVIERA	CODE
2-Door Coupe Hardtop	49487

THE BODY NUMBER is the production serial number of the body. The prefix letter denotes the plant in which the body was built (refer to the assembly plant codes on the VIN plate).

THE PAINT CODE furnishes the key to the paint colors used on the car. A one letter code indicates the bottom and top colors respectively.

COLOR	CODE
Regal Black	10
Cameo Yellow	40
Polar White	50
Twilight Blue	51
Signal Red	52
Crystal Blue	53
Turquoisemist	55
Verde Green	57
Limegreen	59
Burnished Brown	61
Champagnemist	63
Trumpet Gold	65
Burgundy Mist	67
Silver Mist	69
Embassy Gold	75
Antique Gold	77
Azure Blue	80
Sunset Silver	81
Olive Beige	82
Deep Gray Mist	83
Copper Mist	85

ENGINE NUMBER

Along with the VIN number the engine block is stamped with an engine production code. The code has a series of letters that identify the engine and a numeric production date code. The production code is stamped on the right side of the engine block. The production prefix code for 1969 is:

Transmissions

MODELS	TRANSMISSIONS
43327-69	(1)(3)
43537-69	(1)(3)
43327-69	(1)(3)(4)(5)
43537-69	(1)(3)(4)(5)
44437-39-67-69	(1)(3)(4)(5)
43437	(1)(2)(3)
43535-36	(1)(3)
44456-66	(1)(4)(5)
44637-67	(1)(2)(5)
45237-39-69	(1)(3)(5)
45437-39-67-69	(5)
46437-39-69	(1)(5)
46637-39-69	(1)(5)
48257-39-69	(5)
48457-39-67-69	(5)
49487	(5)
49487 G.S.	(5)
(1)	Manual 3 Speed
(2)	Manual 4 Speed
(3)	ST "300"
(4)	TH "350"
(5)	TH "400"

1969 BUICK

THE TRIM NUMBERS: N=Notch Seats B=Bucket Seats

Models	Material	Black	Blue	Buckskin	Burgundy	Green	Gold	Parchment	Peal
3327	CLOTH & VINYL	108		103					
	VINYL	118	111					114	
3435-36	VINYL		121	126					125
3369	CLOTH & VINYL	108	101	103					
	VINYL	128	121					124	
3437	VINYL	128-188B	121-188B	186B				124	185B
3537	VINYL	128-178N	121-171N	176N		170N		124	175N
3569	CLOTH & VINYL	138	131	133		130			
	VINYL	128	121					124	
4437	CLOTH & VINYL	148	141	143					
	VINYL	178N-188B	171N-181B	176N-186B		170N			175N-185B
4439	CLOTH & VINYL		151N	153N	157N	150N			
	VINYL	178N		176N					175N
4467	VINYL	168-178N-188B	171N	176N	187B			164	185B
4469	CLOTH & VINYL		141	143	147	140			
	VINYL	168		166					
4456-66	VINYL		191	196	197	190			195
4637	VINYL	168-188B		186B				164	185B
4667	VINYL	168-188B			187B			164	185B
5200	CLOTH & VINYL	408	401	403	407	400			
5437-6437	CLOTH & VINYL		411	413		410			
	VINYL	428-438B	421	426					425
5439-6439	CLOTH & VINYL		411	413		400			
	VINYL	428	421	426		410			425
5469-6469	CLOTH & VINYL		411	413		410			
	VINYL	428	421	426					425
5467	VINYL	428	421	426	427				
6637	VINYL	458N-478B	451N	453N				455N	
6639	CLOTH & VINYL	468N						464N	
	VINYL	458N	451N	453N					455N
6667	VINYL	458N							
8200	CLOTH & VINYL	608	601	603					
	VINYL	618						614	
8457	CLOTH & VINYL	648N	641N					644N	
	VINYL	638N		633N		630N			
8439	CLOTH & VINYL	628-648N	621-641N			620		624-644N	
	VINYL	638N-639N-658N	631N-632N	633N-636N					
8467	VINYL	638N	631N	633N-636N	637N				
8469	CLOTH & VINYL	628	621			620		624	
	VINYL	638N-639N	631N-632N	633N-636N					
9000	CLOTH & VINYL	678N						674N	
	VINYL (BENCH)	669-688N	691N	686N	687N	680N		666B	685N
	VINYL BUCKET	668-698					692N	664N-694	

Series	Engine Code# Prefix	CID	Use	Comp.	Carb.	HP
*	?	250	Standard	8.5:1	2-bbl	155*
*	RO	350	Optional	9.0:1	2-bbl	230
*	RP	350	Optional	10.25:1	4-bbl	280
44400	RO	350	Standard	9.0:1	2-bbl	230
44400	RP	350	Optional	10.25:1	4-bbl	280
44456,66	RR	400	Optional	10.25:1	4-bbl	340
43435,36	RO	350	Standard	9.0:1	2-bbl	230
43435,36	RP	350	Optional	10.25:1	4-bbl	280
**	RP	350	Standard	10.25:1	4-bbl	280
45000	RO	350	Standard	9.0:1	2-bbl	230
45000	RP	350	Optional	10.25:1	4-bbl	280
45000	RW	350	Export	8.0:1	2-bbl	230
44600	RR	400	Standard	10.25:1	4-bbl	340
44600	RS	400	Stage 1	10.25:1	4-bbl	350
46000	RD	430	Standard	10.25:1	4-bbl	360
***	RD	430	Standard	10.25:1	4-bbl	360
***	RE	430	Export	8.75:1	4-bbl	?

*   43327, 43369, 43537, 43569
**   43437, 43327(California GS)
*** 48000, 49000

VEHICLE IDENTIFICATION NUMBER

```
1960 CADILLAC
* 60K123456 *
```

Commonly referred to as the VIN NUMBER, this series of numbers and letters is stamped into the top left frame support next to the radiator support, and enclosed by asterisks. The number is also on the top surface of engine block forward of valve cover on left side.

EXAMPLE

*60	K	123456 *
Year	Body Style	Prod. Number

FIRST TWO DIGITS identifies the model year.

THIRD DIGIT, a letter, identifies the body style.

Style		Code
6467	Eldorado Biarritz	E
6437	Eldorado Seville	H
6267	Convertible	F
6237	Sixty-Two Coup	G
6229	Sixty-Two Sedan Six Window	K
6239	Sixty-Two Sedan Four Window	A
6337	Coupe DeVille	J
6329	Sedan Deville Six Window	L
6339	Sedan DeVille Four Window	B
6029	Fleetwood Sixty Special	M
6723	Fleetwood Seventy-Five Sedan	R
6733	Fleetwood Seventy-Five Limousine	S
6929	Eldorado Brougham	P
6890	Commercial Chassis	Z

LAST 6 DIGITS: Represent the BASIC PRODUCTION NUMBERS.

CADILLAC BODY NUMBER PLATE

Complete identification of each body is provided by a plate riveted to the cowl at the left of center under the hood.

```
CADILLAC DIV. GENERAL MOTORS CORP.
DETROIT, MICHIGAN
STYLE 60 - 6229   BODY FW-4
TRIM 12           PAINT 10
TOP 2 ACC. CEKMNSKY
THIS CAR FINISHED WITH
MAGIC MIRROR ACRYLIC LACQUER
BODY BY FISHER
```

THE STYLE NUMBER is a combination year and body style. In the number plate illustrated, 60 represents the model year 1960; 6229 represents 6-window 62 series sedan.

SERIES 62

Eldorado Biarritz	6467
Eldorado Seville	6437
Convertible	6267
Sixty-Two Coupe	6237
Sixty-Two Sedan Six Window	6229
Sixty-Two Sedan Four Window	6239
Coupe DeVille	6337
Sedan DeVille Six Window	6329
Sedan DeVille Four Window	6339

SERIES 60

Fleetwood Sixty Special 6029

SERIES 75

Fleetwood Seventy-Five Sedan	6723
Fleetwood Seventy-Five Limousine	6733
Eldorado Brougham	6929
Commercial Chassis	6890

THE TRIM NUMBER furnishes the key to trim color and material for each model SERIES.

Style 60-6029

Black (Cloth) w/White (Leather)	60
Grey (Cloth & Leather)	61
Blue (Cloth & Leather)	63
Plum (Cloth & Leather)	64
Fawn (Cloth & Leather)	65
Turquoise (Cloth & Leather)	66
Green (Cloth & Leather)	67
Grey (Cloth)	71
Blue (Cloth)	72
Tan (Cloth)	74
Grey w/White (Leather)	95
Blue w/White (Leather)	96
Green w/White (Leather)	97

*Export Car

Style 60-6229, 37, 39

Black (Cloth) w/White (Coated Fabric)	30
Grey (Cloth) w/Grey (Coated Fabric)	31
Blue (Cloth) w/Blue (Coated Fabric)	33
Plum (Cloth) w/Plum (Coated Fabric)	34
Fawn (Cloth) w/Fawn (Coated Fabric)	35
Turquoise (Cloth) w/Turquoise (Coated Fabric)	36
Green (Cloth) w/Green (Coated Fabric)	37

Style 60-6267

Black w/White (Leather)	20,20
Black (Leather)	21,21
Grey (Leather)	22,22
Blue (Leather)	23,23
Saddle (Leather)	25,25
Green (Leather)	27,27
Red w/White (Leather)	28,28
Red (Leather)	29,29

Style 60-6329, 37, 39

Silver & Black (Cloth) w/White (Leather)	4
Grey (Cloth & Leather)	4
Blue & Black (Cloth) w/Blue (Leather)	4
Plum (Cloth & Leather)	4
Fawn (Cloth & Leather)	4
Turquoise & Black (Cloth) w/Turquoise (Leather)	4
Green (Cloth & Leather)	4
Grey w/White (Leather)*	9
Blue w/White (Leather)*	9
Green w/White (Leather)*	9

*Export Car

Style 60-6437

White (Leather)	50, 50
Blue (Cloth & Leather)	53, 53
Pink (Cloth & Leather)	54, 54
Silver Beige (Leather)	55, 55
Green (Cloth & Leather)	57, 57
Mauve (Cloth & Leather)	58, 58
Red w/White (Leather)	59, 59

Style 60-6467

White (Leather)	10,10
Black (Leather)	11,11
Grey (Leather)	12,12
Blue (Leather)	13,13
Silver Beige (Leather)	15,15
Green (Leather)	17,17
Red (Leather)	19,19

Style 60-6723, 33
(6733 All Cloth Trim)

Grey (Cloth) 80, 81, 90
Fawn (Cloth) ....:............ 84, 85

Style 60-6733
(Leather Front Compartment and
Cloth Rear Compartment)

Gray(Leather and Cloth) 80,81,90
Black (Leather) 80E,81E,90E
w/Gray (Cloth)
Fawn (Leather) 84,85
Black (Leather) 84E,85E
w/Fawn (Cloth)

THE PAINT CODE furnished the key to the paint colors used on the car. A two number code indicated the color of the car. A two tone car has two sets of numbers (example 10-12). In the example the number 10 is the bottom color ebony, the number 12 is the top color olympic white.

COLOR	Code
Ebony (Black)	10
Olympicwhite	12
Platinum Grey	14
Aleutian Grey	16
Hampton Blue	22
Pelham Blue	24
York Blue	26
Arroyo Turquoise	29
Inverness Green	32
Glencoe Green	36
Beaumont Beige	44
Palomino	45
Fawn	46
Persian Sand	48
Pompeian Red	50
Lucerne Blue	94
Carrara Green	96
Champagne	97
Siena Rose	98
Heather	99

THE TOP NUMBER furnished the convertible top color code.

COLOR	Code
White	1
Black	2
Lt. Gold	4
Med. Blue	5
Lt. Sandalwood	6
Med. Pink	7
Lt. Blue	8

THE ACCESSORY CODE indicates the options that were installed in the car at the factory.

ENGINE NUMBER

The serial number of all 1960 Cadillac engines is stamped on the lower left hand side of the cylinder block, between the two welch plugs, just above the edge of the oil pan. This number is also stamped on top of the frame, on the left hand side bar just behind the radiator, and on the lubrication plate attached to the front face of the left door lock pillar. The engine serial number on the frame is placed between two stars.

Each Cadillac engine carries an engine unit number prefix, which indicates the type of engine, followed by numbers in numerical sequence, denoting the order in which engines were built, regardless of type, staring with number 1. The letters L.C. are added as a suffix to the engine unit number on all engines built to low compression specifications. Engines assembled with .010" oversized pistons may be identified by an asterisk stamped on the block ahead of the engine unit number.

The unit number on all engines is stamped on the bell housing portion of the crankcase behind the left hand cylinder block, directly above the cast rib, and numbered at right angles with the crankshaft.

06X - 6029, 6267, 6237, 6229, 6239, 6339
Without air conditoning, and 3 2-BBL carb.

06K - 6029, 6267, 6237, 6229, 6239, 6337, 6329, 6339
With air conditioning, and 4-BBL carb.

0QX - 6467, 6437
Without Air conditioning, and 3 2-BBL carb.

0QK - 6467, 6437, 6929
With Air Conditioning, and 3 2-BBL carb

07X - 6723, 6733, 6890
Without Air conditioning, and 3 2-BBL carb.

07K - 6723, 6733, 6890
With Air Conditioning, and 4-BBL carb.

BASIC ENGINE IN SERIES

Compression Ratio10.50 to 1
Horsepower:
Standard Engine
Developed at 4800 R.P.M.325 HP

Three 2-Barrel Carburetor Engine
Developed at 4800 R.P.M.345HP

Piston Displacement 390 Cu. In.:
Standard Engine
Torque, at 3100 R.P.M.430 Lbs. - Ft.

Three 2-Barrel Carburetor Engine:
Torque, at 3400 R.P.M.430 Lbs.-Ft.

VEHICLE IDENTIFICATION NUMBER

1961 CADILLAC
* 61K123456 *

Commonly referred to as the VIN NUMBER, this series of numbers and letters is stamped into the top left frame support next to the radiator support, and enclosed by asterisks. The number is also on the top surface of engine block forward of valve cover on left side.

EXAMPLE

*61	K	123456 *
Year	Body	Prod.
	Style	Number

FIRST TWO DIGITS identifies the model year.

THIRD DIGIT, a letter, identifies the body style.

Style	Code
6239 Sixty-Two Sedan Four Window	A
6299 Sixty-Two Sedan Short Deck	C
6229 Sixty-Two Sedan Six Window	K
6237 Sixty-Two Coupe	G
6267 Sixty-Two Convertible	F
6339 Sedan DeVille Four Window	B
6329 Sedan DeVille Six Window	L
6337 Coupe DeVille	J
6367 Eldorado Biarritz	E
6039 Sixty Special Sedan	M
6723 Fleetwood Sedan Nine Passenger	R
6733 Fleetwood Imperial Limousine	S
6890 Commercial	Z

LAST 6 DIGITS: Represent the BASIC PRODUCTION NUMBERS.

CADILLAC BODY NUMBER PLATE

Complete identification of each body is provided by a plate riveted to the cowl at the left of center under the hood.

CADILLAC DIV. GENERAL MOTORS CORP.
DETROIT, MICHIGAN
STYLE 61 - 6229   BODY FW-4
TRIM 20   PAINT12
TOP 2 ACC. CEKMNSKY
THIS CAR FINISHED WITH
MAGIC MIRROR ACRYLIC LACQUER
BODY BY FISHER

THE STYLE NUMBER is a combination year and body style. In the number plate illustrated, 61 represents the model year 1961; 6229 represents 6-window 62 series sedan.

SERIES 62

Sixty-Two Sedan Short Deck	6299
Eldorado Biarritz	6367
Convertible	6267
Sixty-Two Coupe	6237
Sixty-Two Sedan Short Deck	6229
Sixty-Two Sedan Six Window	6229
Sixty-Two Sedan Four Window	6239
Coupe DeVille	6337
Sedan DeVille Six Window	6329
Sedan DeVille Four Window	6339

SERIES 60

Fleetwood Sixty Special	6039

SERIES 75

Fleetwood Seventy-Five Sedan	6723
Fleetwood Seventy-Five Limousine	6733
Commercial Chassis	6890

THE TRIM NUMBER furnishes the key to trim color and material for each model SERIES.

Style 61-6029

Black (Cloth) w/White (Leather)	60
Gray (Cloth & Leather)	61
Blue (Cloth & Leather)	63
Sandalwood (Cloth & Leather)	64
Fawn (Cloth & Leather)	65
Turquoise (Cloth & Leather)	66
Green (Cloth & Leather)	67
Rose (Cloth & Leather)	69
Gray (Cloth)	71
Blue (Cloth)	72
Fawn (Cloth)	75

Style 61-6229,37,39

Black (Cloth) w/White (Coated Fabric)	30
Grey (Cloth) w/Grey (Coated Fabric)	31
Blue (Cloth) w/Blue (Coated Fabric)	33
Plum (Cloth) w/Plum (Coated Fabric)	34
Fawn (Cloth) w/Fawn (Coated Fabric)	35
Turquoise (Cloth) w/Turquoise (Coated Fabric)	36
Green (Cloth) w/Green (Coated Fabric)	37

Style 61-6267

Black w/White (Leather)	20,20B
Black (Leather)	21,21B
Blue (Leather)	23,23B
Sandalwood (Leather)	24,24B
Saddle (Leather)	25,25B
Green (Leather)	27,27B
Maroon w/White (Leather)	28,28B
Maroon (Leather)	29,29B

Style 61-6329,37,39,99

Black (Cloth) w/White (Leather)	40
Gray (Cloth & Leather)	41
Blue (Cloth & Leather)	43
Sandalwood (Cloth & Leather)	44

Turquoise (Cloth & Leather)	4
Green (Cloth & Leather)	4
Rose (Cloth & Leather) *	49

Style 61-6367

White (Leather)	10,10
Black (Leather)	11,11
Blue (Leather)	13,13
Sandalwood (Leather)	14,14
Copper (Leather)	15,15
Turquoise (Leather)	16,16
Mauve (Leather)	18,16
Maroon (Leather)	19,19

Style 61-6723,33
(6733 All Cloth Trim)

Gray (Cloth)	80,81,9
Fawn (Cloth)	84,85

Style 61-6733
(Leather Front Compartment and Cloth Rear Compartment)

Gray (Leather and Cloth)	80,81,9
Black (Leather) w/Gray (Cloth)	80E,81E,90E
Fawn (Leather)	84,8
Black (Leather) w/Fawn (Cloth)	84E,85

THE PAINT CODE furnished the key to the paint colors used on the car. A two number code indicated the color of the car. A two tone car has two sets of numbers (example 10-12). In the example the number 10 is the bottom color ebony, the number 12 is the top color olympic white.

Color	Code
Ebony (Black)	1
Olympic White	12
Platinum	14
Aleutian Gray	16
Bristol Blue	22
Dresden Blue	24
York Blue	26
San Remo Turquoise	29
Concord Green	32
Lexington Green	34

Granada Green 36
Laredo Tan 44
Tunis Beige 46
Fontana Rose 48
Pompeian Red 50
Nautilus Blue 94
Jade 96
Aspen Gold 97
Topaz 98
Shell Pear 99

THE TOP NUMBER furnished the convertible top color.

Color	Code
White	1
Black	2
Lt. Gold	4
Med. Blue	5
Lt. Sandalwood	6
Med. Pink	7
Lt. Blue	8

ENGINE NUMBER

The serial number of all 1961 Cadillac engines is stamped on the lower left hand side of the cylinder block, between the two welch plugs, just above the edge of the oil pan. This number is also stamped on top of the frame, on the left hand side bar just behind the radiator, and on the lubrication plate attached to the front face of the left door lock pillar. The engine serial number on the frame is place between two stars.

Each Cadillac engine carries an engine unit number prefix, which indicates the type of engine, followed by numbers in numerical sequence, denoting the order in which engines were built, regardless of type, starting with number 1. The letters L.C. are added as a suffix to the engine unit number on all engines built to low compression

specifications. Engines assembled with .010" oversized pistons may be identified by an asterisk stamped on the block ahead of the engine unit number.

The unit number on all engines is stamped on the bell housing portion of the crankcase behind the left hand cylinder block, directly above the cast rib, and numbered at right angles with the crankshaft.

16X 6039, 6267, 6237,
6229, 6239, 6337,
6329, 6339,6367, 6299
without air conditioning

16K 6039, 6267, 6237,
6229, 6239, 6337,
6329, 6339, 6367,6299
with airconditioning

17X 6723, 6733, 6890
with air conditioning

17K 6723, 6733, 6890
with air conditioning

BASIC ENGINE IN SERIES

Compression Ratio 10.50 to 1
Standard Engine
Developed 325 HP at 4800 R.P.M.

Piston Displacement 390 Cu. In.:
Standard Engine
Torque, 430 Lbs.-Ft. at 3100 R.P.M.

1962 CADILLAC

VEHICLE IDENTIFICATION NUMBER

```
1962 CADILLAC
* 62K123456 *
```

Commonly referred to as the VIN NUMBER, this series of numbers and letters is stamped into the top left frame support next to the radiator support, and enclosed by asterisks. The number is also on the top surface of engine block forward of valve cover on left side.

EXAMPLE

*62	K	123456 *
Year	Body Style	Prod. Number

FIRST TWO DIGITS identifies the model year.

THIRD DIGIT, a letter, identifies the body style.

Style	Code
6289 Sixty-Two Sedan Short Deck	A
6339 Sedan DeVille Four Window	B
6389 Sixty-Two Sedan four Window Park Avenue	D
6367 Eldorado Biarritz	E
6267 Sixty-Two Convertible	F
6247 Sixty-Two Coupe	G
6347 Coupe DeVille	J
6229 Sixty-Two Sedan Six Window	K
6329 Sedan DeVille Six Window	L
6039 Fleetwood Sixty Special	M
6239 Sixty-Two Sedan HT (4 Window)	N
6723 Fleetwood "75" Sedan Nine Passenger	R
6733 Fleetwood "75" Limousine	S
6890 Commercial	Z

LAST 6 DIGITS: Represent the BASIC PRODUCTION NUMBERS.

CADILLAC BODY NUMBER PLATE

Complete identification of each body is provided by a plate riveted to the cowl at the left of center under the hood.

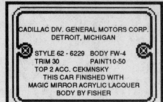

CADILLAC DIV. GENERAL MOTORS CORP.
DETROIT, MICHIGAN
STYLE 62 - 6229 BODY FW-4
TRIM 30 PAINT10-50
TOP 2 ACC. CEKMNSKY
THIS CAR FINISHED WITH
MAGIC MIRROR ACRYLIC LACQUER
BODY BY FISHER

THE STYLE NUMBER is a combination year and body style. In the number plate illustrated 62 represents the model year 1962; 6229 represents 6-window 62 series sedan.

SERIES 62	Code
Eldorado Biarritz	6367
Convertible	6267
Sixty-Two Coupe	6247
Sixty-Two Sedan Six Window	6229
Sixty-Two Sedan Four Window	6239
Coupe DeVille	6347
Sedan DeVille Six Window	6329
Sedan DeVille Four Window	6339
Sixty-Two Sedan Short Deck	6289
Sixty-Two four Window Park Avenue	6389

SERIES 60	Code
Fleetwood Sixty Special	6039

SERIES 75	Code
Fleetwood Seventy-Five Sedan	6723
Limousine	6733
Commercial Chassis	6890

THE TRIM NUMBER furnishes the key to trim color and material for each model SERIES.

Black (Cloth) w/White (Leather)	60
Lt. Gray (Cloth & Leather)	61
Lt. Blue (Cloth & Leather)	63
Med. Fawn (Cloth & Leather)	65
Lt. Turquoise (Cloth & Leather)	66
Lt. Green (Cloth & Leather)	67
Lt. Rose (Cloth & Leather)	69
Lt. Gray (Cloth)	71
Med. Fawn (Cloth)	75
Dk. Maroon (Cloth)	79

Styles 62-6229,39,47,89

Black (Cloth) w/White (Coated Fabric)	30
Lt. Gray (Cloth) w/Lt. Gray (Coated Fabric)	31
Lt. Blue (Cloth) w/Lt. Blue (Coated Fabric)	33,33A
Lt. Sandalwood (Cloth) w/Lt. Sandalwood (Coated Fabric)	34
Lt. Gold (Cloth) w/Lt. Gold (Coated Fabric)	35
Lt. Turquoise (Cloth) w/Lt.Turquoise (Coated Fabric)	36,36A
Lt. Green (Cloth) w/Lt. Green (Coated Fabric)	37,37A
Lt. Rose (Cloth) w/Lt. Rose (Coated Fabric)	39

Style 62-6267

White (Leather) w/Black Trim	20,20B
Black (Leather)	21,21B
Lt. Blue (Leather)	23,23B
Lt. Gold (Leather)	24,24B
Med. Saddle Tan (Leather)	25,25B
Lt. Green (Leather)	27,27B
White (Leather) w/Red Trim	28,28B
Med. Red (Leather)	29,29
Lt. Sandalwood (Leather)	26,26B

Style 62-6329,39,47,89

Black (Cloth) w/ White Leather	40

Gray (Cloth & Leather)	4
Blue (Cloth & Leather)	4?
Sandalwood (Cloth & Leather)	4
Turquoise (Cloth & Leather)	4
Green (Cloth & Leather)	4
Rose (Cloth & Leather) *	4?

Styles 62-6339,47

White (Leather)	50,50?
Black (Leather)	51,51?
Lt. Sandalwood (Leather)	54,54?
Med. Red (Leather)	59,59?

Style 62-6367

White (Leather)	10,10?
Black (Leather)	11,11?
Black & White (Cloth) w/Black (Leather)	12,12?
Med. Blue (Leather)	13,13?
Lt. Sandalwood (Leather)	14,14?
Med. Saddle Tan (Leather)	15,15?
Turquoise (Leather)	16,16?
Med. Pink (Leather)	18,18?
Med. Red (Leather)	19,19?

Styles 62-6723,33
(6733 All Cloth Trim)

Lt Gray (Cloth)	80,81,9?
Med. Fawn (Cloth)	84,8?

Style 62-6733
(Leather Front Compartment and Cloth Rear Compartment)

Gray (Leather & Cloth)	80G,81G, 90?
Black (Leather) w/Gray (Cloth)	80,81,9?
Fawn (Leather & Cloth)	80F,85?
Black (Leather) w/ Fawn (Cloth)	84,8?

THE PAINT CODE furnished th? key to the paint colors used on th? car. A two tone car has two sets o? numbers (example 10-50). In th? example the number 10 is the bo?tom color ebony, the number 50 i? the top color pompeian red.

COLOR	Code
White*	1
Black*	2
Concord Blue*	3
Sandalwood*	4
Med. Saddle Tan (Bronze)*	5
Pink (Heather)*	8
Red*	9
Ebony (Black)	10
Olympic White	12
Nevada Silver	14
Aleutian Gray	16
Newport Blue	22
Avalon Blue	24
York Blue	26
Turquoise	29
Sage	32
Granada Green	36
Sandalwood	44
Maize	45
Driftwood Beige	46
Laurel	48
Pompeian Red	50
Burgundy	52
Silver ""Fire-Frost""	61
Gold ""Fire-Frost""	64
Neptune Blue	94
Pinehurst Green	96
Victorian Gold	97
Bronze	98
Heather	99

THE TOP NUMBER furnished the code to convertible top color.

COLOR	CODE
White	1
Black	2
Lt. Gold	4
Med. Blue	5
Lt. Sandalwood	6
Med. Pink	7
Lt. Blue	8

ENGINE NUMBER

The serial number of all 1962 Cadillac engines is stamped on the lower left hand side of the cylinder block, between the two welch plugs, just above the edge of the oil pan. This number is also stamped on top of the frame, on the left hand side bar just behind the radiator, and on the lubrication plate attached to the front face of the left door lock pillar. The engine serial number on the frame is placed between two stars.

Each Cadillac engine carries an engine unit number prefix, which indicated the type of engine, followed by numbers in numerical sequence, denoting the order in which engines were built, regardless of type, starting with number 1. The letters L.C. are added as a suffix to the engine unit number on all engines built to low compression specifications. Engines assembled with .010" oversized pistons may be identified by an asterisk stamped on the block ahead of the engine unit number.

The unit number on all engines is stamped on the bell housing portion of the crankcase behind the left hand cylinder block, directly above the cast rib, and numbered at right angles with the crankshaft.

26X	6039, 6229, 6239, 6329, 6339, 6289, 6267, 6367, 6347, 6247, 6389 Without Air Conditioning
26K	6039, 6229, 6239, 6329, 6339, 6289, 6267, 6367, 6347, 6247, 6389 With Air Conditioning
27X	6723, 6733, 6890 Without Air Conditioning
27K	6723, 6733, 6890 With Air Conditioning

BASIC ENGINE IN SERIES

Compression Ratio 10.50 to 1
Standard Engine
Developed 325 HP at 4800 R.P.M.

Piston Displacement 390 Cu. In.:
Standard Engine
Torque, 430 Lbs.-Ft. at 3100 R.P.M.

VEHICLE IDENTIFICATION NUMBER

```
   1963 CADILLAC
   * 63K123456 *
```

Commonly referred to as the VIN NUMBER, this series of numbers and letters is stamped into the top left frame support next to the radiator support, and enclosed by asterisks. The number is also on the top surface of engine block forward of valve cover on left side.

EXAMPLE

*63	K	123456 *
Year	Body Style	Prod. Number

FIRST TWO DIGITS identifies the model year.

THIRD DIGIT, a letter, identifies the body style.

Style	Code
6339 Sedan DeVille Four Window	B
6389 (4 Window Park Av)	D
6367 Eldorado Biarritz	E
6267 Sixty-Two Convertible	F
6257 Sixty-Two Coupe	G
6357 Coupe DeVille	J
6229 Sixty-Two Sedan Six Window	K
6329 Sedan DeVille Six Window	L
6039 Fleetwood Sixty Special	M
6239 Sixty-Two Sedan HT (4 Window)	N
6723 Fleetwood "75" Sedan Nine Passenger	R
6733 Fleetwood "75" Limousine	S
6890 Commercial	Z

LAST 6 DIGITS: Represent the BASIC PRODUCTION NUMBERS.

CADILLAC BODY NUMBER PLATE

Complete identification of each body is provided by a plate riveted to the cowl at the left of center under the hood.

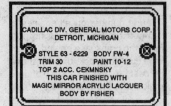

```
CADILLAC DIV. GENERAL MOTORS CORP.
         DETROIT, MICHIGAN
   STYLE 63 - 6229   BODY FW-4
   TRIM 30        PAINT 10-12
   TOP 2 ACC. CEKMNSKY
   THIS CAR FINISHED WITH
 MAGIC MIRROR ACRYLIC LACQUER
        BODY BY FISHER
```

THE STYLE NUMBER is a combination year and body style. In the number plate illustrated, 63 represents the model year 1963; 6229 represents 6-window 62 series sedan.

SERIES 62	Code
Eldorado Biarritz	6367
Convertible	6267
Sixty-Two Coupe	6257
Sixty-Two Sedan Six Window	6229
Sixty-Two Sedan Four Window	6239
Coupe DeVille	6357
Sedan DeVille Six Window	6329
Sedan DeVille Four Window	6339
Sedan Park Av	6389

SERIES 60	Code
Fleetwood Sixty Special	6039

SERIES 75	Code
Fleetwood Seventy-Five Sedan	6723
Limousine	6733
Commercial Chassis	6890

THE TRIM NUMBER furnishes the key to trim color and material for each model SERIES.

Style 63-6039

Black (Cloth) w/White (Leather)	60
Lt. Gray (Cloth & Leather)	61
Dk. Blue (Cloth & Leather)	62A
Lt. Blue (Cloth & Leather)	63
Lt. Sandalwood (Cloth & Leather)	64
Lt. Beige (Cloth & Leather)	65A
Lt. Turquoise (Cloth & Leather)	66
Lt. Green (Cloth & Leather)	67
White (Leather)	70
Black (Leather)	71
Lt. Gray (Cloth)	72
Lt. Sandalwood (Leather)	74
Lt. Beige (Cloth)	75
Med. Red (Leather)	79

Styles 62-6229,39,47,89

Black (Cloth) w/White (Coated Fabric)	30
Lt. Gray (Cloth) w/Lt. Gray (Coated Fabric)	31
Lt. Blue (Cloth) w/Lt. Blue (Coated Fabric)	33,33A
Lt. Sandalwood (Cloth) w/Lt. Sandalwood (Coated Fabric)	34
Lt. Gold (Cloth) w/Lt. Gold (Coated Fabric)	35
Lt. Turquoise (Cloth) w/Lt.Turquoise (Coated Fabric)	36,36A
Lt. Green (Cloth) w/Lt. Green (Coated Fabric)	37,37A
Lt. Rose (Cloth) w/Lt. Rose (Coated Fabric)	39

Style 62-6267

White (Leather) w/Black Trim	20,20B
Black (Leather)	1,21B
Lt. Blue (Leather)	23,23B

Styles 63,6329,39,57,89

Black (Cloth) w/White (Leather)	40
Lt. Gray (Cloth & Leather)	4
Dk. Blue (Cloth & Leather)	4?
Lt. Blue (Cloth & Leather)	4?
Lt. Sandalwood (Cloth & Leather)	44
Lt. Turquoise (Cloth & Leather)	4
Lt. Green (Cloth & Leather)	4?
Lt. Rose (Cloth & Leather)	4?

Styles 63-6339,57,89

White (Leather)	50,50
Black (Leather)	51,51
Lt.Sandalwood (Leather)	54,54B
Med. Red (Leather)	59,59B

Style 63-6367

White (Leather)	18,18B
Black (Leather)	11,11B
Lt. Blue (Leather)	13,13B
Lt. Sandalwood (Leather)	14,14B
Lt. Tan (Leather)	15,15B
Beryl (Lt. Aquamarine) (Leather)	16,16B
Emerald (Lt. Green) (Leather)	17,17B
Med. Red (Leather) (Leather Front Compartment and Cloth Rear Compartment)	19,19B

Styles 63-6723,33
(6733 All Cloth Trim)

Lt. Gray (Cloth)	80,81,90
Med. Fawn (Cloth)	84,85

Style 63-6733
(Leather Front Compartment and Cloth Rear Compartment)

Black (Leather) w/Gray (Cloth)	80,81,9?
Gray (Leather & Cloth)	90G
Black (Leather) & Lt. Beige (Cloth)	84,8?
Lt. Beige (Leather & Cloth)	84F,85F
Lt. Beige(Leather&Cloth)	84f,85F

THE PAINT CODE furnished the key to the paint colors used on the car. A two number code indicated the color of the car. A two tone car has two sets of numbers (example 10-12). In the example the number 10 is the bottom color ebony, the number 12 is the top color aspen white.t

COLOR	Code
Ebony (Black)	10
Aspen White	12
Nevada Silver	14
Cardiff Gray	16
Kenton Blue	22
Basque Blue	24
Somerset Blue	26
Turino Turquoise	29
Basildon Green	32
Brewster Green	36
Bahama Sand	44
Fawn	46
Palomino	47
Friar Rose	48
Matador Red	50
Royal Maroon	52
Silver Frost	92
Frost Aquamarine	94
Frost Green	96
Frost Gold	97
Frost Red	98
Leather	99
Leather	99

THE TOP NUMBER furnished the code to convertible top color.

COLOR	Code
White	1
Black	2
Lt. Gold	4
Med. Blue	5
Lt. Sandalwood	6
Med. Pink	7
Lt. Blue	8
Silver Blue	9

ENGINE NUMBER

The serial number of all 1963 Cadillac engines is stamped on the lower left hand side of the cylinder block, just between the two welch plugs, just above the edge of the oil pan. This number is also stamped on top of the frame, on the left hand side bar just behind the radiator, and on the lubrication plate attached to the front face of the left door lock pillar. The engine serial number on the frame is placed between two stars.

Each Cadillac engine carries an engine unit number prefix, which indicates the type of engine, followed by numbers in numerical sequence, denoting the order in which engines were built, regardless of type, starting with number 1. The letters L.C. are added as a suffix to the engine unit number on all engines built to low compression specifications. Engines assembled with .010" oversized pistons may be identified by an asterisk stamped on the block ahead of the engine unit number.

The unit number on all engines is stamped on the bell housing portion of the crankcase behind the left hand cylinder block, directly above the cast rib, and numbered at right angles with the crankshaft.

36X 6039,6229,6257,
6267,6239,6329,
6339,6357, 6367,6389

36K 6039,6229,6257,
6267,6239,6329,
6339,6357, 6367,6389
With Air Conditioning

37X 6723,6733,6890

37K 6723,6733,6890
With Air Conditioning

BASIC ENGINE IN SERIES

Compression Ratio 10.50 to 1
Standard Engine
Developed 325 HP at 4800 R.P.M.

Piston Displacement 390 Cu. In.:
Standard Engine
Torque, 430 Lbs.-Ft. at 3100 R.P.M.

VEHICLE IDENTIFICATION NUMBER

```
1964 CADILLAC
* 64K123456 *
```

Commonly referred to as the VIN NUMBER, this series of numbers and letters is stamped into the top left frame support next to the radiator support, and enclosed by asterisks. The number is also on the top surface of engine block forward of valve cover on left side.

EXAMPLE

*64	K	123456 *
Year	Body Style	Prod. Number

FIRST TWO DIGITS identifies the model year.

THIRD DIGIT, a letter, identifies the body style.

Style	Code
6339 Sedan DeVille Four Window	B
6367 Eldorado	E
6267 Sixty-Two Convertible	F
6257 Sixty-Two Coupe	G
6357 Coupe DeVille	J
6229 Sixty-Two Sedan Six Window	K
6329 Sedan DeVille Six Window	L
6039 Fleetwood Sixty Special	M
6239 Sixty-Two Sedan HT (4 Window)	N
6723 Fleetwood "75" Sedan Nine Passenger	R
6733 Fleetwood "75" Limousine	S
6890 Commercial	Z

LAST 6 DIGITS: Represent the BASIC PRODUCTION NUMBERS.

CADILLAC BODY NUMBER PLATE

Complete identification of each body is provided by a plate riveted to the cowl at the left of center under the hood.

```
CADILLAC DIV. GENERAL MOTORS CORP.
DETROIT, MICHIGAN
STYLE 64 - 6229   BODY FW-4
TRIM 40          PAINT10-12
TOP 2 ACC. CEKMNSKY
THIS CAR FINISHED WITH
MAGIC MIRROR ACRYLIC LACQUER
BODY BY FISHER
```

THE STYLE NUMBER is a combination of year and body style. In the plate illustration, 64 represents the model year: 1964, 6329 represents 6 window Sedan DeVille.

SERIES 62	Code
Eldorado	6367
Convertible	6267
Sixty-Two Coupe	6257
Sixty-Two Sedan Six Window	6229
Sixty-Two Sedan Four Window	6239
Coupe DeVille	6357
Sedan DeVille Six Window	6329
Sedan DeVille Four Window	6339
Sedan Park Av	6389

SERIES 60	Code
Fleetwood Sixty Special	6039

SERIES 75	Code
Fleetwood Seventy-Five Sedan	6723
Limousine	6733
Commercial Chassis	6890

THE TRIM NUMBER furnishes the key to trim color and material for each model SERIES.

Style 64-6039

Black (Cloth)	60
w/White (Leather)	
Lt. Gray (Cloth & Leather)	61
Midnight Blue	62
(Cloth & Leather)	
Lt. Blue (Cloth & Leather)	63
Lt. Sandalwood	64
(Cloth & Leather)	
Lt. Beige (Cloth & Leather)	65A
Lt. Turquoise (Cloth & Leather)	66
Lt. Green (Cloth & Leather)	67
Lt. Gray (Cloth)	71
Lt. Beige (Cloth)	75
White (Leather)	80
Black (Leather)	81
Lt. Sandalwood (Leather)	84
Med. Red (Leather)	89

Styles 64-6229,39,57

Black (Cloth) w/White	30
(Coated Fabric)	
Lt. Gray (Cloth) w/Lt.	31
Gray (Coated Fabric)	
Midnight Blue(Cloth)	32
w/Midnight Blue (Coated Fabric)	
Lt. Blue (Cloth) w/Lt.	33
Blue (Coated Fabric)	
Lt. Sandalwood (Cloth)	34
w/Lt. Sandalwood	
(Coated Fabric)	
Lt. Turquoise (Cloth)	36
w/Lt.Turquoise	
(Coated Fabric)	
Lt. Green (Cloth)	37
w/Lt. Green (Coated Fabric)	

Style 62-6267

White (Leather)	20,20B
Black (Leather)	21,21B
Lt. Blue (Leather)	23,23B
Lt. Sandalwood (Leather)	24,24B
Lt. Tan (Leather)	25,25B
Lt. Lime w/White(Leather)	26,26B
Lt. Green (Leather)	27,27B
White (Leather)	28,28B
Med. Red (Leather)	29,29B

Style 64-6329,39,57

Black (Cloth)	4
w/White (Leather)	
Lt. Gray (Cloth & Leather)	4
Midnight Blue	4
(Cloth & Leather)	
Lt. Blue (Cloth & Leather)	43
Lt. Sandalwood	4
(Cloth & Leather)	
Lt. Turquoise	4
(Cloth & Leather)	
Lt. Green (Cloth & Leather)	4
Lt. Lime (Cloth & Leather)	4

Styles 64-6339,57

White (Leather)	50,50
Black (Leather)	51,51
Lt. Sandalwood (Leather)	54,54
Med. Red (Leather)	59,59

Style 64-6367

White (Leather)	10,10
Black (Leather)	11,11
Lt. Blue (Leather)	13,13
Lt. Sandalwood (Leather)	14,14
Lt. Tan (Leather)	15,15
Lt. Aquamarine (Leather)	16,16
Dk. Green (Leather)	17,17
Med. Red (Leather)	19,19

Styles 64-6723,33
(6733 All Cloth Trim)

Med. Gray (Cloth)	9
Lt. Gray (Cloth)	91,9
Lt. Beige (Cloth)	94,9

Style 64-6733
(Leather Front Compartment and Cloth Rear Compartment)

Black (Leather)	9
w/Med. Gray (Cloth)	
Lt. Gray (Leather)	90
w/Med. Gray (Cloth)	

lack (Leather) 91,92
/Lt. Gray (Cloth)
t. Gray (Cloth) 91G,92G
  Leather) .
lack (Leather) 94,95
/Lt. Beige
t. Beige (Leather) 94F,95F
/Med. Gray (Cloth)

HE PAINT CODE furnished the
ey to the paint colors used on
e car. A two number code
dicated the color of the car. A
/o tone car has two sets of
umbers (example 10-12). In the
xample the number 10 is the
ottom color ebony, the number
2 is the top color olympic white.

OLOR	Code
ony (Black)	10
spen White	12
evada Silver	14
ardiff Gray	16
eacon Blue	22
ruce Blue	24
merset Blue	26
urino Turquoise	29
eacrest Green	32
ne	34
le Green	36
ahama Sand	44
erra Gold	46
alomino	47
atador Red	50
oyal Maroon	52
remist Blue	92
remist Aquamarine	94
remist Green	96
remist Saddle	97
remist Red	98

HE TOP NUMBER furnished the
de to convertible top color.

COLOR	Code
White	1
Black	2
Aquamarine	3
Lt. Lime	4
Sandalwood	5
Lt. Blue	8
Silver Blue	9

ENGINE NUMBER

The serial number of all 1964 Cadillac engines is stamped on the lower left hand side of the cylinder block, between the two welch plugs, just above the edge of the oil pan. This number is also stamped on top of the frame, on the left hand side bar just behind the radiator, and on the lubrication plate attached to the front face of the left door lock pillar. The engine serial number on the frame is placed between two stars.

Each Cadillac engine carries an engine unit number prefix, which indicates the type of engine, followed by numbers in numerical sequence, denoting the order in which engines were built, regardless of type, starting with number 1. The letters L.C. are added as a suffix to the engine unit number on all engines built to low compression specifications. Engines assembled with .010" oversized pistons may be identified by an asterisk stamped on the block ahead of the engine unit number.

The unit number on all engines is stamped on the bell housing portion of the crankcase behind the left hand cylinder block, directly above the cast rib, and numbered at right angles with the crankshaft.

44X 6039,6329,6339,
        6357,6367,6267

44K 6039,6329,6339,
        6357,6367,6267
        With Air Conditioning

46X 6229,6257,6239

46K 6229,6257,6239
        With Air Conditioning

47X 6723,6733, 6890

47K 6723,6733, 6890
        With Air Conditioning

BASIC ENGINE IN SERIES

Compression Ratio 10.50 to 1
Standard Engine
Developed 340 HP at 4600 R.P.M.

Piston Displacement 429 Cu. In.:
Standard Engine
Torque, 480 Lbs.-Ft. at 3000 R.P.M.

VEHICLE IDENTIFICATION NUMBER

```
1965 CADILLAC
*N5100001*
```

Commonly referred to as the VIN NUMBER, this series of numbers and letters is stamped into the top surface of frame R/H side rail forward of front coil suspension. (May be obscured by rubber splash shield.) This number is also located on the rear portion of the block behind the left cylinder bank.

EXAMPLE

* N 5 100001 *

First character "N", represents the Model Identity Number

Second character "5", represents the Model Year: 1965

Style	Code
68339 Sedan DeVille Four Window	B
68467 Eldorado Conv	E
68367 DeVille Convertible	F
68257 Calais Coupe	G
68357 Coupe DeVille	J
68269 Calais Sedan	K
68369 Sedan DeVille Six Window	L
68069 Fleetwood Sixty Special (Brougham Option)	M
68239 Calais Hardtop Sedan	N
69723 Fleetwood Seventy- Five Sedan	R
69733 Fleetwood "75" Limousine	S
69890 Commercial	Z

The last six digits are the basic production code.

CADILLAC BODY NUMBER PLATE

Complete identification of each body is provided by a plate attached to the top surface of shroud, left under hood, near cowl.

```
CADILLAC DIV. GENERAL MOTORS CORP.
DETROIT, MICHIGAN
09C
ST 65 - 68369    FWD 19 BODY
TR 346           40-60 PAINT
AEYKMSNL

BODY BY FISHER
```

THE STYLE NUMBER is a combination of year and body style. In the plate illustrated, "65" represents the model year: 1965. "68369" represents the style: 4-Door Sedan DeVille.

Calais Series	Code
Calais Hardtop Sedan	68239
Calais Coupe	68257
Calais Sedan	68269

DeVille Series	Code
Hardtop Sedan DeVille	68339
Coupe DeVille	68357
DeVille Convertible	68367
Sedan DeVille	68369

Fleetwood Series	Code
Fleetwood Sixty Special (Brougham Option)	68069
Fleetwood Eldorado Convertible	68467
Fleetwood "75" Sedan	69723
Fleetwood "75" Limousine	69733
Commercial Chassis	69890

THE TRIM NUMBER furnishes the key to trim color and material for each model style. - A "B" following indicates bucket seats.

Style 65-68069

Black (Cloth) w/Black (Leather)	010
Lt. Gray (Cloth & Leather)	016
Lt. Gray (Cloth)	018
Lt. Blue (Cloth & Leather)	020
Lt. Blue (Cloth)	021
Midnight Blue (Cloth)	026
White (Leather)	052
White (Leather) w/Med. Carpet & Dk. Blue	053 (A)
White (Leather) w/Dk. Red Carpet & Dk. Red	054 (B)
White (Leather) w/Med. Turquoise Carpet &Dk. Turquoise	055 (A)
Lt. Sandalwood (Leather)	081
Med. Red (Leather)	099

Styles 65-68239,57,69"

Black (Cloth) w/White (Coated Fabric)	210
Lt. Gray (Cloth) w/Lt. Gray (Coated Fabric)	216
Lt. Blue (Cloth) w/Lt. Blue (Coated Fabric)	220
Midnight Blue (Cloth) w/Midnight Blue (Coated Fabric)	226
Lt. Turquoise (Cloth) w/Lt. Turquoise (Coated Fabric)	228
Lt. Green (Cloth) w/Lt. Green (Coated Fabric)	230
Lt. Sandalwood (Cloth) w/Lt. Sandalwood (Coated Fabric)	241

Styles 65-68339,57"

Black (Cloth) w/White (Leather)	310
Dk. Gray (Cloth) w/Lt. Gray (Leather)	319
Lt. Blue (Cloth & Leather)	320
Midnight Blue (Cloth & Leather)	326
Lt. Turquoise (Cloth & Leather)	328
Lt. Green (Cloth & Leather)	230
Lt. Sandalwood (Cloth & Leather)	341
Dk. Bronze (Cloth) w/Med. Bronze (Leather)	346

Styles 65-68339,57"

Black (Leather)	351,351B
White (Leather)	352,352B
White (Leather)	353,353B(A)

w/Med. Blue Carpet & Dk. Blue White (Leather)	354,354B (B)
w/Dk. Red Carpet & Dk. Red White (Leather)	355,355B (A)
w/Med. Turquoise Carpet & Dk. Turquoise Lt. Sandalwood (Leather)	381,381B
Med. Red (Leather)	388,388B

Style 65-68367

Black (Leather)	351,351B
White (Leather)	352,352B
White (Leather) w/Med. Blue Carpet & Dk. Blue	353,353B
White (Leather) w/Dk. Red Carpet & Dk. ReD	354,354B
Med. Bronze (Leather)	386,386B
Med. Red (Leather)	388,388B

Style 65-68467

Black (Leather)	451,451B
White (Leather) w/Black Carpet	452,452B
White (Leather) w/Red Carpet	454,454B
Med. Gray-Blue (Leather)	461,461B
Med. Blue-Green (Leather)	476,476B
Lt. Sandalwood (Leather)	481,481B
Lt. Tan (Leather)	483,483B
Med. Red (Leather)	488,488B

Style 65-69723

Lt. Gray (Cloth)	716
Lt. Gray (Cloth) w/ Med. Gray (cloth)	718
Med. Gray (Cloth)	719
Midnight Blue (Cloth)	726
Lt. Beige (Cloth)	744

Style 65-69733
(Leather Front Compartment and Cloth Rear Compartment)

Black (Leather)......................716
w/ Lt. Gray (Cloth)
Lt. Gray.................716G
Leather & Cloth)
Black (Leather)......................718
w/Lt. Gray (Cloth)
Lt. Gray.................718G
Leather & Cloth)
Black (Leather) 719
Lt. Gray (Leather).................719G
w/Med.Gray (Cloth)
Black (Leather) 726
w/Midnight Blue (Cloth)
Midnight Blue 726M
Leather & Cloth)

THE PAINT CODE furnished the key to the paint colors used on the car. A two number code indicated the color of the car. A two tone care has two sets of numbers (example 46-90). In the example the number 46 is the bottom color Samoan Bronze, the number 90 is the top color Peacock Firemist.

Color	Code
Sable (Black)	10
Aspen White	12
Starlight Silver	16
Ascot Gray	18
Hampton Blue	20
Tahoe Blue	24
Ensign Blue	26
Alpine Turquoise	28
Cascade Green	30
Inverness Green	36
Cape Ivory	40
Sandalwood	42
Sierra Gold	44
Samoan Bronze	46
Matador Red	48
Claret Maroon	49
Peacock Firemist	90
Sheffield Firemist	92
Jade Firemist	96
Saddle Firemist	97
Crimson Firemis	98

THE TOP NUMBER furnished the code to convertible top color.

COLOR	Code
White	1
Black	2
Blue	3
Brown	5
Sandalwood	6

ENGINE NUMBER

The serial number of all 1965 Cadillac engines is stamped on the lower left hand side of the cylinder block, between the two welch plugs, just above the edge of the oil pan. This number is also stamped on top of the frame, on the left hand side bar just behind the radiator, and on the lubrication plate attached to the front face of the left door lock pillar. The engine serial number on the frame is placed between two stars.Each Cadillac engine carries an engine unit number prefix, which indicates the year of the engine followed by numbers in numerical sequence, denoting the order in which engines were built, regardless of type, starting with number 1. The letters L.C. areadded as a suffix to the engine unit number on all engines built to low compression specifications. Ensembled with .010" oversized pistons may be identified by an asterisk stamped on the block ahead of the engine unit number.

The unit number on all engines is stamped on the bell housing portion of the crankcase behind the left hand cylinder block, directly above the cast rib, and numbered at right angles with the crankshaft.

BASIC ENGINE IN SERIES

Compression Ratio 10.50 to 1 HP Standard Engine
Developed 340 HP at 4600 R.P.M.
Piston displacement 429 Cu. In.: Standard Engine
Torque, 480 LBS.-FT. at 3000 R.P.M.

VEHICLE IDENTIFICATION NUMBER

```
1966 CADILLAC
*N6100001*
```

Commonly referred to as the VIN NUMBER, this series of numbers and letters is stamped into the top surface of frame R/H side rail forward of front coil suspension. (May be obscured by rubber splash shield.) This number is also located on the rear portion of the block behind the left cylinder bank.

EXAMPLE

* N 6 100001 *

First character "N", represents the Model Identity Number

Second character "6", represents the Model Year: 1966

Style	Code
68339 Sedan DeVille Hardtop	B
68169 Fleetwood Sedan	D
68467 Eldorado Conv	E
68367 DeVille Convertible	F
68257 Calais Coupe	G
68357 Coupe DeVille	J
68269 Calais Sedan	K
68369 Sedan DeVille Six Window	L
68069 Fleetwood Sixty Special Sedan	M
68239 Calais Hardtop Sedan	N
68169 Fleetwood Brougham Sedan	P
69723 Fleetwood Seventy-Five Sedan	R
69733 Fleetwood "75" Limousine	S
69890 Commercial	Z

The last six digits are the basic production code.

CADILLAC BODY NUMBER PLATE

Complete identification of each body is provided by a plate attached to the top surface of shroud, left under hood, near cowl.

```
CADILLAC DIV. GENERAL MOTORS CORP.
DETROIT, MICHIGAN
09C
ST 66 - 68369    FWD 19 BODY
TR 346       12-20 PAINT
PEYKMSNR

BODY BY FISHER
```

THE STYLE NUMBER is a combination of year and body style. In the plate illustrated, "66" represents the model year: 1966. "68369" represents the style: 4-Door Sedan DeVille.

Calais Series	Code
Calais Hardtop Sedan	68239
Calais Coupe	68257
Calais Sedan	68269

DeVille Series	Code
Hardtop Sedan DeVille	68339
Coupe DeVille	68357
DeVille Convertible	68367
Sedan DeVille	68369

Fleetwood Series	Code
Fleetwood Sixty Special	68069
Fleetwood Broughman Sedan	68169

Fleetwood Eldorado Convertible	68467
Fleetwood "75" Sedan	69723
Fleetwood "75" Limousine	69733
Commercial Chassis	69890

THE TRIM NUMBER furnishes the key to trim color and material for each model style. - A "B" following indicates bucket seats.

Styles 68069,68169

Black Dartmoor (Cloth) w/Black (Leather)	011
Lt. Gray Delmont (Cloth)	016
Med. Blue Dartmoor (Cloth) w/Med. Blue (Leather)	020
Med. Blue Delmont (Cloth)	021
Midnight Blue Damask (Cloth) w/Midnight Blue(Leather)	026
Med. Turquoise Damask (Cloth)w/Lt.Turquoise (Leather)	028
Med. Turquoise Delmont (Cloth)	029
Med. Green Delmont (Cloth)	030
Med. Beige Dartmoor (Cloth) w/Med. Beige (Leather)	042
Med. Beige Delmont (Cloth)	043
Med. Gold Damask) (Cloth) w/Med. Gold (Leather)	044

Med. Crimson Damask (Cloth) w/Med. Crimson Black (Leather)	047
Black (Leather)	051
White (Leather) w/Black	052 (A)
White (Leather) w/Med. Blue	053 (A)
White (Leather) w/Dk. Red	054 (A)
White (Leather) w/Med. Turquoise	055 (A)
Med. Blue (Leather)	060
Antique Dk. Saddle (Leather)	083
Lt. Gold (Leather)	084
Med. Red (Leather)	088

Styles 68239,57,69

Black Delrio (Cloth) w/Black (Coated Fabric)	211
Dk. Gray Danbury (Cloth) w/Lt. Gray (Coated Fabric)	216
Dk. Blue Danbury (Cloth) w/Lt. Blue (Coated Fabric)	226
Dk. Turquoise Delrio (Cloth) w/Lt. Turquoise (CoatedFabric)	228

Styles 68339,57,69

Black Desmond (Cloth) 311
w/Black (Leather)
Lt. Gray Danube (Cloth) 316
w/Lt. Gray (Leather)
Med. Blue Danube (Cloth) 320
w/Med. Blue (Leather)
Med. Turquoise Desmond 328
(Cloth) w/Med. Turquoise
(Leather)
Med. Green Danube 330
(Cloth) w/Med. Green
(Leather)
Med. Beige Danube 342
(Cloth) w/ Med. Beige
(Leather)
Med. Gold Desmond 344
(Cloth) w/Lt. Gold
(Leather)
Dk. Copper Desmond 346
(Cloth) w/Dk. Copper
(Leather)
Black (Leather) 351,351B
White (Leather) 325,352B
w/Black
White (Leather) .... 353 (A)
w/Med. Blue
White (Leather) .... 354 (A)
w/Dk. Red
White (Leather) .... 355 (A)
w/Med. Turquoise
Med. Blue (Leather) 360
Med. Turquoise (Leather) 368
Dk. Green (Leather) 371
Antique Dk. Saddle 383,383B
(Leather)
Lt. Gold (leather) 384
Med. Red (Leather) 388,388B

Style 68467

Black (Leather) 451,451B
White (Leather) 452,452B
w/Black
White (Leather) .... 457 (A)
w/Med. Vermillion
White (Leather) .... 458 (A)
w/Midnight Blue
Midnight Blue 466,466B
(Leather)
Dk. Green (Leather) 471,471B
Antique Dk. Saddle 483,483B
(Leather)
Lt. Gold (Leather) 484,484B
Med. Vermillion 489,489B
(Leather)

Style 69723

Lt. Gray Delmont (Cloth) 716
Med. Gray Decordo (Cloth) ... 719
Med. Blue Delmont (Cloth) ... 721
Midnight Blue Damask 726
(Cloth)
Med. Beige Dresden 743
(Cloth)

Style 69733
Leather Front Compartment
and Cloth Rear Compartment

Black (Leather) 716
w/Lt. Gray Delmont
(Cloth)
Lt. Gray (Leather) 716G
w/Lt. Gray Dresden
(Cloth)
Black (Leather) 719
w/Med. Gray Decordo
(Cloth)
Lt. Gray (Leather) 719G
w/Med. Gray Decordo
(Cloth)

Style 69723

Black (Leather)w/Lt. 719
Gray Delmont (Cloth)
Med. Gray Decordo 721
(Cloth)Black (Leather) w/
Med.Blue Delmont (Cloth)

Midnight Blue 721M
(Leather) w/Med. Blue
Dresden (Cloth)
Black (Leather) 726
w/Midnight Blue
Damask (Cloth)
Midnight Blue (Leather) 726M
Black (Leather) w/Med. 743
BeigeDresden (Cloth)
Med. Beige (Leather) w/ 743F
Med. Beige Dresden (Cloth)

THE PAINT CODE furnished the
key to the paint colors used on
the car. A two number code indicates the color of the car. In
1966 two-tone was not a factory
option. In the example 46 is the
color code - fawn. The second
number is the top color.

Color	Code
Sable (Black)	10
Strathmore White	12
Starlight Silver	16
Summit Gray	18
Mist Blue	20
Marlin Blue	24
Nocturne Blue	26
Caribbean Aqua	28
Cascade Green	30
Inverness Green	36
Cape Ivory	40
Sandalwood	42
Antique Gold	44
Autumn Rust	46
Flamenco Red	48
Claret Maroon	49
Cobalt Firemist	90
Crystal Firemist	92
Tropical Green Firemist	96
Ember Firemist	98

THE TOP NUMBER furnished the
code to convertible top color.

COLOR	Code
White	1
Black	2
Blue	3
Brown	5
Sandalwood	6

ENGINE NUMBER

The serial number of all 1966
Cadillac engines is stamped on
the lower left hand side of the
cylinder block, between the two
welch plugs, just above the edge
of the oil pan. This number is
also stamped on top of the frame,
on the left hand side bar just
behind the radiator, and on the
lubrication plate attached to the
front face of the left door
lockpillar. The engine serial
number on the frame is place
between two stars.

Each Cadillac engine carries an
engine unit number prefix, which
indicates the year, followed by
numbers in numerical sequence,
denoting the order in which
engines were built, regardless of
type, starting with number 1. The
letters L.C. are added as a suffix
to the engine unit number on all
engines built to low compression
specifications.

BASIC ENGINE IN SERIES

Compression Ratio 10.50 to 1
Standard Engine
Developed 340 HP at 4600
R.P.M.

Piston Displacement 429 Cu. In.:
Standard Engine
Torque, 480 Lbs.-Ft. at 3000
R.P.M.

VEHICLE IDENTIFICATION NUMBER

```
1967 CADILLAC
*N7100001*
```

Commonly referred to as the VIN NUMBER, this series of numbers and letters is stamped into the top surface of frame R/H side rail forward of front coil suspension. (May be obscured by rubber splash shield.) This number is also located on the rear portion of the block behind the left cylinder bank.

EXAMPLE

* N 7 100001 *

First character "N", represents the Model Identity Number

Second character "7", represents the Model Year: 1967

Style	Code
68349 Sedan DeVille Hardtop	B
68367 DeVille Convertible	F
68257 Calais Coupe	G
69347 Fleetwood Eldorado	H
68347 Coupe DeVille	J
68369 Calais Sedan	K
68369 Sedan DeVille Six Window	L
68069 Fleetwood Sixty Special Sedan	M
68249 Calais Hardtop Sedan	N
68169 Fleetwood Brougham Sedan	P
69723 Fleetwood Seventy- Five Sedan	R
69733 Fleetwood "75" Limousine	S
69890 Commercial	Z

The last six digits are the basic productiob code.

CADILLAC BODY NUMBER PLATE

Complete identification of each body is provided by a plate attached to the top surface of shroud, left under' hood, near cowl.

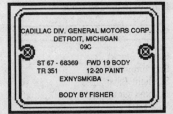

```
CADILLAC DIV. GENERAL MOTORS CORP.
DETROIT, MICHIGAN
09C
ST 67 - 68369   FWD 19 BODY
TR 351          12-20 PAINT
EXNYSMKIBA

BODY BY FISHER
```

THIS STYLE NUMBER is a combination of year and body style. In the plate illustrated, "67" represents the model year: 1967. "68369 represents the style: 4-door Sedan DeVille.

Calais Series	Code
Calais Hardtop Sedan	68249
Calais Coupe	68247
Calais Sedan	68269

DeVille Series	Code
Hardtop Sedan DeVille	68349
Coupe DeVille	68347
DeVille Convertible	68367
Sedan DeVille	68369

Fleetwood Series	Code
Fleetwood Sixty Special	68069
Fleetwood Broughman Sedan	68169
Fleetwood Eldorado Convertible	68347

Fleetwood "75" Sedan 69723
Fleetwood "75" Limousine 69733
Commercial Chassis 69890

THE TRIM NUMBER furnishes the key to trim color and material for each model style. - A "B" following indicates bucket seats.

Styles 68069, 68169

Black Damascus (Cloth)	010
w/ Black (Leather)	
Black Dartmoor (Cloth)	011
w/Black (Leather)	
Lt. Gray Delmont (Cloth)	016
Med. Blue Dartmoor	020
(Cloth) w/Med. Blue (Leather)	
Med. Blue Delmont (Cloth)	021
Dark Blue Diplomat	025
(Cloth) w/Med. Blue(Leather)	
Midnight Blue Damask	026
(Cloth) w/Midnight Blue(Leather)	
Med. Turquoise Damask	028
(Cloth) w/Lt. Turquoise (Leather)	
Med. Turquoise Delmont	029
(Cloth)	
Med. Green Delmont (Cloth)	030
Med. Covert Damascus	040
(Cloth) w/Med. Covert(Leather)	
Med. Beige Dartmoor (Cloth)	042
w/Med. Beige (Leather)	
Med. Beige Delmont (Cloth)	043

Med. Gold Damask (Cloth)	04
w/Med. Beige (Leather)Med. Crin son Damask	047
(Cloth) w/Med. Crimson (Leather)	
Dark Maroon Diplomat	04
(Cloth) w/Dark Maroon (Leather)	
Black (Leather)	05
White (Leather) w/Black	052 (A
White (Leather)	053 (A
w/Med. Blue	
White (Leather) w/Dk. Red	054(A
White (Leather) w/Med.	055 (A
Turquoise	
Med. Blue (Leather)	06
Dark Green (Leather)	07
Light Sandalwood (Leather)	08
Med. Saddle (Leather)	08
Med. Red (Leather)	08
Dark Maroon (Leather)	08

Styles 68247, 49, 69

Black Duet (Cloth)	21
w/Black (Coated Fabric)	
Dark Blue Duet (Cloth)	22
w/Med. Blue (CoatedFabric)	
Dark Aqua Duet (Cloth)	22
w/Med. Aqua (CoatedFabric)	
Dark Green Duet (Cloth)	23
w/Med. Green(Coated Fabric)	
Dark Covert Duet (Cloth)	24
w/Med. Covert (Coated Fabric)	
Dark Beige Duet (Cloth)	24
w/Med. Beige (Coated Fabric)	

Black (Coated Fabric)   251
Dark Beige (Coated Fabric)   282

Styles 68339,57,69

Black Duchess (Cloth) 311
w/Black (Leather)
Med. Blue Duchess (Cloth) ... 320
w/Med. Blue (Leather)
Dark Blue Darien (Cloth) 326
w/Dark Blue(Leather)
Med. Aqua Darien (Cloth) 328
w/Med. Aqua (Leather)
Med. Green Duchess 330
(Cloth) w/Med. Green (Leather)
Med. Covert Darien (Cloth) ... 340
w/Med. Covert (Leather)
Med. Beige Duchess (Cloth)   344
w/Med. Beige(Leather)
Dark Maroon Duet (Cloth) 349
w/Dark Maroon (Leather)
Black (Leather) 351,351B
White (Leather) 352
w/Black Carpet and Beltline trim.
White (Leather)w/Med. Blue   353
Carpet and Belt Line Trim
White (Leather)w/Dark 354
Red Carpet and Belt Line Trim
White (Leather) w/Med. 355
Aqua Carpet and Belt Line Trim
Med. Blue (Leather) 360
Light Sandalwood (Leather) .. 382
Med. Saddle (Leather) 385
Med. Red (Leather) 388,388B

Style 68367

Black (Leather) 351,351B
White (Leather) w/ 352,352B
Black Carpet and Belt Line Trim
White (Leather) 353
White (Leather) 354
w/Dark Red Carpet and
Belt Line Trim
White (Leather) 355
w/Med. Aqua Carpet and Belt
Line Trim
Med. Blue (Leather) 360
Med. Aqua (Leather) 368
Med. Green (Leather) 371
Med. Covert (Leather) 380
Light Sandalwood 382,382B
Med. Saddle (Leather) 385
Med. Red (Leather) 388
Dark Maroon (Leather) 389
Turquoise (Leather)

Style 69347

Black Dalmatian (Cloth) 410
Black Darien (Cloth) 411
w/Black (Coated Fabric)
Dark Blue Darien (Cloth) 426
w/Dark Blue (Coated Fabric)
Dark Aqua Darien (Cloth) 429
w/Dark Aqua (Coated Fabric)
Dark Green Darien (Cloth) 431
w/Dark Green (Coated Fabric)
Med. Beige Darien (Cloth) 444
w/Med. Beige (Coated Fabric)
Dark Maroon Darien (Cloth) .. 449
w/Dark Maroon (Coated Fabric)
Black (Leather) 451,451B
White (Leather) w/ 452
Black Carpet and Belt Line Trim
Dark Blue (Leather) 466
Dark Aqua (Leather) 469
Dark Green (Leather) 471
Light Sandalwood 482,482B
(Leather)
Med. Saddle (Leather) 485
Med. Red (Leather) 488
Dark Maroon (Leather) 489

Style 69723

Light Gray Devonshire 716
(Cloth)
Med. Gray Decordo (Cloth) ... 719
Med. Blue Devonshire (Cloth) 721
Dark Blue Damascus (Cloth)   726
w/Dark Blue (Leather)
Med. Beige Devonshire 743
(Cloth)

Style 69733
Leather Front Compartment
and Cloth Rear Compartment

Black (Leather) w/Light Gray
Devonshire (Cloth)716
Light Gray (Leather) w/ 716G
Light Gray Devonshire (Cloth)
Black (Leather) 719
w/Med. Gray Decordo (Cloth)
Light Gray (Leather) 721M
w/Med. Gray Devonshire (Cloth)
Decordo (Cloth) 719G
Black (Leather) w/ 721
Med. Blue Devonshire (Cloth)
Dark Blue (Leather) w/ 726
Med. Blue Damascus (Cloth)

Dark Blue (Leather) w/ 726M
Dark Blue Damascus (Cloth)
Black (Leather) w/Med. Beige
Devonshire (Cloth)743
Black (Leather) w/Dark Blue Med.
Beige (Leather) 743F
w/Med. Beige Devonshire
(Cloth)

THE PAINT CODE indicates the
color used, as well as the convertible or roof panel option colors in
the example 12 indicates Grecian
White and 20 indicates Black top.

Color	Code
Sable (Black)	10
Grecian White	12
Regal Silver	16
Summit Gray	18
Venetian Blue	20
Marina Blue	24
Admiralty Blue	26
Capri Aqua	28
Pinecrest Green	30
Sherwood Green	36
Persian Ivory	40
Sudan Beige	42
Baroque Gold	43
Doeskin	44
Flamenco Red	48
Regent Maroon	49
Atlantis Blue Firemist	90
Crystal Firemist	92
Tropic Green Firemist	96
Olympic Bronze Firemis	97

Style 68367
CONVERTIBLE TOPS COLOR
OPTIONS

White .... Option #1
Black .... Option #2
Dark Blue .... Option #3
Dark Brown .... Option #5
Sandalwood .... Option #6

ROOF PANEL COVERING OP-
TIONS

White .... Option #1
Black .... Option #2
Dark Blue .... Option#3
Dark Brown .... Option #5
Sandalwood .... Option #6

ENGINE NUMBER

The serial number of all 1967 Cadillac engines is stamped on the lower
left hand side of the cylinder block,
between the two welch plugs, just
above the edge of the oil pan. This
number is also stamped on top of
the frame, on the left hand side bar
just behind the radiator, and on the
lubrication plate attached to the
front face of the left door lockpillar.
The engine serial number on the
frame is place between two stars.

Each Cadillac engine carries an
engine unit number prefix, which
indicates style code, followed by
numbers in numerical sequence,
denoting the order in which engines were built, regardless of type,
starting with number 1. The letters
L.C. are added as a suffix to the
engine unit number on all engines
built to low compression specifications. Engines assembled with
.010" oversized pistons may be
identified by an asterisk stamped
on the block ahead of the engine
unit number.

The unit number on all engines is
stamped on the bell housing portion of the crankcase behind the left
hand cylinder block, directly above
the cast rib, and numbered at right
angles with the crankshaft.

BASIC ENGINE IN SERIES

Compression Ratio 10.50 to 1
Standard Engine
Developed 340 HP at 4600 R.P.M.

Piston Displacement 429 Cu. In.:
Standard Engine
Torque, at 480 Lbs.-Ft. 3000
R.P.M.

VEHICLE IDENTIFICATION NUMBER

```
┌─────────────────────────┐
│   1968 CADILLAC         │
│      *N8100001*         │
└─────────────────────────┘
```

Commonly referred to as the VIN NUMBER, this series of letters and numbers is stamped on a steel plate and riveted to the cowl bar at the lower left corner of the windshield. Also stamped on a pad on the rear upper portion of the cylinder block behind the intake manifold, and on the left side of the transmission case. (Minus Model Identity Symbol)

EXAMPLE

* N 8 100001 *

First character "N", represents the Model Identity Number

Second character "8" represents the model year: 1968

Style	Code
68349 Sedan DeVille Hardtop	B
68367 DeVille Convertible	F
68247 Calais Coupe	G
69347 Fleetwood Eldorado	H
68347 Coupe DeVille	J
68369 Sedan DeVille -Six Window	L
68069 Fleetwood Sixty Special Sedan	M
68249 Calais Hardtop Sedan	N
68169 Fleetwood Brougham Sedan	P
69723 Fleetwood Seventy- Five Sedan	R
69733 Fleetwood "75" Limousine	S
69890 Commercial	Z

The last six digits are the basic production code.

CADILLAC BODY NUMBER PLATE

Complete identification of each body is provided by a plate attached to the top surface of shroud, left under hood, near cowl.

```
┌──────────────────────────────────┐
│ CADILLAC DIV. GENERAL MOTORS CORP.│
│        DETROIT, MICHIGAN          │
│              09C                  │
│  ST 68-68367    FWD 123456        │
│                 BODY              │
│  TR 351         12-20 PAINT       │
│                                   │
│        BODY BY FISHER             │
└──────────────────────────────────┘
```

THE STYLE NUMBER is a combination of year and body style. In the plate illustrated, "68" represents the model year: 1968. 68367 represents the style: DeVille convertible.

Calais Series	CODE
Calais Hardtop Sedan	68249
Calais Coupe	68247

DeVille Series	CODE
Hardtop Sedan DeVille	68349
Coupe DeVille	68387
DeVille Convertible	68367
Sedan DeVille	68369

Fleetwood Series	Code
Fleetwood Sixty Special	68069
Fleetwood Broughman Sedan	68169
Fleetwood "75" Sedan	69723
Fleetwood "75"	

Limousine	69733
Commercial Chassis	69890
Feetwood Eldorado	69347

THE TRIM NUMBER furnishes the key to trim color and material for each model style. - A "B" following indicates bucket seats.

Style 68069, 68169

Black DuBarry (Cloth)	010
w/ Black (Leather)	
Black Damsel (Cloth)	011
w/ Black (Leather)	
Lt. Gray Dunstan (Cloth)	016
Med. Blue Dunstan (Cloth)	021
Dk. Blue DuBarry (Cloth)	026
w/ Dk. Blue (Leather)	
Dk. Aqua DuBarry (Cloth)	029
w/ Dk. Aqua (Leather)	
Dk. Green Damsel (Cloth)	031
w/ Dk. Green (Leather)	
Med. Covert DuBarry (Cloth)	040
w/ Med. Covert (leather)	
Lt. Beige Dunstan (Cloth)	043
Dk. Maroon Damsel (Cloth)	049
w/ Dk. Maroon (Leather)	
Black (leather)	051
White (Leather)	052
w/ Black Carpet	
Dk. Blue (Leather)	066
Dk. Green (Leather)	071
Lt. Sandalwood (leather)	082
Med. Saddle (Leather)	085

Med. Red (leather)	088
Dk. Maroon (Leather)	089

Style 68247, 49

Black Dakarta (Cloth)	211
w/ Black (Coated Fabric)	
Dk. Blue Dakarta (Cloth)	226
w/ Dk. Blue (Coated Fabric)	
Dk. Aqua Dakarta (Cloth)	229
w/ Dk. Aqua (Coated Fabric)	
Dk. Green Dakarta (Cloth)	231
w/ Dk. Green (Coated Fabric)	
Med. Covert Dakarta (Cloth)	240
w/ Med. Covert (Coated Fabric)	
Lt. Beige Dakarta (Cloth)	244
w/ Lt. Beige (Coated Fabric)	
Black (Coated Fabric)	251
Lt. Sandalwood	282
(Coated Fabric)	

Style 68347, 49, 69

Black Domino (Cloth)	311
w/ Black (Leather)	
Med. Blue Domino (Cloth)	320
w/ Dk. Blue (Leather)	
Dk. Blue Decor (Cloth)	326
w/ Dk. Blue (Leather)	
Dk. Aqua Decor (Cloth)	329
w/ Dk. Aqua (Leather)	
Dk. Green Domino (Cloth)	331
w/ Dk. Green (Leather)	
Med. Covert Decor (Cloth)	340
w/ Med. Covert (Leather)	

t. Beige Domino (Cloth) 344
w/ Lt. Beige (Leather)
k. Maroon Decor (Cloth) 349
w/ Dk. Maroon (Leather)
Black (Leather) 351
White (Leather) 352
w/ Black Carpet
White (Leather) 353
w/ Dk. Blue Carpet
White (Leather) 354
w/ Dk. Red Carpet
k. Blue (Leather) 366
t. Sanalwood (Leather) 382
Med. Sandalwood (Leather) 385
Med. Red (Leather) 388

Style 68367

Black (Leather) 351,351B
White (leather) 352
w/ Black Carpet
White (Leather) 353
w/ Dk. Blue Carpet
White (Leather) 354
w/ dk. Red Carpet
k. Blue (Leather) 366
k. Aqua (Leather) 369
k. Green (Leather) 371
Med. Covert (Leather) 380
t. Sandalwood 382,382B
Leather)
Med. Saddle (Leather) 385
Med. Red (Leather) 388

Style 39347

Black Deauville (Cloth) 410
w/ Black (Coated Fabric)
Black Diamond (Cloth) 411
w/ Black (Coated Fabric)
k. Blue Deauville (Cloth) 426
w/ Dk. Blue (Coated Fabric)
k. Aqua Diamond (Cloth) 429
w/ Dk. Aqua (Coated Fabric)
k. Green Deauville (Cloth) .. 431
w/ Dk. Green (Coated Fabric)
ed. Covert Diamond (Cloth) 440
w/ Med. Covert (Coated Fabric)
Beige Deauville (Cloth) 444
w/ Lt. Beige (Coated Fabric)
Maroon Diamond (Cloth) 449
w/ Dk. Maroon (Coated Fabric)
ack (Leather) 451,451B
White (Leather)w/ Black 452
arpet & Belt LIne Trim

White (Leather) w/ Dk. Blue .. 453
Carpet & Belt Line Trim
Whitre (Leather) w/ Dk. Red   454
Carpet & Belt Line Trim
Dk. Blue (Leather) 466
Dk. Aqua (Leather) 469
Dk. Green (Leather) 471
Med. Covert (Leather) 480
Lt. Sanalwood 482,482B
(Leather)
Med. Saddle (Leather) 485
Med. Red (Leather) 488
Dk. Maroon (Leather) 489

Style 39723

Lt. Gray Dunstan (Cloth) 716
Med. Gray Decordo (Cloth) ... 719
Med. Blue Dunstan (Cloth) ... 721
Dk. DuBarry (Cloth) ....
726
Lt. Beige Dunstan (Cloth) 743

Style 69733
Leather Front Compartment &
Cloth Rear Compartment

Black (Leather) w/ Gray 716
Dunstan (Cloth)
Lt. Gray (Leather) w/Lt. 716G
Gray Dunstan (Cloth)
Black (Leather) w/ Med. 719
Gray Decordo (Cloth)
Lt. Gray (Leather) w/ Med.   719G
Gray Decordo (Cloth)
Black (Leather) w/ Med. 721
Blue Dunstan (Cloth)
Black (Leather) w/ Dk. 726
Blue DuBarry (Cloth)
Black (Leather) w/ Lt. 743
Beige Dunstan (Cloth)

THE PAINT CODE indicates the
color used, as well as the
convertable or roof panel option
colors in the exable 12 indicates
Grecian White and 20 indicated
Black Top.

COLOR   Code

Sable Black 10
Grecian White 12
Regal Silver 16
Summit Gray 18

Arctic Blue 20
Normandy Blue 24
Emperor Blue 26
Caribe Aqua 28
Silver Pine Green 30
Ivanhoe Green 36
Kashmir Ivory 40
Sudan Beige 42
Baroque Gold 43
Chestnut Brown 44
San Mateo Red 48
Regent Maroon 49
Specre Blue Firemist 90
Topaz Gold Firemist 94
Monterey Green Firemist 96
Rosewood Firemist 97
Madeira Plum Firemist 98

CONVERTIBLE TOP
COLOR OPTIONS

White .... Option #1
Black .... Option #2
Dk. Blue .... Option #3
Dk. Brown .... Option #4
Sandalwood .... Option #5

ROOF PANEL
COVERING OPTIONS

White .... Option #1
Black .... Option #2
Dk. Blue .... Option #3
Dk. Brown .... Option #4
Sandalwood .... Option #5

ENGINE NUMBER

The serial number of all 1968 Cadillac engines is stamped on the lower
left hand side of the cylinder block,
between the two welch plugs, just
above the edge of the oil pan. This
number is also stamped on top of
the frame, on the left hand side bar
just behind the radiator, and on the
lubrication plate attached to the
front face of the left door lockpillar.
The engine serial number on the
frame is place between two stars.

Each Cadillac engine carries an
engine unit number prefix, which
indicates style code, followed by
numbers in numerical sequence,

denoting the order in which engineswere built, regardless of type,
starting with number 1. The letters
L.C. are added as a suffix to the
engine unit number on all engines
built to low compression specifica
tions.   Engines assembled with
.010" oversized pistons may be
identified by an asterisk stamped
on the block ahead of the engine
unit number.

The unit number on all engines is
stamped on the bell housing portion of the crankcase behind the left
hand cylinder block, directly above
the cast rib, and numbered at right
angles with the crankshaft.

BASIC ENGINE IN SERIES

Compression Ratio 10.50 to 1
Standard Engine
Developed 375 HP at 4400 R.P.M.

Piston Displacement 472 Cu. In.:
Standard Engine
Torque,   525 Lbs.-Ft. at 3000
R.P.M.

VEHICLE IDENTIFICATION NUMBER

```
1969 CADILLAC
*N9100001*
```

Commonly referred to as the VIN NUMBER, this series of letters and numbers is stamped on a steel plate and riveted to the cowl bar at the lower left corner of the windshield. Also stamped on a pad on the rear upper portion of the cylinder block behind the intake manifold, and on the left side of the transmission case. (Minus Model Identity Symbol)

EXAMPLE

* N 9 100001 *

First character "N", represents the Model Identity Number

Second character "9" represents the model year: 1969

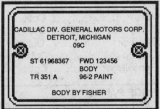

Style	Code
68349 Sedan DeVille Hardtop	B
68367 DeVille Convertible	F
68247 Calais Coupe	G
69347 Fleetwood Eldorado	H
68347 Coupe DeVille	J
68369 Sedan DeVille -Six Window	L
68069 Fleetwood Sixty Special Sedan	M
68249 Calais Hardtop Sedan	N
68169 Fleetwood Brougham Sedan	P
69723 Fleetwood Seventy-Five Sedan	R
69733 Fleetwood "75" Limousine	S
69890 Commercial	Z

The last six digits are the basic production code.

CADILLAC BODY NUMBER PLATE

Complete identification of each body is provided by a plate attached to the top surface of shroud, left under hood, near cowl.

```
CADILLAC DIV. GENERAL MOTORS CORP.
DETROIT, MICHIGAN
09C
ST 61968367      FWD 123456
                 BODY
TR 351 A         96-2 PAINT

BODY BY FISHER
```

THE STYLE NUMBER is a combination of year and body style. In the plate illustrated, "69" represents the model year: 1969. 68367 represents the style: DeVille convertible.

Calais Series	CODE
Calais Hardtop Sedan	68249
Calais Coupe	68247

DeVille Series	CODE
Hardtop Sedan DeVille	68349
Coupe DeVille	68357
DeVille Convertible	68367
Sedan DeVille	68369

Fleetwood Series	CODE
Fleetwood Sixty Special	68069
Fleetwood Broughman Sedan	68169
Fleetwood "75" Sedan	69723
Fleetwood Eldorado	69347
Fleetwood "75" Limousine	69733
Commercial Chassis	69890

The Trim Number indicates the key to trim color and material for each style. A "B" following indicates bucket seats.

Style 68069

Black Devereaux (Cloth) w/ Black (Leather)	011,011S
Lt. Gray DuBonnet (Cloth)	016,016S
Dk. Blue DuBonnet (Cloth)	026,026S
Med. Aqua Devereaux (Cloth)	029,029S
Dk. Green DuBonnet (Cloth) w/ Dk. Green (Leather)	031,031S
Lt. Flax DuBonnet (Cloth)	042,042S
Med. Gold Devereaux W/ Antique Med. Gold (Leather)	046,046S
Dk. Cordovan Dumont w/ Dk. Mauve (Leather)	047,047S
Dk. Maroon Devereaux w/ Dk. Marron (Leather)	049,049S
Black (Leather)	051,051S
White (leather) w/ Black Carpet	052,052S
Dk. Blue (leather)	066,066S
Dk. Green (Leather)	071,071S

Antique Lt. Flax (Leather)	082,082
Antique Med. Gold (Leather)	084,084
Antique Dk. Cordovan (Leather)	086,086
Dk. Mauve (Leather)	087,087
Med. Red (Leather)	088,088

Style 68247,49

Black Decameron (Cloth) w/ Black (Coated Fabric)	21
Dk. Blue Decameron (Cloth) w/ Dk. Blue (Coated Fabric)	22
Med. Aqua Decameron (Cloth)w/ Med Aqua (Coated Fabric)	22
Dk. Green Decameron (Cloth) w/ Dk. Green (Coated Fabric)	23
Lt. Flax Decameron (Cloth) w/ Antiqe Lt. Flax (Coated Fabric)	24
Med. Gold Decameron (Cloth) w/ Antique Med. Gold (Coated Fabric)	24
Black (Coated Fabric)	25
Antiqe Lt. Fax (Coated Fabric)	28

Style 6834,49,69

Black Dardanelle (Cloth) w/ Black (Leather)	311,311

Dk. Blue Delphine 326,326S
Pattern Cloth) & Flair (Plain
Cloth) w/ Dk Blue (Leather)
Med. Aqua Delphine 329,329S
Pattern Cloth) & Flair (Plain
Cloth) w/ Med. Aqua (Leather)
Dk. Green Dardanelle .. 331,331S
Cloth) w/ Dk. Green (Leather)
Lt. Flax Delphine 342,342S
Pattern Cloth) & Flair (Plain
Cloth) w/ Antique Lt. Flax
Leather)
Med. Gold Dardanelle 344,344S
Cloth) w/ Med. Gold (Leather)
Dk. Cordovan 346,346S
Dardanelle (Cloth) w/ Antique
Cordovan (Leather)
Dk. Mauve Delphine 347,347S
Pattern Cloth) & Flair (Plain
Cloth) w/ Dk. Mauve (Leather)
Black (Leather) 351,351S
White (Leather) 352,352S
w/ Black Carpet
Dk. Blue (Leather) 366,366S
Dk. Green (Leather) 371,371S
Antique Lt. Flax 382,382S
Leather)
Antique Med. Gold 384,384S
Leather)
Antique Dk. Cordovan 386,386S
Leather)
Dk. Mauve (Leather) ... 387,387S
Med. Red (Leather) 388,388S

Style 68367

Black (Leather) 351,351S
White (Leather) 352,352S
w/ Black Carpet
White (Leather) 353,353S
w/ Dk. Blue Carpet
White (Leather) 354,354S
w/ Med. Red Carpet
Dk. Blue (Leather) 366,366S
Dk. Green (Leather) 371,371S
Antique Lt. Flax 382,382S
Leather)
Antique Med. Gold 384,384S
Leather)
Antique Dk. Cordovan 386,386S
Leather)
Dk. Mauve (Leather) 387,387S
Med. Red (Leather) 388,388S

Style 69347

Black Dominion (Cloth) 410
w/ Black (Coated Fabric)
Black Dubonnet (Cloth) 411
w/ Black (Coated Fabric)
Dk. Blue Dubonnet (Cloth) 426
w/ Dk. Blue (Coated Fabric)
Med. Aqua Dubonnet 429
(Cloth) w/Med. Aqua
(Coated Fabric)
Dk. Green Dubonnet (Cloth) 431
w/ Dk. Green (Coated Fabric)
Lt. Flax Dubonnet (Cloth) 442
w/ Antique Lt. Flax
(Coated Fabric)
Med. Gold Dubonnet (Cloth) 444
w/ Antique Med. Gold
(Coated Fabric)
Dk. Cordovan Dubonnet 446
(Cloth) w/ Antique Dk.
Cordovan (Coated Fabric)
Dk. Mauve (Cloth) 447
w/ Dk. Mauve (Coated Fabric)
Black (Leather) 451,451B
White (Leather) 452
w/ Black Carpet
Dk. Blue (Leather) 466
Dk. Green (Leather) 471
Antique Lt. Flax 482,482B
(Leather)
Antique Me. Gold (Leather) 484
Antique Dk. Cordovan 486
(Leather)
Dk. Mauve (Leather) 487
Med. Red (Leather) 488

Style 69723

Lt. Gray Dunstan (Cloth) 716
Med. Gray Decordo (Cloth) 719
Med. Blue Dunstan (Cloth) ... 721
Dk. Blue DuBarry (Cloth) 726
Lt. Beige Dunstan (Cloth) 743

Style 60733

Black (Leather) 716
w/ Lt. Gray Dunstan (Cloth)
Lt. Gray (Leather) 716G
w/ Lt. Gray Dunstan (Cloth)
Black (Leather) 719
w/ Med. Gray Decordo (Cloth)
L:t. Gray (Leather) 719G
w/ Med. Gray Decordo (Cloth)

Black (Leather) 721
w/ Med. Blue Dunstan (Cloth)
Black (Leather) 726
w/ Dk. Blue DuBarry (Cloth)
Black (Leather) 743
w/ Lt. Beige Dunstan (Cloth)

THE PAINT CODE furnished the
key to the paint colors used on
the car. A two number code
indicated the color of the car. A
two-toned car has two sets of
numbers (example 10-12). In the
example the number 10 is the top
color Sable, the number 12 is the
top color Cottilion White.

COLOR	Code
Sable Black	10
Cotillion White	12
Patina Silver	16
Phantom Gray	18
Astral Blue	24
Athenian Blue	26
Persian Aqua	28
Palmetto Green	30
Rampur Green	36
Colonial Yellow	40
Cameo Beige	42
Shalimar Gold	44
Cordovan	46
Wisteria	47
San Mateo Red	48
Empire Maroon	49
Saphire Blue Firemist	90
Chalice Gold Firemist	94
Biscay Aqua Firemist	96
Nutmeg Brown Firemist	97
Chateau Mauve Firemist	99

**COVERTIBLE TOP
COLOR OPTIONS**

White .... Option J
Black .... Option B
Dk. Blue .... Optiob L
Lt. Flax .... Option M
Dk. Cordovan .... Option N

**1969 ROOF COVERING
OPTIONS**

White .... Option J
Black .... Option K
Dk. Blue .... Option L

Lt. Flax .... Option M
Dk. Cordovan .... Option N
Med. Gold .... Option R

ENGINE NUMBER

The serial number of all 1969 Cadillac engines is stamped on the lower left hand side of the cylinder block, between the two welch plugs, just above the edge of the oil pan. This number is also stamped on top of the frame, on the left hand side bar just behind the radiator, and on the lubrication plate attached to the front face of the left door lockpillar. The engine serial number on the frame is place between two stars.

Each Cadillac engine carries an engine unit number prefix, which indicates style code, followed by numbers in numerical sequence, denoting the order in which engineswere built, regardless of type, starting with number 1. The letters L.C. are added as a suffix to the engine unit number on all engines built to low compression specifications. Engines assembled with .010" oversized pistons may be identified by an asterisk stamped on the block ahead of the engine unit number.

The unit number on all engines is stamped on the bell housing portion of the crankcase behind the left hand cylinder block, directly above the cast rib, and numbered at right angles with the crankshaft.

BASIC ENGINE IN SERIES

Compression Ratio 10.50 to 1
Developed 375 HP at 4400 R.P.M.

Piston Displacement 472 Cu. In.:
Standard Engine
Torque, 525 Lbs.-Ft. at 3000 R.P.M.

VEHICLE IDENTIFICATION NUMBER

CHEVROLET
01511T1001555

Commonly referred to as the VIN NUMBER, this series of numbers and letters is stamped on a plate attached to the left front door hinge pillar.

Corvette VIN Embossed on Stainless Steel Plate Welded to top of Steering Column Mast under Hood.

EXAMPLE

0	1411	T	1001555
Year	Series Body Style	Assy Plant	Production Number

FIRST DIGIT: Identifies the year, 0 for 1960.

SECOND AND THIRD DIGITS: Identify the series.

SERIES	Code
Corvair 6 cyl	05
CorvairDeluxe	07
Corvette	08
Biscayne 6 cyl	11
Biscayne 8 cyl	12
Biscayne Fleetmstr 6 cyl	13
Biscayne Fleetmstr 6 cyl	14
Bel Air 6 cyl	15
Bel Air 8 cyl	16
Impala 6 cyl	17
Impala 8 cyl	18

FOURTH AND FIFTH DIGITS: Identify the Body Style.

STYLE	Code
2-Dr Sedan	11
4-Dr Sedan	19
Utility Sedan	21
Club Coupe	27
2-Dr Sport Coupe	37
4-Dr Sport Sedan	39
Convertible	67
4-Dr Sedan	69

2-Door Station Wagon 6 Pass	15
4-Door Station Wagon 6 Pass	35
4-Door Station Wagon 9 Pass	45

SIXTH DIGIT: A letter identifies the Assembly Plant.

ASSEMBLY PLANT	Code
Atlanta	A
Baltimore	B
Flint	F
Janesville	J
Kansas City	K
Los Angeles	L
Norwood	N
Oakland	O
St. Louis	S
Tarrytown	T
Willow Run	W
Framingham	G

FISHER BODY NUMBER PLATE

Complete identification of each body is provided by a plate riveted to the top of the cowl on the left side of the car.

*Exception: Corvair body tag is located on left rear wheel housing inside the engine compartment.

CHEVROLET DIVISION
GENERAL MOTORS CORP.
CORRESPONDENCE PERTAINING TO THE
BODY MUST BEAR THESE NUMBERS

STYLE No.	60 1511
BODY No.	T 101555
TRIM No.	810
PAINT No.	936

BODY BY FISHER

THE STYLE NUMBER is a combination of the year, series, and body style.

CORVAIR	Std	Deluxe
Club Coupe	527	727
4-Dr Sedan	569	769

CORVAIR MONZA	Code
Club Coupe	927

CORVETTE	Code
Convertible	0867

BISCAYNE	6 cyl	8 cyl
2-Dr Sedan	1111	1211
4-Dr Sedan	1119	1219

	6 cyl	8 cyl
2-Dr Utility Sedan	1121	122
2-Dr Sedan Delivery	1170	127
2-Dr Sedan Pickup	1180	128
2-Dr Station Wagon	1115	121
4-Dr Station Wagon	1135	123

FLEETMASTER	6 cyl	8 cyl
2-Dr Sedan	1311	141
4-Dr Sedan	1319	141

BEL AIR	6 cyl	8 cyl
2-Dr Sedan	1511	161
4-Dr Sedan	1519	161
2-Dr Sport Coupe	1537	163
4-Dr Sport Coupe	1539	163
4-Dr Station Wagon	1535	163
4-Dr Station Wagon	1545	164

IMPALA

	6 cyl	8 cyl
4-Dr Sedan	1719	1819
2-Dr Sport Coupe	1737	1837
4-Dr Sport Sedan	1739	1839
2-Dr Convertible	1767	1867
4-Dr Station Wagon	1735	1835

THE BODY NUMBER is the production serial number of the body. The prefix letter denotes the plant in which the body was built.

ASSEMBLY PLANT   Code

	Code
Atlanta	A
Baltimore	B
Flint	F
Janesville	J
Kansas City	K
Los Angeles	L
Norwood	N
Oakland	O
St. Louis	S
Tarrytown	T
Willow Run	W
Framingham	G

THE TRIM NUMBER furnishes the key to trim color and material for each model SERIES.

D=Dark, M=Medium, L=LIGHT, I=IMITATION, W=WOVEN

D Gray Cloth	
Silver I-Leather	800
D Gray I-Leather	
Silver I-Leather	801
D Gray I-Leather	
Met. Silver I-Leather	802
D Gray I-Leather	
Met. Silver Leather	803
D Gray I-Leather	
L, D Gray Cloth	806
D Gray I-Leather	
L, D, Gray W-Plastic	807
Black, White I-Leather	
White, Black Cloth	809
Black I-Leather	
White I-Leather	810
Black, White I-Leather	
White, Black Cloth	811
Green I-Leather	
M Green Cloth	817
Green I-Leather	
M Green I-Leather	818
M Green I-Leather	
L Green I-Leather	819
M Green I-Leather	
L, M Green Cloth	822
M Green I-Leather	
L, M Green W-Plastic	823
M & L Green I-Leather	
L, M Green Cloth	825
M & L Green I-Leather	
L, M Green I-Leather	826
M & L Green Cloth	
M, L Green I-Leather	827

L Blue I-Leather	
M Blue Cloth	833
L Blue I-Leather	
M Blue I-Leather	834
M Blue I-Leather	
L Blue I-Leather	835
M Blue I-Leather	
L, M Blue Cloth	838
M Blue I-Leather	
L, M Blue W-Plastic	839
M & L Blue I-Leather	
L, M Blue Cloth	841
M & L Blue I-Leather	
L, M Blue I-Leather	842
M & L Blue I-Leather	
L, M Blue Cloth	843
M Turquoise I-Leather	
L, M Turquoise Cloth	849
L, M Turquoise I-Leather	
M Turquoise W-Plastic	850
M & L Turquoise I-Leather	
L, M Turquoise I-Leather	852
M & L Turquoise I-Leather	
L, M Turquoise I-Leather	853
M & L Turquoise I-Leather	
L, M Turquoise I-Leather	854
M Copper I-Leather	
L, M Copper Cloth	862
M Copper I-Leather	
M Copper W-Plastic	863
M & L Copper I-Leather	
L, M Cooper Cloth	865
M & L Copper I-Leather	
L, M Copper I-Leather	866
M & L Copper I-Leather	
L, M Copper Cloth	867
Red, White I-Leather	
White, RedCloth	873
Red & White I-Leather	
White, Red I-Leather	874
Red, White I-Leather	
White, Red Cloth	875

THE PAINT CODE furnishes the key to the paint colors on the car.

COLOR	Code
Tuxedo Black	900
Cascade Green	903
Jade Green	905
Horizon Blue	910
Royal Blue	912
Tasco Turquoise	915
Suntan Copper	920
Roman Red	923
Crocus Cream	925
Ermine White	936
Fawn Beige	938
Sateen Silver	940
Shadow Gray	941

TWO-TONE

Ermine White	
Tuxedo Black	950
Ermine White	
Cascade Green	953
Cascade Green	

Jade Green	955
Ermine White	
Horizon Blue	960
Horizon Blue / Royal Blue	962
Ermine White	
Tasco Turquoise	963
Fawn Beige	
Suntan Copper	970
Ermine White	
Roman Red	973
Ermine White	
Sateen Silver	984
Sateen Silver	
Shadow Gray	988

ENGINE NUMBER

All Chevrolet Engines are stamped with a Plant Code, Production Date, and Engine Type Code.

Note:

1. Corvette Engines have the last six digits of the VIN stamped on the block next to the engine number.

2. Corvair Engines are stamped on the top of the block forward of the generator.

3. 8 cylinder engines are stamped on the right front of the engine block.

4. 6 cylinder engines are stamped on the right side of the block at the rear of the distributor.

EXAMPLE

T	01	01	A
PLANT	MONTH	DAY	CODE

ENGINE PLANTS   CODE

	CODE
Tonawanda	T
Flint	F

Chevrolet and Corvette

Code	Cid	Description	Model
A	235	6 cyl w/ 3 Speed Trans	11-15-1700
AE	235	6 cyl w/ H.D. Clutch	11-15-1700
AF	235	6 cyl w/ A/C	11-15-1700
AG	235	6 cyl w A/C,/H.D. Clutch	11-15-1700
AJ	235	6 cyl w/ PS,A/C, H.D. Clutch	11-15-1700
AK	235	6 cyl w/ PS	11-15-1700
AM	235	6 cyl w/ PS, H.D. Clutch	11-15-1700
AP	235	6 cyl w/ 3 Speed Trans	1300
AR	235	6 cyl w/ H.D. Clutch	1300
AS	235	6 cyl w/ PS	1300
AT	235	6 cyl w/ PS, H.D. Clutch	1300
AZ	235	6 cyl w/ PS,A/C	11-15-1700
B	235	6 cyl w/ PG	11-13-15-1700
BE	235	6 cyl w/ PS,PG	11-13-15-1700
BG	235	6 cyl w/ PG,A/C	11-13-15-1700
BH	235	6 cyl w/ PG,A/C,PS	11-15-1700
C	283	8 cyl	12-14-16-1800
CD	283	8 cyl w/ Overdrive	12-14-16-1800
CF	283	8 cyl w/ 4BC	12-14-16-1800
CG	283	8 cyl w/ Overdrive, 4BC	12-14-16-1800
CL	283	8 cyl w/ A/C	12-14-16-1800
CM	283	8 cyl w/ A/C, 4BC	12-14-16-1800
D	283	8 cyl w/ PG	12-14-16-1800
DB	283	8 cyl w/ PG, 4BC	12-14-16-1800
DK	283	8 cyl w/ PG,A/C	12-14-16-1800
DM	283	8 cyl w/ PG,A/C, 4BC	12-14-16-1800
E	283	8 cyl w/ Turboglide	12-14-16-1800
EB	283	8 cyl w/ Turboglide, 4BC	12-14-16-1800
EG	283	8 cyl w/ Turboglide, A/C	12-14-16-1800
EJ	283	8 cyl w/ Turboglide, A/C., 4BC	12-14-16-1800
F	348	8 cyl	12-14-16-1800
FA	348	8 cyl w/ 3/2BC	12-14-16-1800
FE	348	8 cyl w/ 3/2BC, High Perf	12-14-16-1800
FG	348	8 cyl w/ High Perf	12-14-16-1800
FH	348	8 cyl w/ 3/2BC, Special High Perf	12-14-16-1800
FJ	348	8 cyl w/ Special High Perf	12-14-16-1800
G	348	8 cyl w/ PG	12-14-16-1800
GB	348	8 cyl w/ PG, 3/2BC	12-14-16-1800
GD	348	8 cyl w/ PG, 3/2BC, High Lift Cam	12-14-16-1800
H	348	8 cyl w/ Turboglide	12-14-16-1800
HA	348	8 cyl w/ Turboglide, 3/2BC	12-14-16-1800
CQ	283	8 cyl	12-14-16-1800
CR	283	8 cyl w/ Fuel Injection	12-14-16-1800
CS	283	8 cyl w/ Fuel Injection, High Lift Cam	CORVETTE
CU	283	8 cyl w/ Dual 4BC, High Lift Cam	CORVETTE
DG	283	8 cyl w/ Powerglide	CORVETTE
DJ	283	8 cyl w/ Powerglide, Dual 4BC	CORVETTE
CT	283	8 cyl w/ M.T., 2/4BC	CORVETTE

CORVAIR

Code	Cid	Description	Model
YC	145	6 cyl w/ Manual Trans	5-7-900
YN	145	6 cyl w/ Manual Trans, High Perf	5-7-900
YH	145	6 cyl w/ Manual Trans	5-735
YL	145	6 cyl w/ Manual Trans, A/C	5-7-900
YM	145	6 cyl w/ Manual Trans, A/C, High Perf	5-7-900
Y	145	6 cyl w/ Manual Trans, High Perf	5-735
YR	145	6 cyl w/ Turbo Charged, 4-SPD	927-967
ZB	145	6 cyl w/ Automatic Trans	5-700
ZB	145	6 cyl w/ Automatic Trans	5-735
ZD	145	6 cyl w/ Automatic Trans, A/C	5-700
ZF	145	6 cyl w/ Automatic Trans, High Perf	5-7-900
ZG	145	6 cyl w/ Automatic Trans, A/C,High Perf	5-7-900
ZH	145	6 cyl w/ Automatic Trans	900
ZJ	145	6 cyl w/ Automatic Trans, A/C	900
ZK	145	6 cyl w/ Automatic Trans, High Perf	5-735
ZL	145	6 cyl w/ Automatic Trans	935
V	145	6 cyl w/ Manual Trans	F.C.
W	145	6 cyl w/ Automatic Trans	F.C.

Engine	Com	HP
145 Corvair	8.0:1	95
145 Corvair	8.0:1	80
235 pass	8.25:1	135
283 pass (1)	8.5:1	170
283 pass-vette (2)	9.5:1	230
283 vette (3)	9.5:1	245
283 vette (4)	9.5:1	270
283 vette (5)	9.5:1	250
283 vette (6)	10.5:1	290
348 pass (2)	9.5:1	250
348 pass (7)	(A)	(B)
348 pass (8)	9.5:1	280
348 pass (9)	11.25:1*	335

(1) 2-bbl
(2) 4-bbl
(3) vette 2 / 4-bbl
(4) vette 2 / 4-bbl & sp. cam
(5) vette F.I.
(6) vette F.I. & sp. cam
(7) 4-bbl & sp. cam
(8) 3 / 2-bbl
(9) 3 / 2-bbl & sp. cam
(A) 11.25:1 M.T., 11.0:1 Auto
(B) 320 w/ M.T., 305 w/ Auto
* 3 or 4 spd M.T.

VEHICLE IDENTIFICATION NUMBER

CHEVROLET
11511T1001555

Commonly referred to as the VIN NUMBER, this series of numbers and letters is stamped on a plate attached to the left front door hinge pillar.

EXAMPLE

1	1411	T	1001555
Year	Series Body Style	Assy Plant	Production Number

Corvair VIN Embossed on a Stainless Steel Plate Welded to Left Hand Center Pillar Post Facing.

Corvette VIN Embossed on Stainless Steel Plate Welded to top of Steering Column Mast under Hood.

FIRST DIGIT: Identifies the year, 1 for 1961.

SECOND AND THIRD DIGITS: Identifiy the series.

SERIES	Code
Corvair 6 cyl	05
Corvair Deluxe	07
Corvair Monza	09
Corvette	08
Biscayne 6 cyl	11
Biscayne 8 cyl	12
Biscayne Fleetmstr 6 cyl	13
Biscayne Fleetmstr 8 cyl	14
Bel Air 6 cyl	15
Bel Air 8 cyl	16
Impala 6 cyl	17
Impala 8 cyl	18

FOURTH AND FIFTH DIGITS: Identify the Body Style.

Style	Code
2-Dr Sedan	11
Utility Sedan	21
Club Coupe	27
2-Dr Sport Coupe	37
4-Dr Sport Sedan	39
Convertible	67
4-Dr Sedan	69
4-Dr Station Wagon 6 Pass	35
4-Dr Station Wagon 9 Pass	45

SIXTH DIGIT: A letter identifies the Assembly Plant.

ASSEMBLY PLANT	Code
Atlanta	A
Baltimore	B
Flint	F
Janesville	J
Kansas City	K
Los Angeles	L
Norwood	N
Oakland	O
St. Louis	S
Tarrytown	T
Willow Run	W
Framingham	G

FISHER BODY NUMBER PLATE

Complete identification of each body is provided by a plate riveted upper right part of dash panel.

*Exception: Corvair body tag is located on the left rear wheel housing inside the engine compartment.

THE STYLE NUMBER is a combination of the year, series, and body style.

CORVAIR	500	700
Club Coupe	527	727
4-Dr Sedan	569	769
4-Dr Station Wagon	535	735

MONZA	CODE
2-Dr Club Coupe	927
4-Dr Sdan	969

CHEVROLET DIVISION
GENERAL MOTORS CORP.
CORRESPONDENCE PERTAINING TO THE BODY MUST BEAR THESE NUMBERS

STYLE No.   61 15 11
BODY No.   T 1001555
TRIM No.   810
PAINT No.   936

BODY BY FISHER

CORVETTE	CODE
Convertible	0867

BISCAYNE	6 cyl	8 cyl
2-Dr Sedan	1111	1211
2-Dr Utility Sedan	1121	1221
4-Dr Station Wagon	1135	1235
2-Dr Sedan	1311	1411
4-Dr StationWagon 9 Pass	1145	1245
4-Dr Sedan (Biscayne Fleetmaster)	1369	1469

BEL AIR	6 cyl	8 cyl
2-Dr Sedan	1511	1611
4-Dr Sedan	1569	1669
2-Dr Sport Coupe	1537	1637
4-Dr Sport Coupe	1539	1639
4-Dr Station Wagon	1535	1635
4-Dr Station Wagon	1545	1645

IMPALA	6 cyl	8 cyl
4-Dr Sedan	1769	1869
2-Dr Sport Coupe	1737	1837
2-Dr Sedan	1711	1811
4-Dr Sport Sedan	1739	1839
2-Dr Convertible	1767	1867
4-Dr Station Wagon	1735	1835
4-Dr Station Wagon 9 Pass	1745	1845

* Super Sport Was an option no model.

THE BODY NUMBER is the p duction serial number of the bo The prefix letter denotes the plan which the body was built.

ASSEMBLY PLANT	Co
Atlanta	
Baltimore	
Flint	
Janesville	
Kansas City	
Los Angeles	
Norwood	
Oakland	
St. Louis	
Tarrytown	
Willow Run	
Framingham	

THE TRIM NUMBER furnishes key to trim color and material each model SERIES.

D=Dark, M=Medium, L=Light, I=Imitation, W=Woven

LGray Cloth, LGray .... M Gray, I- Leather 800
L Gray, D Gray I- Leather 801
L Gray, M Gray, Black I-Leather 804
L Gray, Ivory Cloth, L Gray, M Gray, Ivory, I- Leather 806
G Cloth, L Grey, M Gray, I-Leather 807
L Gray Cloth, L Gray, Gray, M Gray, Ivory 1,I-Leather 809
L Gray, M Gray, Ivory I- Leather 810
L Gray Cloth, M Gray, Ivory, I-Leather 811
M Fawn Cloth, Metallic M Fawn I-Leather 816
L& M Green Cloth, L & M Green, I-Leather 817
L & M Green I- Leather 818
Red Cloth, Red I- Leather 820
M Green Cloth, Metallic M Green I-Leather 821
L Blue Cloth, L & M & D I- Leather 822
823D Green Cloth, L & M Green I-Leather 823
L & M Green Cloth, L & M Green I-Leather 825
L& M Green I- Leather 826
M Green Cloth, L & M Green I-Metallic M Blue I-Leather 827
M Blue Cloth, I- Metallic M Blue I-Leather 829
L Gray Cloth, Black I-Leather 830
M Green Cloth, Metallic M Green and L Green I-Leather 831
Metallic M Green Fiber Rib I-Leather, Metallic M Green and L Green I- Leather 832
L M Blue Cloth, L M Blue I-Leather 833
L M Blue I-Leather 834
M Blue Cloth, Metallic M Blue and L Blue I-Leather 836
Metallic M Blue Fiber Rib I-Leather, Metallic M Blue and L Blue I-Leather 837
M D Blue Cloth, M D Blue I-Leather 838
M Blue Cloth, L M Blue I-Leather 839
L M Blue Cloth, L M Blue I-Leather 841
M Blue Cloth, L M Blue I-Leather 842
M Blue Cloth, L M Blue I-Leather 843
L Gray Cloth, Ivory I-Leather 844
M Green Cloth, Metallic M Green I-Leather 847
L M Turquoise, L M Turquoise I-Leather 849
M Turquoise Cloth, M D Turquoise I-Leather 850
L M Turquoise Cloth, L M Turquoise I-Leather 852
M Turquoise Cloth, L M Turquoise I-Leather 853
M Turquoise Cloth, L M Turquoise I-Leather 854
Metallic M Fawn I-Leather 855

Red I-Leather 856
Metallic M Green I-Leather 857
Metallic M Blue I-Leather 858
Ivory I-Leather 859
L M Fawn Cloth, L M D Fawn I-Leather 862
L M Fawn Cloth, L M D Fawn I-Leather 863
L M Fawn Cloth L M Fawn I-Leather 865
L M Fawn I- Leather 866
L M Fawn Cloth L M I-Leather 867
Black I-Leather 869
Red Cloth, Ivory, Red I-Leather 873
Ivory, Red I-Leather 874
Ivory Cloth, Ivory, Red I-Leather 875
M Gray Cloth, L Gray and Ivory I-Leather 885
M Gray Cloth, L Gray and Ivory I-Leather 886
M Green Cloth, Metallic M Green I-Leather 887
M Blue Cloth, Metallic M Blue I-Leather 888
Red Cloth, Red I- Leather 889
Metallic L Gray Fiber Rib I-Leather, L Gray and Ivory I-Leather 895
M Gray Cloth, L Gray and Ivory I-Leather 896
M Green Cloth, Metallic M Green I-Leather 897
M Blue Cloth, Metallic M Blue I-Leather 898
Red Cloth, Red I- Leather 899

Bucket Seats

M Fawn Cloth, Metallic M Fawn I-Leather 845
Red Cloth, Red I- Leather 846
M Green Cloth, Metallic M Green I-Leather ...847
M Blue Cloth, Metallic M Blue I-Leather 848
L Gray Cloth, Black I-Leather .870
L Gray Cloth, Ivory I-Leather ..871
Black I-Leather 878
Ivory I-Leather 879
Metallic M Fawn I-Leather 880
Red I-Leather 881
Metallic M Green I-Leather 882
Metallic M Blue I- Leather 883

THE PAINT CODE furnishes the key to the paint colors on the car.

PAINT	Code
Tuxedo Black	900
Seafoam Green	903
Arbor Green	905
Jewel Blue	912
Midnight Blue	914
Twilight Turquoise	915
Seamist Turquoise	917
Fawn Beige	920
Roman Red	923
Coronna Cream	925
Ermine White	936
Almond Beige	938
Sateen Silver	940
Shadow Gray	941
Honduras Maroon	948

Two-Tone

	Code
White / Black	950
White / Seafoam Green	953
S. Green / A. Green	955
White / Jewel Blue	959
J. Blue / M. Blue	962
White / T. Turquoise	963
S. Turquoise / T. Turquoise	965
A. Beige / F. Beige	970
White / Red	973
White / Silver	984

ENGINE NUMBER

All Chevrolet Engines are stamped with a Plant Code, Production Date, and Engine Type Code.

Notes:

1. Corvette Engines have the last six digits of the VIN stamped on the block next to the engine number.

2. Corvair Engines are stamped on the top of the block forward of the generator.

3. 8 cylinder engines are stamped on the right front of the engine block.

4. 6 cylinder engines are stamped on the right side of the block at the rear of the distributor.

EXAMPLE

I	01	01	A
PLANT	MONTH	DAY	CODE

ENGINE PLANTS	Code
Tonawanda	T
Flint	F

Code	Cid	Description	Model
Chevrolet and Corvette			
A	235	6 cyl w/ 3 Speed Trans	11-15-1700
AE	235	6 cyl w/ H.D. Clutch	11-15-1700
AF	235	6 cyl w/ C.A.C	11-15-1700
AG	235	6 cyl w/ C.A.C. and H.D. Clutch	11-15-1700
AJ	235	6 cyl w/ Power Steering, C.A.C., H.D. Clutch	11-15-1700
AK	235	6 cyl w/ Power Steering	11-15-1700
AM	235	6 cyl w/ Power Steering, H.D. Clutch	11-15-1700
AP	235	6 cyl w/ 3 Speed Trans	1300
AR	235	6 cyl w/ H.D. Clutch	1300
AS	235	6 cyl w/ Power Steering	1300
AT	235	6 cyl w/ Power Steering, H.D. Clutch	1300
AZ	235	6 cyl w/ Power Steering, C.A.C.	11-15-1700
B	235	6 cyl w/ Powerglide	11-13-15-1700
BE	235	6 cyl w/ Powerglide, Power Steering	11-13-15-1700
BG	235	6 cyl w/ Powerglide, C.A.C.	11-13-15-1700
BH	235	6 cyl w/ Powerglide, Power Steering, C.A.C.	11-15-1700
C	283	8 cyl	12-14-16-1800
CD	283	8 cyl w/ Overdrive	12-14-16-1800
CF	283	8 cyl w/ 4BC	12-14-16-1800
CG	283	8 cyl w/ Overdrive, 4BC	12-14-16-1800
CL	283	8 cyl w/ C.A.C.	12-14-16-1800
CM	283	8 cyl w/ C.A.C., 4BC	12-14-16-1800
D	283	8 cyl w/ Powerglide	12-14-16-1800
DB	283	8 cyl w/ Powerglide, 4BC	12-14-16-1800
DK	283	8 cyl w/ Powerglide, C.A.C.	12-14-16-1800
DM	283	8 cyl w/ Powerglide, C.A.C., 4BC	12-14-16-1800
E	283	8 cyl w/ Turboglide	12-14-16-1800
EB	283	8 cyl w/ Turboglide, 4BC	12-14-16-1800
EG	283	8 cyl w/ Turboglide, C.A.C.	12-14-16-1800
EJ	283	8 cyl w/ Turboglide, C.A.C., 4BC	12-14-16-1800
F	348	8 cyl	12-14-16-1800
FA	348	8 cyl w/ 3/2BC	12-14-16-1800
FH	348	8 cyl w/ 3/2BC, Special High Perf	12-14-16-1800
FJ	348	8 cyl w/ Special High Perf	12-14-16-1800
FL	348	8 cyl w/High Perf	12-14-16-1800
GD	348	8 cyl w/ Powerglide, 3/2BC, High Lift Cam	12-14-16-1800
GE	348	8 cyl w/ Powerglide, High Perf	12-14-16-1800
H	348	8 cyl w/ Turboglide	12-14-16-1800
HA	348	8 cyl w/ Turboglide, 3/2BC	12-14-16-1800
Q	409	8 cyl w/High Perf, M.T.	12-14-16-1800
QA	409	8 cyl w/ S. High Perf	12-14-16-1800
CQ	283	8 cyl	12-14-16-1800
CR	283	8 cyl w/ Fuel Injection	12-14-16-1800
CS	283	8 cyl w/ Fuel Injection, High Lift Cam	CORVETTE
CU	283	8 cyl w/ Dual 4BC, High Lift Cam	CORVETTE
DG	283	8 cyl w/ Powerglide	CORVETTE
DJ	283	8 cyl w/ Powerglide, Dual 4BC	CORVETTE
CT	283	8 cyl w/ M.T., 2/4BC	CORVETTE
CORVAIR			
YC	145	6 cyl w/ Manual Trans	5-7-900 (exc. STA WAG)
YN	145	6 cyl w/ Manual Trans, High Perf	5-7-900 (exc. STA WAG)
YH	145	6 cyl w/ Manual Trans	5-735
YL	145	6 cyl w/ Manual Trans, C.A.C.	5-7-900 (exc. STA WAG)
YM	145	6 cyl w/ Manual Trans, C.A.C., High Perf	5-7-900 (exc. STA WAG)
Y	145	6 cyl w/ Manual Trans, High Perf	5-735
YR	145	6 cyl w/ Turbo Charged, 4-SPD	927-967
ZB	145	6 cyl w/ Automatic Trans	5-700 (exc. STA WAG)
ZB	145	6 cyl w/ Automatic Trans	5-735
ZD	145	6 cyl w/ Automatic Trans, C.A.C.	5-700 (exc. STA WAG)
ZF	145	6 cyl w/ Automatic Trans, High Perf	5-7-900 (exc. STA WAG)
ZG	145	6 cyl w/ Automatic Trans, C.A.C.,High Perf	5-7-900 (exc. STA WAG)
ZH	145	6 cyl w/ Automatic Trans	900 (exc. STA WAG)
ZJ	145	6 cyl w/ Automatic Trans, C.A.C.	900 (exc. STA WAG)
ZK	145	6 cyl w/ Automatic Trans, High Perf	5-735
ZL	145	6 cyl w/ Automatic Trans	935
V	145	6 cyl w/ Manual Trans	F.C.
W	145	6 cyl w/ Automatic Trans	F.C.

Engine	Com	HP
145 Corvair	8.0:1	95
145 Corvair	8.0:1	80
235 pass	8.25:1	13
283 pass (1)	8.5:1	17
283 pass-vette (2)	9.5:1	23
283 vette (3)	9.5:1	24
283 vette (4)	9.5:1	27
283 vette (5)	11.0:1	27
283 vette (6)	11.0:1	31
348 pass (2)	9.5:1	25
348 pass (7)	9.5:1	30
348 pass (8)	9.5:1	28
348 pass (7)*	11.0:1	30
348 pass (7)*	11.25:1	34
348 pass (9)	11.25:1	35
409 pass (2)	11.25:1	36

(1) 2-bbl
(2) 4-bbl
(3) 2 / 4-bbl
(4) 2 / 4-bbl & sp. cam
(5) F.I.
(6) F.I. & sp. cam
(7) 4-bbl
(8) 3 / 2-bbl
(9) 3 / 2-bbl & sp. cam
* special cam

1962 CHEVROLET

VEHICLE IDENTIFICATION NUMBER

CHEVROLET
21511T1001555

Commonly referred to as the VIN NUMBER, this series of numbers and letters is stamped on a plate attached to the left front door hinge pillar.

CORVETTE VIN Embossed on Stainless Steel Plate Welded to Top of Steering Column Mast under Hood.

CORVAIR VIN Embossed on a Stainless Steel Plate Welded to Left Hand Center Pillar Post Facing.

CHEVY II VIN Embossed on a Stainless Steel Plate Welded to Left Front Door Hinge Pillar Post Facing.

EXAMPLE

2	1411	T	1001555
Year	Series Body Style	Assy Plant	Production Number

FIRST DIGIT: Identifies the year 2 for 1962.

SECOND AND THIRD DIGITS: Identify the series.

SERIES	Code
Chevy II 4 cyl	01
Chevy II	02
Chevy II 6 cyl	03
Chevy II & Nova 6 cyl	04
Corvair Monza	09
Corvair 6 cyl	05
Corvair Deluxe	07
Corvette	08
Biscayne 6 cyl	11
Biscayne 8 cyl	12
Bel Air 6 cyl	15
Bel Air 8 cyl	16
Impala 6 cyl	17
Impala 8 cyl	18

FOURTH AND FIFTH DIGITS: Identify the Body Style.

STYLE	Code
2-Dr Sedan	11
4-Dr Sedan	19
Club Coupe	27
2-Dr Sport Coupe	37
4-Dr Sport Sedan	39
Convertible	67
4-Dr Sedan	69
2-Dr Station Wagon 6 Pass	15
4-Dr Station Wagon 6 Pass	35
4-Dr Station Wagon 9 Pass	45
2-Dr Spt. Cpl	47

CHEVROLET DIVISION
GENERAL MOTORS CORP.
CORRESPONDENCE PERTAINING TO THE BODY MUST BEAR THESE NUMBERS

STYLE No.	62 1511
BODY No.	T 101555
TRIM No.	810
PAINT No.	936

BODY BY FISHER

SIXTH DIGIT: A letter identifies the Assembly Plant.

ASSEMBLY PLANT	Code
Atlanta	A
Baltimore	B
Flint	F
Janesville	J
Kansas City	K
Los Angeles	L
Norwood	N
Oakland	O
St. Louis	
Tarrytown	
Willow Run	
Framingham	

FISHER BODY NUMBER PLATE

Complete identification of eac body is provided by a plate riveted t the top of the cowl on the left side the car.

Exception: Corvair body tag is located on the left rear wheel housing inside the engine compartment.

The Style Number is a combination of the year, series, and body style.

CORVAIR

	Std	Deluxe	Monza
Club Coupe	527	727	927
4-Dr Sedan	569	769	969
4-Dr St. Wagon	535	735	935
Convertible			967

CORVETTE   CODE

Convertible 0867

CHEVY II 100 .... 4 cyl ..... 6 cyl

	4 cyl	6 cyl
2-Dr Sedan	0111	0211
4-Dr Sedan	0169	0269
4-Dr Station Wagon	0135	0235

CHEVY II 300 .... 4 cyl ..... 6 cyl

	4 cyl	6 cyl
2-Dr Sedan	0311	0411
4-Dr Sedan	0369	0469
4-Dr Station Wagon	0345	0445

NOVA 400   Code

	Code
4-Dr Sedan	0449
2-Dr Sport Coupe	0437
2-Dr Conv	0467
4-Dr Station Wagon	0435
2-Dr Sedan	0441

BISCAYNE   6 cyl ... 8 cyl

	6 cyl	8 cyl
2-Dr Sedan	1111	1211
4-Dr Sedan	1169	1269
4-Dr Station Wagon	1135	1235

BEL AIR   6 cyl   8 cyl

	6 cyl	8 cyl
2-Dr Sedan	1511	1611
2-Dr Sport Coupe	1537	1637
4-Dr St. Wagon	1535	1635
4-Dr St. Wagon	1545	1645
4-Dr Sedan	1569	1669

IMPALA   6 cyl   8 cyl

	6 cyl	8 cyl
4-Dr Sedan	1769	1869
4-Dr Sport Sedan	1739	1839
2-Dr Convertible	1767	1867
4-Dr St. Wagon	1735	1835
4-Dr St. Wagon	1745	1845
2-Dr Sport Coupe	1747	1847

THE BODY NUMBER is the production serial number of the body. The prefix letter denotes the plant in which the body was built.

ASSEMBLY PLANT   Code

	Code
Atlanta	A
Baltimore	B
Flint	F
Janesville	J
Kansas City	K
Los Angeles	L
Norwood	N
Oakland	O
St. Louis	S
Tarrytown	T
Willow Run	W
Framingham	G

THE TRIM NUMBER furnishes the key to trim color and material for each model SERIES.

D=Dark, M=Medium, L=Light, I=Imitation, W=Woven

Trim	Code
M Blue Cloth, Metallic D Blue I-Leather, L Blue I-Leather	731
M Blue Cloth, Metallic M Blue I-Leather	735
M Blue Cloth, Metallic M Blue I-Leather	738
D Blue Cloth, Metallic M Blue I-Leather	739
D Blue Pattern I-Leather, Metallic M Blue and Ivory I-Leather	742
M Aqua Cloth, Metallic M Aqua I-Leather	745
M Aqua Cloth, Metallic M Aqua I-Leather	748
M Aqua Cloth, Metallic M Aqua I-Leather	749
D Aqua Cloth, Metallic M Aqua I-Leather	750
M Aqua Cloth, Metallic D Aqua and L Aqua I-Leather	751
M Aqua Cloth, Metallic M Aqua I-Leather	752
D Aqua Pattern I-Leather, Metallic M Aqua and Ivory I-Leather	753
Metallic D Aqua I-Leather, Metallic M Aqua I-Leather	754
M Fawn Cloth, Metallic M Fawn I-Leather	756
M Fawn Cloth, Metallic D Fawn and L Fawn I-Leather	757
M Fawn Cloth, Metallic M Fawn I-Leather	759
M Fawn Cloth, Metallic M Fawn I-Leather	760
Metallic D Fawn Pattern I-Leather, Metallic M Fawn I-Leather	761
M Fawn Cloth, Metallic M Fawn I-Leather	762
D Fawn Cloth, Metallic M Fawn I-Leather	763
Metallic M Fawn I-Leather, Metallic D Fawn I-Leather	765
D Fawn Pattern I-Leather, Metallic M Fawn and Ivory I-Leather	766
D Red Cloth, M Red and Ivory I-Leather	772
M Red Pattern I-Leather, M Red and Ivory I-Leather	774
M Red Cloth, M Red I-Leather	776
D Red Pattern I-Leather, M Red I-Leather	777
M Red Cloth, M Red I-Leather	778
M Red Cloth, M Red I-Leather	779
M Red. Cloth, D Red and Ivory I-Leahter	780
M Red. Cloth, M Red I-Leather	782
D Gold Cloth, M Gold and Ivory I-Leather	787
L Gold Pattern I-Leather, M Gold and Ivory I-Leahter	789
Lt. Gold Cloth, L Gold I-Leather	793
Black Pattern I-Leather, Black I-Leather	814
M Green Serenade Cloth, M Green I-Leather	823
M Green Samarra Cloth, w/ M Green Parma Cloth-M Green I-Leather	826
M Green Pattern I-Leather-M Green I-Leather	829
M Blue Pattern I-Leather-M Blue I-Leather	836
M Blue Serenade Cloth-M Blue I-Leather	839
M Blue Samarra Cloth w/ M Blue Parma Cloth - M Blue I-Leather	842
M Aqua Pattern I-Leather-M Aqua I-Leather	847
M Aqua Sernade Cloth-M Aqua I-Leather	850
M Aqua Strand Cloth-M Aqua & L Aqual-Leather	852
M Aqua Samarra Cloth w/ M Aqua Parma Cloth -M Aqua I-Leather	853
M Aqua Pattern I-Leather-M Aqua & L Aqua I-Leather	855
M Fawn Strand Cloth -M Fawn & L Fawn I-Leather	860
M Fawn Pattern I- Leather-M Fawn & L Fawn I-Leather-	861
M Fawn Sernade Cloth-M Fawn I-Leather	863
M Fawn I-Leather-D Fawn I-Leather	865
M Fawn Samarra Cloth w/ M Fawn Parma Cloth-Med. Fawn I-Leather	866
M Fawn Pattern I-Leather-M Fawn I-Leather	870
M Red Serenade Cloth-M Red I-Leather	872
M Red Samarra Cloth w/ M Red Parma Cloth-M Red I-Leather	874
M Red Strand Cloth-M Red I-Leather	876
M Red Pattern I- Leather-M Red I-Leather	877
M Red Pattern I-Leather-M Red I-Leather	886
L Gold Samarra Cloth w/ L Gold Parma Cloth-L Gold I-Leather	892
L Gold Pattern I-Leather-L Gold I-Leather	894

Bucket Seats

Trim	Code
Black Pattern I-Leather-Black I-Leather	815
M Green Pattern I-Leather-	
M Green I-Leather	821
M Green Pattern I-Leather-M Green I-Leather	827
M Blue Pattern I-Leather-M Blue I-Leather	831
M Blue Pattern I-Leather-M Blue I-Leather	843
M Aqua Pattern I-Leather-M Aqua I-Leather	845
M Aqua Pattern I-Leather-M Aqua I-Leather	854
M Fawn Pattern I-Leather-M Fawn I-Leather	856
M Fawn Pattern I-Leather-M Fawn I-Leather	867
M Red Pattern I-Leather-M Red I-Leather	875
M Red Pattern I-Leather-M Red I-Leather	879
L Gold Pattern I-Leather-L Gold I-Leather	890
L Gold Pattern I-Leather-L Gold I-Leather	891
Black I-Leather	712
Black I-Leather	715
Metallic M Aqua I-Leather	719
D Aqua I-Leather, Leather, Metallic M Aqua I-Leather	721
D Aqua Pattern I-Leather, Metallic M Aqua and Ivory I-Leather	722
Metallic M Blue I-Leather	732
Metallic M Blue I-Leather	736
D Blue I-Leather, Metallic M Blue and Ivory I-Leather	740
D Blue Pattern I-Leather, Metallic M Blue and Ivory I-Leather	741
Metallic M Aqua I-Leather	755
Metallic M Fawn I-Leather	758
D Fawn I-Leather, Metallic M Fawn and Ivory I-Leather	767
Metallic M Fawn I-Leather	769
D Fawn I-Leather, Metallic M Fawn and Ivory I-Leather	770
M Red I-Leather M Red and Ivory I-Leather	775
Metallic Red I-Leather	781
Metallic Red I-Leather	785
Metallic Red Pattern I-Leather, M Red and Ivory I-leather	786
L Gold I-Leather, M Gold and Ivory I-Leather	790
L Gold Pattern I- Leather, M Gold and Ivory I-Leather	791
L Gold I-Leather	795
L Gold I-Leather	799

THE PAINT CODE furnishes the key to the paint colors on the car.

PAINT   Code

	Code
Tuxedo Black	900
Surf Green	903
Laurel Green	905
Silver Blue	912
Nassau Blue	914
Twilight Turquoise	917
Twilight Blue	918
Autumn Gold	920
Roman Red	923

Coronna Cream 925
Anniversary Gold 927
Ermine White 936
Adobe Beige 938
Satin Silver 940
Honduras Maroon 948

TWO-TONE ....

White / Black 950
White / S. Green 953
Surf Green / L. Green 955
White / S. Blue 959
Silver Blue / N. Blue 962
White / T. Blue 963
T. Turquoise / T. Blue 965
Adobe Beige / A. Gold 970
White / Red 973
White / Satin Silver 984

ENGINE NUMBER

All Chevrolet Engines are stamped with a Plant Code, Production Date, and Engine Type Code.

Notes:

1. Corvette Engines have the last six digits of the vin stamped on the block next to the engine number.

2. Corvair Engines are stamped on the top of the block forward of the generator.

3. 8 cylinder engines are stamped on the right front of the engine block.

4. 6 cylinder engines are stamped on the right side of the block at the rear of the disjtributor.

EXAMPLE

I   01   01   A
PLANT .MONTH ....DAY .. CODE

ENGINE PLANT	Code
Tonawanda	T
Flint	F

BASIC ENGINE DATA

Models	Cu. In. Displ.	Comp Ratio	H.P.	Carburetor	Transmission
6 Cyl PASS	235	8.25	135	Single Barrel	3-Speed, OD PG
8 Cyl PASS	.283	8.5	170	2-Barrel	3-Speed, OD PG
8 Cyl PASS	327	10.5	250	4-Barrel	3 or 4-Speed PG
8 Cyl PASS	327	10.5	300	Large 4-Barrel	3 or 4-Speed PG
8 Cyl PASS	409	11.0	380	Large 4-Barel	3 or 4-Speed
8 Cyl PASS	409	11.0	409	Dual 4-Barrel	3 or 4-Speed
8 Cyl CORVETTE	327	10.5	250	4-Barrel	3 or 4-Speed PG
8 Cyl CORVETTE	327	10.5	300	Large 4-Barrel	3 or 4-Speed PG
8 Cyl CORVETTE	327	11.25	340	Large 4-Barrel	3 or 4-Speed
8 Cyl CORVETTE	327	11.25	360	Fuel Injection	3 or 4-Speed
6 Cyl CORVAIR	145	8.0	80	Dual 1-Barrel	3 or 4-Speed PG
6 Cyl CORVAIR	145	9.0	84	Dual 1-Barrel	PG
6 Cyl CORVAIR	145	9.0	102	Dual 1-Barrel	3 or 4-Speed PG
6 Cyl CORVAIR	145	8.0	150	Single Side Draft w/Turbocharge	3 or 4-Speed
4 Cyl CHEVY II	153	8.5	90	Single Barrel	3-Speed, PG
6 Cyl CHEVY II	194	8.5	120	Single Barrel	3-Speed, PG

ENGINE CODES

CHEVY II	Code
153 4-Cyl	
man	E,EP,EK,ES
PG	EG,EQ,EL,ET
man, HD clutch	ER,EB
194 6-Cyl	
man	H,HL,HT
man, HD clutch	HB
PG	HF,HU,HM
230 6-Cyl	
PG	BT,BU
man	LP,LR
283 8-Cyl	
3-spd, man	CH
3-spd man, A/C	CJ
4-spd man	CF
4-spd man, A/C	CG
PG	DE
PG, A/C	DF

CORVAIR	Code
man	YC,YH,
man, high p.	Y,YN,
man, A/C	YL
man, high p., A/C	YM

	Code
4-spd, turbo	YR
AT	ZB,ZH,ZL
AT, A/C	ZD,ZJ
AT, high p.	ZF,ZK
AT,A/C,high p.	ZG

CHEVROLET	Code
235 6-Cyl	
man	A,AE
man,A/C	AF,AG,AJ
man,PS	AK,AM,AZ
PG	B,BE
PG,A/C	BG,BH
283 8-Cyl	
man	C,CL
overdrive	CD
PG	D,DK
327 8-Cyl	
man	R,RA,RB
PG	S,SA,SB
409 8-Cyl	
4-bbl	QA
2 / 4-bbl	QB

CORVETTE	Cod
327 8-Cyl	
2 / 4-bbl	Q
man	R
man high p.	RD,R
fuel inj.	R
PG	S
PG,high p.	S

VEHICLE IDENTIFICATION NUMBER

```
CHEVROLET
31511T1001555
```

Commonly referred to as the VIN NUMBER, this series of numbers and letters is stamped on a plate attached to the left front door hinge pillar.

CORVETTE VIN Embossed on a Stainless steel Plate Welded to R/H side Hinge Pillar Cross-Brace under Glove Box.

CORVAIR VIN Embossed on a Stainless Steel Plate Welded to Left Hand Center Pillar Post Facing.

CHEVY II VIN Embossed on a Stainless Steel Plate Welded to Left Front Door Hinge Pillar Post Facing.

EXAMPLE

3	1511	T	1001555
Year	Series Body Style	Assy Plant	Production Number

FIRST DIGIT: Identifies the year, 3 for 1963

SECOND AND THIRD DIGITS: Identify the series.

SERIES	Code	
	6-CYL	8-CYL
Chevy II 100	01	02
Chevy II 300	03	04
Nova 400	-	04

SERIES	Code
Corvair 6 cyl	05
Corvair Deluxe	07
Corvair Monza	09
Corvette	08
Biscayne 6 cyl	11
Biscayne 8 cyl	12
Bel Air 6 cyl	15
Bel Air 8 cyl	16

	Code
Impala 6 cyl	17
Impala 8 cyl	18

FOURTH AND FIFTH DIGITS: Identify the Body Style.

STYLE	Code
2-Dr Sedan	11
4-Dr Sedan	19
Club Coupe	27
2-Dr Sport Coupe	37
4-Dr Sport Sedan	39
Convertible	67
4-Dr Sedan	69
4-Dr Station Wagon 6 Pass	35
4-Dr Station Wagon 9 Pass	45

SIXTH DIGIT: A letter identifies the Assembly Plant.

ASSEMBLY PLANT	Code
Atlanta	A
Baltimore	B
Flint	F
Janesville	J
Kansas City	K
Los Angeles	L
Norwood	N
Oakland	O
St. Louis	S
Tarrytown	T
Willow Run	W
Framingham	G

CHEVROLET DIVISION
GENERAL MOTORS CORP.
CORRESPONDENCE PERTAINING TO THE BODY MUST BEAR THESE NUMBERS

STYLE No.	63 1511
BODY No.	T 1001555
TRIM No.	749
PAINT No.	936

BODY BY FISHER

FISHER BODY NUMBER PLATE

Complete identification of each body is provided by a plate riveted to the top of the cowl on the left side of the car.

*Exception: Corvair body tag is located on left rear wheel housing inside the engine compartment.

HE STYLE NUMBER is a combition of the year, series, and body tyle.

CORVAIR	STD	DELUXE
Club Coupe	527	727
-Dr Sedan		769
Monza 2-Dr Club Coupe		927
Monza 4-Dr Sedan		969
Monza Convertible		967
-Dr Station Wagon		735

BEL AIR	6 cyl	8 cyl
-Dr Sedan	1511	1611
-Dr Sedan	1569	1669
-Dr Station Wagon	1535	1635
-Dr Station Wagon	1545	1645

CORVETTE	Code
Convertible	0867
Spt-Cpe	0837

BISCAYNE	6 cyl	8 cyl
2-Dr Sedan	1111	1211
4-Dr Sedan	1169	1269
2-Dr Sedan Deliver	1170	1270
2-Dr Sedan Pickup	1180	1280
4-Dr St. Wagon	1135	1235

IMPALA	6 cyl	8 cyl
4-Dr Sedan	1769	1869
2-Dr Sport Coupe	1747	1847
4-Dr Sport Sedan	1739	1839
2-Dr Convertible	1767	1867
4-Dr Station Wagon	1735	1835
4-Dr Station Wagon	1745	1845

Note: "SS" does not change style #

CHEVY II 100	4 cyl	6 cyl
2-Dr Sedan	0111	0211
4-Dr Sedan	0169	0269
4-Dr Station Wagon	0135	0235

CHEVY II 300	6 cyl	8 cyl
2-Dr Sedan	0311	0411
4-Dr Sedan	0369	0469
4-Dr Station Wagon	0345	0445

NOVA 400	Code
4-Dr Sedan	0449
2-Dr Sport Coupe	0437
2-Dr Conv	0467
4-Dr Station Wagon	0435

Note: "SS" does not change style #

THE BODY NUMBER is the production serial number of the body. The prefix letter denotes the plant in which the body was built.

ASSEMBLY PLANT	Code
Atlanta	A
Baltimore	B
Flint	F
Janesville	J
Kansas City	K
Los Angeles	L
Norwood	N
Oakland	O
St. Louis	S
Tarrytown	T
Willow Run	W
Framingham	G

THE TRIM NUMBER furnishes the key to trim color and material for each model SERIES.

D=Dark, M=Medium, L=Light, I=Imitation, W=Woven

MATERIAL	Code	Models
M Saddle Cloth, M Saddle I-Leather	707	437-49
M Saddle Pattern I-Leather, M Saddle I-Leather	709	435-67
Metallic M Aqua I-Leather, L Aqua I-Leather	720	527
M Blue Cloth, L Blue I-Leather	731	727-79
M Blue Cloth, L Blue I-Leather	738	311-45-69 411-45-69
M Blue Cloth, Metallic M Blue I-Leather	739	437-49
M Blue Pattern I-Leather, Metallic Med. Blue I-Leather	742	435
Med. Aqua Cloth, L Aqua I-Leather	749	311-45-69 411-45-69
M Aqua Cloth, Metallic M Aqua I-Leather	750	437-49
M Aqua Cloth, L Aqua I-Leather	751	727-69
M Aqua Cloth, Metallic M Aqua I-Leather	752	111-69 211-69
M Aqua Pattern I-Leather, Metallic M Aqua I-Leather	753	435-67
I-Leather, Metallic M Aqua I-Leather	754	135-235
M Fawn Cloth, L Fawn I-Leather	757	727-69
M Fawn Cloth, Metallic M Fawn I-Leather	760	111-69 211-69
Metallic M Fawn Pattern I-Leather, Metallic M Fawn I-Leather	761	135-235
M Fawn Cloth, Light Fawn I-Leather	762	311-45-69 411-45-69
M Fawn Cloth, Metallic M Fawn I-Leather	763	437-49
Metallic M Fawn I-Leather, L Fawn I-Leather	764	527
Metallic M Fawn I-Leather	765	111-69 211-69
M Red Cloth, M Red I-Leather	772	437-49
M Red. Pattern I-Leather, M Red I-Leather	774	435
M Red Cloth, M Red I-Leather	776	111-69 211-69
M Red Pattern I-Leather, M Red I-Leather	777	135-235
Med. Red Cloth, Med. Red I-Leather	778	311-45-69 411-45-69
M Red Cloth, Ivory I-Leather	780	727-69
M Red I-Leather, Ivory I-Leather	783	527
Black Savarine Cloth, Black Sparta Cloth	811	1739-47 1839-47
Black I-Leather	814	1767-1867

	Code	Models
M Green Cloth, M Green I-Leather	823	1511-35-45-69 1611-35-45-69
M Green Savarine Cloth, M Green Sparta Cloth	826	1735-39-45-47-69 1835-39-45-47-69
M Green I-Leather	829	1767-1867
Metallic M Blue I-Leather	836	1767-1867
M Blue Cloth, Metallic M Blue I-Leather	839	1511-35-45-69 1611-35-45-69
M Blue Savarine Cloth, M Blue Sparta Cloth	842	1735-39-45-47-69 1835-39-45-47-69
Metallic M Aqua I-Leather	847	1767-1867
M Aqua Cloth, M Aqua I-Leather	850	1511-35-45-69 1611-35-45-69
M Aqua Cloth, Metallic M Fawn Ribbed I-Leather	852	1111-69 1211-69
M Aqua Savarine Cloth, M Aqua Sparta Cloth	853	1735-39-45-47-69 1835-39-45-47-69
Metallic M Aqua Pattern I-Leather, Metallic M Aqua Ribbed I-Leather	855	1135-1235
M Saddle Savarine Cloth M Saddle Sparta Cloth	857	1735-39-45-47-69 1835-39-45-47-69
M Saddle I-Leather	859	1767-1867
M Fawn Cloth, Metallic M Fawn Ribbed I-Leather	860	1111-69 1211-69
Metallic M Fawn Pattern I-Leather, Metallic M Fawn Ribbed Imitation Leather	861	1135-1235
M Fawn Cloth, Metallic M Fawn I-Leather	863	1511-35-45-69 1611-35-45-69
Metallic M Fawn I-Leather, Metallic M Fawn Ribbed I-Leather	865	1111-69 1211-69
M Fawn Savarine Cloth M Fawn Sparta Cloth	866	1735-39-45-47-69 1835-39-45-47-69
Metallic M Fawn I-Leather	870	1767-1867
M Red Cloth, M Red Imitation Leather	872	1511-35-45-69 1611-35-45-69
M Red Savarine Cloth, M Red Sparta Cloth	874	1735-39-45-47-69 1835-39-45-47-69
M Red Cloth, M, Red Ribbed I-Leather	876	1111-69

M Red Pattern I-Leather,
M Red Ribbed I-Leather 877 1135-1235
M Red I-Leather 886 1767-1867

Bucket Seats

Black I-Leather 702 437
M Saddle I-Leather 705 927-67-69
M Saddle I-Leather 708 437
M Saddle Pattern I-Leather,M Saddle I-Leather .. 710 467
Black I-Leather 712 927-67-69
Black I-Leather 714 467
M Aqua I-Leather, Metallic M Aqua I-Leather 721 437
M Aqua Pattern I-Leather,
Metallic Med. Aqua I-Leather 722 467
Ivory I-Leather 727 927-67-69
Metallic M Blue I-Leather 732 927-67-69
M Blue I-Leather,Metallic M Blue I-Leather 740 437
M Blue I-Leather, Metallic M Blue I-Leather 741 467
Metallic M Aqua I-Leather 755 927-67-69
Metallic M Fawn I-Leather 758 927-67-69
M Fawn I-Leather, Metallic M Fawn I-Leather 767 437
M Fawn I-Leather, Metallic M Fawn I-Leather 770 467
M Red I-Leather 775 437
M Red I-Leather 781 927-67-69
M Red I-Leather 786 467
Black I-Leather 812 1747-1847
Black I-Leather 815 1767-1867
Metallic M Green I-Leather 821 1767-1867
Metallic M Green I-Leather 827 1747-1847
Metallic M Blue I-Leather 831 1767-1867
Metallic M Blue I-Leather 843 1747-1847
Metallic M Aqua I-Leather 845 1767-1867
Metallic M Aqua I-Leather 854 1747-1847
Metallic M Fawn I-Leather 856 1767-1867
M Saddle I-Leather 858 1767-1867
M Saddle I-Leather 862 1767-1867
Metallic M Fawn I-Leather 867 1747-1847
M Red I-Leather 875 1747-1847
M Red I-Leather 879 1767-1867

1211-69

THE PAINT CODE furnishes the key to the paint colors on the car.

PAINT	Code
Tuxedo Black	900
Laurel Green	905
Ivy Green	908
Silver Blue	912
Monaco Blue	914
Daytona Blue	916
Azure Aqua	918
Marine Aqua	919
Autumn Gold	920
Ember Red	922
Riverside Red	923
Saddle Tan	932
Cordovan Brown	934
Ermine White	936
Adobe Beige	938
Satin Silver	940
Sebring Silver	941
Palomar Red	948
White / Black	950
White / L. Green	954
White / S. Blue	959
Silver Blue / M. Blue	962
White / A. Aqua	963
Azure Aqua / M. Aqua	967
Adobe Beige / A. Gold	970
Adobe Beige / Saddle Tan	971
Adobe Beige / C. Brown	972
White / Red	973
White / Satin Silver	984

ENGINE NUMBER

All Chevrolet Engines are stamped with a Plant Code, Production Date, and Engine Type Code.

Note:

1. Corvette Engines have the last six digits of the VIN stamped on the block next to the engine number.

2. Corvair Engines are stamped on the top of the block forward of the generator.

3. 8 cylinder engines are stamped on the right side of the block at the rear of the distributor.

EXAMPLE

I	01	01	A
PLANT	MONTH	DAY	CODE

ENGINE PLANTS	Code
Tonawanda	T
Flint	F

BASIC ENGINE DATA

MODEL	CID	COMP	HP	CARBURETOR	TRANSMISSION
6 Cyl PASS.	230	8.5	140	Single Barrel	3-SPD.,OD,PG
8 Cyl PASS.	283	8.5	195	2-Barrel	3-SPD.,OD.,PG
8-Cyl PASS.	327	10.5	250	4-Barrel	3-SPD., 4-SPD.,PG
8 Cyl PASS.	327	10.5	300	Lg. 4-Barrel	3-SPD., 4-SPD.,PG
8 Cyl PASS.	409	11.0	340	Lg. 4-Barrel	3-SPD., 4-SPD.,PG
8 Cyl PASS.	409	11.0	400	Lg. 4-Barrel	3-SPD., 4-SPD.
8 Cyl PASS.	409	11.0	425	Dual 4-Barrel	3-SPD., 4-SPD.
8 Cyl CORVETTE	327	10.5	250	4-Barrel	3-SPD., 4-SPD., PG
8 Cyl CORVETTE	327	10.5	300	Lg. 4-Barrel	3-SPD., 4-SPD., PG
8 Cyl CORVETTE	327	11.25	340	Lg. 4-Barrel	3-SPD., 4-SPD.
8 Cyl CORVETTE	327	11.25	360	Fuel Injection	3-SPD., 4-SPD.
6 Cyl CORVAIR	145	8.0	80	Dual Sg. Barrel	3-SPD.,4-SPD.,PG
6 Cyl CORVAIR	145	9.0	102	Dual Sg. Barrel	3-SPD., 4-SPD.
6 Cyl CORVAIR	145	8.0	150	Single Side Draft w/Turbocharger	3-SPD., 4-SPD.
6 Cyl CORVAIR	145	9.0	84	Dual Sg. Barrel	PG
4 Cyl CHEVY II	153	8.5	90	Single Barrel	3-SPD., PG
6 Cyl CHEVY II	194	8.5	120	Single Barrel	3-SPD., PG

ENGINE CODES

CORVAIR

145 6-cyl
man	YC,YN
man, A/C	YL,YM
4-spd, turbo	Y
AT	Z,ZH,ZF
AT, A/C	ZD,ZG

CORVETTE

327 8-cyl
man	RC,RD
spec. high p.	RE
FI	RF
PG	SC,SD

CHEVY II

153 4-Cyl
man	E,EP,EK,ES
PG	EG,EQ,EL,ET
man, HD clutch	ER,EB

194 6-Cyl
man	H,HL,HT
man, HD clutch	HB
PG	HF,HU,HM

230 6-Cyl
PG	BT,BU
man	LP,LR

283 8-Cyl
3-spd, man	CH
3-spd man, A/C	CJ
4-spd man	CF
4-spd man, A/C	CG
PG	DE
PG, A/C	DF

CHEVROLET

230 6-cyl
man	A,AE
PG	B

283 8-cyl
man	C,CB,CD,CL
PG	D,DK

327 8-cyl
man	R,RA,RB,RK
PG	SA,SB,SG
man, high p.	XE

409 8-cyl
man	QA,QB,QC
PG	QG

427 8-cyl
Z11	QM

1964 CHEVROLET

VEHICLE IDENTIFICATION NUMBER

> **CHEVROLET**
> **41511T101555**

Commonly referred to as the VIN NUMBER, this series of numbers and letters is stamped on a plate attached to the left front door hinge pillar.

CORVETTE VIN Embossed on a Stainless Steel Plate Welded to R/H side Hinge Pillar Cross-Brace under Glove Box.

CHEVELLE & Chevy II VIN Embossed on a Stain-less Steel Plate Welded to Left Front Door Hinge Pillar Post Facing.

CORVAIR VIN Embossed on a Stainless Steel Plate Welded to Left Hand Center Pillar Post.

FIRST DIGIT: Identifies the year, 4 for 1964.

SECOND AND THIRD DIGITS: Identify the series.

SERIES	Code
Corvair 6 cyl.	05
Corvair Deluxe	07
Monza	09
Monza Spyder	06
Corvette	08
Biscayne 6 cyl	11
Biscayne 8 cyl	12
Bel Air 6 cyl	15
Bel Air 8 cyl	16
Impala 6 cyl	17
Impala 8 cyl	18
Impala SS 6 cyl	13
Impala SS 8 cyl	14
Chevy II 100 4 cyl	01
Chevy II 100 6 cyl	02
Nova 6 cyl	04

EXAMPLE

4	1511	T	101555
Year	Series Body Style	Assy Plant	Production Number

Chevelle 300 6 cyl	53
Chevelle 300 8 cyl	54
Malibu 6 cyl	55
Malibu 8 cyl	56
Malibu SS 6 cyl	57
Malibu SS 8 cyl	58

Fourth and Fifth Digits: Identify the Body Style.

MODEL	Code
2-Dr Sedan	11
4-Dr Sedan	19
Club Coupe	27
2-Dr Sport Coupe	37
4-Dr Sport Sedan	39
Convertible	67
4-Dr Sedan	69

> **CHEVROLET DIVISION**
> **GENERAL MOTORS CORP.**
> CORRESPONDENCE PERTAINING TO THE BODY MUST BEAR THESE NUMBERS
>
> STYLE No.   64 1511
> BODY No.   T 101555
> TRIM No.   701
> PAINT No.   936
>
> BODY BY FISHER

Dr Station Wagon 6 Pass. 15
Dr Station Wagon 6 Pass. ...35
Dr Station Wagon 9 Pass. ...45
Dr Sports Coupe 47

IXTH DIGIT: Identifies the As-
embly Plant

Assembly Plant	Code
Atlanta	A
Baltimore	B
Atlanta BOP	C
Flint	F
Framingham	G
Fremont	H
Janesville	J
Kansas City	K
Los Angeles	L
Norwood	N
Oakland	-O
Arlington	R
St. Louis	S
Tarrytown	T
Southgate	U
Willow Run	W
Wilmington	Y

LAST SIX DIGITS: Production
sequence number

FISHER BODY NUMBER PLATE

Complete identification of each
body is provided by a plate riveted
to the top of the cowl on the left side
of the car.

Exception: Corvair body tag is
located on left rear wheel housing
inside the engine compartment.

THE STYLE NUMBER is a combination of the series, and body
style.

Chevy II 100	Code
2-Dr Sedan, 6 Pass. 4 Cyl	111
4-Dr Sedan, 6 Pass. 4 Cyl	169
2-Dr Sedan, 6 Pass. 6 Cyl	211
4-Dr Sedan, 6 Pass. 6 Cyl	269
4-Dr St.Wagon, 2 Seat 6 Cyl	235

Nova 6 Cyl	Code
2-Dr Sport Coupe	437
2-Dr Sedan, 6 Pass.	411
4-Dr Sedan, 6 Pass.	469
4-Dr Station Wagon, 2 Seat	435

Corvair 500	Code
2-Dr Coupe, 5 Pass.	527

Corvair 700	Code
4-Dr Sedan, 6 Pass.	769

Monza 900	Code
2-Dr Coupe, 4 Pass.	927
2-Dr Convertible, 4 Pass.	967
4-Dr Sedan, 5 Pass.	969

Monza Spyder 600	Code
2-Dr Coupe, 4 Pass.	627
2-Dr Convertible, 4 Pass.	667

Biscayne	6 Cyl	8 Cyl
2-Dr Sedan	1111	1211
4-Dr Sedan	1169	1269
4-Dr Station Wagon, 6 Pass.	1135	1235

Bel Air	6 Cyl	8 Cyl
2-Dr Sedan	1511	1611
4-Dr Sedan	1569	1569
4-Dr Station Wagon, 6 Pass.	1535	1535
4-Dr Station Wagon, 9 Pass.	1545	1645

Impala	6 Cyl	8 Cyl
4-Dr Sedan	1769	1869
2-Dr Sport Coupe	1747	1847
4-Door Sport Sedan	1739	1839
4-Dr Station Wagon, 6 Pass.	1735	1835
4-Dr Station Wagon, 9 Pass.	1745	1845
Convertible	1767	1867

Impala SS	6 Cyl	8 Cyl
2-Dr Sport Coupe	1347	1447
Convertible	1367	1467

Chevelle 300	6 Cyl	8 Cyl
2-Dr Sedan, 6-Pass.	5311	5411
4-Dr Sedan, 6-Pass.	5369	5469
2-Dr Station Wagon, 2-Seat	5315	5415
4-Dr Station Wagon, 2-Seat	5335	5435

Malibu	6 Cyl	8 Cyl
4-Dr Sedan, 6-Pass.	5569	5669

	6 Cyl	8 Cyl
2-Dr Sport Coupe, 5-Pass.	5537	5637
2-Dr Convertible, 5-Pass.	5567	5667
4-Dr Station Wagon, 2-Seat	5535	5635
4-Dr Station Wagon, 3-Seat	5545	5645

Malibu SS	6 Cyl	8 Cyl
2-Dr Sport Coupe, 4-Pass.	5737	5837
2-Dr Sedan Convertible, 4-Pass.	5767	5867

THE BODY NUMBER is the
production serial number of the
body. The prefix letter denotes the
plant in which the body was built.

Assembly Plant	Code
Atlanta	A
Baltimore	B
Atlanta BOP	C
Flint	F
Framingham	G
Fremont	H
Janesville	J
Kansas City	K
Los Angeles	L
Norwood	N
Oakland	-
Arlington	R
St. Louis	S
Tarrytown	T
Southgate	U
Willow Run	W
Wilmington	Y

THE PAINT CODE furnishes the
key to the paint colors on the car.

COLOR	Code
Tuxedo Black	900
Meadow Green	905
Bahama Green	908
Silver Blue	912
Daytona Blue	916
Azure Aqua	918
Lagoon Aqua	919
Almond Fawn	920
Ember Red	922
Riverside Red	923
Saddle Tan	932
Ermine White	936
Desert Beige	938
Satin Silver	940
Goldwood Yellow	943
Palomar Red	948
B. Green / M. Green	952
White / M. Green	954
White / S. Blue	959
Daytona Blue / S. Blue	960
White / L. Aqua	965
Desert Beige / Saddle Tan	971
Desert Beige / E. Red	975
Daytona Blue / S. Silver	982
Azure Aqua / White	988
Desert Beige / P. Red	993
Satin Silver / P. Red	995

THE TRIM NUMBER furnishes the key to trim color and material for each model SERIES.

D=Dark, M=Medium, L=Light, I=Imitation, W=Woven

Material	Code	Models
M Saddle Cloth, M Saddle I-Leather	701	411-69
M Saddle Cloth, M Saddle I-Leather	703	435
M Saddle Starette Cloth, M Saddle I-Leather	707	5637-69-80
M Saddle I-Leather	709	5635-45-67
Metallic M Aqua I-Leather	720	527
M Blue Scotia Cloth, Metallic M Blue I-Leather	731	769
M Blue Pacific Cloth, M Metallic Blue I-Leather	734	411-69
M Blue Imitation Leather, M Metallic Blue I-Leather	736	435
M Blue Solaire Cloth, M Metallic Blue I-Leather	738	5411-15-35-69
M Blue Starette Cloth, M Metallic Blue I-Leather	739	5637-69
M Metallic Blue I-Leather	742	5635-45-67
M Aqua Pacific Cloth, M Metallic Aqua I-Leather	745	411-69
M Aqua I-Leather, M Metallic Aqua I-Leather	747	435
M Aqua I-Leather, M Metallic Aqua I-Leather	748	5480
M Aqua Solaire Cloth, M Metallic Aqua I-Leather	749	5411-15-35-69
Aqua Starette Cloth, M Metallic Aqua I-Leather	750	5637-69-80
M Red Scotia Cloth, M Red I-Leather	751	769
M Aqua Savona Cloth, M Metallic Aqua I-Leather	752	211-69
M Metallic Aqua I-Leather	753	5635-45-67
M Metallic Aqua I-Leather	754	235
M Fawn Scotia Cloth, L Fawn I-Leather	757	769
M Fawn Savona Cloth, L Fawn I-Leather	760	211-69
L Fawn I-Leather	761	235
M Fawn Solaire Cloth, L Fawn I-Leather	762	5411-15-35-69
M Fawn Starette Cloth, L Fawn I-Leather	763	5637-69-80
L Fawn I-Leather	764	527
L Fawn I-Leather	766	5635-45-67
L Fawn Pattern I-Leather, L Fawn I-Leather	767	5480
M Fawn Pacific Cloth, L Fawn I-Leather	768	411-69
L Fawn Pattern I-Leather L Fawn I-Leather	769	435
M Red Starette Cloth, M Red I-Leather	772	5637-69-80
M Red I-Leather	774	5635-45-67
M Red Savona Cloth, M Red I-Leather	776	211-69
M Red Pattern I-Leather	777	235
M Red Solaire Cloth, M Red I-Leather	778	5411-15-35-69
M Red Scotia Cloth, M Red I-Leather	780	769
M Red Pattern I-Leather	783	527
M Red Pacific Cloth, M Red I-Leather	791	411-69
M Red Pattern I-Leather, M Red I-Leather	793	435
M Red Pattern I-Leather, M Red I-Leather	794	5480
Black Sabrina Cloth, Black Sardis Cloth	811	1839-47
Black I-Leather	814	1867
M Metallic Olive I-Leather	823	1611-35-45-69
M Olive Sabrina Cloth, M Olive Sardis Cloth	826	1839-47-69
M Metallic Olive I-Leather	829	1835-45-67
M Metallic Blue I-Leather	836	1835-45-67
M Blue Shelburne Cloth, M Metallic Blue I-Leather	839	1611-35-45-69
M Blue Sabrina Cloth, M Blue Sardis Cloth	842	1839-47-69
M Metallic Aqua I-Leather	847	1835-45-67
M Aqua Shelburne Cloth, M Metallic Aqua I-Leather	850	1611-35-45-69
M Aqua Sapphire Cloth, M Metallic Aqua Pattern I-Leather	852	1211-69
M Aqua Sabrina Cloth, M Aqua Sardis Cloth	853	1839-47-69
M Metallic Aqua Pattern I-Leather, M Metallic Aqua Pattern I-Leather	855	1235
M Saddle Sabrina Cloth, M Saddle Sardis Cloth	857	1839-47-69
M Saddle I-Leather	859	1835-45-67
M Fawn Sapphire Cloth, L Fawn Pattern I-Leather	860	1211-69
L Fawn Pattern I-Leather	861	1235
M Fawn Shelburne Cloth, L Fawn I-Leather	863	1611-35-45-69
M Fawn Sabrina Cloth, M Fawn Sardis Cloth	866	1839-47-69
L Fawn I-Leather	870	1835-45-67
M Red Shelburne Cloth, M Red I-Leather	872	1611-35-45-69
M Red Sabrina Cloth, M Red Sardis Cloth	874	1837-47-69
M Red Sapphire Cloth, M Red Pattern I-Leather	876	1211-69
M Red Pattern I-Leather, M Red Pattern I-Leather	877	1235
M Red I-Leather	886	1835-45-67

Bucket Seats

M Saddle I-Leather	705	927-67-69, 627-67
M Saddle I-Leather	710	5837-67
Black I-Leather	712	927-67-69, 627-67
Black I-Leather	714	5837-67
L Fawn I-Leather	717	5680
Metallic M Aqua I-Leather	722	5837-67
Metallic M Aqua I-Leather	724	5680
M Red I-Leather	726	5680
Ivory I-Leather	727	927-67-69, 627-67
Ivory I- Leather	729	5837-67
Metallic M Blue I-Leather	732	927-67-69, 627-67
M Metallic Blue I-Leather	741	5837-67
M Metallic Aqua I-Leather	755	927-67-69, 627-67
L Fawn I-Leather	758	927-67-69, 627-67
L Fawn I-Leather	770	5837-67
M Red I-Leather	781	927-67-69, 627-67
M Red I-Leather	786	5837-67
M Silver I-Leather	805	1447-67
Black I-Leather	815	1447-67
M Metallic Blue I-Leather	831	1447-67
Ivory I-Leather	845	1447-67
L Fawn I-Leather	856	1447-67
M Saddle I-Leather	862	1447-67
Ivory I-Leather	878	1447-67
M Red I-Leather	879	1447-67

ENGINE NUMBER

All Chevrolet Engines are stamped with a Plant Code, Production Date, and Engine Type Code.

Note:

1. Corvette Engines have the last six digits of the VIN stamped on the block next to the engine number.

2. Corvair Engines are stamped on the top of the block forward of the generator.

3. 8 cylinder engines are stamped on the right front of the engine block.

4. 6 cylinder engines are stamped on the right side of the block at the rear of the distributor.

EXAMPLE

```
T        01      01      A
PLANT .. MONTH ...DAY ... CODE
```

ENGINE PLANTS	CODE
Tonawanda ....T
Flint ....F

BASIC ENGINE DATA

Model	CID	COMP.	H.P.	Carburetor	Transmission
6 Cyl PASS.	230	8.5	140	Single Barrel	3-SPD., OD,PG
6 Cyl PASS.	230	8.5	125	Single Barrel	3-SPD., OD.,PG, Econ. Carb.
8 Cyl PASS.	283	9.25	195	2-Barrel	3-PSD., OD,PG
8 Cyl PASS.	327	10.5	250	4-Barrel	3-SPD., 4-SPD.,PG
8 Cyl PASS.	327	10.5	300	Large 4-Barrel	3-SPD., 4-SPD.,PG
8 Cyl PASS.	409	10	340	4-Barrel	3-SPD., 4-SPD.,PG
8 Cyl PASS.	409	11	400	Large 4-Barrel	3-SPD., 4-SPD., C.R. 4-SPD.
8 Cyl PASS.	409	11	425	Dual 4-Barrel	3-SPD., 4-PSD., C.R. 4-SPD.
8 Cyl CORVETTE	327	10.5	250	4-Barrel	3-SPD., 4-PSD.,PG
8 Cyl CORVETTE	327	10.5	300	Large 4-Barrel	3-SPD., 4-SPD.,PG
8 Cyl CORVETTE	327	11.25	365	Large 4-Barrel	3-SPD., 4-SPD.
8 Cyl CORVETTE	327	11.25	375	Fuel Injection	3-SPD., 4-SPD.
CORVAIR	164	8.25	95	Dual 1-Barrel	3-SPD., 4-SPD.,PG
CORVAIR	164	9.25	110	Dual 1-Barrel	3-SPD., 4-SPD.,PG
SPYDER	164	8.25	150	Single Side Draft	3-SPD., 4-SPD.
4 Cyl CHEVY II	153	8.5	90	Single Barrel	3-SPD., P.G.
6 Cyl CHEVY II	194	8.5	120	Single Barrel	3-SPD., P.G
6 Cyl CHEVY II	194	8.5	140	Single Barrel	3-SPD., P.G.
8 Cyl CHEVY II	283	9.25	195	2 Barrel	3-SPD., 4-SPD.,P.G.
6 Cyl CHEVELLE	194	8.5	120	Single Barrel	3-SPD., P.G., O.D.
6 Cyl CHEVELLE	230	8.5	140	Single Barrel	3-SPD., P.G., O.D.
6 Cyl CHEVELLE	230	8.5	155	Single Barrel	3-SPD, P.G.
8 Cyl CHEVELLE	283	9.25	195	2 Barrel	3-SPD., 4-SPD., P.G., O.D.
8 Cyl CHEVELLE	283	9.25	220	4 Barrel	3-SPD., 4-SPD., P.G., O.D.
8 Cyl Malibu SS	327	10.5	250	4 Barrel	3-SPD, 4-SPD, P.G.
8 Cyl Malibu SS	327	10.5	300	4 Barrel	3-SPD, 4-SPD,P.G.

ENGINE CODES

CHEVROLET

230 6-cyl	
man	A,AE,AF,AG
PG	B,BQ
283 8-cyl	
man	C,CB
PG	D
327 8-cyl	
man	R,RB
PG	SB
man, high p.	XE
409 8-cyl	
man	QA,QE,QQ,QC,QN
PG	QG,QR

CHEVY II

153 4-Cyl	
man	E,EP,EK,ES
PG	EG,EQ,EL,ET
man, HD clutch	ER,EB
194 6-Cyl	
man	H,HL,HT
man, HD clutch	HB
PG	HF,HU,HM
230 6-Cyl	
PG	BT,BU
man	LP,LR
283 8-Cyl	
3-spd, man	CH
3-spd man, A/C	CJ
4-spd man	CF
4-spd man, A/C	CG
PG	DE
PG, A/C	DF

CHEVELLE

194 6-Cyl	
man	G,GH,GJ,GB,GF,GG
man, A/C	GK,GL,GM,GN
PG	K,KB
PG,A/C	KJ,KH
230 6-Cyl	
man	LL,LM,LN
PG	BN,BL
PG,A/C	BM,BP
283 8-Cyl	
man	J,JA,JH
PG	JD,JG
327 8-Cyl	
man	JQ,JR,JS,JT
PG	SR,SS

CORVAIR

145 6-cyl	
man	YC,YN
man, A/C	YL,YM
4-spd, turbo	Y
AT	Z,ZH,ZF
AT, A/C	ZD,ZG

CORVETTE

327 8-cyl	
man	RC,RD,RT
man, A/C	RP,RQRR,RU
spec. high p.	RE
FI	RF,RX
PG	SC,SD,SK,SL

VEHICLE IDENTIFICATION NUMBER

CHEVROLET
164375T101555

Commonly referred to as the VIN NUMBER, this series of numbers and letters is stamped on a plate attached to the left front door hinge pillar.

Chevrolet, Chevelle, and Chevy II VIN Embossed on a Stainless Steel Plate Riveted to Left Front Door Hinge Post Facing.

Corvair VIN Embossed on a Stainless Steel Plate Riveted to Left Side-Rail near Battery in Engine Compartment.

Corvette VIN Embossed on a Stainless Steel Plate Riveted to Right Side Dash Pillar Brace under Glove Box.

FIRST DIGIT: Identifies Chevrolet Division.

NEXT FOUR DIGITS: Identify the Model number.

Biscayne / Bel-Air 5000
Impala 6000
Chevelle, Malibu 3000
Chevy II, Nova 1000
Corvair 0000
Corvette 9000

SIXTH DIGIT: 5, for 1965.

SEVENTH DIGIT: Identifies the Assembly Plant.

EXAMPLE

1	6437	5	T	101551
Man. Symbol	Model	Year	Assy Plant	Production Number

ASSEMBLY PLANT	Code
Atlanta, Ga.	A
Baltimore, Md.	B
Southgate, Calif.	C
Flint, Mich.	F
Framingham, Mass.	G
Janesville, Wis.	J
Kansas City, Mo.	K
Los Angeles, Calif.	L
Norwood, Ohio	N
Arlington, Tex. GMAD	R
St. Louis, Mo.	S
Tarrytown, N.Y.	T
Willow Run, Mich.	W
Wilmington, Del.	Y
Fremont, Calif.	Z
Oshawa, Ont., Can.	1
Ste. Therese, Que., Can.	2
Pontiac, Mich.	P

LAST SIX DIGITS: Production sequence number.

CHEVROLET DIVISION
GENERAL MOTORS CORP.
CORRESPONDENCE PERTAINING TO THE
BODY MUST BEAR THESE NUMBERS

STYLE No.   65 15411
BODY No.   T 1001555
TRIM No.   810
PAINT No.   936

BODY BY FISHER

FISHER BODY NUMBER PLATE

Complete identification of each body is provided by a plate riveted to the top of the cowl.

*Exception: Corvair body tag is located on left rear wheel housing inside the engine compartment.

THE BODY NUMBER is the production serial number of the body. The prefix letter denotes the plant in which the body was built.

ASSEMBLY PLANT — Code

Atlanta, Ga.	A
Baltimore, Md.	B
Southgate, Calif.	C
Flint, Mich.	F
Framingham, Mass.	G
Janesville, Wis.	J
Kansas City, Mo.	K
Los Angeles, Calif.	L
Norwood, Ohio	N
Arlington, Tex. GMAD	R
St. Louis, Mo.	S
Tarrytown, N.Y.	T
Willow Run, Mich.	W
Wilmington, Del.	Y
Fremont, Calif.	Z
Oshawa, Ont., Can.	1
Ste. Therese, Que., Can.	2
Pontiac, Mich.	P

LAST SIX DIGITS: Production sequence number.

THE STYLE NUMBER is a combination of the series, and body style.

CHEVROLET - 15-1600 SERIES

Series	Style No.	6 Cyl.	8 Cyl.	Description
Biscayne		15311	15411	2-Door Sedan, 6-Passenger
		15369	15469	4-Door Sedan, 6-Passenger
		15335	15435	4-Door station Wagon, 2-Seats
Bel Air		15511	15611	2-Door Sedan, 6-Passenger
		15569	15669	4-Door Sedan, 6-Passenger
		15535	15635	4-Door Station Wagon, 2-Seats
		15545	16645	4-Door Station Wagon, 3-Seats
Impala		16369	16469	4-Door Sedan, 6-Passenger
		16339	16439	4-Door Sport Sedan, 6-Passenger
		16337	16437	2-Door Sport Coupe, 5-Passenger
		16367	16467	2-Door Convertible, 5-Passenger
		16335	16435	4-Door Station Wagon, 2-Seats
		16345	16445	4-Door Station Wagon, 3-Seats
Impala SS		16537	16637	2-Door Sport Coupe, 4-Passenger
		16567	16667	2-Door Convertible, 4-Passenger

CHEVELLE - 13000 SERIES

Series	Style No.	6 Cyl.	8 Cyl.	Description
Chevelle 300		13111	13211	2-Door Sedan, 6-Passenger
		13169	13269	4-Door Sedan, 6-Passenger
		13115	13215	2-Door Station Wagon, 2-Seat
Chevelle 300 (Deluxe)		13311	13411	2-Door Sedan, 6-Passenger
		13369	13469	4-Door Sedan, 6-Passenger
		13335	13435	4-Door Station Wagon, 2-Seat
Malibu		13569	13669	4-Door Sedan, 6-Passenger
		13537	13637	2-Door Sport Coupe, 5-Passenger
		13567	13667	2-Door Convertible, 5-Passenger
		13535	13635	4-Door Station Wagon, 2-Seat
Malibu SS		13737	13837	2-Door Sport Coupe, 4-Passenger
		13767	13867	2-Door Convertible, 4-Passenger

CHEVY II - 11000 SERIES

Series	Style No.	L4	6 CYL.	8 CYL.	Description
Standard		11111	11311	11411	2-Door Sedan, 6-Passenger
		11169	11369	11469	4-Door Sedan, 6-Passenger
		-	11335	11435	4-Door Station Wagon, 2-Seat
Nova		-	11569	11669	4-Door Sedan, 6-Passenger
		-	11537	11637	2-Door Sport Coupe, 5-Passenger
		-	11535	11635	4-Door Station Wagon, 2-Seat
Nova SS		-	11737	11837	2-Door Sport Coupe, 4-Passenger

CORVAIR - 10000 SERIES

Series	Style No.	Description
Standard	10137	2-Door Sport Coupe, 5-Passenger
	10139	4-Door Sport Sedan, 6-Passenger
Monza	10537	2-Door Sport Coupe, 4-Passenger
	10567	2-Door Convertible, 4-Passenger
	10539	4-Door Sport Sedan, 5-Passenger
Corsa	10737	2-Door Sport Coupe, 4-Passenger
	10767	2-Door Convertible, 4-Passenger

CORVETTE - 19000 SERIES

Series	Style No.	Description
Corvette	19437	2-Door Sport Coupe, 2-Passenger
	19467	2-Door Convertible, 2-Passenger

THE TRIM NUMBER furnishes the key to trim color and material for each model SERIES.

D=Dark, M=Medium, L=Light, I=Imitation, W=Woven

Material	Code	Models
D Saddle Cloth, M Saddle I-Leather	710	11637-39
M Saddle Pattern I-Leather, M Saddle I-Leather	703	11635
M Saddle Ramada Cloth, M Saddle I-Leather	707	13637-69
M Saddle Pattern I-Leather, M Saddle I-Leather, M Saddle I-Leather	709	13635-67
L Fawn Pattern I-Leather, L Fawn I-Leather	717	13680
M Turquoise Pattern I-Leather	723	10139-37
M Turquoise Pattern I-Leather, M Turquoise I-Leather	724	13680
M Red Pattern I-Leather, M Red I-Leather	726	13680
D Blue Romany Cloth w/D Blue Sardis Cloth, M Blue I-Leather	734	11637-69
D Blue Pattern I-Leather, M Blue I-Leather	736	11635
M Blue Ramada Cloth, M Blue I-Leather	739	13637-69
D Turquoise Romany Cloth w/D Turquoise Sardis Cloth, M Turquoise I-Leather	745	11637-69
D Tuquoise Pattern I-Leather, M Turquoise I-Leather	747	11635
M Turquoise Pattern I-Leather, M Turquoise I-Leather	748	13480
M Turquoise Radiant Cloth, M Turquoise I-Leather	749	13411-35-69
M Turquoise Ramada Cloth, M Turquoise I-Leather	750	13637-69-80
M Turquoise Rialto Cloth, M Turquoise I-Leather	751	13211-69
M Turquoise Regatta Cloth, M Turquoise I-Leather	752	11411-69
M Turquoise Pattern I-Leather, M Turquoise I-Leather	753	13635-67
M Turquoise Pattern I-Leather	754	11435
M Turquoise Pattern I-Leather, M Turquoise I-Leather	755	13215
M Fawn I-Leather	758	11411-69
M Fawn I-Leather	759	13211-69
L Fawn Regatta Cloth, L Fawn I-Leather	760	11411-69
L Fawn Pattern I-Leather	761	11435
L Fawn Radiant Cloth, L Fawn I-Leather	762	13411-35-69
L Fawn Ramada Cloth, L Fawn I-Leather	763	13637-69-80
L Fawn Rialto Cloth, L Fawn I-Leather	764	13211-69
L Fawn Pattern I- Leather, L Fawn I-Leather	765	13215
L Fawn Pattern I-Leather, L Fawn I-Leather	766	13635-67
L Fawn Pattern I-Leather, L Fawn I--Leather	767	13480
M Fawn Romany Cloth w/M Fawn Sardis Cloth, L Fawn I-Leather	768	11637-69
M Fawn Pattern Imitation Leather, L Fawn I-Leather	769	11635
L Fawn Pattern I-Leather	771	10139-37
M Red Ramada Cloth, M Red I-Leather	772	13637-69-80
M Red Pattern I-Leather, M Red I-Leather	774	13635-37
M Red Regatta Cloth, M Red I-Leather	776	11411-69
M Red Pattern I-Leather	777	11435
M Red Radiant Cloth, M Red I-Leather	778	13411-35-69
M Red Rialto Cloth, M Red I-Leather	780	13211-69
M Red Pattern I-Leather, M Red Imitation Leather	781	13215
M Red Pattern I-Leather	782	10139-37
D Red Romany Cloth w/D Red Sardis Cloth, M Red I-Leather	791	11637-69
M Red Pattern I-Leather, M Red I-Leather	793	11635
M Red Pattern I-Leather, M Red I-Leather	794	13480
Black Regency Cloth, Black Regency I-Leather	811	16437-39-69
Black I-Leather	814	16435-45-67-37-39
M Green Regina Cloth, M Green I-Leather	823	15611-35-45-69
M Green Regency Cloth, M Green I-Leather	826	16437-39-69
M Green I-Leather	829	16435-45-67
M Blue I-Leather	836	16435-45-67
M Blue Regina Cloth, M Blue I-Leather	839	15611-35-45-69
M Blue Regency Cloth, M Blue I-Leather	842	16437-39-69

Material	Code	Models
M Turquoise I-Leather	847	16435-45-67
M Turquoise Regina Cloth, M Turquoise I-Leather	850	15611-35-45-69
M Turquoise Renfrew Cloth, M Turquoise I-Leather	852	15411-69
M Turquoise Regency Cloth, M Turquoise I-Leather	853	16437-39-69
M Turquoise Pattern I-Leather, M Turquoise I-Leather	855	15435
M Saddle Regency Cloth, M Saddle I-Leather	857	16437-39-69
M Saddle I-Leather	859	16435-45-67
L Fawn Renfrew Cloth, L Fawn I-Leather	860	15411-69
L Fawn Pattern I-Leather, L Fawn I-Leather	861	15435
L Fawn Regina Cloth, L Fawn I-Leather	863	15611-35-45-69
M Fawn I-Leather	865	15411-69
L Fawn Regency Cloth, L Fawn I-Leather	866	16437-39-69
L Fawn I-Leather	870	16435-45-67
M Red Regina Cloth, M Red I-Leather	872	15611-35-45-69
M Red Regency Cloth, M Red I-Leather	874	16437-39-69
M Red Renfrew Cloth, M Red I-Leather	876	15411-69
M Red Pattern I-Leather, M Red I-Leather	877	15435
M Red I-Leather	886	16435-45-67

BUCKET SEATS

Material	Code	Models
M Saddle I- Leather	702	11837
M Saddle I- Leather	706	10537-39-67, 10737-67
M Saddle Pattern I-Leather, M Saddle I-Leather	710	13837-67
Black I-Leather	712	71211837
Black I-Leather	713	10537-39-67, 10737-67
Black Pattern I-Leather, Black I-Leather	714	13837-67
L Fawn I-Leather	718	11837
M Blue I-Leather	732	11837
M Blue I-Leather	733	10537-39-67, 10737-67
M Blue Pattern I-Leather, M Blue I-Leather	741	13837-67
M Turquoise I-Leather	744	11837
L Fawn Pattern I- Leather, L Fawn I-Leather	770	13837-67
L Fawn I-Leather	773	10537-39-67, 10737-67
M Red I-Leather	785	10537-39-67, 10737-67
M Red Pattern I-Leather, M Red I-Leather	786	13837-67
M Red I-Leather	787	11837
Ivory Pattern I-Leather, Ivory I-Leather	792	13837-67
M Slate I-Leather	795	10537-39-67, 10737-67
Ivory Pattern I-Leather, Ivory I-Leather	796	13837-67
Ivory I-Leather	797	10537-39-67, 10737-67
Ivory I-Leather	798	10537-67
M Slate Pattern Imitation Leather, M Slate I-Leather	799	13837-67
Ivory I-Leather	802	16637-67
M Slate I-Leather	805	16637-67
Black I-Leather	815	16637-67
M Blue I-Leather	831	16637-67
Ivory I-Leather	845	16637-67
L Fawn I-Leather	856	16637-67
M Saddle I-Leather	862	16637-67
M Red I-Leather	879	16637-6
Black Fabric & Vinyl	817	16439
Blue Fabric & vinyl	843	16439
Fawn Fabric L-Fawn Vinyl	858	16439

THE PAINT CODE gives the key to he exterior color.

PAINT	Code
Tuxedo Black	A
Ermine White	C
Mist Blue	D
Danube Blue	E
Nassau Blue	FF
Glen Green	GG
Willow Green	H
Cypress Green	J
Artesian Turquoise	K
Tahitian Turquoise	L
Milano Maroon	MM
Madeira Maroon	N
Evening Orchid	P
Silver Pearl	QQ
Regal Red	R
Sierra Tan	S
Rally Red	UU
Cameo Beig	V
Glacier Gray	W
Goldwood Yellow	XX
Crocus Yellow	Y

ENGINE NUMBER

All Chevrolet Engines are stamped with a Plant Code, Production Date, and Engine Type Code.

Note:

1. Corvette Engines have the last six digits of the VIN stamped on the block next to the engine number.

2. Corvair Engines are stamped on the top of the block forward of the generator.

3. 8 cylinder engines are stamped on the right front of the engine block.

4. 6 cylinder engines are stamped on the right side of the block at the rear of the distributor.

EXAMPLE

T	01	01	A
PLANT	MONTH	DAY	CODE

ENGINE PLANTS

	Code
Tonawanda	T
Flint	F

BASIC ENGINE DATA

Model	CID	Comp.	H.P.	Carburetor	Transmission
6 Cyl PASS.	230	8.5	140	1-Barrel	3-SPD., O.D.,P.G.
6 Cyl PASS.	230	8.5	125	1-Barrel	3-SPD., O.D.
8 Cyl PASS.	283	9.25	195	2 Barrel	3-SPD., O.D.,P.G.
8 Cyl PASS.	283	9.25	220	4 Barrel	3-SPD., 4-SPD.,P.G.
8 Cyl PASS.	327	10.5	250	4 Barrel	3-SPD., 4-SPD.,P.G.
8 Cyl PASS.	327	10.5	300	Large 4-Barrel	3-spd., 4-spd.,P.G.
8 Cyl PASS.	396	10.25	325	4 Barrel	3-SPD., 4-SPD.,P.G.
8 Cyl PASS.	396	11	425	4-Barrel	3-SPD., 4-SPD.,P.G.
8 Cyl PASS.	409	10	340	4-Barrel	3-SPD., 4-SPD.,P.G.
8 Cyl PASS.	409	11	400	Large 4-Barrel	3-SPD., 4-SPD., C.R. 4-SPD.
8 Cyl CORVETTE	327	10.5	250	4 Barrel	3-SPD., 4-SPD.,P.G.
8 Cyl CORVETTE	327	10.5	300	Large 4-Barrel	3-SPD., 4-SPD.,P.G.
8 Cyl CORVETTE	327	11	350	Large 4-Barrel (Hyd. Lifters)	3-SPD., 4-SPD.
8 Cyl CORVETTE	327	11	365	Large 4-Barrel (Mech. Lifters)	3-SPD., 4-SPD.
8 Cyl CORVETTE	327	11	375	F.I. (Mech. Lifters)	3-SPD., 4-SPD.
8 Cyl CORVETTE	396	11	425	4 Barrel	4-SPD.
Turbo-Air CORVAIR	164	8.25	95	2 Single Barrel	3-SPD., 4-SPD.,P.G.
Turbo-Air CORVAIR	164	9.25	110	2 / 1-Barrel	3-SPD., 4-SPD.,P.G.
Turbo-Air CORSA	164	9.25	140	4 / 1-Barrel	3 SPD., 4-SPD.
Turbo-Charged CORSA	164	8.25	180	Single Side Draft	3-SPD., 4-SPD.
4 Cyl CHEVY II	153	8.5	90	Single Barrel	3-SPD., P.G.
6 Cyl CHEVY II	194	8.5	120	Single Barrel	3-SPD., P.G.
6 Cyl CHEVY II	230	8.5	140	Large 1-Barrel	3-SPD., P.G.
8 Cyl CHEVY II	283	9.25	195	2-Barrel	3-SPD., 4-SPD.,P.G.
8 Cyl CHEVY II	283	9.25	220	4-Barrel	3-SPD., 4-SPD.,P.G.
8 Cyl CHEVY II	327	10.5	250	4-Barrel	3-SPD., 4-SPD.,P.G.
8 Cyl CHEVY II	327	10.5	300	Large 4-Barrel	3-SPD., 4-SPD.,P.G.
6 Cyl CHEVELLE	194	8.5	120	Single Barrel	3-SPD., P.G., O.D
6 Cyl CHEVELLE	230	8.5	140	Single Barrel	3-SPD., P.G., O.D.
6 Cyl CHEVELLE	230	8.5	155	Single Barrel	-
8 Cyl CHEVELLE	283	9.25	195	2-Barrel	3-SPD., 4-SPD., P.G., O.D
8 Cyl CHEVELLE	327	10.5	250	4-Barrel	3-SPD., 4-SPD.,P.G
8 Cyl CHEVELLE	327	10.5	300	Large 4-Barrel	3-SPD., 4-SPD.,P.G.
8 Cyl CHEVELLE	327	11	350	Large 4-Barrel (Hyd. Lifters)	3-SPD., 4-SPD.
8 Cyl CHEVELLE	327	11	375	Large 4-Barrel	3-SPD., 4-SPD.

ENGINE	CODES

CHEVY II

153 4-cyl	OA,OC,OH,OG,OJ
194 6-cyl	OK,OM,OR,OQ,OT
230 6-cyl	PV,PX
283 8-cyl 195 HP	PD,PF,PL
	PM,PN,PP
220 HP	PE,PG,PK,PB
327 8-cyl 250 HP	ZA,ZK,ZE,ZM
300 HP	ZB,ZL,ZF,ZN

CHEVELLE

194 6-cyl	AA,AG,AC,AH
	AL,AR,AK,AN
230 6-cyl	CA,CB,CC,CD
283 8-cyl 195 HP	DA,DB,DE
220 HP	DG,DH
327 8-cyl 250 HP	EA,EE
300 HP	EB,EF
350 HP	EC,ED

CHEVROLET

230 6-cyl	FA,FL,FE,FF
	FM,FR,FK,FP
283 8-cyl	GA,GC,GF,GK,GL
327 8-cyl 250 HP	HA,HC
300 HP	HB,HD
396 8-cyl 325 HP	IA,LF,IG,IC,II,
	LB,IV,LC,IW
425 HP	IE
409 8-cyl 340 HP	JB,JC,JE,JF
400 HP	JA,JD

CORVETTE

327 8-cyl 250 HP	HE,HI,HO,HQ
300 HP	HF,HJ,HP,HR
350 HP	HT,HU,HV,HW
365 HP	HH,HK,HL,HM
375 HP	HG,HN
396 8-cyl 425 HP	IF

CORVAIR

164 6-cyl 95 HP	RA,RE,RG
	RJ,RS,RV
110 HP	RD,RF,RH
	RK,RU,RX
140 HP	RB,RM,RN
180 HP	RL

1966 CHEVROLET

VEHICLE IDENTIFICATION NUMBER

CHEVROLET
15411 T101555

Commonly referred to as the VIN NUMBER, this series of numbers and letters is stamped on a plate attached to the left front door hinge pillar.

Chevrolet, Chevelle, and Chevy II VIN Embossed on a Stainless Steel Plate Riveted to Left Front Door Hinge Post Facing.

Corvair VIN Embossed on a Stainless Steel Plate Riveted to Left Side-Rail near Battery in Engine Compartment.

Corvette VIN Embossed on a Stainless Steel Plate Riveted to Right Side Dash Pillar Brace under Glove Box.

FIRST DIGIT: Identifies Chevrolet Division.

NEXT FOUR DIGITS: Identify the Model number.

Biscayne / Bel-Air	5000
Impala	6000
Chevelle, Malibu	3000
Chevy II, Nova	1000
Corvair	0000
Corvette	9000

SIXTH DIGIT: 6, for 1966.

SEVENTH DIGIT: Identifies the Assembly Plant.

EXAMPLE

1	5411	6	T	101551
Man. Symbol	Model	Year	Assy Plant	Production Number

Assembly Plant	Code
Atlanta, Ga.	A
Baltimore, Md.	B
Southgate, Calif.	C
Flint, Mich.	F
Framingham, Mass.	G
Janesville, Wisc.	J
Kansas City, Mo.	K
Lordstown, Ohio	U
Los Angeles, Calif.	L
Norwood, Ohio	N
Arlington, Tex. GMAD	R

St. Louis, Mo.	S
Tarrytown, N.Y.	T
Willow Run, Mich.	W
Wilmington, Del.	Y
Fremont, Calif.	Z
Oshawa, Ont., Can.	1
Ste. Therese, Que., Can.	2
Pontiac, Mich.	P

LAST SIX DIGITS: Production sequence number.

CHEVROLET DIVISION
GENERAL MOTORS CORP.
CORRESPONDENCE PERTAINING TO THE BODY MUST BEAR THESE NUMBERS

STYLE No.	66 15411
BODY No.	T 101555
TRIM No.	810
PAINT No.	936

BODY BY FISHER

FISHER BODY NUMBER PLATE

Complete identification of each body is provided by a plate riveted to the top of the cowl.

Exception: Corvair body tag is located on left rear wheel housing inside the engine compartment.

THE BODY NUMBER is the production serial number of the body. The prefix letter denotes the plant in which the body was built.

ASSEMBLY PLANT Code

Plant	Code
Atlanta, Ga.	A
Baltimore, Md.	B
Southgate, Calif.	C
Flint, Mich.	F
Framingham, Mass.	G
Janesville, Wis.	J
Kansas City, Mo.	K
Los Angeles, Calif.	L
Norwood, Ohio	N
Arlington, Tex. GMAD	R
St. Louis, Mo.	S
Tarrytown, N.Y.	T
Willow Run, Mich.	W
Wilmington, Del.	Y
Fremont, Calif.	Z
Oshawa, Ont., Can.	1
Ste. Therese, Que., Can.	2
Pontiac, Mich.	P
Lordstown, Ohio	U

LAST SIX DIGITS: Production sequence number.

THE STYLE NUMBER is a combination of the series, and body style.

CHEVROLET - 15-1600 SERIES

Series	Style No.	6 Cyl.	8 Cyl.	Description
Biscayne		15311	15411	2-Door Sedan, 6-Passenger
		15369	15469	4-Door Sedan, 6-Passenger
		15335	15435	4-Door station Wagon, 2-Seats
Bel Air		15511	15611	2-Door Sedan, 6-Passenger
		15569	15669	4-Door Sedan, 6-Passenger
		15535	15635	4-Door Station Wagon, 2-Seats
		15545	16645	4-Door Station Wagon, 3-Seats
Impala		16369	16469	4-Door Sedan, 6-Passenger
		16339	16439	4-Door Sport Sedan, 6-Passenger
		16337	16437	2-Door Sport Coupe, 5-Passenger
		16367	16467	2-Door Convertible, 5-Passenger
		16335	16435	4-Door Station Wagon, 2-Seats
		16345	16445	4-Door Station Wagon, 3-Seats
Impala SS		16737	16837	2-Door Sport Coupe, 4-Passenger
		16767	16867	2-Door Convertible, 4-Passenger
Caprice			16639	4-Door Sedan, 6-Passenger
			16647	2-Door Coupe, 5-Passenger
			16645	4-Door Station Wagon, 3-Seat
			16635	4-Door Station Wagon, 2-Seat

CHEVELLE - 13000 SERIES

Series	Style No.	6 Cyl.	8 Cyl.	Description
Chevelle 300		13111	13211	2-Door Sedan, 6-Passenger
		13169	13269	4-Door Sedan, 6-Passenger
Chevelle 300 (Deluxe)		13311	13411	2-Door Sedan, 6-Passenger
		13369	13469	4-Door Sedan, 6-Passenger
		13335	13435	4-Door Station Wagon, 2-Seat
Malibu		13569	13669	4-Door Sedan, 6-Passenger
		13517	13617	2-Door Sport Coupe, 5-Passenger
		13567	13667	2-Door Convertible, 5-Passenger
		13535	13635	4-Door Station Wagon, 2-Seat
		13539	13639	4-Door Sedan, 6-Passenger
Chevelle 396 SS			13817	2-Door Sport Coupe, 5-Passenger
			13867	2-Door Convertible, 5-Passenger

CHEVY II - 11000 SERIES

Series	Style No.	L4	6 CYL.	8 CYL.	Description
Standard		11111	11311	11411	2-Door Sedan, 6-Passenger
		11169	11369	11469	4-Door Sedan, 6-Passenger
		-	11335	11435	4-Door Station Wagon, 2-Seat
Nova		-	11569	11669	4-Door Sedan, 6-Passenger
		-	11537	11637	2-Door Sport Coupe, 5-Passenger
		-	11535	11635	4-Door Station Wagon, 2-Seat
Nova SS		-	11737	11837	2-Door Sport Coupe, 4-Passenger

CORVAIR - 10000 SERIES

Series	Style No.	Description
Standard	10137	2-Door Sport Coupe, 5-Passenger
	10139	4-Door Sport Sedan, 6-Passenger
Monza	10537	2-Door Sport Coupe, 4-Passenger
	10567	2-Door Convertible, 4-Passenger
	10539	4-Door Sport Sedan, 5-Passenger
Corsa	10737	2-Door Sport Coupe, 4-Passenger
	10767	2-Door Convertible, 4-Passenger

CORVETTE - 19000 SERIES

Series	Style No.	Description
Corvette	19437	2-Door Sport Coupe, 2-Passenger
	19467	2-Door Convertible, 2-Passenger

THE TRIM NUMBER furnishes the key to trim color and material for each model SERIES.

REGULAR SEATS

Material	Code	Models
L Fawn Pattern I-Leather	701	10137-39
M Fawn Raeburn Cloth, L Fawn I-Leather	704	13211-69
M Fawn Rideau Cloth, L Fawn I-Leather	706	13411-69
L Fawn Pattern I-Leather, L Fawn I-Leather	707	13435-80
L Fawn Renville Cloth, L Fawn I-Leather	708	13617-39-69
M Fawn I-Leather, L Fawn I-Leather	709	13635-67, 13817-67
M Fawn I-Leather, L Fawn I-Leather	710	13680
M Fawn Ravona Cloth, L Fawn I-Leather	714	11411-69
L Fawn Pattern I-Leather	715	11435
L Fawn Rosemere Cloth, L Fawn I-Leather	716	11637-69
M Fawn Pattern I-Leather, L Fawn I-Leather	717	11635
M Blue Pattern I-Leather	721	10137-39
M Blue Raeburn Cloth, M Blue I-Leather	724	13211-69
M Blue Rideau Cloth, M Blue I-Leather	726	13411-69
M Blue Pattern I-Leather, M Blue I-Leather	727	13435-80
D Blue Renville Cloth, M Blue I-Leather	728	13617-39-69
D Blue I-Leather, M Blue I-Leather	729	13635-67, 13817-67
D Blue I-Leather, M Blue I-Leather	730	13680
M Blue Ravona Cloth, M Blue I-Leather	733	11411-69
M Bright Blue I-Leather	732	13817-67
M Blue Pattern I-Leather	734	11435
M Blue Rosemere Cloth, M Blue I-Leather	735	11637-69
D Blue Pattern I-Leather, M Blue I-Leather	736	11635
M Red Pattern I-Leather	739	10137-39
M Red Raeburn Cloth, M Red I-Leather	742	13211-69
M Red Rideau Cloth, M Red I-Leather	744	13411-69
M Red Pattern I-Leather, M Red I-Leather	745	13435-80
M Red Renville Cloth, M Red I-Leather	746	13617-39-69
M Red I-Leather	747	13635-67, 13817-67
M Red I-Leather	748	13680
M Red Ravona Cloth, M Red I-Leather	752	11411-69
M Red Pattern I-Leather	753	11435
M Red Rosemere Cloth, M Red I-Leather	754	11637-69
M Red Pattern I-Leather, M Red I-Leather	755	11635
Black I-Leather	761	13617-39-67, 13817-67
D Turquoise Renville Cloth, M Turquoise I-Leather	775	13617-39-69
D Turquoise I-Leather, M Turq. I-Leather	776	13635-67, 13817-67
M Turquoise I-Cloth, M Turquoise I-Leather	779	11637-69
D Turquoise Pattern I-Leather, M Turquoise I-Leather	780	11635
Black Regis Cloth, Black I-Leather	811	16437-39-69
Black I-Leather	814	16435-37-39-45-67, 16635-45
Black Rivoli Cloth, Black I-Leather	817	16639
Black Rivoli Cloth, Black I-Leather	818	16639 (Astro Bench Seat)
D Green Regis Cloth, M Green I-Leather	826	16437-39-69
D Green I-Leather, M Green I-Leather	829	16435-45-67, 16635-45
M Blue Pattern I-Leather, M Blue I-Leather	832	15435
M Blue I-Leather	833	15635-45
M Blue Rivoli Cloth, M Blue I-Leather	834	16639 (Astr BenchSeat)
D Blue I-Leather, M Blue I-Leather	836	16435-45-67, 16635-45
M Blue Rochelle Cloth, D Blue I-Leather	839	15611-69
M Blue Ranier Cloth, M Blue I-Leather	840	15411-69
D Blue Regis Cloth, M Blue I-Leather	842	16437-39-69
M Blue Rivoli Cloth, M Blue I-Leather	843	16639-47
D Turquoise I-Leather, M Turquoise I-Leather	847	16435-45-67, 16635-45
M Turquoise Rochelle, Cloth, D Tuquoise I-Leather	850	15611-69
D Turquoise Regis Cloth, D Tuquoise I-Leather, M Turquoise I-Leather	853	16437-39-69
M Turquoise I-Leather	854	15635-45
M Fawn Rivoli Cloth, L Fawn I-Leather	857	16639-47
M Fawn Ranier Cloth, L Fawn I-Leather	860	15411-69
L Fawn Pattern Imitation Leather, L Fawn I-Leather	861	15435
M Fawn Rochelle Cloth, D Fawn I-Leather	863	15611-69
Fawn Regis Cloth, L Fawn I-Leather	866	16437-39-69
M Fawn I-Leather	867	15635-45
M Fawn Rivoli Cloth, L Fawn I-Leather	868	16639 (Astro Bench Seat)
M Fawn I-Leather, L Fawn I-Leather	870	16435-45-67, 16635-45
M Red I-Leather	871	16435-45-67, 16635-45
M Red Rochelle Cloth, M Red I-Leather	872	15611-69
M Red Regis Cloth, M Red I-Leather	874	16437-39-69
M Red Ranier Cloth, M Red I-Leather	876	15411-69
M Red Pattern I-Leather, M Red I-Leather	877	15435
M Red I-Leather	878	15635-45

BUCKET SEATS

Material	Code	Models
L Fawn Imitation Leather	702	10537-39-67, 19737-67
M Fawn I-Leather, L Fawn I-Leather	711	13680
L Fawn I-Leather, M Fawn I-Leather	712	13617-67, 13817-67
L Fawn I-Leather	718	11837
M Bright Blue I-Leather, M Bright Blue I-Leather	722	10537-39-67, 10737-67
M Bright Blue I-Leather, D Bright Blue I-Leather	731	13617-67, 13817-67
M Bright Blue I-Leather	737	11837
M Red I-Leather	740	10537-39-67, 10737-67
M Red I-Leather	749	13680
M Red I-Leather	750	13617-67, 13817-67
M Red I-Leather	756	11837
Black I-Leather	758	10537-39-67, 10737-67
Black I-Leather	762	13680
Black I-Leather	763	13617-67, 13817-67
Black I-Leather	765	11837
M Turquoise I-Leather, D Turq. I-Leather	777	13817-67
M Turquoise I-Leather	781	11837
M Bronze I-Leather	788	10537-39-67, 10737-67
M Bronze I-Leather	790	13617-67, 13817-67
M Bright Blue I-Leather	792	10537-39-67, 10737-67
Ivory I-Leather	795	10537-39-67, 10737-67
Ivory I-Leather	797	13817-67
Black I-Leather	813	16837-67
Black I-Leather	815	16647
Black Rivoli Cloth, Black I-Leather	816	16647
D Green I-Leather, M Green I-Leather	830	16837-67
M Blue I-Leather	831	16647
D Blue I-Leather, M Blue I-Leather	837	16837-67
M Blue Rivoli Cloth, M Blue I-Leather	841	16647
D Bright Blue I-Leather, M Bright Blue I-Leather	844	16837-67

Turquoise I-Leather, M Turq. I Leather 846 16837-67
1 Turquoise I-Leather 848 16647
Fawn I-Leather 856 16647
1 Fawn Rivoli Cloth, L Fawn I-Leather 864 16647
1 Fawn I-Leather, L Fawn I-Leather 869 16837-67
1 Red I-Leather 873 16837-67
led I-Leather 879 16647
vory I-Leather 855 16837-67
1 Bronze I-Leather 891 1664

THE PAINT CODE gives the key to the exterior color.

PAINT COMBINATION CHART

Model Usage	Chevy Code	Color
Pass., Corvette .... A, 900		Tuxedo Black
Pass., Corvette .... C, 972		Ermine White
Pass. .... D		Mist Blue
Pass. .... E		Danube Blue
Pass. .... F		Marina Blue
Pass. .... H		Willow Green
Pass. .... K		Artesian Turquoise
Pass. .... L		TropicTurquoise
Pass. .... M		Aztec Bronze
Pass. .... N		Madeira Maroon
Pass. .... R		Regal Red
Pass. .... T		Sandalwood Tan
Pass. .... V		Cameo Beige
Pass. .... W		Chateau Slate
Pass. .... Y		Lemonwood Yellow
Corvette 974		Rally Red
Corvette 976		Nassau Blue
Corvette 978		Laguna Blue
Corvette 980		Trophy Blue
Corvette 982		Mosport Green
Corvette 984		Sunfire Yellow
Corvette 986		Silver Pearl
Corvette 988		Milano Maroon

n two tone combinations on Passenger Models, first letter indicates
the lower color, second letter the upper code.
Note: Two Tone Color Code. Basic color is color indicated. 2nd color
s code 526 Ivory.

ENGINE NUMBER

All Chevrolet Engines are stamped with a Plant Code, Production Date, and Engine Type Code.

Notes:

1. Corvette Engines have the last six digits of the VIN stamped on the block next to the engine number.

2. Corvair Engines are stamped on the top of the block forward of the generator.

3. 8 cylinder engines are stamped on the right front of the engine block.

4. 6 cylinder engines are stamped on the right side of the block at the rear of the distributor.

EXAMPLE

T	01	01	A
PLANT	MONTH	DAY	CODE

ENGINE PLANTS	Code
Tonawanda	T
Flint	F

ENGINE	CODES

CHEVY II

153 4-cyl	OA,OC,OH
194 6-cyl	ZY,ZV,ZX, OK,OM,OR,ZY,OS
230 6-cyl	PC,PI,PV,PX
283 8-cyl 195 HP	PD,PF,PL, PM,PN,PP, PE,PG,PQ, PS,PU,PO
220 HP	QC,QF,QD,QE, QA,QB,PK,PB
327 8-cyl 275 HP	ZA,ZB,ZK,ZE, ZD,ZC,ZF
350 HP	ZG,ZH,ZI,ZJ

CHEVELLE

194 6-cyl	AA,AG,AC,AH AL,AR,AY,AX, AS,AT,AW,AU
230 6-cyl	CA,CB,CC,CD, BN,BO,BL,BM
283 8-cyl 195 HP	DA,DB,DE, DI,DK,DJ
220 HP	DG,DH,DL,DM
327 8-cyl 275 HP	EA,EE,EB,EC
250 HP	ZM
396 8-cyl 325HP	EH,EM,ED,EK
360 HP	EJ,EN,EF,EL

CHEVROLET

250 6-cyl	FV,FY,GP,GQ,FZ, GR,FA,FL,FE,FF, FM,FR,FK,FP
283 8-cyl 195 HP	GA,GF,GC, GK,GT,GS
220 HP	GX,GZ,GW,GL
327 8-cyl 275 HP	HA,HC,HB,HF
396 8-cyl 325 HP	IA,IB,IG, IC,IV,IN,IO
427 8-cyl 390 HP	II,IH,IJ
425 HP	ID

CORVETTE

327 8-cyl 300 HP	HH,HR,HE, HO,HP
350 HP	HT,HD,HK
427 8-cyl 390 HP	IM,IL
425 HP	IP,IK

CORVAIR

164 6-cyl 95 HP	RA,RE,RG RJ,RS,RV
110 HP	RD,RF,RH RK,RU,RW
140 HP	RB,RM,RN, RQ,RX,RR, RZ,RY,RT
180 HP	RL

BASIC ENGINE DATA

Model	CID	Comp.	H.P.	Carburetor	Transmission
6 Cyl PASS.	250	8.5	155	Single Barrel	3-SPD., P.G.
8 Cyl PASS.	283	9.25	195	2-Barrel	3-SPD., O.D.,P.G.
8 Cyl PASS.	283	9.25	220	4-Barrel	3-SPD., 4-SPD.,P.G.
8 Cyl PASS.	327	10.5	275	4-Barrel	3-SPD., 4-SPD.,P.G.
8 Cyl PASS.	396	10.5	325	4-Barrel	3-SPD., 4-SPD.,
8 Cyl PASS.	427	10.5	390	4- Barrel	3-SPD., 4-SPD.,TH
8 Cyl PASS.	427	11	425	4-Barrel	3-SPD., 4-SPD.
8 Cyl CORVETTE	327	10.5	300	Large 4-Barrel	3-SPD., 4-SPD.,P.G.
8 Cyl CORVETTE	327	11	350	Large 4-Barrel (Hyd. Lifters)	3-SPD., 4-SPD.
8 Cyl CORVETTE	427	10.25	390	Large 4-Barrel (Hyd. Lifters)	4-SPD.
8 Cyl CORVETTE	427	11	425	Fuel Inj. (Mech. Lifters)	4-SPD.
Turbo CORVAIR	164	8.25	95	2 /1 -Barrel	3-SPD., 4-SPD.,P.G.
Turbo CORVAIR	164	9.25	110	2 / 1-Barrel	3-SPD., 4-SPD.,P.G.
Turbo CORVAIR	164	9.25	140	4 / 1-Barrel	3-SPD., 4-PSD.,P.G.
Turbo-Charged CORSA	164	8.25	180	Single Side Draft	3-SPD., 4-SPD.
4 Cyl CHEVY II	153	8.5	90	Single Barrel	3-SPD., P.G
6 Cyl CHEVY II	194	8.5	120	Single Barrel	3-SPD., P.G.
6 Cyl CHEVY II	230	8.5	140	Single Barrel	3-SPD., P.G.
8 Cyl CHEVY II	283	9.25	195	2-Barrel	3-SPD., 4-SPD.,P.G.
8 Cyl CHEVY II	283	9.25	220	4-Barrel	3-SPD., 4-SPD.,P.G.
8 Cyl CHEVY II	327	10.5	250	4-Barrel	3-SPD., 4-SPD.,P.G.
8 Cyl CHEVY II	327	11	350	Large 4-Barrel	3-SPD., 4-SPD.
6 Cyl CHEVELLE	194	8.5	120	Single Barrel	3-SPD., P.G., O.D.
6 Cyl CHEVELLE	230	8.5	140	Single Barrel	3-SPD., P.G., O.D.
8 Cyl CHEVELLE	283	9.25	195	2-Barrel	3-SPD., 4-SPD., P.G., O.D.
8 Cyl CHEVELLE	283	9.25	220	4-Barrel	3-SPD., 4-SPD., P.G., O.D.
8 Cyl CHEVELLE	327	10.5	250	4- Barrel	3-SPD., 4-SPD.,P.G.
8 Cyl CHEVELLE	396	10.25	325	4- Barrel	3-SPD., 4-SPD.,P.G.
8 Cyl CHEVELLE	396	10.25	360	4-Barrel	3-SPD., 4-SPD.,P.G.

VEHICLE IDENTIFICATION NUMBER

CHEVROLET
154117T101555

Commonly referred to as the VIN NUMBER, this series of numbers and letters is stamped on a plate attached to the left front door hinge pillar.

Chevrolet Chevelle, Camaro, and Chevy II VIN Embossed on a Stainless Steel Plate Riveted to Left Front Door Hinge Post Facing.

Corvair VIN Embossed on a Stainless Steel Plate Riveted to Left Side-Rail near Battery in Engine Compartment.

Corvette VIN Embossed on a Stainless Steel Plate Riveted to Right Side Dash Pillar Brace under Glove Box.

FIRST DIGIT: Identifies Chevrolet Division.

NEXT FOUR DIGITS: Identify the Model number.

Biscayne / Bel-Air	5000
Impala	6000
Chevelle, Malibu	3000
Chevy II, Nova	1000
Camaro	2000
Corvair	0000
Corvette	9000

SIXTH DIGIT: #7, for 1967.

SEVENTH DIGIT: Identifies the Assembly Plant.

Assembly Plant	Code
Atlanta, Ga.	A
Baltimore, Md.	B
Southgate, Calif.	C
Doraville	D
Flint, Mich.	F
Framingham, Mass.	G
Janesville, Wisc.	J
Kansas City, Mo.	K
Lordstown, Ohio	U
Los Angeles, Calif.	L
Norwood, Ohio	N
Arlington, Tex. GMAD	R
St. Louis, Mo.	S
Tarrytown, N.Y.	T
Willow Run, Mich.	W
Wilmington, Del.	Y
Fremont, Calif.	Z
Oshawa, Ont., Can.	1
Ste. Therese, Que., Can.	2
Pontiac, Mich.	P

LAST SIX DIGITS: Production sequence number.

EXAMPLE

1	5411	7	T	101551
Man. Symbol	Model	Year	Assy Plant	Production Number

FISHER BODY NUMBER PLATE

Complete identification of each body is provided by a plate riveted to the top of the cowl.

*Exception: Corvair body tag is located on left rear wheel housing inside the engine compartment.

THE BODY NUMBER is the production serial number of the body The prefix letter denotes the plant in which the body was built. Refer to the Assembly Plants and codes that are in the VIN plate.

LAST SIX DIGITS: Production sequence number.

THE STYLE NUMBER is a combination of the series, and body style.

```
        CHEVROLET DIVISION
        GENERAL MOTORS CORP.
    CORRESPONDENCE PERTAINING TO THE
    BODY MUST BEAR THESE NUMBERS

    STYLE No.     67 15411
    BODY No.      T 1001555
    TRIM No.      810
    PAINT No.     936

          BODY BY FISHER
```

CHEVELLE

	Model Number		
Series	6 Cyl.	8 Cyl	Description
Chevelle 300	13111	13211	2-Dr Sedan, 6-Pass.
	13169	13269	4-Dr Sedan, 6-Pass.
Chevelle 300 Deluxe	13311	13411	2-Dr Sedan, 6-Pass.
	13369	13469	4-Dr Sedan, 6-Pass.
	13335	13435	4-Dr Station Wagon, 2-Seat
Malibu	13569	13669	4-Dr sedan, 6-Pass.
	13539	13639	4-Dr Sport Sedan, 6-Pass.
	13517	13617	2-Dr Sport Coupe, 5-Pass.*
	13567	13667	2-Dr Convertible, 5-Pass.*
	13535	13635	4-Dr Station Wagon, 2-Seat
Super Sport 396	-	13817	2-Dr Sport Coupe, 5-Pass.*
	-	13867	2-Dr Convertible, 5-Pass.*
Concours	13735	13835	4-Dr Station Wagon, 2-Seat

*4-Passenger when optional bucket seats are specified.

CHEVY II

	Model Number			
Series	L-4	6 Cyl.	V-8	Description
100	11111	11311	11411	2-Dr Sedan, 6-Pass.
	11169	11369	11469	4-Dr Sedan, 6-Pass.
	-	11335	11435	4-Dr Station Wagon, 2-Seat
Nova	-	11569	11669	4-Dr Sedan, 6-Pass.
	-	11537	11637	2-Dr Sport Coupe, 5-Pass.
	-	11535	11635	4-Dr Station Wagon, 2-Seat
Nova SS	-	11737	11837	2-Dr Sport Coupe, 4-Pass.

CAMARO

	Model Number		
Series	6 Cyl.	8 Cyl	Description
Camaro	12337	12437	2-Dr Sport Coupe, 4-Pass.
	12367	12467	2-Dr Convertible, 4-Pass.

CHEVROLET

	Model Number		
Series	6 Cyl.	8 Cyl	Description
Biscayne	15311	15411	2-Dr Sedan, 6-Pass.
	15369	15469	4-Dr Sedan, 6-Pass.
	15335	15435	4-Dr Station Wagon, 2-Seat
Bel Air	15511	15611	2-Dr Sedan, 6-Pass.
	15569	15669	4-Dr Sedan, 6-Pass.
	15535	15635	4-Dr Station Wagon, 2-Seat
	15545	15645	4-Dr Station Wagon, 3-Seat
Impala	16387	16487	2-Dr Sport Coupe, 5-Pass.
	16367	16467	2-Dr Convertible, 5-Pass.
	16369	16469	4-Dr Sedan, 6-Pass.
	16339	16439	4-Dr Sport Sedan, 6-Pass.
	16335	16435	4-Dr Station Wagon, 2-Seat
	16345	16445	4-Dr Station Wagon, 3-Seat
Impala Super Sport	16787	16887	2-Dr Sport Coupe, 4-Pass.
	16767	16867	2-Dr Convertible, 4-Pass.
Caprice	-	16647	2-Dr Custom Coupe, 5-Pass.
	-	16639	4-Dr Custom Sedan, 6-Pass.
	-	16635	4-Dr Custom Wagon, 2-Seat
	-	16645	4-Dr Custom Wagon, 3-Seat

*4-Passenger when optional bucket front seats are specified.

CORVETTE

Model Number	Description
19437	2-Door Sport Coupe, 2-Pass.
19467	2-Door Convertible, 2-Pass.

CORVAIR

Series	Model Number	Description
Standard	10139	4-Dr Sport Sedan, 6-Pass.
	10137	2-Dr Sport Coupe, 5-Pass.
Monza	10539	4-Dr Sport Sedan, 5-Pass.
	10537	2-Dr Sport Coupe, 4-Pass.
	10567	2-Dr Convertible, 4-Pass.

THE TRIM NUMBER furnishes the key to trim color and material for each model SERIES.

D=Dark, M=Medium, L= Light, I=Imitation, W=Woven

Material	Code	Models
M Fawn -Leather	703	10137-39
Plum Royale Cloth, Antique Plum I-Leather	705	13639
M Fawn I-Leather	719	11411-69
M Fawn I-Leather	720	13211-69
M Blue Pattern I-Leather, M Blue I-Leather	721	10137-39
M Bright Blue I-Leather	723	13617-35-67
		13817-35-67
M Blue R-Cloth, M Blue I-Leather	724	13211-69
M Blue Rio Cloth, M Blue I-Leather	726	13411-69
M Blue Pattern I-Leather, M Blue I-Leather	727	13435-80
M Blue Roncina Cloth, M Blue I-Leather	728	13617-39-69
M Blue I-Leather	729	
		13635-39-67-80
		13817-35-67
M Blue Royale Cloth, M Blue I-Leather	730	13639
M Blue Rosemont Cloth, M Blue I-Leather	733	11411-69
M Blue Pattern I-Leather, M Blue I-Leather	734	11411-35-69
M Blue Rocalla Cloth, M Blue I-Leather	735	11637-69
M Blue Pattern I-Leather, M Blue I-Leather	736	11635-37
D Maroon Roncina Cloth, D Maroon I-Leather	746	13617-39-69
M Red I-Leather	747	13617-35-67
		13817-35-67
Black Pattern I-Leather, Black I-Leather	751	10137-39
D Maroon Rocalla Cloth, D Maroon I-Leather	754	1166
Black Pattern I-Leather, Black I-Leather	757	13211-6
Black Roncina Cloth, Black I- Leather	759	13617-39-69
Black I-Leather	761	
		13617-35-39-67-80,
		13817-35-67
Black Royale Cloth, Black I-Leather	762	13639
Black Rio Cloth, Black I-Leather	764	13411-69
Black Pattern I-Leather, Black I-Leather	766	13435-80
M Fawn Redmond Cloth, M Fawn I-Leather	768	13211-69
M Fawn Rio Cloth, M Fawn I-Leather	769	13411-69
M Fawn Pattern I-Leather, M Fawn I-Leather	770	13435-80
M Fawn Rosemont Cloth, M Fawn I-Leather	771	11411-69
M Fawn Pattern I-Leather, M Fawn I-Leather	774	11635
M Turquoise Roncina Cloth M Turquoise I-Leather	775	13617-39-69
M Turquoise I-Leather	776	13635-67
		13817-35-67
M Gold Roncina Cloth, M Gold I-Leather	782	13617-39-69
M Gold I-Leather	783	13635-67-80
		13817-35-67
Black Pattern I-Leather, Black I-Leather	785	11635-37
Black Rocalla Cloth, Black I-Leather	786	11669
Black Pattern I-Leather, Black I-Leather	791	11411-35-69
M Gold Royale Cloth, M Gold I-Leather	794	13639
M Fawn Raleigh Cloth, M Fawn I-Leather	801	15411-69
M Fawn Pattern I-Leather, M Fawn I-Leather	802	15435
M Fawn Ramsgate Cloth, M Fawn Pattern I-Leather	803	15611-69
M Fawn Pattern I-Leather, M Fawn I-Leather	804	15635-45
Black Romaine Cloth, Black I-Leather	811	16439-69-87
Black Pattern I-Leather, Black I-Leather	812	15411-35-69
Black I-Leather	814	
		16435-39-45-67-87,
		16635-45
Black Rhapsody Cloth, Black I-Leather	817	16639-47
Black Ramsgate Cloth, Black I-Leather	819	15611-69
Black Pattern I-Leather, Black I-Leather	820	15635-45
M Blue Pattern I-Leather, M Blue -Leather	832	15435
M Blue Pattern I-Leather, M Blue I-Leather	833	15635-45
M Blue I-Leather	836	
		16435-39-45-67
		16635-45

Material	Code	Models
M Blue Ramsgate Cloth, M Blue I-Leather	839	15611-69
M Blue Raleigh Cloth, M Blue I-Leather	840	15411-69
M Blue Romaine Cloth, M Blue I-Leather	842	16439-69-87
M Blue Rhapsody Cloth, M Blue I-Leather	843	16639-47
M Bright Blue I-Leather	845	16467-87
M Turquoise I-Leather	847	16435-45-67
		16635-45
M Turquoise Ramsgate Cloth, M Turquoise I-Leather	850	15611-69
M Turquoise Romaine Cloth, M Turquoise I-Leather	853	16439-69-87
M Turquoise Pattern I-Leather, M Turquoise I-Leather	854	15635-45
Plum Rhapsody Cloth, Ant. Plum I-Leather	860	16639-47
M Fawn I-Leather	865	15411-69
M Red I-Leather	871	
		16435-45-67-87
		16635-45
D Maroon Romaine Cloth, D Mroon I-Leather	874	16439-69-87
M Gold Rhapsody Cloth, M Gold I-Leather	887	16639-47
M Gold Romaine Cloth, M Gold I-Leather	888	16439-69-87
M Gold I-Leather	889	16435-45-67
		16635-45
Parchment I-Leather	894	16467-87

BUCKET SEATS

Material	Code	Models
L Yellow I-Leather	707	12637-67
M Gold I-Leather	709	12437-67
M Gold I-Leather	711	12637-67
M Gold I-Leather	712	12637-67
M Gold I-Leather	713	10537-39-67
M Bright Blue I-Leather	716	10537-39-67
M Blue I-Leather	717	12437-67
M Bright Blue I-Leather	722	10537-39-67
M Bright Blue I-Leather	731	13617-67
		13817-67
M Bright Blue I-Leather	732	12637-67
M Bright Blue I-Leather	737	11837
M Blue I-Leather	738	13617-67
		13817-67
M Red I-Leather	741	12437-67
M Red I-Leather	742	12637-67
M Red I-Leather	749	11837
M Red I-Leather	750	13617-67-80
		13817-67
Black I-Leather	758	10537-39-67
Black I-Leather	760	12437-67
Black I-Leather	763	13617-67-80
		13817-67
Black I-Leather	765	12637-67
Black I-Leather	767	12637-67
M Turquoise I-Leather	778	13817-67
M Turquoise I-Leather	779	12637-67
Black I-Leather	780	11837
M Gold I-Leather	781	11837
M Gold I-Leather	784	13617-67-80
		13817-67
Parchment I-Leather	797	12637-67
Black I-Leather	810	16867-87
Black I-Leather	813	16867-87
Black I-Leather	815	16647
Black Rhapsody Cloth, Black I-Leather	818	16639-47
Black I-Leather	821	16639
M Blue Rhapsody Cloth, M Blue I-Leather	834	16639-47
M Blue I-Leather	835	16639
M Blue I-Leather	837	16647
M Bright Blue I-Leather	844	16867-87
M Bright Blue I-Leather	848	16867-87
Plum Rhapsody Cloth, Ant.Plum I-Leather	862	16639-47
M Red I-Leather	870	16867-87
M Red I-Leather	873	16867-87
M Gold I-Leather	884	16639

VEHICLE IDENTIFICATION NUMBER

CHEVROLET
154118T101555

Commonly referred to as the VIN NUMBER, this series of numbers and letters is stamped on a plate attached to the left front door hinge pillar.

Chevrolet, Chevelle, Chevy II, Camaro and Corvair VIN Stamped on Plate on top of Instrument Panel Visible through Windshield near Left Door.

Corvette VIN Stamped on Plate on Inner Vertical Surface of Left Windshield Pillar Visible through Windshield.

FIRST DIGIT: Identifies Chevrolet Division.

NEXT FOUR DIGITS: Identify the Model number.

Biscayne / Bel-Air	5000
Impala	6000
Chevelle, Malibu	3000
Chevy II, Nova	1000
Camaro	2000
Corvair	0000
Corvette	9000

SIXTH DIGIT: 8, for 1968.

SEVENTH DIGIT: Identifies the Assembly Plant.

ASSEMBLY PLANT	Code
Atlanta, Ga.	A
Baltimore, Md.	B
Southgate, Calif.	C
Doraville	D
Flint, Mich.	F
Framingham, Mass.	G
Janesville, Wisc.	J
Kansas City, Mo.	K
Lordstown, Ohio	U
Los Angeles, Calif.	L
Norwood, Ohio	N
Arlington, Tex. GMAD	R
St. Louis, Mo.	S
Tarrytown, N.Y.	T
Willow Run, Mich.	W
Wilmington, Del.	Y
Fremont, Calif.	Z
Oshawa, Ont., Can.	1
Ste. Therese, Que., Can.	2
Pontiac, Mich.	P

LAST SIX DIGITS: Production sequence number.

EXAMPLE

1	5411	8	T	101551
Manf. Symbol	Model	Year	Assy Plant	Production Number

FISHER BODY NUMBER PLATE

Complete identification of each body is provided by a plate riveted to the top of the cowl.

*Exception: Corvair body tag is located on left rear wheel housing inside the engine compartment.

THE BODY NUMBER is the production serial number of the body. The prefix letter denotes the plant in which the body was built. Refer to the Assembly Plants and codes that are in the VIN plate.

LAST SIX DIGITS: Production sequence number.

THE STYLE NUMBER is a combination of the series, and body style.

```
+--------------------------------------------------+
|          CHEVROLET DIVISION                      |
|          GENERAL MOTORS CORP.                    |
|       CORRESPONDENCE PERTAINING TO THE           |
|       BODY MUST BEAR THESE NUMBERS               |
|                                                  |
|       STYLE No.    68 5411                       |
|       BODY No.     T 101555                      |
|       TRIM No.     810                           |
|       PAINT No.    936                           |
|                                                  |
|              BODY BY FISHER                      |
+--------------------------------------------------+
```

CHEVELLE

Series	Model Number 6-Cyl.	V-8	Description
300	13127	13227	2-Dr Pillar Coupe, 5-Pass.
Nomad	13135	13235	4-Dr Station Wagon, 2-Seat
300 Deluxe	13327	13427	2-Dr Pillar Coupe, 5-Pass.
	13369	13469	4-Dr Sedan, 6-Pass.
	13337	13437	2-Dr Sport Coupe, 5-Pass.
Custom Nomad	13335	13435	4-Dr Station Wagon, 2-Seat
Malibu	13569	13669	4-Dr Sedan, 6-Pass.
	13539	13639	4-Dr Sport Sedan, 6-Pass.
	13537	13637	2-Dr Sport Coupe, 5-Pass.*
	13567	13667	2-Dr Convertible, 5-Pass.*
	13535	13635	4-Dr Station Wagon, 2-Seat
SS 396	-	13837	2-Dr Sport Coupe, 5-Pass.*
	-	13867	2-Dr Convertible, 5-Pass.*
Concours	13735	13835	4-Dr Station Wagon, 2-Seat

*4-Passenger when optional front bucket seats are ordered.

CHEVY II

Model Number 6-Cyl.	V-8	Description
11327	11427	2-Dr Sport Coupe, 5-Pass.
11369	11469	4-Dr Sedan, 6-Pass.

CAMARO

Model Number 6-Cyl.	V-8	Description
12337	12437	2-Dr Sport Coupe, 4-Pass.
12367	12467	2-Dr Convertible, 4-Pass.

CORVETTE

Model Number	Description
19437	2-Door Sport Coupe, 2-Passenger
19467	2-Door Convertible, 2-Passenger

CORVAIR

Series	Model Number	Description
Standard	10137	2-Door Sport Coupe, 5 Passenger
Monza	10537	2-Door Sport Coupe, 4-Passenger
	10567	2-Door Convertible, 4-Passenger

CHEVROLET

Series	Model Number 6-Cyl.	V-8	Description
Biscayne	15311	15411	2-Dr Sedan, 6-Pass.
	15369	15469	4-Dr Sedan, 6-Pass.
	15335	15435	4-Dr Station Wagon, 2-Seat
Bel Air	15511	15611	2-Dr Sedan, 6-Pass.
	15569	15669	4-Dr Sedan, 6-Pass.
	15535	15635	4-Dr Station Wagon, 2-Seat
	15545	15645	4-Dr Station Wagon, 3-Seat
Impala	16387	16487	2-Dr Sport Coupe, 5-Pass.
	-	16467	2-Dr Convertible, 5-Pass.
	16369	16469	4-Dr Sedan, 6-Pass.
	16339	16439	4-Dr Sport Sedan, 6-Pass.
	-	16435	4-Dr Station Wagon, 2-Seat
	-	16445	4-Dr Station Wagon, 3-Seat
Impala Custom	16347	16447	2-Dr Custom Sport Coupe, 5-Pass.*
Caprice	-	16647	2-Dr Custom Sport Coupe, 5-Pass.*
		16639	4-Dr Custom Sport Sedan, 6-Pass.
		16635	4-Dr Custom Wagon, 2-Seat
		16645	4-Dr Custom Wagon, 3-Seat

THE TRIM NUMBER furnishes the key to trim color and material for each model SERIES.

D=Dark, M=Medium, L=Light, I=Imitation, W=Woven

Material	Code	Models
Black Pattern I-Leather, Black I-Leather	703	10137-39
D Blue Pattern I-Leather, D Blue I-Leather	706	10137-39
M Gold Pattern I-Leather, M Gold I-Leather	709	10137-39
Black I-Leather	713	12437-67
Black I-Leather	715	12437
D Blue I-Leather	718	12437
D Blue I-Leather	720	12437
M Gold I-Leather	723	12437
M Red I-Leather	724	12437-67
M Turquoise I-Leather	727	12437
Black I-Leather	731	11427-69
Black Pattern I-Leather, Black I-Leather	733	11427-69
Black Random Cloth, Black I-Leather	734	11427-69
D Blue Rancona Cloth, Black I-Leather	737	11427-69
Gold Rancona Cloth, M Gold I-Leather	741	11427-69
M Gold Random Cloth, M Gold I-Leather	742	11427-69
D Blue Random Cloth, D Blue I-Leather	739	11427-69
M Gold Pattern I-Leather, M-Gold I-Leather	752	13227
M Green Richmond Cloth, M Green I-Leather	753	13639
M Gold I-Leather	754	13637-39-67 13837-67
M Teal I-Leather	755	13637-39-67 13837-67
M Saddle Pattern I-Leather, M Saddle I-Leather	758	13480
D Blue Pattern, D Blue I-Leather	759	13480
Black Pattern I-Leather, Black I-Leather	760	13480
Black Pattern I-Leather, Black I-Leather	761	13227-35
Black Ramara Cloth, Black I-Leather	762	13427-37-69
Black Pattern I-Leather, Black I-Leather	763	13427-35-37-69
Black Rapture Cloth, Black I-Leather	764	13637-39-69
Black I-Leather	765	13635-37-39-45-67-69-80 13835-37-45-67
Black Richmond Cloth, Black I-Leather	768	13639
D Blue Ramara Cloth, D Blue I-Leather	770	13427-37-69
D Blue Pattern I-Leather, D Blue I-Leather	771	13435
D Blue Rapture Cloth, D Blue I-Leather	772	13637-39-69
D Blue I-Leather	773	13635-45-80
D Blue Richmond Cloth, D Blue I-Leather	776	13639
D Blue Pattern I-Leather, D Blue I-Leather	777	13227-35
M Gold Rapture Cloth, M Gold I-Leather	779	13637-39-69
M Gold Richmond Cloth, M Gold I-Leather	780	13639
M Saddle Pattern I-Leather,	781	13435
Ant. M Saddle I-Leather	782	13635-45-80
M Turquoise I-Leather	786	13635-45
M Gold Ramara Cloth, M Gold I-Leather	788	13427-37-69
M Green Rapture Cloth, M Green I-Leather	791	13637-39-69
Parchment I-Leather	793	16637
M Red I-Leather	795	13637
M Saddle Pattern I-Leather, M Saddle I-Leather	799	13235
Black Pattern I-Leather, Black I-Leather	802	15411-35-69
Black Richelieu Cloth, Black I-Leather	803	15611-69
Black Pattern I-Leather, Black I-Leather	804	15611-35-45-69
Black Radiance Cloth, Black I-Leather	805	16439-47-69-87
Black I-Leather	806	16435-39-45-47-67-87, 16635-45
Black Reverie Cloth, Black I-Leather	807	16639-47
Black Reverie Cloth, Black I-Leather	808	16639-47
Black Pattern I-Leather, Black I-Leather	811	15611-69
Black I-Leather	813	16447-87
Black I-Leather	814	16639
D Blue I-Leather	815	16639-47
D Blue Pattern Cloth, D Blue I-Leather	816	15411-69
D Blue Pattern Vinyl, D Blue I-Leather	817	15435
D Blue Richelieu Cloth, D Blue I-Leather	818	15611-69
D Blue Pattern I-Leather, D Blue I-Leather	819	15635-45
D Blue Radiance Cloth, D Blue I-Leather	820	16439-47-69-87 16639-47-69-87
D Blue I-Leather	821	16435-39-45 16635-45
D Blue Reverie Cloth, D Blue I-Leather	822	16639-47
D Blue Reverie Cloth, D Blue I-Leather	823	16639-47
M Gold I-Leather	830	16447-67-87
M Gold Rampart Cloth, M Gold I-Leather	831	15411-69
M Gold Richelieu Cloth, M Gold I-Leather	832	15611-69
M Gold Radiance Cloth, M Gold I-Leather	833	16439-47-69-87
M Gold Reverie Cloth, M Gold I-Leather	834	16639-47
M Gold Reverie Cloth, M Gold I-Leather	835	16639-47
M Saddle Pattern I-Leather, M Saddle I-Leather	837	15435
M Saddle Pattern I-Leather, Ant. M Saddle I-Leather	838	15635-45
Ant. M Saddle I-Leather	839	16435-45 16635-45
M Gold I-Leather	841	16447-87
M Turquoise I-Leather	842	16439-47-69-87
M Turquoise Richelieu Cloth, M Turquoise I-Leather	843	15611-69
M Turquoise Pattern I-Leather, M Turquoise I-Leather	844	15635-45
M Turquoise I-Leather	845	16435-45 16635-45
M Green Reverie Cloth, M Green I-Leather	852	16639-47
M Green Radiance Cloth, M Green I-Leather	853	16439-47-69-87
M Green Reverie Cloth, M Green I-Leather	856	16639-47
Parchment I-Leather	858	16447-67-87
M Teal I-Leather	861	16447-87
M Teal I-Leather	864	16447-67-87
M Red I-Leather	866	16467

BUCKET SEATS

Material	Code	Models
Black I-Leather	704	10537-39-67
D Blue I-Leather	707	10537-39-67
M Gold I-Leather	710	10537-39-67
Black I-Leather	712	12437-67
Black I-Leather	714	12437-67
D Blue I-Leather	717	12437-67
D Blue I-Leather	719	12437-67
M Gold I-Leather	721	12437-67
M Gold I-Leather	722	12437-67
M Red I-Leather	725	12437-67
M Turquoise I-Leather	726	12437-67
Parchment I-Leather	730	12437-67
Black I-Leather	735	11427
D Blue I-Leather	740	11427
M Gold I-Leather	745	11427
M Gold I-Leather	756	13637-67 13837-67
M Teal I-Leather	757	13637-67 13837-67
Black I-Leather	766	13637-67-80 13837-67-80
D Blue I-Leather	774	13680
M Saddle I-Leather	783	13680-13880
Parchment I-Leather	794	13637-67 13837-67
Black I-Leather	809	16639

Black I-Leather 812 16447-67-87
D Blue I-Leather 824 16647
M Gold I-Leather 836 16447-67-87
M Gold I-Leather 840 16639-47
M Green I-Leather 857 16647
Parchment I-Leather 859 16447-67-87
M Teal I-Leather 862 16447-67-87
M Red I-Leather 868 16447-67-87

THE PAINT CODE gives the key to the exterior color.

1968 PAINT COMBINATION CHART

Model Usage	Chevy Code	Color
Pass., Corvette	A-900	Tuxedo Black
Pass.	C	Ermine White
Pass.	D	Grotto Blue
Pass.	E	Fathom Blue
Pass.	F	Island Teal
Pass.	G	Ash Gold
Pass.	H	Grecian Green
Pass.	K	Tripoli Turquoise
Pass.	L	Teal Blue
Pass.	N	Cordovan Maroon
Pass.	P	Seafrost Green
Pass.	R	Metador Red
Pass.	T	Palomino Ivory
Pass.	V	Sequoia Green
Pass.	Y	Butternut Yellow
Corvette	972	Polar White
Corvette	974	Rally Red
Corvette	976	LeMans Blue
Corvette	978	International Blue
Corvette	983	British Green
Corvette	984	Safari Yellow
Corvette	986	Silverstone Silver
Corvette	988	Cordovan Maroon
Corvette	992	Corvette Bronze

In two tone combinations on Passenger Models, first letter indicates the lower color, second letter the upper code.

ENGINE NUMBER

All Chevrolet Engines are stamped with a Plant Code, Production Date, and Engine Type Code.

Note:

1. Corvette Engines have the last six digits of the VIN stamped on the block next to the engine number.

2. Corvair Engines are stamped on the top of the block forward of the generator.

3. 8 cylinder engines are stamped on the right front of the engine block.

4. 6 cylinder engines are stamped on the right side of the block at the rear of the distributor.

EXAMPLE

T   01   01   A
PLANT.. MONTH ...DAY ...CODE

ENGINE PLANTS   CODE

Tonawanda ....T
Flint ....F

BASIC ENGINE DATA

Engine	CID	Comp.	H.P.	Carburetor	Transmission
Super Thrift (153-4 cyl.)	153	8.5	90	Single Barrel	3-SPD., P.G.
Turbo-Air (164)	164	8.25	95	2 Single Barrel	3-SPD., 4-SPD., P.G.
Turbo-Air (164 Hi-Per.)	164	9.25	110	2 Single Barrel	3-SPD., 4-SPD.,
Turbo-Air (164 Sp. Hi-Per)	164	9.25	140	4 Single Barrel	3-SPD., 4-SPD., P.G.
Turbo-Thrift (230-6 cyl.)	230	8.5	140	Single Barrel	3-SPD., 4-SPD., O.D., P.G.
Turbo-Thrift (250-6 cyl.)	250	8.5	155	Single Barrel	3-SPD., 4-SPD., O.D., P.G.
Turbo-Fire (307-8 cyl.)	307	9.0	200	2 Barrel	3-SPD., 4-SPD., O.D., P.G.
Turbo-Fire (327-8 cyl.)	327	8.75	210	2 Barrel	3-SPD., 4-SPD., P.G.
Turbo-Fire (327-8 cyl.)	327	8.75	250	4 Barrel	3-SPD.,4-SPD., TH
Turbo-Fire (327-8 cyl.)	327	10.0	275	2 Barrel	3-SPD., 4-SPD., P.G., TH
Turbo-Fire (327-8 cyl.)	327	10.0	300	4 Barrel	3-SPD., 4-SPD., TH
Turbo-Fire (327-8 cyl.)	327	11.0	325	4 Barrel	3-SPD., 4-SPD.
Turbo-Fire (327-8 cyl.)	327	11.0	350	4 Barrel	4-SPD.
Turbo-Fire (350-8 cyl.)	350	10.25	295	4 Barrel	3-SPD., 4-SPD., P.G.
Turbo-Jet (396-8 cyl.)	396	10.25	325	4 Barrel	3-SPD., 4-SPD., P.G., TH
Turbo-Jet (396-8 cyl.)	396	10.25	350	4 Barrel	3-SPD., 4-SPD., P.G., TH
Turbo-Jet (396-8 cyl.)	396	11.0	375	4-Barrel	3-SPD., 4-SPD., P.G., TH
Turbo-Jet (427-8 cyl.)	427	10.25	385	4 Barrel	3-SPD., 4-SPD., TH
Turbo-Jet (427-8 cyl.)	427	10.25	390	4 Barrel	3-SPD., 4SPD., TH
Turbo-Jet (427-8 cyl.)	427	10.25	400	3 x 2 Barrel	4-SPD., TH
Turbo-Jet (427-8 cyl.)	427	11.0	435	3 x 2 Barrel	4-SPD.

ENGINE	CODES

CHEVY II

153 4-cyl	OA,OC,OH
230 6-cyl	BA,BB,BC,BD,BF,BH
250 6-cyl	CM,CN,CQ,CR
307 8-cyl	DA,DB,DE
327 8-cyl 275 HP	EE,EA
325HP	EP,ML,MM
350 8-cyl	MU,MS
396 8-cyl 350 HP	MX
375 HP	MQ,MR

CHEVELLE

230 6-cyl	BA,BB,BC,BD,BF,BH
250 6-cyl	CM,CQ,CN,CR,
307 8-cyl	DA,DB,DE,DN
327 8-cyl 250 HP	EI,EH,EJ
275 HP	EE,EA,EO
325 HP	EP,ES
396 8-cyl 325HP	EK,ET,ED
350 HP	EF,EU,EL
375 HP	EG

CHEVROLET

250 6-cyl	CA,CB,CC,CJ,CK,
	CM,CN,CQ,CR,CS,C
307 8-cyl	DO,DP,DR,DS,
	DQ,DH
327 8-cyl 250 HP	HJ,HM,HI,
	HL,HK,HN
275 HP	HA,HC,HB,
	HF,HG,HH
396 8-cyl 325 HP	IA,IV,IG,
427 8-cyl 385 HP	IH,IJ,IC,IE,IS
425 HP	ID,IO

CORVETTE

327 8-cyl 300 HP	HE,HO
350 HP	HT
427 8-cyl 390 HP	IL,IQ,
400 HP	IM,IO
435 HP	IT,IR,IU

CAMARO

230 6-cyl	BA,BB,BC,
	BD,BF,BH
250 6-cyl	CM,CN,CQ,CR
302 8-cyl	MO
327 8-cyl 210 HP	ME,MA
275 HP	EE,EA
350 8-cyl	MU,MS
396 8-cyl 325 HP	MY,MW
350 HP	MR,MX
375 HP	MQ,MT

CORVAIR

164 6-cyl 95 HP	RJ,RE,RS,RV
110 HP	RK,RF,RU,RW
164 6-CYL 140 HP	RY,RZ

VEHICLE IDENTIFICATION NUMBER

CHEVROLET
154119T101555

Commonly referred to as the VIN NUMBER, this series of numbers and letters is stamped on a plate attached to the left front door hinge pillar.

Chevrolet, Chevelle, Chevy II, Camaro and Corvair-1969-VIN Stamped on Plate on top of Instrument Panel Visible through Windshield near Left Door.

Corvette VIN Stamped on Plate on Inner Vertical Surface of Left Windshield Pillar Visible through Windshield.

FIRST DIGIT: Identifies Chevrolet Division.

NEXT FOUR DIGITS: Identify the Model number.

MODEL	Code
Corvair	0000
Nova	1000
Camaro	2000
Chevelle	3000
Chevrolet	5000
Impala	6000
Corvette	9000

SIXTH DIGIT:9, for 1969.

SEVENTH DIGIT: Identifies the Assembly Plant.

ASSEMBLY PLANT	Code
Atlanta, Ga.	A
Baltimore, Md.	B
Southgate, Calif.	C
Doraville	D
Flint, Mich.	F
Framingham, Mass., GMAD	G
Janesville, Wisc.	J
Kansas City, Mo.	K
Lordstown, Ohio	U
Los Angeles, Calif.	L
Norwood, Ohio	N
Arlington, Tex. GMAD	R
St. Louis, Mo.	S
Tarrytown, N.Y.	T
Willow Run, Mich.	W
Wilmington, Del.	Y
Fremont, Calif.	Z
Oshawa, Ont., Can.	1
Ste. Therese, Que., Can.	2
Pontiac, Mich.	P

LAST SIX DIGITS: Production sequence number.

EXAMPLE

1	5411	9	T	101551
Man. Symbol	Model	Year	Assy Plant	Production Number

FISHER BODY NUMBER PLATE

Complete identification of each body is provided by a plate riveted to the top of the cowl.

Exception: Corvair body tag is located on left rear wheel housing inside the engine compartment.

THE BODY NUMBER is the production serial number of the body. The prefix letter denotes the plant in which the body was built. Refer to the Assembly Plants and codes that are in the VIN plate.

LAST SIX DIGITS: Production sequence number.

THE STYLE NUMBER is a combination of the series, and body style.

```
┌─────────────────────────────────────────────┐
│                                               │
│         CHEVROLET DIVISION                    │
│         GENERAL MOTORS CORP.                  │
│    CORRESPONDENCE PERTAINING TO THE           │
│    BODY MUST BEAR THESE NUMBERS               │
│                                               │
│  ○   STYLE No.    69 15411               ○    │
│      BODY No.     T 1001555                    │
│      TRIM No.     810                          │
│      PAINT No.    936                          │
│                                               │
│             BODY BY FISHER                    │
│                                               │
└─────────────────────────────────────────────┘
```

CHEVELLE

Series	6-Cyl.	V-8	Description
Nomad	13135	13235	4-Dr Station Wagon, 2-Seat
300 Deluxe	13369	13469	4-Dr Sedan, 6-Pass.
	13327	13427	2-Dr Pillar Coupe, 5-Pass.
	13337	13437	2-Dr Sport Coupe, 5-Pass.
	13335	13435	4-Dr Station Wagon, 2-Seat (Greenbrier)
	13336	13436	4-Dr Station Wagon, 2-Seat (Greenbrier)
	13346	13446	4-Dr Station Wagon, 3-Seat (Greenbrier)
Malibu	13569	13669	4-Dr Sedan, 6-Pass.
	13539	13639	4-Dr Sport Sedan, 6-Pass.
	13537	13637	2-Dr Sport Coupe, 5-Pass.*
	13567	13667	2-Dr Convertible, 5-Pass.*
	13536	13636	4-Dr Station Wagon, 2-Seat (Concours)
	13546	13646	4-Dr Station Wagon, 3-Seat (Concours)
Super Sport	-	13837	2-Dr Sport Coupe, 5-Pass.*
Concours	-	13836	4-Dr Station Wagon, 2-Seat
Estate Wagon	-	13846	4-Dr Station Wagon, 3-Seat

*4-Passenger when optional bucket seats are ordered.

NOVA

4 Cyl.	6-Cyl.	V-8	Description
11127	11327	11427	2-Dr Sport Coupe, 5-Pass.
11169	11369	11469	4-Dr Sedan, 6-Pass.

CAMARO

6-Cyl.	V-8	Description
12337	12437	2-Dr Sport Coupe, 4-Pass.
12367	12467	2-Dr Convertible, 4-Pass.

CORVETTE

Model Number	Description
19437	2-Dr Sport Coupe, 2-Passenger
19467	2-Dr Convertible, 2-Passenger

CORVAIR

Series	Model Number	Description
Standard	10137	2-Dr Sport Coupe, 5 Passenger
Monza	10537	2-Dr Sport Coupe, 4-Passenger
	10567	2-Dr Convertible, 4-Passenger

CHEVROLET

Series	6-Cyl.	V-8	Description
Biscayne	15311	15411	2-Dr Sedan, 6-Pass.
	15369	15469	4-Dr Sedan, 6-Pass.
	15336	15436	4-Dr Station Wagon, 2-Seat (Brookwood)
Bel Air	15511	15611	2-Dr Sedan, 6-Pass.
	15569	15669	4-Dr Sedan, 6-Pass.
	15536	15639	4-Dr Station Wagon, 2-Seat (Townsman)
	15546	15646	4-Dr Station Wagon, 3-Seat (Townsman)
Impala	16369	16469	4-Dr Sedan, 6-Pass.
	16339	16439	4-Dr Sport Sedan, 6-Pass.
	16337	16437	2-Dr Sport Coupe, 5-Pass.*
	-	16467	2-Dr Convertible, 5-Pass.*
	-	16436	4-Dr Station Wagon, 2-Seat (Kingswood)
	-	16446	4-Dr Station Wagon, 3-Seat (Kingswood)
Impala Custom	-	16447	2-Dr Sport Coupe, 5-Pass.*
Caprice	-	16639	4-Dr Sport Sedan, 6-Pass.
	-	16647	2-Dr Sport Coupe, 5-Pass.*
	-	16636	4-Dr Station Wagon, 2-Seat (Estate Wagon)
	-	1646	4-Dr Station Wagon, 3-Seat (Estate Wagon)

THE TRIM NUMBER furnishes the key to trim color and material for each model SERIES.

D=Dark, M=Medium, L=Light, I=Imitation, W=Woven

Material	Code	Models
Black Pattern Ctd. Fab. Black Ctd. Fab.	700	10137
Met. D Blue Pattern Ctd. Fab., Met. D Blue Ctd. Fab.	703	10137
Met. M Green Pattern Ctd. Fab., Met. M Green Ctd. Fab.	708	10137
Black Pattern Ctd. Fab., Black Ctd. Fab.	731	11427-69 71427-69
Black Ctd. Fab.	732	11427-69 71427-69 (CUS)
M Blue Rancona Cloth, Met. M Blue Ctd. Fab.	735	11427-69 71427-69
M Blue Remington Cloth, Met. M Blue Ctd. Fab.	736	11427-69 71427-69 (CUS)
M Green Rancona Cloth, Met. M Green Ctd. Fab.	742	11427-69 71427-69
M Green Remington Cloth, Met. M Green Ctd. Fab	743	11427-69 71427-69 (CUS)
Midnight Green Remington Cloth, Aff Midnight Green Ctd. Fab.	744	11427-69 71427-69 (CUS)
Aff Midnight Green	745	11427-69 71427-69 (CUS)
Black Pattern Ctd. Fab.	750	13235-36
Black Ctd. Fab., Black Ransom Cloth	751	13427-37-69
Black Ctd. Fab., Black Pattern Ctd.Fab.	752	13427-35-36-37-46-69-80
Black Ctd. Fab., Black Rior Cloth	753	13637-39-69
Black Ctd. Fab. Black Richmond Cloth, Black Ctd. Fab.	754	13639 (CUS)
Black Ctd. Fab.	755	13636-37-39-46-67-69-80 13836-46
Met. M Blue Pattern Ctd. Fab., Met. M Blue Ctd. Fab.	759	13235-36
M Blue Ransom Cloth, M Blue Ctd. Fab.	760	13427-37-69
Met. M Blue Pattern Ctd. Fab., Met. D Blue Ctd. Fab.	761	13435-36-46-80
D Blue Rior Cloth, Met. D Blue Ctd. Fab.	762	13637-39-69
D Blue Richmond Cloth, Met. D Blue Ctd. Fab.	763	13639 (CUS)
Met. D Blue Coated Fab.	764	13636-46-80
Ant. M Saddle Ctd. Fab.	770	13636-46-80
M Saddle Pattern Ctd. Fab., Ant. M Saddle Ctd. Fab.	772	13235-36
M Saddle Pattern Ctd. Fab., Ant. M Saddle Ctd. Fab.	773	13435-36-46-80
M Turq. Rior Cloth, Met. M Turq. Ctd. Fab.	779	13637-39-69
Midnight Green Rior Cloth, Aff Midnight Green Ctd. Fab.	782	13637-39-69
M Green Rior Cloth, Met. M Green Ctd. Fab.	783	13637-39-69
Met. M Green Ctd. Fab.	784	13637-39
M Green Ransom Cloth, Met. M Green Ctd. Fab.	786	13427-37-69
M Red Ctd. Fab.	787	13637-67
Aff Parchment Ctd. Fab., (Black Carpet, etc.)	790	13637-67
Midnight Green Richmond Cloth, Aff Mid. Green Ctd. Fab.	794	13639 (CUS)
Aff Mid. Green Ctd. Fab.	795	13636-37-39-46

Material	Code	Models
Black Pattern Ctd. Fab., Black Ctd. Fab.	802	15411-36-69
Black Radmere Cloth, Black Ctd. Fab.	803	15611-69
Black Pattern Ctd. Fab., Black Ctd. Fab.	804	15611-36-46-69
Black Reveille Cloth, Black Ctd. Fab.	805	16437-39-47-69
Black Ctd. Fab.	806	16436-37-39-46-47-67-69, 16636-46
Black Regale Cloth, Black Ctd. Fab.	807	16639-47
Black Prima Cloth, Black Ctd. Fab.	808	16639-47
Black Prima Cloth, Black Ctd. Fab.	813	16639-47
Met. M Blue Pattern Ctd. Fab., Met. M Blue Ctd. Fab.	815	15436
M Blue Rampart Cloth, Met. M Blue Ctd. Fab.	816	15411-69
M Blue Radmere Cloth, Met. M Blue Ctd. Fab.	818	15611-69
Met. M Blue Pattern Ctd. Fab., Met. M Blue Ctd. Fab.	819	15611-36-46-69
D Blue Reveille Cloth Met. D Blue Ctd. Fab.	820	16437-39-47-69
Met. D Ctd. Fab.	821	16436-37-39-46-47-49 16636-46
M Blue Regale Cloth, Met. M Blue Ctd. Fab.	822	16639-47
D Blue Prima Cloth, Met. D Blue Ctd. Fab.	826	16639-47
Ant. M Saddle Ctd. Fab.	830	16436-46 16636-46
M Saddle Pattern Ctd. Fab., Ant. M Saddle Ctd. Fab.	831	15436
M Gold Reveille Cloth, Ant. M Gold Ctd. Fab.	837	16437-39-47
M Saddle Pattern Ctd. Fab., Ant. M Saddle Ctd. Fab.	838	15636-46
M Gold Regale Cloth, Ant. M Gold Ctd. Fab.	840	16639-47
M Turq. Reveille Cloth, Met. M Turq. Ctd. Fab.	844	16437-39-47-69
M Turq. Regale Cloth, Met. M Turq. Ctd. Fab.	846	16639-47
Midnight Green Radmere Cloth, Aff. Midnight Green Ctd. Fab.	848	15611-69
M Green Rampart Cloth, M Green Ctd. Fab.	849	15411-69
M Green Radmere Cloth, Met. M Green Ctd. Fab.	850	15611-69
Met. M Green Pattern Ctd. Fab., Met. M Green Ctd. Fab.	851	15636-46
M Green Reveille Cloth, Green Ctd. Fab.	852	16437-39-47-69
Met. M Green Ctd. Fab.	853	16437-47-67
Midnight Green Prima Cloth, Aff. Midnight Green Ctd. Fab.	855	16639-47
M Green Regale Cloth, Met. M Green Ctd. Fab.	856	16639-47
Aff. Parchment Ctd. Fab., (Black Carpet, etc.)	858	16437-47-67
Midnight Green Reveille Cloth, Aff. Midnight Green Ctd. Fab.	860	16437-39-47-69
Aff. Midnight Green Ctd. Fab.	861	16436-46 16636-46
M Red Ctd. Fab.	866	16437-47-67 16647

BUCKET SEATS

	Code	Models
Black Ctd. Fab.	701	10537-67
Met. D Blue Ctd. Fab.	704	10537-67
Met. M Green Ctd. Fab.	707	10537-67
Black Ctd. Fab.	711	12437-67
Black Ctd. Fab.	712	12437-67 (CUS)
Black Radcliffe Cloth, Black Ctd. Fab.	713	12437 (CUS)
Met. D Blue Ctd. Fab.	715	12437-67
Met. D Blue Ctd. Fab.	716	12437-67 (CUS)

M Red Ctd. Fab. 718 12437-67
M Red Ctd. Fab. 719
.... 12437-67 (CUS)
Met. M Green Ctd. Fab. 721 12437-67
Met. M Green Ctd. Fab. 722
.... 12437-67 (CUS)
Aff. Mid. Green Ctd. Fab. 723 12437-67
Aff. Mid. Green Ctd. Fab. 725
.... 12437-67 (CUS)
Ivory Ctd. Fab., (Black Carpet, etc.) 727 12437-67
Black Radcliffe Cloth, Ivory Ctd. Fab. ...... 729 .... 12437 (CUS)
Black Ctd. Fab. .... 733 .... 11427, 71427
Met. M Blue Ctd. Fab. .... 737 .... 11427, 71427
M Red Ctd. Fab. .... 746 .... 11427, 71427
Black Ctd. Fab. 756 13637-67-80
Met. D Blue Ctd. Fab. 765 13637-67-80
Ant. M Saddle Ctd. Fab. 771 13680
Met. M Green Ctd. Fab. 785 13637
M Red Ctd. Fab. 788 13637-67
Aff. Parchment Ctd. Fab., (Black Carpet, etc.) 791 13637-67
Aff. Mid. Green Ctd. Fab. 796 13637
Black Ctd. Fab. 809 16437-67
Black Ctd. Fab. 812 16437-47-67
.... 16647
M D Blue Ctd. Fab. 824 16647
Met. M Green Ctd. Fab. 854 16647
Aff. Mid. Green Ctd. Fab. 857 16647
Aff. Parchment Ctd. Fab., (Black Carpet, etc.) 859 16437-47-67
Met. M Green Ctd. Fab. 862 16647
M Red Ctd. Fab. 867 16437-47-67
.... 16647

Paint Code - gives key to exterior color.

1969 PAINT COMBINATION CHART

Model Usage	Chevy Code	Color
Pass., Corvette	10-900	Tuxedo Black
Pass.	40	Butternut Yellow
Pass.	50	Dover White
Pass.	51	Dusk Blue
Pass.	52	Garnet Red
Pass.	53	Glacier Blue
Pass.	55	Azure Turquoise
Pass., Corvette	57-983	Fathom Green
Pass.	59	Frost Green
Pass.	61	Burnished Brown
Pass.	63	Champagne
Pass.	65	Olympic Gold
Pass., Corvette	67-988	Burgundy
Pass., Corvette	69-986	Cortez Silver
Pass., Corvette	71-976	LeMans Blue
Camaro, Corvette	72-990	Hugger Orange
Camaro, Corvette	76-984	Daytona Yellow
Camaro	79	Rallye Green
Corvette	972	Can - Am White
Corvette	974	Monza Red
Corvette	980	Riverside Gold

ENGINE NUMBER

All Chevrolet Engines are stamped with a Plant Code, Production Date, and Engine Type Code.

Note:

1. Corvette Engines have the last six digits of the VIN stamped on the block next to the engine number.

2. Corvair Engines are stamped on the top of the block forward of the generator.

3. 8 cylinder engines are stamped on the right front of the engine block.

4. 6 cylinder engines are stamped on the right side of the block at the rear of the distributor.

EXAMPLE

T	01	01	A
PLANT	MONTH	DAY	CODE

ENGINE PLANTS   Code

Tonawanda .... T
Flint .... F

ENGINE	CODES
CHEVY II	
153 4-cyl	AA,AB
230 6-cyl	AM,AN,AO, AP,HQ,AR
250 6-cyl	BB,BC,BD, BE,BF,BH
307 8-cyl	DA,DC,DE,DD
350 8-cyl	HA,HB,HC, HD,HE,HF, HQ,HR,HS,HP
396 8-cyl	JF,JH,JI,JL,JU JM,KA,KC,KE
CHEVELLE	
230 6-cyl	AM,AN,AD, AP,AQ,AR
250 6-cyl	BB,BC,BD, BE,BF,BH
307 8-cyl	DA,DC,DE,DD
350 8-cyl	HA,HB,HC,HP,HS, HD,HE,HF,HR
396 8-cyl	JA,JC,JD,JE,JK, KF,KG,KH,KB, JV,KD,KI

CHEVROLET	
250 6-cyl	BA,BG,BJ,BL BO,BP,BQ
327 8-cyl	FA,FB,FC,FH,FG,FJ, FK,FL,FY,FZ,GA,GB
350 8-cyl	GE,HD,HF,HG,HH, HI,HJ,HK,HL,HM, HN,HD,HP,HT,HU, HY,IA,IL,IM,IN,IP, IQ,IR,IS,IT,IV,IW, IX,IY,IZ
396 8-cyl	JN,JO,JP, JQ,JT,JR
427 8-cyl	LA,LB,LC,LD, LE,LF,LG,LH, LI,LJ,LK,LS, LY,LZ,MA, MB,MC,MD

CORVETTE	
350 8-cyl	HW,HX,HY,HZ,GD
427 8-cyl	LL,LM,LN,LO, LP,LQ,LR,LT, LU,LV,LW,LX, ME,MG,MH,MI, MJ,MK,MS,MR

CAMARO	
230 6-cyl	AM,AN,AO, AP,AQ,AR
250 6-cyl	BB,BC,BD, BE,BF,BH
302 8-cyl	DZ
307 8-cyl	DA,DC,DD,DE
350 8-cyl	HA,HB,HC, HD,HE,HF, HQ,HR,HS
396 8-cyl	JB,JF,JG,JH, JI,JJ,JL,JM, JU,KA,KC,KE
427 8-cyl	ME,MG,MN, MO,ML,MM

CORVAIR	
164 6-cyl 95 HP	AC,AE
110 HP	AD,AF
140 HP	AG,AH

BASIC ENGINE DATA

Engine	CID	Comp.	H.P.	Carburetor	Transmission
Super Thrift (153-4 cyl.)	153	8.5	90	Single Barrel	3-SPD., P.G.
Turbo-Air (164)	164	8.25	95	2 Single Barrel	3-SPD., 4-SPD., P.G.
Turbo-Air (164 Hi-Per.)	164	9.25	110	2 Single Barrel	3-SPD., 4-SPD., P.G.
Turbo-Air (164 Sp. Hi-Per.)	164	9.25	140	4 Single Barrel	3-SPD., 4-SPD., P.G.
Turbo-Thrift (230-6 cyl.)	230	8.5	140	Single Barrel	3-SPD., P.G. T.H.
Turbo-Thrift (250-6 cyl.)	250	8.5	155	Single Barrel	3-SPD., P.G., T.H.
Turbo-Fire (307-8 cyl.)	307	9.0	200	2-Barrel	3-SPD., 4-SPD., P.G., T.H.
Turbo-Fire (302-8 cyl.)	302	11.0	290	4-Barrel	4-SPD.
Turbo-Fire (327-8 cyl.)	327	9.0	210	2-Barrel	3-SPD., 4-SPD., P.G., T.H.
Turbo-Fire (327-8 cyl.)	327	9.0	235	2-Barrel	3-SPD., 4-SPD., P.G., T.H.
Turbo-Fire (350-8 cyl.)	350	9.0	255	4-Barrel	3-SPD., 4-SPD., P.G., T.H.
Turbo-Fire (350-8 cyl.)	350	10.25	300	4-Barrel	3-SPD., 4-SPD., P.G., T.H.
Turbo-Fire (350-8 cyl.)	350	11.0	350	4-Barrel	4-SPD.
Turbo-Jet (396-8 cyl.)	396	9.0	265	2-Barrel	3-SPD., 4-SPD., T.H.
Turbo-Jet (396-8 cyl.)	396	10.25	325	4-Barrel	3-SPD., 4-SPD., TH400
Turbo-Jet (396-8 cyl.)	396	10.25	350	4-Barrel	3-SPD., 4-SPD., TH400
Turbo-Jet (396-8 cyl.)	396	11.0	375	4-Barrel	3-SPD., 4-SPD., TH400
Turbo-Jet (427-8 cyl.)	427	10.25	335	4-Barrel	3-SPD., 4-SPD., TH400
Turbo-Jet (427-8 cyl.)	427	10.25	390	4-Barrel	3-SPD., 4-SPD., TH400
Turbo-Jet (427-8 cyl.)	427	10.25	400	3 x 2-Barrel	4-SPD., TH400
Turbo-Jet (427-8 cyl.)	427	11.0	425	4-Barrel	3-SPD., 4-SPD., TH400
Turbo-Jet (427-8 cyl.)	427	12.5	430	4-Barrel	4-SPD., TH400
Turbo-Jet (427-8 cyl.)	427	11.0	435	3 x 2-Barrel	4-SPD., TH400

VEHICLE IDENTIFICATION NUMBER

OLDSMOBILE
608A001555

Commonly referred to as the VIN NUMBER, this series of numbers and letters is stamped on a plate attached to the left front door hinge pillar.

EXAMPLE

60	8	A	001555
YEAR	SERIES	ASSY PLANT	PRODUCTION NUMBER

FIRST AND SECOND DIGITS: Identify the year, 60 for 1960.

THIRD DIGIT: Identifies the series, 7 for Dynamic 88 (3200 Series), 8 for Super 88 (3500 Series) and 9 for 98 (3800 Series).

FOURTH DIGIT: (letter) Identifies the Assembly Plant.

ASSEMBLY PLANT	CODE
Atlanta, Georgia	A
Framingham, Mass.	B
South Gate, CA	C
Kansas City, Kansas	K
Linden, NJ	L
Lansing, MI	M
Arlington, TX	T
Wilmington, Del.	W

LAST 6 DIGITS: Represent the Basic Production Numbers.

FISHER BODY NUMBER PLATE

Complete identification of each body is provided by a plate under the hood below the left windshield wiper transmission.

The Style Number is a Combination of the Year, Series (35 for 3500, Super 88), and Body Style (39 for Holiday Sedan).

DYNAMIC "88"	CODE
2-Door Sedan	3211
4-Door Sedan	3219
Fiesta Station Wagon	3235

	CODE
Fiesta 3-Seat Station Wagon	3245
Holiday Coupe	3237
Holiday Sedan	3239
Convertible Coupe	3267

SUPER "88"	CODE
4-Door Sedan	3519
Fiesta Station Wagon	3535
Fiesta 3-Seat Station Wagon	3545
Holiday Coupe	3537
Holiday Sedan	3539
Convertible Coupe	3567

"98"	CODE
4-Door Sedan	3819
Holiday Coupe *	3837
Holiday Sedan *	3839
Convertible Coupe *	3867

* Equipped with electric windows and electric 2-Way Seat.

THE BODY NUMBER is the production serial number of the body. The prefix letter denotes the plant in which the body was assembled.

ASSEMBLY PLANT	CODE
Lansing	LA
Doraville	BA
Framingham	BF
Kansas City	BK
Linden	BL
South Gate	BC
Wilmington	BW
Arlington	BT

OLDSMOBILE DIV. GENERAL MOTORS CORP.
LANSING MICHIGAN

STYLE 60-3539   **BODY** BA 001555
TRIM 345   **PAINT** AC
ACC.00

BODY BY FISHER

LAST SIX DIGITS: Represent the Basic Production Numbers.

THE PAINT CODE furnishes the key to the paint colors used on the car. A two letter code indicates the bottom and top colors respectively.

COLOR	CODE
Ebony Black	A
Charcoal Mist Iridescent	B
Provincial White	C
Platinum Mist Iridescent	D
Gulf Blue Iridescent	F
Resden Blue Iridescent	H
Palmetto Mist Iridescent	J
Fern Mist Iridescent	K
Garnet Mist Iridescent	L
Citron	M
Cordovan Iridescent	N
Golden Mist Iridescent	P
Shell Beige	R
Copper Mist Iridescent	S
Turquoise Iridescent	T

HE TRIM NUMBER furnishes the key to trim color and material for ach model series

ERIES AND MODELS	TRIM NO.	COLOR
YNAMIC 88		MOROCCEEN
-Door Sedan	311	L-Gray
elebrity Sedan	312	L-Green
loliday SceniCoupe	313	L-Blue
loliday SportSedan	314	L-Fawn
	316	L-Turquoise
YNAMIC 88		MOROCCEEN
onvertible Coupe	321	L-Gray
	322	L-Green
	323	L-Blue
	325	D-Red
YNAMIC 88		MOROCCEEN
iesta 2-Seat	391	L-Gray
iesta 3-Seat	392	L-Green
	393	L-Blue
	394	L-Fawn
	395	D-Red
SUPER 88		PATTERN CLOTH
Celebrity Sedan	331	M-Gray
	332	M-Green
	333	M-Blue
	334	M-Fawn
	336	M-Turquoise
SUPER 88		MOROCCEEN
Holiday SceniCoupe		
Holiday SportSedan	341	D-Gray
	342	M-Green
	343	M-Blue
	344	M-Fawn
	345	M-Red
SUPER 88		LEATHER
Convertible Coupe	351	D-Gray
	352	M-Green
	353	M-Blue
	355	M-Red
SUPER 88		PATTERN CLOTH
Fiesta 2-Seat	390	D-Gray
Fiesta 3-Seat	396	M-Fawn
	397	M-Green
	398	M-Blue
	399	M-Red
NINETY-EIGHT		PATTERN CLOTH
Celebrity Sedan	361	M-Gray
	362	M-Green
	363	M-Blue
	364	M-Fawn
	366	M-Turquoise
NINETY-EIGHT		LEATHER
Holiday SceniCoupe		
Holiday SportSedan	371	D-Gray
Celebrity Sedan with	372	M-Green
Cust. Trim Option K-5	373	M-Blue
	374	M-Fawn
	375	M-Red
NINETY-EIGHT		MOROCCEEN
Convertible Coupe	381	M-Gray
	382	M-Green
	383	M-Blue
	384	M-Fawn
	385	M-Red

ENGINE NUMBER

The engine unit number is stamped on the left cylinder head. A prefix letter code identifies the engine followed by a production sequence number.

Two engines rated at 371 cid, are available on the 88 Series. One engine has a compression ratio of 9.75:1 and is designed to use premium fuel. The other engine has a compression ration of 8.75:1 and is designed to use regular fuel. Both engines have the letter "C" Prefix Code, and the Premium Fuel Version has a suffix "H".

The S88 and 98 Series, use a 394 cid engine identified by a prefix "D" to the engine unit number. This engine has a compression ratio of 9.75:1, and is also designed for premium fuel.

Low compression export option engines will also use a "C" or "D" prefix and will be identified by the letter "E" as a suffix to the engine unit number.

Engine	Comp.	H.P.	CID
371	8.75:1	240	371
371	9.75:1	260	371
394	9.75:1	315	394

1961 OLDSMOBILE

VEHICLE IDENTIFICATION NUMBER

```
OLDSMOBILE
618A001555
```

Commonly referred to as the VIN NUMBER, this series of numbers and letters is stamped on a plate attached to the left front door hinge pillar.

EXAMPLE

61	8	A	001555
YEAR	SERIES	ASSEMBLY PLANT	PRODUCTION NUMBER

FIRST AND SECOND DIGITS: Identify the year 61 for 1961.

THIRD DIGIT: Identifies the Series.

MODEL	SERIES	CODE
F85	3000	0
DELUXE F-85	3100	1
88	3200	2
SUPER 88	3500	5
STARFIRE	3600	6
98	3800	8

FOURTH DIGIT: (letter) Identifies the Assembly Plant.

ASSEMBLY PLANT	CODE
Atlanta, Ga.	A
Framingham, Mass.	B
South Gate, Calif.	C
Kansas City, Kans.	K
Linden, N.J.	L
Lansing, Mich.	M
Arlington, Tex.	T
Wilmington, Del.	W

Last 6 Digits: Represent the Basic Production Numbers

FISHER BODY NUMBER PLATE

Complete identification of each body is provided by a plate under the hood below the left windshield wiper transmission.

The Style Number is a Combination of the Series and Body Style.

DYNAMIC "88"	CODE
2-Door Sedan	3211
4-Door Sedan	3269
Fiesta Station Wagon	3235
Fiesta 3-Seat Station Wgn	3245
Holiday Coupe	3237
Holiday Sedan	3239
Convertible Coupe	3267

SUPER "88"	CODE
4-Door Sedan	3569
Fiesta Station Wagon	3535
Fiesta 3-Seat Station Wgn	3545
Holiday Coupe	3537
Holiday Sedan	3539
Convertible Coupe	3567

"98"	CODE
4-Door Sedan	3819
Holiday Coupe*	3837
Holiday Sedan*	3829
Convertible Coupe*	3867
Sport Sedan	3839

* Equipped with electric windows and electric 2-Way Seat.

STARFIRE	CODE
Convertible Coupe	3667

F-85	CODE
4-Door Sedan	3019
Club Coupe	3027
Station Wagon 2-seat	3035
Station Wagon 3-seat	3045

F-85 DELUXE	CODE
Sport Coupe Cutlass	3117
4-Door Sedan	3119

```
OLDSMOBILE DIV. GENERAL MOTORS CORP.
LANSING MICHIGAN

STYLE 61-3539      BODY BA 001555
TRIM 345           PAINT AC
ACC.00

BODY BY FISHER
```

Station Wagon 2-seat	3135
Station Wagon 3-seat	3145

THE BODY NUMBER is the production serial number of the body. The prefix letter denotes the plant in which the body was assembled.

ASSEMBLY PLANT	CODE
Lansing	LA
Doraville	BA
Kansas City	BK
Linden	BL
South Gate	BC
Wilmington	BW
Arlington	BT

LAST SIX DIGITS: Represent the Basic Production Numbers.

THE PAINT CODE furnished the key to the paint colors used on the car. A two letter code indicates the bottom and top colors respectively.

COLOR	CODE
Ebony Black	A
Twilight Mist	E
Provincial White	C
Platinum Mist	D
Azure Mist	F
Glacier Blue	H
Tropic Mist	J
Alpine Green	K
Garnet Mist	L
Cordovan Mist	N
Turquoise Mist	P
Aqua	Q
Sandalwood	R
Autumn Mist	S
Fawn Mist	T

HE TRIM CODE furnishes the key to interior color and material.

ERIES AND MODELS	TRIM NO.	COLOR
YNAMIC 88		
Door Sedan	311	Lt. Gray
elebrity Sedan	312	Med. Green
	313	Med. Blue
	314	Med. Fawn
	305*	Med. Red
oliday Coupe	310	Lt. Gray
oliday Sedan	317	Med. Green
	318	Med. Blue
	319	Med. Fawn
	315	Med. Red
oliday Coupe	921	Dk. Gray
oliday Sedan	922	Dk. Green
Starglo Trim Option)	923	Dk. Blue
	924	Dk. Fawn
	925	Dk. Red
onvertible Coupe	321	Dk. Gray
	322	Dk. Green
	323	Dk. Blue
	324	Dk. Fawn
	325	Dk. Red
-Seat Fiesta	391	Dk. Gray
-Seat Fiesta	392	Dk. Green
	393	Dk. Blue
	394	Dk. Fawn
	395	Dk. Red
	387	Dk. Turquoise
SUPER 88		
Celebrity Sean	331	White
	332	Lt. Green
	333	Lt. Blue
	334	Lt. Fawn
	335	Lt. Red
Holiday Coupe	341	Dk. Gray
	342	Dk. Green
	343	Dk. Blue
	344	Lt. Fawn
	345	Dk. Red
Convertible Coupe	351	Dk. Gray
	352	Dk. Green
	353	Dk. Blue
	354	Dk. Fawn
	355	Dk. Red
2-Seat Fiesta	390	White
3-Seat Fiesta	397	Lt. Green
	398	Lt. Blue
	396	Med. Fawn
	399	Med. Red
	388	Med. Turquoise
NINETY-EIGHT		
4-Door Sedan	361	Med. Gray
	362	Med. Green
	363	Med. Blue
	364	Med. Fawn
	366	Med. Turquoise

Holiday Sedan	301	Lt. Gray
	302	Med. Green
	303	Med. Blue
	304	Med. Fawn
	306	Med. Turquoise
Holiday Coupe	371	Lt. Gray
Sport Sedan	372	Med. Green
	373	Med. Blue
	374	Med. Fawn
	375	Med. Red
Convertible Coupe	381	Lt. Gray
	382	Med. Green
	383	Med. Blue
	384	Med. Fawn
	385	Med. Red

*Not available on Dynamic 88 2-Door Sedan.

F-85		
4-Door Sedan	901*	Lt. Gray
Club Coupe	902	Med. Green
	903*	Med. Blue
	904*	Med. Fawn
	905	Med. Red
Station Wagon	911	Lt. Gray
2-Seat	912	Med. Green
3-Seat	913	Med. Blue
	904	Med. Fawn
	905	Med. Red
DeLuxe	971	Lt. Gray
Sport Coupe	972	Med. Green
	973	Med. Blue
	974	Med. Fawn
	975	Med. Red
DeLuxe	951	Dk. Gray
4-Door sedan	952	Dk. Green
	953	Dk. Blue
	954	Dk. Fawn
	965	Dk. Red
DeLuxe Station Wagon	951	Dk. Gray
2-Seat	952	Dk. Green
3-Seat	953	Dk. Blue
	964	Dk. Fawn
	965	Dk. Red

*Only combinations 901, 903 and 904 available on Club Coupe.

ENGINE NUMBER

The engine unit number is stamped on the left cylinder head (a production number only). Each engine is stamped with a prefix letter code for identification.

F 85 series is stamped on the right cylinder head.

ENGINE IDENTIFICATION

SERIES	CODE	CARB	COMP.	C.I.D.	HP
88 standard	F	2 Bbl.	8.5:1	394	250
88 option	G	2 Bbl.	10.0:1	394	275
88 option	G	4 Bbl.	10.0:1	394	325
S 88 & 98	G	4 Bbl.	10.0:1	394	325
Starfire	G	4 Bbl.	10.25:1	394	330
F-85 standard	S	2 Bbl.	8.75:1	215	155
F-85 option*	S	4 Bbl.	10.25:1	215	185

1) If no Suffix code exists, it is a standard engine.
2) E,H, Suffix indicates an Export engine
3) G, Hi-Comp. L, Low-Comp.

* Standard on Cutlass

VEHICLE IDENTIFICATION NUMBER

```
OLDSMOBILE
628A001555
```

Commonly referred to as the VIN NUMBER, this series of numbers and letters is stamped on a plate attached to the left front door hinge pillar.

EXAMPLE

62	8	A	001555
YEAR	SERIES	ASSEMBLY PLANT	PRODUCTION NUMBER

FIRST AND SECOND DIGITS: Identify the year 62 for 1962.

THIRD DIGIT: Identifies the series.

MODEL	SERIES	CODE
F85	3000	0
F85 DIX	3100	1
88	3200	2
SUPER 88	3500	5
STARFIRE	3600	6
98	3800	8

FOURTH DIGIT: (letter) Identifies the Assembly Plant.

ASSEMBLY PLANT	CODE
Atlanta, Ga.	A
South Gate, Calif.	C
Kansas City, Kans.	K
Linden, N.J.	L
Lansing, Mich.	M
Arlington, Tex.	T
Wilmington, Del.	W

LAST 6 DIGITS: Represent the Basic Production Numbers.

FISHER BODY NUMBER PLATE

Complete identification of each body is provided by a plate under the hood below the left windshield wiper transmission.

The Style Number is a Combination of the Series and Body Style

DYNAMIC "88"	CODE
4-Door Sedan Celebrity	3269
Fiesta Station Wagon	3235
Fiesta 3-Seat Station Wgn	3245
Holiday Coupe	3247
Holiday Sedan	3239
Convertible Coupe	3267

SUPER "88"	CODE
4-Door Sedan Celebrity	3569
Fiesta Station Wagon	3535
Holiday Coupe	3547
Holiday Sedan	3539

STARFIRE	CODE
Starfire Coupe	3647
Convertible	3667

"98"	CODE
4-Door Sedan	3819
Holiday Coupe*	3847
Holiday Sedan*	3829
Convertible Coupe*	3867
Sports Sedan	3839

*Equipped with electric windows and electric 2-Way Seat.

F-85	CODE
4-Door Sedan	3019
Club Coupe	3027
2-Seat Station Wagon	3035
3-Seat Station Wagon	3045
Sprots Convertible	3067

F-85 DELUXE	CODE
Cutlass Coupe	3127
Deluxe 4-Door Sean	3119
Deluxe 2-Seat Station Wgn	3135
Cutlass Convertible	3167
Cutlass 2-Door Coupe	3117

JET FIRE	CODE
2-Door Hardtop Coupe	3147

THE BODY NUMBER is the production serial number of the body. The prefix letter denotes the plant in which the body was assembled.

LAST SIX DIGITS: Represent the Basic Production Numbers.

ASSEMBLY PLANT	CODE
Lansing, Mich.	LA
Doravill	BA
Framingham	BF
Kansas City	BK
Linden	BL
South Gate	BC
Wilmington	BW
Arlington	BT

```
OLDSMOBILE DIV. GENERAL MOTORS CORP.
LANSING MICHIGAN

STYLE 62-3539        BODY BA 001555
TRIM 345             PAINT AC
ACC.00

BODY BY FISHER
```

THE PAINT CODE furnished the ket to the paint colors used on the car. A two letter code indicates the bottom and top colors respectively.

COLOR	CODE
Ebony Black	A
Heather Mist	B
Provincial White	C
Sheffield Mist	D
Cirrus Blue	H
Willow Mist	J
Surf Green	K
Garnet Mist	L
Cameo Cream	M
Royal Mist	N
Pacific Mist	P
Sand Beige	R
Sahara Mist	T
Sunset Mist	X

THE TRIM CODE furnishes the key to interior color and material.

SERIES / MODELS	TRIM NO.	COLOR
DYNAMIC 88		
Celebrity Sedan	300	Dk. Gray
	311	Dk. Gray
	312	Dk. Green
	313	Dk. Blue
	314	Dk. Fawn
	305	Dk. Red
Holiday Coupe	310	Med. Gray
Holiday Sedan	317	Med. Green
	318	Med. Blue
	319	Med. Fawn
	315	Med. Red
Holiday Coupe	923	Med. Blue
Holiday Sedan	924	Med. Fawn
Optional	925	Med. Red
(Morocceen Trim)		
Convertible Coupe	321	Med. Gray
	322	Med. Green
	323	Med. Blue
	324	Med. Fawn
	325	Med. Red
Fiesta, 2-Seat "	391	Med. Gray
Fiesta, 3-Seat "	392	Med. Green
	393	Med. Blue
	394	Med. Fawn
	395	Med. Red
	387	Med. Aqua
F-85		
Club Coupe	900	Med. Gray
	908	Med. Blue
	904	Med. Fawn
4-Door Sedan	911	Med. Gray
	902	Med. Green
	903	Med. Blue
	904	Med. Fawn
	905	Med. Red
Sports Convertible	981	Med. Gray
	983	Mee. Blue
	984	Med. Fawn
	985	Med. Red
Station Wagon	911	Med. Gray
2-Seat	913	Med. Blue
3-Seat	904	Med. Fawn
Cutlass Coupe	971	Med. Gray
	973	Med. Blue
	974	Med. Fawn
	975	Med. Red
Cutlass Convertible	991	Med. Gray
	993	Med. Blue
	994	Med. Fawn
	995	Med. Red
DeLuxe	951	Med. Gray
4-Door Sedan	952	Med. Green
	953	Med. Blue
	954	Med. Fawn
	965	White

SERIES / MODELS	TRIM NO.	COLOR
DeLuxe Station Wagon	950	Med. Gray
2-Seat	952	Med. Green
	958	Med. Blue
	964	Lt. Fawn
	965	White
STARFIRE		
Hardtop Coupe	931	Med. Gray
Convertible Coupe	933	Med. Blue
	934	Med. Fawn
	935	Med. Red
NINETY-EIGHT		
Town Sedan	361	Med. Gray
	362	Med. Green
	363	Med. Blue
	364	Med. Fawn
	365	Med. Red
Holiday Sedan	301	Med. Gray
	302	Med. Green
	303	Med. Blue
	304	Med. Fawn
	945	Med. Red
Holiday Sports Coupe	371	Med. Gray
Holiday Sports Sedan	372	Med. Green
	373	Med. Blue
	374	Med. Fawn
	375	Med. Red
Convertible Coupe	381	Dk. Gray
	383	Dk. Blue
	384	Dk. Fawn
	385	Dk. Red
SUPER 88		
Celebrity Sedan	331	Med. Gray
	332	Med. Green
	333	Med. Blue
	334	Med. Fawn
	335	Med. Red
Holiday Coupe	341	Med. Gray
Holiday Sedan	342	Med. Green
	343	Med. Blue
	344	Med. Fawn
	345	Med. Red
"Fiesta, 2-Seat "	390	White
	397	Lt. Green
	398	Lt. Blue
	396	Lt. Fawn
	399	White
	388	Lt. Aqua

ENGINE NUMBER

The engine unit number is stamped on the left cylinder head (a production number only). Each engine is stamped with a prefix letter code for identification.

F 85 series is stamped on the right cylinder head.

ENGINE IDENTIFICATION

Series	Prefix (Code Letter)	Suffix (Code Letter)	Carburetor Type	Compression Ratio	HP
394 CID					
88	F	—	2-Bbl.	10.25:1	280
88 (Opt. W4)	F	L	2-Bbl.	8.75:1	260
88 (Opt. W3)	G	—	4-Bbl.	10.25:1	330
S88 & 98	G	—	4-Bbl.	10.25:1	330
Starfire	G	S	4-Bbl.	10.50:1	345
215 CID					
F-85 (stand.)	S		2-Bbl.	8.75:1	155
F-85 (opt.) Cutlass	G		4-Bbl.	10.25:1	185
Jetfire	T		Turbo Charged	10.25:1	215

1) If no Suffix code exists, it is a standard engine
2) E,H, Suffix indicates an Export engine
3) G, Hi-Comp. L, Low-Comp.

VEHICLE IDENTIFICATION NUMBER

Commonly referred to as the VIN NUMBER, this series of numbers and letters is stamped on a plate attached to the left front door hinge pillar.

```
OLDSMOBILE
638A001555
```

EXAMPLE

63	8	A	001555
YEAR	SERIES	ASSEMBLY PLANT	PRODUCTION NUMBER

FIRST AND SECOND DIGITS: Identify the year.

THIRD DIGIT: Identifies the series.

MODEL	SERIES	CODE
F85 Std.	30	0
F85 Deluxe	31	1
Dynamic 88	32	2
Super 88	35	5
Starfire	36	6
98	38	8
Custom 98	39	9

FOURTH DIGIT: (letter) Identifies the Assembly Plant.

ASSEMBLY PLANT	CODE
Atlanta, Ga.	A
South Gate, Calif.	C
Kansas City, Kans.	K
Linden, N.J.	L
Lansing, Mich.	M
Arlington, Tex.	T
Wilmington, Del.	W

LAST 6 DIGITS: Represent the Basic Production NUmbers.

FISHER BODY NUMBER PLATE

Complete identification of each body is provided by a plate under the hood below the left windshield wiper transmission.

F 85 lcoated on cowl.

The Style Number is a Combination of the Series and Body Style.

F 85 STANDARD	CODE
4- Door Sedan	3019
Club Coupe	3027
Station Wagon	3035

F 85 DELUXE	CODE
Cutlass Coupe	3117
4- Door Sedan	3119
Station Wagon	3135
Cutlass Convertible	3167

JET FIRE	CODE
2-Door Hardtop Coupe	3147

DYNAMIC 88	CODE
2-Seat Fiesta Station Wgn	3235
Holiday Sedan	3239
3-Seat Fiesta Station Wgn	3245
Holiday Coupe	3247
Convertible Coupe	3267
Celebrity Four Door Sedan	3269

SUPER 88	CODE
2-Seat Fiesta Station Wgn	3535
Holiday Sedan	3539
Holiday Coupe	3547
Celebrity Four Door Sedan	3569

```
OLDSMOBILE DIV. GENERAL MOTORS CORP.
LANSING MICHIGAN

STYLE 63-3539          BODY BA 001555
TRIM 345               PAINT AC
ACC.00

        BODY BY FISHER
```

STARFIRE	CODE
Coupe	3657
Convertible	3667

"98"	CODE
Four Door Town Sedan	3819
Luxury Sedan	3829
Sports Sedan	3839
Holiday Coupe	3847
Convertible Coupe	3867
Custom Sports Coupe	3947

THE BODY NUMBER is the production serial number of the body. The prefix letter denotes the plant in which the body was assembled.

LAST SIX DIGITS: Represent the Basic Production Numbers.

ASSEMBLY PLANT	CODE
Lansing	LA
Doravill	BA
Kansas City	BK
Linden	BL
South Gate	BC
Wilmington	BW
Arlington	BT

THE PAINT CODE furnished t key to the paint colors used on car. A two letter code indicates t bottom and top colors respec tively.

COLOR	CO
Ebony Black	
Provincial White	
Sheffied Mist	
Wedgewood Mist	
Cirrus Blue	
Willow Mist	
Barktone Mist	
Regal Mist	
Pacific Mist	
Sand Beige	
Saddle Mist	
Sahara Mist	
Holiday Red	
Midnight Mist	
Antique Rose	

THE TRIM CODE furnishes the key to interior color and material.

MODELS	TRIM NO.	COLOR
NINETY-EIGHT		
Luxury Sedan	391	Silver
	392	Med. Green
	393	Med. Blue
	394	Med. Fawn
	396	Med. Aqua
Town Sedan	361	Silver
	362	Med. Green
	363	Med. Blue
	364	Med. Fawn
	366	Me.d Aqua
Holiday Sports Sedan	371	Med. Gray
Holiday Sports Coupe	372	Med. Green
	373	Med. Blue
	374	Med. Fawn
	375	Med. Red
Convertible Coupe	383	Med. Blue
	385	Med. Red
	387	White
	388	Med. Saddle
Custom Sports Coupe	960	Black
	963	Med. Blue
	965	Med. Red
	967	Black
	968	Med. Saddle
	969	Lt. Rose
SUPER 88		
Holiday Sedan	341	Silver
Holiday Coupe	342	Med. Green
	343	Med. Blue
	344	Med. Fawn
	345	Med. Red
Celebrity Sedan	351	Silver
	352	Med. Green
	353	Med. Blue
	354	Med. Fawn
	355	Med. Red
"Fiesta, 2-Seat "	982	Med. Green
	983	Med. Blue
	985	Med. Red
	986	
	987	White
	988	Med. Saddle
DYNAMIC 88		
Holiday Coupe	311	Dk. Gray
Holiday Sedan	313	Dk. Blue
	314	Dk. Fawn
	315	Dk. Red
Holiday Coupe	322	Dk. Green
Holiday Sedan	323	Dk. Blue
(Optional	324	Dk. Fawn
All-Morocceen Trim)	325	Dk. Red
Celebrity Sedan	300	
	301	Charcoal

MODELS	TRIM NO.	COLOR
	302	Dk. Green
	303	Dk. Blue
	304	Dk. Fawn
	305	Dk. Red
Celebrity Sedan Custom interior trim-Y69)	311	Charcoal
	312	Dk. Green
	313	Dk. Blue
	327	White
	325	Dk. Red
"Fiesta, 2-Seat " "Fiesta, 3-Seat "	971	Charcoal
	972	Dk. Green
	973	Dk. Blue
	975	Dk. Red
	978	Dk. Saddle
Convertible Coupe	331	Charcoal
	332	Dk. Green
	333	Dk. Blue
	335	Dk. Red
	338	Dk. Saddle
STARFIRE Coupe Convertible	990	Black
	993	Med. Blue
	995	Med. Red
	997	White
	998	Med. Saddle
	999	Lt. Rose
F-85		
DeLuxe 4-Door Sedan	931	Platinum
	932	Med. Green
	933	Med. Blue
	934	Med. Fawn
	945	Med. Red
DeLuxe 4-Door Sedan	922	Med. Green
	923	Med. Blue
	924	Med. Fawn
"DeLuxe Station Wagon," 2-Seat	931	Platinum
	932	Med. Green
	933	Med. Blue
	944	Med. Fawn
	945	Med. Red
Cutlass Coupe Cutlass Convertible	950	Black
	953	Med. Blue
	955	Med. Red
	957	White
	958	Med. Saddle
Club Coupe 4-Door Sedan	901	Platinum
	904	Med. Fawn
	912	Med. Green
	913	Med. Blue
	915	Med. Red
"Station Wagon, 2-Seat "	911	Platinum
		913-Blue
		914-Fawn
		915-Red
JETFIRE Hardtop Coupe	950	Black
		953-Blue
		955-Red
		957-White
		958-Saddle

ENGINE NUMBER

The engine unit number is stamped on the left cylinder head (a production number only). Each engine is stamped with a prefix letter code for identification.

F 85 series is stamped on the right cylinder head.

ENGINE IDENTIFICATION

Series	Prefix Code Letter	Suffix Code Letter	Carb Type	Comp Ratio	CID	HP
3000 & 3100	S	—	2 bbl.	8.75:1	215	155
3000 & 3100	S	G	4 bbl.	*10.75:1	215	195
High Comp.	S	G	4 bbl.	10.25:1	215	185
3147	S	T	Turbo charged	10.25:1	215	215
3200						
Std. Comp.	H	—	2 bbl.	10.25:1	394	280
Optional	H	L	2 bbl.	8.75:1	394	260
Optional	J		4 bbl.	10.25:1	394	330
3500 & 3800	J		4 bbl.	10.25:1	394	330
3600 & 3900	J	S	4 bbl.	10.5:1	394	345

*High compression ratio F-85 4 bbl. engines with Hydra Matic Transmissions ONLY.

1) If no Suffix code exists, it is a standard engine
2) E,H, Suffix indicates an Export engine
3) G, Hi-Comp. L, Low-Comp.

VEHICLE IDENTIFICATION NUMBER

Commonly referred to as the VIN NUMBER, this series of numbers and letters is stamped on a plate attached to the left front door hinge pillar.

```
OLDSMOBILE
834M001002
```

EXAMPLE

8	3	4	M	001002
Cyl	Series	Year	Assembly Plant	Production Number

THE FIRST DIGIT identifies the Engine Type: 6 (6 cyl), 8 (8 cyl).

THE SECOND DIGIT identifies the Series Designation.

MODEL	SERIES	CODE
F85 Standard	30	0
F85 Deluxe	31	1
F85 Cutlass	32	2
88 Jetstar	33	3
Dynamic 88	34	4
Super 88	35	5
Starfire	36	6
Jetstar I	34	7
"98"	38	8
"98" Custom	39	9

The third digit identifies the Model Year: 4 - 1964

The fourth character identifies the Assembly Plant:

Assembly Plant	CODE
Atlanta	A
Baltimore	B
Southgate	C
Kansas City, Mo.	D
Fremont	F
Kansas City, Kans.	K
Linden	L
Lansing	M
Arlington	T

LAST 6 DIGITS: Represent the Basic Production Numbers.

FISHER BODY NUMBER PLATE

Complete identification of each body is provided by a plate on the cowl under the hood.

The Style Number is a Combination of the Series and Body Style.

F 85 STANDARD	CODE
Club Coupe	3027
St. Wgn	3035
4-Door Sedan	3069

F 85 DELUXE	CODE
V6 Sport Coupe	3127
St. Wgn	3135
4-Door Sedan	3169

CUTLASS	CODE
Sports Coupe	3227
Holiday Coupe	3237
Convertible	3267

VISTA-CRUISER	STD.	CUST.
St. Wgn. 2-Seat	3055	3255
St. Wgn. 3-Seat	3065	3265

JETSTAR 88	CODE
Holiday Sedan	3339
Holiday Coupe	3347
Convertible	3367
Celebrity 4-Door Sedan	3369

JETSTAR I	CODE
Sports Coupe	3457

DYNAMIC 88	CODE
2-Seat Fiesta StWgn	3435
Holiday Sedan	3439
3-Seat Fiesta StWgn	3445
Holiday Coupe	3447
Convertible	3467
Celebrity 4-Door Sedan	3469

SUPER 88	CODE
Holiday Sedan	3539
Celebrity 4-Door Sedan	3569

STARFIRE	CODE
Coupe	3657
Convertible	3667

98	CODE
4-Door Town Sedan	3819
Luxury Sedan	3829
Holiday Sports Sedan	3839
Holiday Sports Coupe	3847
Convertible	3867
Custom Sports Coupe	3947

THE BODY NUMBER is the production serial number of the body. The prefix letter denotes the plant in which the body was assembled.

OLDSMOBILE DIV. GENERAL MOTORS CORP.
LANSING MICHIGAN

STYLE 64-3539   BODY BA 001555
TRIM 345   PAINT AC
ACC.00

BODY BY FISHER

LAST SIX DIGITS: Represent the Basic Production Number

ASSEMBLY PLANT	COD
Lansing	L
Blatimore	B
Fremont	B
Kansas City, Mo.	K
Atlanta	B
Kansas City, Kans.	B
Linden	B
South Gate	B
Arlington	B

THE PAINT CODE furnished the key to the paint colors used on the car. A two letter code indicates the bottom and top colors respectively.

COLOR	CODE
Ebony Black	A
Provincial White	C
Sheffield Mist	D
Jade Mist	E
Wedgewood Mist	F
Bermuda Blue	H
Fern Mist	
Tahitian Yellow	H
Regal Mist	L
Pacific Mist	F
Aqua Mist	C

Cashmere Beige	R
Saddle Mist	S
Holiday Red	V
Midnight Mist	W

THE TRIM CODE furnishes the key to interior color and material.

MODEL	TRIM	COLOR
98		
	360	Black
	370L	Black
	351	Silver
	341	Silver
	381	Silver
	342	Med. Green
	362	Med. Green
	352	Dk. Green
	372L	Dk. Green
	382	Dk. Green
	353	Blue
	343	Blue
	363	Blue
	373L	Blue
	383	Blue
	365	Maroon
	385	Maroon
	375L	Red
	356	Aqua
	346	Aqua
	366	Aqua
	386	Aqua
	377L	White
	358	Saddle
	348	Saddle
	368	Saddle

Starfire

330	Black
332L	Dk. Green
333L	Blue
335L	Red
337L	White
338L	Saddle

Super 88

321	Silver
311	Silver
322	Med. Green
312	Med. Green
323	Dk. Green
313	Dk. Green
326	Aqua
316	Aqua
328	Saddle
318	Saddle

Dynamic 88

970	Black
990v	Black
981	Silver
971	Silver
982	Med. Green
972	Med. Green
982v	Med. Green
312	Med. Green
992v	Med. Green
983	Blue
993v	Blue
973	Blue
313	Blue

995v	Maroon
315v	Maroon
994v	Red
986	Aqua
976	Aqua
996v	Aqua
316	Aqua
997v	White
317v	White
988	Saddle
978	Saddle
998v	Saddle
318v	Saddle

Jetstar 88

970v	Black
990v	Black
981	Siver
971	Siver
982	Med. Green
972	Med. Green
992v	Dk.Green
983	Blue
993v	Blue
973	Blue
995v	Maroon
994v	Red
986	Aqua
976	Aqua
997v	White
988	Saddle
978	Saddle
998v	Saddle

Jetstar I

302v	Silver
303v	Blue
305v	Red
307v	White
308v	Saddle

F85 Deluxe

960v	Black
940	Black
920	Black
930v	Black
922	Med. Green
962v	Dk. Green
942	Dk. Green
963v	Blue
943	Blue
923	Blue
935v	Maroon
965v	Red
945v	Red
926	Aqua
967v	White
947v	White
968v	Saddle
948	Saddle
928	Saddle
938v	Saddle

F85

901	Black
911	Black
902	Silver
912v	Silver
903	Blue
913v	Blue
915v	Maroon
906	Aqua
918v	Saddle

ENGINE NUMBER

The engine unit number is stamped with a production sequence number on the left cylinder head (394 engine), which follows the engine identification code letter. 330 engine is stamped on the right cylinder head. V-6 engine is stamped on right front cylinder head, year (K, 1964), compression (H, standard, J, low), and production date code.

ENGINE IDENTIFICATION

Series	Prefix Code Letter	Suffix Code Letter	Carb. Type	Comp. Ratio	CID	HP
3000 & 3100 (V-6)	KH	—	1-Bbl.	9.0:1	225	155
3000 & 3100 (V-6) Export Low Comp.	KJ	—	1-Bbl.	8.3:1	225	-
3000 & 3100 (V-8) Not Avail. in 3300 Series	T		2-Bbl.	8.75:1	330	230
3000 & 3100 (V-8) Export Low Comp.	T	E	2-Bbl.	8.3:1	330	-
3200 (V-8) Opt. in 3000-3100-3300	T	G	4-Bbl.	10.25:1	330	290
3200 (V-8) Export Low Comp.	T	H	4-Bbl.	8.3:1	330	-
3300 (V-8) Not Avail. in 3000 3100-3200	T	K	2-Bbl.	10.25:1	330	245
3300 (V-8) Export Low Comp.	T	E	2-Bbl.	8.3:1	330	-
3400 (V-8)	H		2-Bbl.	10.25:1	394	280
3400 (V-8) Export Low Comp.	H	E	2-Bbl.	8.3:1	394	-
3400 (V-8) Domestic Low Comp.	H	L	2-Bbl.	8.75:1	394	260
3400-3500-3800	J		4-Bbl.	10.25:1	394	330
3500-3800 Export Low Comp.	J	E	4-Bbl.	8.3:1	394	-
3457-3600-3900	J	S	4-Bbl.	10.5:1	394	345
442 Option			4-Bbl.		330	310

VEHICLE IDENTIFICATION NUMBER

Commonly referred to as the VIN NUMBER, this series of numbers and letters is stamped on a plate attached to the left front door hinge pillar.

```
OLDSMOBILE
333275M600819
```

EXAMPLE

3	3327	5	M	600819
Mfg.	Series Type	Year	Assembly Plant	Production Number

FIRST DIGIT: Manufacturer's Symbol (3) = Oldsmobile

SECOND THRU FIFTH DIGITS: Identity the series & Body Style. Refer to the Fisher Body Plate, same as style Number.

SIXTH DIGIT: Model Year 5 - 1965

SEVENTH DIGIT: Indicates the Assembly Plant.

Assembly Plant	Code
Lansing, Mich.	M
Arlington, Tex.	R
Atlanta, Ga.	D
Baltimore, Md.	B
South Gate, Calif.	C
Fremont, Calif.	Z
Kansas City, Mo.	K
Kansas City, Kans.	X
Linden, N.J.	E

LAST SIX DIGITS: Sequential Production Number.

FISHER BODY NUMBER PLATE

Complete identification of each body is provided by a plate on the cowl under the hood.

The Style Number follows the year code, it is a Combination of the Series and Body Style. Third digit indicates engine type, odd number is a 6-cyl, even number is an 8-cyl.

F 85 STANDARD	Code
V-6 Club Coupe	33327
V-6 StWgn 2-Seat	33335
V-6 4-Door Sedan	33369
V-8 Club Coupe	33427
V-8 StWgn 2-Seat	33435
V-8 Vista-Cruiser SW 2 Seat	33455
V-8 Vista-Cruiser SW 3 Seat	33465
V-8 4-Door Sedan	33469
V-6 Sports Coupe	33527

F 85 DELUXE	Code
V-6 StWgn 2-Seat	33535
V-6 4-Door Sedan	33569
V-8 StWgn 2-Seat	33635
V-8 4-Door Sedan	33669
V-8 Vista-Cruiser 2-Seat	33855
V-8 Vista-Cruiser 3-Seat	33865

CUTLASS	Code
V-8 Sports Coupe	33827
V-8 Holiday Coupe	33837
V-8 Convertible	33867

JETSTAR 88	Code
Holiday Coupe	35237
Holiday Sedan	35239
Convertible	35267
Celebrity Sedan	35269

JETSTAR I	Code
Sports Coupe	35457

DYNAMIC 88	Code
Holiday Coupe	35637
Holiday Sedan	35639

	Code
Convertible	35667
Celebrity Sedan	35669

DELTA 88	Code
Holiday Coupe	35837
Holiday Sedan	35839
Celebrity Sedan	35869

STARFIRE	Code
Coupe	36657
Convertible	36667

98	Code
Holiday Sports Coupe	38437
Holiday Sports Sedan	38439
Convertible	38467
Town Sedan	38469
Luxury Sedan	38669

THE BODY NUMBER is the production serial number of the body. The prefix letter denotes to the plant in which the body was assembled.

Assembly Plants	Code
F 85 Bodies	
Lansing	LA
Baltimore	BA
Fremont	BF
Kansas City	KC

All 88 and 98 Bodies	Code
Lansing	L
Doraville	B.
Kansas City	B
Linden	B
South Gate	B
Arlington	B

All 98 series will be assembled a Lansing

THE PAINT CODE furnished the key to the paint colors used on the car. A two letter code indicates the bottom and top colors respectively.

COLOR	Code
Ebony Black	A
Nocturne Mist	B
Provincial White	C
Lucerne Mist	D
Royal Mist	E
Laurel Mist	H
Forest Mist	J
Ocean Mist	K
Turquoise Mist	L
Burgundy Mist	N
Target Red	R
Mohave Mist	T
Almond Beige	V
Sterling Mist	W
Saffron Yellow	Y

OLDSMOBILE DIV. GENERAL MOTORS CORP.
LANSING MICHIGAN

STYLE 65-33327   **BODY** BA 001555
TRIM 345   **PAINT** AC
ACC. 00

BODY BY FISHER

THE TRIM CODE furnishes the key to the trim color and material.

MODEL	TRIM	COLOR
98		
	360	Black
	370L	Black
	351	Silver
	361	Silver
	381	Silver
	272L	Dk. Green
	382	Green
	362	Green
	352	Green
	353	Blue
	363	Blue
	373L	Blue
	383	Blue
	384	Fawn
	354	Fawn
	364	Fawn
	365	Red
	375L	Red
	356	Turquoise
	366	Turquoise
	386	Turquoise
	377L	White
Starfire		
	340L	Black
	341L	Silver
	343L	Blue
	344L	Fawn
	345L	Red
	347L	White

MODEL	TRIM	COLOR
Delta 88		
	320	Black
	321V	Silver
	322	Green
	323	Blue
	324	Fawn
	325	Red
	326	Turquoise
Dynamic 88		
Jetstar 88		
	971V	Silver
	981	Silver
	992V	Dk. Green
	972	Green
	973	Blue
	983	Blue
	993V	Blue
	974	Fawn
	984	Fawn
	994V	Fawn
	975V	Red
	985V	Red
	995V	Red
	976	Turquoise
	986	Turquoise
	977V	White
Jetstar I		
	310V	Black
	313V	Blue
	314V	Fawn
	315V	Red
	317V	White

MODEL	TRIM	COLOR
Vista Cruiser		
	960	Black
	962	Green
	963	Blue
	913	Blue
	964V	Fawn
	914	Fawn
	965V	Red
	915	Red
	967V	White
F85 Cutlas		
	300V	Black
	940V	Black
	950V	Black
	951V	Silver
	924V	Fawn
	302	Green
	303	Blue
	943V	Blue
	953V	Blue
	304	Fawn
	944V	Fawn
	954V	Fawn
	945V	Red
	955V	Red
	307V	White
	947V	White
	957V	White

MODEL	TRIM	COLOR
F85 Deluxe		
	300V	Black
	940V	Black
	942V	Dk. Green
	302	Green

ENGINE NUMBER

The engine unit number on V-6 stamped on the right cylinder head consists of two letters (L, 1966: plus H for standard or J for low comp.) and three number date code. V-8 engines are stamped with a production sequence code and a prefix letter to identify the engine

ENGINE IDENTIFICATION CHART

Series	Prefix Code Letter	Carb Type	Comp Ratio	CID	Suffix Code	HP
33300 & 33500 (F-85 V-6)	LH	1 bbl.	9.0:1	225	-	155
3300 & 33500 (F-85 V-6 Export Low Comp.)	LJ	1 bbl.	7.6:1	225	-	-
"33400, 33600 & 33800" (F-85 V-8)	T	2 bbl.	9.0:1	330	-	250
"33400, 33600 & 33800 (F-85" V-8 Export Low Comp.)	T	2 bbl.	8.3:1	330	E	-
"33827, 33837, 33867 & L-74" & L-76 Optional	T	4 bbl.	10.25:1	330	G	260
All F-85 Series with Low Comp. Export Option	T	4 bbl.	8.3:1	330	H	-
35200 (Jetstar 88 Std. V-8) (High Comp.)	U	2 bbl.	10.25:1	330	-	260
35200 (Jetstar 88 Low Comp. V-8) (Export Option)	U	2 bbl.	8.3:1	330	E	-
35200 (Jetstar 88 Std. V-8 (High Comp. L-74 or L-76 Option)	U	4 bbl.	10.25:1	330	G	315
35200 (Jetstar 88 Low Comp. V-8) (Export Low Comp. Option)	U	4 bbl.	8.3:1	330	H	-
35200 (Jetstar 88 Low Comp. Domestic) (L-65)	U	2 bbl.	9.0:1	330	L	250
35600 & 35800 (Std. Comp.) Dynamic 88 & Delta 88	M	2 bbl.	10.25:1	425	-	310
35600 & 35800 (Export Low Compression)	M	2 bbl.	8.3:1	425	E	-
35600 & 35800 Domestic Low Comp. Option (L-65)	M	2 bbl.	9.0:1	425	L	300
"35400, 36600, 38400, 38600" & L-74 Option Std. Comp.	N	4 bbl.	10.25:1	425	-	360
Export Low Compression	N	4 bbl.	8.3:1	425	E	-
"35400, 36600 & L-75 & L-77" Option	N	4 bbl.	10.5:1	425	S	370
442 Option	V	4 bbl.	10.25:1	400	-	345

VEHICLE IDENTIFICATION NUMBER

Commonly referred to as the VIN NUMBER, tjhis series of numbers and letters is stamped on a plate attached to the left front door hinge pillasr.

```
OLDSMOBILE
333276M600819
```

EXAMPLE

3	3327	6	M	600819
Mfg.	Series Type	Year	Assembly Plant	Production Number

FIRST DIGIT: Manufacturer's Symbol (3) = Oldsmobile

SECOND THRU FIFTH DIGITS: Identity the series & Body Style. Refer to the Fisher Body Plate, same as style Number.

SIXTH DIGIT: Model Year 6 - 1966

SEVENTH DIGIT: Indicates the Assmebly Plant.

ASSEMBLY PLANT | Code

	Code
Lansing, Mich.	M
Atlanta, Ga.	D
South Gate, Calif.	C
Fremont, Calif.	Z
Linden, N.J.	E
Kansas City, Kan.	X

LAST SIX DIGITS: Sequential Production Number.

FISHER BODY NUMBER PLATE

Complete identification of each body is provided by a plate on the cowl under the hood.

The Style Number follows the year code, is a Combination of the Series and Body Style. Third digit indicates engine type, odd number iis a 6-cyl, even number is an 8-cyl.

F 85 STANDARD	Code
V-6 Club Coupe	33307
V-6 StWgn 2-Seat	33335
V-6 4-Door Sedan	33369
V-8 Club Coupe	33407
V-8 St Wgn 2-Seat	33435
V-8 Vista Cruiser SW	
•2-Seat	33455
V-8 Vista Cruiser SW	
•3-Seat	33465
V-8 4-Door Sedan	33469

F 85 DELUXE	Code
V-6 Holiday Coupe	33517
V-6 StWgn 2-Seat	33535
V-6 Holiday Sedan	33539
V-6 4-Ddor Sedan	33569
V-8 Holiday Coupe	33617
V-8 StWgn 2-Seat	33635
V-8 Holiday Sedan	33639
V-8 4-Door Sedan	33669

CUTLASS	Code
V-8 Sports Coupe	33807
V-8 Holiday Coupe	33817
V-8 Holiday Sedan	33839
V-8 Convertible	33867
V-8 Celebrity Sedan	33869
V-8 Custom Vista Cruiser	
S.W. 2-Seat	33855
V-8 Custom Vista Cruiser	
S.W. 3-Seat	33865

JETSTAR 88	Code
Holiday Coupe	35237
Holiday Sedan	35239
Celebrity Sedan	35269

STARFIRE	Code
Coupe	35457

DYNAMIC 88	Code
Holiday Coupe	35637

Holiday Sedan	3563
Celebrity Sedan	3566
Convertible	3566

DELTA 88	Code
Holiday Coupe	3583
Holiday Sedan	3583
Convertible	3586
Celebrity Sedan	3586

98	Code
Holiday Coupe	3843
Holiday Sedan	3843
Convertible	3846
Town Sedan	3846
Luxury Sedan	3866

TORONADO	Code
Sport Coupe	3948
Sport Coupe Custom	3968

```
OLDSMOBILE DIV. GENERAL MOTORS CORP.
           LANSING MICHIGAN

STYLE 66-38469      BODY LA1
TRIM 054            PAINT TT


        BODY BY FISHER 0000000000
```

MODEL	TRIM	COLOR
	*15	Red
	346	Turquoise
	356	Turquoise
	*46	Turquoise
	*16	Turquoise
	917	White
	*17	White
	358	Bronze
	918	Bronze
	*18	Bronze
Jetstar 88		
Dynamic 88		
	320	Black
	*10	Black
	301	Silver
	*11	Green
	302	Green
	312	Green
	*42	Green
	303	Blue
	313	Blue
	323	Blue
	*43	Blue
	*13	Blue
	304	Fawn
	314	Fawn
	*44	Fawn
	305	Red
	325	Red
	*15	Red
	306	Turquoise
	316	Turquoise
	*46	Turquoise
	327	White
	*17	White
	328	Bronze
	*18	Bronze
Vista Cruiser		
	970	Black
	*10	Black
	973	Blue
	933	Blue
	*43	Blue
	*13	Blue
	974	Fawn
	934	Fawn
	*14	Fawn
	935	Red
	*15	Red
	976	Turquoise
	936	Turquoise
	*46	Turquoise
	*16	Turquoise
	978	Bronze
	*18	Bronze
Cutlass		
	900	Black
	980	Black
	80	Black
	960	Black
	990	Black
	*10	Black
	972	Green
	*42	Green
	973	Blue
	903	Blue
	983	Blue
	963	Blue

THE BODY NUMBER is the production serial nubmer of the body. The prefix letter denotes the plant in which the body was assembled.

Assembly Plants — Code

F 85 bodies
Lansing .... LAN
Fremont .... BF

All 88 and 98
Lansing .... LAN
Doraville .... BA
Kansas City .... BK
Linden .... BL
South Gate .... BC

All 98 series will be assembled at Lansing.

TRIM CODE furnishes the key to interior color and matieral.

MODEL	TRIM	COLOR
Toronado		
	50	Black
	10	Black
	*10	Black
	52	Green
	12	Green
	*42	Green
	*12	Green
	53	Blue
	13	Blue
	*43	Blue
	*13	Blue

MODEL	TRIM	COLOR
	54	Fawn
	14	Fawn
	*14	Fawn
	56	Turquoise
	16	Turquoise
	*16	Turquoise
	46	Turquoise
	58	Bronze
	18	Bronze
	*18	Bronze
	59	Plum
	19	Plum
	*49	Plum
	*19	Plum
	390	Black
	370	Black
	380	Black
	*40	Black
	*10	Black
	391	Silver
	361	Silver
	*41	Silver
	362	Green
	*42	Green
	393	Blue
	363	Blue
	373	Blue
	383	Blue
	*43	Blue
	*13	Blue
	394	Fawn
	364	Fawn
	374	Fawn
	*44	Fawn
	395	Red
	385	Red
	*45	Red
	*15	Red
	396	Turquoise

MODEL	TRIM	COLOR
	366	Turquoise
	376	Turquoise
	*46	Turquoise
	387	White
	*17	White
	378	Bronze
	*48	Bronze
Starfire		
	330	Black
	30	Black
	*10	Black
	333	Blue
	*13	Blue
	335	Red
	*15	Red
	337	White
	*17	White
	38	Bronze
	*18	Bronze
Delta 88		
	350	Black
	910	Black
	*10	Black
	341	Silver
	*41	Silver
	342	Green
	352	Green
	*42	Green
	343	Blue
	353	Blue
	913	Blue
	*43	Blue
	*13	Blue
	344	Fawn
	354	Fawn
	*14	Fawn
	*44	Fawn
	355	Red
	915	Red

MODEL	TRIM	COLOR
	993	Blue
	*43	Blue
	*13	Blue
	974	Fawn
	*14	Fawn
	944	Fawn
	*44	Fawn
	905	Red
	985	Red
	965	Red
	995	Red
	*15	Red
	976	Turquoise
	906	Turquoise
	946	Turquoise
	*46	Turquoise
	987	White
	967	White
	*17	White
	978	Bronze
	908	Bronze
	88	Bronze
	*18	Bronze
	*48	Bronze
F 85 Deluxe		
	950	Black
	990	Black
	*10	Black
	952	Green
	*12	Green
	953	Blue
	993	Blue
	*13	Blue
	944	Fawn
	954	Fawn
	*44	Fawn
	*14	Fawn
	955	Red
	995	Red
	*15	Red
	946	Turquoise
	*46	Turquoise
F85 Std.		
	923	Blue
	933	Blue
	*43	Blue
	*13	Blue
	924	Fawn
	934	Fawn
	*44	Fawn
	*14	Fawn
	935	Red
	*15	Red
	936	Turquoise
	*16	Turquoise

Color	Code
Tropic Turquoise	L
Autumn Bronze	M
Burgundy Mist	N
Target Red	R
Sierra Mist	T
Almond Beige	V
Silver Mist	W

ENGINE NUMBER

The L-6 engine has a DATE-CODE stamped on the right side of the engine block, directly to the rear of the distributor.

The date code consists of a letter, four digits and two letters. The first letter stands for source identification. The first two digits show the month and the second two digits show the day the unit was built. The last two letters show transmission or option usage.

F ... Source Code (Flint)
T ... Source Code (Tonawanda)

07.. July - Month
12.. Day of Month

V-8 engines have the engine unit number stamped on a machined pad at the front of the right cylinder head.

V-8 engines used in F-85 Series (33400, 33600 and 33800) have a "W" prefix and the starting unit number is 001001.

Engines in the Jetstar 88 Series (35200) have a "X" prefix and also have a starting number of 001001.

Engines in "442" series have a "V" prefix and have a starting unit number of 100001.

Engines used in all other series (35400 through 38600) have an "M" prefix for 2-bbl. and "N" prefix for 4-bbl. carburetor equipped engines with a starting unit number of 500001.

THE PAINT CODE furnishes the key to exterior colors.

COLOR	Code
Ebony Black	A
Nocturne Mist	B
Provincial White	C
Lucerne Mist	D
Royal Mist	E
Laurel Mist	H
Forest Mist	J
Ocean Mist	K

ENGINE IDENTIFICATION

SERIES	PREFIX CODE	SUFFIX CODE	COMP. RATIO	CARBURETOR	CID	HP
33300 & 33500 L-6 (man. T.)	F or T	VA, VB, VD, VC	8.5:1	1-bbl.	250	155
Export	F or T	VJ	7.25:1	1-bbl.	250	-
L-6 (Auto. Y.)	F or T	VE, VF, VG	8.5:1	1-bbl.	250	155
Export	F or T	VK	7.25:1	1-bbl.	250	-
33400, 33600 &33800	W	-	9.0:1	2-bbl.	330	250
Export	W	E	8.3:1	2-bbl.	330	
33807, 33867 Stand. & Optional 33839, 33869	W	G	10.25:1	4-bbl.	330	320
Export (all F 85 L.C.)	W	H	8.3:1	4-bbl.	330	-
L.C. Domestic	W	L	9.0:1	4-bbl.	330	310
442	V	-	10.25:1	4-bbl	400	350
442 Optional	V	-	10.25:1	3 / 2-bbl.	400	360
35200	X	-	10.25:1	2-bbl.	330	260
Export	X	E	8.3:1	2-bbl	330	-
35200 Optional	X	G	10.25:1	4-bbl.	330	320
Export	X	H	8.3:1	4-bbl.	330	-
35200 L.C. Domestic	X	L	9.0:1	2-bbl.	330	310
35600 &35800	M	-	10.25:1	2-bbl.	425	310
Export	M	E	8.3:1	2-bbl.	425	-
L.C. Domestic	M	L	9.0:1	2-bbl.	425	300
35400, 38400 & 38600	N	-	10.25:1	4-bbl.	425	365
Export	N	E	8.3:1	4-bbl.	425	
35400	N	S	10.5:1	4-bbl.	425	375
3900	N	T	10.5:1	4-bbl.	425	385

VEHICLE IDENTIFICATION NUMBER

Commonly referred to as the VIN NUMBER, this series of numbers and letters is stamped on a plate attached to the left front door hinge pillar.

OLDSMOBILE
333077M100001

EXAMPLE

3	3307	6	M	100001
Mfg.	Series	Year	Assembly Plant	Production Number

FIRST DIGIT: Manufacturer's Symbol (3) = Oldsmobile

SECOND THRU FIFTH DIGITS: Identity the series & Body Style. Refer to the Fisher Body Plate, same as style Number.

SIXTH DIGIT: Model Year
7 - 1967

SEVENTH DIGIT: Indicates the assembly plant.

ASSEMBLY PLANT   Code

Lansing, Mich.	M
Atlanta, Ga.	D
South Gate, Calif.	C
Fremont, Calif.	Z
Linden, N.J.	E
Kansas City, Kan.	X

LAST SIX DIGITS: Sequential Production Number.

FISHER BODY NUMBER PLATE

Complete identification of each body is provided by a plate on the cowl under the hood.

The Style Number follows the year code, is a Combination of the Series and Body Style. First digit 3, indicates Oldsmobile Division. Third digit indicates engine type, odd number iis a 6-cyl, even number is an 8-cyl.

F 85 STANDARD	Code
6 Cyl.	
Club Coupe	3307
Station Wagon	3335
Town Sedan	3369
V-8	
Club Coupe	3407
Station Wagon	3435
Vista Cruiser 3-Seat Std	3465
Town Sedan	3469

CUTLASS	Code
6 Cyl.	
Holiday Coupe	3517
Station Wagon	3535
HolidaySedan	3539
Convertible	3567
Town Sedan	3569
V-8	
Holiday Coupe	3617
Station Wagon	3635
Holiday Sedan	3639
Convertible	3667
Town Sedan	3669

CUTLASS SUPREME	Code
Sports Coupe	*3807
Holiday Coupe	*3817
Holiday Sedan	3839
Vista Cruiser 2-Seat Cust.	3855
Vista Cruiser 3-Seat Cust.	3865
Convertible	*3867
Town Sedan	3869

DELMONT 88 "330"	Code
Holiday Sedan	5239
Town Sedan	5269
Holiday Coupe	5287

DELTA 88 CUSTOM	Code
Holiday Sedan	5439
Holiday Coupe	5487

DELMONT 88 "425"	Code

Holiday Sedan	5639
Convertible	5667
Town Sedan	5669
Holiday Coupe	5687

DELTA 88	Code
Holiday Sedan	5839
Convertible	5867
Town Sedan	5869
Holiday Coupe	5887

"98"	Code
Holiday Sedan	8439
Holiday Coupe	8457
Convertible	8467
Town Sedan	8469
Luxury Sedan	8669

TORONADO	Code
Toronado Std	9487
Toronado Deluxe	9687

*Available with 4-4-2 Option

OLDSMOBILE DIV. GENERAL MOTORS CORP. LAN

STYLE 67 33307   **BODY** 001555
TRIM 345 A   **PAINT** AC
ACC.00

BODY BY FISHER

THE TRIM CODE provides the key to identifing the interior material and color.

MODEL	TRIM	COLOR
Toronado		
	090	Black
	080	Black
	060	Black
	*60	Black
	*40	Black
	*10	Black
	083	Blue
	063	Blue
	*43	Blue
	094	Champagne
	084	Champagne
	064	Champagne
	*34	Champagne
	*14	Champagne
	095	Garnet
	085	Garnet
	*35	Garnet
	*15	Garnet
	086	Turquoise
	066	Turquoise
	*46	Turquoise
	089	Dubonnet
	*49	Dubonnet
98		
	020	Black
	030	Black
	040	Black
	050	Black
	*10	Black
	*40	Black
	*80	Black
	011	Pewter
	021	Pewter
	041	Pewter
	*41	Pewter
	013	Blue
	023	Blue
	033	Blue
	043	Blue
	*13	Blue
	*43	Blue
	014	Gold
	045	Gold
	*44	Gold
	*45	Gold
	025	Burgundy
	035	Burgundy
	045	Burgundy
	*15	Burgundy
	*45	Burgundy
	016	Turquoise
	026	Turquoise
	046	Turquoise
	*46	Turquoise
	038	Yellow
	*18	Yellow
Delta Custom		
	330	Black
	340	Black
	380	Black
	*30	Black
	*40	Black
	341	Pewter

THE BODY NUMBER is the production serial number of the body. The prefix letter denotes the plant in which the body was assembled.

Assembly Plants	Code
F 85 bodies	
Lansing	LAN
Fremont	BF
Framingham	FRA
All 88 and 98 bodies	
Lansing	LAN
Doraville	BA
Kansas City	BK
Linden	BL
South Gate	BC

All 98 series will be assembled at Lansing.

All 94 and 96 Series will be built at Lansing, Michigan and have code letters "EUC" for Body Unit Number(s) prefix.

THE PAINT CODE gives key to exterior color.

COLOR	Code
Ebony Black	A
Provincial White	C
Crystal Blue	D
Midnight Blue	E
Gold	G
Aspen Green	H
Aquamarine	K
Tahoe Turquoise	L
Burgundy Mist	N
Pewter	P
Spanish Red	R
Champagne	S
Cameo Ivory	T
Antique Pewter	V
Saffron	Y

Toronado

Ebony Black	A
Turquoise Frost	B
Provincial White	C
Crystal Blue	D
Bimini Blue	F
Gold	G
Aspen Green	H
Emerald Green	J
Tahoe Turquoise	L
Pewter	P
Dubonnet	U
Antique Pewter	V
Sauterne	W
Garnet Red	X
Florentine Gold	Z

Toronado/442 stripes

Black	A
White	C
Dark Blue	E
Dark Green	J
Dk. Turquoise	L
Maroon	N
Red	R
Beige	T
Dark Taupe	V
Dark Yellow	Y

1967 OLDSMOBILE

MODEL	TRIM	COLOR
	381	Pewter
	*41	Pewter
	382	Green
	*42	Green
	343	Blue
	383	Blue
	*33	Blue
	*43	Blue
	344	Champagne
	384	Champagne
	*14	Champagne
	*34	Champagne
	345	Burgundy
	*35	Burgundy
	386	Turquoise
	*16	Turquoise
Delta 88		
	350	Black
	360	Black
	370	Black
	*10	Black
	*40	Black
	351	Pewter
	361	Pewter
	*41	Pewter
	352	Green
	362	Green
	*42	Green
	353	Blue
	363	Blue
	373	Blue
	*13	Blue
	*43	Blue
	354	Champagne
	364	Champagne
	374	Champagne
	*14	Champagne
	365	Red
	375	Red
	*15	Red
	356	Turquoise
	366	Turquoise
	*46	Turquoise
	378	Yellow
	*18	Yellow
Delmont 88	300	Black
	310	Black
	320	Black
	*10	Black
	*40	Black
	311	Pewter
	*41	Pewter
	302	Green
	*42	Green
	303	Blue
	313	Blue
	323	Blue
	*13	Blue
	*43	Blue
	304	Champagne
	314	Champagne
	324	Champagne
	*14	Champagne
	325	Red
	*15	Red
	305	Burgundy
	315	Burgundy
	*45	Burgundy
	306	Turquoise
	316	Turquoise

MODEL	TRIM	COLOR
	*46	Turquoise
	328	Yellow
	*18	Yellow
Vista Cruiser		
	910	Black
	990	Black
	*10	Black
	*40	Black
	913	Blue
	993	Blue
	*13	Blue
	914	Champagne
	994	Champagne
	*14	Champagne
	995	Burgundy
	*15	Burgundy
	995	Turquoise
	*46	Turquoise
Station Wagon		
	913	Blue
	933	Blue
	*13	Blue
	914	Champagne
	934	Champagne
	*14	Champagne
	935	Red
	*15	Red
Cutlass Supreme		
	390	Black
	920	Black
	940	Black
	950	Black
	970	Black
	980	Black
	*10	Black
	*30	Black
	*40	Black
	393	Blue
	923	Blue
	943	Blue
	953	Blue
	973	Blue
	*33	Blue
	*43	Blue
	934	Champagne
	944	Champagne
	984	Champagne
	*14	Champagne
	954	Gold
	*44	Gold
	395	Red
	975	Red
	*35	Red
	945	Burgundy
	955	Burgundy
	*15	Burgundy
	936	Turquoise
	946	Turquoise
	956	Turquoise
	*16	Turquoise
	*46	Turquoise
	978	Yellow
	*38	Yellow
Cutlass		
	920	Black
	930	Black
	*10	Black
	*40	Black

MODEL	TRIM	COLOR
	923	Blue
	933	Blue
	*13	Blue
	*43	Blue
	934	Champagne
	*14	Champagne
	935	Red
	965	Red
	*15	Red
	936	Turquoise
	*16	Turquoise
	938	Yellow
	*18	Yellow
F85	910	Black
	*10	Black
	903	Blue
	*43	Blue
	914	Champagne
	*14	Champagne
	905	Red
	915	Red
	*15	Red
	*45	Red

ENGINE NUMBER

The L-6 Engine has a DATE-CODE stamped on the right side of the engine block, directly to the rear of the distributor. The date code consists of a letter, four digits and two letters. The first letter stands for source identification. The first two digits show the month and the second two digits show the day the unit was built. The last two letters show transmission or option.

V-8 engines have the engine unit number stamped on a machined pad at the front of the right cylinder head. All 94 and 96 Series have the 425 cu. in. 4 bbl. carburetor equipped engine with the letter "T" suffix and letter "R" prefix.

ENGINE IDENTIFICATION

Series	Prefix Code Letter	Suffix Code Letter	Carb. Type	Comp. Ratio	CID	HP
33300 & 33500 (F-85 L-6)						
With: Manual Transmission	F	VA	1 bbl.	8.5:1	250	155
Manual Transmission	F	VB	1 bbl.	8.5:1	250	155
Manual Transmission	F	VD	1 bbl.	8.5:1	250	155
Manual Transmission	F	VC	1 bbl.	8.5:1	250	155
Manual Transmission Export	F	VJ	1 bbl.	7.25:1	250	-
Jetaway	F	VE	1 bbl.	8.5:1	250	155
Jetaway	F	VF	1 bbl.	8.5:1	250	155
Jetaway	F	VH	1 bbl.	8.5:1	250	155
Jetaway Export	F	VJ	1 bbl.	7.25:1	250	-
Jetaway	F	VG	1 bbl.	8.5:1		
33400-33600 & 33855 & 65						
Low Compression	W	—	2 bbl.	10.25:1	330	260
33400-33600 & 33855 & 65						
Export Low Comp.	W	E	2 bbl.	9.0:1	330	250
33800 Exc. 55 & 65 (Opt. 33400 33600 & 33855 & 65) H.C.	W	G	4 bbl.	10.25:1	330	320
"33400, 33600 & 33800 (V-8)" (Low Comp. Export Option)	W	H	4 bbl.	8.3:1	330	-
4-4-2 (400 cu. in.)	V	G	4 bbl.	10.50:1	400	350
4-4-2 (400 cu. in.)	V	—	2 bbl.	10.50:1	400	300
442 Option			3 / 2 bbl.	10.50:1	400	360
35200 (High Compression)	X	—	2 bbl.	10.25:1	330	260
35200 (High compression)	X	G	4 bbl.	10.25:1	330	320
35200 (Low Comp. Export Option)	X	E	2 bbl.	8.3:1	330	-
5600 and 5800 (High Comp.)	P	—	2 bbl.	10.25:1	425	310
5600 and 5800 (Low Comp.)	P	L	2 bbl.	9.0:1	425	300
5600 and 5800 (Low Comp. Export Option)	P	E	2 bbl.	8.3:1	425	-
High Compression	R	—	4 bbl.	10.25:1	425	365
Delta 88 Custom	R	S	4 bbl.	10.50:1	425	375
Low Comp. Export Option	R	E	4 bbl.	8.3:1	425	-
Toronado	R	T	4 bbl.	10.50:1	425	385

VEHICLE IDENTIFICATION NUMBER

Commonly referred to as the VIN NUMBER, this series of numbers and letters is stamped on a plate riveted to top of instrument panel visible through windshied.

```
OLDSMOBILE
333778M100001
```

EXAMPLE

3	3377	8	M	100001
Mfg.	Series	Year	Assembly Plant	Production Number

FIRST DIGIT: Manufacturer's Symbol (3) = Oldsmobile

SECOND THRU FIFTH DIGITS: Identity the series & Body Style. Refer to the Fisher Body Plate, same as style Number.

SIXTH DIGIT: Model Year 8 - 1968

SEVENTH DIGIT: Indicates the Assembly plant.

ASSEMBLY PLANT	Code
Lansing, Mich.	M
Fremont, Calif.	Z
Framingham, Mass.	G
Kansas City, Kans.	X
Linden, N.J.	E
South Gate, Calif.	C
Oshawa, Canada	1

LAST SIX DIGITS: Sequential Production Number.

FISHER BODY NUMBER PLATE

Complete identification of each body is provided by a plate on the cowl under the hood.

The Style Number follows the year code, is a Combination of the Series and Body Style. First digit 3, indicates Oldsmobile Division. Third digit indicates engine type, odd number iis a 6-cyl, even number is an 8-cyl.

F 85	Code
Six Town Sedan	3169
Six Club Coupe	3177
V-8 Town Sedan	3269
V-8 Club Coupe	3277

CUTLASS SIX	Code
2-Seat Station Wagon	3535
Holiday Sedan	3539
Convertible	3567
Town Sedan	3569
Sports Coupe	3577
Holiday Coupe	3587

CUTLASS V-8	Code
2-Seat Station Wagon	3635
Holiday Sedan	3639
Convertible	3667
Town Sedan	3669
Sports Coupe	3677
Holiday Coupe	3687

```
OLDSMOBILE DIV. GENERAL MOTORS CORP.
              LAN

STYLE 68 33377      BODY 001555
TRIM 345 A          PAINT AC
ACC.00

         BODY BY FISHER
```

CUTLASS SUPREME	Code
V-8 Holiday Sedan	4239
V-8 Town Sedan	4269
V-8 Holiday Coupe	4287

4-4-2	Code
V-8 Convertible	4467
V-8 Sports Coupe	4477
V-8 Holiday Coupe	4487

VISTA CRUISER	Code
V-8 2-Seat	4855
V-8 3-Seat	4865

DELMONT 88	Code
Holiday Sedan	5439
Convertible	5467
Town Sedan	5469
Holiday Coupe	5487

DELTA 88	Code
Holiday Sedan	6439
Town Sedan	6469
Holiday Coupe	6487
Custom Holiday Sedan	6639
Custom Holiday Coupe	6687

98	Code
Holiday Sedan	8439
Holiday Coupe	8457
Convertible	8467
Town Sedan	8469
Luxury Sedan	8669

TORONADO	Code
Holiday Coupe	9487

MODEL	TRIM	COLOR
	15	Garnet
	939	Teal
	999	Teal
	19	Teal
	390	Black
	960	Black
	970	Black
	990	Black
	10	Black
	30	Black
	394	Gold
	964	Gold
	974	Gold
	994	Gold
	14	Gold
	34	Gold
	44	Gold
	393	Blue
	963	Blue
	973	Blue
	993	Blue
	43	Blue
	977	Parchment
	37	Parchment
	395	Garnet
	965	Garnet
	975	Garnet
	995	Garnet
	15	Garnet
	35	Garnet
	399	Teal
	969	Teal
	999	Teal
	19	Teal
	396	Turquoise
	966	Turquoise
	46	Turquoise
Cutlass Supreme		
	390	Black
	960	Black
	970	Black
	980	Black
	10	Black
	30	Black
	394	Gold
	964	Gold
	974	Gold
	34	Gold
	44	Gold
	393	Blue
	963	Blue
	973	Blue
	33	Blue
	43	Blue
	977	Parchment
	987	Parchment
	17	Parchment
	37	Parchment
	395	Garnet
	965	Garnet
	975	Garnet
	15	Garnet
	35	Garnet
	399	Teal
	969	Teal
	989	Teal
	19	Teal
	396	Turquoise
	966	Turquoise
	46	Turquoise

THE BODY NUMBER is the production serial number of the body. The prefix letter denotes the plant in which the body was assembled.

Assembly Plants	Code
F 85 bodies	
Lansing	LAN
Fremont	BF
Framingham	FRA
Oshawa, Ontario, Can	OS
All 88 and 98 bodies	
Lansing	LAN
Atlanta	ATL
Kansas City	BK
Linden	BL
South Gate	BC

All 98 series will be assembled at Lansing.

All 94 and 96 Series will be built at Lansing, Michigan and have code letters "EUC" for Body Unit Number(s) prefix.

LAST SIX DIGITS: Represent the Basic Production Numbers.

THE TRIM CODE is the key to interior color and material.

MODEL	TRIM	COLOR
F85		
	910	Black
	10	Black
	914	Gold
	14	Gold
	903	Blue
	43	Blue
	917	White
	17	White
	916	Turquoise
	16	Turquoise
Cutlas		
	934	Gold
	944	Gold
	14	Gold
	34	Gold
	923	Blue
	943	Blue
	953	Blue
	13	Blue
	33	Blue
	43	Blue

MODEL	TRIM	COLOR
	947	White
	957	Parchment
	17	Parchment
	37	Parchment
	945	Garnet
	35	Garnet
	939	Teal
	949	Teal
	19	Teal
	39	Teal
	926	Turquoise
	46	Turquoise
Vista Cruiser StWgn Custom		
	930	Black
	990	Black
	10	Black
	934	Gold
	994	Gold
	14	Gold
	993	Blue
	13	Blue
	43	Blue
	995	Garnet

1968 OLDSMOBILE

MODEL	TRIM	COLOR
442		
	940	Black
	950	Black
	10	Black
	30	Black
	944	Gold
	34	Gold
	943	Blue
	953	Blue
	13	Blue
	33	Blue
	947	Parchment
	957	Parchment
	17	Parchment
	37	Parchment
	945	Garnet
	35	Garnet
	949	Teal
	39	Teal
Delmont		
	300	Black
	320	Black
	10	Black
	50	Black
	304	Gold
	324	Gold
	14	Gold
	344	Gold
	354	Gold
	64	Gold
	302	Blue
	312	Blue
	323	Blue
	343	Blue
	353	Blue
	13	Blue
	43	Blue
	53	Blue
	327	Parchment
	357	Parchment
	17	Parchment
	57	Parchment
	305	Garnet
	315	Garnet
	325	Garnet
	15	Garnet
	45	Garnet
	309	Teal
	329	Teal
	349	Teal
	359	Teal
	19	Teal
	49	Teal
	69	Teal
	306	Turquoise
	316	Turquoise
	346	Turquoise
	356	Turquoise
	46	Turquoise
	66	Turquoise
Delta		
	340	Black
	350	Black
	10	Black
	344	Gold
	354	Gold
	44	Gold
	343	Blue
	353	Blue
	13	Blue

MODEL	TRIM	COLOR
	357	Parchment
	17	Parchment
	349	Teal
	359	Teal
	49	Teal
	346	Turquoise
	356	Turquoise
	46	Turquoise
Delta Custom		
	360	Black
	370	Black
	10	Black
	362	Gold
	42	Gold
	363	Blue
	43	Blue
	367	Parchment
	377	Parchment
	17	Parchment
	37	Parchment
	369	Teal
	49	Teal
	366	Turquoise
	46	Turquoise
98		
	900	Black
	010	Black
	020	Black
	030	Black
	040	Black
	050	Black
	070	Black
	10	Black
	40	Black
	80	Black
	012	Gold
	022	Gold
	032	Gold
	042	Gold
	12	Gold
	42	Gold
	024	Gold
	044	Gold
	44	Gold
	013	Blue
	023	Blue
	033	Blue
	043	Blue
	13	Blue
	43	Blue
	027	Parchment
	037	Parchment
	17	Parchment
	019	Teal
	029	Teal
	049	Teal
	49	Teal
	016	Turquoise
	026	Turquoise
	046	Turquoise
	46	Turquoise
Toronado		
	030	Black
	060	Black
	10	Black
	30	Black
	080	Black
	090	Black
	60	Black

MODEL	TRIM	COLOR
	70	Black
	062	Gold
	082	Gold
	42	Gold
	62	Gold
	067	Parchment
	087	Parchment
	17	Parchment
	57	Parchment
	085	Garnet
	55	Garnet
	069	Teal
	089	Teal
	49	Teal
	69	Teal
	086	Turquoise
	66	Turquoise
	068	Buckskin
	088	Buckskin
	098	Buckskin
	18	Buckskin
	38	Buckskin
	58	Buckskin
	78	Buckskin

ENGINE NUMBER

The L-6 Engine has a DATE-CODE stamped on the right side of the engine block, directly to the rear of the distributor. The date code consists of, four digits and two letters. The last two letters identify the engine.

V-8 engines have the engine unit number stamped on a machined pad at the front of the right cylinder head.

THE PAINT CODE is the key to the exterior color.

COLOR	Code
Ebony Black	A
Twillight Teal	B
Provincial White	C
Sapphire Blue	D
Nocturne Blue	E
Teal Frost	F
Willow Gold	G
Ocean Turquoise	K
Teal Blue	L
Cinnamon Bronze	M
Burgundy	N
Silver Green	P
Scarlet	R
Jade Gold	S
Ivory	T
Juneau Gray	V
Silver Beige	W
Buckskin	X
Saffron	Y
Peruvian Silver	Z

ENGINE SPECIFICATIONS

Engines	H.P.	C.I.D.	Comp	Carb
400-hp Rocket 455 V-8*	400	455	10.25:1	4-bbl.
390-hp Hurst / Olds	390	455	10.50:1	4-bbl.
375-hp Rocket 455 V-8	375	455	10.25:1	4-bbl.
365-hp Rocket 455 V-8	365	455	10.25:1	4-bbl.
320-hp Rocket 455 V-8	320	455	10.25:1	2-bbl.
310-hp Rocket 455 V-8	310	455	9.00:1	2-bbl.
360-hp Rocket 400 V-8*	360	400	10.50:1	4-bbl.
350-hp Rocket 400 V-8	350	400	10.50:1	4-bbl.
325-hp Rocket 400 V-8	325	400	10.50:1	4-bbl.
290-hp Rocket 400 V-8	290	400	9.00:1	2-bbl.
310-hp Rocket 350 V-8	310	350	10.25:1	4-bbl.
250-hp Rocket 350 V-8	250	350	9.00:1	2-bbl.
155-hp Action-Line 6	155	250	8.50:1	1-bbl.

* With Force-Air Induction System.

Engine Code	Auto	Man
250 6-cyl.	VF,VE	VB,VA
350 2-bbl	QA,QB	QI
Delmont 88	TB,TD,TN	TL
4-bbl.	QN,QP	QV
400 2-bbl.	QL	
4-bbl.	QR,QS,QT	QW,QU
455 2-bbl. L.C.	UC,UD	UJ
H.C.	UA,UB	
4-bbl.	UN,UO	
Toronado	US,UT,UV,UW	

VEHICLE IDENTIFICATION NUMBER

Commonly referred to as the VIN NUMBER, this series of numbers and letters is stamped on a plate riveted to top of instrument panel visible through windshied.

```
OLDSMOBILE
333179M100001
```

EXAMPLE

3	3317	9	M	100001
Mfg.	Series	Year	Assembly Plant	Production Number

FIRST DIGIT: Manufacturer's Symbol (3) = Oldsmobile

SECOND THRU FIFTH DIGITS: Identity the series & Body Style. Refer to the Fisher Body Plate, same as style Number.

SIXTH DIGIT: Model Year
9 - 1969

SEVENTH DIGIT: Indicates the Assembly plant.

ASSEMBLY PLANT	Code
South Gate, California	C
Atlanta, Georgia	D
Linden, New Jersey	E
Lansing, Michigan	M
Kansas City, Kansas	X
Fremont, California	Z
Oshawa, Canada	1

LAST SIX DIGITS: Sequential Production Number.

FISHER BODY NUMBER PLATE

Complete identification of each body is provided by a plate on the cowl under the hood.

The Style Number follows the year code, is a Combination of the Series and Body Style. First digit 3, indicates Oldsmobile Division. Third digit indicates engine type, odd number iis a 6-cyl, even number is an 8-cyl.

F 85 6-CYL.	Code
Sports Coupe	3177

F 85 V-8	Code
Sports Coupe	3277

CUTLASS 6-CYL.	Code
Station Wagon	3535
Holiday Sedan	3539
Convertible	3567
Town Sedan	3569
Sports Coupe	3577
Holiday Coupe	3587

CUTLASS V-8	Code
Station Wagon	3635
Holiday Sedan	3639
Convertible	3667
Town Sedan	3669
Sports Coupe	3677
Holiday Coupe	3687

```
OLDSMOBILE DIV. GENERAL MOTORS CORP.
              LAN

STYLE 69 33317      BODY 001555
TRIM 345 A          PAINT AC
ACC.00

          BODY BY FISHER
```

CUTLASS SUPREME	Code
Holiday Sedan	4239
Town Sedan	4269
Holiday Coupe	4287

4-4-2	Code
Convertible	4467
Sports Coupe	4477
Holiday Coupe	4487

VISTA CRUISER	Code
2-Seat	4855
3-Seat	4865

DELTA 88	Code
Holiday Coupe	5437
Holiday Sedan	5439
Convertible	5467
Town Sedan	5469

DELTA 88 CUSTOM	Code
Holiday Coupe	6437
Holiday Sedan	6439
Town Sedan	6469

DELTA 88 ROYALE	Code
Holiday Coupe	6647

"98"	Code
Holiday Sedan	8439
Holiday Coupe	8457
Convertible	8467
Town Sedan	8469
Luxury Sedan	8639
Luxury Sedan	8669

TORONADO	Code
Deluxe Coupe	9487

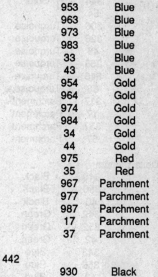

MODEL	TRIM	COLOR
	12	Green
	953	Blue
	963	Blue
	973	Blue
	983	Blue
	33	Blue
	43	Blue
	954	Gold
	964	Gold
	974	Gold
	984	Gold
	34	Gold
	44	Gold
	975	Red
	35	Red
	967	Parchment
	977	Parchment
	987	Parchment
	17	Parchment
	37	Parchment
442		
	930	Black
	940	Black
	10	Black
	30	Black
	942	Green
	12	Green
	933	Blue
	943	Blue
	333	Blue
	13	Blue
	33	Blue
	43	Blue
	334	Gold
	934	Gold
	944	Gold
	14	Gold
	34	Gold
	44	Gold
	935	Red
	35	Red
	937	Parchment
	947	Parchment
	17	Parchment
	37	Parchment
Delta		
	300	Black
	310	Black
	10	Black
	350	Black
	60	Black
	302	Green
	312	Green
	12	Green
	342	Green
	352	Green
	62	Green
	303	Blue
	313	Blue
	323	Blue
	43	Blue
	13	Blue
	353	Blue
	53	Blue
	304	Gold
	314	Gold
	324	Gold
	14	Gold
	44	Gold
	354	Gold

THE BODY NUMBER is the production serial number of the body. The prefix letter denotes the plant in which the body was assembled.

Assembly Plants — **Code**

F 85 bodies
Lansing...................LAN
Fremont .... BF
Framingham .... FRA
Oshawa, Ontario, Can.............OS

All 88 and 98 bodies
Lansing .... LAN
Atlanta .... ATL
Kansas City .... BK
Linden .... BL
South Gate .... BC

All 98 series will be assembled at Lansing.

All 94 and 96 Series will be built at Lansing, Michigan and have code letters "EUC" for Body Unit Number(s) prefix.

LAST SIX DIGITS: Represent the Basic Production Numbers.

THE TRIM CODE is the key to Interior Colors.

MODEL	TRIM	COLOR
F85		
	900	Black
	10	Black
	902	Green
	12	Green
	903	Blue
	43	Blue
	904	Gold
	14	Gold
	907	Parchment
	17	Parchment
		Parchment
		Parchment
Cutlass		
	910	Black
	930	Black
	940	Black
	942	Black
	10	Black
	12	Black
	30	Black
	912	Green
	942	Green
	12	Green
	333	Blue
	923	Blue
	933	Blue
	943	Blue
	13	Blue
	33	Blue
	43	Blue
	334	Gold
	924	Gold
	934	Gold
	944	Gold

MODEL	TRIM	COLOR
	14	Gold
	34	Gold
	44	Gold
	935	Red
	35	Red
	937	Parchment
	947	Parchment
	17	Parchment
	37	Parchment
Custom-Vista Cruiser StWgn		
	910	Black
	990	Black
	10	Black
	912	Green
	992	Green
	12	Green
	913	Blue
	993	Blue
	13	Blue
	914	Gold
	994	Gold
	14	Gold
	915	Red
	995	Red
	15	Red
Cutlass Supreme		
	950	Black
	960	Black
	970	Black
	980	Black
	10	Black
	30	Black
	40	Black
	952	Green
	962	Green
	982	Green

MODEL	TRIM	COLOR	MODEL	TRIM	COLOR
	344	Gold		043	Blue
	54			053	Blue
	306	Turquoise		13	Blue
	326	Turquoise		43	Blue
	46	Turquoise		63	Blue
	356	Turquoise		014	Gold
	346	Turquoise		024	Gold
	66	Turquoise		034	Gold
	317	Parchment		044	Gold
	17	Parchment		054	Gold
	357	Parchment		14	Gold
	57	Parchment		44	Gold
				64	Gold
Delta Custom				018	Sandlewood
	340	Black		028	Sandlewood
	350	Black		048	Sandlewood
	40	Black		058	Sandlewood
	342	Green		48	Sandlewood
	352	Green		68	Sandlewood
	42	Green	**Toronado**		
	343	Blue		060	Black
	353	Blue		10	Black
	13	Blue		080	Black
	344	Gold		090	Black
	354	Gold		60	Black
	14	Gold		70	Black
	346	Turquoise		082	Green
	356	Turquoise		62	Green
	46	Turquoise		083	Blue
	357	Parchment		63	Blue
	17	Parchment		064	Gold
Delta Royale				084	Gold
	360	Black		14	Gold
	370	Black		54	Gold
	30	Black		067	Parchment
	40	Black		087	Parchment
	362	Green		17	Parchment
	42	Green		57	Parchment
	363	Blue		77	Parchment
	43	Blue			
	364	Gold			
	374	Gold			
	34	Gold			
	44	Gold			
	367	Parchment			
	377	Parchment			
	17	Parchment			
	37	Parchment			
98					
	030	Black			
	070	Black			
	380	Black			
	390	Black			
	020	Black			
	040	Black			
	050	Black			
	10	Black			
	40	Black			
	60	Black			
	012	Green			
	022	Green			
	032	Green			
	042	Green			
	052	Green			
	12	Green			
	42	Green			
	62	Green			
	013	Blue			
	023	Blue			
	033	Blue			

Convertible Top

White	1
Black	2
Blue	3
Gold	6

Vinyl Roof Color

Black	2
Blue	3
Antique Parchment	5
Sable	8
Green	9
Burgundy	7

THE PAINT CODE gives the key to the Exterior Color.

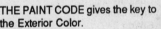

COLOR	Code
Ebony Black	10
Saffron	40
Cameo White	50
Trophy Blue	51
Crimson	52
Nassau Blue	53
Tahitian Turquoise	55
Glade Green	57
Meadow Green	59
Sable	61
Topaz	65
Burgundy Mist	67
Platinum	69
Aztec Gold	75
Autumn Gold	*77
Powder Blue	*80
Flamingo Silver	*81
Covert Beige	*82
Deauville Gray	*83
Chestnut Bronze	*85
Amethyst	**01
Caribbean Turquoise	**02
Nugget Gold	**03

*Exclusive Toronado Colors
** Special Order Toronado Colors

ENGINE NUMBER

The L-6 Engine has a DATE-CODE stamped on the right side of the engine block, directly to the rear of the distributor. The date code consists of, four digits and two letters. The last two letters identify the engine.

V-8 engines have the engine unit number stamped on a machined pad at the front of the right cylinder head.

ENGINES

Engines	400-HP Rocket 455 V-8 H.C.	390-HP Rocket 455 V-8 H.C.	375-HP Rocket 455V-8 H.C.	365-HP Rocket 455 V-8 H.C.	310-HP Rocket 455 V-8 (Reg.-Fuel)	360-HP Rocket 400 V-8 (Force-Air)	350-HP Rocket H.C. 400 V-8 H.C.
Displacement (Cu. In.)	455	455	455	455	455	400	400
Compression Ratio	10.25:1	10.25:1	10.25:1	10.25:1	9.0:1	10.50:1	10.50:1
Carburetor (No.) Barrels	4	4	4	4	2	44	4

Engines	325-HP Rocket 400 V-8 H.C.	325-HP Rocket 350 V-8 H.C. (Force-Air)	310-HP Rocket 350 V-8 H.C.	250-HP Rocket 350 V-8 (Reg.-Fuel)	155-HP Action-Line 6 (Reg.-Fuel)
Displacement (Cu. In.)	400	350	350	350	250
Compression Ratio	10.50:1	10.50:1	10.25:1	9.0:1	8.50:1
Carburetor (No.) Barrels	4	4	4	2	1

ENGINE CODES

250 Man	VA,VB,VD,VJ
250 Auto	VE,VF,VK,VL
350 2-bbl Auto	QA,QB,QJ,TB, TD,TC
350 2-bbl Man	QI,TL
350 4-bbl Auto	QN,QP
350 4-bbl Man	QV
350 H.C.	QX
400 4-bbl Auto	QR,QS
400 4-bbl Man	QW
400 H.C. Auto	QT
400 H.C. Man	QU
455 2-bbl Auto	UC,UD
455 2-bbl Man	UJ
455 4-bbl Auto	UN,UO,UW, UL,US,UT,UV

VEHICLE IDENTIFICATION NUMBER

```
PONTIAC
360 P1555
```

Commonly referred to as the VIN NUMBER, this series of numbers and letters is stamped on the plate attached to the left front door hinge pillar.

EXAMPLE

3	60	P	1555
Series	Year	Assy Production	Number
		Plant	

First Digit: Identifies the series, 1 for 2100 (CATALINA), 3 for 2300 (VENTURA), 4 for 2400 (STAR CHIEF), 7 for 2700 (BONNEVILLE SAFARI), 8 for 2800 (BONNEVILLE).

Second and Third Digit indicates the model year, 60 for 1960.

Fourth Digit, a letter, identifies the assembly plant.

ASSEMBLY PLANT	Code
Pontiac, Mich.	P
South Gate, CA.	S
Linden	L
Wilmington, Del.	W
Kansas City, Kans.	K
Doraville	D
Arlington, Tx.	A
Euclid	E

FINAL DIGITS: Represent the production sequence number.

FISHER BODY NUMBER PLATE

Complete identification of each body is provided by a plate riveted to the cowl at the left of center under the hood.

THE STYLE NUMBER is a combination of the year, division, series, and body style. In the number plate illustrated, 60 represents the model year 1960; the first digit 2 indicates Pontiac Motor Division; the second digit 3 indicates Series 2300; 37 indicates the 2-Door Sport Coupe body style.

CATALINA - 2100	Code
Coupe-Convertible	2167
Sport Coupe - 2 Door	2137
Sport Sedan - 2 Door	
- 4 Window	2111
Sedan - 4 Door, 6 Window	2119
Vista - 4 Door, 4 Window	2139
Safari Station Wagon - 4 Door 2 Seat; 2nd. Seat Folding	2135
Safari Station Wagon - 4 Door 3 Seat; 2nd. Seat Folding	2145

VENTURA - 2300	Code
Sport Coupe	2337
Vista - 4 Door, 4 Window	2339

STAR CHIEF - 2400	Code
Sport Sedan	2411
Sedan - 4 Door, 6 Window	2419
Vista - 4 Door, 4 Window	2439

BONNEVILLE - 2700/2800	Code
Safari Station Wagon - 4 Door 2 Seat; 2nd Seat Folding	2735
Coupe - Convertible	2867
Sport Coupe - 2 Door	2837
Vista - 4 Door, 4 Window	2839

THE BODY NUMBER is the production serial number of the body. The prefix letter denotes the plant in which the body was built.

ASSEMBLY PLANT	Code
Pontiac, Mich.	PO
South Gate, CA.	BC
Linden	BL
Wilmington, Del.	BW
Kansas City, Kans.	BK
Doraville	BA
Arlington, Tx.	BT
Euclid	EP

THE TRIM NUMBER furnishes the key to trim color and material for each model SERIES.

Model	Color	Code

Cloth and Imitation Leather

2111-19 201
Dark and Medium Grey Polaris Cloth with Ivory Imitation Leather

2111-19 202
Dark and Medium Blue Polaris Cloth with .... Light Blue Imitation Leather

2111-19 203
Dark and Medium Yellow Green Polaris Cloth with Light Yellow Green Imitation Leather.

2111-19 204
Dark and Medium Fawn Polaris Clothe with Light Fawn Imitation Leather

2137-39 206
Dark and Medium Blue Parade Cloth with Ivory Imitation Leather

2137-39 207
Dark and Medium Blue Parade Cloth with .... Light Blue Imitation Leather

2137-39 208
Dark and Medium Yellow Green Parade Cloth with Light Yellow Green Imitation Leather

2137-39 209
Dark and Medium Fawn Parade Cloth with ... Light Fawn Imitation Leather

2137-39 210
Dark and Medium Maroon Parade Cloth with Ivory Imitation Leather

2419 224
Dark Grey Pomeroy Cloth with Metallic Silver and Medium Grey Imitation Leather

2419 225
Dark Blue Pomeroy Cloth with Light Blue .. and Metallic Medium Blue Imitation Leather

2419 226
Dark Yellow Green Pomeroy Cloth with .... Light Yellow Green and Metallic Medium Yellow Green Imitation Leather

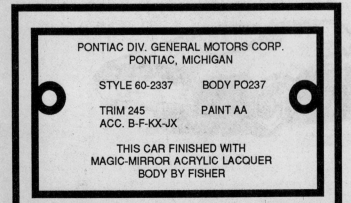

```
PONTIAC DIV. GENERAL MOTORS CORP.
PONTIAC, MICHIGAN

STYLE 60-2337      BODY PO237

TRIM 245           PAINT AA
ACC. B-F-KX-JX

THIS CAR FINISHED WITH
MAGIC-MIRROR ACRYLIC LACQUER
BODY BY FISHER
```

2419 227
Dark Fawn Pomeroy Cloth with
Light Fawn and Metallic Medium
Fawn Imitation Leather

2411-39 229
Tri-Tone Grey Palermo Cloth with
Metallic Silver and Medium Grey
Imitation Leather

2411-39 230
Tri-Tone Blue Palermo Cloth with
Light Blue and Metallic Medium
Blue Imitation Leather

2411-39 231
Tri-Tone Yellow Green Palermo
Cloth with Light Yellow Green and
Metallic Medium Yellow Green
Imitation Leather

2411-39 232
Tri-Tone Fawn Palermo Cloth
with Light....... Fawn and Metallic
Medium Fawn Imitation Leather

2837-39 245
Tri-Tone Grey Penngate Cloth
and Medium Grey Penobscot
Cloth with Metallic Silver Imitation
Leather

2837-39 246
Tri-Tone Blue Penngate Cloth
and Dark Blue Penobscot Cloth
with Light Blue Imitation Leather

2837-39 247
Tri-Tone Yellow Green Penngate
Cloth and Dark Yellow Green
Penobscot Cloth with Light Yellow
Green Imitation Leather

2837-39 248
Tri-Tone Fawn Penngate Cloth
and Dark Fawn Penobscot Cloth
with Light Fawn Imitation Leather

2837-39 249
Tri-Tone Maroon Penngate Cloth
and Dark Maroon Penobscot
Cloth with Metallic Light Maroon
Imitation Leather.

2167 212
Ivory and Metallic Medium Grey

2167 213
Light Blue and Metallic Medium
Blue

2167 214
Light Yellow Green and Metallic
Medium Yellow Green

2167 215
Light Fawn and Metallic Medium
Fawn

2167 216
Ivory and Metallic Maroon

2135-45 218
Ivory and Metallic Medium Grey

2135-45 219
Light Blue and Metallic Medium
Blue

2135-45 220
Light Yellow Green and Metallic
Medium Yellow Green

2135-45 221
Light Fawn and Metallic Medium
Fawn

2135-45 221
Light Fawn and Metallic Medium
fawn

2135-45 222
Ivory and Metallic Medium
Maroon

2411-39 237
Light Blue with Metallic Dark Blue
and Medium Blue

2411-39 238
Light Yellow Green with Metallic
Dark Yellow Green and Medium
Yellow Green

2411-39 239
Light Fawn with Metallic Dark
Fawn and Medium Fawn

2337-39 241
Ivory with Metallic Dark Grey and
Medium Grey

2337-39 242
Light Fawn with Metallic Dark
Fawn and Medium Fawn

2337-39 243
Ivory with Metallic Dark Maroon
and Medium Maroon

2837-39 252
Light Blue with Metallic Dark Blue
and Medium Blue

2837-39 253
Light Yellow Green with Metallic
Dark Yellow Green and Medium
Yellow Green

2837-39 254
Light Fawn with Metallic Dark
Fawn and Medium Fawn

2837-39 255
Metallic Light Maroon with
Metallic Dark Maroon and
Medium Maroon

2735 260
Light Blue with Metallic dark blue
and Medium Blue

2735 261
Light Yellow Green with Metallic
Dark Yellow Green and Medium
Yellow Green

2735 261
Light Yellow Green with Metallic
Dar Yellow Green and Medium
Yellow Green

2735 262
Light Fawn with Metallic Dark
Fawn and Medium Fawn

2111-19 299
Metallic Dark Grey with Metallic
Medium Grey and Ivory

Genuine Leather and Imitation Leather

2867 266
Metallic Dark Blue and Medium
Blue Genuine Leather with Light
Blue Imitation Leather

2867 267
Metallic Dark Fawn and Medium
Fawn Genuine Leather with Light
Fawn Imitation Leather

2867 268
Metallic Dark Maroon and
Medium Maroon Genuine Leather
with Metallic Light Maroon
Imitation Leather

2867 276
Metallic Dark Blue and Medium
Blue Genuine Leather with
Metallic Light Maroon Imitation
Leather

2867 277
Metallic Dark Fawn and Medium
Fawn Genuine Leather with Light
Fawn Imitation Leather

2867 278
Metallic Dark Maroon and
Medium Maroon Genuine Leather
with Metallic Light Maroon
Imitation Leather

THE PAINT CODE furnishes the key to the paint colors used on the car. A two letter code indicates the bottom and top colors respectively. Two-Tone color combinations are made-up of the first letter of each basic color. Example: CA - means the lower body is Shelltone Ivory and the upper body is Regent Black.

Color	Code
Regent Black	AA
Black Pearl	BB
Shelltone Ivory	CC
Richmond Grey	DD
Newport Blue	FF
Skymist Blue	HH
Fairway Green	JJ
Berkshire Green	KK
Coronado Red	LL
Stardust Yellow	MM
Mahogany	NN
Shoreline Gold	PP
Palomino Beige	RR
Sierra Copper	SS
Caribe Turquoise	TT

ENGINE NUMBER

Along with the VIN number the engine block is stamped with an engine production code. The code has a letter and number that identify the engine. The production code is stamped on the right front of the engine block directly below the VIN number. The production code for 1960 is:

CODE	MODEL	TRANS	CID	HP	COMP	CARB
A2	21-23-24-S	M	389	215	8.6:1	2-BBL
B2	27-28-S	M	389	281	8.6:1	4-BBL
C2	ALL-O	M	389	318	10.75:1	3/2-BBL
P4	ALL-O	M	389	-	10.25:1	4-BBL
F4	ALL(425A)-O	M	389	330	10.75:1	4-BBL
M4	ALL(425A)-O	M	389	345	10.75:1	3/2-BBL
R2	21-23-24-E	M	389	-	7.8:1	2-BBL
G4	21-23-24-O	M	389	-	8.6:1	2-BBL
H4	27-28-O	M	389	-	8.6:1	4-BBL
A1	21-23-24-S	A	389	283	10.25:1	2-BBL
B1	21-23-24-27-28	A	389	303	10.25:1	4-BBL
E3	ALL(425E)-O	A	389	215	8.6:1	2-BBL
C1	ALL-O	A	389	318	10.75:1	3/2-BBL
P1	ALL-O	A	389	-	10.25:1	4-BBL
F1	ALL(425A)-O	A	389	330	10.75:1	4-BBL
M1	ALL(425A)-O	A	389	345	10.75:1	3/2-BBL
J1	21-23-24-E	A	389	-	8.6:1	2-BBL
K1	21-23-24-E	A	389	-	7.8:1	2-BBL
L1	27-28-E	A	389	-	8.6:1	4-BBL
N1	27-28-E	A	389	-	7.8:1	4-BBL

NOTE: S - STANDARD, O - OPTIONAL, E - EXPORT.

1961 PONTIAC

VEHICLE IDENTIFICATION NUMBER

PONTIAC
361P1555

Commonly referred to as the VIN NUMBER, this series of numbers and letters is stamped on the plate attached to the left front door hinge pillar.

EXAMPLE

3	61	P	1555
Series	Year	Assy Plant	Production Number

First Digit: Identifies the series, 1 for 2100 (TEMPEST), 3 for 2300 (CATALINA), 5 for 2500 (VENTURA), 6 for 2600 (STAR CHIEF), 7 for 2700 (BONNEVILLE SAFARI), 8 for 2800 (BONNEVILLE).

Second and Third Digit indicates the model year, 60 for 1960.

Fourth Digit, a letter, identifies the assembly plant.

ASSEMBLY PLANT	Code
Pontiac, Mich.	P
South Gate, CA.	S
Linden	L
Wilmington, Del.	W
Kansas City, Kans.	K
Doraville	D
Arlington, Tx.	A
Euclid	E

FINAL DIGITS: Represent the production sequence number.

FISHER BODY NUMBER PLATE

Complete identification of each body is provided by a plate riveted to the cowl at the left of center under the hood.

THE STYLE NUMBER is a combination of the year, division, series, and body style. In the number plate illustrated, 61 represents the model year 1961; the first digit 2 indicates Pontiac Motor Division; the second digit 3 indicates Series 2300; 37 indicates the 2-Door Sport Coupe body style.

TEMPEST - 2100	Code
Sport Coupe - 2 Door Std	2127
Sport Coupe - 2 Door Cust	2117
Sedan - 4 Door, 6 Window	2119
2 Seat; 2nd. Seat Folding	2135

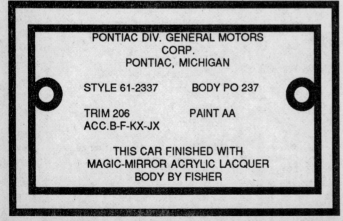

PONTIAC DIV. GENERAL MOTORS CORP.
PONTIAC, MICHIGAN

STYLE 61-2337   BODY PO 237

TRIM 206   PAINT AA
ACC.B-F-KX-JX

THIS CAR FINISHED WITH
MAGIC-MIRROR ACRYLIC LACQUER
BODY BY FISHER

CATALINA - 2300	Code
Coupe-Convertible	2367
Sport Coupe - 2 Door	2337
Sport Sedan - 2 Door - 4 Window	2311
Sedan - 4 Door, 6 Window	2369
Vista - 4 Door, 4 Window	2339
Safari Station Wagon - 4 Door 2 Seat; 2nd. Seat Folding	2335
Safari Station Wagon - 4 Door 3 Seat; 2nd. Seat Folding	2345

VENTURA - 2500	Code
Sport Coupe	2537
Vista - 4 Door, 4 Window	2539

STAR CHIEF - 2600	Code
Sedan - 4 Door, 6 Window	2669
Vista - 4 Door, 4 Window	2639

BONNEVILLE - 2700/2800	Code
Safari Station Wagon - 4 Door 2 Seat; 2nd Seat Folding	2735
Coupe - Convertible	2867
Sport Coupe - 2 Door	2837
Vista - 4 Door, 4 Window	2839

THE BODY NUMBER is the production serial number of the body. The prefix letter denotes the plant in which the body was built.

ASSEMBLY PLANT	Code
Pontiac, Mich.	PO
South Gate, CA.	BC
Linden	BL
Wilmington, Del.	BW
Kansas City, Kans.	BK
Doraville	BA
Arlington, Tx.	BT
Euclid	EP

THE TRIM NUMBER furnishes the key to trim color and material for each model SERIES.

Model	Color	Code
Cloth and Imitation Leather		
2119	Mediium Blue Potomac Cloth with Metallic Dark Blue Imitation Leather	262
2119	Medium Green Potomac Cloth with Metallic Dark Green Imitation Leather	263
2119	Medium Fawn Potomac Cloth with Metallic Dark Fawn Imitation Leather	264
2119	Medium Maroon Potomac Cloth with Metallic Dark Maroon Imitation Leather	265
2311-69	Medium Grey Parana Cloth with Metallic Dark Grey, Metallic Medium Grey, and Ivory Imitation Leather	201

2311-69 202
Medium Blue Parana Cloth with
Metallic Dark Blue, Metallic Me-
dium Blue, and Light Blue
Imitation Leather

2311-69 203
Medium Green Parana Cloth with
Metallic Dark Green, Metallic
Medium Green, and Light Green
Imitation Leather

2311-69 204
Medium Fawn Parana Cloth with
Metallic Dark Fawn, Metallic Medium Fawn, and Light Fawn Imitation Leather

2337-39 206
Medium Grey Picardy Cloth with
Metallic Dark Grey, Metallic Me-
dium Grey, and Ivory Imitation
Leather

2337-39 207
Medium Blue Picardy Cloth with
Metallic Dark Blue, Metallic Me-
dium Blue, and Light Blue
Imitation Leather

2337-39 208
Medium Green Picardy Cloth with
Metallic Dark Green, Metallic Medium Green, and Light Green Imitation Leather

2337-39 209
Medium Fawn Picardy Cloth with
Metallic Dark Fawn, Metallic Medium Fawn, and Light Fawn Imitation Leather

2337-39 210
Medium Maroon Picardy Cloth
with Metallic Dark Maroon,
Metallic Medium Maroon, and
Ivory Imitation Leather

2669-39 229
Medium and Dark Grey Paragon
Cloth with Metallic Medium Grey,
and Ivory Imitation Leather

2669-39 230
Medium and Dark Blue Paragon
Cloth with Metallic Medium Blue,
and Pale Blue Imitation Leather

2669-39 213
Medium and Dark Green Paragon
Cloth with Metallic Medium
Green, and Pale Green Imitation
Leather

2837-39 243
Dark Grey Provencal Cloth with
Dark Grey Pennwyl Cloth, and
Metallic Silver Imitation Leather

2837-39 244
Dark Blue Provencal Cloth with
Dark Blue Pennwyl Cloth, and
Plae Blue Imitation Leather

2837-39 245
Dark Green Provencal Cloth with
Dark Green Pennwyl Cloth, and
Pale Green Imitation Leather

2837-39 246
Dark Fawn Provencal Cloth with
Dark Fawn Pennwyl Cloth, and
Light Fawn Imitation Leather

2837 247
Dark Maroon Provencal Cloth
with Dark Maroon Pennwyl Cloth,
and Metallic Light Maroon
Imitation Leather

Imitation Leather

2119 271
Metallic Medium Grey with
Metallic Silver, and Metallic Dark
Grey

2119-35 272
Metallic Medium Blue with
Metallic Dark Blue, and Light Blue

2119-35 273
Metallic Medium Green with Me-
tallic Dark Green, and Light
Green

2119-35 274
Metallic Medium Fawn with Metal-
lic Dark Fawn, and Light Fawn

2119-35 275
Metallic Medium Maroon with Metallic Dark Maroon, and Ivory

2135 298
Metallic Grey Pattern with Metallic
Silver, and Metallic Dark Grey

2311-69 299
Metallic Medium Grey with
Metallic Dark Grey, and Ivory

2335-45 218
Metallic Medium Grey with
Metallic Dark Grey, and Ivory

2335-45 219
Metallic Medium Blue with
Metallic Dark Blue, and Light Blue

2335-45 220
Metallic Medium Green with Me-
tallic Dark Green, and Light
Green

2335-45 221
Metallic Medium Fawn with Metal-
lic Dark Fawn, and Light Fawn

2335-45 222
Metallic Medium Maroon with Metallic Dark Maroon, and Ivory

2367 212
Metallic Medium Grey with
Metallic Dark Grey, and Ivory

2367 213
Metallic Medium Blue with
Metallic Dark Blue, and Light Blue

2367 214
Metallic Medium Green with Me-
tallic Dark Green, and Light
Green

2367 215
Metallic Medium Fawn with Me-
tallic Dark Fawn, and Light Fawn

2367 216
Metallic Medium Maroon with Metallic Dark Maroon, and Ivory

2537-39 224
Metallic Dark Grey with Metallic
Medium Grey, and Ivory

2537-39 225
Metallic Dark Blue lwith Metallic
Medium Blue, and Light Blue

2537-39 226
Metallic Dark Green with Metallic
Medium Green, and Light Green

2537-39 227
Metallic Dark Fawn with Metallic
Medium Fawn, and Light Fawn

2537-39 228
Metallic Dark Maroon with
Metallic Medium Maroon, and
Ivory

2639-69 241
Metallic Dark Fawn with Metallic
Medium fawn, and Light Fawn

2639-69 239
Metallic Dark Blue with Metallic
Medium Blue, and Pale Blue

2639-69 240
Metallic Dark Green with Metallic
Mediium Green, and Pale Green

2639-69 242
Metallic Dark Maroon with
Metallic Medium Maroon, and
Ivory

2735 291
Metallic Dark Green with Metallic
Medium Green, and Pale Green

2735 292
Metallic Dark Fawn with Metallic
Medium Fawn, and Cream

2735 293
Metallic Dark maroon with
Metallic Medium Maroon, and
Metallic Light Maroon

2837-39 249
Metallic Dark Blue with Metallic
Medium Blue, and Pale Blue

2837-39 250
Metallic Dark Green with Metallic
Medium Green, and Pale Green

2837-39 251
Metallic Dark Fawn with Metallic
Medium Fawn, and Light Fawn

2837-39 252
Metallic Dark Maroon with
Metallic Medium Maroon, and
Metallic Light Maroon

Genuine Leather and Imitation Leather

2867 253-283
Metallic Silver and Ivory Genuine
Leather with Metallic Dark Blue
Imitation Leather

2867 254-284
Metallic Dark Green and Metallic
Mediium Green Genuine Leather
with Pale Green Imitation Leather

2867 255-285
Metallic Dark Fawn and Metallic
Medium Fawn Genuine Leather
with Cream Imitation Leather

2867 256-286
Metallic Dark Maroon and Metallic
Medium Maroon Genuine Leather
with Metallic Light Maroon
Imitation Leather.

THE PAINT CODE furnishes the
key to the paint colors used on the
car. A two letter code indicates the
bottom and top colors respectively.
Two-Tone color combinations are
made-up of the first letter of each
basic color. Example: CA - means
the lower body is Shelltone Ivory
and the upper body is Regent
Black.

Color	Code
Regent Black	AA
Shelltone Ivory	CC
Richmond Gray	DD
Bristol Blue	EE
Richelieu Blue	FF
Tradewind Blue	HH
Jadestone Green	JJ
Seacrest Green	KK
Coronado Re	LL
Bamboo Cream	MM
Cherrywood Bronze	NN
Rainier Turquoise	PP
Fernando Beige	RR
Dawnfire Mist	SS
Mayan Gold	TT

ENGINE NUMBER

Along with the VIN number the engine block is stamped with an engine production code. The code has a letter and number that identifiy the engine. The production code is stamped on the right front of the engine block directly below the VIN number. The production codes for 1961 are:

A1 389 cid/H/M 10.25:1 comp. 2BC Tri-powered long exhaust man. standard Catalina, Ventura

A2 S/M 389cid 8.6:1 comp. 2BC standard Catalina, Ventura

A2 Same exc. heavy transmission standard Star Chief

B1 389cid H/M 10.25.1 wmp 4BC special Catalilna, Ventura

A5 H/M 10.25.1 comp. 2BC standard Star Chief

B4 389cid S/M 8.6:1 comp. 4BC special Catalina, Ventura St Star Chief St Bonneville (27)

B4 Same exc. heavy transmission special Star Chief St Bonneville (28)

B5 389cid H/M 8.6:1 comp. 4BC special Star Chief standard Bonneville (27) standard Boneville (28) standard (HD)

C4 389cid /SM 10.75:1 comp. Tri-power Spl All

E3 389 H/M 8.6:1 comp. 2BC Economy Catalina, Ventura

E7 389 H/M 8.6:1 comp. 2BC Economy Star Chief, Bonneville (27 & 28)

F4 389 S/M 10.75.1 comp. 4BC long ex man. Tri-powered/all except Tempest

G4 389 S/M 806:1 comp. 2BC Spl Catalina/Std. police & taxi, Ventura and Star Chief

H4 389 S/M 8.6:1 comp. 2BC Spl Bonneville (27 & 28) St HD

M4 389 S/M 10.75:1 comp. Tri-powered carb. long ex. man Tri-powered/All except Tempest

P4 389 S/M 10..25:1 1BC Spl. Police, Catalina

S1 389 H/M 10.25-1 2BC Air Cond. Ventura, Catalina

S5 AC Star Chief same as S1

T5 389 H/M 10.25:1 Comp 1BC AC Star Chief, Bonneville (27 & 28)

T1 389 H/M 10.25:1 Comp 2BC AC Catalina Ventura

W3 389 H/M 8.6:1 Coomp 2BC AC Catalina Ventura

W7 389 H/M 8.6:1 Comp 2BC AC Star Chief Bonneville (27 & 28)

RC4 389 S/M 10.75:1 Comp Tri Powered Special all

RM4 Same as RC4 exc. long ex. man All

C0 389 H/M 10.25:1 Comop Tri-powered Spl. Catalina Ventura

I9 H/M Same as C0 Spl. 26, 27, 28, 2890

P0 389 H/m 10.25:1 4BC Long ex man spl. Police/23

F0 389 H/M 10.75:1 Commop 4BC long ex man tri-powered 23 & 25

M0 Same Tri-powered

U9 Same as F0 Tri 26, 27 & 28

V9 Same as Mo Tri. 26, 27 & 28

RC0 389 H/M 10.75:1 Tri-power long exhaust Spl 23, 25

RI9 Same as RC0, Spl. 26, 27, 28, 2890

RM0 Same as RC0, Tri. 23, 25

RV9 Same as RC0, Tri. 26, 27, 28

DS, ZS, XS, OS, 195 CID Tempest Man. T.

YS, AYS, 215 V-8 Tempest Man. T.

DA, ZA, XA, OA, 195 CID Tempest auto. T.

YA, AYA, 215 CID Tempest Auto. T.

TEMPEST ENGINES

CID	HP	CARB
195-4	110	1-BBL
195-4	120	1-BBL
195-4	130	1-BBL
195-4	140	1-BBL
195-4	155	4-BBL
215 V-8	155	2-BBL

PONTIAC ENGINES

389 V-8	215	2-BBL
389 V-8	230	2-BBL
389 V-8	267	2-BBL
389 V-8	283	2-BBL
389 V-8	235	4-BBL
389 V-8	303	4-BBL
389 V-8	333	4-BBL
389 V-8	318	3 / 2-BBL
389 V-8	348	3 / 2-BBL

VEHICLE IDENTIFICATION NUMBER

PONTIAC
362P1555

Commonly referred to as the VIN NUMBER, this series of numbers and letters is stamped on the plate attached to the left front door hinge pillar.

EXAMPLE

3	62	P	1555
Series	Year	Assy Plant	Production Number

FIRST DIDIT: identifies the series

1	21	Tempest
3	23	Catalina
6	26	Star Chief
7	27	Bonneville Safari
8	28	Bonneville
9	29	Grand Prix

SECOND AND THIRD DIGIT: indicates the model year 62 for 1962

FOURTH DIGIT: identifies the assembly plant.

ASSEMBLY PLANT   Code

Pontiac, Mich.	P
South Gate, CA	S
Linden	L
Wilmington, Del.	W
Kansas City, Kans.	K
Doraville	D
Arlington, Tx.	A

FINAL DIGITS: production sequence number

FISHER BODY NUMBER PLATE

PONTIAC DIV. GENERAL MOTORS CORP.
PONTIAC, MICHIGAN

STYLE 62-2337   BODY PO 237

TRIM 243   PAINT AA
ACC.B-F-KX-JX

THIS CAR FINISHED WITH
MAGIC-MIRROR ACRYLIC LACQUER
BODY BY FISHER

Complete identification of each body is provided by a plate riveted to the cowl at the left of center under the hood.

THE STYLE NUMBER is a combination of the year, division, series and body style. In the number plate illustrated, 62 represents the model year 1962; the first digit 2 indicates Pontiac Motor Division; the second digit 3 indicates Series 2300; 37 indicates the 2-Door Sport Coupe body style.

TEMPEST - 2100   Code

Sport Coupe - 2 Door Std	2127
Sport Coupe- 2 Door Cust	2117
Sedan - 4 Door, 6 Window	2119
2 Seat; 2nd. Seat Folding	2135
Convertible	2167

CATALINA - 2300   Code

Coupe-Convertible	2367
Sport Coupe - 2 Door	2347
Sport Sedan - 2 Door - 4 Window	2311
Sedan - 4 Door, 6 Window	2369
Vista - 4 Door, 4 Window	2339
Safari Station Wagon - 4 Door 2 Seat; 2nd. Seat Folding	2335
Safari Station Wagon - 4 Door 3 Seat; 2nd. Seat Folding	2345

STAR CHIEF - 2600   Code

Sedan - 4 Door, 6 Window	2669
Vista - 4 Door, 4 Window	2639

BONNEVILLE - 2700/2800 Code

Safari Station Wagon - 4 Door 2 Seat; 2nd Seat Folding	2735
Coupe - Convertible	2867
Sport Coupe - 2 Door	2847
Vista - 4 Door, 4 Window	2839

GRAND PRIX - 2900   Code

Sport Coupe - 2 Door	2947

THE BODY NUMBER is the production serial number of the body. The prefix letter denotes the plant in which the body was built.

ASSEMBLY PLANT   Code

Pontiac, Mich.	PO
South Gate, CA.	BC
Linden	BL

Wilmington, Del.	BW
Kansas City, Kans.	BK
Doraville	BA
Arlington, Tx.	BT
Euclid	EP

THE TRIM NUMBER furnishes the key to trim color and material for each model SERIES.

Model	Color	Code
6839-47 Medium and Dark Blue Cloth		256
2839-47 Medium and Dark Aqua		257
2839-47 Medium and Dark Green Cloth		258
2839-47 Medium and Dark Fawn Cloth		259
2839-47 Medium and Dark Fawn Cloth		260

1962 Cloth and Imitation Leather

2119-27 Medium and Dark Blue Pavilion Cloth with Metallic Medium Blue Imitation Leather		201
2119-27 Medium and Dark Fawn Pavilion Cloth with Metallic Medium Fawn Imitation Leather		204

THE PAINT CODE furnishes the key to the paint colors used on the car. A two letter code indicates the bottom and top colors respectively. Two-Tone color combinations are made-up of the first letter of each basic color. Example: CA - means the lower body is Cameo Ivory and the upper body is Starlight Black.

Color	Code
Starlight Black	AA
Cameo Ivoryvory	CC
Silvermist Grey	DD
Ensign Bluee	EE
Yorktown Blue	FF
Kimberley Blue	HH
Silverleaf Green	JJ
Aquamarine	PP
Seafoam Aqua	QQ
Caravan Gold	TT
Yuma Beige	RR
Burgundy	NN
Belmar Red	LL
Mandalay Red	VV
Bamboo Cream	MM

ENGINE NUMBER

Along with the VIN number the engine block is stamped with an engine production code. The production code is stamped on the right front of the engine block directly below the VIN number.

TEMPEST ENGINES

CID	HP	CARB
195-4	110	1-BBL
195-4	115	1-BBL
195-4	120	1-BBL
195-4	140	1-BBL
195-4	166	4-BBL
215 V-8	185	2-BBL

PONTIAC ENGINES

389 V-8	215	2-BBL
389 V-8	230	2-BBL
389 V-8	267	2-BBL
389 V-8	283	2-BBL
389 V-8	235	4-BBL
389 V-8	303	4-BBL
389 V-8	333	4-BBL
389 V-8	318	3 / 2-BBL
389 V-8	348	3 / 2-BBL
421 V-8	405	2 / 4-BBL*

* 11.0:1 Comp. Ratio

PONTIAC ENGINES

CODE	TRANS.	MODEL APPLICATION	OPTIONS
01A	S/M	Std.-23	(3)(6)(9)
01A*	S/M	Std.-26	(3)(6)(9)
02B	S/M	Std.-28 Spl. Equip.-26	(3)(7)
02B**	S/M	Std.-27 Spl. Equip.-23	(3)(7)
03B	S/M	Spl.Equip.23-26 Std.Pol.&Taxi	(3)(6)
04B	S/M	Std.-2840-2890;Spl.Equip.27-28	(3)(7)
05A	S/M		
06B	S/M	Spl. Police-Std.-29	(2)(7)
08B	S/M	425A-23-26-27-28-29	(1)(7)(9)
10B	S/M	Spl. Equip.-23-26-27-28-29	(1)(8)
11B	S/M	425A-23-26-27-28—29	(1)(8)(9)
15H	10 H/M	Std.-23	(2)(5)
16K	10 H/M	Spl. Equip.-23	(2)(7)
16KJ	10 H/M	Std.29	(2)(5)
17H	10 H/M	Air Cond.-23	(2)(5)
18K	10 H/M	Air Cond.-23-29	(2)(7)
20L	10 H/M	425E-23-29	(3)(6)
21L	10 H/M	425E-Air Cond.-23-29	(3)(6)
23H	A/T		
25J	10 H/M	425A-23-29	(1)(7)(9)
27J	10 H/M	Spl. Equip.-23-29	(1)(8)
28J	10 H/M	425-23-29	(1)(8)(9)
35M	315 H/M	Std.-26 Taxi & Police	(2)(5)
36P	315 H/M	Std.-27-28;Spl. Equip.-26	(2)(7)
37M	315 H/M	Air Cond.-26 Taxi & Police	(2)(5)
38P	315 H/M	Air Cond.-26-27-28	(2)(7)
39N	315 H/M	Spl. Police	(2)(7)
40R	315 H/M	425E—26-27-28 & Taxi	(3)(6)
41R	315 H/M	425E-Air Cond. 26-27-28& Taxi	(3)(6)
44M	A/T		
45P	A/T		
47N	315 H/M	425A-26-27-28	(1)(7)(9)
49N	315 H/M	Spl. Equip.-26-27-28	(1)(8)
50N	315 H/M	425-26-27-28	(1)(8)(9)

(1)	10.75:1 Compression Ratio (Cyl. Hd. & Valves)
(2)	10.25:1 Compression Ratio (Pistons)
(3)	8.6:1 Compression Ratio (Pistons)
(4)	7.81 Compression Ratio (Pistons)
(5)	2BBL. Carb.(1 1/2 Throttle Bore)
(6)	2BBL. Carb.(1 1/4 Throttle Bore)
(7)	4BBL. Carburetor
(8)	Tri-Power Carburetor
(9)	Long Exhaust Manifold

TEMPEST ENGINES

CODE	TRANS	APPLICATION	OPTIONS
83Z	S/M	195	
84Z	S/M	195	
89Z	S/M	195 - 4 Std.	(2)(4)
88Z	S/M	195 - 4 Export	(1)(4)
87Z	S/M	195 - 4 Spec. Order	(3)(5)
86Z	S/M	195 - 4 Spec. Order	(3)(4)
85Z	S/M	195 - 4 Taxi	(2)(4)
79Y	Auto	195 - 4 Std.	(2)(4)
78Y	Auto	195 - 4 Export	(1)(4)
77Y	Auto	195 - 4 Spec. Order	(3)(5)
76Y	Auto	195 - 4 Spec. Order	(3)(4)
97Y	Auto	215 V - 8 Spec. Order	(3)(5)
96Y	S/M	195	
91Z	S/M	195	

(1)	7.6:1 Comp. Ratio
(2)	8.6:1 Comp. Ratio
(3)	10.25:1 Comp. Ratio
(4)	1 - Barrel Carb.
(5)	4 - Barrel Carb.

1963 PONTIAC

VEHICLE IDENTIFICATION NUMBER

| PONTIAC |
| 363P1555 |

Commonly referred to as the VIN NUMBER, this series of numbers and letters is stamped on the plate attached to the left front door hinge pillar.

EXAMPLE

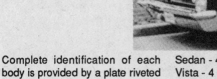

| 3 | 63 | P | 1555 |
| Series | Year | Assy Plant | Production Number |

FIRST DIDIT: identifies the series

1	21	Tempest
2	22	Le Mans
3	23	Catalina
6	26	Star Chief
8	28	Bonneville
9	29	Grand Prix

SECOND AND THIRD DIGIT: indicates the model year 63 for 1963

FOURTH DIGIT: identifies the assembly plant.

ASSEMBLY PLANT	Code
Pontiac, Mich.	P
South Gate, CA	S
Linden	L
Wilmington, Del.	W
Kansas City, Kans.	K
Doraville	D
Arlington, Tx.	A

FINAL DIGITS: production sequence number

FISHER BODY NUMBER PLATE

PONTIAC DIV. GENERAL MOTORS CORP.
PONTIAC, MICHIGAN

STYLE 63-2347   BODY PO 237

TRIM 243   PAINT AA
ACC.B-F-KX-JX

THIS CAR FINISHED WITH
MAGIC-MIRROR ACRYLIC LACQUER
BODY BY FISHER

Complete identification of each body is provided by a plate riveted to the cowl at the left of center under the hood.

THE STYLE NUMBER is a combination of the year, division, series and body style. In the number plate illustrated, 63 represents the model year 1963; the first digit 2 indicates Pontiac Motor Division; the second digit 3 indicates Series 2300; 47 indicates the 2-Door Sport Coupe body style.

TEMPEST - 2100	Code
Sport Coupe - 2 Door Std	2127
Sport Coupe- 2 Door Cust	2117
Sedan - 4 Door, 6 Window	2119
2 Seat; 2nd. Seat Folding	2135
Convertible	2167

LE MANS - 2200	Code
Sport Coupe - 2 Door	2217
Convertible	2267

CATALINA - 2300	Code
Coupe-Convertible	2367
Sport Coupe - 2 Door	2347
Sport Sedan - 2 Door	
- 4 Window	2311

	Code
Sedan - 4 Door, 6 Window	2369
Vista - 4 Door, 4 Window	2339
Safari Station Wagon - 4 Door 2 Seat; 2nd. Seat Folding	2335
Safari Station Wagon - 4 Door 3 Seat; 2nd. Seat Folding	2345

STAR CHIEF - 2600	Code
Sedan - 4 Door, 6 Window	2669
Vista - 4 Door, 4 Window	2639

BONNEVILLE - 2800	Code
Safari Station Wagon - 4 Door 2 Seat; 2nd Seat Folding	2835
Coupe - Convertible	2867
Sport Coupe - 2 Door	2847
Vista - 4 Door, 4 Window	2839

GRAND PRIX - 2900	Code
Sport Coupe - 2 Door	2957

THE BODY NUMBER is the production serial number of the body. The prefix letter denotes the plant in which the body was built.

ASSEMBLY PLANT	Code
Pontiac, Mich.	PO
South Gate, CA.	BC
Linden	BL
Wilmington, Del.	BW
Kansas City, Kans.	BK
Doraville	BA
Arlington, Tx.	BT
Euclid	EP

The Trim Code furnishes the key to interior color and material.

Model	Color	Code

Cloth andImitation Leather

2119-27 201
Blue Prelude Cloth with Med. Blue and Light Blue

Imitation Leather

2119-27 20
Aqua Prelude Cloth with Med. Aqua and Light Aqua Imitation Leather

2119-27 20
Fawn Prelude Cloth with Med. Fawn and Light Fawn Imitation Leather

2119-27 20
Maroon Prelude Cloth with Med. Maroon and Ivory Imitation Leather

2311-69 22
Med. Blue Pennant Cloth with Med. Blue and Light Blue Imitation Leather

2311-69 22
Med. Aqua Pennant Cloth with Med. Aqua and Light Aqua Imitation Leather

2311-69 23
Med. Gawn Pennant Cloth with Med. Fawn and Light Fawn Imitation Leather

2339-47 23
Blue Palomar Cloth with Med. Blue and Light Blue Imitation Leather

2339-47 23
Aqua Palomar Cloth with Med. Aqua and Light Aqua Imitation Leather

2339-47 23
Med. Fawn Palomar Cloth with Med. Fawn and Light Fawn Imitation Leather

2339-47 23
Med. Maroon Palomar Cloth with med. Maroon and Ivory Imitation Leather

2369 230
Med. Green Pennant Cloth with
Med. Green and
Light Green Imitation Leather

2369 232
Med. Maroon Pennant Cloth with
Med. Maroon and
Ivory Imitation Leather

2639-69 253
Med. Blue premiereCloth with
Med. Blue and Dark
Blue Imitation Leather

2639-69 254
Med. Aqua Premiere Cloth with
med. Aqua and Dark
Aqua Imitation Leather

2639-69 255
Med.Fawn Premier Cloth with
Med. Fawn and Dark
Fawn Imitation Leather

2639-69 256
Med. Maroon Premiere Cloth with
Med. Maroon and
Dark Maroon Imitation Leather

2839-69 261
Blue Patrician Stripe and Blue
Parma Cloth with
Dark Blue Imitation Leather

2839-47 262
Aqua Patrician Stripe and aqua
Parma Cloth with
Dark Aqua Imitation Leather

2839-47 264
Dark Fawn Patrician stripe and
Med. Fawn Parma
Cloth with Dark Fawn Imitation
Leather

2839-47 265
Dark Maroon Patrician Stripe and
Med. Maroon Parma
Cloth with Dark Maroon Imitation
Leather

Imitation Leather

2119-35 206
Silver (Black Ribbed) with med.
Gray and Ivory

2117-19-35-67 208
Med.Blue with Dark Blue and
Light Blue

2117-19-35-67 209
Med.Aqua with Dark Aqua and
Light Aqua

2117-19-35 210
Med. Green with Dark Green and
Light Green

2117-19-35 211

Med. Fawn with Dark Fawn and
Light Fawn

2117-19-35-67 212
Med. Maroon with Dark Maroon
and Ivory

2135 207
Med. Maroon (Black Ribbed) with
Med. Maroon and
Ivory

2117-67 213
Black

2217-67 214
Light Fawn

2117-67 215
Red

2117-67 216
Bronze

2117-67 217
Dark Blue

2311-69 299
Med. Gray with Dark Gray and
Silver

2335-45 243
Med. Blue with Dark Blue and
Light Blue

2335-45 244
Med. Aqua with Dark Aqua and
Light Aqua

2335-45 245
Med. Green with Dark Green and
Light Green

2335-45 246
Med. Fawn with Dark Fawn and
Light Fawn

2335-45 247
Med. Maroon with Dark Maroon
and Ivory

2339-47-69 238-294
Med. Blue with Dark Blue and
Light Blue

2339-47-69 239-295
Med. Aqua with Dark Aqua and
Light Aqua

2339-47-69 240
Med. Green with Dark Green and
Light Green

2339-47-69 241
Med. Fawn with Dark Fawn and
Light Fawn

2339-47-69 242-296
Med. Maroon with Dark Maroon
and Ivory

2367 248
Med. Blue with Dark Blue and
Light Blue

2367 249
Med. Aqua with Dark Aqua and
Light Aqua

2367 251
Med. Fawn with Dark Fawn and
Light Fawn

2367 252
Med. Maroon with Dark Maroon
and Ivory

2639-69 257
Med. Blue and Dark Blue

2639-69 258
Med. Aqua and Dark Aqua

2639-69 259
Med. Fawn and Dark Fawn

2639-69 260
Med. Maroon and Dark Maroon

2835 279
Med. Blue and Dark Blue

2835 280
Med. Fawn and Dark Fawn

2835 281
Med. Maroon and Dark Maroon

2839-47 218-266
Black

2839-47 219-267
Med. Blue and Dark Blue

2839-47 220-268
Med. Aqua and Dark Aqua

2839-47 221-269
Med. Fawn and Dark Fawn

2839-47 222-270
Med. Maroon and Dark Maroon

2839-47 223-289
Light Fawn with Black Carpet

2839-47 224-290
Light Fawn with Med. Maroon
Carpet

2839-47 225-291
Light Fawn with Saddle Carpet

2957 282
Black

2957 283
Light Fawn with Black Carpet

2957 284
Light Fawn with Saddle Carpet

2957 285
Light Fawn with Red Carpet

2957 286
Med. Red

2957 287
Dark Aqua

THE PAINT CODE furnishes the
key to the paint colors used on the
car. A two letter code indicates the
bottom and top colors respectively

Color	Code
Starlight Black	A
Cameo Ivory	C
Silvermist Gray	D
Yorktown Blue	F
Kimberley Blue	H
Silverleaf Green	J
Marimba Red	L
Cordovan	K
Aquamarine	P
Marlin Aqua	Q
Yuma Beige	R
Saddle Bronze	S
Caravan Gold	T
Grenadier Red	V
Nocturne Blue	W

ENGINE NUMBER

Along with the VIN number the engine block is stamped with an engine production code. The production code is stamped on the engine block directly below the VIN number. The production codes for 1963 are:

APPLICATION	ENGINE CODE	CARB.	COMP.	CID	HP	TRANS.
PONTIAC						
Std. 23-26	01A	2-bbl	8.6:1	389	215	Man.
Std.-28 Spec. Eqptt. 23-26	02B	4-bbl	8.6:1	389	235	Man.
Spec. Eqpt.-23-26						
Std. Police-Taxi	03B	2-bbl	8.6:1	389	215	Man
Spec. Eqpt.-28	04B	4-bbl	8.6:1	389	235	Man.
Export-23-26	05A	2-bbl	7.6:1	389	215	Man.
Spec. Police-Std. 29 &						
All 4 spd. SM	06B	4-bbl	10.25:	389	235	Man.
Spec. Eqpt.-23-26-28-29	07B	Tri-Carb	10.25:	389	313	Man.
421 H.O.-23-26-28-29	08B	4-bbl	10.75:1	421	353	Man.
421 H.O.-23-26-28-29	11B	Tri-Carb	10.75:1	421	370	Man.
421 S.D. 23-29	12B	4-bbl	11.5:1	421	N.A.	Man.
421 S.D. 23-29	13B	Dual 4-bbl	11.5:1	421	N.A.	Man.
Std. 23	15H	2-bbl	10.25:	389	267	Auto
Spec. Eqpt.-23 Std.-29	16K	4-bbl	10.25:	389	303	Auto
Air Cond.-23	17H	2-bbl	10.25:	389	267	Auto
Air Cond.-23-29	18K	4-bbl	10.25:	389	303	Auto
Economy-23-29	20L	2-bbl	8.6:1	389	230	Auto
Economy-A/C-23-29	21L	2-bbl	8.6:1	389	230	Auto
-	22B	4-bbl	10.25:1	421	320	Auto
Export-23-29	23H	2-bbl	7.6:1	389	267	Auto
421 H.O.-23-29	25G	4-bbl	10.75:1	421	353	Auto
Spec. Eqpt.-23-29	266	Tri-Carb	10.25:	389	313	Auto
421 H.O.-23-29	28G	Tri-Carb	10.75:1	421	370	Auto
-	34J	4-bbl	10.75:1	421	320	Auto
Std.-26 Taxi-Police	35M	2-bbl	10.25:	389	283	Auto
Std.-28-Spec. Eqpt.-26	36P	4-bbl	10.25:	389	303	Auto
Air Cond.-26 Taxi-Police	37M	2-bbl	10.25:	389	283	Auto
Air Cond.-26-28	38P	4-bbl	10.25:	389	303	Auto
Spec. Police	39N	4-bbl	10.25:	389	303	Auto
Economy-26-28 Taxi-Police	40R	2-bbl	8.6:1	389	230	Auto
Economy A/C 26-28 Taxi	41R	2-bbl	8.6:1	389	230	Auto
-	43N	4-bbl	8.6:1	421	320	Auto
Export-26	44M	2-bbl	7.6:1	389	283	Auto
Export-28	45P	4-bbl	7.6:1	389	303	Auto
421 H.O.-26-28	47Q	4-bbl	10.75:1	421	353	Auto
Spec. Eqpt.-26-28	48N	Tri-Carb	10.25:	389	313	Auto
421 H.O.-26-28	50Q	Tri-Carb	10.75:1	421	370	Auto
421 S.H.O.	-	2 / 4-bbl	13.0:1	421	-	-
TEMPEST						
Std.	89Z	1-bbl	8.6:1	195	115	Man.
Export	88Z	1-bbl	7.6:1	195	115	Man.
Spec. Eqpt.	87Z	4-bbl	10.25:1	195	166	Man.
Spec. Eqpt.	86Z	1-bbl	10.25:1	195	120	Man.
Std. Taxi-Spec. Eqpt.	85Z	1-bbl	8.6:1	195	115	Man.
Spec. Eqpt.	84Z	4-bbl	10.25:1	195	166	Man.
Spec. Eqpt.	83Z	1-bbl	10.25:1	195	120	Man.
Spec. Eqpt.	82Z	1-bbl	7.6:1	195	115	Man.
Std.	79Y	1-bbl	8.6:1	195	115	Auto
Export	78Y	1-bbl	7.6:1	195	115	Auto
Spec. Eqpt.	77Y	4-bbl	10.25:1	195	166	Auto
Spec. Eqpt.	76Y	1-bbl	10.25:1	195	140	Auto
Spec. Eqpt.	68X	2-bbl	8.6:1	326	250	Man.
Spec. Eqpt.	70X	4-bbl	10.25:1	326	280	Man.
Spec. Eqpt.	71X	2-bbl	10.00:1	326	260	Man.
Spec. Eqpt.	60O	2-bbl	10.25:1	326	260	Auto
Spec. Eqpt.	69O	2-bbl	8.6:1	326	250	Auto
-	59O	4-bbl	10.25:1	326	280	Auto

VEHICLE IDENTIFICATION NUMBER

PONTIAC
834P1001

Commonly referred to as the VIN NUMBER, this series of numbers and letters is stamped on the plate attached to the left front door hinge pillar.

VIN consists of Engine Type Symbol, Series Identify Symbol, Model Year Symbol, Assembly Plant Symbol and a sequential Production Number.

THE FIRST DIGIT: identifies the Engine Type: 6—6 cylinder; 8—8 cylinder

THE SECOND DIGIT: identifies the Series:

Tempest	0
Tempest Custom	1
LeMans	2
Catalina	3
Star Chief	6
Bonneville	8
Grand Prix	9

THE THIRD DIGIT: identifies Model Year: 4 = 1964

THE FOURTH DIGIT: identifies the Assembly Plant:

Assembly Plant	Code
Pontiac	P
Linden-BOP	L
South Gate-BOP	S
Kansas City-BOP	K
Doraville-BOP	D
Fremont-BOP	F
Arlington-BOP	A
Baltimore-Chev.	B
Kansas City-Chev.	M

FINAL DIGITS: production sequence number

FISHER BODY NUMBER PLATE

PONTIAC DIV. GENERAL MOTORS CORP.
000 PONTIaC, MICHIGAN
STYLE 64-2311   BODY PO 000
TRIM 000   PAINT 000
ACC. 0-0-00-00
THIS CAR FINISHED WITH MAGIC-MIRROR ACRYLIC LACQUER BODY BY FISHER

Complete identification of each body is provided by a plate riveted to the cowl at the left of center under the hood.

THE STYLE NUMBER is a combination of the year, division, series and body style. In the examples— 64 is the model year 1964, 2 represents Pontiac division, 3 indicates series 2300—Catalinia and 11 represents body style, 2 door sport sedan.

TEMPEST - 2000	Code
Sedan - 4 Door	2069
Sport Coupe - 2 Door	2027
Safari Stn. Wgn. 2-Seat	2035

TEMPEST CUST.- 2100	Code
Sport Coupe - 2 Door Std	2127
Sedan - 4 Door	2169
Safari Stn. Wag. 2-Seat	2135
Convertible	2167

LE MANS - 2200	Code
Sport Coupe - 2 Door	2227
Hardtop Sports Coupe	2237
Convertible	2267

*NOTE: GTO is an option not a model.

CATALINA - 2300	Code
Coupe-Convertible	2367
Sport Coupe - 2 Door	2347
Sport Sedan - 2 Door - 4 Window	2311
Sedan - 4 Door, 6 Window	2369
Vista - 4 Door, 4 Window	2339
Safari Station Wagon - 4 Door	
2 Seat; 2nd. Seat Folding	2335
Safari Station Wagon - 4 Door	
3 Seat; 2nd. Seat Folding	2345

STAR CHIEF - 2600	Code
Sedan - 4 Door, 6 Window	2669
Vista - 4 Door, 4 Window	2639

BONNEVILLE - 2800	Code
Safari Station Wagon - 4 Door	
2 Seat; 2nd Seat Folding	2835
Coupe - Convertible	2867
Sport Coupe - 2 Door	2847
Vista - 4 Door, 4 Window	2839

GRAND PRIX - 2900	Code
Sport Coupe - 2 Door	2957

THE BODY NUMBER is the production serial number of the body. The prefix letter denotes the plant in which the body was built.

ASSEMBLY PLANT	Code
Pontiac, Mich.	PC
South Gate, CA.	BC
Linden	BL
Wilmington, Del.	BW
Kansas City, Kans.	BK
Doraville	BA
Arlington, Tx.	BT
Euclid	EF

THE TRIM CODE furnishes the key to interior color and material.

Cloth and Imitation Leather

Model	Code

2027-69 201
Med. Blue Pembroke Cloth with Med. Blue and Dark Blue Imitation Leather

2027-69 202
Med. Aqua Pembrook Cloth with Med. Aqua and Dark Aqua Imitation Leather

2027-69 203
Light Saddle IPembrook Cloth with Light Saddle and Dark Saddle Imitation Leather

2027-69 204
Med. Maroon Pembroke Cloth with Med. Maroon and Dark Marooon Imitation Leather

2311-69 221
Med. Blue Prentice Cloth with Dark Blue and Med. Blue Imitation Leather

2311-69 222
Med. Aqua Prentice Cloth with Dark Aqua and Med. Aqua Imitation Leather

2311-69 225
Med. Maroon Prentice Cloth with Dark Maroon and Med. Maroon Imitation Leather

2339-47 286
Med. Blue Prewntice Cloth with Dark Blue and Med. Blue Imitation Leather

2339-47 288
Med. Aqua Prentice Cloth with Dark Aqua and Med. Aqua Imitation Leather

2339-47 291
Med. Olive PrenticeCloth with Dark Olive and Med. Olive Imitation Leather

2339-47 297
Light Saddle Prentice Cloth with Dark Saddle and Light Saddle Imitation Leather

2339-47 298
Med. Maroon Prentice Cloth with Dark Maroon and Med. Maroon Imitation Leather

2369-69 223
Med. Olive Prentice Cloth with Dark Olive Imitation Leather

2369-47 224
Light Saddle Prentice Cloth with Dark Saddle Imitation Leather

2639-69 241
Med. Blue Cloth with Dark Blue Imitation Leather

2639-69 242
Med. Aqua Cloth with Dark Aqua Imitation Leather

2639-69 243
Med. Fawn Cloth with Dark Fawn Imitation Leather

2639-69 244
Light Maroon Cloth with Dark Rose Imitation Leather

2839-47 249
Dark Blue Preston Cloth with Med. Blue Imitation Leather

2839-47 250
Dark Aqua Preston Cloth with Med. Aqua Imitation Leather

2839-47 251
Black Preston Cloth with Black Imitation Leather

2839-47 252
Dark Rose Preston Cloth with Light Maroon Imitation Leather

2839 293
Black Preston Cloth with Black Imitation Leater

Imitation Leather

2035-69 205
Med. Gray with Silver Pattern and Dark Gray

2035 206
Light Saddle with Light Saddle and Dark Saddle

2035 207
Med. Red Pattern and Med. Red

2127-35-67-69 208
Med. Blue and Dark Blue

2127-35-67-69 209
Med. Aqua and Dark Aqua

2127-35-67-69 212
Med. Maroon and Dark Maroon

2127-35-69 211
Light Saddle and Dark Saddle

2135-69 210
Med. Olive and Dark Olive

2227-67 214
Black

2227-67 215
Dark Blue

2227-67 216
Light Saddle

2227-67 217
Dark Aqua

2227-67 218
Medium Red

2227-67 219
Parchment

2311-69 299
Silver Pattern with Dark Gray and Med.Gray

2335-45 231
Med. Blue Pattern and Dark Blue

2335-45 232
Med. Aqua Pattern and Dark Aqua

2335-45 233
Med. Olive Pattern and Dark Olive

2335-45 234
Light Saddle Pattern and Dark Saddle

2335-45 235
Med. Maroon Pattern and Dark Maroon

2339-47-69 226
Med. Blue and Dark Blue and Light Blue

2339-47 227
Med. Aqua with Dark Aqua and Light Aqua

2339-47-69 229
Light Saddle and Parchment

2339-47-69 230
Med. Maroon with Dark Maroon and Ivory

2347 258-282
Black

2347 276
Med. Blue with Dark Blue and Light Blue

2347 280
Medium Red

2367 236
Dark Blue with Med. Blue and Light Blue

2367 237
Dark Aqua with Med. Aqua and Light Aqua

2367 238
Light Saddle

2367 239
Medium Red

2367 240
Black

2639-69 245
Med. Blue and Dark Blue

2639-69 246
Med. Aqua and Dark Aqua

2639-69 247
Med. Fawn and Dark Fawn

2639-69 248
Light Maroon and Dark Rose

2835 278
Dark Blue and Med. Blue

2835 279
Light Saddle

2835 281
Dark Rose and Light Maroon

2839-47 253
Black

2839-47 254
Dark Blue and Med. Blue

2839-47 255
Dark Aqua and Med. Aqua

2839-47 256
Light Saddle

2839-47 257
Dark Rose and Light Maroon

2839-47 259-292
Parchment

2847 267
Parchment

2847 283
Black

2847 284
Dark Blue and Med. Blue

2847 287
Medium Red

2957 268
Black

2957 269
Dark Blue

2957 270
Light Saddle

2957 271
Dark Aqua

2957 272
Medium Red

2957 273-274-275
Parchment

Genuine Leather and Imitation Leather

2867 260-290
Black Genuine Leather with Black Imitation Leather

2867 261-289
Med. Blue Genuine Leather with Dark Blue Imitation Leather

2867 262
Med. Aqua Genuine Leather with Dark Aqua Imitation Leather

2867 263
Light Maroon Genuine Leather with Dark Parchment Imitation Leather

2867 264-265-294
Parchment Genuine Leather with Parchment Imitation Leather

2867 266-295
Light Saddle Genuine Leather with Light Saddle Imitation Leather

2867 296
Med. Red Genuine Leather with Med. Red Imitation Leather

THE PAINT CODE furnishes the key to the paint colors used on the car. A two letter code indicates the bottom and top colors respectively

Color	Code
Starlight Black	A
Cameo Ivory	C
Silvermist Grey	D
Yorktown Blue	F
Skyline Blue	H
Pinehurst Green	J
Marimba Red	L
Surnfire Red	N
Aquamarine	P
Gulfstream Aqua	Q
Alamo Beige	R
Saddle Bronze	S
Singapore Gold	T
Grenadier Red	V
Nocturne Blue	W

ENGINE NUMBER

Along with the VIN number the engine block is stamped with an engine production code. The production code is stamped on the engine block directly below the VIN number. The production codes for 1964 are:

H. P.	ENGINE CODE	TRANS.	MODEL	APPLICATION	COMP.	CARB.
TEMPEST						
140	80Z,84Z,85Z	SM	215	Standard	8.6:1	1-bbl
140	81Z	SM	215	Spec. Equip.	8.6:1	1-bbl
-	82Z	SM	215	-	6.9:1	1-bbl
-	87Y	A	215	-	6.9:1	1-bbl
140	88Y,89Y,83Y	A	215	Standard	8.6:1	1-bbl
250	925	SM	326	Spec. Equip	8.6:1	2-bbl
280	945	SM	326HO	Spec. Equip.	10.5:1	4-bbl
250	96O	A	326	Spec. Equip.	8.6:1	2-bbl
280	971	A	326HO	Spec. Equip.	10.5:1	4-bbl
348	76X	SM	389	GTO	10.75:1	3/2-bbl
348	77J	A	389	GTO	10.75:1	3/2-bbl
325	78X	SM	389	GTO	10.75:1	4-bbl
325	79J	A	389	GTO	10.75:1	4-bbl

HP	ENGINE CODE	CID	TRANS.	APPLICATION	MODELS	COMP.	CARB.
PONTIAC							
215	01A	389	SM	Standard	23	8.6:1	2-bbl (4)
215	01A	389	SM	Standard	26	8.6:1	2-bbl (4)
215	02B	389	SM	1-R.P.O.	23	8.6:1	2-bbl (4)
215	02B	389	SM	1-R.P.O.		8.6:1	2-bbl (4)
215	02B	389	SM	Std. Police		Police	2-bbl (4)
						8.6:1	2-bbl (4)
215	02B	389	SM	Std. Taxi		8.6:1	2-bbl (4)
215	02B	389	SM	Trail Prov.	23 26	8.6:1	2-bbl (4)
239	03A	389	SM	Export	23	7.9:1	2-bbl (4)
239	03A	389	SM	Export	26	7.9:1	2-bbl (4)
306	23B	389	SM	Spec. Police		Police	4-bbl
						10.5:1	4-bbl
306	23B	389	SM	Standard	29 2835 (1)	10.5:1	4-bbl
306	23B	389	SM	1-R.P.O.	23 W51 OPT 26	10.5:1	4-bbl
235	22B	389	SM	Standard	(2)		4-bbl
330	32B	389	SM	1-R.P.O.	23 W51 OPT 29 26 2835 (1)	10.75:1	3 x 2-bbl
320	35B	421	SM	421	23 W51 OPT 29 26 2835 (1)	10.5:1	4-bbl
350	44B	421	SM	421	23 W51 OPT 29 26 2835 (1)	10.75:1	3 x 2-bbl
370	45B	421	SM	421 H.O.	23 W51 OPT 29 26 2835 (1)	10.75:1	3 x 2-bbl
283	10A	389	SM	1-R.P.O.	23	10.5:1	2-bbl (3)
283	10A	389	SM	1-R.P.O.	26	10.5:1	2-bbl (3)
283	10A	389	SM	Standard	23 W51 OPT 26	10.5:1	2-bbl (3)
350	49N	421	315 HM	421	26 2835 (1)	10.75:1	3 x 2-bbl
370	50Q	421	315 HM	421 H.O.	26 2835 (1)	10.75:1	3 x 2-bbl
350	34N	389	315 HM	1-R.P.O.	26 2835 (1)	10.75:1	3 x 2-bbl
230	08R	389	315 HM	2-425E	26 2835 (1)	Taxi	2-bbl (4)
						8.6:1	2-bbl (4)
						Police	2-bbl (4)
230	09R	389	315 HM	2-425E A/C	26 2835 (1)	Taxi	2-bbl (4)
						8.6:1	2-bbl (4)
303	27P	389	315 HM	Standard	2835 (1)	10.5:1	4-bbl
303	27P	389	315 HM	1-R.P.O.	26	10.5:1	4-bbl
303	27P	389	315 HM	Standard	(2)	10.5:1	4-bbl
303	28P	389	315 HM	A/C	26 2835 (1)	10.5:1	4-bbl
303	28P	389	315 HM	A/C	(2)	10.5:1	4-bbl
306	29N	389	315 HM	1-R.P.O.	(2)	Police	4-bbl
						10.5:1	4-bbl
283	17M	389	315 HM	1-R.P.O.	26	10.5:1	2-bbl (3)
283	17M	389	315 HM	1-R.P.O.		Taxi	2-bbl (3)
						10.5:1	2-bbl (3)
						Police	2-bbl (3)
283	18M	389	315 HM	A/C	26	10.5:1	2-bbl (3)
283	18M	389	315 HM	A/C		Taxi	2-bbl (3)
						10.5:1	2-bbl (3)
						Police	2-bbl (3)
320	43N	421	315 HM	421	26 2835 (1)	10.5:1	4-bbl
230	04L	389	375 RHM	2-425E	23 W51 OPT 29	8.6:1	2-bbl (4)
230	05L	389	375 RHM	2-425 A/C	23 W51 OPT 29	8.6:1	2-bbl (4)
370	46G	421	375 RHM	421 H.O.	23 W51 OPT 29	10.75:1	3 x 2-bbl
350	47S	421	375 RHM	421	23 W51 OPT 29	10.75:1	3 x 2-bbl
303	25K	389	375 RHM	1-R.P.O.	23 W51 OPT	10.5:1	4-bbl
303	25K	389	375 RHM	Standard	29	10.5:1	4-bbl
303	26K	389	375 RHM	A/C	23 W51 OPT	10.5:1	4-bbl
303	26K	389	375 RHM	A/C	29	10.5:1	4-bbl
267	11H	389	375 RHM	Standard	23 W51 OPT	10.5:1	2-bbl (3)
267	12H	389	375 RHM	A/C	23 W51 OPT	10.5:1	2-bbl (3)
320	38S	421	375 RHM	421	23 W51 OPT 29	10.5:1	4-bbl
350	336	389	375 RHM	1-R.P.O.	23 W51 OPT 29	10.75:1	3 x 2-bbl
-	13L	389	A/T	-		7.6:1	2-bbl
-	19R	389	A/T	-		7.6:1	2-bbl
-	30R	389	A/T	-		7.6:1	2-bbl

"(1) 2839, 2847, 2867"
"(2) 2840, 2850, 2890"
"(3) 11/16"" Bore"
"(4) 7/16"" Bore"
@ Special Exhaust Manifolds

VEHICLE IDENTIFICATION NUMBER

> **PONTIAC**
> 252695P100001

VIN consists of Manufacturer's Symbol, Series and Body Style Code, Model Year Symbol, Assembly Plant Symbol and a sequential Production Number.

THE FIRST DIGIT: 2, identifies Pontiac Division.

SECOND AND THIRD: identify the Series.

Tempest	33
Tempest Custom	35
Tempest LeMans	37
Catalina	52
Star Chief	56
Bonneville	62
Grand Prix	66

FOURTH AND FIFTH DIGIT: identify the body style in each series, (Example, 27 is a 2-Door Sports Coupe).

THE SIXTH DIGIT: identifies the Model Year, :5—1965.

THE SEVENTH DIGIT: identifies the Assembly Plant.

Assembly Plant	Code
Pontiac, Mich.	P
Linden, N.J.	E
Southgate, Cal.	C
Kansas City, Ks.	X
Doraville, Ga.	D
Fremont, Cal.	Z
Arlington, Tex.	R
Baltimore, Md.	B
Kansas City, Mo.	K

FINAL DIGITS: production sequence number

FISHER BODY NUMBER PLATE

Complete identification of each body is provided by a plate riveted to the cowl at the left of center under the hood.

THE STYLE NUMBER is a combination of the year, Division, series and body style. In the examples-65 is the model year 1965, 2 represents Pontiac division, 52 indicates series 5200—Catalinia and 11 represents body style, 2 door sedan.

TEMPEST - 3300	Code
Sedan - 4 Door	3369

Sport Coupe - 2 Door	3327
Safari Stn. Wgn. 2-Seat	3335

TEMPEST CUST.- 3500	Code
Sport Coupe - 2 Door Std	3527
Sedan - 4 Door	3569
Safari Stn. Wag. 2-Seat	3535
Convertible	3567
Hardtop Coupe - 2 Door	3537

LE MANS - 3700	Code
Sport Coupe - 2 Door	3727
Hardtop Sports Coupe	3737
Convertible	3767
Sedan - 4Door	3769

*NOTE: GTO is an option not a model.

CATALINA - 5200	Code
Coupe-Convertible	5267
Sport Coupe - 2 Door	5237
Sport Sedan - 2 Door	
- 4 Window	5211
Sedan - 4 Door, 6 Window	5269
Vista - 4 Door, 4 Window	5239
Safari Station Wagon - 4 Door 2 Seat; 2nd. Seat Folding	5235
Safari Station Wagon - 4 Door 3 Seat; 2nd. Seat Folding	5245

STAR CHIEF - 5600	Code
Sedan - 4 Door, 6 Window	5669
Vista - 4 Door, 4 Window	5639

BONNEVILLE - 6200	Code
Safari Station Wagon - 4 Door 2 Seat; 2nd Seat Folding	6235
Coupe - Convertible	6267
Sport Coupe - 2 Door	6237
Vista - 4 Door, 4 Window	6239

GRAND PRIX - 6600	Code
Sport Coupe - 2 Door	6657

THE BODY NUMBER is the production serial number of the body. The prefix letter denotes the plant in which the body was built.

ASSEMBLY PLANT	Code
Pontiac, Mich.	PO
South Gate, CA.	BC
Linden	BL
Wilmington, Del.	BW
Kansas City, Kans.	BK
Doraville	BA
Arlington, Tx.	BT
Euclid	EP

> PONTIAC DIV. GENERAL MOTORS CORP.
> 000 PONTIAC, MICHIGAN
>
> STYLE 65-25211   P 000BODY
> TRIM 000   000PAINT
> ACC. 0-0-00-00
>
> BODY BY FISHER

TRIM CODE furnishes the key to the interior color and material.

Model	Color	Code

Cloth and Imitation Leather

3327-69 201
Blue Paloma Pattern Cloth with Blue Imit. Leather

3327-69 202
Turquoise Paloma Pattern Cloth with Turquoise Imit. Leather

3327-69 203
Gold Paloma Pattern Cloth with Gold Imit. Leather

3327-69 204
Red Paloma Pattern Cloth with Red Imit. Leather

3769 265
Blue Charcoal Preston Cloth with Blue Charcoal Imit. Leather

3769 298
Burgundy Preston Cloth with Burgundy Imit. Leather

5211-69 219
Blue Pompei Pattern Cloth with Blue Imit. Leather

5211-69 220
Turquoise Pompeei Pattern Cloth with Turquoise Imit. Leather

5211-69 223
Red Pompei Pattern Cloth with Red Imit. Leather

5237-39 292
Blue Pompei Pattern Cloth with Blue Imit. Leather

5237-39 293
Turquoise Pompei Pattern Cloth with Turquoise Imit. Leather

5237-39 295
Bronze Pompei Pattern Cloth with Gold Imit. Leather

5237-39 296
Red Pomppei Pattern Cloth with Red Imit. Leather

5239 294
Green Pompei Pattern Cloth with Green Imit. Leather

5269 221

Green Pompei Pattern Cloth with Green Imit. Leather

5269 222
Bronze Pompei Pattern Cloth with Gold Imit. Leather

5639-69 242
Blue Palmetto Pattern Cloth with Blue Imit. Leather

5639-69 243
Turquoise Palmetto Pattern Cloth with Turquoise Imit. Leather

5639-69 244
Gold Palmetto Pattern Cloth with Gold Imit. Leather

5639-69 245
Red Palmetto Pattern Cloth with Red Imit. Leather

6237-39 246
Blue Province Pattern Cloth with Blue Imit. Leather

6237-39 248
Gold Province Pattern Cloth with Gold Imit. Leather

6237-39 249
Black Province Pattern Cloth with Black Imit. Leather

6239 247
Turquoise Province Pattern Cloth with Turquoise Imit. Leather

6239 250
Plum Province Pattern Cloth with Plum Imit. Leather

6239 262
Blue Charcoal Plaza Bolster and Pontchartrain Pattern Cloth with Blue Charcoal Imit. Leather

6239 263
Gold Plaza Bolster and Pontchartrain Pattern Cloth with Parchment Imit. Leather

6239 264
Plum Plaza Bolster and Pontchartrain Pattern Cloth with Plum Imit. Leather

6657 259-290
Blue Charcoal Pontchartrain Pattern Cloth with Blue Charcoal Imit. Leather

6657 291
Gold Pontchartrain Pattern Cloth with .... Parchment Imit. Leather

1965 Imitation Leather

3327-35-69 208
Silver Brigade Pattern and Med. Gray

3335 205
Turquoise Brigade Pattern and Med. Turquoise

3335 206
Gold Brigade Pattern and Gold

2334 207
Red Brigade Pattern and Med. Red

3527-35-37-67-69 209
Med. Blue and Dark Blue

3527-35-37-69 210
Med. Turquoise and Dark Turquoise

3527-35-37-67-69 211
Gold and Bronze

3527-35-37-67-69 212
Med. Red and Burgundy

3727-37-67 213
Black

3727-37-67 214
Turquoise

3727-37-67 215
Gold

3727-37-67 216
Red

3727-37-67 217
Blue

3727-37-67 218
Parchment

5211-69 299
Silver Brigade Pattern and Med. Gray

5235-45 224
Blue Saxony Pattern and Med. Blue

5235-45 225
Turquoise Saxony Pattern and Med. Turquoise

5235-45 226
Green Saxony Pattern and Med. Green

5235-45 227
Gold Saxony Pattern and Gold

5235-45 228
Red Saxony Pattern and Med. Red

5237 (2+2) 233
Black

5237 (2+2) 234
Red

5237 (2+2) 235
Blue Charcoal

5237 (2+2) 236
Parchment

5237 237
Med. Blue and Dark Blue

5237 238
Med. Turquoise and Dark Turquoise

5237 239
Gold and Bronze

5237 240
Red

5237 241
Black

5239-69 237
Med. Blue and Dark Blue

5239-69 238
Med. Turquoise and Dark Turquoise

5239-69 239
Gold and Bronze

5239-69 240
Red

5267 229
Med. Blue and Dark Blue

5267 230
Med. Turquoise and Dark Turquoise

5267 231
Gold and Bronze

5267 232
Red

5267 (2+2) 233
Black

5267 (2+2) 234
Red

5267 (2+2) 235
Blue Charcoal

5267 (2+2) 236
Parchment

5267 297
Black

5639 - 69 237
Med. Blue and Dark Blue

5639 - 69 238
Med. Turquoise and Dark Turquoise

5639 - 69 239
Gold and Bronze

5639 - 69 240
Red

6235 278
Dark Turquoise and Med. Turquoise

6235 279
Slate

6235 280
Red

6237 - 39 251
Dark Blue and Med. Blue

6237 - 39 252
Dark Turquoise and Med. Turquoise

6237 - 39 253
Gold

6237 - 39 254
Red

6237 - 39 255-260
Black

6237 - 39 256-257-261
Parchment

6267 266-273
Dark Blule and Mmed. Blue

6267 267
Dark Turquoise and Med. Turquoise

6267 268
Gold

6267 269-275
Red

6267 270-276
Black

6267 271-272-277
Parchment

6657 258-281
Black

6657 282
Turquoise

6657 283
Slate

6657 284
Gold

6657 285
Red

6657 286
Blue Charcoal

6657 287
Plum

6657 288-289
Parchment

ENGINE NUMBER

Along with the VIN number the engine block is stamped with an engine production code. The production code is stamped on the engine block directly below the VIN number. The production codes for 1965 are:

THE PAINT CODE furnishes the key to the paint colors used on the car. A two letter code indicates the bottom and top colors respectively

Color	Code
Starlight Black	A
Blue Charcoal	B
Cameo Ivory	C
Fontaine Blue	D
Nightwatch Blue	E
Palmetto Green	H
Reef Turquoise	K
Teal Turquoise	L
Burgundy	N
Iris Mist	P
Montero Red	R
Capri Gold	T
Mission Beige	V
Bluemist Slate	W
Mayfair Maize	Y

HORSE POWER	ENGINE CODE	C.I.D.	TRANS. TYPE	USAGE	MODELS	COMP. RATIO	CARB.
TEMPEST							
140	ZK	215	SM	Standard	"33, 35, 37"	8.6:1	1-bbl
140	ZR	215	SM	Standard	"33, 35, 37"	8.6:1	1-bbl
140	ZS	215	SM	Standard	Taxi	8.6:1	1-bbl
					Police		1-bbl
140	ZS	215	SM	Optional	"33, 35, 37"	8.6:1	1-bbl
140	ZN	215	SM	Optional	"33, 35, 37"	8.6:1	1-bbl
					Taxi		1-bbl
					Police		1-bbl
-	ZD	215	SM	-	-	6.9:1	4-bbl
-	ZE	215	A	-	-	6.9:1	4-bbl
360	WS	389	SM	Optional	GTO	10.75:1	3 x 2-bbl
335	WT	389	SM	Standard	GTO	10.75:1	4-bbl
250	WP	326	SM	Optional	"33, 35, 37"	9.2:1	2-bbl
					Taxi		2-bbl
					Police		2-bbl
285	WR	326 H.O.	SM	Optional	"33, 35, 37"	10.5:1	4-bbl
					Taxi		4-bbl
					Police		4-bbl
140	ZL	215	A	Optional	"33, 35, 37"	8.6:1	1-bbl
					Taxi		1-bbl
					Police		1-bbl
140	ZM	215	A	Optional	"33, 35, 37"	8.6:1	1-bbl
					Taxi		1-bbl
					Police		1-bbl
360	YR	389	A	Optional	GTO	10.75:1	3 x 2-bbl
335	YS	389	A	Optional	GTO	10.75:1	4-bbl
250	YN	326	A	Optional	"33, 35, 37"	9.2:1	2-bbl
					Taxi		2-bbl
					Police		2-bbl
285	YP	326 H.O.	A	Optional	"33, 35, 37"	10.5:1	4-bbl
					Taxi		4-bbl
					Police		4-bbl

HORSE POWER	ENGINE CODE	C.I.D.	TRANS. TYPE	USAGE	MODELS	COMP. RATIO	CARB.
PONTIAC							
256	WA	389	SM	Standard	252 266	8.6:1	2-bbl
256	WB	389	SM	Optional	252 266	8.6:1	2-bbl
256	WB	389	SM	Std. Police	Police	8.6:1	2-bbl
256	WB	389	SM	Std. Taxi	Taxi	8.6:1	2-bbl
290	WC	389	SM	Optional	252 266	10.5:1	2-bbl
290	WC	389	SM	Spec. Police	Police	10.5:1	2-bbl
276	WD	389	SM	Standard	(3)	8.6:1	4-bbl
333	WE	389	SM	Standard	256 (2)	10.5:1	4-bbl
333	WE	389	SM	Optional	252 266 Police	10.5:1	4-bbl
338	WF	389	SM	Optional	252 256 266 (2) Police	10.75:1	3 x 2-bbl
338	WG	421	SM	Standard	(1)	10.5:1	4-bbl
338	WG	421	SM	Optional	252 256 266 (2)	10.5:1	4-bbl
356	WH	421	SM	Optional	252 (1) 256 266 (2)	10.75:1	3 x 2-bbl
356	WJ	421	SM	421 H.O.	252 (1) 256 266 (2) Police	10.75:1	3 x 2-bbl
256	YA	389	HM	Reg. Fuel	252 256 266 (2) Police	8.6:1	2-bbl
256	YB	389	HM	Reg. Fuel A/C	252 256 266 (2)	8.6:1	2-bbl
290	YC	389	HM	Standard	252 266 Taxi Police	10.5:1	2-bbl
290	YD	389	HM	Std. A/C	252 266 Taxi Police	10.5:1	2-bbl
325	YE	389	HM	Standard	256 (2)	10.5:1	4-bbl
325	YE	389	HM	Optional	252 266 (3) Police	10.5:1	4-bbl
325	YF	389	HM	A/C	252 256 266 (2) (3) Police	10.5:1	4-bbl

HORSE POWER	ENGINE CODE	C.I.D.	TRANS. TYPE	USAGE	MODELS	COMP. RATIO	CARB.
338	YH	421	HM	Optional	252 (1) 256 266 (2)	10.75:1	4-bbl
356	YJ	421	HM	Optional	252 (1) 256 266 (2)	10.75:1	3 x 2-bbl
376	YK	421	HM	421 H.O.	252 (1) 256 266 (2) Police	10.75:1	3 x 2-bbl
338	YG	389	HM	Optional	252 256 266 (2) Police	10.75:1	3 x 2-bbl
-	XB	389	A/T	-	-	7.6:1	2-bbl
-	XC	389	A/T	-	-	7.6:1	4-bbl

(1) 2+2 Option
"(2) 6235, 37, 39, 67"
"(3) 6240, 50, 90"
@ Special Exhaust Manifolds

** Note - 2-bbl Carb had 11/16 Bore

VEHICLE IDENTIFICATION NUMBER

```
PONTIAC
252696P100001
```

VIN consists of Manufacturer's Symbol, Series and Body Style Code, Model Year Symbol, Assembly Plant Symbol and a sequential Production Number.

THE FIRST DIGIT: 2, identifies Pontiac Division.

SECOND AND THIRD: identify the Series.

Tempest	33
Tempest Custom	35
Tempest LeMans	37
Catalina	52
Star Chief	56
Bonneville	62
Grand Prix	66

FOURTH AND FIFTH DIGIT: identify the body style in each series, (Example, 27 is a 2-Door Sports Coupe).

THE SIXTH DIGIT: identifies the Model Year, :6—1966.

THE SEVENTH DIGIT: identifies the Assembly Plant.

Assembly Plant	Code
Pontiac, Mich.	P
Linden, N.J.	E
Southgate, Cal.	C
Kansas City, Ks.	X
Doraville, Ga.	D
Fremont, Cal.	Z
Arlington, Tex.	R
Baltimore, Md.	B
Kansas City, Mo.	K
Lordstown, O	U

FINAL DIGITS: production sequence number

FISHER BODY NUMBER PLATE

Complete identification of each body is provided by a plate attached to the left side of cowl under hood.

THE STYLE NUMBER is a combination of the year, division, series and body style. 66 Represents the model year: 1966; 42 represents the Series — GTO; 07 represents the body style — Sports Coupe

```
GENERAL MOTORS CORPORATION
000

ST 66 4207  PO 123456   BODY
TR 123-A           A-A  PAINT


        BODY BY FISHER
```

Series	Body Style	Code
Tempest 233	Sports Coupe	23307
	Four Door Sedan	23369
	Station Wagon	23335
Tempest Custom 235	Sports Coupe	23507
	Four Door Sedan	23569
	Hardtop Coupe	23517
	Four Door Hardtop	23539
	Convertible	23567
	Statiton Wagon	23535
Tempest LeMans 237	Sports Coupe	23707
	Hardtop Coupe	23717
	Four Door Hardtop	23739
	Convertible	23767
Tempest— G.T.O. 242	Sports Coupe	24207
	Hardtop Coupe	24217
	Convertible	24267
Catalina 252	Two Door Sedan	25211
	Four Door Sedan	25269
	Hardtop Coupe	25237
	Four Door Hardtop	25239
	Convertible	25267
	Station Wagon-2 seat	25235
	Station Wagon-3 seat	25245
2+2 254	Hardtop Coupe	25437
	Convertible	25467
Star Chief Executive 256	Hardtop Coupe	25637
	Four Door Hardtop	25639
	Four Door Sedan	25669
Bonneville 262	Hardtop Coupe	26237
	Four Door Hardtop	26239
	Convertible	26267
	Station Wagon-3 seat	26245
Grand Prix	Hardtop Coupe	26657

THE BODY NUMBER is the production serial number of the body. The prefix letter denotes the plant in which the body was built.

ASSEMBLY PLANT Code

Pontiac, Mich. ....PO
South Gate, CA. ....BC
Linden ....BL
Wilmington, Del. ....BW
Kansas City, Kans. ....BK
Doraville ....BA
Arlington, Tx. ....BT
Euclid ....EP

TRIM CODE furnishes the key to the interior color and material.

Model Color Code

Cloth and Imitation Leather

3307-69 201
Blue Parcrest Cloth with Blue Imit. Leather

3307-69 202
Turquoise Parcrest Cloth with Turquoise Imit. Leather

3307-69 203
Fawn Parcrest Cloth with Fawn Imit. Leather

3307-69 204
Red Parcrest Cloth with Red Imit. Leather

3739 228
Black Parada Cloth with Black Imit. Leather

5211-69 501
Blue Panama Cloth with Blue Imit. Leather

5211-69 502
Turquoise Panama Cloth with Turquoise Imit. Leather

5211-69 503
Red Panama Cloth with Red. Imit. Leather

5269 505
Fawn Panama Cloth with Fawn Imit. Leather

5269 539
Black Panama Cloth with Black Imit. Leather

5237-39 506
Blue Panama Cloth with Blue Imit. Leather

5237-39 507
Turquoise Panama Cloth with Turquoise Imit. Leather

5237-39 508
Fawn Panama Cloth with Fawn Imit. Leather

5237-39 509
Red Panama Cloth with Red Imit. Leather

5237-39 540
Black Panama Cloth with Black Imit. Leather

5239-69-5639-69 534
Blue Pennington Cloth with Blue Imit. Leather

5239-69-5639-69 535
Turquoise Pennington Cloth with Turquoise Imit. Leather

5239-69-5639-69 538
Black Pennington Cloth with Black Imit. Leather

6237-39 542
Blue Prestige Cloth with Blue Imit. Leather

6237-39 543
Fawn Prestige Cloth with Fawn Imit. Leather

6237-39 544
Black Prestige Cloth with Black Imit. Leather

6239 545
Turquoise Prestige Cloth with Turquoise Imit. Leather

6239 546
Plum Prestige Cloth with Plum Imit. Leather

6657 ....*587
Black Palais Cloth with Black Imit. Leather

6657 ....*588
Fawn Palais Cloth with Fawn Imit. Leather

6657 589
Black Palais Cloth with Black Imit. Leather

6657 590
Fawn Palais Cloth with Fawn Imit. Leather

Cloth

6237 569
Fawn Palais Cloth

6237 586
Plum Palais Cloth

6237 593
Black Palais Cloth

6237 556
Gunmetal Palais Cloth

6239 557
Fawn Palais Cloth

6239 558
Plum Palais Cloth

6239 559
Black Palais Cloth

6267 596
Fawn Palais Cloth

6267 597
Black Palais Cloth

Imitation Leather

3307 205
Black

3307-69 210
Slate

3335 207
Turquoise

3335 208
Fawn

3335 209
Red

3335 210
Slate

3507-17-35-39-67-69 213
Blue

3507-17-35-39-69 214
Turquoise

3507-17-35-39—67-69 215
Fawn

3507-17-35-39-67-69 216
Red

37,4207-17-67 ....*219
Blue

37,4207-17-67 ....*220
Turquoise

37,4207-17-67 ....*221
Fawn

37,4207-17-67 ....*222
Red

37,4207-17-67 ....*223
Black

37,4207-17-67 ....*224
Parchment

3739 231
Black

3739 232
Blue

3739 233
Fawn

5211-69 599
Slate

5235-45 511
Blue

5235-45 512
Turquoise

5235-45 513
Fawn

5235-45 514
Red

5235-45 515
Black

5267 516
Blue

5267 517
Turquoise

5267 518
Fawn

5267 519
Red

5267 520
Black

5437-67 ....*521
Black

5437-67 ....*522
Red

5437-67 ....*523
Blue

5437-67 ....*524
Parchment

5237-39-69,5639-69 525
Blue

5237-39-69,5639-69 526
Turquoise

5237-39-69,5639-69 527
Fawn

5237-39-69,5639-69 528
Red

5237-39,5639 529
Black

6237-39 547
Blue

6237-39 548
Turquoise

6237-39 549
Fawn

6237-39 550
Red

6237-39 551
Black

6237-39 552
Parchment

6237 ....*554
Black

6237 ....*555
Parchment

6237 560
Blue

6245 561
Black

6245 562
Fawn

6657 ....*578
Black

6657 ....*579
Turquoise

6657 ....*580
Blue

6657 ....*581
Fawn

6657 ....*582
Red

6657 ....*583
Gunmetal

6657 ....*584
Plum

6657 ....*585

Parchment

6657 591
Black

6657 592
Parchment

.............................271-272-277

Genuine and Imitation Leather

6267 563
Blue

6267 564
Turquoise

6267 565
Fawn

6267 566
Red

6267 567
Black

6267 568
Parchment

6267 ....*570
Blue

6267 ....*571
Red

6267 ....*572
Black

6267 ....*573
Parchment

Genuine Leather

6267 266-273
Dark Blue

6267 267
Dark Turquoise

6267 268
Med. Fawn

6267 269-275
Med. Red

6267 271-272-277
Parchment

The PAINT CODE furnishes the key to exterior color.

COLOR	CODE
Starlight Black*	A
Blue Charcoal	B
Cameo Ivory*	C
Fontaine Blue	D
Nightwatch Blue	E
Palmentto Green	H
Reef Turquoise	K
Marina Turquoise	L
Burgundy	N
Barrier Blue	P
Montero Red*	R
Martinique Bronze	T
Mission Beige	V
Platinum	W
Candlelite Cream	Y

*Pin Stripe Colors

TEMPEST

HP	ENGINE CODE	CID	TRANS	USAGE	MODELS	COMP	CARB
165	ZK	230	SM	Standard	(1)(2)(3)(5)	9.0:1	1-bbl
207	ZD	230	SM	Optional	(1)(2)(3)(5)	10.5:1	4-bbl
165	ZS	230	SM	Optional	(1)(2)(3)(5)	9.0:1	1-bbl
250	WP	326	SM	Optional	(1)(2)(3)(5)	9.2:1	2-bbl
250	WX	326	SM	Optional	(1)(2)(3)(5)	9.2:1	2-bbl
285	WR	326	SM	Optional	(1)(2)(3)	10.5:1	4-bbl
360	WV	389	SM	Optional	(4)	10.75:1	3 x 2-bbl
335	WW	389	SM	Optional	(4)	10.75:1	4-bbl
360	WS	389	SM	Optional	(4)	10.75:1	3 x 2-bbl
335	WT	389	SM	Standard	(4)	10.75:1	4-bbl
165	ZN	230	Auto.	Standard	(1)(2)(3)(5)	9.0:1	1-bbl
207	ZE	230	Auto.	Optional	(1)(2)(3)(5)	10.5:1	4-bbl
165	ZM	230	Auto.	Optional	(1)(2)(3)(5)	9.0:1	1-bbl
250	YN	326	Auto.	Optional	(1)(2)(3)(5)	9.2:1	2-bbl
285	YP	326	Auto.	Optional	(1)(2)(3)	10.5:1	4-bbl
250	XF	326	Auto.	Optional	(1)(2)(3)(5)	9.2:1	2-bbl
285	XG	326	Auto.	Optional	(1)(2)(3)	10.5:1	4-bbl
335	XE	389	Auto.	Optional	(4)	10.75:1	1-bbl
360	YR	389	Auto.	Optional	(4)	10.75:1	3 x 2-bbl
335	YS	389	Auto.	Standard	(4)	10.75:1	1-bbl
360	XS	389	-	Optional	-	10.75:1	3 x 2-bbl
-	ZF	230	SM	-	-	7.6:1	1-bbl
-	ZG	230	Auto	-	-	7.6:1	1-bbl

(1) 233 except 23335   (2) 235 except 23535   (3) 237   (4) 242

PONTIAC

HP	ENGINE CODE	CID	TRANS	USAGE	MODELS	COMP	CARB
256	WA	389	SM	Standard	(1)(4)	8.6:1	2-bbl
256	WB	389	SM	Standard	(2)(7)(9)	8.6:1	2-bbl
256	WB	389	SM	Optional	(1)(4)	8.6:1	2-bbl
260	XA	389	SM	Export	(1)(2)(4)	7.6:1	2-bbl
290	WC	389	SM	Std. Hwy. Pat.	(10)	10.5:1	2-bbl
290	WC	389	SM	Optional	(1)(2)(4)	10.5:1	2-bbl
333	WE	389	SM	Standard	(5)(6)(8)	10.5:1	4-bbl
333	WE	389	SM	Optional	(1)(2)(4)(9)(10)	10.5:1	4-bbl
338	WG	421	SM	Standard	(3)	10.5:1	4-bbl
338	WK	421	SM	Optional	(1)(2)(4)(5)(6)(8)(10)	10.5:1	4-bbl
356	WH	421	SM	Optional	(1)(20(3)(4)(5)(6)(8)(10)	10.75:1	3/2-bbl
376	WJ	421	SM	421 H.O.	(1)(3)(4)(5)(6)(10)	10.75:1	3/2-bbl
256	YA	389	Auto	Reg. Fuel	(1)(2)(4)(5)(6)(8)(9)	8.6:1	2-bbl
290	YU	389	Auto	Optional	(1)(2)(4)(9)(10)	10.5:1	2-bbl
290	YC	389	Auto	Standard	(1)(2)(4)(9)(10)	10.5:1	2-bbl
290	YD	389	Auto	Air. Cond.	(1)(2)(4)(9)(10)	10.5:1	2-bbl
260	XB	389	Auto	Export	(1)(2)(4)	7.6:1	2-bbl
290	YV	389	Auto	Air. Cond.	(1)(2)(4)(9)(10)	10.5:1	2-bbl
325	YL	389	Auto	Police	(10)	10.5:1	4-bbl
325	YW	389	Auto	Optional	(1)(2)(4)(5)(6)(7)(8)(9)	10.5:1	4-bbl
325	YE	389	Auto	Optional	(1)(2)(4)(5)(6)(7)(8)(9)	10.5:1	4-bbl
325	YF	389	Auto	Air Cond.	(1)(2)(4)(5)(6)(7)(8)(9)	10.5:1	4-bbl
325	YX	389	Auto	Air Cond.	(1)(2)(4)(5)(6)(7)(8)(9)	10.5:1	4-bbl
293	XC	389	Auto	Export	(5)(6)(8)	7.6:1	4-bbl
338	YZ	421	Auto	Police	(10)	10.5:1	4-bbl
338	YT	421	Auto	Optional	(1)(2)(4)(5)(6)(8)	10.5:1	4-bbl
338	YH	421	Auto	Standard	(3)	10.5:1	4-bbl
356	YM	421	Auto	Police	(10)	10.75:1	3/2-bbl
356	YJ	421	Auto	Optional	(1)(2)(3)(4)(5)(6)(8)	10.75:1	3/2-bbl
376	YK	421	Auto	421 H.O.	(1)(3)(4)(5)(6)(9)(10)	10.75:1	3/2-bbl

(1) 252 except 35,45   (4) 256   (7) 26240, 50, 90   (10) Police / Hwy. Patrol
(2) 25235, 45   (5) 262 except 35,40,50,90   (8) 26235
(3) 254   (6) 266   (9) Police

VEHICLE IDENTIFICATION NUMBER

PONTIAC
252697P109038

VIN consists of Manufacturer's Symbol, Series and Body Style Code, Model Year Symbol, Assembly Plant Symbol and a sequential Production Number.

THE FIRST DIGIT: 2, identifies Pontiac Division.

SECOND AND THIRD: identify the Series.

Catalina	52
Executive	56
Bonneville	62
Grand Prix	66
Tempest	33
Tempest Custom	35
LeMans	37
Tempest Safari	39
GTO	42
Firebird	23

NOTE: '66 Tempest and Le-Mans Sprint option does not change VIN Catalina 2+2 option does not change VIN.

FOURTH AND FIFTH DIGIT: identify the body style in each series, (Example, 27 is a 2-Door Sports Coupe).

THE SIXTH DIGIT: identifies the Model Year, :5—1965.

THE SEVENTH DIGIT: identifies the Assembly Plant.

Assembly Plant	Code
Pontiac, Mich	P
Linden, N.J.	E
Southgate, Cal	C
Kansas City, Ks.	X
Framington, Mass	G
Fremont, Cal.	Z
Arlington, Tex.	R
Baltimore, Md.	B
Kansas City, Mo.	K
Van Nuys, Cal.	L
Atlanta, Ga.	A
Oshawa, Ont., Can.	1

FINAL DIGITS: production sequence number

FISHER BODY NUMBER PLATE

Complete identification of each body is provided by a plate attached to the left side of cowl under hood

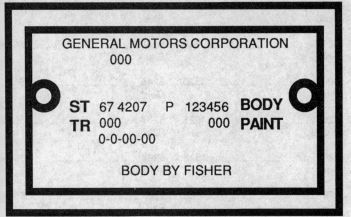

```
┌─────────────────────────────────────────┐
│  ┌───────────────────────────────────┐  │
│  │   GENERAL MOTORS CORPORATION      │  │
│  │            000                    │  │
│ ○│                                   │○ │
│  │ ST 67 4207  P 123456  BODY        │  │
│  │ TR 000            000  PAINT       │  │
│  │    0-0-00-00                      │  │
│  │                                   │  │
│  │       BODY BY FISHER              │  │
│  └───────────────────────────────────┘  │
└─────────────────────────────────────────┘
```

THE STYLE NUMBER is a combination of the year, series, and body code. 67 rep. model year: 1967; 42 rep. series 242—GTO; 07 rep. body style— sports coupe.

Series	Model	Style No.
Catalina 25200	2-Door Sedan	25211
	4-Door Sedan	25269
	Hardtop Coupe	25287
	4-Door Hardtop	25239
	Convertible	25267
	2-Seat Station Wagon	25235
	3-Seat Station Wagon	25245
Executive 25600	Hardtop Coupe	25687
	4-Door Ssedan	25669
	4-Door Hardtop	25639
	2-Seat Station Wagon	25635
	3-Seat Station Wagon	25645
Bonneville 26200	Hardtop Coupe	26287
	4-Door Hardtop	26239
	Convertible	26267
	Station Wagon	26245
Grand Prix 26600	Hardtop Coupe	26657
	Convertible	26667
Tempest 23300	Sports Coupe	23307
	4-Door Sedan	23369
	Station Wagon	23335
Tempest Custom 23500	Sports Coupe	23507
	Hardtop Coupe	23517
	4-Door Hardtop	23539
	4-Door Sedan	23569
	Convertible	23567
	Station Wagon	23535
LeMans 23700	Sports Coupe	23707
	Hardtop Coupe	23717
	4-Door Sedan	23739
	Station Wagon	23767
Tempest Safari 23935	2-Seat Station Wagon	23935
G.T.O. 24200	Sports Coupe	24207
	Hardtop Coupe	24217
	Convertible	24267
Firebird 22300	Sport Coupe	22337
	Convertible	22367

NOTE: TEMPEST SPRINT or LE MANS option does not change style or Catalina 2+2

THE BODY NUMBER is the production serial number of the body. The prefix letter denotes the plant in which the body was built.

Assembly Plant	Code
Pontiac	P
Arlington	R
Baltimore	B
Freemont	Z
Kansas City, Ks.	X
Kansas City, Mo.	K
Linden	E
Southgate	C
Lordstown	U
Framingham	G

THE TRIM CODE furnishes the key to the interior color and material.

Model	Color	Code

Cloth and Imitation Leather

3307-69 201
Blue Paharra Cloth with Blue Imit. Leather

3307-69 202
Turquoise Paharra Cloth with Turquoise Imit. Leather

3307-69 203
Gold Paharra Cloth with Gold Imit. Leather

3369 205
Black Paharra Cloth with Black Imit. Leather

3739 228
Black Prevue Cloth with Black Imit. Leather

3739 229
Blue Prevue Cloth with Blue Imit. Leather

5211-69 501
Blue Poncaire Cloth with Blue Imit. Leather

5211-69 502
Turquoise ..... Poncaire Cloth with Turquoise Imit. Leather

5211 503
Black Poncaire Cloth with Black Imit. Leather

5269 504
Burgundy Poncaire Cloth with Burgundy Imit. Leather

5269 505
Gold Poncaire Cloth with Gold Imit. Leather

5239-87 506
Blue Poncaire Cloth with Blue Imit. Leather

5239-87 507
Turquoise Poncaire Cloth with Turquoise Imit. Leather

5239-87 508
Gold Poncaire Cloth with Gold Imit. Leather

5239-87 509
Burgundy Poncaire Cloth with Burgundy Imit. Leather

5239-87 510
Black Poncaire Cloth with Black Imit. Leather

5239-69,5639-69 534
Blue Pristine Cloth with Blue Imit. Leather

5239-69,5639-69 535
Turquoise Pristine Cloth with Turquoise Imit. Leather

5239-69,5639-69 538
Black Pristine Cloth with Black Imit. Leather

6239-87 542
Blue Parella ICloth with Blue Imit. Leather

6239-87 543
Gold Parella Cloth with Gold Imit. Leather

6239-87 544
Black Parella Cloth with Black Imit. Leather

6239 545
Turquoise Parella Cloth with Turquoise Leather

6239 546
Burgundy Parella Cloth with Burgundy Imit. Leather

6239 556
Black Plaza and Princessa Cloth with Black Imit. Leather

6239 557
Gold Plaza and Princessa Cloth with Gold Imit. Leather

6239 558
Burgundy Plaza and Princessa Cloth with Burgundy Imit. Leather

6239 559
Blue Plaza and Princessa Cloth with Blue Imit. Leather

6287 569
Gold Plaza and Princessa Cloth with Gold Imit. Leather

6287 586
Burgundy Plaza and Princessa Cloth with Burgundy Imit. Leather

6287 593
Black Plaza and Princessa Cloth with Black Imit. Leather

6657 587-589
Black Princessa Cloth with Black Imit. Leather

6657 588-590
Gold Princessa Cloth with Gold Imit. Leather

Imitation Leather

3335 210
Black

3507-17-39-69,3935 213
Blue

3507-17-39-69,3935 214
Turquoise

3507-17-39-69,3935 215
Gold

3507-17-39-69,3935 217
Black

3567 213
Blue

3567 217
Black

3567 218
Red

3707-17-67 219
Blue

3707-17-67 220
Turquoise

3707-17-67 221
Gold

3707-17-67 223
Black

3707-17-67 224
Parchment

3707-17-67 225
Red

3739 231
Black

2739 232
Blue

3739 233
Gold

4207-17-67 219
Blue

4207-17-67 220
Turquoise

4207-17-67 221
Gold

4207-17-67 223
Black

4207-17-67 224
Parchment

4207-17-67 225
Red

5211-69 599
Black

5235-45 511
Blue

5235-45 512
Turquoise

5235-45 513
Gold

5235-45 514
Burgundy

5245-45 515
Black

5239-69,5639-69 525
Blue

5239-69,5639-69 526
Turquoise

5239-69,5639-69 527
Gold

5239,5639 528
Burgundy

5239-69,5639-69 529
Black

5267 516
Blue

5267 518
Gold

5267 519
Red

5267 520
Black

5267 ....*521
Black

5267 ....*522
Red

5267 ....*523
Blue

5267 ....*524
Parchment

5287 ....*521
Black

5287 ....*522
Red

5287 ....*523
Parchment

5287,56878 ....*524
Blue

5287,56878 525
Turquoise

5287,5687 526
Gold

5287,5687 527
Burgundy

5287,5687 528
Black

5635-45 529
Blue

5635-45 530
Gold

5635-45 532
Black

6239 536
Blue

6239 547
Turquoise

6239 548
Gold

6239 549
Burgundy

6239 550
Black

6239 552
Parchment

6245 560
Blue

6245 561
Black

6245 562
Gold

6267 563
Blue

6267 564
Turquoise

6267 566
Red

6267 567
Black

6267 568
Parchment

6267 ....*572
Black

6267 ....*573
Parchment

6287 547
Blue

6287 548
Turquoise

6287 549
Gold

6287 550
Burgundy

6287 551
Black

6287 552
Parchment

6287 ....*554
Black

6287 ....*555
Parchment

6657 ....*579
Turquoise

6657 ....*580
Blue

6657 ....*581
Gold

6657 ....*583
Black

6657 ....*584
Burgundy

6657 ....*585
Parchment

6657 591
Black

6657 592
Parchment

6667 ....*580
Blue

6667 ....*583
Black

6667 ....*585
Parchment

6667 ....*594
Red

FIREBIRD

2337-67 250
Blue (Dark Metallic) 270*

2337-67 251
Gold (Medium Metallic) 271*

2337-67 252
Red

2337-67 253
Black 272*

2337-67 274
Parchmment (Afflair)

CUSTOM INTERIORS

2337-67 255
Blue (Med. Bright Metallic) .. 265*

2337-67 256
Turquoise (Dark Metallic)

2337-67 257
Gold (Medium Metallic) 267*

2337-67 258
Red

2337-67 259
Black 269*

2337-67 260
Parchment (Afflair)

*NOTE:Strato bench seat-regular
production option-available in
coupes only.

The PAINT CODE furnishes the
key to exterior color and striping.

PONTIAC-TEMPEST

COLOR	CODE
Starlight Black	A
Cameo Ivory	C
Montreux Blue	D
Fathom Blue	E
Tyrol Blue	F
Signet Gold	G
Linden Green	H
Gulf Turquoise	K
Mariner Turquoise	L
Plum Mist	M
Burgundy	N
Silver glaze	P
Regimental Red	R
Champagne	S
Montego Cream	T

FIREBIRD

Starlight Black	A
Cameo Ivory	C
Montreux Blue	D
Fathom Blue	E
Tyrol Blue	F
Signet Gold	G
Linden Green	H
Gulf Turquoise	K
Mariner Turquoise	L
Plum Mist	M
Burgundy	N
Silver glaze	P
Regimental Red	R
Champagne	S
Montego Cream	T

ENGINE NUMBER

Along with the VIN the engine block is stamped with an Engine Code. The codes for 1967 are:

PONTIAC ENGINE CHART

HP	ENGINE CODE	C.I.D.	TRANS.	CARB.	COMP.
265	WA	400	Manual	2-bbl	8.6:1
265	WB	400	Manual	2-bbl	8.6:1
333	WD	400	Manual	4-bbl	10.5:1
333	WE	400	Manual	4-bbl	10.5:1
260	XB	400	Automatic	2-bbl	7.9:1
293	XC	400	Automatic	4-bbl	7.9:1
350	XH	400	Automatic	4-bbl	10.5:1
350	XJ	400	Automatic	4-bbl	10.5:1
350	XY	400	Manual	4-bbl	10.5:1
350	XZ	400	Manual	4-bbl	10.5:1
265	YA	400	Automatic	2-bbl	8.6:1
265	YB	400	Automatic	2-bbl	8.6:1
290	YC	400	Automatic	2-bbl	10.5:1
290	YD	400	Automatic	2-bbl	10.5:1
325	YE	400	Automatic	4-bbl	10.5:1
325	YF	400	Automatic	4-bbl	10.5:1
333	WY	400	MANUAL	4-bbl	10.5:1
360	WG	428	Manual	QUADRAJET	10.5:1
376	WJ@	428	Manual	QUADRAJET	10.75:1
376	Y3@	428	Automatic	QUADRAJET	10.75:1
360	Y2	428	Automatic	QUADRAJET	10.5:1
376	XK@	428	Manual	QUADRAJET	10.75:1
360	Y2	428	Automatic	QUADRAJET	10.5:1
376	YK@	428	Automatic	QUADRAJET	10.75:1
360	YY	428	Manual	QUADRAJET	

@ Special Exhaust Manifolds

TEMPEST ENGINE CHART

HP	ENGINE CODE	C.I.D.	TRANS.	CARB.	COMP.
215	ZD	230	Manual	QUADRAJET	10.5:1
215	ZE	230	Automatic	QUADRAJET	10.5:1
155	ZF	230	Manual	1-bbl	7.9:1
155	ZG	230	Automatic	1-bbl	7.9:1
165	ZK	230	Manual	1-bbl	9.0:1
215	ZL	230	Automatic	QUADRAJET	10.5:1
165	ZM	230	Automatic	1-bbl	9.0:1
165	ZN	230	Automatic	1-bbl	9.0:1
215	ZR	230	Manual	QUADRAJET	10.5:1
165	ZS	230	Manual	1-bbl	9.0:1
250	WP	326	Manual	2-bbl	9.2:1
285	WR	326	Manual	4-bbl	10.5:1
250	WX	326	Manual	2-bbl	9.2:1
250	XF	326	Automatic	2-bbl	9.2:1
285	XG	326	Automatic	4-bbl	10.5:1
285	XR	326	Manual	4-bbl	10.5:1
250	YN	326	Automatic	2-bbl	9.2:1
285	YP	326	Automatic	4-bbl	10.5:1
360	WS	400	Manual	QUADRAJET	10.75:1
335	WT	400	Manual	QUADRAJET	10.75:1
360	WV	400	Manual	QUADRAJET	10.75:1
335	WW	400	Manual	QUADRAJET	10.75:1
255	XL	400	Automatic	2-bbl	8.6:1
255	XM	400	Automatic	2-bbl	8.6:1
360	XS	400	Manual	QUADRAJET	10.75:1
360	YR	400	Manual	QUADRAJET	10.75:1
335	YS	400	Automatic	QUADRAJET	10.75:1
360	YZ	400	Automatic	QUADRAJET	10.75:1
360	XP	400	Automatic	QUADRAJET	10.75:1
250	YO	326	Automatic	2-bbl	9.2:1
285	YP	326	Automatic	4-bbl	10.5:1

FIREBIRD ENGINE CHART

HP	ENGINE CODE	C.I.D.	TRANS.	CARB.	COMP.
165	ZK	230	Manual	1-bbl	9.0:1
165	ZS	230	Manual	1-bbl	9.0:1
165	ZN	230	Automatic	1-bbl	9.0:1
165	ZM	230	Automatic	1-bbl	9.0:1
215	ZD	230	Manual	QUADRAJET	10.5:1
215	ZR	230	Manual	QUADRAJET	10.5:1
215	ZE	230	Automatic	QUADRAJET	10.5:1
215	ZL	230	Automatic	QUADRAJET	10.5:1
155	ZF	230	Manual	1-bbl	7.6:1
155	ZG	230	Automatic	1-bbl	7.6:1
250	WC	326	Manual	2-bbl	9.2:1
250	WH	326	Manual	2-bbl	9.2:1
325	WI	400	Manual	4-bbl	10.75:1
325	WZ	400	Manual	4-bbl	10.75:1
250	YJ	326	Automatic	2-bbl	9.2:1
250	XI	326	Automatic	2-bbl	9.2:1
285	WK	326	Manual	4-bbl	10.5:1
285	WO	326	Manual	4-bbl	10.5:1
285	YM	326	Automatic	4-bbl	10.5:1
285	XO	326	Automatic	4-bbl	10.5:1
325	WZ	400	Manual	QUADRAJET	10.75:1
325	WU	400	Manual	QUADRAJET	10.75:1
325	YT	400	Automatic	QUADRAJET	10.75:1
325	WL	400	Manual	QUADRAJET	10.75:1
325	WQ	400	Manual	QUADRAJET	10.75:1
325	XN	400	Automatic	QUADRAJET	10.75:1
265	YB	400	Automatic	2-bbl	8.6:1
290	YC	400	Automatic	2-bbl	10.5:1
290	YD	400	Automatic	2-bbl	10.5:1
325	YE	400	Automatic	4-bbl	10.5:1
325	YF	400	Automatic	4-bbl	10.5:1
360	YH	428	Automatic	4-bbl	10.5:1
376	YK	428	Automatic	4-bbl	10.75:1
360	YY	428	Manual	4-bbl	10.5:1

VEHICLE IDENTIFICATION NUMBER

```
PONTIAC
252698P109038
```

Embossed on a Plate Located on left edge of insturment panel, visible through wimdshield. VIN also stamped on all transmissions and engines.

THE FIRST DIGIT: 2, identifies Pontiac Division.

SECOND AND THIRD: identify the Series.

Catalina	52
Executive	56
Bonneville	62
Grand Prix	66
Tempest	33
Tempest	35
Lemons	37
Tempest Safari	39
GTO	42
Firebird	23

NOTE: Tempest Lemans Spirit does not change VIN.

FOURTH AND FIFTH DIGIT: identify the body style in each series, (Example, 27 is a 2-Door Sports Coupe).

THE SIXTH DIGIT: identifies the Model Year, :8—1968.

THE SEVENTH DIGIT: identifies the Assembly Plant.

Assembly Plant	Code
Pontiac, Mich.	P
Linden, N.J.	E
Southgate, Cal.	C
Kansas City, Ks.	X
Framington, Mass.	G
Fremont, Cal.	Z
Arlington, Tex.	R
Baltimore, Md.	B
Kansas City, Mo.	K
Van Nuys, Cal.	L
Atlanta, Ga.	A
Oshawa, Ont., Can.	1

FINAL DIGITS: production sequence number

FISHER BODY NUMBER PLATE

Complete identification of each body is provided by a plate attached to the left side of cowl under hood

THE BODY NUMBER is the production serial number of the body. The prefix letter denotes the plant in which the body was built.

Assembly Plant	Code
Pontiac	P
Arlington	R
Baltimore	B
Freemont	Z
Kansas City, Ks.	X
Kansas City, Mo.	K
Linden	E
Southgate	C
Lordstown	U
Framingham	G

THE STYLE NUMBER is a combination of the year, series, and body code. 67 rep. model year: 1967; 42 rep. series 242—GTO; 07 rep. body style— sports coupe.

SERIES	MODEL	STYLE NUMBER
Catalina 25200	4-Door Sedan	25269
	Hardtop Coupe	25287
	4-Door Hardtop	25239
	Convertible	25267
	2-Seat Station Wagon	25235
	3-Seat Station Wagon	25245
	2-Door Sedan	25211
Executive 25600	Hardtop Coupe	25687
	4-Door sedan	25669
	4-Door Hardtop	25639
	2-Seat Station Wagon	25635
	3-Seat Station Wagon	25645
Bonneville	Hardtop Coupe	26287
	4-Door Hardtop	26239
	Convertible	26267
	Station Wagon	26245
	4-Door Sedan	26269
Grand Prix 26600	Hardtop Coupe	26657
Tempest 23300	Sports Coupe	23327
	4-Door Sedan	23369
Tempest Custom 23500	Sports Coupe	23527
	Hardtop Coupe	23537
	4-Door Hardtop	23539
	4-Door Sedan	23569
	Convertible	23567
	Station Wagon	23535
LeMans 23700	Sports Coupe	23727
	Hardtop Coupe	23737
	4-Door Sedan	23739
	Convertible	23767
Tempest Safari 23935	2-Seat Stastion Wagon	23935
GTO 24200	Hardtop Coupe	24237
	Convertible	24267
Firebird	Coupe	22337
	Convertible	22367

GENERAL MOTORS CORPORATION
000

ST 68 24237 APL 123456 **BODY**
TR 000A   AA **PAINT**

BODY BY FISHER

THE TRIM CODE: Furnishes the key to the interior color and material.

CLOTH AND IMITATION LEATHER

201	3327-69	Blue Paray cloth and Blue Imit. Leather
202	3327-69	Turquoise Paray cloth and Turquoise Imit. Leather
203	3327-69	Gold Paray cloth and Gold Imit. Leather
228	3739	Black Ponciva cloth and Black Imit, Leather
501	5211-69	Blue Patrice cloth and Blue Imit. leather
503	5211	Black Patrice cloth and Black Imit. leather
505	5211	Gold Patrice cloth and Gold Imit. leather
506	5239-87	Blue Patrice cloth and Blue Imit. leather
507	5239-87	Turquoise Patrice cloth and Turquoise Imit. leather
508	5239-87	Gold Patrice cloth and Gold Imit. leather
509	5239-87	Burgandy Patrice cloth and Burgandy Imit. leather
510	5239-87	Black Patrice cloth and Black Imit. leather
534	5239-69,5639-69	Blue Pierette cloth and Blue Imit. leather
535	5239-69,5639-69	Turquoise Pierette cloth and Turquoise Imit. leather
539	5239-69,5639-69	Gold Pierette cloth and Gold Imit. leather
538	5239-69,5639-69	Black Pierette cloth and Black Imit. leather
502	5269	Turquoise Patrice cloth and Turquoise Imit. leather
504	5269	Burgandy Patrice cloth and Burgandy Imit. leather
542	6239-87	Turquoise Princessa cloth and Turquoise Imit. leather
543	6239-87	Gold Princessa cloth and Gold Imit. leather
544	6239-87	Black Princessa cloth and Black Imit. leather
545	6239-87	Teal Princessa cloth and Teal Imit. leather
546	6239	Burgandy Princessa cloth and Burgandy Imit. leather
556	6239-87	Black parisien and Prima bolster cloth and Black Imit. leather
558	6239-87	Burgandy parisien and Prima bolster cloth and Burgandy Imit. leather
559	6239-87	Blue parisien and Prima bolster cloth and Blue Imit. leather
587-589(2)	6657	Black Promenade cloth and Black Imit. leather
588-590(2)	6657	Black Promenade cloth and Black Imit. leather

F
I
R
E
B
I
R
D

IMITATION LEATHER

250	2337-67	Teal (Std. Interior)
251	2337-67	Gold (Std. Interior)
252	2337-67	Red (Std. Interior)
253-272(2)	2337-67	Black (Std. Interior)
261	2337-67	Turquoise (Std. Interior)
262-273(2)	2337-67	Parchment (Std. Interior)
255	2337-67	Teal Knit and Teal (Custom Interior)
256	2337-67	Turquoise Knit and Turquoise (Custom Interior)
257	2337-67	Gold Knit and Gold (Custom Interior)
258	2337-67	Red Knit and Red (Custom Interior)
259-269(2)	2337-67	Black Knit and Black (Custom Interior)
260-275(2)	2337-67	Parchment Knit and Parchment (Custom Interior)
206	3327	Black
206	3369	Black
213	3527-35-37-39-69	Blue
214	3527-35-37-39-69	Turquoise
215	3527-35-37-39-69	Gold
217	3527-35-37-39-69	Black
213	3567	Blue
217	3567	Black
218	3567	Red
219(1)	3727-37-67,4237-67	Teal
220(1)	3727-37-67,4237-67	Turquoise
221(1)	3727-37-67,4237-67	Gold
223(1)	3727-37-67,4237-67	Black
224(1)	3727-37-67,4237-67	Parchment
225(1)	3727-37-67,4237-67	Red
235(3)	3727-37-67,4237-67	Black
236(3)	3727-37-67,4237-67	Parchment
231(3)	3739	Black
232(3)	3739	Teal
233(3)	3739	Parchment
213	3935	Blue
214	3935	Turquoise
215	3935	Gold
217	3935	Black
599	5211-69	Black
511	5235-45	Blue
512	5235-45	Truquoise
513	5235-45	Gold
514	5235-45	Burgandy
515	5235-45	Black
526	5235-45,5635-45	Turquoise
529	5235-45,5635-45	Black
533	5235-45,5635-45	Teal
525	5239-69,5639-69	Blue
526	5239-69,5639-69	Turquoise
527	5239-69,5639-69	Gold
528	5239,5639	Parchment
529	5239-69,5639-69	Black
516	5267	Blue
518	5267	Gold
519	5267	Red
520	5267	Black
521(1)	5267-87	Black
524(1)	5267-87	Parchment
525	5287,5687	Blue
526	5287,5687	Turquoise
527	5287,5687	Gold
528	5287,5687	Parchment
529	5287,5687	Black
547	6239	Turquoise
548	6239	Teal
549	6239	Gold
550	6239	Burgandy
551	6239	Black
552	6239	Parchment
560	6245	Teal
561	6245	Black
562	6245	Gold
563	6267	Turquoise
564	6267	Teal
566	6267	Red
567-572(1)	6267	Black
568-573(1)	6267	Parchment
547	6287	Turquoise
548	6287	Teal
549	6287	Red
550	6287	Burgandy
551-554(1)	6287	Black
552-555(1)	6287	Parchment
579(1)	6657	Teal
580(1)	6657	Turquoise
581(1)	6657	Gold
584(1)	6657	Burgandy
585(1)	6657	Parchment
583(1)	6657	Black
591(2)	6657	Black
592(2)	6657	Parchment

GENUINE AND IMITATION LEATHER

570	5267,6267	Black
571	5267,6267	Saddle
593(2)	6657	Black
594(2)	6657	Saddle

(1) Denotes Bucket Seats
(2) Denotes Strato bench seat-regular production option
(3) Denotes Notch back bench seat-regular production option

The PAINT CODE furnishes the key to exterior color and striping.

Color	Code
Starlight Black	A
Cameo Ivory	C
Alpine Blue	D
Aegena Blue	E
Nordic Blue	F
April Gold	G
Autumn Bronze	I
Merdian Turquoise	K
Aleutian Blue	L
Flambeau Burgandy	N
Springmist Green	P
Verdoro Green	Q
Solar Red	R
Primavera Beige	T
Nightshade Green	V
Mayfair Maize	Y

ENGINE CODES

The engine code is stamped along with the VIN on the block.

PONTIAC ENGINE CHART

HP	ENGINE CODE	CID	TRANS	CARB	COMP
290	WA	400	Manual	2-bbl	10.5:1
290	WB	400	Manual	2-bbl	10.5:1
265	YA	400	Automatic	2-bbl	8.6:1
290	YC	400	Automatic	2-bbl	10.5:1
340	YE	400	Automatic	QUADRAJET	10.5:1
350	XZ	400	Manual	QUADRAJET	10.5:1
350	XH	400	Automatic	QUADRAJET	10.5:1
350	XZ	400	Manual	4-bbl	10.5:1
375	WG	428	Manual	QUADRAJET	10.5:1
390	WJ@	428	Manual	QUADRAJET	10.75:1
375	YH	428	Automatic	QUADRAJET	10.5:1
390	YK@	428	Automatic	QUADRAJET	10.75:1

@ Special Exhaust Manifolds

TEMPEST ENGINE CHART

HP	ENGINE CODE	CID	TRANS	CARB	COMP
215	ZD	250	Manual	4-bbl	10.5:1
175	ZK	250	Manual	1-bbl	9.0:1
175	ZN	250	Automatic	1-bbl	9.0:1
215	ZO	250	Manual	QUADRAJET	10.5:1
215	ZE	250	Automatic	QUADRAJET	10.5:1
265	WD	350	Manual	2-bbl	9.2:1
265	YN	350	Automatic	2-bbl	9.2:1
320	WR	350	Manual	QUADRAJET	10.5:1
320	YP	350	Automatic	QUADRAJET	10.5:1
265	XM	400	Automatic	2-bbl	8.6:1
360	WT	400	Manual	QUADRAJET	10.75:1
350	YS	400	Automatic	QUADRAJET	10.75:1
360	WS	400	Manual	QUADRAJET	10.75:1
350	YZ	400	Automatic	QUADRAJET	10.75:1
360	XS	400	Manual	QUADRAJET	10.75:1
360	XP	400	Automatic	QUADRAJET	10.75:1
265	WP	350	Manual	2-bbl	9.2:1

FIREBIRD ENGINE CHART

HP	ENGINE CODE	CID	TRANS	CARB	COMP
175	ZK	250	Manual	1-bbl	9.0:1
175	ZN	250	Automatic	1-bbl	9.0:1
215	ZD	250	Manual	QUADRAJET	10.5:1
215	ZE	250	Automatic	QUADRAJET	10.5:1
265	WC	350	Manual	2-bbl	9.2:1
265	YJ	350	Automatic	2-bbl	9.2:1
320	WK	350	Manual	QUADRAJET	10.5:1
320	YM	350	Automatic	QUADRAJET	10.5:1
335	XN	400	Automatic	QUADRAJET	10.75:1
335	WQ	400	Manual	QUADRAJET	10.75:1
335	WI	400	Manual	QUADRAJET	10.75:1
335	WZ	400	Manual	QUADRAJET	10.75:1
330	YW	400	Automatic	QUADRAJET	10.75:1
330	YT	400	Automatic	QUADRAJET	10.75:1

VEHICLE IDENTIFICATION NUMBER

```
PONTIAC
252699P109038
```

Embossed on a Plate Located on left edge of insturment panel, visible through wimdshield. VIN also stamped on all transmissions and engines.

THE FIRST DIGIT: 2, identifies Pontiac Division.

SECOND AND THIRD: identify the Series.

Catalina	52
Executive	56
Bonneville	62
Grand Prix	66
Tempest	33
Tempest	35
Lemons	37
Tempest Safari	39
GTO	42
Firebird	23

NOTE: Tempest Lemans Spirit does not change VIN.

FOURTH AND FIFTH DIGIT: identify the body style in each series, (Example, 27 is a 2-Door Sports Coupe).

THE SIXTH DIGIT: identifies the Model Year, :9—1969.

THE SEVENTH DIGIT: identifies the Assembly Plant.

Assembly Plant	Code
Pontiac, Mich.	P
Linden, N.J.	E
Southgate, Cal.	C
Kansas City, Ks.	X
Framington, Mass.	G
Fremont, Cal.	Z
Arlington, Tex.	R
Baltimore, Md.	B
Kansas City, Mo.	K
Van Nuys, Cal.	L
Atlanta, Ga.	A
Oshawa, Ont., Can.	1

FINAL DIGITS: production sequence number

FISHER BODY NUMBER PLATE

Complete ID of body is provided by a plate attached to left side of cowl under hood.

THE BODY NUMBER is the production serial number of the body. The prefix letter denotes the plant in which the body was built.

Assembly Plant	Code
Pontiac	P
Arlington	R
Baltimore	B
Freemont	Z
Kansas City, Ks.	X
Kansas City, Mo.	K
Linden	E
Southgate	C
Lordstown	U
Framingham	G

THE STYLE NUMBER is a combination of the year, series, and body code. 69 rep. model year: 1969; 42 rep. series 242—GTO; 07 rep. body style— sports coupe.

SERIES	MODEL	STYLE NUMBER
Catalina 25200	4-Door Sedan	25269
	Hardtop Coupe	25237
	4-Door Hardtop	25239
	Convertible	25267
	2-Seat Station Wagon	25236
	3-Seat Station Wagon	25246
Executive 25600	Hardtop Coupe	25637
	4-Door sedan	25669
	4-Door Hardtop	25639
	2-Seat Safari	25636
	3-Seat Safari	25646
Bonneville	Hardtop Coupe	26237
	4-Door Hardtop	26239
	4-Door sedan	26269
	Convertible	26267
	3-Seat Station Wagon	26246
Grand Prix 27600	Hardtop Coupe	27657
Tempest 23300	Sports Coupe	23327
	4-Door Sedan	23369
Custom S 23500	Sports Coupe	23527
	Hardtop Coupe	23537
	4-Door Hardtop	23539
	4-Door Sedan	23569
	Convertible	23567
	Station Wagon	23535
LeMans 23700	Sports Coupe	23727
	Hardtop Coupe	23737
	4-Door Sedan	23739
	Convertible	23767
LeMans Safari 23936	2-Seat Stastion Wagon	23936
GTO 24200	Hardtop Coupe	24237
	Convertible	24267
Firebird 22300	Coupe	22337
	Convertible	22367

THE TRIM CODE: Furnishes the key to the interior color and material.

IMITATION LEATHER

CODE	MODEL	COLOR
200	2337-67	Blue
202	2337-67	Gold
206	2337-67	Green
207	2337-67	Parchment
208	2337-67	Black
210	2337-67	Blue Knit
212	2337-67	Gold Knit
214	2337-67	Red Knit
216	2337-67	Green Knit
217-227(2)	2337-67	Parchment
		Knit
218-228(2)	2337-67	Black Knit
249	3327-69	Black
241	3527-35-37-39-67-69	Blue
222	3527-35-37-39-69	Gold
246	3527-35-37-39-69	Green
248	3527-35-37-39-67-69	Black
250(1)	3727-37-67,4237-67	Blue
252(1)	3727-37-67,4237-67	Gold
254(1)	3727-37-67,4237-67	Red
256(1)	3727-37-67,4237-67	Green
257(1)	3727-37-67,4237-67	Parchment
258(1)	3727-37-67,4237-67	Black
267(2)	3727-37-67,4237-67	Parchment
268(2)	3727-37-67,4237-67	Black
260(2)	3739	Blue
262(2)	3739	Gold
266(2)	3739	Green
531	5236-37-39-46-67-69	Blue
532	5236-37-39-46-67-69	Gold
535	5236-46	Burgandy
536	5236-37-39-46-69	Green
538	5236-37-39-46-67-69	Black
552	5236-37-39-46-69	Gold
556	5236-37-39-46-69	Green
557	5236-37-39-46	Parchment
558	5236-37-39-46-69	Black
550	5237-39-69	Blue
239(1)	5237	Black
534	5267	Red
599	5269(Pol-Taxi)	Black
552	5636-37-39-46-69	Gold
556	5636-37-39-46-69	Green
557	5636-37-39-46	Parchment
558	5636-37-39-46-69	Black
550	5637-39-69	Blue
539(1)	6237-67	Black
560	6237-39-46-67	Blue
562	6237-39-46	Gold
565	6237-39	Burgandy
566	6237-39-46-67	Green
567	6237-39-67	Parchment
568	6237-39-46-67	Black
570	6239-69	Blue
572	6239-69	Gold
575	6239	Burgabdy
577	6239	Parchment
578	6239-69	Black
564	6267	Red
280(1)	7657	Blue
282(1)	7657	Gold
285(1)	7657	Burgandy
286(1)	7657	Green
287(1)	7657	Parchment
288(1)	7657	Black

GENERAL MOTORS CORPORATION
000

ST 69 24237 APL 123456 **BODY**
TR 000A AA **PAINT**
0-0-00-00

BODY BY FISHER

CLOTH AND IMITATION LEATHER

231	3327-69	Blue
232	3327-69	Gold
236	3327-69	Green
238	3739	Black
511	5237	Blue
512	5237	Gold
515	5237	Burgandy
516	5237	Green
518	5237	Black
540	5239-87,5669	Blue
542	5239-87,5669	Gold
546	5239-87,5669	Green
548	5239-87,5669	Black
501	5269	Blue
502	5269	Gold
505	5269	Burgandy
506	5269	Green
508	5269	Black
510	6237	Blue
513	6237	Gold
519	6237	Black
580	6237	Blue
586	6237	Green
588	6237	Black
520	6239-69	Blue
523	6239-69	Gold
526	6239-69	Green
529	6239-69	Black
590	6239	Blue
595	6239	Burgandy
596	6239	Green
598	6239	Black
270(1)	7657	Blue
272(1)	7657	Gold
276(1)	7657	Green
278(1)	7657	Black

GENUINE AND IMITATION LEATHER

293(1)	2337-67	Gold
563	6267	Gold
569	6267	Black
292(1)	7657	Gold
296(1)	7657	Green
298(1)	7657	Black

(1) Denotes Bucket Seats
(2) Denotes Notch back bench seat

Trim combination numbers will be found on the body number plate attached to the dash, under the hood.

The PAINT CODE furnishes the key to exterior color and striping.

Color	Code
Starlight Black	A
Expresso Brown	B
Cameo White	C
Warwick Blue	D
Liberty Blue	E
Antique Gold	G
Limelight Green	H
Crystal Turquoise	K
Midnight Green	M
Burgandy	N
Palladium Silver	P
Verdoro Green	Q
Matador Red	R
Champagne	S
Mayfair Maize	Y
Castilian Bronze	J
Claret Red	L
Nocturne Blue	V

ENGINE CODES

The engine code is stamped along with the VIN on the right hand side of block.

PONTIAC and GRAN PRIX ENGINE CHART

HP	ENGINE CODE	CID	TRANS	CARB	COMP
290(a)	WA	400	Manual	2-bbl	10.5:1
290	WD	400	Manual	2-bbl	10.5:1
265(a)	YA	400	Automatic	2-bbl	8.6:1
265	YB	400	Automatic	2-bbl	8.6:1
290(a)	WB	400	Manual	2-bbl	10.5:1
290	WE	400	Manual	2-bbl	10.5:1
290(a)	YE	400	Automatic	2-bbl	10.5:1
290	YD	400	Automatic	2-bbl	10.5:1
360	WG	428	Manual	4-bbl	10.5:1
360(a)	YL	428	Automatic	4-bbl	10.5:1
360	YH	428	Automatic	4-bbl	10.5:1
390	WJ	428	Manual	4-bbl	10.75:1
360(b)	XK	428	Automatic	4-bbl	10.5:1
"360(a,c)"	XE	428	Automatic	4-bbl	10.5:1
360(c)	XJ	428	Automatic	4-bbl	10.5:1
390	YK	428	Automatic	4-bbl	10.75:1
350(d)	WX	400	Manual	4-bbl	10.5:1
350(d)	XH	400	Automatic	4-bbl	10.5:1
370(d)	WF	428	Manual	4-bbl	10.5:1
370(d)	XF	428	Automatic	4-bbl	10.5:1
390(d)	WL	428	Manual	4-bbl	10.75:1
390(d)	XG	428	Automatic	4-bbl	10.75:1
265(d)	YF	400	Automatic	2-bbl	8.6:1
340	XZ	400	Automatic	4-bbl	10.5:1

(a) Early production small valve engines
(b) Police Freeway Enforcer
(c) Police Highway Patrol
(d) Grand Prix

TEMPEST and GTO ENGINE CHART

HP	ENGINE CODE	CID	TRANS	CARB	COMP
175(a)	ZK	250	Manual	1-bb	9.0:1
175	ZC	250	Manual	1-bbl	9.0:1
175(a)	ZN	250	Automatic	1-bbl	9.0:1
175	ZN	250	Automatic	1-bbl	9.0:1
215(a)	ZE	250	Automatic	4-bbl	10.5:1
215	ZL	250	Automatic	4-bbl	10.5:1
265(a)	XR	350	Automatic	2-bbl	9.2:1
265	XS	350	Automatic	2-bbl	9.2:1
"265(a,)"	YN	350	Automatic	2-bbl	9.2:1
265	YU	350	Automatic	2-bbl	9.2:1
265(a)	WP	350	Manual	2-bbl	9.2:1
265	WU	350	Manual	2-bbl	9.2:1
330	XU	350	Automatic	4-bbl	10.5:1
330	WV	350	Manual	4-bbl	10.5:1
350	YS	400	Automatic	4-bbl	10.75:1
350	WT	400	Manual	4-bbl	10.75:1
366	YZ	400	Automatic	4-bbl	10.75:1
366	WS	400	Manual	4-bbl	10.75:1
265(a)	XM	400	Automatic	2-bbl	8.6:1
265	XM	400	Automatic	2-bbl	8.6:1
370	XP	400	Automatic	4-bbl	10.75:1
370	WW	400	Manual	4-bbl	10.75:1
330	WR	350	Manual	4-bbl	10.5:1
330	XT	350	Automatic	4-bbl	10.5:1
265	XX	400	Automatic	2-bbl	8.6:1
230	ZD	250	Manual	4-bbl	10.5:1
175	ZF	250	Automatic	1-bbl	9.0:1
230	ZH	250	Manual	4-bbl	10.5:1

(a) Early production small valve engine

FIREBIRD ENGINE CHART

HP	ENGINE CODE	CID	TRANS	CARB	COMP
175(a)	ZK	250	Manual	1-bbl	9.0:1
175	ZC	250	Manual	1-bbl	9.0:1
175(a)	ZN	250	Automatic	1-bbl	9.0:1
175	ZN	250	Automatic	1-bbl	9.0:1
230(a)	ZD	250	Manual	4-bbl	10.5:1
230	ZH	250	Manual	4-bbl	10.5:1
215(a)	ZE	250	Automatic	4-bbl	10.5:1
215	ZL	250	Automatic	4-bbl	10.5:1
265(a)	WC	350	Manual	2-bbl	9.2:1
265	WM	350	Manual	2-bbl	9.2:1
265(a)	XL	350	Automatic	2-bbl	9.2:1
265	XB	350	Automatic	2-bbl	9.2:1
265(a)	YJ	350	Automatic	2-bbl	9.2:1
265	YE	350	Automatic	2-bbl	9.2:1
325	WN	350	Manual	4-bbl	10.5:1
325	XC	350	Automatic	4-bbl	10.5:1
330	WZ	400	Manual	4-bbl	10.75:1
330	YT	400	Automatic	4-bbl	10.75:1
335	WQ	400	Manual	4-bbl	10.75:1
335	YW	400	Automatic	4-bbl	10.75:1
345	WH	400	Manual	4-bbl	10.75:1
345	XN	400	Automatic	4-bbl	10.75:1
325	WK	350	Manual	4-bbl	10.5:1
330	WZ	400	Manual	4-bbl	10.75:1
325	XD	350	Automatic	4-bbl	10.5:1
265	YU	350	Automatic	2-bbl	9.2:1
175	ZF	250	Automatic	1-bbl	9.0:1

(a) Early production small valve engines

VEHICLE IDENTIFICATION NUMBER

0A71Y100551

VEHICLE IDENTIFICATION NUMBER LOCATIONS

FULL SIZED FORD VIN Die Stamped into Top of R/H Side-Rail of Frame Forward of Front Suspension Member.

THUNDERBIRD VIN Die Stamped into Top Surface of Front Fender Cross-Brace to the Right of Hood Lock Plate.

FALCON VIN Die Stamped into Top Surface of Left Hand Brace extending from top of Firewall to Left Front Wheelhouse.

1st Digit - MODEL YEAR

The number "0" designates 1960

2nd Digit - ASSEMBLY PLANT

Atlanta	A
Chester	C
Chicago	G
Lorain	H
Los Angeles	J
Louisville	U
Mahwah	E
Dallas	D
Dearborn	F
Kansas City	K
Norfolk	N
Pilot Plant	S
San Jose	R
Twin City	P
Metuchem	T
Wixom	Y

3rd and 4th Digit - MODEL

"The model code number identifies the product line seris and the particular body style: the first of the two digits shows the product line, and the second digit shows a two-door style by an odd number or a four-door style by an even number."

FAIRLANE	CODE
2-Dr. Club Sedan	31
4-Dr. Town Sedan	32
2-Dr. Business Sedan	33

FAIRLANE 500	CODE
2-Dr. Club Sedan	41
4-Dr. Town Sedan	42

GALAXIE	CODE
2-Dr. Club Sedan	51
4-Dr. TownSedan	52
4-Dr. Town Victoria	54
Starliner	
2-Dr. Club Victoria	53
Sunliner Convertible	55

STATION WAGONS	CODE
2-Dr. Ranch Wagon	61
4-Dr. Ranch Wagon	62
4-Dr. 6-PS. Country sedan	64
4-Dr. 9-Ps. Country Sedan	66
4-Dr. 9-Ps. Country Squire	68

2 Door Courier 69
(Commercial Ranch Wagon)

Thunderbird	CODE
Tudor Hardtop	71
Convertible	73

PASSENGER CARS	CODE
2-Door	11
4-Door	12

STATION WAGONS	CODE
2-Door	21
4-Door	22
Ranchero	27

5th digit - Engine

6 Cyl.r 223 C.I.	V
8 Cyl. 292 C.I. (Dual)	W

8 Cyl. 352 Cubic Inch (Dual)	X
8 Cyl. 352 C.I. (4-V)	Y
8 Cyl. 292 C.I. (Dual-L.C.)	T
" Export, 84 Octane"	
8 Cyl. 352 C.I.	G
"(4-V L.C. Export, 84 Octane)"	

FALCON	CODE
6 Cyl. OHV 144 C.I.	S
6 Cyl. OHV 144 C.I.	D
(L.C. - 84 octane)	

THUNDERBIRD	CODE
352 Cubic Inch V-8	Y
430 Cubic Inch V-8	J

PATENT PLATE

"The Patent Plate is located on the front body pillar on all passenger and Thunderbird models, and on the lock face of left front door on Falcon models."

"Indicated in the body specifications are Body Type, Exterior Paint Color, Trim Scheme, Production Date, Transmission Type and Rear Axle Ratio."

0F52W		100001		WARRENTY Number		Made in USA
54A	BM1	32	17K		8	3
BDY	CLR	TRM	DT	DSD	AX	TR

BODY TYPE 63A
BODY COLOR.........................AA
TRIM SCHEME 56
PRODUCT DATE 11-L
TRANSMISSION TYPE 4
REAR AXLE RATIO 8

EXAMPLE

Thunderbird, Hardtop...........63A
Raven Black lower.....................AA
body, Raven Black upper body

First Digit "5" represents...........5
material - All Vinyl

Second digit 6
represents color - Black & White

Eleventh Day of Month............11

Month of Year L
November

Cruise-o-Matic............................4

Rear axle Ratio of......................8
2.91 to 1

ENGINE MODELS AND PISTON DISPLACEMENT (Cubic Inches)

Mileage Maker Six...................223
Thunderbird 292 V-8...............292
Thunderbird 352 V-8...............352
Thunderbird 352 Sp. V-8.........352
Thunderbird 352 Super v-8.....352
Thunderbird 430 Sp. V-8.......430
Police Interceptor 352 Sp.V-8 352
Falcon 6....................................144

COMPRESSION RATIO

Mileage Maker Six...............8.4:1
Thunderbird 292 V-8.............8.8:1
Thunderbird 352 V-8.............8.9:1
Thunderbird 352 ....9.6:1
Special V-8
Thunderbird 352................10.6:1
 Super V-8
Thunderbird 430 ....10.5:1
Sp. V-8
Falcon 6................................8.7:1
Police interceptor.................9.6:1
352 Sp. V-8

BRAKE HORSEPOWER

Mileage Maker Six...................145
Thunderbird 292 V-8...............185
Thunderbird 352 V-8...............235
Thunderbird 352 Sp.V-8.........300
Thunderbird 352 Super v-8....360
Tunderbird 430 Sp. V-8.........350
Police Interceptor 352 Sp.V-8 300

BODY TYPE CODES

BODY MODEL	BODY TYPE	CODE
Galaxie Town Sedan	54A	52
Fairlane 500 Town Sedan	58A	42
Falcon 4-Door Sedan	58A	12
Fairlane Town Sedan	58E	32
Falcon 2-Door Ranch Wagon	59	21
2-Door Ranch Wagon	59C	61
2-Door Commercial Ranch Wagon	59E	69
Wagon "Coure.r"		
Galaxie Club Sedan	62A	51
Starliner Club Victoria	63A	53
Thunderbird Hard Top	63A	71
Fairlane "500" Club Sedan	64A	41
Falcon Tudor Sedan	64A	11
Fairlane Club Sedan	64F	31
Fairlane Business Coupe	64G	33
Falcon 4-dr. Station Wagon	71A	22
Station Wagon Country Sedan (9 pass.)	71E	66
Station Wagon Country Sedan (6 pass.)	71F	64
Station Wagon Country Country Squire	71G	68
4-Door Ranch Wagon	71H	62
Galaxie Town Victoria	75A	54
Thunderbird Convertable	76A	54
Galaxie Convertible	76A	73
Sunliner Convertible	76B	55

MONTH CODES

MONTH	1ST YR.	2ND YR.
January	A	N
February	B	P
March	C	Q
April	D	R
May	E	S
June	F	T
July	G	U
August	H	V
September	J	W
October	K	X
November	L	Y
December	M	Z

REAR AXLE RATIO CODES

REAR AXLE RATIO	REGULAR	LOCKING
3.10 :1	3	C
3.56 :1	1	A
3.70 :1	9	
3.89 :1	2	B
2.91 :1	8	
3.78 :1	4	
3.22 :1	6	
3.50 :1	J	

TRANSMISSION TYPE CODES

TRANSMISSION	CODE
Standard	1
Overdrive	2
Fordomatic (2-Speed)	3
Cruise-O-Matic	4

TRIM SCHEME CODES

TRIM SCHEME	CODE
Passenger Car	
Gray Vinyl & Gray Block	31
Blue Vinyl & Blue Block	32
Blue Vinyl & Blue Modern	32
Blue Vinyl & Blue Nylon	32
Blue Vinyl & Blue Nylon	32
Blue Vinyl & Blue Block Thong Nylon Fabric	32
Green Vinyl & Green Block Stripe Pattern Material	33
Green Vinyl & Green Modern Stripe Fabric	33
Green Vinyl & Green Nylon Faced Fabric	33
Green Vinyl & Green Nylon Striped Tweed Fabric	33
Green Vinyl & Green Block Thong Nylon Fabric	33
Beige Vinyl & Beige Block Stripe Pattern Material	34
Beige Vinyl & Beige Nylon Faced Fabric	34
Beige Vinyl & Beige Nylon Striped Tweed Fabric	34
Red Vinyl & Red Nylon Striped Tweed Fabric	35
White Vinyl & Black & Silver Nylon Faced Fabric	36
Black Vinyl & Black Nylon Striped Tweed Fabric	36
Green All Vinyl	43
Turquoise Vinyl & Turquoise Nylon Faced Fabric	37
Turquoise Vinyl & Nylon Striped Tweed Fabric	37
Turquoise Vinyl & Turquois	37
Block Thong Nylon Fabric	
Yellow Vinyl & Yellow Nylon Striped Tweed Fabric	38
Orchid Vinyl & Orchid Nylon Striped Tweed Fabric	39
Blue All Vinyl	42
Beige All Vinyl	44
Beige Vinyl & Beige Wicker Vinyl	44
Beige Vinyl & Beige Tweed Print Vinyl	44
Black & Red all Vinyl	45
White Vinyl & Red Tweed Print Vinyl	45
White & Red all Vinyl	45
Black all Vinyl	46
Turquoise all Vinyl	47
Yellow & Black all Vinyl	48
Orchid all Vinyl	49
Blue Vinyl & Blue Striped Thong Woven Plastic	62
Blue Vinyl & Blue Dash Pattern Woven Plastic	62
Green Vinyl & Green Striped Thong Woven Plastic	63
Green Vinyl & Green Dash Pattern Woven Plastic	63
Turquoise Vinyl & Turquoise Dash Pattern Woven Plastic	67

THUNDERBIRD

Dark & Light Blue all Vinyl	52
Dark & Light Green all Vinyl	53
Dark & Light Beige all Vinyl	54
Red & White all Vinyl	55
Black & White all Vinyl	56
Dark & Light Turquoise all Vinyl	57
Dark Blue Vinyl & Light Blue Nylon Cord Fabric	72
Dark Green Vinyl & Light Green Nylon Cord Fabric	73
Dark Beige Vinyl & Light Beige Nylon Cord Fabric	74
Black Vinyl & Light Gray Nylon Cord Fabric	76
Dark Turquoise Vinyl & Light Turquoise Nylon Cord Fabric	72
Light Beige all Genuine Leather	84
Red all Genuine Leather	85
Black all Genuine Leather	86
Turquoise all Genuine Leather	87

FALCON

Light Gray Vinyl & Gray Bar Pattern Material	11
Light Gray Vinyl & Gray Nylon Tweed Fabric	21
Light Blue Vinyl & Blue Nylon Tweed Fabric	22
Light Green Vinyl & Green Nylon Tweed Fabric	23

EXTERIOR PAINT - TWO TONE COLOR COMBINATIONS

LOWER BODY / UPPER BODY	CODE
Raven Black / Monte Carlo Red	AJ
Raven Black / Corinthian White	AM
Raven Black / Corinthian White	AR
Kingston Blue / Skymist Blue	BF
Kingston Blue / Chorinthian White	BM
Kingston Blue / Diamond Blue	BN
Aquamarine / Sultana Turquoise	CK
Aquamarine / Chorinthian White	CM
Acapulco Blue / Skymist Blue	EF (1)
Belmont Blue / Skymist Blue	EF (2)
Acapulco Blue / Chorinthian White	EM (1)

8 - 2

Belmont Blue.....................EM (2)
Chorinthian White
Acapulco Blue....................EN (1)
Diamond Blue
Skymist Blue.......................FB
Kingston Blue
Skymist Blue......................FE (1)
Acapulco Blue
Skymist Blue......................FE (2)
Belmont Blue
Skymist Blue......................FE
Chorinthian White
Yosemite Yellow....................GM
Chorinthian White
Beachwood Brown.................HM
Chorinthian White
Monte Carlo Red....................JA
Raven Black
Monte Carlo Red....................JM
Chorinthian White
Sultana Turquoise...................KC
Aquamarine
Sultana Turquoise...................KM
Chorinthian White
Chorinthian White..................MA
Raven Black
Chorinthian White..................MB
Kingston Blue
Chorinthian White..................MC
Aquamarine
Chorinthian White.............ME (1)
Acapulco Blue
Chorinthian White..................MF
Skymist Blue
Chorinthian White..................MH
Beachwood Brown
Chorinthian White..................MJ
Monte Carlo Red
Chorinthian White..................MK
Sultana Turquoise
Chorinthian White..................MR
Moroccan Ivory
Chorinthian White..................MS
Briarcliffe Green
Chorinthian White..................MT
Meadowdale Green
Chorinthian White..................MU
Springdale Rose
Chorinthian White..................MV
Plam Springs Rose
Chorinthian White..................MW
Adriatic Green
Chorinthian White..................MX
Royal Burgandy
Chorinthian White..................MY
Gunpowder Gray
Chorinthian White..................MZ
Platinum
Diamond Blue.........................NB
Kingston Blue
Diamond Blue.....................NE (1)
Acapulco Blue
Orchid Gray.........................QM
Chorinthian White
Moroccan Ivory.......................RA
Raven Black
Moroccan Ivory.......................RM
Chorinthian White
Briarcliffe Green.....................SM
Chorinthian White
Briarcliffe Green.....................ST
Meadowvale Green
Briarcliffe Green.....................SW
Adriatic Green

Meadowvale Green..................TM
Chorinthian White
Meadowvale Green..................TS
Briarcliffe Green
Meadowvale Green..................TW
Adriatic Green
Springdale Rose.....................UM
Chorinthian White
Palm Springs Rose..................VM
Chorinthian White
Adriatic Green.......................WM
Chorinthian White
Adriatic Green.......................WS
Briarcliffe Green
Adriatic Green.......................WT
Meadowvale Green
Adriatic Green.......................WZ
Platinum
Royal Burgandy.....................XM
Chorinthian White
Gunpoweder Gray..................YM
Chorinthian White
Platinum...............................ZA
Raven Black
Platinum...............................ZM
Chorinthian White
Platinum...............................ZW
Adriatic Green
(1) Thunderbird Only
(2) Pasenger & Falcon

EXTERIOR PAINT BODY COLOR CODES - SOLID COLORS

Passenger and Falcon

Raven Black.................................A
Aquamarine.................................C
Belmont Blue...............................E
Skymist Blue................................F
Yosemite Yellow..........................G
Beachwood Brown........................H
Monte Carlo Red...........................J
Sultana Turquoise.........................K
Corinthian White..........................M
Orchid Gray.................................Q
Meadowvale Green.......................T
Adriatic Green.............................W
Platinum.....................................Z
Prime...P
Special......................................S

Thunderbird

Raven Black.................................A
Kingston Blue...............................B
Aquamarine.................................C
Acapulco Blue..............................E
Skymist Blue................................F
Beachwood Brown........................H
Monte Carlo Red...........................J
Sultana Turquoise.........................K
Corinthian White..........................M
Diamond Blue...............................N
Moroccan Ivory.............................R
Briarcliffe Green...........................S
Meadowvale Green.......................T
Springdale Rose...........................U
Palm Springs Rose........................V
Adriatic Green.............................W
Royal Burgandy............................X
Gunpowder Gray..........................Y
Platinum.....................................Z

VEHICLE IDENTIFICATION NUMBER

1 A 7 1 W 1 0 0 5 5

VEHICLE IDENTIFICATION NUMBER LOCATIONS

FULL SIZED FORD VIN Die Stamped into Top of R/H Side-Rail of Frame Forward of Front Suspension Member.

THUNDERBIRD VIN Die Stamped into Top Surface of Front Fender Cross-Brace to the Right of Hood Lock Plate.

FALCON VIN Die Stamped into Top Surface of Left Hand Brace extending from top of Firewall to Left Front Wheelhouse.

1961 Model	1
Assembled at Atlanta Plant	A
Thunderbird-Tudor Hardtop	71
8cyl. OHV Engine	W
2-venturi carb	292 CID
Vehicle Production Number	100551

1st Digit - MODEL YEAR

The numbner "1" designates 1961

ASSEMBLY PLANT - 2nd digit

Atlanta	A
Chester	C
Chicago	G
Lorain	H
Los Angeles	J
Louisville	U
Mahwah	E
Dallas	D
Dearborn	F
Kansas City	K
Norfolk	N
Pilot Plant	S
San Jose	R
Twin City	P
Metuchem	T
Wixom	Y

3rd and 4th Digit - MODEL

The model code number identifies the product line seris and the particular body style: the first of the two digits shows the product line, and the second digit shows a two-door style by an odd number or a four-door style by an even number.

0F52W		100001		WARRENTY Number		Made in USA
54A	BM1	32	17K		8	3
BDY	CLR	TRM	DT	DSD	AX	TR

FAIRLANE	CODE
2-Dr. Club Sedan	31
4-Dr. Town Sedan	32

FAIRLANE 500	CODE
2-Dr. Club Sedan	41
4-Dr. Town Sedan	42

GALAXIE	CODE
2-Dr. Club Sedan	51
4-Dr. Town Sedan	52
2-Dr. Club Victoria Starliner	53
4-Dr. Town Victoria	54
Sunliner Convertible	55
2-Dr. Club Victoria	57

STATION WAGONS	CODE
2-Dr. Ranch Wagon	6
4-Dr. Ranch Wagon	62
4-Dr. 6-Ps. Country Sedan	64
4-Dr. 9-Ps. Country Sedan	66
4-Dr. 6-Ps. Country Squire	67
4-Dr. 9-Ps.	68

FALCON	CODE
2-Door Sedan	11
4-Dr. Sedan	12
2-Dr. Wagon	21
4-Dr. Wagon	22
Ranchero Wagon	27
Country Squire	
Falcon Sedan Delivery	29

THUNDERBIRD   CODE

Tudor Hardtop.....................71
Convertible..........................73

th Digit - ENGINE

ENGINE   CODE

Cyl. 223 CI.........................V
Cyl. 292 CI (Dual)................W
Cyl. 352 CI (Dual)................X
Cyl. 390 CI (4-V)..................Z
Cyl. 292 CI (Dual................T
LC Export, 84 Octane)
Cyl. 390 CI (4-V...................R
LC Export, 84 Octane)
Cyl. OHV 170 CI....................E
Low Comp)
Cyl. 390 (4-V) HP..................Z
Cyl. 390 (8-V) HP..................Z
Cyl. 390..............................Z
4-V) Police
Cyl. OHV 144 CI....................S
Cyl. OHV 144CI.....................D
LC 84 Octane)
Cyl. OHV 170 CI....................U

PATENT PLATE

The Patent Plate is located on the front body pillar on all passenger and Thunderbird models, and on the lock face of left front door on Falcon models.

Indicated in the body specifications are Body Type, Exterior Paint Color, Trim Scheme, Production Date, Transmission Type and Rear Axle Ratio.

EXAMPLE

BODY TYPE 63A
BODY COLOR........................AA
TRIM SCHEME 56
PRODUCT DATE...................11-L
TRANSMISSION TYPE 4
REAR AXLE RATIO 8

Thunderbird, Hardtop.............63A
Raven Black lower body, ...AA
Raven Black upper body
First Digit "5" represents........56
material - All Vinyl
Second digit "6" represents
color - Black & White
Eleventh Day of Month.............11
Month of Year - November.........L
Cruise-o-Matic...........................4
Rear axle Ratio of 2.91 to 1........8

ENGINE MODELS AND PISTON DISPLACEMENT (Cubic Inches)

Falcon..................................144
Falcon..................................170
Mileage Maker Six..................223
292 V-8................................292
352 V-8................................352
390 V-8................................390
390 High Performance V-8......390
390 Police Special V-8............390

COMPRESSION RATIO

144.................................8.7:1
170.................................8.7:1
Mileage Maker Six.............8.4:1
292 V-8............................8.8:1
352 V-8............................8.9:1
390 V-8............................9.6:1
390 High Performance V-8 10.6:1
390 Police Special V-8........9.6:1

BRAKE HORSEPOWER

144.....................................85
170....................................101
Mileage Maker Six...............135
292 V-8..............................175
352 V-8..............................220
390 V-8..............................300
390 V-8 (4-V) HP.................375
390 V-8 (6-V) HP.................401
390 Police Special V-8..........330

BODY TYPE CODES

BODY MODEL	BODY TYPE	SERIES
Galaxie Town Sedan Fairlane	54A	52
500 Town Sedan	58A	42
Falcon 4-Dr. Sedan	58A	12
Fairlane Town Sedan	58	E32
2-Dr. Ranch Wagon(Falcon)	59A	21
2-Dr. Ranch Wagon	59C	61
Galaxie Club Sedan	62A	51
Galaxie Club Victoria(Starliner)	63A	53
Thunderbird Hard Top	63A	71
Fairlane "500" Club Sedan	64A	41
Falcon Tudor Sedan	64A	11
Fairlane Club Sedan	64F	31
Galaxie Club Victoria	65A	57
Ranchero(Falcon)	66A	27
4-Dr. Ranch Wagon(Falcon)	71A	22
Station Wagon "Country Squire" (6 pass.)	71J	67
Station Wagon Country Sedan (9 Ps.)	71E	66
Station Wagon "Country Sedan" (6 pass.)	71F	64
Station Wagon "Country Squire"	71G	68
4-Dr. Ranch Wagon	71H	62
Galaxie Town Victoria	75A	54
Thunderbird Convertible	76A	73
Galaxie Convertible Coupe(Sunliner)	76B	55

Falcon Sedan...........78A...........29
Delivery
Falcon Futura..........64A...........17

MONTHS OF THE YEAR CODES

MONTH	1st YR.	2nd YR.
January	A	N
February	B	P
March	C	Q
April	D	R
May	E	S
June	F	T
July	G	U
August	H	V
September	J	W
October	K	X
November	L	Y
December	M	Z

REAR AXLE RATIO CODES

REAR AXLE RATIO	REGULAR	LOCKING
3.00:1	6	
3.10:1	3	C
3.56:1	1	A
3.50:1		J
3.89:1	2	B
2.91:1	8	H
4.00:1	4	
3.20:1	5	

TRANSMISSION TYPE CODES

TRANSMISSION	CODE
3-Sp. Manual	1
Overdrive	2
Fordomatic (2-Speed)	3
Cruise-O-Matic	4
4-Sp. Manual	5

TRIM SCHEME CODES

TRIM SCHEME	CODE

Passenger Car

Brown Morocco Grain Vinyl.........4
& Brown Strawgrain Vinyl
Gray Vinyl & Gray Stripe............11
Nylon Fabric
Blue Vinyl & Blue Stripe.............12
Nylon Fabirc
Green Vinyl & Green.................13
Stripe Nylon Fabirc
Gray Metallic Vinyl & Gray..........21
Slat Pattern Nylon Fabric
Blue Metallic Vinyl & Blue..........22
Slat Pattern Nylon Fabric
Green Metallic Vinyl & Green.......23
Slat Pattern Nylon Fabric
Brown Metallic Vinyl & Brown.....24
Slat Pattern Nylon Fabric
Turquoise Metallic Vinyl &..........27
Turquoise Slat Pattern
Nylon Fabric

White Metallic Vinyl & Black......30
Shimmer Pattern Nylon Cloth
Blue Metallic Vinyl &.................32
Dark Blue Shimmer
Pattern Nylon Cloth
Green Metallic Vinyl & Dark.......33
Green Shimmer Pattern
Nylon Cloth
Brown Metallic Vinyl.................34
& Dark Brown Shimmer
Pattern Nylon Cloth
White Metallic Vinyl & Red.........35
Shimmer Pattern Nylon Cloth
Turquoise Metallic Vinyl &.........37
Dark Turquoise Shimmer
Pattern Nylon Cloth
Yellow Metallic Vinyl & Black.....38
Shimmer Pattern Nylon Cloth
Black Vinyl & Gray.....................51
Crown Pattern Vinyl
Light Blue Vinyl & Blue..............62
Striped Pattern Woven Plastic
Light Green Vinyl & Green..........63
Striped Pattern Woven Plastic
Medium Blue Metallic Vinyl &.....72
Blue Block Pattern Nylon Cloth
Medium Green Metallic..............73
Vinyl & Green Block
Pattern Nylon Cloth
Medium Turquoise Metallic........77
Vinyl & Turquoise Block
Pattern Nylon Cloth
Brown Morocco Grain Vinyl &....84
Brown Stripe Print Vinyl
White Morocco Grain Vinyl........85
& Red Stripe Print Vinyl
Light Blue Morocco Grain..........92
Vinyl & Medium Blue
Metallic Pleated Vinyl
Light Brown Morocco Grain.......94
Vinyl & Medium Brown
Metallic Pleated Vinyl
White Morocco Grain Vinyl........95
& Red Metallic Pleated Vinyl
White Morocco Grain Vinyl........96
& Black Pleated Vinyl
Light Turquoise Morocco...........97
Grain Vinyl & Medium
Turquoise Metallic Pleated Vinyl
Yellow Morocco Grain Vinyl.......98
& Black Pleated Vinyl

FALCON

Gray Vinyl & Gray Block............11
Stripe Nylon Cloth
Light Brown Vinyl & Medium......24
Brown Tweed Nylon Cloth
Light Gray Metallic Vinyl &.........41
Gray Pteated Tweed Nylon Cloth
Light Blue Metallic Vinyl............42
& Blue Pteated Tweed
Nylon Cloth
Light Green Metallic..................43
Vinyl & Green Pteated
Tweed Nylon Cloth
Light Turquoise Metallic.............47
Vinyl & Turquoise Pteated
Tweed Nylon Cloth
Light Beige Vinyl & Brown..........54
Western Vinyl
Light Blue Metallic Vinyl &.........72
Medium Blue Pleated Vinyl

White Metallic Vinyl &...............75
Red Pleated Vinyl
Whitye Metallic Vinyl &...............76
Black Pleated Vinyl

THUNDERBIRD

Medium Blue Metallic...............52
All Vinyl
Medium Green Metallic...............53
All Vinyl
White Metallic All Vinyl...............54
Red All Vinyl...............55
Black All Vinyl...............56
Turquoise Metallic All Vinyl.......57
Light Blue Morocco...............72
Grain & Medium Blue
Nylon Bedford Cord Fabric
Light Green Morocco...............73
Grain & Medium Green
Nylon Bedford Cord Fabric
Light Beige Pearl Grain.............74
& Medium Beige Nylon
Bedford Cord Fabric
Black Vinyl & Medium Graye.....76
Nylon Bedford Cord Fabric
Medium Turquoise Metallic........77
Vinyl & Medium Turquoise
Nylon Bedford Cord Fabric
Blue All Genuine Leather...........82
Light Beige All Genuine.............84
Leather
Red All Genuine Leather...........85
Black All Genuine Leather..........86
Turquoise All Genuine...............87
Leather

ADDED TRIM FOR 1961 FALCON APPLICATION

APPLICATION TRIM SCHEME	CODE
X(58A, 64A)	11A
Light Gray Vinyl & Gray Bar Pattern	
X(59A, 71A)	23A
Light Green Vinyl & Green Block Pattern Fabric	
X(59A, 71A)	26A
Silver Vinyl & Gray Block Pattern Fabric	
X(58A,64A)	41A
Light Gray Vinyl & Gray Nylon Tweed Fabric	
X(58A, 64A)	43A
Light Green Vinyl & Green Nylon Tweed Fabric	
X(59A, 66A, 71A)	54A
Light Beige Vinyl & Beige Western Vinyl	
X(59A, 66A, 71A)	75A
White and Red all Vinyl	
X(59A, 66A, 71A)	76A
White and Black all Vinyl	

EXTERIOR PAINT BODY COLOR CODES - SOLID COLORS

Passenger and Falcon

COLOR	CODE
Raven Black	A
Aquamarine	C
Starlight Blue	D
Laurel Green	E
Desert Gold	F
Chesapeake Blue	H
Monte Carlo Red	J
Algiers Bronze	K
Corinthian White	M
Silver Gray	Q
Cambridge Blue	R
Mint Green	S
Garden Turquoise	W

Thunderbird

Raven Black	A
Aquamarine	C
Starlight Blue	D
Laurel Green	E
Desert Gold	F
Chesapeake Blue	H
Monte Carlo Red	J
Corinthian White	M
Diamond Blue	N
Nautilus Gray	P
Silver Gray	Q
Cambridge Blue	R
Mint Green	S
Honey Beige	T
PalmSprings Rose	V
Garden Turquoise	W
Heritage Burgundy	X
Mahogany	Y
Fieldstone Tan	Z

VEHICLE IDENTIFICATION NUMBER

2A83X100551

VEHICLE IDENTIFICATION NUMBER LOCATIONS

FULL SIZED FORD VIN Die Stamped into Top of R/H Side-Rail of Frame Forward of Front Suspension Member.

FAIRLANE VIN Die stamped into side of Left Front Inner Fender Apron near top.

THUNDERBIRD VIN Die Stamped into Top Surface of Front Fender Cross-Brace to the Right of Hood Lock Plate.

FALCON VIN Die Stamped into Top Surface of Left Hand Brace extending from top of Firewall to Left Front Wheelhouse.

1962 Mode	I2
Assembled at Atlanta Plant	A
Thunderbird-Tudor Hardtop	83
8cyl. OHV Engine	X
2-venturi carb	352 CID
Vehicle Production Number	100551

1ST Digit - MODEL YEAR

The number "2" designates 1962

2 nd Digit - ASSEMBLY PLANT

Atlanta	A
Chicago	G
Los Angeles	J
Louisville	U
Mahwah	E
Dallas	D
Dearbom	F
Kansas City	K
Norfolk	N
Pilot Plant	S
San Jose	R
Twin City	P
Wayne	W
Wixom	Y
Loraain	H
Metuchen	T
St. Louis	Z

3rd & 4th Digit - MODEL

The model code number identifies the product line seris and the particular body style: the first of the two digits shows the product line, and the second digit shows a two-door style by an odd number or a four-door style by an even number

BDY	CLR	TRM	DT	DSD	AX	TR
54A	YM	5Y	17K	33	1	1

SERIAL NUMBER

2S63X100001

FAIRLANE	CODE
2-Dr. Club Sedan	31
4-Dr. Town Sedan	32

FAIRLANE 500	CODE
2-Dr. Club Sedan	41
4-Dr. Town Sedan	42
Sports Coupe	47

FAIRLANE	CODE
2-Dr. Club Sedan	31
4-Dr. Town Sedan	32

FAIRLANE 500	CODE
2-Dr. Club Sedan	41
4-Dr. Town Sedan	42
Sports Coupe	47

GALAXIE	CODE
2-Dr. Club Sedan	51
4-Dr. Town Sedan	52

GALAXIE	CODE
2-Dr. Club Sedan	61
4-Dr. Town Sedan	62
2-Dr. Club Victoria	63
4-Dr. Town Victoria	64
2-Dr. Convertible	65

GALAXIE 500XL	CODE
Tudor Hardtop	67
Convertible	69
4-Dr. 9-Ps. Country Squire	78

STATION WAGONS — CODE

-Dr. Ranch Wagon...................71
-Dr. 6-Ps. Country Sedan.......72
-Dr. 9-Ps. Country Sedan.......74
-Dr. 6-Ps. Country Squire.......76

FALCON

PASSANGER CARS — CODE

-Door...................................11
-Door...................................12
Tudor Futura........................17

STATION WAGONS — CODE

-Door...................................21
-Door...................................22
Ranchero..............................27
Fordor Squire.......................26
Sedan Delivery.....................29

THUNDERBIRD — CODE

Tudor Hardtop......................83
Convertible...........................85

5th Digit - ENGINE

ENGINE — CODE

GALAXIE

6 Cyl. 223 C.I. V
8 Cyl. 292 C.I. (2-V)..................W
8 Cyl. 352 C.I. (2-V)..................X
8 Cyl. 390 C.I.(4-V)...................Z
8 Cyl. 292 C.I. ....T
(2-V-L.C. Export, 84 Octane)
8 Cyl. 390 C.I. ....R
(4-V,L.C. Export, 84 Octane)
8 Cyl. 390 C.I. ....M
(6-V,High Performance)
8 Cyl. 390 C.I. ....Q
(4-V,HI-PO)
390 4-V Police..........................P
406 4-V Hi Performance............B
406 6-V High Performance........G

FALCON

6 Cyl. 170 CI Export...................E
6 Cyl. OHV 144 C.I.....................S
6 Cyl.OHV 144 C I......................D
(L.C.-84 octane)
6 Cyl. OHV 170 C.I.....................U

FAIRLANE

6 Cyl. 170 CI..............................U
8 Cyl. 221 C.I.(L.C. Export).........C
6 Cyl. 170 C.I.(L.C. Export)........E
8 Cyl. 221 C.I............................L
8 Cyl. 260 CI ....F

Thunderbird

8 Cyl. 390 CI 4-V........................Z
8Cyl. 390 CI 6-V.........................M

PATENT PLATE

The Patent Plate is located on the front body pillar on Galaxie and Thunderbird models, and on the lock face of left front door on Fairlane and Falcon models. The rating for the Falcon Bus models is attached to the left front door hinge pillar.

The following diagram of the Patent Plate specifies, in the Serial Number: the Model Year, Assembly Plant, Series and Body Style, Engine Type and numerical sequence of assembly.
Indicated in the body specifications are Body Type, Exterior Paint Color, Trim Scheme, Production Date, Transmission Type and Rear Axle Ratio.

EXAMPLE

BODY TYPE CODE..............63A
BODY COLOR CODE............AA
TRIM SCHEME CODE............56
PRODUCT DATE CODE....11-G
REAR AXLE RATIO CODE........1
TRANSMISSION TYPE CODE..3

Thunderbird, Hardtop.............63A
Raven Black lower body, Raven Black upper body....................AA
First Digit "5" represents material - All Vinyl.................................56
Second digit "6" represents color .... Black & White
Eleventh Day of Month............11
Month of Year - July..................G
Rear axle Ratio of 3.00 to 1.......1
Fordomatic (2 speed) 3

ENGINE MODELS AND PISTON DISPLACEMENT (Cubic Inches)

Falcon.......................................144
Falcon.......................................170
Mileage Maker Six....................223
292 V-8.....................................292
352 Special V-8........................352
390 Special V-8........................390
390 H.P. V-8.............................390
390 Super H.P. V-8...................390
390 Police Interceptor V-8.....390
221 V-8.....................................221
260 V-8.....................................260
390 Sports V-8.........................390
406 High Performance V-8......406
406 Super High.........................406
Performance V-8

COMPRESSION RATIO

144...8.7:1
170...8.7:1
Mileage Maker Six...............8.4:1
292 V-8..................................8.8:1
352 V-8..................................8.9:1
390 Special V-8...................9.6:1
390 H.P. V-8.......................10.6:1
390 Super H.P. V-8...........11.1:1
390 Police Interceptor V-8...9.6:1
221 V-8..................................8.7:1
260 V-8..................................8.7:1
390 Sports V-8.................10.5:1

406 HP V-8.........................11.4:1
406 Super HP V-8..............11.4:1

BRAKE HORSEPOWER

144...85
170...101
138...135
170...175
352 V-8.......................................220
390 Special V-8........................300
390 H.P. V-8.............................375
390 Super H.P.V-8...................401
330...303
221 V-8......................................145
260 V-8......................................164
390 Sports V-8.........................340
406 HP.......................................385
406 Super HP...........................405

BODY TYPE CODES

BODY MODEL	BODY TYPE	SERIES
Fairlane Town Sedan	54A	32
Galaxie "500" Town Sedan	54A	62
Fairlane "500" Town Sedan	54B	42
Galaxie Town Sedan	54B	52
Falcon 4-Dr. Sedan	58A	12
Falcon 4-door Ranch Wagon	59A	21
Fairlane Club Sedan	62A	31
Galaxie "500" Club Sedan	62A	61
Fairlane "500" Club Sedan	62B	41
Galaxie Club Sedan	62B	51
Failane 500 Sports Coupe	62C	47
Falcon Tudor "Futura".	62C	17
Thunderbird Hard Top	63A	83
Thunderbird Hard Top(Landau)	63B	83
Falcon Tudor Sedan	64A	11
Falcon Tudor Sedan (Futura)	64C	17
Galaxie 500XL Tudor Hardtop	65B	67
Ranchero(Falcon)	66A	27
Galaxie "500" Club Victoria	65A	63
4-Door Ranch Wagon(Falcon)	71A	22
Station Wagon "Country Squire"" (9 pass.)	71A	78
Station Wagon "Country Sedan"	71B	72
Falcon 4-Dr\ Super Deluxe Wagon	71B	26
Station Wagon "Country Sedan" (9 pass.)	71C	74
Falcon 4-Dr.	71B	26
Super Deluxe Wagon 4-Door Ranch Wagon	71D	71
Station Wagon Country Squire (6 Passenger)	71E	76
Galaxie 500 Town Victoria	75A	64
Thunderbird Convertable	S(76A)	85
Thunderbird Convertable	S(76B)	85
Sports Roadster Galaxie "500"	76A	65
"Sunliner" Falcon Sedan Delivery	78A	29
Galaxie 500XL Tudor Convertible	76B	69

MONTHS OF THE YEAR CODES

MONTH	1st YR.	2nd YR.
January	A	N
February	B	P
March	C	Q
April	D	R
May	E	S
June	F	T
July	G	U
August	H	V
September	J	W
October	K	X
November	L	Y
December	M	Z

REAR AXLE RATIO CODES

REAR AXLE RATIO	REGULAR	LOCKING
3.00 : 1	1	A
3.20 : 1	3	B
3.50 : 1	5	E
33..0 : 1	7	G
4.00 : 1	9	Falcon
3.10 : 1	2	
3.25 : 1	4	
3.56 : 1	6	
3.89 : 1	8	
4.11 : 1		
3.10 : 1		B
3.20 : 1		C
3.25 : 1		D
3.50 : 1		E
3.56 : 1		F
3.80 : 1		G
3.89 : 1		H

TRANSMISSION TYPE CODES

TRANSMISSION	CODE
3-Speed Manual	1
Overdrive	2
Fordomatic (2-Speed)	3
Cruise-O-Matic	4
4 Speed Manual	5

ENGINE CODES

ENGINE	CODE
6 Cyl. 223 C. I. OHV	V
8 Cyl. 292 C. I. OHV (2-V)	W
8 Cyl. 352 C. I. OHV (2-V)	X
8 Cyl. 390 C. I. OHV (4-V)	Z
6 Cyl. 170 C. I. OHV	U
6 Cyl. 144 C. I. OHV	S
8 Cyl. 390 C. I. OHV (4-V Sp.)	Q
8 Cyl. 390 C. I. OHV (6-V)	M
8 Cyl. 390 C. I. OHV (2-V)	L
8 Cyl. 390 C. I. OHV (2-V)	F

TRIM SCHEME CODES

TRIM SCHEME	CODE
Passenger Car	
Blue Vinyl & Blue Stripe Nylon Fabirc	12
Green Vinyl & Green Stripe Nylon Fabirc	13
Beige Vinyl & Beige Stripe Nylon Fabirc	14
Red Vinyl & Red Stripe Nylon Fabirc	15
Black Vinyl & Black Stripe Nylon Fabirc	16
Turquoise Vinyl & Turquoise Stripe Nylon Fabirc	17
Chestnut Vinyl & Chestnut Stripe Nylon Fabirc	19
Gray Vinyl & Gray Stripe. Nylon Fabirc	21
Blue Vinyl & Blue Stripe Nylon Fabric	22
Green Vinyl & Green Stripe Nylon Fabric	23
Beige Vinyl & Beige Stripe Nylon Fabric	24
Red Vinyl & Red Stripe Nylon Fabric	25
Turquoise Vinyl & Turquoise Stripe Nylon Fabric	27
Blue Vinyl & Blue Stripe Nylon Fabric	32
Beige Vinyl & Beige Stripe Nylon Fabric	34
Red Vinyl & Red Stripe Nylon Fabric	35
Turquoise Vinyl & Turquoise Stripe Nylon Fabric	37
Chestnut Vinyl	39
Red Vinyl & Red Stripe Nylon Cloth	45
Red Vinyl	55
Black Vinyl	56
Chestnut Vinyl	59
Gray Vinyl & Gray Stripe Nylon Cloth	61
Blue Vinyl & Blue Stripe Nylon Cloth	62
Green Vinyl & Green Stripe Nylon Cloth	63
Beige Vinyl & Beige Stripe Nylon Cloth	64
Turquoise Vinyl & Turquoise Stripe Nylon Cloth	67
Blue Vinyl Woven Plastic	72
Green Vinyl Woven Plastic	73
Beige Vinyl Woven Plastic	74
Red Vinyl Woven Plastic	75
Turquoise Vinyl Woven Plastic	77
Red Vinyl	85
Gray Vinyl & Gray Stripe Nylon Cloth	11
Gray Vinyl & Gray Stripe Nylon Cloth	21
Blue Vinyl & Blue Stripe Nylon Cloth	22
Green Vinyl & Green Stripe Nylon Cloth	23
Beige Vinyl & Beige Stripe Nylon Cloth	24
Turquoise Vinyl & Turquoise Stripe Nylon Cloth	27
Beige Vinyl & Beige Stripe Nylon Cloth	54
Beige Woven Plastic & Beige Vinyl	64
Blue Vinyl	72
Red & White Vinyl	75
Black & White Vinyl	76
Blue Vinyl	82
Beige Vinyl	84
Red Vinyl	85
Black Vinyl	86
Turquoise Vinyl	87

1962 TRIM CODES

TRIM	CODE
FORD	
Green Rib all Vinyl (Police and Taxi)	3
Green Rib all Vinyl (Police and Taxi) - Deviation	03A
Beige Rib all Vinyl (Police and Taxi)	4
Brown Rib all Vinyl (Police and Taxi) - Deviation	04A
Red Rib all Vinyl (Police and Taxi)	5
Red Rib all Vinyl (Policeand Taxi) - Deviation	05A
Red all Vinyl (Police and Taxi) - Deviation	05B
Blue Vinyl & Blue VeniceFabric	12
Green Vinyl & Green Venice Fabric	13
Beige Vinyl & Beige Venice Fabric	14
Black Vinyl & Red Venice Fabric	15
Black Vinyl & Black Venice Fabric	16
Turquoise Vinyl & Turquois Venice Fabric	17
Chestnut Vinyl & Chestnut Venice Fabric	19
Grey Vinyl & Gray Basket Fabric	21
Blue Vinyl & Blue Basket Fabric	22
Green Vinyl & Green Basket Fabric	23
Beige Vinyl & Beige Basket Fabric	24
Beige Vinyl & Beige Basket Fabric	24A
White Vinyl & Red Basket Fabric	25
Turquoise Vinyl & Turquoise Basket Fabric	27
Blue Crush All Vinyl	32
Beige Crush All Vinyl	34
Red Crush All Vinyl	35
Red Crush All Vinyl	35A
Turquoise Crush All Vinyl	37
Chestnut Crush All Vinyl	39
Red Vinyl & Red Venice Fabric	45
Beige Steerhead All Vinyl	54
Beige Steerhead All Vinyl	54A
Black Crush All Vinyl	56
Blue Vinly & Blue Thong Plastic	62
Blue Vinyl & Pogo Stick Plastic	72
Green Vinyl & Green	73
Pogo Stick Plastic	
Light Pearl BiegeVinyl & LightPearl Biege Pogo Stick Plastic	74
Light Pearl Biege	74A
Vinyl & Light Pearl Biege Pogo Stick Plastic	
White Vinyl & Red Pogo Stick Plastic	75
White Vinyl & Red Pogo Stick Plastic	75A
Turquoise Vinyl & Turquoise Pogo Stick Plastic	77
White Vinyl & Red	85
Tweed All Vinyl	
Gray Vinyl & Gray Stripe Frabic	91
Blue Vinyl & Blue Stripe Fabric	92
Green Vinyl & Green Stripe Fabric	93
FAIRLANE	
Green Rib all Vinyl (Police and Taxi)	3
Beige Rib all Vinyl (Police and Taxi)	4
Red Rib all Vinyl (Police and Taxi)	5
Grey Vinyl & Gray Block Stripe Fabric	21
Blue Vinyl & Blue Block Stripe Fabric	22
Green Vinyl & Green Block Stripe Fabric	23
White Vinyl & Red Block Stripe Fabric	25
Blue Crush All Vinyl	52
Gray Vinyl & Gray Scallop Fabric	61
Blue Vinyl & Blue Scallop Fabric	62
Green Vinyl & Green Scallop Fabric	63
Light Pearl Beige Vinyl And Beige Scallop Fabric	64
Turquoise Vinyl & Turquoise Scallop Fabric	67

FALCON

Gray Vinyl & Gray Ladder Bodycloth	1
Gray Vinyl & Gray Arrow Bodycloth	2
Blue Vinyl & Blue Arrowr Bodycloth	2
Green Vinyl & Green Arrow Bodycloth	2
Light Pearl Beige Vinyl & Light Pearl Beige Arrow Bodycloth	2
Turquoise Vinyl & Turquoise Arrow Bodycloth	2
Light Pearl Beige & Medium Beige Steerhead All Vinyl	5
Light Pearl Beige & Beige Thong Plastic	6
Light Blue & Medium Blue Metallic All Vinyl	7
Light Beige & Medium Beige Steerhead All Vinyl	74
White & Red All Vinyl	7
White & Black All Vinyl	7
Light Blue Metallic All Vinyl	8
Light Beige Metallic & Light Pearl Beige All Vinyl	84
Red All Vinyl	85
Black All Vinyl	86
Light Turquiose Metallic All Vinyl	8

THUNDERBIRD

Lt. Silver Blue Met. Vinyl	50
Lt. Blue Met. Vinyl	52
Lt. Pearl Beige Vinyl	54
Red Vinyl	55
Black Vinyl	56
Lt. Turquoise Met. Vinyl	57
Med. Chestnut Vinyl	59
Lt. Silver Blue Met Vinyl&	70
Med. Silver Blue Bedford Cloth	
Lt. Blue Met. Vinyl &	72
Med. Blue Bedford Cloth	
Lt. Pearl Beige Vinyl &	74
Med. Beige Bedford Cloth	
Black Vinyl & Med.	76
Gray Bedford Cloth	
Lt. Turquoise Met. Vinyl &	7
Med. Turquoise Bedford Cloth	
Lt. Silver Blue Met. Leather	80
Med. Blue Leather	82
Lt. Pearlescent Beige Leather	84
Red Leather	85
Black Leather	86
Lt. Turquoise Met. Leather	8
Med. Chestnut Met. Leather	89

EXTERIOR PAINT BODY

COLOR	CODE
Raven Black	A
Ming Green	D
Viking Blue	E
Baffin Blue	F
Oxford Blue	H
Rangoon Red	
Corinthian White	M
Silver Moss	
Silver Gray	C
Tucson Yellow	F
Sandshell Beige	T
Chestmut	V
Fieldstone Tan	Z

VEHICLE IDENTIFICATION NUMBER

3A83X 100551

VEHICLE IDENTIFICATION NUMBER LOCATIONS

FULL SIZED FORD VIN Die Stamped into extension Tob of Top of Cowl R/H Side of Car under hood.

FAIRLANE VIN Die stamped into side of Left Front Inner Fender Apron near top.

THUNDERBIRD VIN Die Stamped into Top Surface of Front Fender Cross-Brace to the Right of Hood Lock Plate.

FALCON VIN Die Stamped into Top Surface of Left Hand Brace extending from top of Firewall to Left Front Wheelhouse.

1963 Model	3
Assembled at Atlanta Plant	A
Thunderbird-Tudor Hardtop	83
8cyl. OHV Engine	X
352 CID 2-venturi carb	
Vehicle Production Number	100551

1st Digit - MODEL YEAR

The number "3" designates 1963

2nd Digit - ASSEMBLY PLANT

Atlanta	A
Chicago	G
Los Angeles	J
Louisville	U
Mahwah	E
Dallas	D
Dearborn	F
Lorain	H
Kansas City	K
Norfolk	N
Pilot Plant	S
Metuchen	T
San Jose	R
Twin City	P
Wayne	W
Wixom	Y
St. Louis	Z

3rd & 4th Digit - MODEL

"The model code number identifies the product line seris and the particular body style: the first of the two digits shows the product line, and the second digit shows a two-door style or a four-door style."

BDY	CLR	TRM	DT	DSD	AX	TR
63A	AA	56	17K	21	1	3

SERIAL NUMBER

3A83X100551

FORD 300	CODE
2-Dr. Sedan	53
4-Dr. Sedan	54

GALAXIE	CODE
2-Dr. Sedan	51
4-Dr. Sedan	52

Galaxie 500	CODE
2 Door Sedan	61
4 Door Sedan	62
2 Door Hardtop	63
4 Door Hardtop	64
2 Door Convertible	65
4-Dr. Hardtop - Fastback	66

GALAXIE 500XL	CODE
2-Dr. Hardtop	67
4-Dr. Hardtop	60
2-Dr. Hardtop Fastbac	68
2-Dr. Convertible	69

FAIRLANE	CODE
2-Dr. Sedan	31
4-Dr. Sedan	32

FAIRLANE 500	CODE
2-Dr. Sedan	41
4-Dr. Sedan	42
2-Dr. Hardtop	43
2-Dr. Hardtop Sport Coupe	47

STATION WAGON	CODE
4-Dr. 6 Ps.	38
4-Dr. Custom 6 Ps.	48
4-Dr. Squire	49
4-Dr. Wagon	72

-Dr. Wagon............74
-Dr. Wagon............76
-Dr. Wagon............78

THUNDERBIRD   CODE
-Dr. Hardtop............83
-Dr. Convertible............85
-Dr. Landau............87
-Dr. Roadster............89

FALCON STANDARD   CODE
SEDAN
-Dr. Sedan............1
-Dr. Sedan............2

FALCON FUTURA   CODE
-Dr. Sedan 19
-Dr. Sedan 19
-Dr. Convertible............15
-Dr. Convertible............15
-Dr. Sedan 16
-Dr. Hardtop............17

STATION WAGONS   CODE
-Dr. Wagon............21
-Dr. Wagon............22
-Dr. Deluxe Wagon............23
-Dr. Deluxe Wagon............24
-Dr. Squire............26

RANCHERO   CODE
-Dr. Ranchero............27

SEDAN DELIVERY   CODE
-Dr. Sedan Delivery............29

5th Digit - ENGINE

ENGINE CODE
Cyl. 223 C.I.............V
Cyl. 352 C.I. (2-V)............X
Cyl. 390 C.I. (4-V))............Z
Cyl. 406 C.I. (4-V H. P.)............B
Cyl. 223 C.I. (Taxi))............E
Cyl. 260 C.I. (2-V))............F
Cyl. 406 C.I. (6-V H. P.)............G
Cyl. 390 C.I.(4-V Interceptor) P
Cyl. OHV 144 C.I.............S
Cyl. OHV 144 C.I.(Low
Compression-84 octane)............2
Cyl. OHV 170 C.I.............U
289 V-8 (2-V)............C
221 V-8............L
221 V-8 (Low Comp.)............3
170 Six (Low Comp.)............4
260 V-8 (Low Comp.)............8
223 Six (Low Comp.)............5
390 V-8 (4-V) (Low Comp.)............9
289 V-8 (4-V) HP............K
390 V-8 (6-V) HP............M
427 V-8 (4-V) HP............Q
427 V-8 (8-V) HP............R
200 I-6............T

PATENT PLATE

The Patent Plate is located on the front body pillar on Galaxie and Thunderbird models, and on the lock face of left front door on Fairlane and Falcon models.

The following diagram of the Patent Plate specifies, in the Serial Number: the Model Year, Assembly Plant, Series and Body Style, Engine Type and numerical sequence of assembly.
Indicated in the body specifications are Body Type, Exterior Paint Color, Trim Scheme, Production Date, Transmission Type and Rear Axle Ratio.

BODY TYPE CODE............63A
BODY COLOR CODE............AA
TRIM SCHEME CODE............56
PRODUCT DATE CODE.....11-G
DISTRIC CODE............21
TRANSMISSION TYPE CODE..1
REAR AXLE RATIO CODE.......3

Thunderbird, Hardtop............63A
Raven Black lower body, Raven Black upper body............AA
First Digit "5" represents material All Vinyl............56
Second digit "6" represents color .... Black & White
Eleventh Day of Month............11
Month of Year - July............G
Distric Code - Atlanta............21
Rear axle Ratio of 3.00 to 1.......1
Fordomatic (2 speed) 3

DISTRICT CODE

DOS units built to a Domestic Special Order, Foreign Special Order, or Pre-Approved Order have the complete order number recorded in this space. Also appearing in this space is the two digit code number of the Distric which orderd the unit. If the unit is regular production, only the Distric code number will appear.

District   Code
Boston............11
Buffalo............12
New York............13
Pitsburg............14
Newark............15
Atlanta............21
Charlotte............22
Philadelphia............23
Jacksonville............24
Richmond............25
Washington............26
Cincinnati............31
Cleveland............32
Detroit............33
Indianoplis............34
Lansing............35
Louisville............36
Chicago............41
Fargo............42
Rockford............43
Twin Cities............44
Davenport............45

Denver............51
Des Moines............52
Kansas City............53
Omaha............54
St. Louis............55
Dallas............61
Huston............62
Memphis............63
New Orleans............64
Oklahoma City............65
Los Angeles............71
San Jose............72
Salt Lake City............73
Seattle............74
Ford of Canada............81
Government............83
Home Office Reserve............84
American Red Cross............85
Transportation Services............89
Export............90-99

ENGINE MODELS AND PISTON DISPLACEMENT (Cubic Inches)

Falcon............144
Falcon & Fairlane............170
Fairlane............200
221 V-8............221
Mileage Maker Six............223
260 V-8............260
352 V-8............352
390 Special V-8............390
406 H. P. V-8 (4-V)............406
406 H. P. V-8 (6-V)............406
390 Police Interceptor V-8............390
289 V-8............289
289 HP............289
390 HP (6V)............390
427 HP (4V)............427
427 HP (8-V)............427

COMPRESSION RATIO

144............8.7:1
170............8.7:1
200............8.9:1
Mileage Maker Six............8.4:1
221 V-8............8.7:1
260 V-8............8.7:1
352 V-8............8.9:1
390 Special V-8............10.5:1
406 HP (4-V)............11.5:1
406 HP (6-V)............11.5:1
390 Police Interceptor V-8 10.5:1
289 (2-V)............8.7:1
289 HP (4-V)............11.0:1
427 HP (4-V)............11.5:1
427 HP (8-V)............11.5:1

BRAKE HORSEPOWER

144............85
170............101
200............116
Mileage Maker Six............138
221 V-8............145
260 V-8............164
352 V-8............220
390 Special V-8............300
406 HP (4-V)............385
406 HP (6-V)............405
390 Police Interceptor V-8............330
289 (2-V)............195

289 HP (4-V)............271
390 HP (6-V)............340
427 HP (4-V)............410
427 HP (8-V)............425

BODY TYPE CODES

BODY MODEL	BODY TYPE

Falcon 2-Dr. Sedan............62A
Falcon 4-Dr. Sedan............54A
Falcon Futura 2-Dr. Sedan...62B
Falcon Futura 4-Dr. Sedan...54B
Falcon Futura Sports Sedan 62C
Falcon Futura 2-Dr. 63B
Hardtop-Bench Seat
Falcon Futura 2-Dr. 63C
Hardtop-Bucket Seat
Falcon 2-Dr. Ranchero............66A
Falcon 2-Dr. Deluxe............66B
Ranchero
Falcon 2-Dr. Super Deluxe.....71D
Squire-Bucket Seat
Falcon Futura Convertible......76A
Falcon Futura Sports............76B
Convertible
Falcon2-Dr. Station Wagon....59A
Falcon 4-Dr. Station Wagon...71A
Falcon Deluxe 2-Dr. 59B
Station Wagon
Falcon Deluxe 4-Dr. Station...71B
Wagon
Falcon Squire............71C
Falcon 2-Dr. Sedan............78A
Delivery
Falcon 2-Dr. Sedan............78B
Deluxe Delivery
Fairlane 2-Dr. Sedan............62A
Fairlane 4-Dr. Sedan............54A
Fairlane 500 2-Dr. Sedan......62B
Fairlane 500 4-Dr. Sedan......54B
Fairlane 500 Hardtop............65A
Fairlane 500 Sports Coupe....65B
Fairlane Ranch Wagon............71D
Fairlane-4-Dr. Squire............71G
(Bucket Seat)
Custom Ranch Wagon............71B
Fairlane Squire............71E
Ford 300 2-Dr. Sedan............62E
Ford 300 4-Dr. Sedan............54E
Galaxie 2-Dr. Sedan............62B
Galaxie 4-Dr. Sedan............54B
Galaxie 500 2-Dr. Sedan............62A
Galaxie 500 4-Dr. Sedan............54A
Galaxie 500 2-Dr. Hardtop.....63B
(Fastback)
Galaxie 500XL 2-Dr. 63C
Hardtop (Fastback)
Galaxie 500 2-Dr. Hardtop....65A
Galaxie Country Squire............71G
(6-Ps.) Bucket Seat
Galaxie Country Squire............71H
(9-Ps.) Bucket Seat
Galaxie 500 4-Dr. Hardtop....75A
Galaxie 500 Convertible............76A
Galaxie 500 XL 2-Dr. 65B
Hardtop
Galaxie 500 XL 4-Dr. 75C
Hardtop
Galaxie 500 XL Convertible............76B
Galaxie Country Sedan............71B
(6-Pass)

GalaxieCountry Sedan...........71C
(9-Pass)
Galaxie Country Squire..........71E
(6-Pass)
Galaxie Country Squire..........71A
(9-Pass)
Thunderbird Hardtop..............63A
Thunderbird Landau...............63B
Thunderbird Convertible........76A
Thunderbird Convertible........76B
Sport Roadster

MONTHS OF THE YEAR

MONTH	1st YR.	2nd YR.
January	A	N
February	B	P
March	C	Q
April	D	R
May	E	S
June	F	T
July	G	U
August	H	V
September	J	W
October	K	X
November	L	Y
December	M	Z

REAR AXLE RATIO CODES

REAR AXLE RATIO	REGULAR	LOCKING
3.00 TO 1	1	A
3.20 TO 1	3	C
3.50 TO 1	5	E
3.80 TO 1	7	G
4.00 TO 1	9*	I
3.10 TO 1	2	B
3.25 TO 1	4	D
3.89 TO 1	8	H
4.11 TO 1	9**	I

* FALCON
** GALAXIE & FAIRLANE

TRANSMISSION TYPE CODES

TRANSMISSION	CODE
Standard	1
Overdrive	2
Fordomatic (2-Speed)	3
Cruise-O-Matic	4
4 Speed	5

TRIM SCHEME CODES

FORD

TRIM SCHEME	CODE
Medium Blue Cloth & Light Blue Crush Vinyl	12
Light Beige Cloth & Pearl Beige Crush Vinyl	14
Red Cloth & Red Crush Vinyl	15
Medium Turquoise Cloth & Light Turquoise Crush Vinyl	17
Light Gold Cloth & Light Gold Crush Vinyl	18
Medium Blue Cloth & Light Blue Crush Vinyl	22
Light Beige Cloth & Pearl Beige Crush Vinyl	24
Red Cloth & Red Crush Vinyl	25
Black Cloth & Black Crush Vinyl	26
Medium Turquoise Cloth & Light Turquoise Crush Vinyl	27
Light Gold Cloth & Light Gold Crush Vinyl	28
Medium Chestnut Cloth & Light Chestnut Crush Vinyl	29
Light Blue Vinyl & Medium Blue Brick Cloth	32
Light Beige Crush Vinyl & Pearl Beige Crush Vinyl	34
Red Vinyl & Red Brick Cloth	35
Light Gold Vinyl & Light Gold Brick Cloth	38
Medium Chestnut Crush Vinyl & Light Chestnut Crush Vinyl	39
Medium Blue Basket Weave Vinyl & Light Blue Crush Vinyl	42
Medium Beige Basket Weave Vinyl & Pearl Beige Crush Vinyl	44
Red Basket Weave Vinyl & Red Crush Vinyl	45
Light Blue Crush Vinyl & Medium Blue Crush Vinyl	52
Pearl Beige Crush Vinyl & Light Beige Steerhead Vinyl	54
Red Crush All Viny	55
Black Crush All Vinyl	56
Light Turquoise Crush Vinyl & Medium Turquoise Crush Vinyl	57
Light Gold Crush Vinyl & Pearl Gold Crush Vinyl	58
Black Vachette Vinyl & Black Crush Vinyl	66
Medium Chestnut Vachette Vinyl & Light Chestnut Crush Vinyl	69
Light Blue Crush Vinyl & Medium Blue Crush Vinyl	72
Pearl Beige Crush Vinyl & Light Beige Steerhead Vinyl	74
Red Crush All Vinyl	75
Light Turquoise Crush Vinyl & Medium Turquoise Crush Vinyl	77
Light Gold Crush Vinyl & Pearl Gold Crush Vinyl	78
Light Rose Beige Crush All Vinyl	80
Red Crush All Vinyl	85
Black Crush All Vinyl	86
Light Turquoise Crush All Vinyl	87
Light Gold Crush All Vinyl	88
Medium Chestnut Crush All Vinyl	89
Medium Blue Vachette Vinyl & Light Blue Crush Vinyl	92
Light Beige Vachette Vinyl & Pearl Beige Crush Vinyl	94
Red Vachette Vinyl & Red Crush Vinyl	95
Medium Turquoise Vachette Vinyl & Light Turquoise Crush Vinyl	97
Light Gold Vachette Vinyl & Pearl Gold Crush Vinyl	98

1963 TRIM CODES

TRIM	CODE
GALAXIE	
54B,62B Medium Green Rib all Vinyl (Police and Taxi)	3
54B,62B Medium Beige Rib all Vinyl (Police and Taxi)	4
54B,62B Red Rib all Vinyl (Police and Taxi)	5
54B,62B Medium Blue Puff Stripe Cloth & Light Blue Crush Vinyl	12
54B,62B Light Beige Puff Stripe Cloth & Pearl Beige Crush Vinyl	14
71B,71C Light Beige Puff Stripe Cloth & Pearl Beige Crush Vinyl	14
54B,62B Red Puff Stripe Cloth & Red Crush Vinyl	15
54B,62B Medium Turquiose Puff Stripe Cloth&Light Turquois Crush Vinyl	17
71B,71C Medium Turquiose Puff Stripe Cloth&Light Turquois Crush Vinyl	17
54B,62B Light Gold Puff Stripe Cloth & Light Gold Crush Vinyl	18
54A,62A,63B,65A,75A Medium Blue Gleam Cloth & Light Blue Crush Vinyl	22
71A,71E Medium Blue Gleam Cloth & Light Blue Crush Vinyl	22
54A,62A,63B,65A,75A Light Beige Gleam Cloth & Pearl Beige Crush Vinyl "71A,71E"	24
54A,62A,63B,65A,75A Light Beige Gleam Cloth & Pearl Beige Crush Vinyl	24
54A,62A,63B,65A,75A Red Gleam Cloth & Red Crush Vinyl	25
71A,71E Red Gleam Cloth & Red Crush Vinyl	25
54A,62A,63B,65A,75A Black Gleam Cloth & Black Crush Vinyl	26
54A,62A,63B,65A,75A Medium Turquiose Gleam Cloth & Light Turquiose Crush Vinyl	27
71A,71E Medium Turquiose Gleam Cloth & Light Turquiose Crush Vinyl	27
54A,62A,63B,65A,75A Light Gold Puff Stripe Cloth & Light Gold Crush Vinyl	28
54A,62A,63B,65A,75A Medium Chestnut Gleam Cloth & Light Chestnut Crush Vinyl	29
54E,62E Light Blue Vinyl & Medium Blue Brick Cloth	32
54E,62E Red Vinyl & Red Brick Cloth	3
54E,62E Light Gold Vinyl & Light Gold Brick Cloth	4
71B,71C Medium Blue Basket Weave Vinyl & Light Blue Crush Vinyl	4
71B,71C Medium Blue Basket Weave Vinyl & Light Blue Crush Vinyl	44
71B,71C Medium Beige Basket Weave Vinyl & Pearl Beige Crush Vinyl	4
71B,71C Red Basket Weave Vinyl & Red Crush Vinyl	4
54A,62A,63B,65A,75A Black Vachette Vinyl & Black Crush Vinyl	6
76A Black Vachette Vinyl & Black Crush Vinyl	6
54A,62A,63B,65A,75A Medium Chestnut Vachette Vinyl & Light Chestnut Crush Vinyl	6
76A Medium Chestnut Vachette Vinyl & Light Chestnut Crush Vinyl	6
63C,65B,75C Light Rose Beige Crush All Vinyl	8
76B Light Rose Beige Crush All Vinyl	8
63C,65B,75C Light Blue Crush All Vinyl	8
76B Light Blue Crush All Vinyl	8
63C,65B,75C Red Crush All Vinyl	8
76B Red Crush All Vinyl	8
63C,65B,75C Black Crush All Vinyl	8
76B Black Crush All Vinyl	8
63C,65B,75C Light Turquoise All Vinyl	8
76B Light Turquoise All Vinyl	8
63C,65B,75C Light Gold All Vinyl	8
76B Light Gold All Vinyl	8
63C,65B,75C Medium Chestnut All Vinyl	8
76B Medium Chestnut All Vinyl	8
54A,62A,63B,65A,75A Medium Blue Vachette Vinyl & Light Blue Crush Vinyl	9
71A,71E Medium Blue Vachette Vinyl & Light Blue Crush Vinyl	9
76A Medium Blue Vachette Vinyl & Light Blue Crush Vinyl	9
71A,71E Light Beige Vachette Vinyl & Pearl Beige Crush Vinyl	9
54A,62A,63B,65A,75A Red Vachette Vinyl & Red Crush Vinyl	9
71A,71E Red Vachette Vinyl & Red Crush Vinyl	9
76A	9

Red Vachette Vinyl & Red
Crush Vinyl
76A..................................97
Medium Turquoise Vachette Vinyl
& Light Turquoise Crush Vinyl
54A,62A,63B,65A,75A..................98
Light Gold Vachette Vinyl &
Pearl Gold Crush Vinyl
76A..................................98
Light Gold Vachette Vinyl &
Pearl Gold Crush Vinyl

FAIRLANE

54A,62A..................................3
Medium Green Rib All Vinyl
(Police & Taxi)
54A,62A..................................4
Medium Beige Rib All Vinyl
(Police & Taxi)
54A,62A..................................5
Red Rib All Vinyl (Police & Taxi)
54A,62A..................................12
Medium Blue Square Puff Cloth
& Light Blue Crush Vinyl
54A,62A..................................15
Red Square Puff Colth And
Red Crush Vinyl
54A,62A..................................18
Light Gold Square Puff Colth &
Light Gold Crush Vinyl
54B,62B,65A..................................22
Medium Blue Wheel Pattern
Cloth & Light Blue Crush Vinyl
54B,62B,65A,71B,71E..................................24
Light Beige Wheel Pattern Cloth
& Pearl Beige Crush Vinyl
54B,62B,65A..................................25
Red Wheel Pattern Cloth &
Red Crush Vinyl
54B,62B,65A..................................27
Medium Turquoise Wheel
Pattern Cloth & Light
Turquoise Crush Vinyl
54B,62B,65A..................................28
Light Gold Wheel Pattern Cloth &
Light Gold Crush Vinyl
54B,62B,65A,71B,71E..................................32
Medium Blue Crush Vinyl &
Light Blue Crush Vinyl
71B,71E..................................34
Light Beige Crush Vinyl &
Pearl Beige Crush Vinyl
54B,62B,65A,71B,71E..................................35
Red Crush All Vinyl
54B,62B,65A..................................38
Light Gold Crush Vinyl & Pearl
Gold Crush Vinyl
54B,62B,65A..................................39
Medium Chestnut Crush Vinyl &
Light Chestnut Crush Vinyl
71D..................................42
Light Blue Preline Vinyl & Light
Blue Crush Vinyl
71D..................................44
Light Beige Preline Vinyl & Light
Beige Crush Vinyl
65B..................................82
Medium Blue Crush Vinyl & Light
Blue Crush Vinyl
65B..................................85
Red Crush All Vinyl
65B..................................86
Black Crush All Vinyl

65Bc..................................88
Light Gold Crush All Vinyl
65B..................................89
Medium Chestnut Crush Vinyl &
Light Chestnut Crush Vinyl

FALCON

54A,62A..................................18
Light Gold Crush Vinyl & Light
Gold Ladder Cloth
54B,62B..................................22
Light Blue Crush Vinyl & Medium
Blue Bar Line Cloth
54B,59B,62B,71B,71C..................................24
Pearl Beige Crush Vinyl &
Medium Beige Bar Line Cloth
54B,62B..................................25
Red Crush Vinyl & Red Bar
Line Cloth
54B,62B..................................27
Light Turquoise Crush Vinyl &
Medium Turquoise Bar Line Cloth
54B,62B..................................28
Light Gold Crush Vinyl & Light
Gold Bar Line Cloth
76A..................................52
Light Blue Crush Vinyl & Medium
Blue Crush Vinyl
59A,71A..................................54
Pearl Beige Crush Vinyl & Light
Beige Steerhead Vinyl
76A..................................55
Red Crush All Vinyl
54B,62B,63B..................................56
Black Crush All Vinyl
59B,66B,71B,71C,78B..................................56
Black Crush All Vinyl
76A..................................56
Black Crush All Vinyl
76A..................................57
Light Turquoise Crush Vinyl &
Medium Turquoise Crush Vinyl
76A..................................58
Light Gold Crush Vinyl & Pearl
Gold Crush Vinyl
54B,62B,63B..................................72
Light Blue Crush Vinyl & Medium
Blue Crush Vinyl
59B,71B,71C..................................72
Light Blue Crush Vinyl & Medium
Blue Crush Vinyl
66A,78A..................................74
Pearl Beige Crush Vinyl & Light
Beige Steerhead Vinyl
54B,62B,63B..................................75
Red Crush All Vinyl
59B,66B,71B,71C,78B..................................75
Red Crush All Vinyl
54B,62B,63B..................................77
Light Turquoise Crush Vinyl &
Medium Turquoise Crush Vinyl
54B,62B,63B..................................78
Light Gold Crush Vinyl & Pearl
Gold Crush Vinyl
62C,63C..................................82
Light Blue Crush Vinyl & Medium
Blue Crush Vinyl
71D..................................82
Light Blue Crush Vinyl & Medium
Blue Crush Vinyl

76B..................................82
Light Blue Crush Vinyl & Medium
Blue Crush Vinyl
62C,63C..................................85
Red Crush All Vinyl
71D..................................85
Red Crush All Vinyl
76B..................................85
Red Crush All Vinyl
62C,63C..................................86
Black Crush All Vinyl
71D..................................86
Black Crush All Vinyl
76B..................................86
Black Crush All Vinyl
62C,63C..................................87
Light Turquoise Crush Vinyl &
Medium Turquoise Crush Vinyl
76B..................................87
Light Turquoise Crush Vinyl &
Medium Turquoise Crush Vinyl
62C,63C..................................88
Light Gold Crush Vinyl & Pearl
Gold Crush Vinyl
76B..................................88
Light Gold Crush Vinyl & Pearl
Gold Crush Vinyl
54A,62A..................................92
Light Blue Crush Vinyl & Medium
Blue Ladder Cloth
54A,62A..................................95
Red Crush Vinyl & Red Ladder
Cloth
54A,62A..................................98
Light Gold Crush Vinyl & Light
Gold Ladder Cloth

EXTERIOR PAINT BODY

COLOR	CODE
Raven Black	A
Ming Green	D
Acapulco Blue	E
Viking Blue	E
Silver Mink	G
Oxford Blue	H
Caspian Blue	H
Castilian Gold	I
Rangoon Red	J
Chalfonte Blue	K
Sahara Rose	L
Corinthian White	M
Diamond Blue	N
Green Mist	O
Silver Moss	P
Silver Gray	Q
Tucson Yellow	R
Cascade Green	S
Sandshell Beige	T
Deep Sea Blue	U
Chestmut	V
Rose Beige	W
Heritage Burgundy	X
Glaicer Blue	Y
Fieldstone Tan	Z

VEHICLE IDENTIFICATION NUMBER

4A83X100551

VEHICLE IDENTIFICATION NUMBER LOCATIONS

FULL SIZED FORD VIN Die Stamped into extension Tab of Top of Cowl R/H Side of Car under hood.

FAIRLANE VIN Die stamped into side of Left Front Inner Fender Apron near top.

THUNDERBIRD VIN Die Stamped into Top Surface of Front Fender Cross-Brace to the Right of Hood Lock Plate.

FALCON VIN Die Stamped into Top of Left Front Inner Fender Apron.

1964 Model	4
Assembled at Atlanta Plant	A
Thunderbird-Tudor Hardtop	83
8cyl. OHV Engine	X
352 CID 2-venturi carb	
Vehicle Production Number	100551

1st Digit - MODEL YEAR
The number "4" designates 1964

2nd Digit - ASSEMBLY PLANT

Atlanta	A
Chicago	G
Los Angeles	J
Louisville	U
Mahwah	E
Dallas	D
Dearborn	F
Lorain	H
Kansas City	K
Norfolk	N
Pilot Plant	S
Metichen	T
San Jose	R
Twin City	P
Wayne	W
Wixom	Y
St. Louis	Z

3rd & 4th Digit - MODEL

"The model code number identifies the product line seris and the particular body style: the first of the two digits shows the product line, and the second digit shows a two-door style by an odd number or a four-door style by an even number."

BDY	CLR	TRM	DT	DSD	AX	TR
63A	AA	56	11G	21	1	3

SERIAL NUMBER

4A83X100551

FORD CUSTOM   **CODE**
2-Dr. Sedan	53
4-Dr. Sedan	54

FORD CUSTOM 500   **CODE**
2-Dr. Sedan	51
4-Dr. Sedan	52

Galaxie 500   **CODE**
2-Dr. Sedan	61
4-Dr. Sedan	62
4-Dr. Hardtop	64
2-Dr. Convertible	65
2-Dr. Fastback	66

GALAXIE 500XL   **CODE**
4-Dr. Fastback	60
2-Dr. Fastback	68
2-Dr. Convertible	69

STATION WAGONS   **CODE**
2-Dr. Wagon	21
4-Dr. Wagon	22
4-Dr. Deluxe Wagon	24
4-Dr. Squire	26

FAIRLANE   **CODE**
2-Dr. Sedan	31
4-Dr. Sedan	32

FAIRLANE 500   **CODE**
2-Dr. Sedan	41
4-Dr. Sedan	42
2-Dr. Hardtop	43
2-Dr. Hardtop Sport Coupe	47

STATION WAGON   **CODE**
4-Dr. 6 Ps.	38
4-Dr. Custom 6 Ps.	48

THUNDERBIRD   **CODE**
2-Dr. Hardtop	83
2-Dr. Convertible	85
2-Dr. Landau	87

FALCON   **CODE**
STANDARD SEDAN
2-Dr. Sedan	1
4-Dr. Sedan	2

FALCON FUTURA   **CODE**
2-Dr. Sedan	19
2-Dr. Hardtop	17
2-Dr. Convertible	15
4-Dr. Sedan	16
2-Dr. Hardtop	11
2-Dr. Hardtop Sprint	13
Convertible	12
Convertible Sprint	14

RANCHERO   **CODE**
2-Dr. Ranchero	27
2-Dr. Deluxe Ranchero	27

SEDAN DELIVERY   **CODE**
2-Dr. Sedan Delivery	29
2-Dr. Deluxe Sedan Delivery	29

STATION WAGONS CODE

4-Dr. 6 Ps. Country Sedan	72
4-Dr. 9 Ps. Country Sedan	74
4-Dr. 6 Ps. Country Squire	76
4-Dr. 9 Ps. Country Squire	78

5th Digit - Engine

ENGINE CODE

6 Cyl. 223 C.I.	V
8 Cyl. 289 C.I. (2-V)	C
8 Cyl. 260 C.I. (2-V)	F
8 Cyl. 289 C.I. (4-V)	D
8 Cyl. 289 C.I. HP (4-V)	K
6 Cyl. 200 C.I. (1-V)	T
6 Cyl. 170 C.I. (1-V)	U
8 Cyl. 427 C.I. (4-V, H.P.)	Q
8 Cyl. 427 C.I. (8-V, H.P.)	R
6 Cyl. 144 C.I.	S
8 Cyl. 352 C.I. (4-V)	X
8 Cyl. 390 C.I. (4-V)	Z
6 Cyl. 223 C.I. (Police)	B
6 Cyl. 223 C.I. (Taxi)	E
8 Cyl. 390 C.I. (4-V, Interceptor)	P
6 Cyl. 289 C.I. (L.C.)	3
6 Cyl. 223 C.I. (L.C.)	5
8 Cyl. 390 V-8 (4-V, L.C.)	9
6 Cyl. 170 C.I. (1-V, L.C.)	4
8 Cyl. 260 C.I. (2-V, L.C.)	6

PATENT PLATE

The Patent Plate is located on the front body pillar on Galaxie and Thunderbird models, and on the lock face of left front door on Fairlane and Falcon models.

The following diagram of the Patent Plate specifies, in the Vehicle Data Line: the Body Type, Exterior Paint Color, Trim Scheme, Production Date, District Code and D.S.O. Numbers, Rear Axle Ratio and Transmission Type.

Indicated in the Vehicle Warranty Number Line, Formally ""Serial Number"" are: the Model Year, Assembly Plant, Series and Body Type, Engine Type and numerical sequence of assembly.

EXAMPLE

BODY TYPE CODE	63A
BODY COLOR CODE	AA
TRIM SCHEME CODE	56
PRODUCT DATE CODE	11-G
DISTRIC CODE	21
TRANSMISSION TYPE CODE	1
REAR AXLE RATIO CODE	3

Thunderbird, Hardtop.............63A
Raven Black lower body, Raven Black upper body....................AA
First Digit "5" represents material - All Vinyl..............56
Second digit "6" represents color....................Black & White

---

Eleventh Day of Month............11
Month of Year - July................G
Distric Code - Atlanta.............21
Rear axle Ratio of 3.00 to 1.......1
Fordomatic (2 speed) 3

DISTRICT CODE

DOS units built to a Domestic Special Order, Foreign Special Order, or Pre-Approved Order have the complete order number recorded in this space. Also appearing in this space is the two digit code number of the Distric which orderd the unit. If the unit is regular production, only the Distric code number will appear.

DISTRICT CODE

Boston	11
Buffalo	12
New York	13
Pitsburg	14
Newark	15
Atlanta	21
Charlotte	22
Philadelphia	23
Jacksonville	24
Richmond	25
Washington	26
Cincinnati	31
Cleveland	32
Detroit	33
Indianopolis	34
Lansing	35
Louisville	36
Chicago	41
Fargo	42
Rockford	43
Twin Cities	44
Davenport	45
Denver	51
Des Moines	52
Kansas City	53
Omaha	54
St. Louis	55
Dallas	61
Huston	62
Memphis	63
New Orleans	64
Oklahoma City	65
Los Angeles	71
San Jose	72
Salt Lake City	73
Seattle	74
Ford of Canada	81
Government	83
Home Office Reserve	84
American Red Cross	85
Transportation Services	89
Export	90-99

ENGINE MODELS AND PISTON DISPLACEMENT (Cubic Inches)

Falcon	144
Falcon	170
Mileage Maker Six	223
289 V-8	289
352 V-8	352
390 V-8	390

---

427 V-8 H.P.(4-V)	427
427 V-8 H.P. (8-V)	427
390 V-8 Police Interceptor	390
200 CI	200
260 V-8	260

COMPRESSION RATIO

144	8.7:1
170	8.7:1
Mileage Maker Six	8.4:1
289 V-8	9.0:1
352 V-8	9.3:1
390 V-8	10.1:1
427 V-8 H.P. (4-V)	11.5:1
427 V-8 H.P. (6-V)	11.2:1
390 Police Interceptor V-8	10.1:1
200	8.7:1
260	8.8:1
289 HP	10.5:1

BRAKE HORSEPOWER

144	85
170	101
Mileage Maker Six	138
289 V-8	195
352 V-8	250
390 V-8 (4-V)	300
427 V-8 H.P. (4-V)	410
427 V-8 H.P. (8-V)	425
390 Police Interceptor V-8	330
200	116
260	164
298 HP	271

BODY TYPE CODES

BODY MODEL	BODY TYPE
Falcon 2-Dr. Sedan	62A
Falcon 4-Dr. Sedan	54A
Falcon Futura 2-Dr. Sedan	62B
Falcon Futura 4-Dr. Sedan	54B
Falcon Futura Convertible (Bench seat)	76A
Falcon Futura Sports Convertible (Bucket seat)	76B
Falcon 2-Dr. Station Wagon	59A
Falcon 4-Dr. Station Wagon	71A
Falcon 2-Dr. Sedan	62D
Falcon 4-Dr. Sedan	54D
Falcon 2-Door Hardtop Futura (Bench Seat)	63B
Falcon 2-Dr. Hardtop (Bucket Seat)	63C
Falcon 2-Dr. Hardtop Sprint (Bucket Seat)	63D
Falcon Ranchero	66A
Falcon Deluxe Ranchero	66B
Falcon Convertible Futura Sprint (Bucket Seat)	76D
Falcon 4-Dr. Deluxe Ranch Wagon	71B
Falcon Squire	71C
Falcon Sedan Delivery	78A
Falcon Delux Sedan Delivery	78B
Fairlane Club Sedan	62A
Fairlane Town Sedan	54A
Fairlane 500 Club Sedan	62B
Fairlane 500 Town Sedan	54B
Fairlane 500 Hardtop	65A
Fairlane 500 Sports Coupe	65B
Fairlane Ranch Wagon	71D

FairlaneCustom Ranch Wagon	71B
Ford Custom 2-Dr. Sedan	62E
Custom 500 4-Dr. Sedan	54B
Ford Custom 4-Dr. Sedan	54E
Ford Custom 4-Dr. Sedan	62B
Galaxie 500 Club Sedan	62A
Galaxie 500 Town Sedan	54A
Galaxie 500 4-Dr. Hardtop	57B
Galaxie 500 Convertible	76A
Galaxie 500 Club Victoria Fastback	63B
Galaxie 500 XL Club Victoria Fastback (bucket seat)	63C
Galaxie 500 XL 4-Door Hardtop (Bucket Seat)	57C
Galaxie 500 XL Convertible	76B
Galaxie Country Sedan (6-Pass)	71B
Galaxie Country Sedan (9-Pass)	71C
Galaxie Country Squire (6-Pass)	71E
Galaxie Country Squire (9-Pass)	71A
Thunderbird Hardtop	63A
Thunderbird Hardtop Landau	63B
Thunderbird Convertible	76A

MONTHS OF THE YEAR CODES

MONTH	1st YR.	2nd YR.
January	A	N
February	B	P
March	C	Q
April	D	R
May	E	S
June	F	T
July	G	U
August	H	V
September	J	W
October	K	X
November	L	Y
December	M	Z

REAR AXLE RATIO CODES

REAR AXLE RATIO	REGULAR	LOCKING
3.00 :1	1	A
3.20 :1	3	C
3.50 :1	5	E
3.80 :1	7	G
4.00 :1	9*	I
3.10 :1	2	B
3.25 :1	4	D
3.89 :1	8	H
4.11 :1	9**	I
2.80: 1	6	F

* FALCON
** GALAXIE

TRANSMISSION TYPE CODES

TRANSMISSION	CODE
Standard	1
Overdrive	2
Fordomatic (2-Speed)	3

Cruise-O-Matic............................4
4 Speed.......................................5
C4 Dual Range Automatic.........6

TRIM SCHEME CODES

FORD

TRIM SCHEME	CODE

Medium Blue Cloth & Light.......12
Blue Crush Vinyl
Light Beige Cloth & Pearl..........14
Beige Crush Vinyl
Red Cloth & Red Crush Vinyl...15
Medium Turquoise Cloth & Light
Turquoise Crush Vinyl..............17
Light Gold Cloth & Light............18
Gold Crush Vinyl
Medium Blue Cloth & Light.......22
Blue Crush Vinyl
Light Beige Cloth & Pearl..........24
Beige Crush Vinyl
Red Cloth & Red Crush Vinyl...25
Black Cloth & Black Crush........26
Vinyl Medium Turquoise Cloth &
Light Turquoise Crush Vinyl......27
Light Gold Cloth & Light............28
Gold Crush Vinyl
Medium Chestnut Cloth &.........29
Light Chestnut Crush Vinyl
Light Blue Vinyl & Medium........32
Blue Brick Cloth
Light Beige Crush Vinyl &.........34
Pearl Beige Crush Vinyl
Red Vinyl & Red Brick Cloth.....35
Light Gold Vinyl & Light............38
Gold Brick Cloth
Medium Chestnut Crush Vinyl &
Light Chestnut Crush Vinyl.......39
Medium Blue Basket Weave Vinyl
& Light Blue Crush Vinyl...........42
Medium Beige Basket Weave
Vinyl & Pearl Beige...................44
Crush Vinyl
Red Basket Weave Vinyl &.......45
Red Crush Vinyl
Light Blue Crush Vinyl &...........52
Medium Blue Crush Vinyl
Pearl Beige Crush Vinyl &........54
Light Beige Steerhead Vinyl
Red Crush All Viny....................55
Black Crush All Vinyl................56
Light Turquoise Crush..............57
Vinyl & Medium Turquoise Crush
Vinyl
Light Gold Crush Vinyl &...........58
Pearl Gold Crush Vinyl
Black Vachette Vinyl &..............66
Black Crush Vinyl
Medium Chestnut Vachette......69
Vinyl & Light Chestnut Crush
Vinyl
Light Blue Crush Vinyl &...........72
Medium Blue Crush Vinyl
Pearl Beige Crush Vinyl &........74
Light Beige Steerhead Vinyl
Red Crush All Vinyl..................75
ight Turquoise Crush Viny.l.......77
& Medium Turquoise Crush Vinyl
Light Gold Crush Vinyl &...........78
Pearl Gold Crush Vinyl

Light Rose Beige Crush 80
All Vinyl
Light Blue Crush All Vinyl.........82
Red Crush All Viny....................85
Black Crush All Vinyl................86
Light Turquoise Crush..............87
All Vinyl
Light Gold Crush All Vinyl........88
Medium Chestnut Crush...........89
All Vinyl
Medium Blue Vachette Vinyl....92
& Light Blue Crush Vinyl
Light Beige Vachette Vinyl 94
& Pearl Beige Crush Vinyl
Red Vachette Vinyl &................95
Red Crush Vinyl
Medium Turquoise Vachette Vinyl
& Light Turquoise.....................97
Crush Vinyl
Light Gold Vachette Vinyl.........98
 & Pearl Gold Crush Vinyl

1964 TRIM CODES

GALAXIE

54B,54E,62B,62E......................3
Medium Green crush vinyl &
Medium Green Rib Vinyl
(Police and Taxi)
54B,54E,62B,62E......................4
Medium Beige crush vinyl &
medium beige Rib Vinyl
(Police and Taxi)
54A,57B,62A,63B......................12
Light Blue crush vinyl & Medium
Blue chain weave cloth
54A,57B,62A,63B......................14
Light Beige crush vinyl & Medium
Beige chain weave cloth
71B,71E....................................14
Light Beige crush vinyl & Medium
Beige chain weave cloth
54A,57B,62A,63B......................15
Red crush vinyl & red chain
weave cloth
54A,62A....................................16
Black crush vinyl & black chain
weave cloth
54A,57B,62A,63B......................17
Light turquoise crush vinyl &
Medium turquoise chain
weave cloth
54B,62B....................................22
Light blue crush vinyl & medium
blue louver pattern cloth
54B,62B....................................24
Light beige crush vinyl & medium
beige louver pattern cloth
54B,62B....................................25
Red crush vinyl & red louver
pattern cloth
54B,62B....................................27
54E,62E....................................32
Light blue crush vinyl & medium
blue bar dot cloth
54E,62E....................................34
Light beige crush vinyl & medium
beige bar dot pattern cloth
54E,62E....................................35
Red crush vinyl & red louver
bar dot cloth
71B,71C....................................42
Medium blue mosaic pattern vinyl

& light blue crush vinyl
71B,71C....................................42
Medium beige mosaic pattern
vinyl & light beige crush vinyl
71B,71C....................................42
Red mosaic pattern vinyl &
red crush vinyl
71B,71C....................................42
Medium turquoise mosaic pattern
vinyl & light turquoise crush vinyl
54B,62B....................................64
Light beige crush all vinyl
54E,62E....................................64
Light beige crush all vinyl
63B..71
Light silver blue crush vinyl &
medium silver blue crush vinyl
76A..71
Light silver blue crush vinyl &
medium silver blue crush vinyl
54A,57B,62A,63B......................72
Light blue crush vinyl & medium
blue crush vinyl
71A,71E....................................72
Light blue crush vinyl & medium
blue crush vinyl
76A..72
Light blue crush vinyl & medium
blue crush vinyl
54A,57B,62A,63B...................... 74
Light beige crush vinyl & medium
beige crush vinyl
76A..74
Light beige crush vinyl & medium
beige crush vinyl
54A,57B,62A,63B......................75
Red crush all vinyl
71A,71E....................................75
Red crush all vinyl
76A..75
Red crush all vinyl
57B,63B....................................76
Black crush all vinyl
71A,71E....................................76
Black crush all vinyl
76A..76
Black crush all vinyl
76A..77
Light turquoise crush vinyl &
medium turquoise crush vinyl
71A,71E....................................79
Medium palpmino crinkle all vinyl
57C,63C....................................80
White crush all vinyl with black
76B..80
White crush all vinyl with black
57C,63C....................................81
Light silver blue crush vinyl &
medium silver blue crush cinyl
76B..81
Light silver blue crush
vinyl & medium silver blue crush
cinyl
57C..63
Light blue crush vinyl & medium
blue crush vinyl
76B..82
Light blue crush vinyl & medium
blue crush vinyl
57C,63C....................................84
Light beige crush all vinyl

76B..84
Light beige crush all vinyl
57C,63C....................................85
Red crush all vinyl
76B..85
Red crush all vinyl
57C,63C....................................86
Black crush all vinyl
76B..86
Black crush all vinyl
57C,63C....................................87
Light turquoise crush vinyl &
medium turquoise crush vinyl
76B..87
Light turquoise crush vinyl &
medium turquoise crush vinyl
57C,63C....................................89
Medium palpmino crinkle all vinyl
76B..89
Medium palpmino crinkle all vinyl

FAIRLANE

54A..4
Medium Beige crush vinyl &
medium beige Rib Vinyl
(Police and Taxi)
54A,62A....................................12
Light blue crush vinyl & medium
blue bar O pattern cloth
54A,62A....................................14
Light beige crush vinyl & medium
beige bar O pattern cloth
54A,62A....................................15
Red crush vinyl & red
bar O pattern cloth
54B,62B,65A..............................22
Light blue crush vinyl & medium
blue ellipse pattern cloth
54A,62B,65A..............................24
Light beige crush vinyl & medium
beige ellipse pattern cloth
54A,62B,65A..............................25
Red crush vinyl & red ellipse
pattern cloth
54A,62B,65A..............................27
Light turquoise crush vinyl &
medium turquoise ellipse
pattern cloth
71D..42
Light blue crush vinyl & medium
blue preline pattern cloth
71D..44
54B,62B,65A,71B....................... 62
54A, 62B,65A............................64
Light beige crush all vinyl
54B,62B,65A,71B.......................65
Red crush all vinyl
65A,71B....................................66
Black crush all vinyl
71B..69
Medium palomino crinkle all vinyl
65B..80
White crush all vinyl with black
65B..81
Light silver blue crush vinyl &
medium silver blue crush cinyl
65B..82
Light blue crush vinyl & medium
blue crush vinyl
76B..85
Red crush all vinyl
65B..86
Black crush all vinyl

...B.................................89
edium palmino crinkle all vinyl

ALCON

.D,62D.............................12
ght Blue crush vinyl & Medium
ue band pattern cloth

A,54D,62A,62D...................14
ght Beige crush vinyl & Medium
eige band pattern cloth

.D,62D.............................15
ed crush vinyl & red band
attern cloth

B,62B.............................22
ght blue vinyl & medium blue
ord stripe pattern cloth

B,62B,71C........................24
ght beige vinyl & medium beige
ord stripe pattern cloth

B,62B.............................25
ed crush vinyl & red cord stripe
attern cloth

B,62B.............................27
ght turquoise crush vinyl &
edium turquoise cord stripe
attern cloth

A,66A,71A,78A....................44
ght beige crush vinyl & medium
eige steerhead pattern vinyl

B,62B,63B,71B,71C................62
ght blue crush vinyl & medium
ue crush vinyl

A.................................62
ght blue crush vinyl & medium
ue crush vinyl

B,62B,63B........................64
ght beige crush all vinyl

A.................................64
ght beige crush all vinyl

B,62B,63B,66B,71B................65
C,78B Red crush all vinyl

A.................................65
ed crush all vinyl

B,66B,71B,71C,78B...............66
ack crush all vinyl

A.................................66
ack crush all vinyl

B.................................67
ght turquoise crush vinyl &
edium turquoise cord stripe
attern cloth

A.................................67
ght turquoise crush vinyl &
edium turquoise cord stripe
attern cloth

B,71C.............................69
edium palmino crinkle all vinyl

3C,63D............................82
ght blue crush vinyl & medium
ue crush vinyl

6B,76D............................82
ght blue crush vinyl & medium
ue crush vinyl

3C,63D............................85
ed crush all vinyl

6B,76D............................85
ed crush all vinyl

3C,63D............................86
ack crush all vinyl

6B,76D............................86
ack crush all vinyl

3C,63D............................87

Light turquoise crush vinyl &
medium turquoise crush vinyl
76B,76D...........................87
Light turquoise crush vinyl &
medium turquoise crush vinyl
63C,63D...........................89
Medium palmino crinkle all vinyl
76B,76D...........................89
Medium palmino crinkle all vinyl

EXTERIOR PAINT BODY COLOR CODES

COLOR	CODE
Raven Black	A
Pagoda Green	B
Ming Green	D
Dynasty Green	D
Acapulco Blue	E
Viking Blue	E
Guardsman Blue	F
Silver Mink	G
Prairie Tan	G
Oxford Blue	H
Caspian Blue	H
Castilian Gold	I
Rangoon Red	J
Chalfonte Blue	K
Silver Smoke Gray	K
Sahara Rose	L
Corinthian White	M
Wimbledon White	M
Diamond Blue	N
Green Mist	O
Silver Moss	P
Phoenician Yellow	R
Tucson Yellow	R
Cascade Green	S
Sandshell Beige	T
Navaho Beige	T
Deep Sea Blue	U
Chestmut	V
Rose Beige	W
Heritage Burgundy	X
Vintage Burgundy	X
Glaicer Blue	Y
Skylight Blue	Y
Fieldstone Tan	Z
Chantilly Beige	Z

VEHICLE IDENTIFICATION NUMBER

5A83X100551

FULL SIZED FORD VIN Die Stamped into extension Tab of Top of Cowl R/H Side of Car under hood.

FAIRLANE VIN Die stamped into side of Left Front Inner Fender Apron near top.

THUNDERBIRD VIN Die Stamped into Top Surface of Front Fender Cross-Brace to the Right of Hood Lock Plate.

MUSTANG VIN Die Stamped into top surface of front inner fender apron.

FALCON VIN Die Stamped into Top of Left Front Inner Fender Apron.

1965 Model..............................5
Assembled at Atlanta Plant........A
Thunderbird-Tudor Hardtop......83
8cyl. OHV Engine.......................X
352 C.I.D., 2V
Vehicle Production.............100551
Number

1st Digit - MODEL YEAR
"The number "5" designates 1965

2nd Digit - ASSEMBLY PLANT
Atlanta..A
Oakville...B
Dallas..D
Mahwah..E
Dearborn..F
Chicago..G
Lorain...H
Los Angeles.......................................J
Kansas City..K
Long Beach...L
Norfolk..N
Twin City...P
San Jose..R
Pilot Plant...S
Metichen...T
Louisville...U
Wayne..W
Wixom..Y
St. Louis..Z

3rd & 4th Digit - MODEL
"The model code number identifies the product line seris and the particular body style: the first of the two digits shows the product line, and the second digit shows a two-door style by an odd number or a four-door style by an even number."

BDY	CLR	TRM	DT	DSD	AX	TR
63A	AA	56	11G	21	1	1

SERIAL NUMBER

5A83X100551

FORD CUSTOM	CODE
2-Dr. Sedan	53
4-Dr. Sedan	54

FORD CUSTOM 500	CODE
2-Dr. Sedan	51
4-Dr. Sedan	52

Galaxie 500	CODE
4-Dr. Sedan	62
4-Dr. Hardtop	64
2-Dr. Convertible	65
2-Dr. Fastback	66

GALAXIE 500XL	CODE
2-Dr. Fastback (1)	68
2-Dr. Convertible (1)	69

(1) Bucket Seats

GALAXIE 500 LTD	CODE
4-Dr. Hardtop	60
2-Dr. Fastback	67

FAIRLANE	CODE
2-Dr. Sedan	3
4-Dr. Sedan	32

FAIRLANE 500	CODE
2-Dr. Sedan	41
4-Dr. Sedan	42
2-Dr. Hardtop	43
2-Dr. Hardtop (Bucket seats)	47
4-Dr. Ranch Wagon	38
4-Dr. Custom Ranch Wagon	48

STATION WAGON

	CODE
-Dr. Ranch Wagon 6 Ps.	71
-Door Custom 9 Ps.	72
-Door 9 Ps.	74

COUNTRY SQUIRE

	CODE
-Dr. 6 Ps.	76
-Dr. 9 Ps.	78

THUNDERBIRD

	CODE
2-Dr. Landau Special	81
2-Dr. Hardtop	83
2-Dr. Convertible	85
2-Dr. Landau	87

FALCON STANDARD SEDAN

	CODE
2-Dr. Sedan	1
2-Dr. Sedan	1
4-Dr. Sedan	2
4-Dr. Sedan	2

FALCON FUTURA

	CODE
2-Dr. Sedan (2)	19
2-Dr. Convertible (2)	15
4-Dr. Sedan (2)	16
2-Dr. Hardtop (1)	11
Convertible (1)	12
Deluxe	27

1) RPO Bucket Seats
2) Bench Seats

STATION WAGONS

	CODE
2-Dr. Wagon	21
4-Dr. Wagon	22
4-Dr. Deluxe Wagon	24
4-Dr. Squire	26

RANCHERO

	CODE
2-Dr. Ranchero	27
2-Dr. Deluxe Ranchero	27
2-Dr. Ranchero	27
(RPO Bucket w/ console)	
2-Dr. Deluxe Ranchero	27
(RPO Bucket w/ console)	

SEDAN DELIVERY

	CODE
2-Dr. Sedan Delivery	29
2-Dr. Deluxe Sedan Delivery	29

MUSTANG

	CODE
2-Door Fastback	9
2-Door Hardtop	7
2-Door Convertible	8
2-Dr. Fastback (Luxury Trim)	9
2-Dr. Hardtop (Luxury Trim)	7
2-Dr. Convertible (Luxury Trim)	8
2-Dr. Hardtop (Bench Seat)	7
2-Dr. Convertible (Bench Seat)	8

5th Digit - Engine

ENGINE	CODE
6 Cyl. 240 C.I.	V
8 Cyl. 289 C.I. (4-V) Prem.	A
8 Cyl. 289 C.I. (2-V)	C
8 Cyl. 289 C.I. (4-V) H. P.	K
6 Cyl. 200 C.I. (1-V)	T
6 Cyl. 170 C.I. (1-V)	U
8 Cyl. 427 C.I. (8-V, H. P.)	R
8 Cyl. 427 C.I. (4-V OH Cam)	L
8 Cyl. 427 C.I. (8-V OH Cam)	M
8 Cyl. 352 C.I. (4-V)	X

8 Cyl. 390 C.I. (4-V)	Z
8 Cyl. 390 C.I.(4-V, Interceptor)	P
8 Cyl. 260 CI (2-V)	F
8 Cyl. 289 CI (4-V) Reg.	D
6 Cyl. 240 CI Police	B
6-Cyl. 240 CI Taxi	E
8 Cyl. 289 C.I. (Low Comp.)	3
6 Cyl. 240 C.I. (Low Comp.)	5
8 Cyl. 390 V-8.	9
(4-V, Low Comp.)	
6 Cyl. 170 C.I.	4
(1-V, Low Comp.)	
6 Cyl. 200 C.I.	2
(1-V, Low Comp.)	

PATENT PLATE

The Patent Plate is located on the left front door lock face panel on all models.

The following diagram of the Patent Plate specifies, in the Vehicle Data Line: the Body Type, Exterior Paint Color, Trim Scheme, Production Date, District Code and D.S.O. Numbers, Rear Axle Ratio and Transmission Type.
Indicated in the Vehicle Warranty Number Line, Formally ""Serial Number"" are: the Model Year, Assembly Plant, Series and Body Type, Engine Type and numerical sequence of assembly.

EXAMPLE

BODY TYPE CODE	63A
BODY COLOR CODE	AA
TRIM SCHEME CODE	56
PRODUCT DATE CODE	11-G
DISTRIC CODE	21
TRANSMISSION TYPE CODE	1
REAR AXLE RATIO CODE	3

Thunderbird, Hardtop	63A
Raven Black lower body, Raven Black upper body	AA
First Digit "5" represents material - All Vinyl	56
Second digit "6" represents color Black & White	
Eleventh Day of Month	11
Month of Year - July	G
Distric Code - Atlanta	21
Rear axle Ratio of 3.00 to 1	1
Fordomatic (2 speed)	3

DISTRICT CODE

DOS units built to a Domestic Special Order, Foreign Special Order, or Pre-Approved Order have the complete order number recorded in this space. Also appearing in this space is the two digit code number of the Distric which orderd the unit. If the unit is regular production, only the Distric code number will appear.

DISTRICT	CODE
Boston	11
Buffalo	12
New York	13
Pitsburg	14
Newark	15
Atlanta	21
Charlotte	22
Philadelphia	23
Jacksonville	24
Richmond	25
Washington	26
Cincinnati	31
Cleveland	32
Detroit	33
Indianoplis	34
Lansing	35
Louisville	36
Chicago	41
Fargo	42
Rockford	43
Twin Cities	44
Davenport	45
Denver	51
Des Moines	52
Kansas City	53
Omaha	54
St. Louis	55
Dallas	61
Huston	62
Memphis	63
New Orleans	64
Oklahoma City	65
Los Angeles	71
San Jose	72
Salt Lake City	73
Seattle	74
Ford of Canada	81
Government	83
Home Office Reserve	84
American Red Cross	85
Transportation Services	89
Export	90-99

ENGINE MODELS AND PISTON DISPLACEMENT (Cubic Inches

170 Six	170
200 Six	200
240 Six	240
260 V-8	260
289 V-8	289
352 V-8	352
390 Special V-8	390
427 H. P. V-8 (8-V)	427

COMPRESSION RATIO

170 Six	9.1:1
200 Six	9.2:1
240 Six	9.2:1
260 V-8	8.8:1
289 V-8 (2-V)	9.3:1
289 V-8 (4-V)	10.0:1
289 V-8 (4-V)HP	10.0:1
352 V-8 (4-V)	9.3:1
390 V-8 (4-V)	10.1:1
289 V-8 (4-V) Reg.	9.0:1
427 V-8 H. P. (8-V)	11.1:1
390 V-8 Police Interceptor	10.1:1

BRAKE HORSEPOWER

170 Six	105
200 Six	120
240 Six	150
260 V-8	164
289 V-8 (2-V)	200
289 V-8 (4-V)	225
289 V-8 H. P.	271
352 V-8	250
289 V-8 (4-V) Reg.	210
390 V-8 (4-V)	300
427 H. P. V-8 (8-V)	425
390 Police Interceptor V-8	330

BODY TYPE CODES

BODY MODEL	BODY TYPE
Falcon 2-Door Sedan	62A
Falcon 2-Dr. Hardtop (Bucket Seat)	63C
Falcon 4-Door Sedan	54A
Falcon Futura 2-Door Sedan	62B
Falcon Futura 4-Door Sedan	54B
Falcon Futura Convertible	76A
Falcon 2-Dr. Convertible (Bucket Seat)	76B
Falcon 2-Door Station Wagon	59A
Falcon 4-Door Station Wagon	71A
Falcon 2-Door Sedan	62D
Falcon 4-Door Sedan	54D
Falcon 2-Door Hardtop	63B
Futura (Bench Seat) Falcon4-Door	71B
Ranch Wagon Falcon 4-Door	
Ranch Wagon Squire	71C
Falcon Sedan Delivery	78A
Falcon Delux Sedan Delivery	78B
Falcon Ranchero	66A
Falcon Delux Ranchero	66B
FalconRanchero (Bucket Seat)	66G
Falcon Delux Ranchero (Bucket Seat)	66H
Fairlane Club Sedan	62A
Fairlane Town Sedan	54A
Failane 500 Club Sedan	62B
Fairlane 500 Town Sedan	54B
Fairlane 500 Hardtop	65A
Fairlane 500 Sports Coupe	65B
Fairlane Ranch Wagon	71D
Fairlane Custom Ranch Wagon	71B
Ford Custom 500 Club Sedan	62B
Ford Custom 500 2-Dr. Sedan	62E
Ford Custom 500 4-Dr. Sedan	54A
Ford Custom 2-Dr. Sedan	54E
Galaxie 500 LTD 4-Dr. Hardtop	54F
Galaxie 500 LTD 4-Dr. Hardtop	63F
Galaxie 500 4-Dr. Hardtop	57B
Galaxie 500 Convertible	76A
Galaxie 500 2-Dr. Hardtop	63B
Galaxie 500XL 2-Dr. Hardtop	63C
Galaxie 500XL Convertible	76B
Galaxie Country Sedan	71B

Galaxie Country Sedan..........71C
(9Ps.)
Galaxie Country Squire..........71E
(6Ps.)
Galaxie Country Squire..........71A
(9Ps.)
Mustang 2-Dr. Fastback.........63A
Mustang 2-Dr. Hardtop...........65A
Mustang 2-Dr. Convertible.....76A
Mustang 2-Dr. Fastback.........63B
(Luxury Trim)
Mustang 2-Dr. Hardtop...........65B
(Luxury Trim)
Mustang 2-Dr. Convertible.....76B
(Luxury Trim)
Mustang 2-Dr. Hardtop...........65C
(Bench Seat)
Mustang 2-Dr. Convertible.....76C
(Bench Seat)

MONTHS OF THE YEAR CODES

MONTH	1st YR.	2nd YR.
January	A	N
February	B	P
March	C	Q
April	D	R
May	E	S
June	F	T
July	G	U
August	H	V
September	J	W
October	K	X
November	L	Y
December	M	Z

REAR AXLE RATIO CODES

REAR AXLE RATIO	REGULAR	LOCKING
2.80 :1	6	F
2.83 :1	2	B
3.00 :1	1	A
3.20 :1	3	C
3.50 :1	5	E
3.80 :1	7	G
3.25 :1	4	D
3.89 :1	8	H
4.00 :1	9*	I
4.11 :1	9**	I

* FALCON
** FORD, FAIRLANE, MUSTANG

TRANSMISSION TYPE CODES

TRANSMISSION	CODE
Standard	1
Overdrive	2
Cruise-O-Matic	4
4 Speed	5
C4 Automatic (XP)	6

ENGINE CODES

Engine	CODE
6 Cyl. 240 C.I. OHV	V
8 Cyl. 352 C.I. OHV (2-V)	X
8 Cyl. 390 C.I. OHV (4-V)	Z
8 Cyl. 390 C.I. OHV (4-V)Police	P
6 Cyl. 170 C.I. OHV	U
6 Cyl. 240 C.I. OHV (Police)	B
6 Cyl. 240 C.I. OHV (Taxi)	E
6 Cyl. 200 C.I. OHV (1V)	T
8 Cyl. 289 C.I. OHV (4V, H. P.)	K
8 Cyl. 289 C.I. OHV (2V)	C
8 Cyl. 289 C.I. OHV (4V)	A
8 Cyl. 427 C.I. OHV (8V, H. P.)	R

1964 TRIM SCHEME CODES

FORD

54B,54E..............................1
Medium Green crush vinyl &
Medium Green Rib Vinyl
(Police and Taxi)
54B,54E,62B,62E...................4
Medium Beige crush vinyl &
medium beige Rib Vinyl
(Police and Taxi)
54E,62E.............................12
Light Blue crinkle vinyl & Medium
Blue plaid stripe cloth
54E,62E.............................15
Red crinkle vinyl & red plaid
stripe cloth
54E,62E.............................19
Medium palomino crinkle
vinyl & Medium palomino
plaid stripe cloth
54E,62E.............................29
Medium palomino crinkle vinyl &
Medium palomino blip stripe cloth
54B,62B.............................32
Light blue crinkle vinyl & medium
blue frost stripe cloth
54B,62B.............................35
Red crinkle vinyl & red frost
stripe cloth
54B,62B.............................37
Light turquoise crinkle vinyl
& medium turquoise frost
stripe cloth
54E,62E.............................39
Medium palomino crinkle vinyl &
Medium palomino frost stripe
cloth
54A,57A,63B........................52
Light Blue crinkle vinyl & Medium
Blue carthage pattern cloth
54A,57B,63B........................55
Red crinkle vinyl & red carthage
pattern cloth
54A.................................56
Black crinkle vinyl & black
carthage pattern cloth
54A,57B,63B........................57
Light turquoise crinkle
vinyl & Medium turquoise
carthage pattern cloth
54A,57B,63B........................58
Light ivy gold crinkle vinyl
& Medium ivy gold carthage
pattern cloth
54A,57B,63B........................59
Medium palomino crinkle vinyl
& Medium palomino carthage
stripe cloth

71A,71B,71C,71E.....................59
Medium palomino crinkle vinyl
& Medium palomino carthage
stripe cloth
54A,57B,63B........................62
Light blue crinkle vinyl & medium
blue crinkle vinyl
71A,71B,71C,71E,76A................62
Light blue crinkle vinyl & medium
blue crinkle vinyl
54A,57B,63B........................65
Red crinkle all vinyl
71A,71B,71C,71E,76A................65
Red crinkle all vinyl
57B,63B............................66
Black crinkle all vinyl
71A,71B,71C,71E,76A................66
Black crinkle all vinyl
76A................................67
Light turquoise crinkle vinyl &
Medium turquoise crinkle vinyl
54A,57B,63B........................68
Light ivy gold crinkle all vinyl
71A,71B,71C,71E,76A................68
Light ivy gold crinkle all vinyl
54A,57B,63B........................69
Medium palomino crinkle all vinyl
71A,71B,71C,71E,76A................69
Medium palomino crinkle all vinyl
63C,76B............................72
Light blue crinkle vinyl & medium
blue crinkle vinyl
63C,76B............................75
Red crinkle all vinyl
63C................................76
Black crinkle all vinyl
63C,76B............................K9
Medium palomino crinkle all vinyl
63C,76B............................L2
White crinkle all vinyl with blue
63C,76B............................L5
White crinkle all vinyl with red
63C,76B............................L6
White crinkle all vinyl with black
63C,76B............................L7
White crinkle all vinyl
with turquoise
63C,76B............................L8
White crinkle all vinyl with ivy gold
63C,76B............................L9
White crinkle all vinyl
with palomino
71D................................N2
Light blue crinkle vinyl & medium
blue blip pattern vinyl
71D................................N5
Red crinkle vinyl & red blip
pattern vinyl
71D................................N9
Medium palomino crinkle vinyl
& Medium palomino blip
pattern vinyl
63C................................P9
Medium palomino crinkle vinyl
& Medium palomino shadow
stripe cloth
54B,54E............................Y5
Red crinkle vinyl & red shadow
block pattern vinyl
54B,54E............................Y9
Medium palomino crinkle vinyl &
Medium palomino shadow
block pattern vinyl

54A................................Z6
Black crinkle all vinyl
54A................................Z9
Medium palomino crinkle all vinyl

FAIRLANE

54A..................................4
Medium Beige crush vinyl
& medium beige Rib Vinyl
(Police and Taxi)
54A,62A.............................12
Light blue crinkle vinyl & medium
blue tartan pattern cloth
54A,62A.............................15
Red crinkle vinyl & red tartan
pattern cloth
54A,62A.............................19
Medium palomino crinkle vinyl &
Medium tartan pattern cloth
54B,62B,65A........................22
Light blue crinkle vinyl & light blue
shasta pattern cloth
54B,62B,65A........................25
Red crinkle vinyl & red shasta
pattern cloth
54B,62B,65A........................27
Light turquoise crinkle vinyl & light
turquoise shasta pattern cloth
54B,62B,65A........................28
Light ivy gold crinkle vinyl & light
ivy gold shasta pattern cloth
54B,62B,65A........................29
Medium palomino crinkle vinyl
& Medium palomino shasta
pattern cloth
65A................................32
Light blue crinkle vinyl & medium
blue crinkle vinyl
54B,62B,65A35
Red crinkle all vinyl
54B,62B,65A........................36
Blue crinkle all vinyl
54B,62B,65A........................39
Medium palomino crinkle all vinyl
71D................................42
Light blue crinkle vinyl & medium
blue basket pattern vinyl
54A,62A,71D........................49
Medium palomino crinkle vinyl
& medium palomino basket
pattern vinyl
71B................................52
Light blue crinkle vinyl & medium
blue crinkle vinyl
71B................................55
Red crinkle all vinyl
71B................................56
Black crinkle all vinyl
71B................................59
Medium palomino crinkle all vinyl
71B................................79
Medium palomino crinkle vinyl
& light palipomino shasta
pattern cloth
65B................................82
Light blue crinkle vinyl & medium
blue ckrukle vinyl
65B................................85
Red crinkle all vinyl
65B................................86
Black crinkle all vinyl
65B................................88
Light ivy gold crinkle all vinyl

5B.....89
edium palomino crinkle all vinyl
5B.....96
lack crinkle vinyl & black shasta
attern cloth
5B.....99
edium palomino crinkle vinyl &
ght palomino shasta pattern
oth
5A.....C2
White crinkle all vinyl with blue
5A.....C5
White crinkle all vinyl with red
5A.....6
White crinkle all vinyl with black
5A.....C7
White crinkle all vinyl with turquoise
5A.....C8
White crinkle all vinyl with ivy gold
5A.....C9
White crinkle all vinyl with palomino
5B.....H2
White crinkle all vinyl with blue
5B.....H5
White crinkle all vinyl with red
5B.....H6
White crinkle all vinyl with black
5B.....H7
White crinkle all vinyl with turquoise
5B.....H8
White crinkle all vinyl with ivy gold
5B.....H9
White crinkle all vinyl with palomino

FALCON

4A,54D,62A,62D.....12
Light Blue crinkle vinyl & Medium Blue T bar pattern cloth
4A,54D,62A,62D.....15
Red crinkle vinyl & red bar pattern cloth
4A,54D,62A,62D.....17
Light turquoise crinkle vinyl & Medium Blue T bar pattern cloth
4A,54D,62A,62D.....19
Light palomino crinkle vinyl & Medium Blue T bar pattern cloth
4B,62B.....22
Light blue crinkle vinyl & medium blue gothic pattern cloth
4B,62B.....25
Red crinkle vinyl & red gothic pattern cloth
4B,62B.....27
Light turquoise crinkle vinyl & medium turquoise gothic pattern cloth
4B,62B.....28
Light ivy gold crinkle vinyl & medium ivy gold gothic pattern cloth
4B,62B,71C.....29
Medium palomino crinkle vinyl & medium palomino gothic pattern cloth
4A,62B,63B,71B,71C.....32
Light Blue crinkle vinyl & Medium Blue crinkle vinyl

54A,62B,63B,71B,71C.....35
Red crinkle all vinyl
63B,71B,71C.....36
Black crinkle all vinyl
63B.....37
Light turquoise crinkle vinyl & Medium turquoise crinkle vinyl
63B,71B,71C.....38
Light ivy gold crinkle all vinyl
54A,62B,63B,71B,71C.....39
Medium palomino crinkle all vinyl
59A,66A,71A,78A.....49
Medium palomino crinkle all vinyl & medium palomino striped rib pattern vinyl
76A.....52
Light blue crinkle vinyl & medium blue crinkle vinyl
76A.....55
Red crinkle all vinyl
76A.....56
Black crinkle all vinyl
76A.....57
Light turquoise crinkle vinyl & medium turquoise crinkle vinyl
76A.....58
Light ivy gold crinkle vinyl
76A.....59
Medium palomino crinkle all vinyl
66B,78B.....62
Light blue crinkle vinyl & medium blue crinkle vinyl
66B,78B.....65
Red crinkle all vinyl
66B,78B.....66
Black crinkle all vinyl
66B,78B.....69
Medium palomino crinkle all vinyl
62C,63C,63D,66H.....82
Light blue crinkle vinyl & medium blue crinkle vinyl
76B,76D.....82
Light blue crinkle vinyl & medium blue crinkle vinyl
63C,63D,66H,76B,76D.....85
Red crinkle all vinyl
63C,63D,66H,76B,76D.....86
Black crinkle all vinyl
63C,63D,76B,76D.....87
Light turquoise crinkle vinyl & medium turquoise crinkle vinyl
63C,63D,76B,76D.....88
Light ivy gold crinkle all vinyl
62C,63C,63D,66G.....89
Medium palomino crinkle all vinyl
66H,76B,76D.....89
Medium palomino crinkle all vinyl

MUSTANG

63A,65A,76A.....22
Medium blue crinkle all vinyl
63A,65A,76A.....25
Red crinkle all vinyl
63A,65A,76A.....26
Black crinkle all vinyl
63A,65A,76A28
Light ivy gold crinkle all vinyl
63A,65A,76A.....29
Medium palomino crinkle all vinyl
63C,65C,76C.....32
Medium blue crinkle all vinyl
63C,65C,76C.....35
Red crinkle all vinyl

63C,65C,76C.....36
Black crinkle all vinyl
63C,65C,76C.....38
Light ivy gold crinkle all vinyl
63C,65C,76C.....39
Medium palomino crinkle all vinyl
65A,76A.....42
White crinkle all vinyl with blue
65A,76A.....45
White crinkle all vinyl with red
65A,76A.....46
White crinkle all vinyl with black
65A,76A.....49
White crinkle all vinyl with palomino
65A.....56
Black crinkle vinyl & black cord pattern cloth
65A.....56A
Black crinkle vinyl & black cord pattern cloth
63B,65B,76B.....62
Light blue crinkle vinyl & white crinkle vinyl
63B,65B,76B.....65
Red crinkle all vinyl
63B,65B,76B.....66
Black crinkle all vinyl
63B,65B,76B.....67
Light turquoise crinkle vinyl & white crinkle vinyl
63B,65B,76B.....68
Light ivy gold crinkle vinyl & white crinkle vinyl
63B,65B,76B.....69
Medium palomino crinkle all vinyl
63A,65A.....76
Black crinkle vinyl & black cord pattern cloth
63A,65A.....79
Medium palomino crinkle vinyl & Light palomino cord pattern cloth
65A,76A.....82
Medium blue crinkle all vinyl
65A,76A.....85
Red crinkle all vinyl
65A,76A.....85A
Red crinkle all vinyl
65A,76A.....86
Black crinkle all vinyl
65A,76A.....86A
Black crinkle all vinyl
65A,76A.....89
Medium palomino crinkle all vinyl
63C,65C.....96
Black crinkle vinyl & black cord pattern cloth
63C,65C.....99
Medium palomino crinkle vinyl & \light palomino shasta pattern cloth
63C,65C,76C.....C2
Medium blue crinkle all vinyl
63C,65C,76C.....C5
Red crinkle all vinyl
63C,65C,76C.....C6
Black crinkle all vinyl
63C,65C,76C.....C8
Light ivy gold crinkle all vinyl
63C,65C,76C.....C9
Medium palomino crinkle all vinyl
63A,65A,76A.....D2
White crinkle all vinyl with blue
63A,65A,76A.....D5
White crinkle all vinyl with blue

63A,65A,76A.....D5
White crinkle all vinyl with red
63A,65A,76A.....D6
White crinkle all vinyl with black
63A,65A,76A.....D8
White crinkle all vinyl with ivy gold
63A,65A,76A.....D9
White crinkle all vinyl with palomino
65A,76A.....46
White crinkle all vinyl with black
65A,76A.....49
White crinkle all vinyl with palomino
65A.....56
Black crinkle vinyl & black cord pattern cloth
65A.....56A
Black crinkle vinyl & black cord pattern cloth
63B,65B,76B.....62
Light blue crinkle vinyl & white crinkle vinyl
63B,65B,76B.....65
Red crinkle all vinyl
63B,65B,76B.....66
Black crinkle all vinyl
63B,65B,76B.....67
Light turquoise crinkle vinyl & white crinkle vinyl
63B,65B,76B.....68
Light ivy gold crinkle vinyl & white crinkle vinyl
63B,65B,76B.....69
Medium palomino crinkle all vinyl
63A,65A.....76
Black crinkle vinyl & black cord pattern cloth
63A,65A.....79
Medium palomino crinkle vinyl & Light palomino cord pattern cloth
65A,76A.....82
Medium blue crinkle all vinyl
65A,76A.....85
Red crinkle all vinyl
65A,76A.....85A
Red crinkle all vinyl
65A,76A.....86
Black crinkle all vinyl
65A,76A.....86A
Black crinkle all vinyl
65A,76A.....89
Medium palomino crinkle all vinyl
63C,65C.....96
Black crinkle vinyl & black cord pattern cloth
63C,65C.....99
Medium palomino crinkle vinyl & \light palomino shasta pattern cloth
63C,65C,76C.....C2
Medium blue crinkle all vinyl
63C,65C,76C.....C5
Red crinkle all vinyl
63C,65C,76C.....C6
Black crinkle all vinyl
63C,65C,76C.....C8
Light ivy gold crinkle all vinyl
63C,65C,76C.....C9
Medium palomino crinkle all vinyl
63A,65A,76A.....D2
White crinkle all vinyl with blue
63A,65A,76A.....D5
White crinkle all vinyl with red

1965 FORD

63A,65A,76A.................................D6
White crinkle all vinyl with black
63A,65A,76A.................................D8
White crinkle all vinyl with ivy gold
63A,65A,76A.................................D9
White crinkle all vinyl with
palomino
63B,65B,76B.................................F2
White crinkle all vinyl with blue
63B,65B,76B.................................F5
White crinkle all vinyl with red
63B,65B,76B.................................F6
White crinkle all vinyl with black
63B,65B,76B.................................F7
White crinkle all vinyl with
turquoise
63B,65B,76B.................................F8
White crinkle all vinyl with ivy gold
63B,65B,76B.................................F9
White crinkle all vinyl with
palomino

EXTERIOR PAINT BODY

COLOR	CODE
Limelight Turquoise	0
Poppy Red (Mustang)	3
Frost Blue	4
Twilight Turquoise	5
Raven Black	A
Pagoda Green	B
White (Pace Car)	C
Honey Gold	C
Dynasty Green	D
Silver Mink	E
Guardsman Blue	F
Lemontree Yellow	G
Caspian Blue	H
Champagne Beige	I
Rangoon Red	J
Silver Smoke Gray	K
Wimbledon White	M
Diamond Blue	N
Prairie Bronze	P
Brittany Blue	Q
Charcoal Green	R
Cascade Green	S
Navaho Beige	T
Patrician Green	U
Sunlight Yellow	V
Rose Beige	W
Vintage Burgundy	X
Silver Blue	Y
Skylight Blue	Y
Chantilly Beige	Z

VEHICLE IDENTIFICATION NUMBER

6A83X100551

VEHICLE IDENTIFICATION NUMBER LOCATIONS

FULL SIZED FORD VIN Die Stamped into extension Tab of Top of Cowl R/H Side of Car under hood.

FAIRLANE VIN Die stamped into top surface of Inner Fender panel & radiator support at L/H side under hood.

THUNDERBIRD VIN Die Stamped into Top Surface of Front Fender Cross-Brace to the Right of Hood Lock Plate under hood.

MUSTANG VIN Die Stamped into top surface left front fender apron.

FALCON VIN Die Stamped into Top surface of Inner Fender panel & radiator support at L/H side under hood.

1966 Model	6
Assembled at Atlanta Plant	A
Thunderbird-Tudor Hardtop	83
8cyl. OHV 352 C.I.D. (2-V)	X
Vehicle Production Number	100551

1st Digit - MODEL YEAR
The number "6" designates 1966

2nd Digit - ASSEMBLY PLANT

Atlanta	A
Oakville	B
Ontario	C
Dallas	D
Mahwah	E
Dearborn	F
Chicago	G
Lorain	H
Los Angeles	J
Kansas City	K
Michigan Truck	L
Norfolk	N
Twin City	P
San Jose	R
Pilot Plant	S
Metichen	T
Louisville	U
Wayne	W
Wixom	Y
St. Louis	Z

BDY	CLR	TRM	DT	DSO	AX	TR
63A	AA	56	26H	33	1	4

WARRANTY NUMBER

6A83Z100551

3rd & 4th Digit - MODEL

The two digit numeral which follows the assembly plant code identifies the body series. This two-digit number is used in conjunction with the Body style code in the vehicle data, which consist of a two-digit number with a letter suffix. The following chart lists the body serial codes, Body Style codes and the body type.

FORD CUSTOM	CODE
2-Dr. Sedan	53
4-Dr. Sedan	54

FORD CUSTOM 500	CODE
2-Dr. Sedan	51
4-Dr. Sedan	52

Galaxie 500	CODE
4-Dr. Sedan	62
4-Dr. Fastback	64
2-Dr. Convertible	65
2-Dr. Fastback	66

GALAXIE 500XL	CODE
2-Dr. Fastback	68
(Bucket seats)	
2-Dr. Convertible	69
(Bucket seats)	

GALAXIE 500 LTD	CODE
-Dr. Hardtop	60
-Dr. Fastback	67

COUNTRY SEDAN	CODE
-DR. 6 Ps.	72
-DR. Custom 9 Ps.	74

GALAXIE 500 7.0 Liter	CODE
-Dr. Fastback	61
-Dr. Convertible	63

FAIRLANE	CODE
-Dr. Sedan	31
-Dr. Sedan	32

FAIRLANE 500	CODE
-Dr. Sedan	41
-Dr. Sedan	42
-Dr. Hardtop	43
-Dr. convertible	45

FAIRLANE 500 XL	CODE
-Dr. Convertible (2)	46
-Dr. Hardtop (2)	47

FAIRLANE 500 GT	CODE
-Dr. Hardtop (2)	40
-Dr. Convertible (2)	44

FAIRLANE WAGONS	CODE
-Dr. Ranch Wagon	38
-Dr. Custom Ranch Wagon	48
-Dr. Squire	49

RANCH WAGON	CODE
-DR. 6 Ps.	71

COUNTRY SQUIRE	CODE
-DR. 6 Ps.	76
-DR. Custom 9 Ps.	78

THUNDERBIRD	CODE
2-Dr. Town Hardtop	81
(Blind quarter roof-Painted)	
2-Dr. Hardtop	83
2-Dr. Convertible	85
2-Dr. Town Landau	87
(Blind quarter roof-Vinyl)	

FALCON STANDARD SEDAN	CODE
2-Dr. Sedan	1
4-Dr. Sedan	2

FALCON FUTURA	CODE
2-Dr. Sedan (1)	11
4-Dr. Sedan (1)	12
2-Dr. Sport Coupe(2)	14

(1) Bench Seat
(2) Bucket Seat

STATION WAGONS	CODE
4-Dr. Wagon	22
4-Dr. Deluxe Wagon	24

RANCHERO	CODE
2-Dr. Ranchero	27
2-Dr. Deluxe Ranchero	27
2-Dr. Rancher	27
(RPO Bucket w/ console)	

MUSTANG	CODE
2-Dr. Fastback (Std. Bucket Seats)	9
2-Dr. Hardtop (Std. Bucket Seats)	7
2-Dr. Convertible (Std. Bucket Seats)	8
2-Dr. Fastback (Luxury Bucket Seats)	9
2-Dr. Hardtop (Luxury Bucket Seats)	7
2-Dr. Convertible (Luxury Bucket Seats)	8
2-Dr. Hardtop (Std. Bench Seats	7
2-Dr. Convertible (Std. Bench Seats)	8

5th Digit - ENGINE

ENGINE	CODE
6 Cyl. 240C.I.	V
6 Cyl. 240 C.I. Police	B
6 Cyl. 240 C.I.(Taxi)	E
8 Cyl. 289 C.I. (4-V) Prem.	A
8 Cyl. 289 C.I. (2-V)	C
8 Cyl. 289 C.I. (4-V, H. P.)	K
6 Cyl. 200 C.I. (1-V)	T
8 Cyl. 427 C.I. (8-V, H. P.)	R
8 Cyl. 410 C.I. (4-V)	M
8 Cyl. 352 C.I. (4-V)	X
8 Cyl. 390 C.I. (4-V)	Z
8 Cyl. 390 C.I. (2-V)	Y
8 Cyl. 390 C.I. (2-V, Special)	H
8 Cyl. 428 C.I. (4-V, Police)	P
8 Cyl. 428 C.I. (4-V)	Q
8 Cyl. 390 C.I. (4-V) GT	S
6 Cyl. 200 C.I. (1-V)	U
8 Cyl. 427 (4-V HP)	W
6 Cyl. 170 (1-V Low Comp.)	4
8 Cyl. 289 (Low Comp.)	3
6 Cyl. 240 (Low Comp.)	5
8 Cyl. 428 C.I.(4-V,Low Comp)	8
6 Cyl. 200 C.I.(1-V,Low Comp.)	2

PATENT PLATE

The Patent Plate is located on the left front door lock face panel on all models.

The following diagram of the Patent Plate specifies, in the Vehicle Data Line: the Body Type, Exterior Paint Color, Trim Scheme, Production Date, District Code and D.S.O. Numbers, Rear Axle Ratio and Transmission Type.

Indicated in the Vehicle Warranty Number Line, Formally ""Serial Number"" are: the Model Year, Assembly Plant, Series and Body Type, Engine Type and numerical sequence of assembly.

BODY TYPE CODE	63A
BODY COLOR CODE	AA
TRIM SCHEME CODE	56
PRODUCT DATE CODE	11-G
DISTRIC CODE	21

TRANSMISSION TYPE CODE	1
REAR AXLE RATIO CODE	3

Thunderbird, Hardtop	63A
Raven Black lower body, Raven Black upper body	AA
First Digit "5" represents material - All Vinyl	56
Second digit "6" represents color - Black & White	
Eleventh Day of Month	11
Month of Year - July	G
Distric Code - Atlanta	21
Rear axle Ratio of 3.00 to 1	1
Fordomatic (2 speed)	3

DISTRICT CODE

DOS units built to a Domestic Special Order, Foreign Special Order, or Pre-Approved Order have the complete order number recorded in this space. Also appearing in this space is the two digit code number of the Distric which orderd the unit. If the unit is regular production, only the distric code number will appear.

DISTRICT	CODE
Boston	11
Buffalo	12
New York	13
Pitsburg	14
Newark	15
Atlanta	21
Charlotte	22
Philadelphia	23
Jacksonville	24
Richmond	25
Washington	26
Cincinnati	31
Cleveland	32
Detroit	33
Indianoplis	34
Lansing	35
Louisville	36
Chicago	41
Fargo	42
Rockford	43
Twin Cities	44
Davenport	45
Denver	51
Des Moines	52
Kansas City	53
Omaha	54
St. Louis	55
Dallas	61
Huston	62
Memphis	63
New Orleans	64
Oklahoma City	65
Los Angeles	71
San Jose	72
Salt Lake City	73
Seattle	74
Ford of Canada	81
Government	83
Home Office Reserve	84
American Red Cross	85
Transportation Services	89
Export	90

ENGINE MODELS AND PISTON DISPLACEMENT (Cubic Inches)

170 Six	170
200 Six	200
240 Six	240
289 V-8	289
352 V-8	352
390 Special V-8 (2V & 4V)	390
427 H. P. V-8 (8-V)	427
428 V-8 (4-V)	428

COMPRESSION RATIO

170 Six	9.1:1
200 Six	9.2:1
240 Six	9.2:1
289 V-8 (2-V)	9.3:1
289 V-8 (4-V)	10.0:1
289 V-8 High Perf.	10.5:1
352 V-8 (4-V) Ford	9.3:1
390 V-8 (4-V)	10.5:1
390 V-8 (2-V) Ford	9.5:1
427 H. P. V-8 (8-V)	11.1:1
428 V-8 (4-V)	10.5:1

BRAKE HORSEPOWER

170 Six	105
200 Six	120
240 Six	155
289 V-8 (2-V)	200
289 V-8 (4-V)	225
289 V-8 H. P.	271
352 V-8	250
390 V-8 (2-V)	265
390 V-8 (4-V)	315
390 V-8 (2-V) Ford	275
390 V-8 (4-V) GT	335
427 HP V-8 (4-V)	410
427 H. P. V-8 (8-V)	425
428 V-8 (4-V)	345
428 Police Interceptor V-8 (4-V)	360

MONTHS OF THE YEAR CODES

MONTH	1st YR.	2nd YR.
January	A	N
February	B	P
March	C	Q
April	D	R
May	E	S
June	F	T
July	G	U
August	H	V
September	J	W
October	K	X
November	L	Y
December	M	Z

REAR AXLE RATIO CODES

A number designates a convential axle, while a letter designates an Equa-Lock axle.

3.00 : 1	1
2.83 : 1	2

3.20 : 1	3
3.25 : 1	4
3.50 : 1	5
2.80 : 1	6
3.89 : 1	8
4.11 : 1	9
3.00 : 1	A
3.20 : 1	C
3.25 : 1	D
3.50:1	E
2.80:1	F
3.89 :1	H
2.83:1	B
4.11:1	I

TRANSMISSION TYPE CODES

TRANSMISSION CODE

3-Speed Manual (2.77)	1
Overdrive	2
3-Speed Manual (3.03)	3
C-6 Automatic (XPL)	4
4 Speed Manual-Shift	5
C-4 Automatic (XP)	6
Cruise-o-matic (FX)	7
Cruise-o-matic (MX)	8

1966 TRIM SCHEME CODES

FORD

Blue cloth and blue vinyl	12
Red cloth and red vinyl	15
Black cloth and black vinyl	16
Aqua cloth and aqua vinyl	17
Palomino cloth and palomino vinyl	19
Blue vinyl	22
Red vinyl	25
Black vinyl	26
Silver cloth and silver vinyl	31
Blue cloth and blue vinyl	32
Red cloth and red vinyl	35
Black cloth and black vinyl	36
Aqua cloth and aqua vinyl	37
Ivy gold cloth and ivy gold vinyl	38
Palomino cloth and palomino vinyl	39
Blue vinyl	42
Red vinyl	45
Black vinyl	46
Aqua vinyl	47
Ivy gold vinyl	48
Silver cloth and silver vinyl	51
Blue cloth and blue vinyl	52
Burgandy cloth and burgandy vinyl	53
Red cloth and red vinyl	55
Black cloth and black vinyl	56
Aqua cloth and aqua vinyl	57
Ivy gold cloth and ivy gold vinyl	58
Blue vinyl	62
Emberglo vinyl	64
Red vinyl	65
Black vinyl	66
Aqua vinyl	67
Ivy gold vinyl	68
Blue vinyl	72
Red vinyl	75
Black vinyl	76
Aqua vinyl	77

Blue vinyl	82
Emberglo vinyl	84
Red viny	85
Black vinyl	86
Blue vinyl	92
Burgandy and burgandy cloth	93
Emberglo vinyl	94
Red viny	95
Black vinyl	96
Burgandy Leather	A3
Blue with Parchment vinyl	B2
Black with Parchment vinyl	B6
Aqua with Parchment vinyl	B7
Gold with Parchment vinyl	B8
Palomino with Parchment vinyl	B9
White with Black viny	D6
White with Black vinyl	E6
Blue with white vinyl	F2
Burgandy with white vinyl	F3
Emberglo with white vinyl	F4
Black with white vinyl	F6
Aqua with white vinyl	F7
Ivy gold with white vinyl	F8
Palomiino with white vinyl	F9
Blue with white vinyl	G2
Burgandy with white vinyl	G3
Emberglo with white vinyl	G4
Black with white vinyl	G6
Aqua with white vinyl	G7
Ivy gold with white vinyl	G8
Palomiino with white vinyl	G9
Blue vinyl	K2
Black vinyl	K6
Blue vinyl	N2
Red vinyl	N5
Green vinyl	O3
Beige vinyl	O4
Blur with parchment vinyl	S2
Red vinyl	X5
Parchment vinyl	XD
Red vinyl	Y5
Black vinyl	Z6
Parchment vinyl	ZD

FAIRLANE, FALCON, MUSTANG

Silver cloth and black vinyl	11
Blue cloth and blue vinyl	12
red cloth and red vinyl	15
Aqua cloth and aqua vinyl	17
Blue vinyl	22
Red vinyl	25
Black vinyl	26
Aqua vinyl	27
Blue cloth and blue vinyl	32
Red cloth and red vinyl	35
Black vinyl	36
Aqua cloth and aqua vinyl	37
Ivy gold and ivy gold vinyl	38
Blur vinyl	42
Emberglo vinyl	44
Red vinyl	45
Black vinyl	46
Aqua vinyl	47
Ivy gold vinyl	48
Blur cloth and blue vinyl	52
Red cloth and red vinyl	55
Aqua cloth and aqua vinyl	57
Blue vinyl	62
Emberglo vinyl	64
Red vinyl	65
Black vinyl	66

Aqua vinyl	67
Ivy gold vinyl	68
Blue vinyl	82
Emberglo vinyl	84
Red vinyl	85
Black vinyl	86
Aqua vinyl	87
Ivy gold vinyl	88
Parchment Cloth and parchment vinyl	1D
Parchment vinyl	2D
Parchment Cloth and parchment vinyl	3D
Parchment vinyl	4D
Parchment Cloth and parchment vinyl	5D
Parchment vinyl	0D
Parchment vinyl W/ Silver	B1
Parchment vinyl W/ Blue	B2
Parchment vinyl W/ Emberglo	B4
Parchment vinyl W/ Red	B5
Parchment vinyl W/ Black	B6
Parchment vinyl W/ Aqua	B7
Parchment vinyl W/ Ivy gold	B8
Parchment vinyl W/ Palomino	B9
Parchment vinyl W/ Blue	C2
Parchment vinyl W/ Burgandy	C3
Parchment vinyl W/ Emberglo	C4
Parchment vinyl W/ Black	C6
Parchment vinyl W/ Aqua	C7
Parchment vinyl W/ Gold	C8
Parchment vinyl W/ Palomino	C9
Parchment vinyl W/ Blue	D2
Parchment vinyl W/ Burgandy	D3
Parchment vinyl W/ Emberglo	D4
Parchment vinyl W/ Black	D6
Parchment vinyl W/ Aqua	D7
Parchment vinyl W/ Gold	D8
Parchment vinyl W/ Palomino	D9
Parchment vinyl W/ Blue	F2
Parchment vinyl W/ Burgandy	F3
Parchment vinyl W/ Emberglo	F4
Parchment vinyl W/ Black	F6
Parchment vinyl W/ Aqua	F7
Parchment vinyl W/ Gold	F8
Parchment vinyl W/ Palomino	F9
White vinyl W/ Silver	H1
White vinyl W/ Blue	H2
White vinyl W/ Emberglo	H4

THUNDERBIRD

Dk. Blue cloth and Dk. Blue vinyl	12
Black cloth and black vinyl	16
Silver Mink vinyl	21
Dk. Blue vinyl	22
Burgandy vinyl	23
Emberglo vinyl	24
Red vinyl	25
Black vinyl	26
Aqua vinyl	27
Ivy gold vinyl	28
Dk. Blue cloth and Dk. Blue vinyl	42
Black cloth and black vinyl	46
Silver Mink vinyl	51
Dk. Blue vinyl	52
Burgandy vinyl	53
Emberglo vinyl	54
Red vinyl	55
Black vinyl	56
Aqua vinyl	57
Ivy gold vinyl	58

Dk. Blue Leather	6?
Red leather	6?
Black leather	6?
Parchment Cloth and parchment vinyl	1D
Parchment Cloth and parchment vinyl	4D
Blue and parchment vinyl	B?
Burgandy and parchment vinyl	B?
Emnerglo and parchment vinyl	B4
Black and parchment vinyl	B6
Turquoise and parchment vinyl	B7
Gold and parchment vinyl	B?
Palomino and parchment vinyl	B9
Silver Mink and white pearl vinyl	G1
Blue and white pearl vinyl	G2
Burgandy and white pearl vinyl	G3
Emberglo and white pearl vinyl	G4
Black and White and white pearl vinyl	G6
Turquoise and white pearl vinyl	G7
Gold and white pearl vinyl	G8
Palomino and white pearl vinyl	G9
Blue and parchment vinyl	K2
Burgandy and parchment vinyl	K3
Emnerglo and parchment vinyl	K4
Black and parchment vinyl	K6
Turquoise and parchment vinyl	K7
Gold and parchment vinyl	K8
Palomino and parchment vinyl	K9
Blue and parchment Leather	LB2
Burgandy and parchment Leather	L3
Emnerglo and parchment Leather	L4
Black and parchment Leather	L6
Turquoise and parchment Leather	L7
Gold and parchment Leather	L8
Palomino and parchment Leather	L9
Silver Mink and white pearl vinyl	P1
Blue and white pearl vinyl	P2
Burgandy and white pearl vinyl	P3
Emnerglo and white pearl vinyl	P4
Black and white pearl vinyl	P6
Turquoise and white pearl vinyl	P7
Gold and white pearl vinyl	P8
Palomino and white pearl vinyl	P9

EXTERIOR PAINT BODY COLOR CODES

A single letter code designates a solid body color and two letters denote a two-tone — the first letter, the lower color and the second letter the upper color.

THUNDERBIRD

Black	A
Light beige Met.	B
Med. Silver Mink Met.	E
Light Blue	F
Brite Blue Met.	G
Light beige	H
Dark blue Met.	K
Ivy Yellow	L
White	M
Platinum	N
Med. Palomino Met.	P
Med. blue Met.	Q
Dk. Green Met.	R
Cascade Green	S
Red	T
Med. Turquoise Met.	U
Emberglo Met.	V
Maroon Met.	X
Med. Sage Gold Met.	Z
Rose Met.	1
Dk. Truquoise Met.	2

FORD

Black	A
Dk. Executive Gray Met.	C
Med. Silver Mink Met.	E
Light Blue	F
Light beige	H
Dark blue Met.	K
White	M
Med. Palomino Met.	P
Dk. Green Met.	R
Red	T
Med. Turquoise Met.	U
Emberglo Met.	V
Maroon Met.	X
Med. Sage Gold Met.	Z
Dk. Truquoise Met.	2
Med. Silver Met.	4
Yellow	8

FALCON, MUSTANG, FAIRLANE

Black	A
Light Blue	F
Light beige	H
Dark blue Met.	K
White	M
Med. Palomino Met.	P
Dk. Green Met.	R
Red	T
Med. Turquoise Met.	U
Emberglo Met.	V
Maroon Met.	X
Lt. Blue Met.	Y
Med. Sage Gold Met.	Z
Med. Silver Met.	4
Red	5
Yellow	8

VEHICLE IDENTIFICATION NUMBER

7A81C100551

VEHICLE IDENTIFICATION NUMBER LOCATIONS

"FAIRLANE, FALCON VIN On the top surface of the radiator and front fender apron support."

THUNDERBIRD VIN On the cowl top panel tab right hand side.

MUSTANG VIN On the top upper flange of the left front fender apron.

1st Digit - MODEL YEAR
The number "7" designates 1967

2nd Digit - ASSEMBLY PLANT

Atlanta	A
Oakville (Canada)	B
Ontario	C
Dallas	D
Mahwah	E
Dearborn	F
Chicago	G
Lorain	H
Los Angeles	J
Kansas City	K
Michigan Truck	L
Norfolk	N
Twin City	P
San Jose	R
Pilot Plant	S
Metichen	T
Louisville	U
Wayne	W
Wixom	Y
St. Louis	Z

3rd & 4th Digit - MODEL

The two digit numeral which follows the assembly plant code identifies the body series. This two-digit number is used in conjunction with the Body style code in the vehicle data, which consist of a two-digit number with a letter suffix.

FORD CUSTOM	CODE
2-Dr. Sedan (1)	50
4-Dr. Sedan (1)	51

FORD CUSTOM 500	CODE
2-Dr. Sedan (1)	52
4-Dr. Sedan (1)	53

Galaxie 500	CODE
4-Dr. Sedan (1)	54
4-Dr. Hardtop (1)	56
2-Dr. Convertible (1)	57
2-Dr. Fastback (1)	55

GALAXIE 500XL	COD[
2-Dr. Hardtop (2)	5
2-Dr. Convertible (2)	5

LTD	COD[
4-Dr. Hardtop (1)	6
2-Dr. Hardtop (1)(3)	6
4-Dr. Sedan	6

A781C		100551		WARRANTY Number		Made in USA
65A	AA	2A	11G	21	1	W
BDY	CLR	TRM	DT	DSD	AX	TR

RANCH WAGON   **CODE**
4-Dr. 6 Ps. 70

COUNTRY SEDAN   **CODE**
4-Dr. 6 Ps. 71
4-Dr. 6 + 4 Ps. 72

COUNTRY SQUIRE   **CODE**
4-Dr. 6 Ps. 73
4-Dr. 6 + 4 Ps. 74
(1) = Bench Seat
(2) = Bucket Seat
(3) = Formal Roof

FAIRLANE   **CODE**
2-Dr. Sedan (1)..................30
4-Dr. Sedan (1)..................31

FAIRLANE 500   **CODE**
2-Dr. Sedan (1)..................33
4-Dr. Sedan (1)..................34
2-Dr. Hardtop (1)................35
2-Dr. convertible (1)............36

FAIRLANE 500 XL   **CODE**
2-Dr. Hardtop (2)................40
2-Dr. convertible (2)............41

FAIRLANE 500 GT   **CODE**
2-Dr. Hardtop (2)................42
2-Dr. convertible (2)............43

STATION WAGONS   **CODE**
4-Door............................32
4-Door............................37
4-Door............................38

RANCHERO   **CODE**
2-Door (1)........................47
2-Door (1)........................48
2-Door (2)........................49
(1) = Bench Seat
(2) = Bucket Seat

THUNDERBIRD   **CODE**
2-Dr. Hardtop (Painted roof).....81
2-Dr. Hardtop
 (Vinyl roof-Landau)............82
4-Dr. Sedan(vinyl roof)..........84

FALCON STANDARD   **CODE**
SEDAN
2-Dr. Club Coupe (1)............10
4-Dr. Sedan (1)..................11

FUTURA   **CODE**
2-Dr. Club Coupe (1)............20
4-Dr. Sedan (1)..................21

SPORT COUPE   **CODE**
2-Door (2)........................22

STATION WAGONS   **CODE**
4-Dr. Wagon......................12
4-Dr. Deluxe Wagon..............23
(1) = Bench Seat
(2) = Bucket Seat

MUSTANG   **CODE**
2-Dr. Fastback (1)................2
2-Dr. Hardtop (1).................1
2-Dr. Convertible (1).............3
2-Dr. Fastback (1)(3).............2
2-Dr. Hardtop (1)(3).............1

2-Dr. Convertible (1)(3)..........3
2-Dr. Hardtop (2).................1
2-Dr. Convertible (2).............3
(1) = Bucket Seat
(2) = Bench Seat
(3) = Luxury Model

5th Digit - ENGINE

ENGINE	CODE
6 Cyl. 240 C.I.	V
6 Cyl. 240 C.I. (Police)	B
6 Cyl. 240 C.I.(Taxi)	E
8 Cyl. 289 C.I. (4-V) Prem.	A
8 Cyl. 289 C.I. (2-V)	C
8 Cyl. 289 C.I. (4-V, H.P.)	K
6 Cyl. 200 C.I. (1-V)	T
8 Cyl. 427 C.I. (8-V, H. P.)	R
8 Cyl. 427 C.I. (4-V, H. P.)	W
8 Cyl. 390 C.I. (4-V)	Z
8 Cyl. 390 C.I. (4-V) GT	S
8 Cyl. 390 C.I. (2-VI)	H
8 Cyl. 428 C.I. (4-V, Police)	P
8 Cyl. 428 C.I. (4-V)	Q
8 Cyl. 289 (Low Com.)	3
6 Cyl. 240 (Low Com.)	5
8 Cyl. 428 C.I.(4-V, Low Com.)	8
6 Cyl. 200 C.I.(1-V, Low Com.)	2
6 Cyl. 170 C.I. (1-V)	U

WARRANTY PLATE

VEHICLE DATA

The vehicle data appears on the second or lower line on the warranty plate. The first two numbers and a letter identify the Body Style. A letter or a number appears next indicating the Exterior Paint Color followed by a number-letter combination designating the interior trim. To the right of this code appears the Data Code indicating the date the car was manufactured. A two digit number next designates the district in which the car was ordered and may appear in conjunction with a Domestic Special Order or Foreign Special Order number when applicable. The final two spaces indicate the Rear Axle Ratio (numbers for regular axles, letters for locking types) and Transmission Type (numbers for manual, letters for automatic.

DISTRICT CODE

DOS units built to a Domestic Special Order, Foreign Special Order, or other special Orders

will have the complete order number in this space. Also appearing in this space is the two digit code number of the Distric which orderd the unit. If the unit is regular production, only the District Code will appear.

DISTRICT	CODE
Boston	11
New York	13
Newark	15
Philadelphia	16
Washington	17
Atlanta	21
Charlotte	22
Jacksonville	24
Richmond	25
Cincinnati	27
Louisville	28
Cleveland	32
Detroit	33
Indianoplis	34
Lansing	35
Buffalo	37
Pittsburgh	38
Chicago	41
Fargo	42
Milwaukee	43
Twin Cities	44
Davenport	45
Denver	51
Des Moines	52
Kansas City	53
Omaha	54
St. Louis	55
Dallas	61
Huston	62
Memphis	63
New Orleans	64
Oklahoma City	65
Los Angeles	71
San Jose	72
Salt Lake City	73
Seattle	74
Phoenix	75
Ford of Canada	81
Government	83
Home Office Reserve	84
American Red Cross	85
Transportation Services	89
Export	90-99

COMPRESSION RATIO

170 Six	9.1:1
150	9.2:1
240 Six	9.2:1
289 V-8 (2-V)	9.3:1
289 V-8 (4-V)	9.8:1
289 V-8 H. P.	10.5:1
390 V-8 (2-V)	9.5:1
390 V-8 (4-V) and G.T	10.5:1
427 H. P. V-8 (4-V)	11.1:1
427 H. P. V-8 (8-V)	11.1:1
428 V-8 (4-V)	10.5:1
428 V-8 (4-V, Police)	10.5:1

BRAKE HORSEPOWER

170 Six	105
200 Six	120
150	155
289 V-8 (2-V)	200
289 V-8 (4-V)	225
289 V-8 H. P.	271
390 V-8 (2-V)	270
390 V-8 (4-V)	315
390 V-8 (4-V) GT	320
427 V-8 (8-V)H.P.	425
427 V-8 (8-V)H. P.	410
428 V-8 (4-V)	345
428 V-8 (4-V) Police	360

MONTHS OF THE YEAR   CODE

MONTH	1st YR.	2nd YR.
January	A	N
February	B	P
March	C	Q
April	D	R
May	E	S
June	F	T
July	G	U
August	H	V
September	J	W
October	K	X
November	L	Y
December	M	Z

REAR AXLE RATIO CODES

A number designates a convential axle, while a letter designates an Equa-Lock axle.

3.00 : 1	1
2.83 : 1	2
3.20 : 1	3
3.25 : 1	4
3.50 : 1	5
2.80 : 1	6
3.36 : 1	7
2.75 : 1	8
4.11 : 1	9
3.10 : 1	0
3.00 : 1	A
2.83 : 1	B
3.20 : 1	C
3.25 : 1	D
2.80 : 1	F
3.50 : 1	E
3.36 : 1	G
2.75 : 1	H
4.11 : 1	I
2.79 : 1	O

TRANSMISSION TYPE CODES

TRANSMISSION	CODE
Standard 3-Speed	1
Overdrive	2
3-Speed Manual	3
4 Speed Manual-Shift	5
Automatic (C-4)	W
Automatic (C-6)	U
Automatic (MX)	Y
Automatic (FX)	X
Automatic (XPL Special, C-6)	Z

1967 TRIM SCHEME CODES

FORD

Blue cloth and Blue vinyl...........1B
Red cloth and red vinyl.............1D
Parchment cloth and parchment vinyl...1U
Black vinyl...........................2A
blue vinyl............................2B
Red vinyl.............................2D
Saddle vinyl..........................2F
Ivy gold vinyl........................2G
Aqua vinyl............................2K
Parchment vinyl W/Black...............2U
Blue cloth and Blue vinyl.............3B
Ivy Gold cloth and Ivy Gold vinyl.....3G
Aqua cloth and Aqua vinyl.............3K
Parchment cloth and Parchment vinyl...3U
Black vinyl (1).......................4A
blue vinyl (1)........................4B
Red vinyl (1).........................4D
Ivy gold vinyl (1)....................4G
Aqua vinyl (1)........................4K
Lt. Silver cloth and Lt. Silver vinyl...4L
Parchment vinyl W/Black (1)...........4U
Black cloth and Black vinyl...........5A
Blue cloth and Blue vinyl.............5B
Ivy Gold cloth and Ivy Gold vinyl.....5G
Aqua cloth and Aqua vinyl.............5K
Parchment cloth and Parchment vinyl...5U
Black vinyl...........................6A
blue vinyl............................6B
Red vinyl.............................6D
Saddle vinyl..........................6F
Ivy gold vinyl........................6G
Aqua vinyl............................6K
Parchment vinyl.......................6U
Black vinyl...........................7A
blue vinyl............................7B
Red vinyl.............................7D
Aqua vinyl............................7K
Parchment vinyl.......................7U
Black vinyl (1).......................8A
blue vinyl (1)........................8B
Red vinyl (1).........................8D
Saddle vinyl..........................8F
Ivy gold vinyl (1)....................8G
Aqua vinyl (1)........................8K
Lt. Silver cloth and Lt. Silver vinyl...8L
Parchment vinyl W/Black (1)...........8U
Black cloth and black vinyl...........9A
Dk. Blue cloth and Dk. Blue vinyl.....9B
Dk. Red cloth and Dk. Red vinyl.......9D
Dk. Ivy gold cloth and Dk. Ivy gold vinyl...9G
Aqua cloth and Aqua vinyl.............9K
Silver cloth and Silver vinyl.........9L
Parchment cloth and Parchment vinyl...9U
Blue vinyl............................CB
Parchment vinyl.......................CU
Blue vinyl............................DB
Parchment vinyl.......................DU
Black cloth and black vinyl...........E1
Dk. Blue cloth and Dk. Blue vinyl.....E2
Parchment cloth and Parchment vinyl...E9
Black vinyl...........................F1
Black cloth and black vinyl...........G1
Dk. Blue cloth and Dk. Blue vinyl.....G2
Parchment cloth and Parchment vinyl...G9
Black Leather.........................HA
Black vinyl...........................H1
Blue vinyl............................JB
Parchment vinyl.......................JU
Black vinyl...........................KA
Black cloth and black vinyl (1)......LA
Blue vinyl............................NB
Red vinyl.............................BD
Parchment vinyl.......................NU
Beige vinyl...........................OE
Parchment.............................OU
Black cloth and black vinyl...........PA
Parchment cloth and Parchment vinyl...PU
Black vinyl...........................RA
Dk. Blue vinyl........................RB
Dk. Red vinyl.........................RD
Saddle vinyl..........................RF
Parchment vinyl.......................RU
Black vinyl...........................SA
Black vinyl...........................UA
Parchment vinyl.......................UU
Parchment cloth and Parchment vinyl...VU
Black vinyl...........................WA
Parchment vinyl.......................WU
Black cloth and Black vinyl...........ZA
Dk. Blue cloth and Dk. Blue vinyl.....ZB
Dk. Red cloth and Dk. Red vinyl.......ZD
Dk. Ivy Gold cloth and Dk. Ivy Gold vinyl...ZG
Aqua cloth and Aqua vinyl.............ZK
Silver cloth and Silver vinyl.........ZL
Parchment cloth and Parchment vinyl...ZU

(1) = Combined with cloth on Thunderbird
(2) = Black Leather on Thunderbird

FAIRLANE, FALCON, MUSTANG

Blue cloth and Blue vinyl...........1B
Red cloth and red vinyl.............1D
Aqua cloth and Aqua vinyl...........1K
Parchment cloth and parchment vinyl...1U
Black vinyl...........................2A
blue vinyl............................2B
Red vinyl.............................2D
Saddle vinyl..........................2F
Ivy gold vinyl........................2G
Aqua vinyl............................2K
Parchment vinyl W/Black...............2U
Blue cloth and Blue vinyl.............3B
Ivy Gold cloth and Ivy Gold vinyl.....3G
Aqua cloth and Aqua vinyl.............3K
Parchment cloth and Parchment vinyl...3U
Black vinyl (1).......................4A
blue vinyl (1)........................4B
Red vinyl (1).........................4D
Ivy gold vinyl (1)....................4G
Aqua vinyl (1)........................4K
Lt. Silver cloth and Lt. Silver vinyl...4L
Parchment vinyl W/Black (1)...........4U
Black cloth and Black vinyl...........5A
Dk. Blue cloth and Blue vinyl.........5B
Aqua cloth and Aqua vinyl.............5K
Parchment cloth and Parchment vinyl...5U
Black vinyl...........................6A
Dk. blue vinyl........................6B
Red vinyl.............................6D
Saddle vinyl..........................6F
Dk. Ivy gold vinyl....................6G
Aqua vinyl............................6K
Parchment vinyl.......................6U
Black vinyl...........................7A
blue vinyl............................7B
Parchment cloth and Parchment vinyl...7U
Black vinyl (1).......................8A
blue vinyl (1)........................8B
Red vinyl (1).........................8D
Saddle vinyl..........................8F
Ivy gold vinyl (1)....................8G
Aqua vinyl (1)........................8K
Parchment vinyl W/Black (1)...........8U
Black cloth and black vinyl...........9A
Dk. Blue cloth and Dk. Blue vinyl.....9B
Black cloth and Black vinyl...........ZA
Dk. Blue cloth and Dk. Blue vinyl.....ZB
Dk. Red cloth and Dk. Red vinyl.......ZD
Dk. Ivy Gold cloth and Dk. Ivy Gold vinyl...ZG
Aqua cloth and Aqua vinyl.............ZK
Silver cloth and Silver vinyl.........ZL
Parchment cloth and Parchment vinyl...ZU

(1) = Combined with cloth on Thunderbird
(2) = Black Leather on Thunderbird

FAIRLANE, FALCON, MUSTANG

Blue cloth and Blue vinyl...........1B
Red cloth and red vinyl.............1D
Aqua cloth and Aqua vinyl...........1K
Parchment cloth and parchment vinyl...1U
Black vinyl...........................2A
blue vinyl............................2B
Red vinyl.............................2D
Saddle vinyl..........................2F
Ivy gold vinyl........................2G
Aqua vinyl............................2K
Parchment vinyl W/Black...............2U
Blue cloth and Blue vinyl.............3B
Ivy Gold cloth and Ivy Gold vinyl.....3G
Aqua cloth and Aqua vinyl.............3K
Parchment cloth and Parchment vinyl...3U
Black vinyl (1).......................4A
blue vinyl (1)........................4B
Red vinyl (1).........................4D
Ivy gold vinyl (1)....................4G
Aqua vinyl (1)........................4K
Lt. Silver cloth and Lt. Silver vinyl...4L
Parchment vinyl W/Black (1)...........4U
Black cloth and Black vinyl...........5A
Dk. Blue cloth and Blue vinyl.........5B
Aqua cloth and Aqua vinyl.............5K
Parchment cloth and Parchment vinyl...5U
Black vinyl...........................6A
Dk. blue vinyl........................6B
Red vinyl.............................6D
Saddle vinyl..........................6F
Dk. Ivy gold vinyl....................6G
Aqua vinyl............................6K
Parchment vinyl.......................6U
Black vinyl...........................7A
blue vinyl............................7B
Parchment cloth and Parchment vinyl...7U
Black vinyl (1).......................8A
blue vinyl (1)........................8B
Red vinyl (1).........................8D
Saddle vinyl..........................8F
Ivy gold vinyl (1)....................8G
Aqua vinyl (1)........................8K
Parchment vinyl W/Black (1)...........8U
Black cloth and black vinyl...........9A
Dk. Blue cloth and Dk. Blue vinyl.....9E
Dk. Red cloth and Dk. Red vinyl.......9D
Aqua cloth and Aqua vinyl.............9K
Parchment cloth and Parchment vinyl W/Black...9U
Parchment vinyl W/Black...............FA
Parchment vinyl W/Blue................FB
Parchment vinyl W/Red.................FD
Parchment vinyl W/Ivy Gold............FG
Parchment vinyl W/Aqua................FK
Black vinyl W/Parchment...............GA
Blue vinyl W/Parchment................GB
Red vinyl W/Parchment.................GD
Ivy Gold vinyl W/Parchment............GG
Saddle vinyl W/Parchment..............GF
Aqua vinyl W/Parchment................GK
Red vinyl.............................LB
Blue vinyl............................LD
Parchment cloth and Parchment vinyl W/Black...LU
Parchment vinyl.......................OU
Parchment vinyl W/Black...............UA
Parchment vinyl W/Blue................UB
Parchment vinyl W/Red.................UD
Parchment vinyl W/Saddle..............UF
Parchment vinyl W/Ivy Gold............UG
Parchment vinyl W/Aqua................UK

THUNDERBIRD

Black vinyl............................2A
Blue vinyl.............................2B
Red vinyl..............................2D
Saddle vinyl.........................2F
Ivy gold vinyl.......................2G
Aqua vinyl...........................2K
Parchment vinyl W/Black.........2U
Black vinyl (1)......................4A
Blue vinyl (1).......................4B
Red vinyl (1)........................4D
Ivy gold vinyl (1)..................4G
Aqua vinyl (1)......................4K
Lt. Silver cloth and
Lt. Silver vinyl.....................4L
Parchment vinyl W/Black (1)....4U
Black cloth and Black vinyl.......5A
Parchment cloth and
Parchment vinyl...................5U
Black vinyl (1)......................8A
Blue vinyl (1).......................8B
Red vinyl (1)........................8D
Ivy gold vinyl (1)..................8G
Aqua vinyl (1)......................8K
Lt. Silver cloth and
Lt. silver vinyl.....................8L
Parchment vinyl (1)...............8U
Black Leather.......................HA
Black Leather.......................LA

(1) = Combined with cloth

EXTERIOR PAINT BODY
COLOR CODES

FORD

Black...................................A
Lt. Aqua..............................B
Dk. Gray Met. C
Med. Beige Met. ....E
Light Blue............................F
Diamond Green......................H
Lime Met..............................I
Dark blue Met. ....K
White..................................M
Platinum..............................N
Pewter Met. ....P
Med. Blue Met. ....Q
Dk. Green Met. ....R
Red.....................................T
Med. Turquoise Met. ....U
Bronze Met. V
Med. Aqua Met. ....W
Maroon Met. X
Dk. Green Met. ....Y
Med. Gold Met. ....Z
Yellow.................................2
Med. Gray Met. 4
Lt. Beige..............................6
Yellow.................................8

VEHICLE IDENTIFICATION NUMBER

8A83Z100551

VEHICLE IDENTIFICATION NUMBER LOCATIONS

The official Vehical. Identification Number (VIN) for title and registration purposes will be stamped on an aluminum tab that will be riveted to the instrument panel close to the windshield on the passenger side of the car and will be visible from outside.

1st Digit - MODEL YEAR
The number "8" designates 1968

2nd Digit - ASSEMBLY PLANT

Atlanta	A
Oakville (Canada)	B
Ontario	C
Dallas	D
Mahwah	E
Dearborn	F
Chicago	G
Lorain	H
Los Angeles	J
Kansas City	K
Michigan Truck	L
Norfolk	N
Twin City	P
San Jose	R
Pilot Plant	S
Metichen	T
Louisville	U
Wayne	W
St. Thomas	X
Wixom	Y
St. Louis	Z

3rd & 4th Digit - MODEL

"The two digit numeral which follows the assembly plant code identifies the body series. This two-digit number is used in conjunction with the Body style code in the vehicle data, which consist of a two-digit number with a letter suffix. The following chart lists the body serial codes and the model.

FORD CUSTOM	CODE
2-Dr. Sedan (1)	50
4-Dr. Sedan (1)	51

FORD CUSTOM 500	CODE
2-Dr. Sedan (1)	52
4-Dr. Sedan (1)	53

8A83Z		100551		WARRANTY Number	Made in USA
65C	AA	4A	11G	21	5 1
BDY	CLR	TRM	DT	DSD	AX TR

Galaxie 500	CODE
4-Dr. Sedan (1)	5
4-Dr. Hardtop (1)	5
2-Dr. Convertible (1)	5
2-Dr. Hardtop (1)	5
2-Dr. Hardtop (3)	5

FORD XL	CODE
4-Dr. Hardtop (2)	60
2-Dr. Convertible (2)	61

LTD	CODE
4-Dr. Hardtop (1)	66
2-Dr. Hardtop (1)(3)	62
4-Dr. Sedan	64

RANCH WAGON	CODE
4-Dr. 6 Ps.	70

CUSTOM RANCH WAGON	CODE
4-Dr. 6 Ps.	71
4-Dr. 10 Ps.	72

COUNTRY SEDAN	CODE
4-Dr. 6 Ps.	73
4-Dr. 10 Ps.	74

COUNTRY SQUIRE	CODE
4-Dr. 6 Ps.	75
4-Dr. 10 Ps.	76

(1) = Bench Seat
(2) = Bucket Seat
(3) = Formal Roof

FAIRLANE	CODE
2-Dr. Hardtop (1)	30
4-Dr. Sedan (1)(3)	31

FAIRLANE 500	CODE
2-Dr. Hardtop (1)	33
4-Dr. Sedan (1)	34
2-Dr. Hardtop (1)	35
2-Dr. convertible (1)	36
2-Dr. Hardtop (2)(3)	33
2-Dr. Hardtop (1)	35
2-Dr. convertible (2)	36

TORINO	CODE
2-Dr. Hardtop (1)(3)	40
4-Dr. Sedan (1)	41

TORINO GT	CODE
2-Dr. Hardtop (2)	42
2-Dr. Hardtop (2)(3)	44
2-Dr. Convertible (2)	43

STATION WAGONS	CODE
4-Dr. Fairlane (1)	32
4-Dr. Fairlane 500 (1)	37
4-Dr. Torino Squire (1)	38

RANCHERO	CODE
2-Door (1)	47
2-Door (1)	48
2-Door (2)	48
2-Door (2)	49

(1) = Bench Seat
(2) = Bucket Seat
(3) = Formal Roof

THUNDERBIRD	CODE
2-Dr. Hardtop (1)	83
2-Dr. Landau Hardtop (1)	84
2-Dr. Hardtop (2)	83
2-Dr. Landau Hardtop (2)	84
4-Dr. Landau (1)	87
4-Dr. Landau (2)	87

(1) = Bucket Seat
(2) = Bench Seat

FALCON STANDARD SEDAN	CODE
2-Dr. Club Coupe (1)	10
4-Dr. Sedan (1)	11

(1) = Bench Seat
(2) = Bucket Seat

FUTURA	CODE
2-Dr. Club Coupe (1)	20
4-Dr. Sedan (1)	21

SPORT COUPE	CODE
2-Door (2)	22

STATION WAGONS	CODE
4-Dr. Wagon	12
4-Dr. Deluxe Wagon	23

MUSTANG	CODE
2-Dr. Fastback (1)(3)	2
2-Dr. Hardtop (1)(3)	1
2-Dr. Convertible (1)(3)	3
2-Dr. Fastback (1)	2
2-Dr. Hardtop (1)	1
2-Dr. Convertible (1)	3
2-Door Hardtop (2)	1
2-Door Fastback (2)	2
2-Door Hardtop (2)(3)	1
2-Door Fastback (2)(3)	2

(1) = Bucket Seat
(2) = Bench Seat
(3) = Luxury Model

5th Digit - ENGINE

ENGINE	CODE
6 Cyl. 240 C.I.	V
6 Cyl. 240 C.I. (Police)	B
6 Cyl. 240 C.I. (Taxi)	E
8 Cyl. 289 C.I. (2-V)	C
6 Cyl. 200 C.I. (1-V)	T
8 Cyl. 427 C.I. (4-V, H. P.)	W
8 Cyl. 390 C.I. (4-V)	Z
8 Cyl. 390 C.I. (4-V)	S
8 Cyl. 390 C.I. (2-V)	Y
8 Cyl. 428 C.I. (4-V, Police)	P
8 Cyl. 428 C.I. (4-V)	Q
6 Cyl. 240 (Low Com.)	5
8 Cyl. 428 C.I. (4-V, Low Com.)	8
6 Cyl. 200 C.I. (1-V, Low Com.)	2
6 Cyl. 170 C.I. (1-V)	U
8 Cyl 302 C.I. (2-V)	F
8 Cyl. 302 C.I. (4-V, Low Com.)	6
8 Cyl. 302 C.I. (2-V)	J
8Cyl. 429 C.I. (4-V)	N

WARRANTY PLATE VEHICLE DATA

Located on the front door hing pillar.

8.	1
A.	2
83	3
Z	4
100551	5
65C	6
AA	7
4A	8
11G	9
21	10
5	11
U	12

MODEL YEAR CODE	1
ASSEMBLY PLANT CODE	2
BODY SERIAL CODE	3
ENGINE CODE	4
CONSECUTIVE UNIT NO.	5
BODY TYPE CODE	6
COLOR CODE	7
TRIM CODE	8
DATE CODE	9
DISTRICT-SPEC. EQUIP. CODE	10
REAR AXLE CODE	11
TRANSMISSION CODE	12

DISTRICT CODE

DOS units built to a Domestic Special Order, Foreign Special Order, or other special Orders will have the complete order number in this space. Also appearing in this space is the two digit code number of the District which orderd the unit. If the unit is regular production, only the District code number will appear.

DISTRICT	Code
Boston	11
New York	13
Newark	15
Philadelphia	16
Washington	17
Atlanta	21
Charlotte	22
Jacksonville	24
Richmond	25
Cincinnati	27
Louisville	28
Cleveland	32
Detroit	33
Indianoplis	34
Lansing	35
Buffalo	37
Pittsburgh	38
Chicago	41
Fargo	42
Milwaukee	43
Twin Cities	44
Davenport	45
Denver	51
Des Moines	52
Kansas City	53
Omaha	54
St. Louis	55
Dallas	61
Huston	62
Memphis	63
New Orleans	64
Oklahoma City	65
Los Angeles	71
San Jose	72
Salt Lake City	73
Seattle	74
Phoenix	75
Ford of Canada	81
Government	83
Home Office Reserve	84
American Red Cross	85
Transportation Services	89
Export	90-99

COMPRESSION RATIO

170 Six	8.7:1
200 Six	8.8:1
240 Six	9.2:1
289 V-8 (2-V)	8.7:1
302 V-8 (4-V)	10.1:1

302 V-8 (2-V)........................9.0:1
390 V-8 (2-V)........................9.5:1
390 V-8 (4-V) Prem. Fuel....10.5:1
390 V-8 (4-V) GT................10.5:1
428 V-8 (4-V) CJ................10.6:1
427 H. P. V-8 (4-V)..............10.9:1
428 V-8 (4-V)......................10.5:1
429 V-8..............................11.0:1

BRAKE HORSEPOWER

170 Six.................................100
200 Six.................................115
240 Six.................................150
289 V-8 (2-V)........................195
302 V-8 (2-V)........................210
302 V-8 (4-V)........................230
390 V-8 (2-V)........................265
390 V-8 (4-V)........................315
390 V-8 (4-V) and GT............325
428 V-8 (4-V) CJ...................335
427 V-8 (8-V)H. P..................390
428 V-8 (4-V)........................340
428 V-8 (4-V) Police.............360
429 V-8.................................360

MONTHS OF THE YEAR

MONTH	1st YR.	2nd YR.
January	A	N
February	B	P
March	C	Q
April	D	R
May	E	S
June	F	T
July	G	U
August	H	V
September	J	W
October	K	X
November	L	Y
December	M	Z

REAR AXLE RATIO CODES

A number designates a convential axle, while a letter designates an Equa-Lock axle.

2.75 : 1.................................1
2.79 : 1.................................2
2.80 : 1.................................3
2.83 : 1.................................4
3.00 : 1.................................5
3.20 : 1.................................6
3.25 : 1.................................7
3.50 : 1.................................8
3.10 : 1.................................9
2.50 : 1.................................0
2.80 : 1.................................C
2.83 : 1.................................D
3.20 : 1.................................F
3.00 : 1.................................E
3.25 : 1.................................G
3.50 : 1.................................H
2.75 : 1.................................A

TRANSMISSION TYPE CODES

TRANSMISSION	CODE
3-Speed Manual	1
4 Speed Manual-Shift	5

C4 Automatic (XP3)................W
C6 Automatic (XPL).................U
Automatic (MX).......................Y
Automatic (FMX).....................X
C6 Automatic (XPL Special)....Z

1968 TRIM SCHEME CODES

FORD

Black cloth and Black vinyl.......1A
Blue cloth and Blue vinyl..........1B
Red cloth and red vinyl.............1D
Med. Ivy Gold cloth and Lt. 1G
Ivy gold vinyl
Med. Aqua cloth and Lt. 1K
aqua vinyl
Lt. Parchment cloth and..........1U
Pastel parchment vinyl
Lt. Nugget Gold cloth and........1Y
Lt. Nugget Gold vinyl
Black vinyl............................2A
Dk. blue vinyl (Mercury)..........2B
Med. Blue cloth and Lt. 2B
Blue vinyl (Ford)
Dk. Red vinyl........................2D
Med. Ivy Gold cloth and Lt. 2G
Ivy gold vinyl
Pastel Parchment vinyl
(Mercury)............................2U
Lt. Parchment cloth and..........2U
Pastel Parchment vinyl (Ford)
Lt. Nuggrt Gold vinyl..............2Y
Black cloth and Black vinyl.......3A
Med. Blue cloth and
Lt. Blue vinyl (Mercury)..........3B
Dk. Blue cloth and
Dk. Blue vinyl (Mercury)..........3B
Dk. Red cloth and
Dk. Red vinyl........................3D
Med. Ivy Gold cloth and Lt. 3G
Ivy Gold vinyl (Mercury)
Dk. Ivy Gold cloth and Dk. 3G
Ivy Gold vinyl (Ford)
Med. Aqua cloth and
Lt. Aqua vinyl (Mercury)..........3K
Lt. Aqua cloth and
Lt. Aqua vinyl (Ford)..............3K
Lt. Nugget Gold cloth and
Lt. Nugget Gold vinyl..............3Y
Black vinyl............................4A
Lt. blue vinyl.........................4B
Dk. Red vinyl........................4D
Lt. Aqua vinyl........................4K
Lt. Nugget Gold and Black.......4K
vinyl
Pastel Parchment vinyl............4U
Lt. Nugget Gold vinyl..............4Y
Black cloth and Black vinyl.......5A
Dk. Blue cloth and
Dk. Blue vinyl (Mercury)..........5B
Med. Blue cloth and
Lt. Blue vinyl (Ford)...............5B
Dk. Ivy Gold cloth and Dk. 5G
Ivy Gold vinyl (Mercury)
Med. Ivy Gold cloth and Lt. 5G
Ivy Gold vinyl (Ford)
Dk. Aqua cloth and Dk. 5K
Aqua vinyl (Mercury)
Med. Aqua cloth and Lt. 5K
Aqua vinyl (Ford)
Lt. Nugget Gold cloth and........5Y

Lt. Nugget Gold vinyl
Black vinyl............................6A
Dk. blue vinyl (Mercury)..........6B
Lt. blue vinyl (Ford)................6B
Dk. Red vinyl........................6D
Dk. Ivy Gold vinyl (Mercury)....6G
Lt. Ivy Gold vinyl (Ford)..........6G
Lt. Aqua vinyl........................6K
Pastel Parchment vinyl............6U
Lt. Nugget Gold vinyl..............6Y
Black vinyl............................7A
Dk. and Lt. blue vinyl..............7B
Dk. Red vinyl........................7D
Dk. and Lt. Ivy Gold vinyl........7G
Pastel Parchment vinyl............7U
Black cloth and black vinyl.......9A
Dk. Blue cloth and Dk. 9B
Blue vinyl
Dk. Red cloth and Dk. 9D
Red vinyl
Dk. Ivy gold cloth and Dk. 9G
Ivy gold vinyl
Lt. Aqua cloth and Lt. 9K
Aqua vinyl
Lt. Nugget Gold cloth and........9Y
Lt. Nugget Gold vinyl
Black cloth and Black vinyl......BA
Dk. Blue cloth and Dk. ....BB
Blue vinyl
Dk. Red cloth and Dk. ....BD
red vinyl
Dk. Ivy gold cloth and Dk. ......BG
Ivy gold vinyl
Lt. Nugget Gold cloth and........BY
Lt. Nugget Gold vinyl
Black Vinyl...........................CA
Dk. Blue vinyl.......................CB
Dk. Red vinyl........................CD
Pastel Parchment and.............CU
Black vinyl
Lt. Nugget Gold vinyl..............CY
Black vinyl...........................DA
Dk. and Lt. Blue vinyl.............BD
Dk. Red vinyl........................DD
Pastel Parchment vinyl............DU
Black cloth and Black vinyl......EA
Dk. Blue cloth and Dk. ....EB
Blue vinyl
Dk. Red cloth and Dk. ....ED
Red vinyl
Dk. Ivy Gold and Dk. Ivy.........EG
Gold vinyl
Lt. Aqua cloth and Lt. ....EK
Aqua vinyl
Lt. Nugget Gold cloth and........EF
Lt. Nugget Gold vinyl
Black vinyl............................FA
Dk. Blue vinyl.......................FB
Dk. Red vinyl........................FD
Lt. Ivy Gold vinyl (Mercury).....FG
Lt. Ivy Gold vinyl (Ford)..........FG
Lt. Nugget Gold vinyl..............FY
Pastel Parchment vinyl............FU
Black vinyl...........................HA
Dk. and Lt. Blue vinyl.............HB
Dk. Red vinyl........................HD
Med, and Lt. Ivy Gold viny.......HG
Pastel Parchment vinyl............HU
Black cloth and Black vinyl......KA
Dk. Blue cloth and Dk. ....KB
Blue vinyl
Dk. Red cloth and Dk. ....KD
Red vinyl

Dk. Ivy Gold cloth and Dk. ......KG
Ivy Gold vinyl
Lt. Nugget Gold cloth and........KY
Lt. Nugget Gold vinyl
Lt. and Med, Beige vinyl..........LE
Black vinyl...........................NA
Dk. and Lt. Blue vinyl
(Mercury)............................NB
Dk. and Lt. Blue vinyl (Ford)....NB
Dk. Red vinyl........................ND
Pastel Parchment vinyl............NU
Black vinyl...........................PA
Dk. and Lt. Blue vinyl..............PB
Dk. Red vinyl........................PD
Med, and Lt. Ivy Gold vinyl......PG
Pastel Parchment vinyl............PU
Black vinyl...........................RA
Lt. Blue vinyl.........................RB
Dk. Red vinyl........................RD
Lt. Ivy Gold vinyl....................RG
Lt. Aqua vinyl........................RK
Lt. Nugget Gold vinyl..............RY
Pastel Parchment vinyl............RU
Black cloth and Black vinyl......SA
Med, cloth and Lt. Blue vinyl....SB
Med. Ivy Gold cloth and Lt. .....SG
Ivy Gold vinyl
Med. Aqua cloth and Lt. ....SK
Lt. Nugget Gold cloth and
Aqua viny
Black cloth and Black vinyl......SY
Lt. Nugget Gold vinyl..............ZA
Dk. Blur cloth and Dk. ....ZB
Lt. Nugget Gold cloth and
Blue vinyl.............................ZY
Lt. Nugget Gold vinyl

FAIRLANE, FALCON, MUSTANG

Black cloth and Black vinyl.......1A
Blue cloth and Blue vinyl..........1B
Med. Ivy Gold cloth and Lt. 1G
Ivy gold vinyl
Lt. aqua vinyl........................1K
Lt. Parchment cloth and 1U
Pastel parchment vinyl
Lt. Nugget Gold vinyl..............1Y
Black vinyl............................2A
Dk. and Lt. blue vinyl..............2B
Red vinyl..............................2D
Med. Saddle vinyl...................2F
Lt. Ivy gold vinyl.....................2G
Lt. Aqua vinyl........................2K
Pastel Parchment vinyl............2U
Lt. Nugget Gold vinyl..............2Y
Black vinyl (Montego)..............3A
Black cloth and Black vinyl
(Fairlane)............................3A
Med. Blue cloth and Lt. Blue vinyl
(Falcon, Fairlane).................3B
Dk. Red vinyl........................3D
Med. Ivy Gold cloth and Lt. 3G
Ivy Gold vinyl
Med. Aqua cloth and Lt. 3K
Aqua vinyl
Lt. Parchment cloth and..........3U
Pastel Parchment vinyl (Falcon)
Lt. Nugget Gold cloth and........3Y
Lt. Nugget Gold vinyl
Black vinyl............................4A
Lt. blue vinyl.........................4B
Dk. Red vinyl........................4D

t. Ivy Gold vinyl.....................4G
t. Aqua vinyl.........................4K
astel Parchment vinyl.............4U
t. Nugget Gold vinyl.................4Y
lack vinyl (Fairlane).................5A
t. and Dk. Blue vinyl...............5B
Fairlane)
k. Red vinyl (Fairlane)............5D
t.. Ivy Gold cloth and Lt. 5G
vy Gold vinyl (Ford)
astel Parchment vinyl.............5U
t. Nugget Gold vinyl................5Y
Fairlane)
lack vinyl...........................6A
k. and Lt. Blue vinyl..............6B
k. Red vinyl........................6D
Med. Saddle vinyl..................6F
Med. and Lt. Ivy Gold vinyl......6G
Dk. and Lt. Aqua vinyl............6K
astel Parchment vinyl.............6U
t. Nugget Gold vinyl................6Y
t. blue vinyl (Cougar)..............7B
Med. Blue cloth and Lt. 7B
Blue vinyl (Fairlane)
k. Red cloth and Dk. 7D
Red vinyl
Med. Ivy Gold cloth and Lt. 7G
vy Gold vinyl
Med. Aqua cloth and Lt. 7K
Aqua vinyl
Nugget Gold cloth and..............7Y
Nugget Gold vinyl
Black vinyl............................8A
k. Blue vinyl........................8B
k. Red vinyl.........................8D
Med. Saddle vinyl W/Black.......8F
Med. and Lt. Ivy Golf vinyl........8G
Dk. and Lt. Aqua vinyl............8K
Pastel Parchment vinyl.............8U
Nugget Gold vinyl....................8Y
Black vinyl............................9A
Dk. Blue vinyl........................9B
Dk. Red vinyl.........................9D
Parchment vinyl......................9U
Lt. Nugget Gold vinyl................9Y
Pastel Parchment vinyl............AA
W/Black
Pastel Parchment vinyl.............AB
W/Blue
Pastel Parchment vinyl............AD
W/Red
Pastel Parchment vinyl.............AF
W/Saddle
Pastel Parchment vinyl............AG
W/Ivy Gold
Pastel Parchment vinyl............AK
W/Aqua
Pastel Parchment vinyl............AY
W/Nugget Gold
Pastel Parchment vinyl............BU
Pastel Parchment vinyl............CU
Pastel Parchment vinyl............DU
Pastel Parchment vinyl ....EU
Pastel Parchment vinyl............FA
W/Black
Pastel Parchment vinyl............FB
W/Blue
Pastel Parchment vinyl............FD
W/Red
Pastel Parchment vinyl............FF
W/Saddle
Pastel Parchment vinyl............FG
W/Ivy Gold

Pastel Parchment vinyl............FK
W/Aqua
Pastel Parchment vinyl............FU
Pastel Parchment vinyl............FY
W/Nugget Gold
Black Vinyl............................HA
Dk. and Lt. Blue vinyl..............HB
Dk. Red vinyl........................HD
Med. and Lt. Ivy Gold vinyl......HG
Dk. and Lt. Aqua vinyl............HK
Pastel Parchment vinyl............HU
Lt. Nugget Gold vinyl...............HY
Pastel Parchment vinyl............JU
Med. Blue cloth and Lt. ....KB
Blue vinyl
Med. Ivy Gold cloth and Lt. .....KG
Ivy Gold vinyl
Pastel Parchment viny
(Fairlane)............................KU
Black vinyl...........................LA
Lt. Blue vinyl........................LB
Dk. Red vinyl........................LD
Pastel Parchment vinyl............LU
Black vinyl...........................MA
Dk. and Lt. Blue vinyl..............MB
Dk. Red vinyl........................MD
Pastel Parchment vinyl............MU
Pastel Parchment vinyl............OU
Black vinyl...........................QA
Dk. and Lt. Blue vinyl..............QB
Pastel Parchment vinyl............QU
Black vinyl...........................RA
Lt. Blue vinyl........................RB
Dk. Red vinyl........................RD
Pastel Parchment vinyl............RU
Pastel Parchment vinyl............TU
Parchment vinyl W/Black.........UA
Parchment vinyl W/Blue...........UB
Parchment vinyl W/Red...........UD
Parchment vinyl W/Saddle.......UF
Parchment vinyl W/Ivy Gold....UG
Parchment vinyl W/Aqua.........UK
Pastel Parchment vinyl............UU
Parchment vinyl
W/Nugget Gold.....................UY
Pastel Parchment vinyl............YU
W/Black
Pastel Parchment vinyl............ZU
W/Black

THUNDERBIRD

Black cloth and Black vinyl.......1A
Dk. Blue cloth and Dk. 1B
Blue vinyl
Dk. Red cloth and Dk. 1D
Red vinyl
Dk. Ivy Gold cloth and Dk. 1G
Ivy Gold vinyl
Lt. Aqua cloth and Lt. 1K
Aqua vinyl
Lt. Nugget cloth and Lt. 1Y
Nugget vinyl
Black vinyl............................2A
Dk. Blue vinyl........................2B
Dk. Red vinyl.........................2D
Med. Saddle vinyl..................2F
Dk. Ivy gold vinyl...................2G
Lt. Aqua vinyl........................2K
Pastel Parchment vinyl............2U
Lt. Nugget Gold vinyl...............2Y
Black cloth and Black vinyl.......3A
Dk. Blue cloth and Dk.............3B
Blue vinyl

Dk. Red cloth and Dk. 3D
Red vinyl
Dk. Ivy Gold cloth and Dk. 3G
Ivy Gold vinyl
Lt. Aqua cloth and Lt. 3K
Aqua vinyl
Lt. Nugget cloth and Lt. 3Y
Nugget vinyl
Black vinyl............................4A
Dk. Blue vinyl........................4B
Med. Saddle vinyl..................4F
Pastel Parchment vinyl............4U
Lt. Nugget Gold vinyl...............4Y
Black Leather........................8A
Med. Saddle Leather...............8F

EXTERIOR PAINT BODY COLOR CODES

FORD

Black......................................A
Maroon...................................B
Med. Beige Met. ....F
Diamond Green.......................H
Dk. Green................................J
Dk. Green................................L
White.....................................M
Diamond Blue.........................N
Light Green..............................O
Pewter Met. ....P
Med. Blue Met. ....Q
Dk. Green Met. ....R
Red..T
Med. Aqua Met. ....U
Lt. Blue..................................V
Yellow....................................W
Dark Blue Met. X
Gold Met. ....Y
Dk. Gray Met. ....Z
Lt. Beige.................................6

THUNDERBIRD

Med. Beige Met. ....F
Diamond Green.......................H
Dk. Green................................J
Dk. Green................................L
Pewter Met. ....P
Lt. Blue..................................V
Dk. Gray Met. ....Z
Lt. Beige.................................6
Rose Met. 2

FAIRLANE, MUSTANG, FALCON

Black......................................A
Maroon...................................B
Bright Blue Met. ....D
Bright Aqua Met. ....F
Lime Green Met. I
White.....................................M
Diamond Blue.........................N
Light Green..............................O
Med. Blue Met. ....Q
Dk. Green Met. ....R
Red..T
Med. Aqua Met. ....U
Yellow....................................W
Dark Blue Met. X
Gold Met.................................Y
Vermillion...............................3
Low Gloss Black......................5
Lt. Beige.................................6

VEHICLE IDENTIFICATION NUMBER

9A83X100551

VEHICLE IDENTIFICATION NUMBER LOCATIONS

The official Vehical Identification Number (VIN) for title and registration purposes will be stamped on an aluminum tab that will be riveted to the instrument panel close to the windshield on the passenger side of the car and will be visible from outside.

1966 Model	9
Assembled at Atlanta Plant	A
Thunderbird-Tudor Hardtop	83
8cyl. OHV Engine	X
352 C.I.D. 2-venturi carb	
Vehicle Production Number	100551

1st Digit - MODEL YEAR
The number "9" designates 1969

2nd Digit - ASSEMBLY PLANT

Atlanta	A
Oakville (Canada)	B
Ontario	C
Dallas	D
Mahwah	E
Dearborn	F
Chicago	G
Lorain	H
Los Angeles	J
Kansas City	K
Michigan Truck	L
Norfolk	N
Twin Cities	P
San Jose	R
Allen Park	S
Metichen	T
Louisville	U
Wayne	W
St. Thomas	X
Wixom	Y
St. Louis	Z

3rd & 4th Digit - MODEL

The two digit numeral which follows the assembly plant code identifies the body series. This two-digit number is used in conjunction with the Body style code in the vehicle data, which consist of a two-digit number with a letter suffix. The following chart lists the body serial codes and the model.

9A83S		100551		WARRANTY Number	Made in USA	
65A	AA	6Y	11G	21	1	1
BDY	CLR	TRM	DT	DSD	AX	TR

FORD CUSTOM	CODE
2-Dr. Sedan (1)	50
4-Dr. Sedan (1)	51

FORD CUSTOM 500	CODE
2-Dr. Sedan (1)	52
4-Dr. Sedan (1)	53

FORD XL

	CODE
4-Dr. Hardtop-Fastback (1)(3)	60
2-Dr. Convertible (1)(3)	61

Galaxie 500

	CODE
4-Dr. Sedan (1)	54
4-Dr. Hardtop (1)	56
2-Dr. Convertible (1)	57
2-Dr. Hardtop-Fastback (1)	55
2-Dr. Hardtop (1)	58

LTD

	CODE
4-Dr. Hardtop (1)(2)	66
2-Dr. Hardtop (1)(2)	62
4-Dr. Sedan (1)(2)	64

RANCH WAGON

	CODE
4-Dr. 6 Ps. (1)	70

CUSTOM 500 RANCH WAGON

	CODE
4-Dr. 6 Ps. (1)	71
4-Dr. Dual Face Rear (1)	72

COUNTRY SEDAN

	CODE
4-Dr. 6 Ps. (1)	73
4-Dr. Dual Face Rear (1)	74

COUNTRY SQUIRE

	CODE
4-Dr. 6 Ps. (1)	75
4-Dr. Dual Face Rear (1)	76

(1) = Bench Seat
(2) = Split Bench
(3) = Bucket Seat

FAIRLANE

	CODE
2-Dr. Hartop-Formal (1)	30
4-Dr. Sedan (1)	31

FAIRLANE 500

	CODE
2-Dr. Hardtop-Formal (1)	33
4-Dr. Sedan (1)	34
2-Dr. Hardtop-Fastback (1)	35
2-Dr. convertible (1)	36
2-Dr. Hardtop-Formal (3)	33
2-Dr. Hardtop-Fastback (3)	35
2-Dr. convertible (3)	36

TORINO

	CODE
2-Dr. Hardtop-Formal (1)	40
4-Dr. Sedan (1)	41

TORINO GT

	CODE
2-Dr. Hardtop-Fastback (1)	42
2-Dr. Hardtop-Formal (1)	44
Convertible (1)	43
2-Dr. Hardtop-Fastback (3)	42
2-Dr. Hardtop-Formal (3)	44
Convertible (3)	43

COBRA

	CODE
2-Dr. Hardtop-Fastback (1)	46
2-Dr. Hardtop-Fastback (3)	46
2-Dr. Hardtop-Formal (1)	45
2-Dr. Hardtop-Formal (3)	45

STATION WAGONS

	CODE
4-Dr. Fairlane (1)	32
4-Dr. Fairlane 500 (1)	37
4-Dr. Torino Squire (1)	38

RANCHERO

	CODE
Ranchero (1)	47
Ranchero 500 (1)	48
Ranchero 500 (3) Opt.	48
Ranchero GT (1)	49
Ranchero GT (3)	49

(1) = Bench Seat
(2) = Split Bench
(3) = Bucket Seat

THUNDERBIRD

	CODE
2-Dr. Hardtop (3)	83
2-Dr. Hardtop (1)	83
2-Dr. Landau (3)(4)	84
2-Dr. Landau (1)(4)	84
4-Dr. Landau (3)	87
4-Dr. Landau (1)	87

(1) = Bench Seat
(2) = Split Bench
(3) = Bucket Seat
(4) = Blind Quarter Roof

FALCON STANDARD SEDAN

	CODE
2-Dr. Sedan (1)	10
4-Dr. Sedan (1)	11

FUTURA

	CODE
2-Dr. Sedan (1)	20
4-Dr. Sedan (1)	21
2-Dr. Sports Coupe (3)	22

STATION WAGONS

	CODE
Standard (1)	12
Futura (1)	23

(1) = Bench Seat
(2) = Split Bench
(3) = Bucket Seat

MUSTANG STANDARD

	CODE
2-Dr. Hardtop-Standard (3)(4)	1
2-Dr. Fastback-Standard (3)(4)	2
2-Dr. Convertible Standard (3)(4)	3
2-Dr. Hardtop-Luxury (3)(4)	1
2-Dr. Fastback-Luxury (3)(4)	2
2-Dr. Convertible-Luxury (3)(4)	3
2-Dr. Hardtop-Standard (1)	1
2-Dr. Hardtop-Luxury (1)	1
2-Dr. Hardtop-Grande (3)	1
2-Dr. Fastback-Mach 1 (4)	2

(1) = Bench Seat
(2) = Split Bench
(3) = Bucket Seat
(4) = Hi-Back Bucket

5th Digit - ENGINE

ENGINE	CODE
6 Cyl. 170 C.I.	U
6 Cyl. 240 C.I.	V
6 Cyl. 240 C.I. (Police)	B
6 Cyl. 240 C.I. (Taxi)	E
6 Cyl. 240 (Low Comp.)	5
6 Cyl.r 250 C.I.	L
6 Cyl. 250 C.I. (Low Comp.)	3
6 Cyl. 200 C.I. (1-V)	T
6 Cyl. 200 C.I. (1-V, Low Com.)	2
8 Cyl. 302 C.I. (4-V) BOSS	G
8 Cyl. 390 C.I. (2-V)	Y
8 Cyl. 390 C.I. (4-V, Improved Perf.)	S

8 Cyl. 428 C.I. (4 -V, Police, Premium Fuel)	P
8 Cyl. 428 C.I. (4-V) CJ	Q
8 Cyl. 428 C.I. (4-V, Ram Air Induction) CJ	R
8 Cyl. 302 C.I. (2-V)	F
8 Cyl. 302 C.I. (4-V, Low Com.)	6
8 Cyl. 302 C.I. (2-V) (Police & Taxi)	D
8 Cyl. 351 C.I. (2-V)	H
8 Cyl. 351 C.I. (4-V)	M
8 Cyl. 429 C.I. (2-V)	K
8 Cyl. 429 C.I. (4-V)	N
8 Cyl. 429 C.I. (4-V) BOSS	Z

WARRANTY PLATE VEHICLE DATA

The Warranty Plate is Located on the lock face of the left front door on all Passenger Cars.

BODY TYPE CODE	65A
EXTERIOR PAINT COLOR CODE	AA
TRIM SCHEME CODE	1A
PRODUCTION DATE CODE	11G
D.S.O. NUMBER (DISTRICT CODE)	21
REAR AXLE RATIO CODE	1
TRANSMISSION TYPE CODE	1

Thunderbird, 2-Dr. Hardtop.....65A
Black lower body, Black upper body..........................AA
First Digit "1" represents material Crinkle Vinyl.....................1A
Second digit "A" represents color ....Charcoal Black
Eleventh Day of Month..............11
Month of Year - July.................G
Atlanta.....21
Rear axle Ratio of 3.00 to 1 (Alphabetical Code f or Limited Slip).....................1
3 Speed Manual........................1

DISTRICT CODE

DOS units built to a Domestic Special Order, Foreign Special Order, or other special Orders will have the complete order number in this space. Also appearing in this space is the two digit code number of the District which orderd the unit. If the unit is regular production, only the district code number will appear.

DISTRICT	CODE
Boston	11
New York	13
Newark	15
Philadelphia	16
Washington	17
Atlanta	21
Charlotte	22
Jacksonville	24
Richmond	25
Cincinnati	27
Louisville	28
Cleveland	32

Detroit	33
Indianoplis	34
Lansing	35
Buffalo	37
Pittsburgh	38
Chicago	41
Fargo	42
Milwaukee	43
Twin Cities	44
Davenport	45
Denver	51
Des Moines	52
Kansas City	53
Omaha	54
St. Louis	55
Dallas	61
Huston	62
Memphis	63
New Orleans	64
Oklahoma City	65
Los Angeles	71
San Jose	72
Salt Lake City	73
Seattle	74
Phoenix	75
Government	83
Home Office Reserve	84
American Red Cross	85
Transportation Services	89
Export	90-99

FORD OF CANADA

Central	B1
Eastern	B2
Atlantic	B3
Midwestern	B4
Pacific	B7
Export	I1-I7

HORSEPOWER

Engine	H.P.
170 Six(1-V)(Falcon)	100
200 Six (1-V)	115
240 Six (V-1)	150
240 Six (V-1)(Police)	150
240 Six (V-1)(Taxie)	150
250 V-8(1-V)	155
302 V-8(2-V)	220
302 V-8(2-V)(P. & T.)	220
351 V-8(2-V)	250
351 V-8(4-V)	290
390 V-8(2-V)	265
302 V-8 (4-V) BOSS	290
390 V-8(4-V)	320
428 V-8(4-V) CJ	335
428 V-8(4-V)(Police)	360
428 V-8(4-V)(CJ Ram Air)	335
429 V-8(2-V)	320
429 V-8(4-V)	360
429 V-8 (4-V) BOSS	370

Engine Compression Ratio

Engine	Comp Ratio
170 Six(1-V)(Falcon)	8.7:1
200 Six (1-V)	8.1:1
240 Six (V-1)	8.8:1
240 Six (V-1)(Police)	9.2:1
240 Six (V-1)(Taxie)	9.2:1
250 V-8(1-V)	9.0:1
302 V-8(2-V)	9.5:1
302 V-8(4-V)(P. & T.)	9.5:1

351 V-8(2-V)......................9.5:1
351 V-8(4-V)......................10.7:1
390 V-8(2-V)......................9.5:1
302 V-8 (4-V) BOSS...........10.5:1
390 V-8(4-V)......................10.5:1
428 V-8(4-V) CJ.................10.6:1
428 V-8(4-V)(Police)...........10.5:1
428 V-8(4-V)(CJ Ram Air) 10.6:1
429 V-8(2-V)......................10.5:1
429 V-8(4-V)......................10.5:1
429 V-8 (4-V) BOSS...........10.5:1

MONTHS OF THE YEAR

MONTH	1st YR.	2nd YR.
January	A	N
February	B	P
March	C	Q
April	D	R
May	E	S
June	F	T
July	G	U
August	H	V
September	J	W
October	K	X
November	L	Y
December	M	Z

REAR AXLE RATIO CODES

	Limited Slip	Conventional
2.50:1	J	1
2.75:1	K	2
2.79:1	L	3
2.80:1	M	4
2.83:1	N	5
3.00:1	O	6
3.10:1	P	7
3.20:1	Q	8
3.25:1	R	9
3.50:1	S	A
3.07:1	T	B
3.08:1	U	C
3.91:1	V	D
4.30:1	W	E

TRANSMISSION TYPE CODES

TRANSMISSION	CODE
3-Speed Manual (3.03)	1
4 Speed Manual-Shift	5
4 Speed Manual-Shift (Close Ratio)	6
C4 Automatic (XP3)	W
C6 Automatic (XPL)	U
Cruise-O-matic (FMX)	X
C6 Automatic (XPL Special)	Z

1969 TRIM SCHEME CODES

FORD
54A,62B....................................3A
charcoal black cloth
54A,62B...................................3B
Lt. Blue corinthian vinyl & Lt. blue decka cloth
54A,62B...................................3G
Dk. ivy gold corinthian vinyl & ivy gold decka cloth
54A,62B...................................3Y
Lt. nugget gold corinthian vinyl & Lt. nugget gold decka pattern cloth
54A,57B,63B,65C (1)..............5A
Charcoal black corinthian vinyl & charcoal black sunda pattern cloth
54A,57B,63B,65C (1)..............5B
Lt. blue Corinthian vinyl & Lt. blue sunda pattern cloth
54A,57B,63B,65C (1)..............5G
Dk. ivy gold corinthian vinyl & Dk. ivy gold sunda pattern cloth
54A,57B,63B,65C (1)..............5K
Lt. aqua corinthian vinyl & Lt. aqua sunda pattern cloth
54A,57B,63B,65C (1)..............5Y
Lt. nugget corinthian vinyl & Lt. nugget sunda pattern cloth
54A,57B,63B,C,65C................6A
Charcoal black corinthian vinyl and charcoal black kiwi pattern vinyl
71B,C,76A,B (1)....................6A
Charcoal black corinthian vinyl and charcoal black kiwi pattern vinyl
54A,57B,63B,C,65C................6B
Lt. blue corinthian vinyl and Lt. blue kiwi pattern vinyl
71B,C,76A,B (1)....................6B
Lt. blue corinthian vinyl and Lt. blue kiwi pattern vinyl
54A,57B,63B,C,65C................6D
Dk. red corinthian vinyl and Dk. red kiwi pattern vinyl
71B,C,76A,B (1)....................6D
Dk. red corinthian vinyl and Dk. red kiwi pattern vinyl
54A,57B,63B,C,65C................6G
Dk. ivy gold corinthian vinyl and Dk. ivy gold kiwi pattern vinyl
71B,C,76A,B (1)....................6G
Dk. ivy gold corinthian vinyl and Dk. ivy gold kiwi pattern vinyl
54A,57B,63B,C,65C................6W
White corinthian vinyl and White kiwi pattern vinyl
71B,C,76A,B (1)....................6W
White corinthian vinyl and White kiwi pattern vinyl
54A,57B,63B,C,65C................6Y
Lt. nugget gold corinthian vinyl and Lt. nugget gold kiwi pattern vinyl
71B,C,76A,B (1)....................6Y
Lt. nugget gold corinthian vinyl and Lt. nugget gold kiwi pattern vinyl
71H,J....................................7A
Charcoal black corinthian vinyl and charcoal black tiber pattern vinyl
71H,J....................................7B
Lt. blue corinthian vinyl and Lt. blue tiber pattern vinyl

71H,J....................................7G
Dk. ivy gold corinthian vinyl and Dk. ivy gold tiber pattern vinyl
71H,J....................................7Y
Lt. nugget gold corinthian vinyl and Lt. nugget gold tiber pattern vinyl
63C,76B (2)..........................8A
Charcoal black corinthian vinyl and charcoal black clarion knitted vinyl
63C,76B (2)..........................8B
Lt. blue corinthian vinyl and Lt. blue clarion knitted vinyl
63C,76B (2)..........................8D
Dk. red corinthian vinyl and Dk. red clarion knitted vinyl
63C (2)...................................8G
Dk. ivy gold corinthian vinyl and Dk. ivy gold clarion knitted vinyl
63C,76B (2)..........................8W
White corinthian vinyl and white clarion knitted vinyl
63C,76B (2)..........................8Y
Lt. nugget gold corinthian vinyl and Lt. nugget gold cimarron and lagoon pattern vinyl
54C,57F,65A (1)....................9A
Charcoal black corinthian vinyl and charcoal black cimarron and lagoon pattern vinyl
54C,57F,65A (1)....................9B
Dk. blue corinthian vinyl and Dk. blue cimarron and lagoon pattern vinyl
54C,57F,65A (1)....................9D
Dk. red corinthian vinyl and Dk. red cimarron and lagoon pattern vinyl
54C,57F,65A (1)....................9G
Dk. ivy gold corinthian vinyl and Dk. ivy gold cimarron and lagoon pattern vinyl
54C,57F,65A (1)....................9K
Lt. aqua corinthian vinyl and Lt. aqua cimarron and lagoon pattern vinyl
54C,57F,65A (1)....................9Y
Lt. nugget gold corinthian vinyl and Lt. nugget gold cimarron and lagoon pattern vinyl
54C,57F,65A (3)....................EA
Charcoal black corinthian vinyl and charcoal black cimarron and lagoon pattern cloth
54C,57F,65A (3)....................EB
Dk. blue corinthian vinyl and Dk. blue cimarron and lagoon pattern cloth
54C,57F,65A (3)....................ED
Dk. red corinthian vinyl and Dk. red cimarron and lagoon pattern cloth
54C,57F,65A (3)....................EG
Dk. ivy gold corinthian vinyl and Dk. ivy gold cimarron and lagoon pattern cloth
54C,57F,65A (3)....................EK
Lt. aqua corinthian vinyl and Lt. aqua cimarron and lagoon pattern cloth
54C,57F,65A (3)....................EY
Lt. nugget gold corinthian vinyl

and Lt. nugget gold cimarron and lagoon pattern cloth
71A,E (1)................................FA
Charcoal black corinthian vinyl and charcoal black kiwi pattern vinyl
71A,E (1)................................FB
Lt. blue corinthian vinyl and Lt. blue kiwi pattern vinyl
71A,E (1)"...............................FD
Dk. red corinthian vinyl and Dk. red kiwi pattern vinyl
71A,E (1)................................FG
Dk. ivy gold corinthian vinyl and Dk. ivy gold kiwi pattern vinyl
71A,E (1)................................FY
Lt. nugget gold corinthian vinyl and Lt. nugget gold kiwi pattern vinyl
71A,E (4)...............................GA
Charcoal black corinthian vinyl and charcoal black kiwi pattern vinyl
71A,E (4)...............................GB
Lt. blue corinthian vinyl and Lt. blue kiwi pattern vinyl
71A,E (4)...............................GD
Dk. red corinthian vinyl and Dk. red kiwi pattern vinyl
71A,E (4)...............................GG
Dk. ivy gold corinthian vinyl and Dk. ivy gold kiwi pattern vinyl
71A,E (4)...............................GY
Lt. nugget gold corinthian vinyl and Lt. nugget gold kiwi pattern vinyl
71A,E (4)...............................HA
Charcoal black corinthian vinyl and charcoal black clarion knitted vinyl
71A,E (4)...............................HY
Lt. nugget gold corinthian vinyl and Lt. nugget gold clarion knitted vinyl
54C,57F (4).............................CA
Charcoal black corinthian vinyl and charcoal black covert pattern cloth
54C,57F (4).............................CB
Dk. blue corinthian vinyl and Dk. blue covert pattern cloth
54C,57F (4).............................CD
Dk. red corinthian vinyl and Dk. red covert pattern cloth
54C,57F (4).............................CG
Dk. ivy gold corinthian vinyl and Dk. ivy gold covert pattern cloth
54C,57F (4).............................CK
Lt. aqua corinthian vinyl and Lt. aqua covert pattern cloth
54C,57F (4).............................CY
Lt. nugget gold corinthian vinyl and Lt. nugget gold covert pattern cloth
54C,57F,65A (1)....................DA
Charcoal black corinthian vinyl and charcoal black covert pattern cloth
54C,57F,65A (1)....................DB
Dk. blue corinthian vinyl and Dk. blue covert pattern cloth
54C,57F,65A (1)....................DD
Dk. red corinthian vinyl and Dk. red covert pattern cloth

54C,57F,65A (1)....................DG
Dk. ivy gold corinthian vinyl and
Dk. ivy gold covert pattern cloth
54C,57F,65A (1)....................DK
Lt. aqua corinthian vinyl and
Lt. aqua covert pattern cloth
54C,57F,65A (1)....................DY
Lt. nugget gold corinthian vinyl
and Lt. nugget gold covert
pattern cloth
54A,57B,71B,C (4)..................JA
Charcoal black corinthian vinyl
and charcoal black clarion
knitted vinyl
54A,57B (4)........................JW
White corinthian vinyl and white
clarion knitted vinyl
71B,C (4)..........................JY
Lt. nugget gold
corinthian vinyl and Lt. nugget
gold clarion
knitted vinyl
71A,E (1)..........................KA
Charcoal black corinthian vinyl
and charcoal black clarion
knitted vinyl
71A,E (1)..........................KY
Lt. nugget gold corinthian vinyl
and Lt. nugget gold clarion
knitted vinyl
54B,E,62B,C (5)....................LE
Med. parchment corinthian vinyl
and Lt. parchment morocco vinyl
54E,62E,71D........................NA
Charcoal black corinthian vinyl
and charcoal black pinta vinyl
54E,62E,71D........................NB
Lt. blue corinthian vinyl andLt.
blue pinta vinyl
54E,62E,71D.........................Y
Lt. nugget gold corinthian vinyl
and Lt. nugget gold pinta vinyl
54B,62B............................PA
Charcoal black corinthian vinyl
and charcoal black pinta vinyl
54B,62B............................PB
Lt. blue corinthian vinyl and
Lt. blue pinta vinyl
54B,62B............................PY
Lt. nugget gold corinthian vinyl
and Lt. nugget gold pinta vinyl
54B,57B,63B,C......................WA
Charcoal black corinthian vinyl
and charcoal black clarion
knitted vinyl
65C,71B,C (1)......................WA
Charcoal black corinthian vinyl
and charcoal black clarion
knitted vinyl
54B,57B,63B,C......................WW
White corinthian vinyl and white
clarion knitted vinyl W/Black
65C,71B,C (1)......................WW
White corinthian vinyl and white
clarion knitted vinyl W/Black
71B,C (1)..........................WY
Lt. nugget gold corinthian vinyl
and Lt. nugget gold clarion
knitted vinyl
54C,57F (4)........................YA
Charcoal black corinthian vinyl
and charcoal black cimarron
and lagoon pattern vinyl

54C,57F (4)........................YB
Dk. blue corinthian vinyl and Dk.
blue cimarron and lagoon
pattern vinyl
54C,57F (4)........................YD
Dk. red corinthian vinyl and Dk.
red cimarron and lagoon
pattern vinyl
54C,57F (4)........................YG
Dk. ivy gold corinthian vinyl and
Dk. ivy gold cimarron and
lagoon pattern vinyl
54C,57F (4)........................YK
Lt. aqua corinthian vinyl and Lt.
aqua heath tricot and
lagoon pattern vinyl
54C,57F (4)........................YY
Lt. nugget gold corinthian vinyl
and Lt. nugget gold heath tricot
and lagoon pattern vinyl
(1) = Full width seat
(2) = Bucket seat
(3) = Split seat
(4) = Reclining seat
(5) = Police and Taxi

FAIRLANE, TORINO

54A,65A............................1A
Charcoal Black corinthian vinyl
with charcoal black kiwi vinyl
and oneida pattern cloth
54A,65A............................1B
Lt. blue corinthian vinyl with Lt.
blue kiwi vinyl and oneida
pattern cloth
54A,65A............................1Y
Lt. nugget gold corinthian vinyl
with Lt. nugget gold kiwi vinyl
and oneida pattern cloth
66A,71D............................2A
Charcoal black corinthian vinyl
with charcoal black corinthian
and gates vinyl
66A,71D............................2B
Lt. blue corinthian vinyl with Lt.
blue corinthian and gates vinyl
66A,71D............................2Y
Lt. nugget gold corinthian vinyl
with Lt. nugget gold corinthian
and gates vinyl
54B,63B,65B........................3A
Charcoal black corinthian vinyl
with charcoal black samara
pattern cloth
54B,63B,65B........................3B
Lt. blue corinthian vinyl with Lt.
blue samara pattern cloth
54B,63B,65B........................3G
Dk. ivy gold corinthian vinyl with
Dk. ivy gold samara pattern cloth
54B................................3K
Lt. aqua corinthian vinyl with Lt.
aqua samara pattern cloth
54B,63B,65B........................3Y
Lt. nugget gold corinthian vinyl
with Lt. nugget gold samara
pattern cloth
71B................................4A
Charcoal black corinthian vinyl
with charcoal black clarion
knitted vinyl
71B................................4Y
Lt. nugget gold corinthian vinyl
with Lt. nugget gold clarion

knitted gates vinyl
54B,63B,65B,66B,71B,76B.......5A
Charcoal black corinthian vinyl
and charcoal black kiwi vinyl
54B,63B,65B,66B,71B,76B.......5B
Lt. blue corinthian vinyl and
Lt. blue kiwi vinyl
63B,65B,66B,71B,76B..............5D
Dk. red corinthian vinyl and
Dk. red kiwi vinyl
63B,65B............................5G
Dk. ivy gold corinthian vinyl
and Dk. ivy kiwi vinyl
63B,65B............................5K
Lt. aqua corinthian vinyl and
Lt. aqua kiwi vinyl
63B,65B,76B........................5W
White corinthian vinyl and
White kiwi vinyl
63B,65B,66B,71B,76B..............5Y
Lt. nugget gold corinthian vinyl
and Lt. nugget gold kiwi vinyl
63F,65F,66C,76F....................6A
Charcoal black corinthian vinyl
and charcoal black kiwi vinyl
63F,65F,66C,76F....................6B
Lt. blue corinthian vinyl and
Lt. blue kiwi vinyl
63F,65F,66C,76F....................6D
Dk. red corinthian vinyl and
Dk. red kiwi vinyl
63F,65F............................6G
Dk. ivy gold corinthian vinyl
and Dk. ivy kiwi vinyl
63F,65F............................6K
Lt. aqua corinthian vinyl and
Lt. aqua kiwi vinyl
63F,65F,76F........................6W
White corinthian vinyl and
White kiwi vinyl
63F,65F,66C........................6Y
Lt. nugget gold corinthian vinyl
and Lt. nugget gold kiwi vinyl
54C,65C............................7A
Charcoal black corinthian vinyl
and charcoal black lagoon
and cimarron pattern cloth
54C,65C............................7B
Lt. blue corinthian vinyl and Lt.
blue lagoon and cimarron
pattern cloth
54C,65C............................7D
Dk. red corinthian vinyl and Dk.
red lagoon and cimarron
pattern cloth
54C,65C............................7G
Dk. ivy gold corinthian vinyl and
Dk. ivy cimarron pattern cloth
54C,65C............................7K
Lt. aqua corinthian vinyl and Lt.
aqua cimarron pattern cloth
54C,65C............................7W
White corinthian vinyl and White
cimarron pattern cloth
54C,65C............................7Y
Lt. nugget gold corinthian vinyl
and Lt. nugget gold cimarron
pattern cloth
63D,65D,66D,76D....................8A
Charcoal black corinthian vinyl
and charcoal black kiwi vinyl
63D,65D,66D,76D....................8B
Lt. blue corinthian vinyl and
Lt. blue kiwi vinyl

63D,65D,66D,76D....................8D
Dk. red corinthian vinyl and
Dk. red kiwi vinyl
63D,65D............................8G
Dk. ivy gold corinthian vinyl
and Dk. ivy kiwi vinyl
63D,65D............................8K
Lt. aqua corinthian vinyl and
Lt. aqua kiwi vinyl
63D,65D,76D........................8W
White corinthian vinyl and
White kiwi vinyl
63D,65D,76D........................8Y
Lt. nugget gold corinthian vinyl
and Lt. nugget gold kiwi vinyl
71E................................9A
Charcoal black corinthian vinyl
and charcoal black kiwi vinyl
71E................................9B
Lt. blue corinthian vinyl and
Lt. blue kiwi vinyl
71E................................9D
Dk. red corinthian vinyl and
Dk. red kiwi vinyl
71E................................9Y
Lt. nugget gold corinthian vinyl
and Lt. nugget gold kiwi vinyl
63B,65B,66B........................EA
Charcoal black corinthian vinyl
and charcoal black clarion
knitted vinyl
63B,65B,66B........................EW
White corinthian vinyl and white
clarion knitted vinyl
63B,65E,66B,76E....................HA
Charcoal black corinthian vinyl
and charcoal black kiwi vinyl
63B,65E,66B,76E....................HB
Lt. blue corinthian vinyl and
Lt. blue kiwi vinyl
63B,65E,66B,76E....................HD
Dk. red corinthian vinyl and
Dk. red kiwi vinyl
63B,65E............................HG
Dk. ivy gold corinthian vinyl
and Dk. ivy kiwi vinyl
63B,65E............................HK
Lt. aqua corinthian vinyl and
Lt. aqua kiwi vinyl
63B,65E,76E........................HW
White corinthian vinyl and
White kiwi vinyl
63B,65E,76E........................HY
Lt. nugget gold corinthian vinyl
and Lt. nugget gold kiwi vinyl
71E................................MA
Charcoal black corinthian vinyl
and charcoal black clarion
knitted vinyl
71E................................NY
Lt. nugget gold corinthian vinyl
and Lt. nugget gold clarion
knitted vinyl
63D,65D,66D........................QA
Charcoal black corinthian vinyl
and charcoal black clarion
knitted vinyl
63D,65D,66D........................QW
White corinthian vinyl and white
clarion knitted vinyl-W/black
63E,65E,66B........................VA
Charcoal black corinthian vinyl
and charcoal black clarion
knitted vinyl

63E,65E,66B.............................VW
White corinthian vinyl and white
clarion knitted vinyl-W/black
63F,65F,66C.............................WA
Charcoal black corinthian vinyl
and charcoal black clarion
knitted vinyl
63F,65F,66C.............................WW
White corinthian vinyl and white
clarion knitted vinyl

BRONCO
96,97,98...................................3
Pastel parchment corinthian
vinyl and Lt. Parchment
matchstick vinyl
96,97,98...................................9
Pastel parchment corinthian vinyl
and Lt. Parchment rosette vinyl
96,97,98...................................94
Pastel parchment corinthian vinyl
and Lt. Parchment rosette vinyl
96,97,98...................................9U
Pastel parchment corinthian vinyl
and Lt. Parchment rosette vinyl

FALCON
54A,62A....................................1A
Charcoal black corinthian vinyl
with charcoal black nimbus
and cadence vinyl
54A,62A....................................1B
Lt. blue corinthian vinyl with Lt.
blue nimbus and cadence vinyl
54A,62A....................................1Y
Lt. nugget gold corinthian vinyl
with Lt. nugget gold nimbus
and cadence vinyl
71A...2A
Charcoal black corinthian vinyl
and charcoal black gates vinyl
71A...2B
Lt. blue corinthian vinyl and
Lt. blue gates vinyl
71A...2Y
Lt. nugget gold corinthian vinyl
and Lt. nugget gold gates vinyl
54B,62B....................................3A
Charcoal black corinthian vinyl
and charcoal black fremont
pattern cloth
54B,62B....................................3B
Lt. blue corinthian vinyl and Lt.
blue fremont pattern cloth
54B,62B....................................3Y
Lt. nugget gold corinthian vinyl
and Lt. fremont pattern cloth
54B,62B,71B..............................4A
Charcoal black corinthian vinyl
and charcoal black kiwi vinyl
54B,62B,71B..............................4B
Lt. blue corinthian vinyl and
Lt. blue kiwi vinyl
54B,62B,71B..............................4D
Dk. red corinthian vinyl and
Dk. red kiwi vinyl
54B,62B,71B..............................4Y
Lt. nugget gold corinthian
vinyl and Lt. kiwi vinyl
62C...8A
Charcoal black corinthian vinyl
and charcoal black kiwi vinyl
62C...8B
Lt. blue corinthian vinyl and

Lt. blue kiwi vinyl
62C...8D
Dk. red corinthian vinyl and
Dk. red kiwi vinyl
62C...8Y
Lt. nugget gold corinthian vinyl
and Lt. kiwi vinyl

EXTERIOR PAINT BODY
COLOR CODES

FORD
Black..A
Maroon.......................................B
Peacock Blue (Bronco)..............D
Bright Blue Met. (Mustang)........D
Med. Beige Met. ....E
Lt. Blue (Bronco).........................F
Dk. Aqua Met. (Excp. Bronco)....F
Chrome Yellow (Bronco)............G
Diamond Green...........................H
Lime Met I
Red (Bronco)...............................J
Dk. Aqua Met. (T/Bird)...............J
Dk. Green(Bronco)......................L
Med. Gray Met. (T/Bird).............L
White..M
Platinum (Diamond Blue)...........N
(Excp. Bronco)
Pewter Met. ....P
Med. Blue Met. ....Q
Dk. Green Met. ....,R
Red...T
Med. Aqua Met...........................U
 (Excp. Bronco)
Med. Green (Bronco)..................U
Lt. Blue.......................................V
Yellow...W
Dark Blue Met. X
Med. Gold Met. ....Y
Signal Flare Red (Bronco)..........Z
Dk. Gray Met. (T/Bird)...............Z
Lt. Ivy Green Met. 4
Dk. Gray Met. 5
(Mustang-Tutone-Hood-Cowl
area)
Lt. Beige.....................................6
Dk. Blue (Bronco).......................7

VEHICLE IDENTIFICATION NUMBER

SERIAL NUMBER

    0 H 3 4 N 5 0 0 5 5 1

VIN Location

Comet - Die stamped into top surface of left hand brace extending from top of firewall to left front wheel base.

Mercury - Die stamped into top of R/H frame side rail forward of cowl underhood.

Lincoln - Die stamped into top face of front compartment lock flange near R/H side.

EXAMPLE

1960 Model Year	0
Assembly Plant Code	H
Body Series Code	34
Engine Code	N
Serial Identification Code	500551

MODEL YEAR
0	1960

ASSEMBLY PLANT | CODE
Lorain	H
Los Angeles	J
Kansas City	K
Metuchen	T
Wayne	W
Wixom	Y
St. Louis	Z
San Jose	R

BODY STYLE CODES

COMET | **CODE**
2-Dr. Sedan	1
4-Dr. Sedan	2
2-Dr. Station Wagon	6
4-Dr. Station Wagon	7

MERCURY | **CODE**
Monterey 2-Dr. Sedan	31
4-Dr. Sedan	32
2-Dr. Cruiser	33
4-Dr. Cruiser	34
2-Dr. Convertible	35
4-Dr. Commuter	37
Country Cruiser (6-8 Ps.)	
Montclair 4-Dr. Sedan	42
2-Dr. Cruiser	43
4-Dr. Cruiser	44
Parklane 2-Dr. Cruiser	53
4-Dr. Cruiser	54
2-Dr. Convertible	55
Colony Park 4-Dr.	57
Country Cruiser (6-8 Ps.)	

LINCOLN | **CODE**
Lincoln 4-Dr. Seda	62
Lincoln 2-Dr. Hardtop	63
Lincoln 4-Dr. Hardtop	64
Premiere 4-Dr. Sedan	72
Premiere 2-Dr. Hardtop	73
Premiere 4-Dr. Hardtop	74
Continental 4-Dr. Sedan	82
Continental 2-Dr. Hardtop	83
Continental 4-Dr. Hardtop	84
Continental 2-Dr. Convertible	85
Lincoln Formal Sedan	92
Lincoln Limousine	99

COMET | **CODE**
4-Dr. Sedan	54A
2-Dr. Station Wagon	59A

2-Dr. Sedan	62A
4-Dr. Station Wagon	71A

MERCURY | **CODE**
Monterey 4-Dr. Sedan	57A
Montclair 4-Dr. Sedan	57B
Parklane 4-Dr. Sedan	57F
Monterey 4-Dr. Sedan	58A
Montclair 4-Dr. Sedan	58B
Monterey 2-Dr. Cruiser	63A
Montclair 2-Dr. Cruiser	63B
Parklane 2-Dr. Cruiser	63F
Monterey 2-Dr. Cruiser	64A
Monterey 2-Dr. Convertible	76A
Parklane 2-Dr. Convertible	76D
Commuter 4-Dr.	77A
Country Cruiser (6-8Ps.)	
Colony Park 4-Dr.	77B
Country Cruiser (6-8Ps.)	

LINCOLN | **CODE**
Lincoln 4-Dr. Sedan	53A
Premiere 4-Dr. Sedan	53B
Continental 4-Dr. Sedan	54A
Lincoln 4-Dr. Landau	57A
Premiere 4-Dr. Landau	57B
Lincoln 2-Dr. Coupe	63A
Premiere 2-Door Coupe	63B
Continental 2-Dr. Coupe	65A
Continental 2-Dr.	68A
Convertible	
Continental 4-Dr. Landau	75A
Lincoln Formal Sedan	23B
Lincoln Limousine	23A

EXTERIOR PAINT CODES

LINCOLN

(A "No Punch" in the paint color space indicates Special Paint)

COLOR	CODE
Presidential Black	A
Marine Blue Poly	B
Sapphire Poly	D
Electric Blue Poly	E
Blue Crystal	F
Tawney Beige	G
Pale Turquoise	I
Cherokee Red	J
Gold Dust Poly	L
Polaris White	M
Platinum	N
Copper Poly	Q
Pastel Yellow	R
Deerfield Green Poly	S
Terre Veree Green Poly	T
Metallic Rose Glow Poly	U
Twilight Pink	V
Killarney Green	W
Maple Leaf Poly	X
Spartan Gray Poly	Y
Silver Poly	Z

MERCURY/COMET

COLOR	CODE
Tuxedo Black	A
Sultana White	M
Med. Valley Green Met.	T
Lt. Inlet Blue	F
Med. Cote D'Azur Blue Met.	E
Signal Red	J
Cloud Silver Metallic	Z
Sun Haze Yellow	R
Polynesian Beige	N
Med. Javelin Bronze Met.	H
Mountain Rose Metallic	U
Summer Rose (Light)	V
Lt. Tucson Turquoise Met.	X
Med. Aztec Turquoise Met.	D
Marine Blue Metallic (Dark)	B
Crystal Turquoise	C
Twilight Turquoise	K
Cameo Green	W

VEHICLE DATE CODES

MONTH	CODE	*CODE
January	A	N
February	B	P
March	C	Q
April	D	R
May	E	S
June	F	T
July	G	U
August	H	V
September	J	W
October	K	X
November	L	Y
December	M	Z

*To be used if 1960 model exceeds 12 months.

Engine Code

MERCURY

ENGINE TYPE	CODE
430 C.I.D. 8 Cyl. 2-V Carb.	M
383 C.I.D. 8 Cyl. 2-V Carb.	N
312 C.I.D. 8 Cyl. 2-V Carb.	P
383 C.I.D 2-V Low Comp.	E
430 C.I.D. 2-V Low Comp.	F

COMET

6 Cyl. OHV 144 Cubic Inch	S
6 Cyl. OHV 144 Cubic Inch Low Compression (84 Octane)	D

LINCOLN

430 C.I.D. 8 Cyl. 2-V	H
430 C.I.D. 2-V (Export)	K

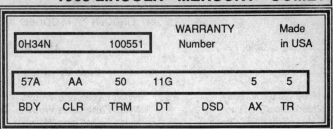

			WARRANTY		Made
0H34N		100551	Number		in USA
57A	AA	50	11G	5	5
BDY	CLR	TRM	DT	DSD	AX	TR

PATENT PLATE

The Patent Plate is riveted to the front body pillar between the front door hinges on the Lincoln and Mercury. The Comet Patent Plate is riveted to the left front door below the door lock. The Patent Plate includes information relative to the type of engine, axle, transmission, trim (exteriorand interior), and body style of the vehicle. It also includes the date (day, month and year) and place of manufacture.

STYLE NUMBER

Body Style Code	57A
Exterior Paint and Tone Code (lower, upper)	M
Trim Code	50
Day and Month of Year Built Code	116
Transmission Code	5
Axle Code	5

ENGINE SPECIFICATIONS

Engine CID	Code	Comp. Ratio	Horsepower
430	H	10.0 : 1	315
430	M	10.0 : 1	310
383	N	8.5 : 1	280
312	P	8.9 : 1	205
144	S	8.7 : 1	90

LINCOLN TRIM CODES

Code	Color	Material

Capri Upholstery

01	Med. Gray/Dk. Gray	Nylon Faille/Cane Weave
02	Med. Blue/Dk. Blue	Nylon Faille/Cane Weave
03	Med. Green/Dk. Green	Nylon Faille/Cane Weave
04	Med. Gray/Dk. Gray	Pavilion Nylon/Starhaze
05	Med. Blue/Dk. Blue	Pavilion Nylon/Starhaze
06	Med. green/Dk. Green	Pavilion Nylon/Starhaze

Fabric/Fabric Upholstery

07	Med. Gray/Dk. Gray	Bristol Nub/Six-Point Matelasse
08	Med. Blue/Dk. Blue	Bristol Nub/Six-Point Matelasse
09	Med. Green/Dk. Green	Bristol Nub/Six-Point Matelasse
10	Med. Brown/Dk. Brown	Bristol Nub/Six-Point Matelasse
11	Dk. Gray/Dk. Gray	Pin Point/Patio Weave Nylon
12	Dk. Blue/Dk. Blue	Pin Point/Patio Weave Nylon
13	Dk. Green/Dk. Green	Pin Point/Patio Weave Nylon

Genuine Leather/Fabric

22	Dk. Blue/Med. Blue	Leather/Brentwood Cord
23	Dk. Green/Med. Green	Leather/Brentwood Cord
24	Starmist White/Champagne	Leather/Brentwood Cord
26	Sand/Black	Leather/Brentwood Cord
27	Huntsman Red/Black	Leather/Brentwood Cord
28	Presidential Black/Black	Leather/Brentwood Cord

Genuine Leather

29	Med. Blue/Dk. Blue	Leather
30	Med. Green/Dk. Green	Leather
31	Starmist White/Huntsman Red	Leather
32	Starmist White/Taos Turquoise	Leather
33	Starmist White/Saturn Gold	Leather
34	Starmist White/Presidential Black	Leather
35	Sand/Desert Buff	Leather
36	Presidential Black	Leather

Genuine Leather Optional

37	Huntsman Red/Starmist White/	Leather
		Presidential Black
38	Bermuda Coral/Starmist White/	Leather
		Presidential Black
39	Flamingo/Starmist White/	Leather
		Presidential Black
40	Taos Turquoise/Starmist White/	Leather
		Presidential Black
42	Saturn Gold/Starmist White/	Leather
		Presidential Black

Genuine Leather/Fabric

44	Dk. Blue/Med. Blue	Leather/Honeycomb Nylon
45	Dk. Green/Med. Green	Leather/Honeycomb Nylon
46	Starmist White/Champagne	Leather/Brentwood Cord
47	Bermuda Coral/Black	Leather/Brentwood Cord
48	Flamingo/Black	Leather/Brentwood Cord
49	Starmist White/Black	Leather/Brentwood Cord

Convertible Top

1		Black
2		White
3		Tan
4		Lt. Blue
5		Lt. Green

COMET TRIM CODES

A two digit number indicates the type of trim and the trim color.

Trim Code	Trim Scheme
01	White Vinyl & Sapphire Tweed B/cloth
02	Green Vinyl & Sapphire Tweed B/cloth
03	Red Vinyl & Sapphire Tweed B/cloth
04	Turquoise Vinyl & Sapphire Tweed B/cloth
05*	Green Vinyl & Green Honeycomb B/cloth
06*	Red Vinyl & Black Honeycomb B/cloth
07*	Turquoise Vinyl & Turquoise Honeycomb B/cloth
08*	White & Black Vinyl
09	Red and Black Vinyl

*Deluxe RPO Trim

VEHICLE IDENTIFICATION NUMBER

SERIAL NUMBER

```
1 H 62 X 5 0 0 5 5 1
```

VIN Location

Lincoln - Right Front inner wheelhouse panel.

Mercury - Top of R/H Frame siderail forward of cowl under hood.

Comet - Top surface of left hand brace.

EXAMPLE

1961 Model Year.........................1
Assembly Plant Code................H
Body Series Code.....................62
Engine Code.............................X
Serial Identification..........500551

MODEL YEAR

1..1961

ASSEMBLY PLANT   CODE

Mahwah......................................E
Lorain..H
Los Angeles..............................J
Kansas City..............................K
San Jose....................................R
Wayne..W
Wixom..Y
St. Louis....................................Z

BODY STYLE CODES

COMET   **CODE**
2-Dr. Sedan...............................11
4-Dr. Sedan...............................12
2-Dr. Sedan (S-22).....................17
2-Dr. Station Wagon.................21
4-Dr. Station Wagon.................22

LINCOLN   **CODE**
Lincoln Continental,
4-Dr. Sedan................................82
Lincoln Continental, 4-Dr.
Convertible.................................86

1H62X	500551	Serial Number
BDY	CLR	TRM	DT	AX	TR
54B	AA	33	11G	3	6

MERCURY   **CODE**
Meteor 4-Dr. Sedan (800)........52
Monterey 4-Dr. Sedan..............62
Meteor 4-Dr. Sedan (600)........42
Meteor 2-Dr. Sedan (800)........51
Meteor 2-Dr. Sedan (600)........41
Meteor 2-Dr. Hardtop (800)......57
Monterey 2-Dr. Hardtop 67
Meteor 4-Dr. Hardtop (800)......54
Monterey 4-Dr. Hardtop...........64
Monterey Convertible...............65
Commuter 4-Dr. 74
(6-9 Ps.)
Colony Park 4-Dr. 76
(6-9 Ps.)

**COMET / MERCURY   CODE
/ LINCOLN**
4-Dr. Sedan..............................54A
Meteor (800) 4-Dr. Sedan......54A
Monterey 4-Dr. Sedan............54B
Meteor (600) 4-Dr. Sedan.....58A
Meteor (800) 2-Dr. Sedan.....62A
Meteor (600) 2-Dr. Sedan.....64A
Meteor (800) 2-Dr. Hardtop...65A
Monterey 2-Dr. Hardtop.........65B
Meteor (800) 4-Dr. Hardtop...75A
Monterey 4-Dr. Hardtop.........75B
Monterey 2-Dr. Convertible....76A
Commuter 4-Dr. Station........71A
Wagon (6-9 Ps.)

Colong Park 4-Dr. 71B
Station Wagon (6-9 Ps.)
Comet 4-Dr. Sedan.................54A
Comet 2-Dr. Sedan.................62A
Comet Commuter 4-Dr. 71A
Station Wagon (6-9 Ps.)
Comet 2-Dr. Sedan.................62A

ENGINE CODES

ENGINE TYPE   CODE

223-C.I.D. 6 Cyl., 1-V Carb. V
292-C.I.D. 8 Cyl., 2-V Carb. ......W
352-C.I.D. 8 Cyl., 2-V Carb. X
390-C.I.D. 8 Cyl., 4-V Carb. ......Z
292-c.I.D. 8 Cyl., 2-V Carb. ....T
(Low Comp. 84 Oct.)
390-C.I.D. 8 Cyl., 4-V Carb. ......R
(Low Comp. 84 Oct.)
430 C.I.D. 3 Cyl. 2-V..................H
430 C.I.D. 8 Cyl. 2-V..................K
(Low Comp. 84 Oct.)
6 Cyl. OHV 144 C.I.D. ....S
6 Cyl. OHV 144 C.I.D. ....D
(Comp. 84 Oct.)
6 Cyl. 170 C.I.D. ....E
(Low Comp. 84 Oct.)
6 Cyl. OHV 170 C.I.D.................U

PATENT PLATE

The Patent Plate is riveted to the front body pillar between the front door hinges on the Lincoln and Mercury. The Comet Patent Plate is riveted to the left front door below the door lock. The Patent Plate includes information relative to the type of engine, axle, transmission, trim (exterior and interior), and body style of the vehicle. It also includes the date (day, month and year) and place of manufacture.

STYLE NUMBER

Body Style Code....................54B
Exterior Paint and
Tone Code (lower, upper)......AA
Trim Code................................33
Day and Month of
YearBuilt Code.....................116
Transmission Code....................3
Axle Code...................................6

TRIM COMBINATION

LINCOLN

TRIM COMBONATION   CODE

Med. Gray Leather and Med.   11
Gray Net Cloth
Med. Blue Met. Leather and   12
Med. Blue Net Cloth
Med. Blue Met. Leather............14
White Leather and Black.........20
Larkspur Cloth
Med. Blue Met. Leather and   22

Med. Blue Larkspur Cloth
Med. Green Met. Leather and
Med. Green Larkspur Cloth......23
Black Leather and Black 26
Larkspur Cloth
Med. Turquoise Met. 27
 Leather and Med. Turquoise
Larkspur Cloth
Med. Rose Met. Leather and
Med. Rose Larkspur Cloth.......29
Med. Gray Broadcloth...............31
Med. (Fawn) Beig Broadcloth 34
Med. Blue Met. Leather............82
Med. Green Met. Leather.........83
Light (Honey) Beige Pearl
Leather...............................84
Red Leather............................85
Black Leather...........................86
Med. Turquoise Met. Leather 87
White and Red Leather.............95
White and Black Leather..........96

COMET

TRIM SCHEME   CODE

White Vinyl and Black..............10*
3-D B/cloth
Blue Vinyl and Blue.................12*
3-D B/cloth
Green Vinyl and Green............13*
3-D B/cloth
Red Vinyl and Black................15*
3-D B/cloth
White Vinyl and Blue-Green.....40
B/cloth
Blue Vinyl and Blue-Green
Tweed B/cloth.........................42
Green Vinyl and Blue-Green
Tweed B/cloth.........................43
Red Vinyl and Red-Gray Tweed
B/cloth..................................45
White and Red Vinyl................75*
White and Black Vinyl.............76*
*Deluxe RPO Trim

MERCURY

Med. Blue Met. and Dk. Blue
Luster Weave Cloth...................1
White Vinyl and Black Luster
Weave Cloth.............................2
Med. Gold Met. Vinyl andDk.
Gold Luster Weave Cloth............3
Med. Blue Met. Vinyl and Dk.
Blue Shadow Weave Cloth.........5
White Vinyl and Black Shadow
Weave Cloth.............................6
Med. Gold Met. Vinyl and Dk.
Gold Shadow Weave Cloth.........8
Med. Turquoise Met....................9
Vinyl and Dk.Turquoise
Shadow Weave Cloth
Med. Green Met. Vinyl and
Dk.Green Shadow
Weave Cloth............................10
Med. Blue Met. Vinyl................11
White and Black Vinyl..............12
White and Red Vinyl................13
White and Med. Gold 14
Met. Vinyl
Med. Turquoise Met. Vinyl.......15
Med. Blue Met. Vinyl and Dk.
Med. Turquoise Vinyl and   37

Blue Country Tweed
Broadcloth...............................24
White Vinyl and Black
Country.................................25
 Tweed Broadcloth
Med. Gold Met. Vinyl and Dk. 27
Gold Country Tweed Broadcloth
Med. Turquoise Met. Vinyl 29
and Dk. Turquoise Country
Tweed Broadcloth
Med. Turquoise Met. Vinyl.......30
 and Dk. Turquoise Luster
 Weave Cloth
Red Vinyl................................32
Black Vinyl..............................33
Med. Blue Vinyl and Med.
BlueOval Tweed Cloth.............34
White Vinyl and Med. Gray......35
Oval Tweed Cloth
Red Vinyl and Med. Gray 36
Oval Tweed Cloth
Med. Turquoise Oval
Tweed Cloth
Brown Rib Morocco Vinyl (Police
and Taxi)................................43
Green Rib Morocco Vinyl (Police
and Taxi)................................44
Red Rib Morocco Vinyl.............45
 (Police and Taxi)

VEHICLE DATE CODES

MONTH	CODE	*CODE
January	A	N
February	B	P
March	C	Q
April	D	R
May	E	S
June	F	T
July	G	U
August	H	V
September	J	W
October	K	X
November	L	Y
December	M	Z

*2 Year Code Letters to be Used
if 1961 Models Exceed 12
Months.

TRANSMISSION CODES

TRASMISSION TYPE
CODE
Standard (S/T)...........................1
Overdrive (O/D).........................2
Two Speed Automatic (2/S)......3
Dual Range (or D/R)
Automatic 4
Single Range (or S/R)
Automatic C

AXLE CODES

RATIO	REGULAR	LOCKING
3.56:1	1	A
3.89:1	2	B
3.10:1	3	C
3.10:1	3	
4.00:1	4	
3.20:1	5	
3.50:1	6	F
2.8:1	7	G

ENGINE SPECIFICATIONS

Engine CID	Comp. Ratio	Horsepower	Cylinders
144	8.7:1	90	I-6
170	8.7:1	101	I-6
223	8.4:1	135	I-6
292	8.8:1	175	V-8
352	8.9:1	220	V-8
390	9.6:1	300	V-8
430	10:01	300	V-8

VEHICLE IDENTIFICATION NUMBER

SERIAL NUMBER

2 H 54 X 500 551

Lincoln - RT, FT, inner wheelhouse panel.

Mercury - Top of RH frame side rail forward of cowl under hood.

Comet - Top surface of left hand brace.

Meteor - Left front inner fender apron under hood.

EXAMPLE

1962 Model Year	2
Assembly Plant Code	H
Body Series Code	54
Engine Code	X
Serial Identification Code	500551

ASSEMBLY / CODE

ASSEMBLY	CODE
Mahwah	E
Dearborn	F
Lorain	H
Los Angeles	J
Kansas City	K
San Jose	R
Metuchen	T
Wayne	W
Wixom	Y
St. Louis	Z

BODY STYLE CODES

METEOR	CODE
4-Dr. Sedan	32
4-Dr. Sedan - Custom	42
2-Dr. Sedan	31
2-Dr. Sedan - Custom	41
2-Dr. Sedan - (S-33)	47

COMET	CODE
4-Dr. Sedan - C/P	2
4-Dr. Sedan - Custom - C/P	12
2-Dr. Sedan - C/P	1
2-Dr. Sedan - Custom - C/P	11
2-Dr. Sedan - Special (S-22)	17
2-Dr. Station Wagon	21
2-Dr. Station Wagon - Custom	23
4-Dr. Station Wagon	22
-Dr. Station Wagon - Custom	24
4-Dr. Station Wagon - Villager	26
4-Dr. Station Wagon - Villager Bucket Seat	26

75A	AA	26	11G	32-0551	1	3
BDY	CLR	TRM	DT	DSD	AX	TR

SERIAL NUMBER

2H54X500551

MERCURY	CODE
4-Dr. Sedan - C/P	52
4-Dr. Sedan - Custom - C/P	62
2-Dr. Sedan	51
2-Dr. Hardtop	53
2-Dr. Hardtop - Custom	63
2-Dr. "S-55" Hardtop	67
4-Dr. Hardtop	54
4-Dr. Hardtop - Custom	64
2-Dr. Convertible	65
2-Dr. "S-55" Convertible	69
4-Dr. Commuter Station Wagon (6 Ps.)	72
4-Dr. Colony Park Station Wagon - Custom (6 Ps.)	76
4-Dr. Commuter Station Wagon (9 Ps.)	72

	CODE
4-Dr. Colony Park Station Wagon - Custom (9 Ps.)	76
4-Dr. Station Wagon - Custom	24
4-Dr. Station Wagon - Villager	26
4-Dr. Station Wagon - Villager Bucket Seat	26

MERCURY	CODE
4-Dr. Sedan - C/P	52
4-Dr. Sedan - Custom - C/P	62
2-Dr. Sedan	51
2-Dr. Hardtop	53
2-Dr. Hardtop - Custom	63
2-Dr. "S-55" Hardtop	67
4-Dr. Hardtop	54
4-Dr. Hardtop - Custom	64

	CODE
2-Dr. Convertible	65
2-Dr. "S-55" Convertible	69
4-Dr. Commuter Station Wagon (6 Ps.)	72
4-Dr. Colony Park Station Wagon - Custom (6 Ps.)	76
4-Dr. Commuter Station Wagon (9 Ps.)	72
4-Dr. Colony Park Station Wagon - Custom (9 Ps.)	76

LINCOLN	CODE
Lincoln Continental 4-Dr. Sedan	82
Lincoln Continental 4-Dr. Convertible	86

ENGINE CODES

ENGINE TYPE	CODE
223-C.I.D. 6 Cyl., 1-V Carb.	V
292-C.I.D. 8 Cyl., 2-V Carb.	W
352-C.I.D. 8 Cyl., 2-V Carb.	X
390-C.I.D. 8 Cyl., 4-V Carb.	Z
390-C.I.D. 8 Cyl., 4-V Carb. Interceptor RPO	P
292-C.I.D. 8 Cyl., 2-V Carb. (Low Comp. 84 Oct.)	T
390-C.I.D. 8 Cyl., 4-V Carb. (Low Comp. 84 Oct.)	R

406-C.I.D. 8 Cyl., 4-V Carb. ......B
406-C.I.D. 8 Cyl., 6-V Carb. ......G
6 Cyl. OHV 170 C.I.D. 1-V.........U
6 Cyl. OHV 170 C.I.D. 1-V ....E
(Low Comp.)
8 Cyl. OHV 221 C.I.D. 2-V.........L
8 Cyl. OHV 221 C.I.D. 2-V.........C
(Low Comp.)
8 Cyl. OHV 260 C.I.D. 2-V.........F
8 Cyl. 430 C.I.D. 2-V ....H
8 Cyl. 430 C.I.D. 2-V...............K
(Low Comp. 84 Oct.)
6 Cyl. OHV 144 C.I.D................S
6 Cyl. OHV 144 C.I.D................D
(Low Comp.)

The Patent Plate is riveted to the front body pillar between the front door hinges on the Lincoln and Mercury. The Comet Patent Plate is riveted to the left front door below the door lock. The Patent Plate includes information relative to the type of engine, axle, transmission, trim (exterior sand interior), and body style of the vehicle. It also includes the date (day, month and year), place manufactured, and the code number of the district ordering the unit.

STYLE NUMBER

Body Style Code......................75A
Exterior Paint and Tone Code(lower, upper)..................AA
Trim Code.............................26
Day and Month of Year
Built Code.............................116
District Code...........................32
DSO Number........................0551
Axle Code................................1
Transmission Code...................3

BODY STYLE

MERCURY	CODE
4-Dr. Sedan	54A
4-Dr. Sedan - Custom	54B
2-Dr. Sedan	62A
2-Dr. Sedan Hardtop	65A
2-Dr. Sedan Hardtop - Custom	65B
"2-Dr. ""S-55"" Hardtop"	65C
4-Dr. Sedan Hardtop	75A
4-Dr. Sedan Hardtop - Custom	75B
2-Dr. Convertible	76A
"2-Dr. ""S-55"" Convertible"	76B
4-Dr. Commuter Station Wagon (6-Ps.)	71A
4-Dr. Colony Park Station Wagon (6-Ps.)	71B
4-Dr. Commuter Station Wagon (9Ps.)	71C
4-Dr. Colony Park Station Wagon (9-Ps.)	71D

COMET	CODE
4-Dr. Sedan	54A
4-Dr. Sedan - Custom	54B
2-Dr. Sedan	62A
2-Dr. Sedan - Custom	62B
2-Dr. Sedan -l (S-22)	62C

2-Dr. Station Wagon..............59A
2-Dr. Station WagonCustom 59B
4-Dr. Station Wagon.............71A
4-Dr. StationWagonCustom 71B
4-Dr. Station
 Wagon -Villager...................71C
4-Dr. Station Wagon - Villager
Bucket Seat...........................71D

METEOR	CODE
4-Dr. Sedan	54A
4-Dr. Sedan - Custom	54B
2-Dr. Sedan	62A
2-Dr. Sedan - Custom	62B
2-Dr. Sedan - (S-33)	62C

LINCOLN	CODE
4-Door Sedan	53
4-Door Convertible	74

INTERIOR TRIM IDENTIFICATION

A two-digit number indicates the color and type of trim.

A new procedure for patent plate identification of deviation trim sets, when Service is affected, has been adopted.

When deviation trim sets are established against an existing trim scheme, patent plate code identification will be mde by adding a numerical suffix after the code if the trim set is not serviced, such as 22-1 or 22-2; and by adding an alphabetical suffix after the code if the trim set is serviced, such as 22-A or 22-B.

LINCOLN TRIM CODES

TRIM COMBONATION	CODE
Med. Silver Blue Broadcloth	30
Lt. Honey Beige Broadcloth	34
Lt. Silver Blue Met. Leather and Lt. Blue Empire Cloth	60
Lt. Pearl Beige Leather and Lt. Beige Empire Cloth	64
White Leather and Black Matelasse Cloth	71
Lt. Blue Met. Leather and Lt. Blue Matelasse Cloth	72
Lt. Green Met. Leather and Lt. Green Matelasse Cloth	73
Lt. Honey Beige Met. Leather and Med. Fawn Matelasse Cloth	74
Black Leather and Black Matelasse Cloth	76
Lt. Turquoise Met. Leather and Lt. Turquoise Matelasse Cloth	77
Med. Chestnut Met. Leather and Med. Chestnut Matelasse Cloth	79

TRIM COMBONATION	CODE
Lt. Blue Met. Leather	82
Lt. Green Metallic Leather	83
Lt. Pearlescent Honey Beige Leather	84
Red Leather	85
Black Leather	86
Light Turquoise Met. Leather	87
Med. Chestnut Met. Leather	89
White and Black Leather	96

MERCURY TRIM CODES

TRIM COMBONATION	CODE
White Vinyl and Black Shadow Weave Cloth	26
Lt. Blue Vinyl and Med. Blue Shadow Weave Cloth	22
Lt. Turquoise Vinyl and Med. Turquoise Shadow Weave Cloth	27
Lt. Green Vinyl and Med. Green Shadow Weave Cloth	23
Lt. Beige Vinyl and Med. Beige Shadow Weave Cloth	24
White and Black Vinyl	96
Lt. and Med. Turquoise Vinyl	97
Light Beige Vinyl	94
Lt. Blue Vinyl and Med. Blue. Corinthian Cloth	12
Lt. Turquoise Vinyl and Med. Turquoise Corinthian Cloth	17
Lt. Green Vinyl and Med. Green Corinthian Cloth	13
Lt. Beige Vinyl and Med. beige Corinthian Cloth	14
Lt. and Med. Blue Vinyl	92
White Vinyl and Black Corinthian Cloth	16
White and Red Vinyl	95

METEOR TRIM CODES

TRIM COMBONATION	CODE
Red Vinyl & Black Lexington Body Cloth	15
Lt. Blue Met. Vinyl & Med. Blue Lexington Body Cloth	12
Lt. Pearlescent Honey Beige Leather	84
Lt. Green Met. Leather and Lt. Green Matelasse Cloth	73
Lt. Honey Beige Broadcloth	34
White Leather and Black Matelasse Cloth	71
Black Leather and Black Matelasse Cloth	76
Med. Chestnut Met. Leather and Med. Chestnut Matelasse Cloth	79
Med. Chestnut Met. Leather	89

DISTRICT CODE

DISTRICT	CODE
Boston	11
Philadelphia	12
New York	13
Washington	14
Atlanta	21
Dallas	22
Jacksonville	24
Memphis	25
Buffalo	31
Cincinnati	32
Cleveland	33
Detroit	34
Pittsburgh	35
Chicago	41
Kansas City	43
St. Louis	44
Twin City	45
Denver	51
Los Angeles	52
Oakland	53
Seattle	54
Ford of Canada	81
Home Office Reserve	84
Export	90-99

EXTERIOR PAINT CODES

LINCOLN

COLOR	CODE
Presidential Black	A
Royal Red	B
Oxford Gray	C
Riviera Turquoise	D
Bermuda Blue	E
Powder Blue	F
Silver Mink	G
Nocturne Blue	H
Castilian Gold	I
Teaberry	L
Sultana White	M
Platinum	N
Scotch Green	P
Jamaica Yellow	R
Highlander Green	S
Champagne	T
Velvet Turquoise	U
Chestnut	V
Black Cherry	X
Desert Frost	Z

MERCURY

COLOR	CODE
Presidential Black	A
Medium Turquoise	B
Ocean Turquoise Met.	D
Pacific Blue Met.	E
Sea Blue	F
Carnival Red	J
Light Aqua	K
Blue Satin Metallic	H
Castilian Gold	I
Sultana White	M
Scotch Green	P
Sheffield Gray Metallic	Q
Jamaica Yellow	R
Champagne	T
Black Cherry Metallic	X
Desert Frost Metallic	Z

VEHICLE DATE CODES

MONTH	CODE	*CODE
January	A	N
February	B	P
March	C	Q
April	D	R
May	E	S
June	F	T
July	G	U

Month	Code	2-Year Code
August	H	V
September	J	W
October	K	X
November	L	Y
December	M	Z

*2 year code letters to be used if 1962 models exceed 12 months.

AXLE CODES

RATIO	REGULAR	LOCKING
3.00:1	1	A
3.20:1	3	-
3.25:1	4	-
3.50:1	5	-
3.56:1	6	B
3.80:1	7	B
3.89:1	8	F
4.00:1	9	-

TRANSMISSION CODES

TRANSMISSION TYPE	CODE
Standard (3-Speed) (S/T)	1
Overdrive (O/D)	2
Two Speed Automatic (2/S)	3
Dual Range Automatic (D/R)	4
Standard (4-Speed) (4/S)	5

ENGINE SPECIFICATIONS

Engine CID	Comp. Ratio	Horsepower	Cylinders
144	8.7:1	85	I-6
170	8.7:1	101	I-6
221	8.7:1	145	V-8
223	8.4:1	138	I-6
260	8.7:1	164	V-8
292	8.8:1	170	V-8
352	8.9:1	220	V-8
390	9.6:1	300	V-8
430	10.0:1	300	V-8
406 4-V	9.6:1	330	V-8
406 6-V	10.9:1	405	V-8

VEHICLE IDENTIFICATION NUMBER

VEHICLE WARRANTY NUMBER

| 3 H 5 4 Y 5 0 0 5 5 1 |

Lincoln - Rt. Front innerWheelhouse Panel.

Mercury - Extension Tab of Top of right cowl under hood.

Comet - Top of left front inner fender apron under hood.

Meteor - Left front inner fender apron under hood.

ASSEMBLY PLANT	CODE
Mahwah	E
Dearborn	F
Lorain	H
Los Angeles	J
Kansas City	K
San Jose	R
Metuchen	T
Wayne	W
Wixom	Y
St. Louis	Z
Pilot Plant	S

MERCURY	CODE
4-Dr. Sedan - C/P	52
4-Dr. Sedan -Custom-C/P	62
2-Dr. Sedan	51
2-Dr. Fastback Hardtop - Custom	66
"2-Dr. ""S-55"" Fastback Hardtop	68
2-Dr. Hardtop	53
2-Dr. Hardtop - Custom	63
"2-Dr. ""S-55"" Hardtop"	67
4-Dr. Hardtop	54
4-Dr. Hardtop - Custom	64
"4-Dr. ""S-55"" Hardtop"	60
2-Dr. Convertible	65
"2-Dr. ""S-55"" Convertible"	69
4-Dr. Colony Park Station Wagon - Custom (6-Ps.)	76
4-Dr. Colony Park Station Wagon - Custom (9-Ps.)	76

METEOR	CODE
4-Dr. Sedan	32
4-Dr. Sedan - Custom	42
2-Dr. Sedan	31
2-Dr. Sedan - Custom	41
2-Dr. Hardtop - Custo	43
"2-Dr. ""S-33"" Hardtop - Custom	47

4-Dr. Station Wagon - Custom (8 Ps.)	48
4-Door Station Wagon (6-Ps.	38
4-Dr. Station Wagon (8-Ps.)	38
4-Dr. Station Wagon - Country Cruiser (6 Ps.)	49
4-Dr. Station Wagon - Custom (6 Ps.)	48
4-Dr. Station Wagon - Country Cruiser (8 Ps.)	49

COMET	CODE
4-Dr. Sedan	2
4-Dr. Sedan - Custom	12
2-Dr. Station Wagon	21
2-Dr. Station Wagon - Custom	23
2-Dr. Sedan	1

75A	AA	26	11G	32-0551	1	5
BDY	CLR	TRM	DT	DSD	AX	TR

SERIAL NUMBER

| 3H54Y500551 |

2-Dr. Sedan - Custom	11
"2-Dr. ""S-22"" Sedan"	17
2-Dr. Hardtop	17
"2-Dr. ""S-22"" Hardtop"	19
4-Dr. Station Wagon	22
4-Dr. Station Wagon - Custom	24
4-Door Station Wagon-Villager	26
4-Door Station Wagon-Villager (Bucket Seat)	26
2-Door Convertible	15
"2-Door ""S-22"" Convertible	15

LINCOLN	CODE
Lincoln Continenta	82
4-Dr. Sedan	
Lincoln Continental	86
4-Dr. Convertible	

ENGINE	CODES

CODE	ENGINE TYPE
8 Cyl. - 390 C.I.D., 2-V Carb	Y
8 Cyl. - 390 C.I.D., 4-V Carb	Z
8 Cyl. - 390 C.I.D., 4-V Carb	P
Interceptor	
8 Cyl. - 390 C.I.D., 4-V Carb	9
(Low Comp.)	
8 Cyl. - 406 C.I.D., 4-V Carb	B
8 Cyl. - 406 C.I.D., 6-V Carb	G
8 Cyl. - 427 C.I.D., 4-V Carb	Q
8 Cyl. - 427 C.I.D., 8-V Carb	R
6 Cyl. - 170 C.I.D., 1-V Carb	U
6 Cyl. - 170 C.I.D., 1-V Carb	4
(Low Comp.)	
6 Cyl. - 200 C.I.D., 1-V Carb	T
8 Cyl. - 221 C.I.D., 2-4 Carb	L
8 Cyl. - 221 C.I.D., 2-V Carb	3
(Low Comp.)	
8 Cyl. - 260 C.I.D., 2-V Carb	F
8 Cyl. - 260 C.I.D., 2-V Carb	8
(Low Comp.)	
430 C.I.D. 8 Cyl. 4-V Carb	N
430 C.I.D. 8 Cyl. 4-V Carb	7
(Low Comp.)	
6 Cyl. - 144 C.I.D., 1-V Carb	S
6 Cyl. - 144 C.I.D., 1-V Carb	2
(Low Comp.)	

STYLE NUMBER

Body Style Code....................75A
Exterior Paint and Tone
Code(lower, upper)..................AA
Trim Code....................26
Day and Month of Year
Built Code....................116
District Code....................32
DSO Number....................0551
Axle Code....................1
Transmission Code....................5

PATENT PLATE

"The Warranty Plate is riveted to the left front door below the door lock. The Warranty Plate includes information relative to the type of engine, axle, transmission, trim (exterior and interior), and body style of the vehicle. It also includes the date "

"(day, month and year) and place of manufacture."

MERCURY	CODE
4-Dr. Sedan	54A
4-Dr. Sedan - Custom	54B
2-Dr. Sedan	62A
2-Dr. Fastback Hardtop - Custom	63B
"2-Dr. ""S-55" Fastback Hardtop	63C
2-Dr. Sedan Hardtop	65A
2-Dr. Sedan Hardtop - Custom	65B
"2-Dr. ""S-55" Hardtop	65C
4-Dr. Colony Park Station Wagon (6 Ps.)	71B
4-Dr. Colony Park Station Wagon (9 Ps.)	71D
4-Dr. Sedan Hardtop	75A
4-Dr. Sedan Hardtop - Custom	75B
"4-Dr. ""S-55" Hardtop	75C
2-Dr. Convertible	76A
"2-Dr. ""S-55" Convertible	76B

LINCOLN	CODE
4-Door Sedan	54A
4-Door Convertible	74A

COMET	CODE
4-Dr. Sedan	54A
4-Dr. Sedan - Custom	54B
2-Dr. Sedan	62A
2-Dr. Sedan - Custom	62B
"2-Dr. ""S-22"" Sedan"	62C
2-Dr. Hardtop	63B
"2-Dr. ""S-22" Hardtop	;63C
2-Dr. Convertible	76A
"2-Dr. ""S-22" Convertible	76B
2-Dr. Station Wagon	59A
2-Dr. Station Wagon - Custom	59B
4-Dr. Station Wagon	71A
4-Dr. Station Wagon - Custom	71B

4-Dr. Station Wagon -
Villager....................71C
4-Dr. Station Wagon - Villager
Bucket Seat....................71D

METEOR	CODE
4-Dr. Sedan	54A
4-Dr. Sedan - Custom	54B
2-Dr. Sedan	62A
2-Dr. Sedan - Custom	62B
2-Dr. Hardtop - Custom	65A
"2-Dr. ""S-33""Hardtop - Custom	65B
4-Dr. Station Wagon - Custom (8 Ps.)	71A
4-Dr. Station Wagon (6 Ps.)	71B
4-Dr. Station Wagon (8 Ps.)	71C
4-Dr. Station Wagon - Country Cruiser (6 Ps.)	71D
4-Dr. Station Wagon - Custom (6 Ps.)	71E
4-Dr. Station Wagon - Country Cruiser (8 Ps.)	71F

LINCOLN

"(A ""No Punch"" in the paint color space indicates Special Paint.)"

COLOR	CODE
Black Satin	A
Oxford Gray	C
Riviera Turquoise	D
Bermuda Blue	E
Silver Mink	G
Nocturne Blue	H
Polynesian Gold	I
Teaberr	L
Ermine White	M
Platinum	N
Inverness Green	O
Scotch Green	P
Spanish Red	Q
Premier Yellow	R
Highlander Green	S
Nassau Beige	T
Rose Metallic	W
Burgundy Frost	X
Autumn Frost	Z

MERCURY

"(A ""No Punch"" in Paint Code Space"
Designates Special Paint)

COLOR	CODE
Presidential Black	A
Peacock Turquois	B
Ocean Turquoise Metallic	D
Pacific Blue Metallic	E
Sea Blu	F
Carnival Red	J
Light Aqua	K
Blue Satin Metallic	H
Castilian Gold	I
Sultana White	M
Scotch Green	P
Sheffield Gray Metallic	Q

Jamaica Yellow	R
Champagne	T
Pink Frost	W
Black Cherry Metallic	X
Cascade Blue	Y
Desert Frost Metallic	Z

TRIM CODES

A two-digit number indicates the type of trim and trim color. If, due to unavailability or other difficulties in production, a particular trim set is not intended for service (minor deviation from intended trim), the warranty plate code will be followed w.

COMET

TRIM	CODE

Stripe Pattern Cloth and Vinyl

Med. Blue/Lt. Blue Met.	12
Med. Beige/Pearl Beige	14
Black/Red	15
Black /White	16
Med. Turquoise/Lt. Turquoise Met.	17

Metallic Rib Cloth and Vinyl

Blue/Lt. Blue Met.	42
Beige /Beige	44
Black/Red	45
Black/White	46
Turquoise/Lt. Turquoise Met.	47

Crush Vinyl and Crush Vinyl

Lt. Blue D/L/Med. Blue D/L	52
Lt. Beige D/L/Pearl Beige	54
Red	55
Black/Pearl Beige	56
Lt. Turquoise D/L/Med. Turquoise D/L	57
Lt. Gold D/L/Lt. Gold Pearl	58

Crush Vinyl and Vachette Vinyl

Lt. Blue Met./Med. Blue Met.	72
Pearl Beige/Lt. Beige Met.	74
White/Red	75
White/Black	76
Lt. TurquoiseMet./Med. Turquoise Met.	77
Lt. Gold Met./Pearl Gold Met.	78
Lt. Blue/Med. Blue	82
Pearl Beige/Lt. Beige	84
Red/Red	85
White Pearl/Black	86

METEOR

*Rib Crush Vinyl and Crush Vinyl

Med. Green/Med. Green	3
Med. Beige/Med. Beige	4
Red/Red	5

Hi-Sheen Body Cloth and Crush Grain Vinyl
Med. Blue/Lt. Blue Met............12

Med. Beige/Pearl Beige	14
Black/Red	15
Black/Black	16
Med. Turquoise/Lt. Turquoise Met.	17

Vachette Ribbed Vinyl and Crush Grain Vinyl

Black/Black	34
Red/Red	35
Lt. Beige Met./Pearl Beige	36

Kirby Pattern Body Cloth and Crush Grain Vinyl

Med. Blue/Lt. Blue Met.	42
Med. Beige/Pearl Beige	44
Black/Red	45
Black/Black	46
Med. Turquoise/Lt. Turquoise Met.	47

Crush Grain Vinyl

Med. Blue Met./Lt. Blue Met.	52
Lt. Beige Met./Pearl Beige	54
Red	55
Black	56
Med. Turquoise Met./ Lt. Turquoise Met.	57
Lt. Gold Met.	58

*Police and Taxi

MERCURY

TRIM	CODE

Block Pattern Cloth and Crush Vinyl

Med. Rose and Lt. Rose D/L	10
Med. Blue and Lt. Blue D/L	12
Med. Beige and Pearl	14
Black and Black	16
Med. Turquoise and Lt. Turquoise D/L	17
Med. Gold and Lt. Pearl Gold	18

Dot Pattern Cloth and Crush Vinyl

Med. Blue and Lt. Blue met.	22
Med. beige and Lt. Pearl Beige	24
Black and Black	26
Med. Turquoise and Lt. Turquoise Met.	27

Crush Grain Vinyl and Crush Grain Vinyl

Lt. Rose D/L and Med. Rose D/L	50
Lt. Blue and Dk. Blue D/L	52
Lt. Beige Pearl and Lt. Beige D/L	54
Red	55
Black	56
Lt. Turquoise D/L and Dk. Turquoise D/L	57
Lt. Gold D/L and Med. Gold D/L	58

Rib Crush Vinyl (Police and Taxi)

Med. Green	3
Med. Beige	4
Red	5

LINCOLN

TRIM COMBONATION   CODE

Trim	Code
Medium Silver Blue Broadcloth	30
Lt. Honey Beige Cloud Pattern Broadcloth adn Pearl Honey Beige Crinkle Leather	64
Black Cloud Pattern Broadcloth and Black Crinkle Leather	66
Lt. Turquoise Cloud Pattern Broadcloth and Lt. Turquoise-Diamond Luster Crinkle Leather	67
Lt. Silver Blue Star Pattern Broadcloth and Lt. Silver Blue Diamond Luster Crinkle Leather	70
Lt. Rose Beige Star Pattern Broadcloth and Lt. Rose Beige-Diamond Luster Crinkle Leather	71
Lt. Blue Star Pattern Broadcloth and Lt. Blue-Diamond Luster Crinkle Leathe	72
Black Star Pattern Broadcloth and White Crinkle Leather	76
Lt. Gold Star Pattern Broadcloth and Pearl Gold Crinkle Leather	78
Lt. Rose Beige-Diamond Luster Crinkle Leathe	81
Lt. Blue-Diamond Luster Crinkle Leather	82
Pearl Honey Beige Crinkle Leather	84
Red Crinkle Leather	85
Black Crinkle Leather	86
Lt. Turquoise-Diamond Luster Crinkle Leather	87
Pearl Gold Crinkle Leather	88
White and Black Crinkle Leather	96

VEHICLE DATE CODES

MONTH	CODE	*CODE
January	A	N
February	B	P
March	C	Q
April	D	R
May	E	S
June	F	T
July	G	U
August	H	V
September	J	W
October	K	X
November	L	Y
December	M	Z

*2 year code letters to be used if 1963 models exceed 12 months.

DSO AND DISTRICT CODES

Units built on a Domestic Special Order, Foreign Special Ordoer, or other special orders will have the complete order number in this space. Also to appear in this space. is the two-digit code number of the Distict which ordered the unit. If the unit is a regular production unit, only the District code number will appear.

DISTRICT	CODE
Boston	11
Philadelphia	12
New York	13
Washington	14
Atlanta	21
Dallas	22
Jacksonville	24
Memphi	25
Buffalo	31
Cincinnati	32
Cleveland	33
Detroit	34
Pittsburgh	35
Chicago	41
Kansas City	43
St. Loui	44
Twin Cities	45
Denver	51
Los Angeles	52
Oakland	53
Seattle	54
Ford of Canada	81
Home Office Reserve	84
Export	90-99

REAR AXLE   CODES

RATIO	REGULAR	LOCKING
3.00:1	1	A
3.10:1	2	B
3.20:1	3	C
3.25:1	4	D
3.50:1	5	E
3.80:1	7	G
3.89:1	8	H
4.00:1	9-Comet	I
4.11:1	9	I
2.89:1	1-Lincoln	
2.89:1		A-Lincoln

TRANSMISSION CODES

TRASMISSION TYPE	CODE
Standard (3 Speed) (3/S)	1
Overdrive (O/D)	2
Automatic (2 Speed) (2/S)	3
Dual Range Automatic (D/R)	4
Standard (4 Speed) (4/S)	5

ENGINE SPECIFICATIONS

ENGINE MODELS AND PISTON DISPLACEMENT - Cubic Inches

Engine	Displacement
I-6	144
I-6	170
I-6	200
V-8	221
Mileage Maker Six	223
260 V-8	260
390 Marauder	390
390 Marauder Super	390
390 Police Interceptor V-8	390
406 Hi-Perf V-8 (4-V)	406
406 Hi-Perf V-8 (6-V)	406
427 Marauder V-8 (4-V)	427
427 Marauder Super V-8 (8-V)	427
430 Lincoln	430

COMPRESSION RATIO

144 I-6	8.7:1
170 I-6	8.7:1
200 I-6	8.7:1
221 V-8	8.7:1
Mileage Maker Six	8.4:1
260 V-8	8.7:1
390 Marauder	8.9:1
390 Marauder Super	10.5:1
390 Police Interceptor V-8	10.5:1
406 Hi-Perf V-8 (4-V)	11.5:1
406 Hi-Perf V-8 (6-V)	11.5:1
427 Marauder V-8 (4-V)	11.5:1
427 Marauder Super V-8 (8-V)	11.5:1
430 Lincoln	10.0:1

BRAKE HORSEPOWER

144 I-6	85
170 I-6	101
200 I-6	116
221 V-8	145
Mileage Maker Six	138
260 V-8	164
390 Marauder	250
390 Marauder Super	300
390 Police Interceptor V-8	330
406 Hi-Perf V-8 (4-V)	385
406 Hi-Perf V-8 (6-V)	405
427 Marauder V-8 (4-V)	410
427 Marauder Super V-8 (8-V)	425
430 Lincoln	320

VEHICLE IDENTIFICATION NUMBER

VEHICLE WARANTY NUMBER

```
4H64Y500551
```

Lincoln - Die Stamped into RightFront Inner WhelhousePanel (may be covered by windshield washer bag).

Comet-VIN Die Stamped into Top of Left Front Inner Fender Apron under Hood.

Mercury-VIN Die Stamped into extension Tab of Top of Right Cowl under Hood.

EXAMPLE

1964 Model Year	4
Assembly Plant Code	H
Body Series Code	64
Engine Code	Y
Serial Identification Code	500551

ASSEMBLY PLANT CODES

Assembly Plant	Code
Mahwah	E
Dearborn	F
Lorain	H
Los Angeles	J
Kansas City	K
San Jose	R
Metuchen	T
Wayne	W
Wixom	Y
St. Louis	Z

BODY STYLE CODES - COMET

BODY SERIES	BODY SERIES CODE	SERIES CODE
4-Dr. Sedan - 202	54A	2
4-Dr. Sedan - 404	54B	12
4-Dr. Sedan - Caliente (Bucket Seat)	54C	22
4-Dr. Sedan - Caliente	54D	22
2-Dr. Sedan - 202	62A	1
2-Dr. Sedan - 404	62B	11
2-Dr. Sedan - 404 (Bucket Seat)	62C	11
2-Dr. Hardtop - Caliente (Bucket Seat)	63C	23
2-Dr. Hardtop - Caliente	63D	23
2-Dr. Hardtop - Cyclone (Bucket Seats)	63E	27

4-Dr. Station Wagon - 202	71A	32
4-Dr. Station Wagon - 404	71B	34
4-Dr. Station Wagon - 404 (Wood Rail)	71C	36
2-Dr. Convertible - Caliente (Bucket Seat)	76B	25
2-Dr. Convertible - Caliente	76D	25

BODY STYLE CODES - MERCURY

4-Dr. Sedan (Monterey)	54A	42
4-Dr. Sedan (Montclair)	54B	52
4-Dr. Sedan (Parklane)	54F	62
4-Dr. Hardtop-Fastback - Monterey	57A	48
4-Dr. Hardtop-Fastback - Parklane Marauder Bucket Seats	57C	68
4-Dr. Hardtop-Fastback - Montclair Marauder	57D	58
4-Dr. Hardtop-Fastback - Parklane	57F	68
2-Dr. Sedan - Monterey	62A	41
2-Dr. Hardtop-Fastback - Monterey	63A	47
2-Dr. Hardtop-Fastback - Parklane	63C	67
Marauder (Bucket Seat)		

2-Dr. Hardtop-Fastback - Montclair Marauder	63D	57
2-Dr. Hardtop-Fastback - Parklane Marauder	63F	67
2-Dr. Hardtop - Monterey	65A	43
2-Dr. Hardtop - Montclair	65B	53
2-Dr. Hardtop - Parklane (Bucket Seat)	65C	63
2-Dr. Hardtop - Parklane	65F	63
4-Dr. - Commuter Station Wagon (6 Ps)	71A	72
4-Dr. - Colony Park Station Wagon (6 Ps)	71B	76
4-Dr. - Commuter Statio Wagon (9 Ps)	71C	72
4-Dr. - Colony Park Station Wagon (9 Ps)	71D	76
4-Dr. Hardtop - Parklane	75F	64
2-Dr. Convertible - Monterey	76A	45
2-Dr. Convertible - Parklane (Bucket Seat)	76C	65
2-Dr. Convertible - Parklane	76F	65

SERIAL NUMBER 4H64Y 500551	OTHER PATENTS PENDING

BODY	COLOR	TRIM	DATE	DIST	DSO	TR	AX
75F	AA	16	11G	32	0551	1	5

ENGINE CODES

Engine Type	Code
6 Cyl. - 170 C.I.D., 1-V Carb.	U
6 Cyl. - 170 C.I.D., 1-V Carb. (Low Comp.)	4
6 Cyl. - 200 C.I.D., 1-V Carb.	T
8 Cyl. - 260 C.I.D., 2-V Carb.	F
8 Cyl. - 260 C.I.D., 2-V Carb Low Comp.	6
8 Cyl. - 289 C.I.D., 4-V Carb.	D
8 Cyl. - 289 C.I.D., 4-V HP Carb.	K
8 Cyl. - 390 C.I.D., 2-V Carb. (Regular)	Y
8 Cyl. - 390 C.I.D., 2-V Carb. (Special)	H
8 Cyl. - 390 C.I.D., 4-V Carb.	Z
8 Cyl. - 390 C.I.D., 4-V Carb.	P
8 Cyl. - 390 C.I.D., 4-V Carb. (Low Comp.)	9
8 Cyl. - 427 C.I.D., 4-V Carb.	Q
8 Cyl. - 427 C.I.D., 8-V Carb.	R
8 Cyl. - 430 C.I.D., 4-V Carb.	N
8 Cyl. - 430 C.I.D., 4-V Carb. (Low Comp.)	7

PATENT PLATE

The Warranty Plate is riveted to the left front door below the door lock. The Warranty Plate includes information relative to the type of engine, axle, transmission, trim (exterior and interior), and body style of the vehicle. It also includes the date (d"

BODY STYLE - LINCOLN

Body Style Codes	Body Code
4-Dr. Sedan	53A
4-Dr. Convertible	74A

BODY STYLE - MERCURY

Body Style Codes	Body Code
4-Dr. Sedan (Monterey. 54A	
4-Dr. Sedan (Montclair)	54B
4-Dr. Sedan (Parklane)	54F
4-Dr. Hardtop-Fastback - Monterey	57A
4-Dr. Hardtop- Fastback - Parklane Marauder (Bucket Seat)	57C
4-Dr. Hardtop-Fastback - Montclair Marauder	57D
4-Dr. Hardtop-Fastback - Parklane Marauder	57F
2-Dr. Sedan Monterey	62A
2-Dr. Hardtop-Fastback - Monterey	63A
2-Dr. Hardtop-Fastback - Parklane Marauder (Bucket Seat)	63C
2-Dr. Hardtop-Fastback - Montclair Marauder	63D
2-Dr. Hardtop-Fastback - Parklane Marauder	63F
2-Dr. Hardtop - Monterey	65A
2-Dr. Hardtop - Montclair	65B
2-Dr. Hardtop - Parklane (Bucket Seat)	65C
2-Dr. Hardtop - Parklan	65F
4-Dr. - Commuter Station Wagon (6 Passenger)	71A
4-Dr. - Colony Park Station Wagon (6 Ps)	71B
4-Dr. - Commuter Station Wagon (9 Ps)	71C
4-Dr. - Colony Park. Station Wagon (9 Ps)	71D
2-Dr. Hardtop - Parklan	75F
2-Dr. Convertible	76A
2-Dr. Convertible	76C
2-Dr. Convertible	76F

BODY STYLE CODES - COMET

2-Dr. Sedan - 202	54A
2-Dr. Sedan - 404	54B
2-Dr. Sedan - Claiente (Bucket Seat)	54C
4-Dr. Sedan - Caliente	54D
2-Dr. Sedan - 202	62A
2-Dr. Sedan - 404	62B
2-Dr. Sedan - 404 (Bucket Seat)	62C
2-Dr. Hardtop - Caliente (Bucket Seat)	63C
2-Dr. Hardtop - Caliente	63D
2 Dr. Hardtop - Cycloner	63E
4-Dr. Station Wagon - 202	71A
4-Dr. Station Wagon - 404	71B
4-Dr. Station Wagon - 404 (Wood Rail)	71C
2-Dr. Convertible - Caliente (Bucket Seat)	76B
2-Dr. Convertible - Caliente	76D

EXTERIOR PAINT CODES LINCOLN

"(A ""No Punch"" in the paint color"
space indicates special paint)

Color	Code
Black Satin	A
Princetone Gray	C
Silver Blue	E
Powder Blue	F
Buckskin	G
Nocturne Blue	H
Fiesta Red	J
Arctic White	M
Platinum	N
Silver Green	O
Burnish Bronz	P
Huron Blue	Q
Encino Yellow	R
Highlander Green	S
Silver Sand	Z

EXTERIOR PAINT CODES MERCURY

Color	Code
Onyx	A
Peacock	B
Silver Turquoise	D
Pacific Blue	F
Palomino	G
Aztec Gold	I
Carnival Red	J
Anniversary Silver	K
Bittersweet	L
Polar White	M
Pecan Frost	P
Yellow Mist	R
Fawn	T
Maize	V
Pink Frost	W
Burgundy	X
Glacier Blue	Y
Platinum Beige	Z

TRIM CODES - MERCURY

Deviation trim sets will use existing trim codes plus a suffix. A trim code with a numeral suffix is not serviced, while a trim code with an alphabetical suffix is serviced."

Trim	Code
Discus Fabric and Crush Vinyl (Bench-Pleated)	
Med. Silver Blue and Lt. Silver Blue Met.	11
Med. Blue and Lt. Blue Met.	12
Med. Beige and Lt. Beige Met.	14
Black and Black	16
Cord Fabric and Crush Vinyl (Bench-Plain)	
Med. Blue and Lt. Blue Met.	22
Med. beige and Lt. Beige Met.	24
Black and Black	26
Stitch Rib Vinyl and Crush Vinyl (Crinkle) (Bench-Plain)	
Med. Blue Met. and Lt. Blue Met.	32
Red and Re	35
Black and Black	36
Med. Palomino and Med. Palomino (*)	39
Ostrich Vinyl and Crush Vinyl (Crinkle) (Bucket-Biscuit)	
Med. Blue Met. and Lt. Blue D/L*	52
Red and Red	55
Black and Black	56
Med. Palomino and Med. Palomino	59
White Pearl and White Pearl	82
(W/Red) White and White Pearl	85
(W/Black) White Pearl and White Pearl	86
(W/Turq.) White Pearl and White Pearl	87
(W/Palomino) White Pearl and White Pearl	89
Caspian Fabric and Crush Vinyl (Bench-Biscuit)	
Med. Silver Blue and Lt. Silver Blue D/L*	61
Med. Blue and Lt. Blue D/L*	62
Med. Beige and Lt. Beige D/L*	64
Black and Black	66
Med. Turquoise and Med. Turquoise Met.	67
Crush Vinyl (Crinkle) (Bench-Pleated)	
Med. and Lt. Blue Met.	72
Red	75
Black	76
Medium Palomino	79
Ostrich Vinyl and Crush Vinyl (*Crinkle) (Bench-Biscuit)	
Lt. Blue Met. and Med. Blue Met.	92
Red and Re	95
Black and Black	96
Lt. Turquoise Met. and Med. Turquoise Met.	97
Med. Palomino and Med. Palomino (*	99

*C/L - Diamond Lustre

DATE CODES

Month	Code	*Code
January	A	N
February	B	P
March	C	Q
April	D	R
May	E	S
June	F	T
July	G	U
August	H	V
September	J	W
October	K	X
November	L	Y
December	M	Z

*2 Year Code Letters to be Used if 1964 Models Exceed 12 Months.

DSO NUMBERS

Domestic Special Orders, Foreign Special orders, and Pre-Approved"

Special Orders have the complete order number recorded in this space. Also to appear in this space is the two-digit code number of the

"District which ordered the unit. If the unit is regular production, only the District code number appears."

DISTRICT CODE

District	Code
Boston	11
New York	15
Philadelphia	16
Washington	17
Atlanta	21
Dalllas	22
Jacksonville	23
Memphis	26
Buffalo	31
Cincinnati	32
Cleveland	33
Detroit	34
Chicago	41
St. Louis	42
Denver	51
Los Angeles	52
Oakland	53
Seattle	54
Ford of Canada	81
Home Office Reserve	84
Export	90-99

TRIM CODES - LINCOLN

Deviation trim sets will use existing trim codes plus 2 suffix. A Trim code with a numeral suffix is not serviced, while a trim code with an alphabetical suffix is serviced.

Trim	Code
Motif Cloth and Crinkle Leather	
(Bench-Biscuit)	
Rose Beige and Rose Beige	20
Blue and Blue	22
Turquoise and Turquoise	27
(Bench-Pleated)	
Rose Beige and Lt. Rose Beige D/	70
Silver Blue and Lt. Silver Blue Met.	71

MERCURY
REAR AXLE CODES

Ratio	Locking	Non-Locking
3.00 : 1	A	1
3.20 : 1	C	3
3.25 : 1	D	4
3.50 : 1	E	5
2.80 : 1	F	6
3.89 : 1	H	8
3.10 : 1	B	2
3.80 : 1	G	7
4.00 : 1 Comet.I		9
4.11 : 1	I	9

LINCOLN
REAR AXLE CODES

Ratio	Locking	Non-Locking
2.89 : 1	A	1
3.11 : 1	C	3

TRANSMISSION CODES

ManualL (3-Speed)(3/S)	1
Overdrive (3-Speed) O/D(O/D)	2
Automatic (2-Speed)(2/S)	3
Dual Range Automatic(D/R)	4
Manual(4-Speed)(4/S)	5
C4 Duyal Range Automatice(3-Speed)(Dir) (XP.)	6

ENGINE MODELS AND PISTON DISPLACEMENT - Cubic Inches

390 V-8 and 290 Marauder V-8 (2-V)	390
390 V-8 Marauder Super(4-V)	390
390 Marauder Interceptor V-8 (4-V)	390
427 MaruaderV-8 (4-V)	427
427Maruader SuperV-8(8-V)	427
430 V-8	430
Comet I-6	170
Cyclone 2-V V-8	260
Cyclone V-8 (4-V)	289
V-8 (4-V)	289

COMPRESSION RATIO

Comet 170 I-6	8.7:1
Comet 200 I-6	8.7:1
Cyclone Super 289 V-8 (4-V)	9.0:1
Cyclone Super 289 V-8 (4-V0 HP	10.5:1
Cyclone 260 V-8 (2-V)	8.8:1
390 V-8 and 390 Maruader V-8 (2-V)	9.4:1
390 Maruader Super V-8 (4-V)	10.1:1
390 Maruader Interceptor V-8 (4-V)	10.1:1
427 Maruader V-8 (4-V)	11.5:1
427 MaruaderV-8 (8-V)	11.2:1
430 V-8	10.0:1

BRAKE HORSEPOWER

Comet 170I-6	101
Comet 200 I-6	116
Cyclone 260 V-8 (2.V)	164
Cyclone Super 289 V-8 (2-V)	210
Cyclone Super 289 V-8 (4-V) HP	271
390 V-8 (2-V)	250
390 Maruader V-8 (2-V)	266
390Marauder V-8 (4-V)	300
390 Marauder Interceptor V-8 (4-V)	330
427 Marauder Super V-8 (4-V)	410
427 Marauder Super V-8 (8-V)	425
430 V-8	320

VEHICLE IDENTIFICATION NUMBER

VEHICLE WARANTY NUMBER

```
5 H 6 2 Z 5 0 0 5 5 1
```

Lincoln-Die Stamped into Right Front Inner Wheelhouse Panel (may be covered by windshield washer bag).

Comet-VIN Die Stamped into Top of left front inner fender apron under hood.

Mercury-VIN Die stamped into extension Tab of Top of Right Cowl under Hood.

EXAMPLE

1964 Model Year	5
Assembly Plant Code	H
Body Series Code	62
Engine Code	Z
Serial Identification Code	500551

ASSEMBLY PLANT CODES

Assembly Plant	Code	Assembly Plant	Code
Atlanta	A	Norfolk	N
Dallas	D	Twin Cities	P
Mahwah	E	San Jose	R
Dearborn	F	Pilot Plant	S
Chicago	G	Metuchen	T
Lorain	H	Louisville	U
Los Angeles	J	Wayne	W
Kansas City	K	Wixom	Y
Michigan Truck	L	St. Louis	Z

SERIAL	NUMBER				
5H62Z 500551					
BODY COLOR TRIM	DATE	DIST	AXLE	TRANS	
50F AA 36	11G	32	1	4	

BODY SERIAL AND STYLE CODES

The two-digit numeral which follows the assembly plant code identifies the series. This two-digit number is used in conjunction with the Body Style Code, in the Vehicle Data, which consists of a two-digit number with a letter suffix. The following chart I

LINCOLN CONTINENTAL

Body Type	Serial Code	Style Code
4-Dr. Sedan		53A
4-Dr. Convertible	86	74A

COMET 202

Body Type	Serial Code	Style Code
4-Dr. Sedan*	2	54A
2-Dr. Sedan*	1	62A
4-Dr. Wagon	32	71A

COMET 404

Body Type	Serial Code	Style Code
4-Dr. Sedan	12	54B
2-Dr. Sedan	11	62B
2-Dr. Sedan**	11	62C
4-Dr. Wagon*	34	71B
4-Dr. (Villager) Wagon*	36	71C

COMET CALIENTE

Body Type	Serial Code	Style Code
4-Dr. Sedan**	22	54
4-Dr. Sedan*	22	54D
2-Dr. Hardto (Fastback)	23	63C
2-Dr. Hardtop* (Fastback)	23	63D
2-Dr. Convertible**	25	76B
2-Dr. Convertible*	25	76D

CYCLONE

Body Type	Serial Code	Style Code
2-Dr. Hardtop** (Fastback)	23	63E

*Bench Seat

MERCURY MONTEREY

Body Type	Serial Code	Style Code
4-Dr. Sedan**	42	50A
2-Dr. Sedan	43	62A
4-Dr. Sedan	44	54A
2-Dr. Convertible	45	76A
2-Dr. Hardtop	47	63A
4-Dr. Hardtop	48	57A
2-Dr. Convertible*	45	76G
2-Dr. H/T Fastback	47	63G

MERCURY MONTCLLAIR

Body Type	Serial Code	Stye Code
4-Dr. Sedan**	52	50B
2-Dr. Hardtop	57	63B
4-Dr. Hardtop	58	57B

MERCURY PARLANE

Body Type	Serial Code	Style Code
4-Dr. Sedan**	62	50F
2-Dr. Convertible	65	76F
2-Dr. Convertible*	65	76C
2-Dr. H/T Fastback	67	63F
2-Dr. H/T Fastback*	67	63C
4-Dr. Hardtop	68	57F

MERCURY COMMUTER

Body Type	Serial Code	Style Code
4-Dr. 6 Ps. Station Wagon	72	71B
4-Dr. 9 Ps. Station Wagon	72	71C

MERCURY COLONYH PARK

Body Type	Serial Code	Style Code
4-Dr. 6 Passenger Station Wagon	76	71A
4-Door 9 Ps. Station Wagon	76	71E

**Reverse Back Window
*Bucket Seats

STYLE NUMBER

Body Style Code......................50F
Exterior Paint and Tone
Code(lower, upper)...................AA
Trim Code...........................36
Day and Month of YearBuilt
Code................................116
District Code.......................32
Transmission Code...................1
Axle Code...........................4

VEHICLE DATA PLATE

The vehicle data appears in a line across the top of the warranty plate. The first two letters and a number identify the Body Style. The following one or two letters identify the Exterior Paint Color. The next code consisting of two numbers, or a letter and a number, identifies the Interior Trim. The Date Code showing the date the car was manufactured, follows the Trim Code and consists of two numbers and a letter. The next code gives the district in which the car was ordered and consists of two numbers. The next to the last code is the Axle Ratio Code and is designated by a number for a conventional axle or a letter for an Equa-Lock axle. The last code in the vehicle data is the Transmission Code and consists of one number.

ENGINE CODES

Engine	Code
Cyl. 390 Cu. In. (2-V Spec.)	H
Cyl. 427 Cu. In. (4-V OH Cam)	L
Cyl. 427 Cu. In. (8-V OH Cam)	M
Cyl. 390 Cu. In. (4-V Spec.)	P
Cyl. 427 Cu. In. (8-V H.P.)	R
Cyl. 390 Cu. In. (2-V)	Y
Cyl. 390 Cu. In. (4-V)	Z
Cyl. *240 Cu. In. (1-V)	5
Cyl. *390 Cu. In. (4-V)	9
cyl. 289 Cu. In. (4-V Prem.)	A
Cyl. 289 Cu. In. (2-V)	C
Cyl. 289 Cu. In. (4-V Hi-Perf.)	K
Cyl. 200 Cu. In. (1-V)	T
Cyl. *200 Cu. In. (1-V)	2
Cyl. *289 Cu. In. (2-V)	3
-Cyl. 430 Cu. In. 4-V Carb.	N
-Cyl. * 430 Cu. In. 4-V Carb.	7

Low Compression

CONSECUTIVE UNIT NUMBER

The assembly plant, with each model year, begins with consecutive unit number 400001 and continues on for each car built. 50001 = Mercury/ Comet.

EXTERIOR PAINT

LINCOLN

Color	Code
Black	A
Dk. Turq. Met.	B
Med. Ivy Gold Met.	C
Med. Silver Mink Met.	E
Lt. Blue	F
Lt. Ivy Gold	G
Dk. Blue Met.	H
Red	J
Lilac Mist Met.	L
White	M
Platinum	N
Palomino Met.	P
Med. Blue Met.	Q
Dk. Ivy Green Met.	R
Dk. Grey Met.	S
Lt. Beige	T
Med. Turq. Met.	U
Maroon Met.	X
Med. Beige Met.	Z
Lt. Aqua	4

COMET / MERCURY

Color	Code

A single letter code designates a solid body color and two letters denote a two-tone—the first letter, the lower color and the second letter, the lower color and the second letter, the upper color."

Color	Code
Black	A
Med. Ivy Gold Met.	C
Med. Turq. Met.	D
Dk. Blue Met.	H
Lt. Beige Met.	I
Red	J
Med. Gray Met.	K
White	M
Lt. Peacock	O
Palomino Met.	P
Dk. Ivy Green Met.	R
Yellow	V
Maroon Met.	X
Med. Blue Met.	Y
Dk. Turq. Met.	5
Med. Ivy Gold Met.	F
Lt. Beige	T

INTERIOR TRIM CODES

Deviation trim sets will use existing

trim codes plus 2 suffix. A trim code

"with a numeral suffix is not serviced,"
while a trim code with an alphabetical suffix is serviced.

COMET

Trim	Code
Beige Vinyl	4
Med. Blue and Lt. Blue Met. Fabric and Vinyl	12
Red Fabric and Vinyl	15
Black Fabric and Vinyl	16
Med. Turq. and Lt. Turq. Met. Fabric and Vinyl	17
Palomino and Med. Palomino Fabric and Vinyl	19
Med. and Lt. Blue Met. Vinyl (Comet), Fabric and Vinyl (Except Comet)	22
Red Vinyl (Comet), Fabric and Vinyl (Except Comet)	25
Black Vinyl	26
Med. and Lt. Turquoise Met. Vinyl (Comet), Fabric and Vinyl (Except Comet)	27
Ivy Gold and Lt. Ivy Gold D/L Fabric and Vinyl	28
Palomino Vinyl (Comet), Fabric and Vinyl (Except Comet)	29
Med. Blue and Lt. Blue Met. Fabric and Vinyl (Comet) Vinyl (Except Comet)	32
Red Fabric and Vinyl (Comet) Vinyl (Except Comet)	35
Black Fabric and Vinyl (Comet) Vinyl (Except Comet)	36
Med. Turquoise and Lt. Turq. Met. Fabric and Vinyl (Comet) Vinyl (Except Comet)	37
Ivy Gold Fabric and Vinyl (Comet) Vinyl (Except Comet)	38
Palomino and Med. Palomino Fabric and Vinyl (Comet) Vinyl (Except Comet)	39
White and Blue Vinyl	42
White and Red Vinyl	45
White and Black Vinyl	46
White and Ivy Gold Vinyl	48
Med. Palomino Vinyl	49
Med. Blue and Lt. Blue Met. Fabric and Vinyl (Comet), Vinyl (Except Comet)	52
Red Fabric and Vinyl (Comet), Vinyl (Except Comet)	55
Black Fabric and Vinyl (Comet), Vinyl (Except Comet)	56
Palomino and Med. Palomino Fabric and Vinyl (Comet), Vinyl (Except Comet)	59
White Pearl (W/Red) Fabric and Vinyl	F2
White Pearl (W/Black) Fabric and Vinyl	F5

Trim Schems	Code
White Pearl (W/Turquoise) Fabric and Vinyl	F6
White Pearl (W/Gold) Fabric and Vinyl	F8
White Pearl (W/Palomino) Fabric and Vinyl	F9
Lt. Blue Met. Vinyl	62
Red Vinyl	65
Black Vinyl	66
Turquoise Vinyl	67
Ivy Gold Met. and D/L Vinyl	68
Med. Palomino Vinyl	69
White Pearl (W/Blue) Vinyl	G2
White Pearl (W/Red) Vinyl	G5
White Pearl (W/Black) Vinyl	G6
White Pearl (W/Turquoise) Vinyl	G7
White Pearl (W/Gold) Vinyl	G8
White Pearl (W/Palomino) Vinyl	G9
Lt. Blue Met. Vinyl	72
Red Vinyl	75
Black Vinyl	76
Lt. Turq. Met. Vinyl	77
Ivy Gold D/L Vinyl	78
Med. Palomino Vinyl	79
White (W/Blue) Vinyl	H2
White (W/Red) Vinyl	H5
White (W/Black) Vinyl	H6
White (W/Turquoise) Vinyl	H7
White (W/Gold) Vinyl	H8
White (W/Palomino) Vinyl	H9
Lt. and Med. Blue Met. Vinyl	82
Red Vinyl	85
Black Vinyl	86
Lt. Turq. Met. Vinyl	87
Lt. Ivy Gold Met. Vinyl	88
Med. Palomino Vinyl	89
Blue Vinyl	92
Red Vinyl	95
Black Vinyl (Except Fairlane) Fabric and Vinyl (Fairlane)	96
Palomino Vinyl (Except Fairlane) Fabric and Vinyl (Fairlane)	99

MERCURY

Trim	Code
Green Vinyl	3
Beige Vinyl	4
Blue and Lt. Blue Met. Fabric & Vinyl	12
Red Fabric & Vinyl	15
Black Fabric & Vinyl	16
Turquoise and Lt. Turq. Met. Fabric & Vinyl	17
Palomino and Med. Palomino Fabric & Vinyl	19
White Pearl (W/Black) Vinyl	D6
Lt. Blue Met. Vinyl	22
Red Vinyl	25
Black Vinyl	26
Med. Palomino Vinyl	29
Blue and Blue Met. Vinyl	32
Burgundy Vinyl	33
Red Vinyl	35
Black Vinyl	36
Turquoise and Tur. Met. Vinyl	37

Trim Schemes	Code
Itvy Gold and Lt. Ivy Gold Vinyl	38
Palomino and Med. Palomino Vinyl	39
White Pearl (W/Blue) Vinyl	E2
White Pearl (W/Burgundy) Vinyl	E3
White Pearl (W/Red) Vinyl	E5
White Pearl (W/Black) Vinyl	E6
White Pearl (W/Turq.) Vinyl	E7
White Pearl (W/Ivy Gold) Vinyl	E8
White Pearl (W/Palomino) Vinyl	E9
Med. Blue Met. Vinyl	42
Red Vinyl	45
Black Vinyl	46
Turquoise Vinyl	47
Lt. Ivy Gold D/L Vinyl	48
Med. Palomino Vinyl	49
Blue and Blue Met. Fabric & Vinyl	52
Red Fabric & Vinyl	55
Black Fabric & Vinyl	56
Turquoise and Turq. Met. Fabric & Vinyl	57
Ivy Gold Fabric & Vinyl	58
Palomino and Med. Palomino Fabric & Vinyl	59
White (W/Black) Vinyl	F6
Blue Met. and Lt. Blue Met. Vinyl	62
Red Vinyl	65
Black Vinyl	66
Med. Turq. and Lt. Turq. Vinyl	67
Lt. Ivy Gold Vinyl	68
Med. Palomino Vinyl	69
White Pearl (W/Blue) Vinyl	G2
White Pearl (W/Blue) with Headrest Vinyl	L2
White Pearl (W/Burgundy)	G3
White Pearl (W/Turq.) with Headrest Vinyl	L7
White Pearl (W/Ivy Gold) Vinyl	G8
White Pearl (W/Ivy Gold) with Headrest Vinyl	L8
White Pearl (W/Burgundy) with Headrest Vinyl	L3
White Pearl (W/Red) Vinyl	G5
White Pearl (W/Red) with Headrest Vinyl	L5
White Pearl (W/Black) Vinyl	G6
White Pearl (W/Black) with Headrest Vinyl	L6
White Pearl (W/Turq.) Vinyl	G7
White Pearl (W/Palomino) Vinyl	G9
White Pearl (W/Palomino) with Headrest Vinyl	L9
Med. Blue Met. Vinyl	72
Blue with Headrest Vinyl	K2
Red Vinyl	75
Red with Headrest Vinyl	K5
Black Vinyl	76
Black with Headrest Vinyl	K6
Turquoise Vinyl	77
Turquoise with Headrest Vinyl	K7
Lt. Ivy Gold D/L Vinyl	78

Trim Schemes	Code
vy Gold with Headrest Vinyl	K8
Med. Palmino Vinyl	79
Med. Palomino with Headrest Vinyl	K9
White Pearl (W/Black) Vinyl	M6
Lt. Blue Met. Vinyl	82
Red Vinyl	85
Black Vinyl	86
Turquoise Vinyl	87
Black Vinyl	88
Turquoise Vinyl	87
Med. Palomino Vinyl	89
Lt. Blue Met. Vinyl (Mercury), Fabric & Vinyl (Ford)	92
Burgundy Fabric & Vinyl	93
Red Vinyl	95
Black Vinyl (Mercury) Fabric and Vinyl (Ford)	96
Turquoise Fabric & Vinyl	97
Med. Palomino Vinyl (Mercury), Fabric & Vinyl (Ford)	99
Palomino Fabric & Vinyl	A9
Palomino with Headrest Fabric & Vinyl	P9
Burgundy Leather	B3
Med. Palomino Leather	B9
Burgundy Leather	C3
Med. Palomino Leather	C9
Red Vinyl	Y5
Palomino Vinyl	Y9
Black Vinyl	Z6
Palomino Vinyl	Z9

LINCOLN

Trim	Code
White Pearl Leather with Blue Complements	12
White Pearl Leather with Beige Complements	14
White Pearl Leather with Red Complements	15
White Pearl Leather with Black Complements	16
White Pearl Leather with Ivy Gold Complements	18
Green Leather	99
Silver Mink Cloth	3
Blue and Lt. Blue Low Met. Cloth and Leather	42
Beige and Pastel Beige Pearl Cloth and Leather	44
Black and Black Cloth and Leather	46
White Leather with Black Complements	26
Burgundy Leather	50
Lt. Silver Mink Low Met. Leather	51
Lt. Blue Low Met. Leather	52
Pastel Beige Pearl Leather	54
Red Leather	55
Black Leather	56
Lt. Aqua Low Met. Leather	57
Lt. Ivy Gold Low Met. Leather	58
Med. Palomino Leather Print	59
Silver Mink Cloth and Lt. Silver Mink Low Met. Leather	61
Blue Cloth and Lt. Blue	62

Trim Schemes

Trim Schemes	Code
Black Cloth and Black Leather	66
Aqua Cloth and Lt. Aqua Low Met. Leather	67
Ivy Gold Cloth and Lt. Ivy Gold Low Met. Leather	68
Silver Mink Cloth and Lt. Silver Mink Low Met. Leather	71
Blue Cloth and Lt. Blue Low Met. Leather	72
Black Cloth and Black & White Pearl Leather	73
Beige Cloth and Pearl Beige Leather	74
Aqua Cloth and Lt. Aqua Low Met. Leather	77
Ivy Gold Cloth and Lt. Ivy Gold Low Met. Leather	78
Burgundy Leather	80
Lt. Silver Mink Low Met. Leather	81
Lt. Blue Low Met. Leather	82
White Pearl & Black Leather	83
Pastel Beige Pearl Leather	84
Red Leather	85
Black Leather	86
Lt. Aqua Low Met. Leather	87
Lt. Ivy Gold Low Met. Leather	88
Med. Palomino Leather Print Leather	89

DATE CODES

A number signifying the date precedes the month code letter. A second-year code letter will be used if the model exceeds 12 months.

Month	1 st Yr.	2nd Yr.
January	A	N
February	B	P
March	C	Q
April	D	R
May	E	S
June	F	T
July	G	U
August	H	V
September	J	W
October	K	X
November	L	Y
December	M	Z

DISTRICT CODES (DSO)

Units built on a Domestic Special Order, Foreign Special Order, or other special orders will have the complete order number in this space. Also to appear in this space is the two-digit code number of the District which ordered the unit. If the unit is a regular production unit, only the District code number will appear.

COMET

District	Code
Boston	11
Phildelphia	16

District	Code
New York	15
Washington	14
Atlanta	21
Dallas	22
Jacksonville	23
Memphis	26
Buffalo	31
Cincinnati	32
Cleveland	33
Detroit	34
Chicago	41
St. Louis	42
Twin Cities	45
Denver	51
Los Angeles	52
Oakland	53
Seattle	54
Ford of Canada	81
Home Office Reserve	84
Export	90-99

LINCOLN

District	Code
Boston	11
Philadelphia	12
New York	13
Washington	14
Atlanta	21
Dallas	22
Jacksonville	24
Memphis	25
Buffalo	31
Cincinnati	32
Cleveland	33
Detroit	34
Chicago	41
St. Louis	44
Twin Cities	45
Denver	51
Los Angeles	52
Oakland	53
Seattle	54
Ford of Canada	81
Home Office Reserve	84
Export	90-99

MERCURY

District	Code
Boston	11
New York	15
Philadelphia	16
Washington	17
Atlanta	21
Dallas	22
Jacksonville	23
Memphis	26
Buffalo	31
Cincinnati	32
Cleveland	33
Detroit	34
Chicago	41
St. Louis	42
Denver	51
Los Angeles	52
Oakland	53
Seattle	54

REAR AXLE RATIO CODES

A number designates a conventional axle, while a letter designates an Equa-Lock differential.

Ratio	Code
3.00:1	1
3.20:1	3
3.25:1	4
3.50:1	5
2.80:1	6
2.89:1	2
2.89:1	1
3.11:1	3
3.89:1	8
4.11:1	9
3.00:1	A
3.20:1	C
2.83:1	B
2.89:1	A
3.11:1	C
3.25:1	D
3.50:1	E
2.80:1	F
3.89:1	H
4.11:1	I

TRANSMISSION CODES

Type	Code
3-Speed Manual-Shift	1
Twin-Range Turbo-Drive	4
4-Speed Manual-Shift	5
C-4 Automatic Dua Range	6

ENGINE MODELS AND PISTON DISPLACEMENT - Cubic Inches

260 V-8	260
289 V-8 (2-V)& (4-V)	289
390 V-8 (2-V and 4-V)	390
427 Hi-Perf V-8 (8-V)	427
430 V-8 (4-V)	430

COMPRESSION RATIO

200 Six	9.2:1
289 V-8 (2-V)	9.3:1
289 V-8 (4-V)	10.0:1
289 V-8 Hi-Perf	10.5:1
390 V-8 (2-V) Monterey and Montclair	9.4:1
390 V-8 (4-V)	10.1:1
390 Police Interceptor V-8 (4-V)	10.1:1
427 Hi-Perf V-8 (8-V)	11.1:1
430 V-8 (4-V)	10.1:1

BRAKE HORSEPOWER

200 Six	120
289 V-8 (2-V)	200
289 V-8 (4-V)	225
289 V-8 Hi-Perf	271
352 V-8 (2-V) Monterey	250
390 V-8 (2-V) Montclair	266
390 V-8 (4-V)	300
390 Police Interceptor V-8 (4-V)	330
427 Hi-Perf V-8 (8-V)	425
430 V-8 (4-V)	320

VEHICLE IDENTIFICATION NUMBER

VEHICLE WARANTY NUMBER

6 H 6 2 Z 5 0 0 5 5 1

Lincoln-VIN Die stamped into Right Front Inner Fender Panel above UPper Suspension Arm Opening Under Hood.

Mercury-VIN Die Stamped into extension Tab of Top of Cowl under hood.

Comet-VIN Die stamped into top surface of Inner Fender Panel and Radiator Support at L/H side of Car under Hood.

EXAMPLE

1964 Model Year	6
Assembly Plant Code	H
Body Series Code	62
Engine Code	Z
Serial Identification	500551

ASSEMBLY PLANT CODES

Assembly Plant	Code Letter
Atlanta	A
Oakville Passenger	B
Ontario Truck	C
Dallas	D
Mahwah	E
Chicago	G
Lorain	H
Los Angeles	J
Kansas City	K

Assembly Plant Letter	Code
Michigan Truck	L
Norfolk	N
Twin Cities	P
San Jose	R
Pilot Plant	S
Metuchen	T
Louisville	U
Wayne	W
Wixom	Y
St. Louis	Z

SERIAL NUMBER
6H62Z 500551

BODY	COLO	TRIM	DATE	DIIST	AXLE	TRANS
50F	AA	26	11G	32	1	4

BODY SERIAL AND STYLE CODES

The two-digit numeral which follows the assembly plant code identifies the body series. This two-digit number is used in conjunction with the Body Style Code, in the Vehicle Data, wich consists of a two-digit number with a letter suffix. The following chart lists the Body Serial Codes, Body Style Codes and the model.

LINCOLN CONTINENTAL

Body Type	SerialCode	Style Code
4-Door Sedan	82	53A
2-Door Hardtop	89	65A
4-Door Convertible	86	74A

COMET 202

Body Type	SerialCode	Style Code
4-Door Sedan*	2	54A
2-Door Sedan*	1	62A
4-Door Wagon*	6	71A

CAPRI

Body Type	SerialCode	Style Code
4-Door Sedan*	12	54B
2-Door Hardtop*	13	63B

COMET CALIENTE

Body Type	Code Serial	Code Style
4-Door (Villager) Wagon*	16	71C
4-Door Sedan*	22	54D
2-Door Hardtop**	23	63C
2-Door Hardtop*	23	63D
2-Door Convertible**	25	76E
2-Door Convertible*	25	76D

CYCLONE

Body Type	Code Serial	Code Style
2-Door Hardtop**	27	63
E2-Door Hardtop** (GT)	27	63H
2-Door Convertible	29	76C
2-Door Convertible** (GT)	29	76H

*Bench Seat
**Bucket Seat

MERCURY MONTEREY

Body Type	Code Serial	Code Style
4-Door Sedan**	42	50A
2-Door Sedan	43	62A
4-Door Sedan	44	54A
4-Door H/T Fastback	48	57A
2-Door Convertible*	45	76C
2-Door H/T Fastback*	47	63C

MERCURY MONTCLAIR

Body Type	Code Serial	Code Style
4-Door Sedan**	52	50B
4-Door Seda	54	54
2-Door H/T Fastbacr	57	63B
4-Door H/T Fastback	58	57B

ENGINE CODES

Engine	Code
8 Cyl. 289 Cu. In. (2-V)	C
8 Cyl. 390 Cu. In. (2-V, Special)	H
8 Cyl. 410 Cu. In. (4-V)	M
8 Cyl. 428 Cu. In. (4-V, Police)	P
8 Cyl. 428 Cu. In. (4-V)	Q
8 Cyl. 427 Cu. In. (8-V, Hi-Perf)	R
8 Cyl. 390 Cu. In. (2-V)	Y
8 Cyl. 289 Cu. In. (2-V)*	3
8 Cyl. 428 Cu. In. (4-V)*	8
6 Cyl. 200 Cu. In. (1-V)	T
6 Cyl. *200 Cu. In. (1-V)	2
8 Cyl. 390 Cu. In. (4-V) GT	S
8 Cyl. 462 Cu. In. (4-V)	G

*Low Compression

EXTERIOR PAINT

COLOR CODES

"A single letter code designates a solid body color and two letters denote two-tone—the first letter, the lower color and the second letter, the upper color."

LINCOLN

Color	Code
Black	A
Lt. Beige Met.	B
Med. Silver Mink Met.	E
Lt. Blue	F
Lt. Beige	H
Dk. Blue Met.	K
Ivy Yellow	L
White	M
Platinum	N
Med. Palomino Met.	P
Med. Blue Met.	Q
Dk. Green Met.	R
Dk. Gray Met.	S
Red	T
Med. Turquoise Met.	U
Emberglo Met.	V
Maroon Met.	X
Med. Sage Gold Met.	Z
Rose Met.	1
Dk. Turquoise Met.	2

COMET

Color	Code
Black	A
Lt. Blue	F
Lt. Beige	H
Dk. Blue Met.	K
White	M
Med. Palomino Met.	P
Dk. Green Met.	R
Red	T
Med. Turquoise Met.	U
Emberglo Met.	V
Maroon Met.	X
Lt. Blue Met.	Y
Med. Sage Gold Met.	Z
Med. Silver Met.	4
Red	5
Yellow	8

MERCURY

Color	Code
Black	A
Dk. Executive Gray Met.	C
Lt. Blue	F
Lt. Beige	H
Dk. Blue Met.	K
White	M
Med. Palomino Met.	P
Dk. Green Met.	R
Red	T
Med. Turquoise Met.	U
Emberglo Met.	V
Maroon Met.	X
Lt. Blue Met.	Y
Med. Sage Gold Met.	Z
Dk. Turquoise Met.	2
Med. Silver Met.	4
Yellow	8

MERCURY S-55

2-Door Covnertible	45	76A
2-Door H/T Fastback	47	63A

MERCURY PARKLANE

4-Door Sedan**	62	50F
2-Door Convertible	65	76F
2-Door Convertible*	65	76C
2-Door H/T Fastback	67	76C
2-Door H/T Fastback*	67	63C
4-Door H/T Fastback	68	57F

MERCURY COMMUTER

4-Door 6 Pass. Station Wagon	72	71B
4-Door 9 Pass. Station Wagon	72	57F

MERCURY COLONY PARK

4-Door 9 Pass. Station WSagon	76	71A
4-Door 6 Pass. Station Wagon	76	71E

STYLE NUMBER

Body Style Code	50F
Exterior Paint and Tone Code(lower, upper)	AA
Trim Code	26
Day and Month of YearBuilt Code	116
District Code	32
Transmission Code	1
Axle Code	4

VEHICLE DATA PLATE

The vehicle data appears in a line across the top of the warranty plate. The first two letters and a number identify the Body Style. The following one or two letters identify the Exterior Paint Color. The next code consisting of two numbers, or a letter and a number, identifies the Interior Trim. The Date Code showing the date the car was manufactured, follows the Trim Code and consists of two numbers and a letter. The next code gives the district in which the car was ordered and consists of two numbers. The next to the last code is the Axle Ratio Code and is designated by a number for a conventional axle or a letter for an Equa-Lock axle. The last code in the vehicle data is the Transmission Code and consists of one number.

INTERIOR TRIM CODES

16 .... White W/Black Leather
26 .... White W/Black Leather
31 .... Silver Mink Cloth
46 . Black Cloth and Black Leather
52 .... Blue Leather
56 .... Black Leather
58 .... Ivy Gold Leather
60 .... Burgundy Cloth and Leather
61 .. Silver Mink Cloth and Leather
62 .... Blue Cloth and Leather
66 .... Black Cloth and Leather
67 .... Aqua Cloth and Leather
68 .... Ivy Gold Cloth and Leather
69 ..... Palomino Cloth and Leather
70 .... Burgundy Cloth and Leather
71 .. Silver Mink Cloth and Leather
72 .... Blue Cloth and Leather
73 . Black Cloth and White Leather
77 .... Aqua Cloth and Leather
78 .... Ivy Gold Cloth and Leather
79 .... Palomino Cloth and Leather
80 .... Burgundy Leather
81 .... Silver Mink Leather
82 .... Blue Leather
83 .... White and Black Leather
84 .... Emberglow Leather
85 .... Red Leather
86 .... Black Leather
87 .... Aqua Leather
88 .... Ivy Gold Leather
89 .... Palomino Leather
5D .... Parchment Leather
6D .. Parchment Cloth and Leather
7G .... Green Cloth and Leather
8D .... Parchment Leather
8G .... Green Leather

MERCURY

Code.................................Trim

12 .... Blue Cloth and Blue Vinyl
15 .... Red Cloth and Red Vinyl
16 .... Black Cloth and Black Vinyl
17 .... Aqua Cloth and Aqua Vinyl
19 .... Palomino Cloth and
Palomino Vinyl
22 .... Blue Vinyl
25 .... Red Vinyl
26 .... Black Vinyl
31 ..... Silver Cloth and Silver Vinyl
32 .... Blue Cloth and Blue Vinyl
35 .... Red Cloth and Red Vinyl
36 ...... Black Cloth and Black Vinyl
37 .... Aqua Cloth and Aqua Vinyl
38 .... Ivy Gold Cloth and Ivy
Gold Vinyl
39 .... Palomino Cloth and
Palomino Vinyl
42 .... Blue Vinyl
45 .... Red Vinyl
46 .... Black Vinyl
47 .... Aqua Vinyl
48 .... Ivy Gold Vinyl
51 ..... Silver Cloth and Silver Vinyl
52 .... Blue Cloth and Blue Vinyl
53 .... Burgundy Cloth and
Burgundy Vinyl
55 .... Red Cloth and Red Vinyl
56 ...... Black Cloth and Black Vinyl

57 ...... Aqua Cloth and Aqua Vinyl
58 .... Ivy Gold Cloth and Ivy
Gold Vinyl
62 .... Blue Vinyl
64 .... Emberglo Vinyl
65 .... Red Vinyl
66 .... Black Vinyl
67 .... Aqua Vinyl
68 .... Ivy Gold Vinyl
72 .... Blue Vinyl
75 .... Red Vinyl
76 .... Black Vinyl
77 .... Aqua Vinyl
82 .... Blue Vinyl
84 .... Emberglo Vinyl
85 .... Red Vinyl
86 .... Black Vinyl
92 .... Blue Vinyl
93 .... Burgundy Cloth and
Burgundy Vinyl
94 .... Emberglo Vinyl
95 .... Red Vinyl
96 .... Black Vinyl
A3 .... Burgundy Leather
B2 ...... Blue with Parchment Vinyl
B3 ...... Burgundy with Parchment
Vinyl
B6 .... Black with Parchment Vinyl
B7 .... Aqua with Parchment Vinyl
B8 ..... Gold with Parchment Vinyl
B9 .... Palomino with Parchment
Vinyl
D6 .... White with Black Vinyl
E6 .... White with Black Vinyl
F2 .... Blue with White Vinyl
F3 .... Burgundy with White Vinyl
F4 .... Emberglo with White Vinyl
F6 .... Black with White Vinyl
F7 .... Aqua with White Vinyl
F8 .... Ivy Gold with White Vinyl
F9 .... Palomino with White Vinyl
G2 .... Blue with White Vinyl
G3 ...... Burgundy with White Vinyl
G4 ...... Emberglo with White Vinyl
G6 .... Black with White Vinyl
G7 .... Aqua with White Vinyl
G8 .... Ivy Gold with White Vinyl
G9 .... Palomino with White Vinyl
K2 .... Blue Vinyl
K6 .... Black Vinyl
N2 .... Blue Vinyl
N5 .... Red Vinyl
03 .... Green Vinyl
04 .... Beige Vinyl
S2 .... Blue with Parchment Vinyl
X5 .... Red Vinyl
XD .... Parchment Vinyl
Y5 .... Red Vinyl
Z6 .... Black Vinyl
ZD .... Parchment Vinyl

COMET

Code.................................Trim

11 ..... Silver Cloth and Black Vinyl
12 .... Blue Cloth and Blue Vinyl
15 .... Red Cloth and Red Vinyl
17 ...... Aqua Cloth and Aqua Vinyl
22 .... Blue Vinyl
25 .... Red Vinyl
26 .... Black Vinyl
27 .... Aqua Vinyl
32 .... Blue Cloth and Blue Vinyl
35 .... Red Cloth and Red Vinyl
36 .... Black Vinyl
37 ...... Aqua Cloth and Aqua Vinyl
38 ..... Ivy Gold Cloth and Ivy Gold
Vinyl
42 .... Blue Vinyl
44 .... Emberglo Vinyl
45 .... Red Vinyl
46 .... Black Vinyl
47 .... Aqua Vinyl
48 .... Ivy Gold Vinyl
52 ..... Blue Cloth and Blue Vinyl
55 .... Red Cloth and Red Vinyl
57 ...... Aqua Cloth and Aqua Vinyl
62 .... Blue Vinyl
64 .... Emberglo Vinyl
65 .... Red Vinyl
66 .... Black Vinyl
67 .... Aqua Vinyl
68 .... Ivy Gold Vinyl
82 .... Blue Vinyl
84 .... Emberglo Vinyl
85 .... Red Vinyl
86 .... Black Vinyl
87 .... Aqua Vinyl
88 .... Ivy Gold Vinyl
1D .... Parchment Cloth and
Parchment Vinyl
2D .... Parchment Vinyl
3D .... Parchment Cloth and
Parchment Vinyl
4D .... Parchment Vinyl
5D .... Parchment Cloth and
Parchmetn Vinyl
OD .... Parchment Vinyl
B1 .... Parchment Vinyl W/Silver
B2 .... Parchment Vinyl W/Blue
B4 . Parchment Vinyl W/Emberglo
B5 .... Parchment Vinyl W/Red
B6 .... Parchment Vinyl W/Black
B7 .... Parchment Vinyl W/Aqua
B8 .... Parchment Vinyl W/Ivy Gold
B9 .. Parchment Vinyl W/Palomino
C2 .... Parchment Vinyl W/Blue
C3 . Parchment Vinyl W/Burgundy
C4 . Parchment Vinyl W/Emberglo
C6 .... Parchment Vinyl W/Black
C7 .... Parchment Vinyl W/Aqua
C8 .... Parchment Vinyl W/Gold
C9 .. Parchment Vinyl W/Palomino
D2 ...... Parchment Vinyl W/Blue
D3 . Parchment Vinyl W/Burgundy
D4 . Parchment Vinyl W/Emberglo
D6 .... Parchment Vinyl W/Black
D7 .... Parchment Vinyl W/Aqua
D8 .... Parchment Vinyl W/Gold
D9 .... Parchment Vinyl W/Palomino
F2 ...... Parchment Vinyl W/Blue
F3 .. Parchment Vinyl W/Burgundy
F4 .. Parchment Vinyl W/Emberglo
F6 .... Parchment Vinyl W/Black
F7 .... Parchment Vinyl W/Aqua
F8 .... Parchment Vinyl W/Ivy Gold
F9 .. Parchment Vinyl W/Palomino

H1 .... White Vinyl W/Silve[r]
H2 .... White Vinyl W/Blu[e]
H4 .... White Vinyl W/Embergl[o]
H5 .... White Vinyl W/Re[d]
H6 .... White Vinyl W/Blac[k]
H7 .... White Vinyl W/Aqu[a]
H8 .... White Vinyl W/Palomin[o]

DATE CODES

A number signifying the date pre
cedes the month code letter. A sec
ond-year code letter will be used [if]
the model exceeds 12 months.

Month	1 st Yr.	2 nd Yr.
January	A	N
February	B	P
March	C	Q
April	D	R
May	E	S
June	F	T
July	G	U
August	H	V
September	J	W
October	K	X
November	L	Y
December	M	Z

DISTRICT CODES (DSO)

Domestic Special Orders, Foreig[n]
Special Orders, Limited Productio[n]
Option, and Pre-Approved Specia[l]
Orders have the complete order
number recorded in this space. Als[o]
to appear in this space is the two
digit code number of the Distric[t]
which ordered the unit. If the unit i[s]
regular production, only the Distric[t]
code number appears.

District	Code
Boston	1
Philadelphia	1[6]
New York	1[5]
Washington	1
Atlanta	2
Dallas	2[ ]
Jacksonville	2[3]
Memphis	2[6]
Buffalo	3
Cincinnati	3
Cleveland	3
Detroit	3[ ]
Chicago	4
St. Louis	4
Twin Cities	4[ ]
Denver	5
Los Angeles	5[ ]
Oakland	5
Seattle	5
Ford of Canada	8
Home Office Reserve	8[ ]
Export	90-9[9]

REAR AXLE RATIO CODES

A number designates a conventional axle, while a letter designates a Locking differential.

Ratio	Code
3.00:1	1
2.83:1	2
3.20:1	3
3.25:1	4
2.89:1 (Locking)	4
3.50:1	5
2.80:1	6
3.89:1	7
2.89:1	8
4.11:1	9
3.00:1	A
2.83:1	L
3.20:1	C
3.25:1	D
3.50:1	E
2.80:1	F
2.89:1	H
3.10:1	O
3.11:1	I

TRANSMISSION CODES

Type	Code
3-Speed Manual Shift	1
4-Speed Manual (303)	3
C-6 Automatic (XPL)	4
4-Speed Manual-Shift	5
C-4 Automatic Dual Range	6
Cruis-o-matic (MX)	8
Multi-Drive (Mercury)	

ENGINE MODELS AND PISTON DISPLACEMENT - Cubic Inches

289 V-8	289
390 V-8	390
240 Six	240
390 V-8 (2-V and 4-V)	390
410 V-8 (4-V)	410
427 Hi-Perf V-8 (8-V)	427
428 V-8 (4-V)	428
462 V-8	462

COMPRESSION RATIO

200 Six	9.2:1
289 V-8 (2-V)	9.3:1
390 V-8 (2-V)	9.5:1
390 V-8 (4-V)	10.5:1
410 V-8 (4-V) Mercury	10.5:1
427 Hi-Perf V-8 (8-V)	11.1:1
428 V-8 (4-V)	10.1:1
462 V-8 (4-V)	10.25:1

BRAKE HORSEPOWER

200 Six	120
289 V-8 (2-V)	200
390 V-8 (2-V)	265
390 V-8 (4-V)	335
390 V-8 (2-V) Mercury Special	275
410 V-8 (4-V) Mercury	330
427 Hi-Perf V-8 (8-V)	425
428 V-8 (4-V)	345
428 Police Interceptor V-8 (4-V)	360
462 V-8 (4-V)	340

VEHICLE IDENTIFICATION NUMBER

VEHICLE WARANTY NUMBER

7 H 6 4 Z 5 0 0 5 5 1

LINCOLN-VIN Die Stamped into Right Front Inner Fender Panel above Upper Suspension Arm Opening under Hood.

MERCURY-VIN Die Stamped into extension Tab of top of Cowl under Hood.

COMET-VIN Die Stamped into Top Surface of Inner Fender Panel & Radiator Support at L/H side of Car under Hood.

COUGER-VIN Die Stamped into Top Surface of Inner Fender Panel & Radiator Support at L/H side of Car under Hood.

1967 Model Year 7
Assembly Plant Code .... H
Body Series Code 64
Engine Code .... Z
Serial Identification 500551
 Code

ASSEMBLY PLANT CODES

Assembly Plant	Code Letter
Atlanta	A
Oakville (Canada)	B
Ontario Truck	C
Dallas	D
Mahwah	E
Dearborn	F
Chicago	G
Lorain	H
Los Angeles	J
Kansas City	K
Michigan Truck	L
Norfolk	N
Twin Cities	P
San Jose	R
Metuchen	T
Louisville	U
Wayne	W
Wixom	Y
St. Louis	Z

SERIAL NUMBER					
7H64Z 500551					
BODYCOLORTRIM	DATE	DIST	AXLE		TRANS
54E AA 2A	11G	32	1		4

STYLE NUMBER

Body Style Code 54E
Exterior Paint and Tone Code(lower, upper) .... AA
Trim Code 2A
Day and Month of YearBuilt Code 116
District Code 32
Transmission Code 1
Axle Code 4

VEHICLE DATA PLATE

The vehicle data appears in a line across the top of the warranty plate. The first two letters and a number identify the Body Style. The following one or two letters identify the Exterior Paint Color. The next code consisting of two numbers, or a letter and a number, identifies the Interior Trim. The Date Code showing the date the car was manufactured, follows the Trim Code and consists of two numbers and a letter. The next code gives the district in which the car was ordered and consists of two numbers. The next to the last code is the Axle Ratio Code and is designated by a number for a conventional axle or a letter for an Equa-Lock axle. The last code in the vehicle data is the Transmission Code and consists of one number.

BODY SERIAL AND STYLE CODES

The two-digit numeral which follows the assembly plant code identifies the body series This two-digit number is used in conjunction with the Body Style Code, in the Vehicle Data, which consists of a two-digit number with a letter suffix. The following chart lists the Body Serial Codes, Body Style Codes and the model.

MERCURY (Full-Size and Intermediate-Size)
Monterey

Body Type	Serial Code	StyleCode
4-Door Sedan (1)	44	54A
4-Door Sedan (3)	44	54B
4-Door Hardtop (1)	48	57A
2-Door Hardtop (1)	47	63A
2-Door Convertible (1)	45	76A
2-Door Hardtop (2)	47	63G
2-Door Convertible (2)	45	76G

Montclair

4-Door Sedan (1)	54	54C
4-Door sedan (1) (3)	54	54D
4-Door Hardtop (1)	58	57B
2-Door Hardtop (1)	57	63B

Parklane

4-Door Sedan (1)	64	54E
4-Door Hardtop (1)	68	57F
2-Door Hardtop (1)	67	63F
2-Door Convertible (1)	65	76F

Brougham

4-Door Sedan (1	61	54J
4-Door Hardtop (1)	62	57C

Marquis

2-Door Hardtop (4)	69	63D

Commuter

4-Door 6 Passenger	72	71B
4-Door 9 Passenger	72	71C

Colony Park STATION WAGON

4-Door 6 Passenger	76	71E
4-Dorr 9 Passenger	76	71A

Comet 202

4-Door Sedan (1)	2	54A
2-Door Sedan (1)	1	62A

Comet Capri

4-Door Sedan (1)	8	54B
2-Door Hardtop (1)	7	63B

Caliente

4-Door Sedan (1)	10	54D
2-Door Hardtop (1)	11	63D
2-Door Convertible (1)	12	76D

Cyclone

2-Door Hardtop (2)	15	63E
2-Door Convertible (2)	16	76C

GT

2-Door Hardotp (2)	17	63H
2-Door Convertible (2)	18	76H

COMET VOYAGER STATION WAGON

4-Door 6 Passenger	3	71A

VILLAGER STATION WAGON

4-Door 6 Passenger	8	71C

(1) Bench Seat
(2) Bucket Seat
(3) Drop Backlite
(4) Split Bench Seat

COUGAR

2-Door Hardtop (Bucket Seat)	91	65A
2-Door Hardtop (Bucket seat) (1)	91	65B
2-Door Hardtop (Bench Seat)	91	65D
2-Door Hardtop (Bench Seat)	91	65C
(1) Luxury Mode	91	65D

LINCOLN CONTINENTAL

4-Door Sedan	82	53A
2-Door Hardtop	89	65A
4-Door Convertible	86	74A

ENGINE CODES

Type	Code
6 Cyl. 200 Cu. In. (1V)	T
6 Cyl. (1) 200 Cu. In. (1V)	2
8 Cyl. 289 Cu. In. (2V)	C
8 Cyl. (1) 289 Cu. In. (2V)	3
8 Cyl. 289 Cu. In. (4V) Prem. Fuel	A
8 Cyl. 390 Cu. In. (2V)	H
8 Cyl. 390 Cu. In. (4V)	S
8 Cyl. 410 Cu. In. (4V)	M
8 Cyl. 428 Cu. In. (4V)	Q
8 Cyl. (1) 428 Cu. In. (4V)	8
8 Cyl. 428 Cu. In. (4V) Police	P
8 Cyl. 462 Cu. In. (4V)	G
8 Cyl. (1) 462 Cu. In. (4V)	7
8 Cyl. 427 Cu. In. (4V) Hi-Perf	W
8 Cyl. 427 Cu. In. (8V) Hi-Perf	R

(1) Low Compression

CONSECUTIVE UNIT NUMBER

Each model year, each assembly plant begins production with number 500001 (Mercury, Comet or Cougar) or 800001 (Lincoln-Continental) and continues on for each unit built.

EXTERIOR PAINT COLOR CODES

Color	Code
Black	A
Lt. Aqua	B
Dk. Gray Met	C
Med. beige Met	E
Lt. Blue	F
Diamond Green	H
Lime Met	I
Dk. Blue Met	K
White	M
Platinum	N
Lt. Green	O
Pewter Met	P
Med. Blue Met	Q
Dk. Green Met	R
Red	T
Med. Turquoise Met	U
Bronze Met	V
Med. Aqua Met	W
Maroon Met	X
Dk. Green Met	Y
Med. Gold Met	Z
Yellow	2
Med. Gray Met	4
Lt. Beige	6
Yellow	8

INTERIOR TRIM CODES

Code	Trim Schemes
1A	Black Cloth and Black Vinyl
1B	Blue Cloth and Blue Vinyl
1D	Red Cloth and Red Vinyl
1G	Ivy Gold Cloth and Ivy Gold Vinyl
1K	Aqua Cloth and Aqua Vinyl
1L	Lt. Silver Cloth and Lt. Silver Vinyl
1U	Parchment Cloth and Parchment Vinyl W/Black
2A	Black Vinyl (1)
2B	Blue Vinyl (1)
2D	Red Vinyl (1)
2F	Saddle Vinyl (1)
2G	Ivy Gold Vinyl (1)
2K	Aqua Vinyl
2L	Silver Leather
2U	Parchment Vinyl W/Black (1)
3B	Blue Cloth and Blue Vinyl
3G	Ivy Gold Cloth and Ivy Gold Vinyl
3K	Aqua Cloth and Aqua Vinyl
3L	Silver Cloth and Silver Vinyl
3U	Parchment Cloth and Parchment Vinyl W/Black
4A	Black Vinyl
4B	Blue Vinyl
4D	Red Vinyl
4G	Aqua Vinyl
4U	Parchment Vinyl
5A	Black Cloth and Black Vinyl (1)
5B	Dk. Blue Cloth and Blue Vinyl (1)
5D	Dk. Red Leather
5F	Saddle Leather
5G	Dk. Ivy Gold Cloth and Ivy Gold Vinyl (1)
5K	Aqua Cloth and Aqua Vinyl
5L	Silver Cloth and Silver Vinyl
5U	Parchment Cloth and Parchment Vinyl W/Saddle (1)
6A	Black Vinyl
6B	Dk. Blue Vinyl
6D	Red Vinyl
6F	Saddle Vinyl
6G	Dk. Ivy Gold Vinyl
6K	Aqua Vinyl
6U	Parchment Vinyl
7A	Black Vinyl (1)
7B	Blue Vinyl (1)
7D	Red Vinyl
7F	Saddle Vinyl
7G	Ivy Gold Vinyl
7U	Parchment Cloth and Parchment Vinyl (1)
8A	Black Vinyl
8B	Blue Vinyl
8D	Red Vinyl
8F	Saddle Vinyl
8U	Parchment Vinyl W/Black
9A	Black Cloth and Black Vinyl
9B	Dk. Blue Cloth and Dk. Blue Vinyl
9G	Dk. Ivy Gold Cloth and Dk. Ivy Gold Vinyl
9K	Aqua Cloth and Aqua Vinyl
9L	Silver Cloth and Silver Vinyl
9U	Parchment Cloth and Parchment Vinyl W/Black
AG	Lt. Ivy Gold Cloth and Lt. Ivy Gold Vinyl
BA	Parchment Vinyl W/Black
BB	Parchment Vinyl W/Blue
BD	Parchment Vinyl W/Red
BF	Parchment Vinyl W/Saddle
BG	Parchment Vinyl W/Ivy Gold (1)
BK	Parchment Vinyl W/Aqua (1)
CA	Prchment Vinyl W/Black
CB	Parchment Vinyl W/Blue
CD	Parchment Vinyl W/Red
CF	Parchment Vinyl W/Saddle
DA	Black Vinyl
DB	Blue Vinyl
DD	Red Vinyl
DG	Lt. Ivy Gold Cloth and Lt. Ivy Gold Vinyl
EG	Lt. Ivy Gold Leather
EK	Lt. Aqua Leather
FA	Parchment Vinyl W/Black
FB	Parchment Vinyl W/Blu
FD	Parchment Vinyl W/Ivy Gold
FG	Parchment Vinyl W/Ivy Gold
FK	Parchment Vinyl W/Aqua
GG	Lt. Ivy Gold Leather
JD	Dk. Red Leather
KA	Black Cloth and Black Vinyl
KB	Dk. Blue Cloth and Dk. Blue Vinyl
KD	Dk. Red Cloth and Dk. Red Vinyl
KG	Ivy Gold Cloth and Ivy Gold Vinyl
KU	Parchment Cloth and Parchment Vinyl W/Saddle
LB	Red Vinyl
LD	Blue Vinyl
LU	Parchment Cloth and Parchment Vinyl W/Black
MA	Parchment Vinyl W/Black
MB	Parchment Vinyl W/Blue
MD	Parchment Vinyl W/Red
MF	Parchment Vinyl W/Saddle
MG	Parchment Vinyl W/Ivy Gold
MK	Parchment Vinyl W/Aqua
SU	Parchment Cloth and Parchment Vinyl W/Black
TD	Dk. Red Leather
UA	Parchment Vinyl W/Black
UB	Parchment Vinyl W/Blue
UD	Parchment Vinyl W/Red
UF	Parchment Vinyl W/Saddle
UG	Parchment Vinyl W/Ivy Gold
UK	Parchment Vinyl W/Aqua

(1) Leather on Lincoln Continental

DATE CODES

A number signifying the date precedes the month code letter. A second-year code letter will be used if the model exceeds 12 months.

Month	1 st Yr.	2 nd Yr.
January	A	N
February	B	P
March	C	Q
April	D	R
May	E	S
June	F	T
July	G	U
August	H	V
September	J	W
October	K	X
November	L	Y
December	M	Z

DISTRICT CODES (DSO)

Units built on a Domestic Special Orders, or other special orders wil have the complete order number in this space. Also to appear in this space is the two-digit code number of the District which ordered the unit. If the unit is regular production only the District code number appears.

District	CODE
Boston	1
Philadelphia	16
New York	15
Washington	1
Atlanta	2
Dallas	2:
Jacksonville	23
Memphis	26
Buffalo	31
Cincinnati	3:
Cleveland	3:
Detroit	34
Chicago	4
St. Louis	4:
Twin Cities	46
Denver	51
Los Angeles	52
Oakland	5:
Seattle	5
Home Office Reserve	84
Export	90-99

REAR AXLE RATIO CODES

A number designates a conventional axle, while a letter designates a locking differential.

Ratio	Code
3.00:1	1
3.25:1	4
3.50:1	5
2.80:1	6
3.89:1	1
2.75:1	8
3.00:1	A
3.25:1	D
2.80:1	F
3.50:1	E
2.75:1	H

TRANSMISSION CODES

Type	Code
3-Speed Manual	3
4-Speed Manual	5
Automatic (C4)	W
Automatic (C6)	U
Automatic (MX)	Y
Automatic (XPL Special) C6	Z

ENGINE MODELS AND PISTON DISPLACEMENT -
Cubic Inches

200 Six	200
289 V-8 (2-V)	289
289 V-8 (4-V)	289
390 V-8 (2-V and 4-V)	390
410 V-8 (4-V)	410
427 Hi-Perf V-8 (8-V)	427
428 V-8 (4-V)	428
462 V-8	462

COMPRESSION RATIO

200 Six	9.2:1
289 V-8 (2-V)	9.3:1
289 V-8 (4-V)	9.8:1
390 V-8 (2-V)	9.5:1
390 V-8 (4-V)	10.5:1
410 V-8 (4-V) Mercury	10.5:1
427 Hi-Perf V-8 (8-V)	11.1:1
428 V-8 (4-V)	11.1:1
428 Police Interceptor V-8 (4-V)	10.5:1
462 V-8 (4-V)	10.5:1

BRAKE HORSEPOWER

200 Six	120
289 V-8 (2-V)	200
289 V-8 (4-V)	225
390 V-8 (2-V)	270
390 V-8 (4-V)	320
410 V-8 (4-V) Mercury	330
427 Hi-Perf V-8 (8-V)	425
428 V-8 (4-V)	345
428 Police Interceptor V-8 (4-V)	360
462 V-8 (4-V)	340
427 Hi-Perf V-8 (4-V)	410

VEHICLE IDENTIFICATION NUMBER

VEHICLE WARANTY NUMBER

8H64Z500551

LINCOLN-VIN Stamped on Metal Tab Riveted to Instrument Panel on Right Hand Side. VIN Visible through Windshield.

MERCURY-VIN Stamped on Metal Tab Aluminum Riveted to Instrument Panel on Right Hand Side.

VIN Visible through Windshield.

1967 Model Year 8
Assembly Plant Code ....H
Body Series Code 64
Engine Code ....Z
Serial Identification 500551
  Code

ASSEMBLY PLANT CODES

Assembly Plant	Code Letter
Atlanta	A
Oakville (Canada)	B
Ontario Truck	C
Dallas	D
Mahwah	E
Dearborn	F
Chicago	G
Lorain	H
Los Angeles	J
Kansas City	K
Michigan Truck	L
Norfolk	N
Twin Cities	P
San Jose	R
Pilot Plant	S
Metuchen	T
Louisville	U
Wayne	W
St. Thomas	X
Wixom	Y
St. Louis	Z

SERIAL	NUMBER
8H64Z	500551

BODY	COLOR	TRIM	DATE	DIST	AXLE		TRANS
54E		AA	2A	11G	32	5	U

STYLE NUMBER

Body Style Code 54E
Exterior Paint and Tone Code(lower, upper) .... AA
Trim Code 2A
Day and Month of YearBuilt Code 116
District Code 32
Axle Code 5
Transmission Code .... U

VEHICLE DATA

The vehicle data appears on the second or lower line on the Warranty Plate. The first two numbers and a letter identify the Body Style. A letter or a number appears next indicating the Exterior Paint Color followed by a number-letter combination designating the Interior Trim. To the right of this code appears the Date Code indicating the date the car was manufactured. A two digit number next designates the district in which the car was ordered and may appear in conjunction with a Domestic Special Order or Foreign Special Order number when applicable. The final two spaces indicate the Rear Axle Ratio (numbers for regular axles, letters for locking-types) and the Transmission type (numbers for manual, letters for automatic).

BODY SERIAL AND STYLE CODES

The two-digit numerla which follows the assembly plant code identifies the body series. This two- digit number is used in conjunction with the Body Style Code, in the Vehicle Data, which consists of a two-digit number with a letter suffix. The following chart lists the Body Serial Codes, Body Style Codes and the Model.

LINCOLN

Serial Code	Style Code	Body Type
4-Door Sedan	82	53A
2-Door Hardtop	80	65A

MONTEGO
Comet

Sports Coupe (1)	1	65A

MONTEGO

4-Door Sedan (1)	6	54B
2-Door Hardtop (1) (3)	7	65B

MONTEGO MX

4-Door Sedan (1)	10	54D
2-Door Hardtop (1) (3)	11	65D
2-Door Convertible (1)	12	76D
2-Door Hardtop (2) (3)	11	65E
2-Door Convertible (2)	12	76B

BROUGHAM

4-Door Sedan	10	54C
2-Door Hardtop (3)	11	65C

CYCLONE

2-Door Hardtop (1)	15	63A
2-Door Hardtop (1) (3)	17	65F
2-Door Hardtop (2)	15	63C
2-Door Hardtop (2) (3)	17	65G
2-Door Hardtop GT (2)	15	63H
2-Door Hardtop GT (2) (3)	17	65H

MONTEGO MX

4-Door Wagon (1)	3	71B
4-Door Wagon (1)	8	71C

(1) Bench Seat
(2) Bucket Seat
(3) Formal Roof

COUGAR

2-Door Hardtop (Bucket Seat)	91	65A
2-Door Hardtop (Bucket Seat)	91	65B
2-Door Hardtop (Bench Seat)	91	65C

(1) Luxury Model

MERCURY

MONTEREY

4-Door Sedan (1) (3)	44	54A
4-Door Sedan (1) (4)	44	54B
4-Door Hardtop (1)	48	57A
2-Door Hardtop (1)	47	63A
2-Door Convertible (1)	45	76A

MONTCLAIR

4-Door Sedan (1) (3)	54	54C
4-Door Sedan (1) (4)	54	54D
4-Door Hardtop (1)	58	57B
2-Door Hardtop (1)	57	63B

PARKLANE

4-Door Sedan (1) (2) (4)	64	54E
4-Door Hardtop (1) (2)	68	57F
2-Door Hardtop (1) (2)	67	63F
2-Door Convertible (1)	65	76F

PARKLANE BROUGHAM

4-Door Sedan (2) (4)	64	54J
4-Door Hardtop (2)	68	57C

MARQUIS

2-Door Hardtop (2)	69	63D

COMMUTER

4-Door 6 Passenger (1)	72	71B
4-Door 10 Passenger (1)	72	71C

COLONY PARK

4-Door 6 Passenger (1)	76	71E
4-Door 10 Passenger (1)	76	71A

(1) Bench Seat
(2) Split Bench
(4) Drop Backlite

ENGINE CODES

Type	Code
8 Cyl. 302 Cu. In. (2V)	F
8 Cyl. 302 Cu. In. (2V) (1)	6
8 Cyl. 390 Cu. In. (2V)	Y
8 Cyl. 390 Cu. In. (2V) Prem. Fuel	X
8 Cyl. 390 Cu. In. (4V)	Z
8 Cyl. 428 Cu. In. (4V)	Q
8 Cyl. 428 Cu. In. (4V) (1)	8
8 Cyl. 428 Cu. In. (4V) Police	P
8 Cyl. 427 Cu. In. (4V) Hi-Perf.	W
6 Cyl. 200 Cu. In. (1V)	T
6 Cyl. (1) 200 Cu. In. (1V)	2
8 Cyl. 302 Cu. In. (4V)	J
8 Cyl. 390 Cu. In. (4V) and GT	S
8 Cyl. 462 CID (4V)	G
8 Cyl. 462 CID (4V) (1)	7
8 Cyl. 460 CID (4V)	A
8 Cyl. 460 CID (4V) (1)	1

(1) Low Compression

CONSECUTIVE UNIT NUMBER

The assembly plant, with each model year, begins with consecutive unit number 800001 and continues on for each car built.
500001 Mercury

EXTERIOR PAINT COLOR CODES

LINCOLN

Color	Code
Black	A
Maroon	B
Med. Beige Met.	E
Med. Green Met.	G
Lt. Green	H
Lime Met.	I
Dk. Aqua Met.	J
Silver Met.	L
White	M
Platinum	N
Pewter Met.	P
Med. Blue Met.	Q
Dk. Green Met.	R
Iris Met.	S
Red	T
Med. Aqua Met.	U
Lt. Blue	V
Yellow	W
Dk. Blue Met.	X
Nugget Bold Met.	Y
Dk. Gray Met.	Z
Lt. Beig.	6

Color	Code
Black	A
Maroon	B
Bright Blue Met.	D
Bright Aqua Met.	F
Lime Green Met.	I
White	M
Diamond Blue	N
Light Green	O
Med. Blue Met.	Q
Dk. Green Met.	R
Red	T
Med. Aqua Met.	U
Yellow	W
Dk. Blue Met.	X
Gold Met.	Y
Vermillion	3
Low Gloss Black	5
Lt. Beige	6
Rose Met.	2

NTERIOR TRIM CODES

MERCURY

Code	Trim
1A	Black Cloth and Black Vinyl
1B	Med. Blue Cloth and Lt. Blue Vinyl
1D	Dk. Red Cloth and Dk. Red Vinyl
1G	Med. Ivy Gold Cloth and Lt. Ivy Gold Vinyl
1K	Med. Aqua Cloth and Lt. Aqua Vinyl
1U	Lt. Parchment Cloth and Pastel Parchment Vinyl
1Y	Lt. Nugget Gold Cloth and Lt. Nugget Gold Vinyl
2A	Black Vinyl
2B	Dk. Blue Vinyl (Mercury)
2B	Med. Blue Cloth and Lt. Blue Vinyl (Ford)
2D	Dk. Red Vinyl
2G	Med. Ivy Gold Cloth and Lt. Ivy Gold Vinyl
2U	Pastel Parchment Vinyl (Mercury)
2U	Lt. Parchment Cloth and Pastel Parchment Vinyl (Ford)
2Y	Lt. Nugget Gold Vinyl
3A	Balck Cloth and Black Vinyl
3B	Med. Blue Cloth and Lt. Blue Vinyl (Mercury)
3B	Dk. Blue Cloth and Dk. Blue Vinyl (Ford)
3D	Dk. Red Cloth and Dk. Red Vinyl
3G	Med. Ivy Gold Cloth and Lt. Ivy Gold Vinyl (Mercury)
3G	Dk. Ivy Gold Cloth and Dk. Ivy Gold Vinyl (Ford)
3K	Med. Aqua Cloth and Lt. Aqua Vinyl (Mercury)
3K	Lt. Aqua Cloth and Lt. Aqua Vinyl (Ford)
3Y	Lt. Nugget Gold Cloth and Lt. Nugget Gold Vinyl
4A	Black Vinyl
4B	Lt. Blue Vinyl
4D	Dk. Red Vinyl
4K	Lt. Aqua Vinyl
4K	Lt. Nugget Gold and Black Vinyl
4U	Pastel Parchment Vinyl
4Y	Lt. Nugget Gold Vinyl
5A	Black Cloth and Black Vinyl
5B	Dk. Blue Cloth and Dk. Blue Vinyl (Mercury)
5B	Med. Blue Cloth and Lt. Blue Vinyl (Ford)
5G	Dk. Ivy Gold Cloth and Dk. Ivy Gold Vinyl (Mercury)
5G	Med. Ivy Gold Cloth and Lt. Ivy Gold Vinyl (Ford)
5K	Lt. Aqua Cloth and Lt. Aqua Vinyl (Mercury)
5K	Med. Aqua Cloth and Lt. Aqua Vinyl (Ford)
5Y	Lt. Nugget Gold Cloth and Lt. Nugget Gold Vinyl
6A	Black Vinyl
6B	Dk. Blue Vinyl (Mercury)
6B	Lt. Blue Vinyl (Ford)
6D	Dk. Red Vinyl
6G	Dk. Ivy Gold Vinyl (Mercury)
6G	Lt. Ivy Gold Vinyl (Ford)
6K	Lt. Aqua Vinyl
6Y	Lt. Nugget Gold Vinyl
7A	Black Vinyl
7B	Dk. and Lt. Blue Vinyl
7D	Dk. Red Vinyl
7G	Med. and Lt. Ivy Gold Vinyl
7U	Pastel Parchment Vinyl
9A	Black Cloth and Black Vinyl
9B	Dk. Blue Cloth and Dk. Blue Vinyl
9D	Dk. Red Cloth and Dk. Red Vinyl
9G	Dk. Ivy Gold Cloth and Dk. Ivy Gold Vinyl
9K	Lt. Aqua Cloth and Lt. Aqua Vinyl
9Y	Lt. Nugget Gold Cloth and Lt. Nugget Gold Vinyl
BA	Black Cloth and Black Vinyl
BB	Dk. Blue Cloth and Dk. Blue Vinyl
BD	Dk. Red Cloth and Dk. Red Vinyl

MERCURY

Code	Trim
BG	Dk. Ivy Gold Cloth and Dk. Ivy Gold Vinyl
BY	Lt. Nugget Gold Cloth and Lt. Nugget Gold Vinyl
CA	Black Vinyl
CB	Dk. Blue Vinyl
CD	Dk. Red Vinyl
CU	Pastel Paprchment and Black Vinyl
CY	Lt. Nugget Gold Vinyl
DA	Balck Vinyl
DB	Dk. and Lt. Blue Vinyl
DD	Dk. Red Vinyl
DU	Pastel Parchment Vinyl
EA	Black Cloth and Black Vinyl
EB	Dk. Blue Cloth and Dk. Blue Vinyl
ED	Dk. Red Cloth and Dk. Red Viny
EG	Dk. Ivy Gold Cloth and Dk. Ivy Gold Viny
EK	Lt. Aqua Cloth and Lt. Aqua Viny
EY	Lt. Nugget Gold Cloth and Lt. Nugget Gold Viny
FA	Black Viny
FB	Dk. Blue Viny
FD	Dk. Red Viny
FG	Lt. Ivy Gold Vinyl (Mercury
FG	Dk. Ivy Gold Vinyl (Ford
FY	Lt. Nugget Gold Viny
FU	Pastel Parchment Viny
HA	Black Viny
HB	Dk. and Lt. Blue Viny
HD	Dk. Red Viny
HG	Med. and Lt. Ivy Gold Viny
HU	Pastel Parchment Viny
KA	Black Cloth and Black Viny
KB	Dk. Blue Cloth and Dk. Red Viny
KD	Dk. Red Cloth and Dk. Red Viny
KG	Dk. Ivy Gold Cloth and Dk. Ivy Gold Viny
KY	Lt. Nugget Gold Cloth and Lt. Nugget Gold Viny
LE	Lt. and Med. Beige Viny
NA	Black Viny
NB	Dk. and Lt. Blue Viny (Mercury
NB	Lt. Blue Vinyl (Ford
ND	Dk. Red Viny
NU	Pastel Parchment Viny
PA	Black Viny
PB	Dk. and Lt. Blue Viny
PD	Dk. Red Viny
PG	Med. and Lt. Ivy Gold Viny
PU	Pastel Parchment Viny
RA	Black Viny
RB	Lt. Blue Viny
RD	Dk. Red Viny
RG	Lt. Ivy Gold Viny
RK	Lt. Aqua Viny
RY	Lt. Nugget Gold Viny
RU	Pastel Parchment Viny
SA	Black Cloth and Black Viny
SB	Med. Blue Cloth and Lt. Blue Viny
SG	Med. Ivy Gold Cloth an Lt. Ivy Gold Viny
SK	Med. Aqua Cloth an Lt. Aqua Viny
SY	Lt. Nugget Gold Cloth an Lt. Nugget Gold Viny
ZA	Black Cloth and Black Viny
ZB	Dk. Blue Cloth and Dk. Blue Viny
ZY	Lt. Nugget Gold Cloth an Lt. Nugget Gold Vin

MONTEGO/COUGAR

Code	Trim
1A	Black Cloth and Black Vin
1B	Med. Blue Cloth and L Blue Viny
1G	Med. Ivy Gold Cloth an Lt. Ivy Gold Viny
1K	Lt. Aqua Viny
1U	Lt. Parchment Cloth an Pastel Parchment Vin

1Y .... Lt. Nugget Gold Vinyl
2A .... Black Vinyl
2B .... Dk. & Lt. Blue Vinyl
2D .... Red Vinyl
2F .... Med. Saddle Vinyl
2G .... Lt. IVy Gold Vinyl
2K .... Lt. Agua Vinyl
2U .... Pastel Parchment Vinyl
2Y .... Lt. Nugget Gold Vinyl
3A .... Black Vinyl (Montego)
3A .... Black cloth and Black Vinyl (Fairlane)
3B .... Lt. Blue Vinyl (Montego)
3B .... Med. Blue Cloth and Lt. Blue Vinyl (Falcon, Fairlane)
3D .... Dk. Red Vinyl
3G .... Med. Ivy Gold Cloth and Lt. Ivy Gold Vinyl
3K .... Med. Aqua Cloth and Lt. Aqua Vinyl
3U .... Pastel Parchment Vinyl (Montego)
3U .... Lt. Parchment Cloth and Pastel Parchment Vinyl (Falcon)
3Y .... Lt. Nugget Cloth and Lt. Nugget Vinyl
4A .... Black Vinyl
4B .... Lt. Blue Vinyl
4D .... Dk. Red Vinyl
4G .... Lt. Ivy Gold Vinyl
4K .... Lt. Aqua Vinyl
4U .... Pastel Parchment Vinyl
4Y .... Lt. Nugget Gold Vinyl
5A ..... Black Cloth and Black Vinyl (Montego)
5A .... Black Vinyl (Fairlane)
5B .... Med. Blue Cloth and Lt. Blue Vinyl (Montego)
5B .. Dk. & Lt. Blue Vinyl (Fairlane)
5D ...... Dk. Red Cloth and Dk. Red Vinyl (Montego)
5D .... Dk. Red Vinyl (Fairlane)
5G .... Lt. Ivy Gold Cloth and Lt. Ivy Gold Vinyl
5K .... Med. Aqua Cloth and Lt. Aqua Vinyl (Montego)
5K . Dk. & Lt. Aqua Vinyl (Fairlane)
5U .. Lt. parchment Cloth and Pastel Parchment Vinyl (Montego)
5U .... Pastel Parchment Vinyl (Fairlane)
5Y .... Lt. Nugget Godl Cloth and Lt. Nugget Gold Vinyl (Montego)
5Y Lt. Nugget Gold Vinyl (Fairlane)
6A .... Black Vinyl
6B .... Dk. & Lt. Blue Vinyl
6D .... Dk. Red Vinyl
6F .... Med. Saddle Vinyl
6G .... Med. & Lt. Ivy Gold Vinyl
6K .... Dk. & Lt. Aqua Vinyl
6U .... Pastel Parchment Vinyl
6Y .... Lt. Nugget Gold Vinyl
7A .... Black Vinyl (Cougar)
7A .... Black Cloth and Black Vinyl (Fairlane, Montego)
7B .... Lt. Blue Vinyl (Cougar)
7B ... Med. Blue Cloth and Lt. Blue Vinyl (Fairlane)
7B ..... Dk. Blue Cloth and Dk. Blue Vinyl (Montego)
7D ...... Dk. Red Cloth and Dk. Red Vinyl

7G .... Med. Ivy Gold Cloth and Lt. Ivy Gold Vinyl
7K .... Med. Aqua Cloth and Lt. Aqua Vinyl
7Y .... Nugget Gold Cloth and Nugget Gold Vinyl
8A .... Black Vinyl
8B .... Dk. Blue Vinyl
8D .... Dk. Red Vinyl
8F ... Med. Saddle Vinyl with Black
8G .... Med. & Lt. Ivy Gold Vinyl
8K .... Dk. & Lt. Aqua Vinyl
8U .... Pastel Parchment Vinyl
8Y .... Nugget Gold Vinyl
9A .... Black Vinyl
9B .... Dk. Blue Vinyl
9D .... Dk. Red Vinyl
9U .... Parchment Vinyl
9Y .... Lt. Nugget Gold Vinyl
AA .... Pastel Parchment Vinyl with Black
AB .... Pastel Parchment Vinyl with Blue
AD .... Pastel Parchment Vinyl with Red
AF .... Pastel Parchment Vinyl with Saddle
AG .... Pastel Parchment Vinyl with Ivy Gold
AK .... Pastel Parchment Vinyl with Aqua
AY .... Pastel Parchment Vinyl
BU .... Pastel Parchment Vinyl
CU .... Pastel Parchment Vinyl
DU .... Pastel Parchment Vinyl
EU .... Pastel Parchment Vinyl
FA .... Pastel Parchment Vinyl with Black
FB .... Pastel Parchment Vinyl with Blue
FD .... Pastel Parchment Vinyl with Red
FF .... Pastel Parchment Vinyl with Saddle
FG .... Pastel Parchment Vinyl with Ivy Gold
FK .... Pastel Parchment Vinyl with Aqua
FU .... Pastel Parchment Vinyl
FY .... Pastel Parchment Vinyl with Nugget Gold
HA .... Black Vinyl
HB .... Dk. & Lt. Blue Vinyl
HD .... Dk. Red Vinyl
HG ..... Med. & Lt. Ivy Gold Vinyl
HK .... Dk. & Lt. Aqua Vinyl
HU .... Pastel Parchment Vinyl
HY .... Lt. Nugget Gold Vinyl
JU .... Pastel Parchment Vinyl
KB .... Med. Blue Cloth and Lt. Blue Vinyl
KG .... Med. Ivy Gold Cloth and Lt. Ivy Gold Vinyl
KU ... Lt. Parchment Cloth and Pastel Parchment Vinyl (Montego)
KU .... Pastel Parchment Vinyl (Fairlane)
LA .... Black Vinyl
LB .... Lt. Blue Vinyl
LD .... Dk. Red Vinyl
LU .... Pastel Parchment Vinyl
MA .... Black Vinyl
MB .... Dk. & Lt. Blue Vinyl

MD .... Dk. Red Vinyl
MU .... Pastel Parchment Vinyl
OU .... Pastel Parchment Vinyl
QA .... Black Vinyl
QB .... Dk. & Lt. Blue Vinyl
QU .... Pastel Parchment Vinyl
RA .... Black Vinyl
RB .... Lt. Blue Vinyl
RD .... Dk. Red Vinyl
RU .... Pastel Parchment Vinyl
TU .... Pastel Parchment Vinyl
UA ..... Parchment Vinyl with Black
UB .... Parchment Vinyl with Blue
UD .... Parchment Vinyl with Red
UF ... Parchment Vinyl with Saddle
UG .... Parchment Vinyl with Ivy Gold
UK ..... Parchment Vinyl with Aqua
UU .... Pastel Parchment with Nugget Gold
UY .... Parchment Vinyl with Nugget Gold
YU .... Pastel Parchment Vinyl
ZU .... Pastel Parchment Vinyl

LINCOLN

1A ..... Black Cloth and Black Vinyl
1B .... Dk. Blue Cloth and Dk. Blue Vinyl
1D .... Dk. Red Cloth and Dk. Red Vinyl
1G .... Dk. Ivy Gold Cloth and Dk. Ivy Gold Vinyl
2A .... Black Leather
2B .... Dk. Blue Leather
2D .... Dk. Red Leather
2F .... Med. Saddle Leather
2G .... Dk. Ivy Gold Leather
2K .... Lt. Aqua Leather
2U .... Pastel Parchment Leather
2Y .... Lt. Nugget Gold Leather
4A ..... Black Cloth and black Vinyl
4B .... Dk. Blue Cloth and Dk. Blue Vinyl
4D .... Dk. Red Cloth and Dk. Red Vinyl
4G .... Dk. Ivy Gold Cloth and Dk. Ivy Gold Vinyl
5A .... Black Leather
5B .... Dk. Blue Leather
5D .... Dk. Red Leather
5F .... Med. Saddle Leather
5G .... Dk. Ivy Gold Leather
5K .... Lt. Aqua Leather
5U ..... Pastel Parchment Leather
5Y .... Lt. Nugget Gold Leather
6A ..... Black Cloth and Black Vinyl
7A .... Black Leather
7B .... Dk. Blue Leather
7G .... Dk. Ivy Gold Leather
7U .... Pastel Parchment Leather
AA ..... Black Cloth and Black Vinyl
AB .... Lt. Blue Cloth and Lt. Blue Vinyl
AG .... Lt. Ivy Gold Cloth and Lt. Ivy Gold Vinyl
AK .... Lt. Aqua Cloth and Lt. Aqua Vinyl
AL .... Lt. Silver Cloth and Lt. Silver Vinyl
AY .... Lt. Nugget Gold Cloth and Lt. Nugget Gold Vinyl

BB .... Lt. Blue Leather
BG .... Lt. Ivy Gold Leather
JA ...... Black Cloth and Black Vinyl
JB .... Lt. Blue Cloth and Lt. Blue Vinyl
JG .... Lt. Ivy Gold Cloth and Lt. Ivy Gold Vinyl
JK .... Lt. Aqua Cloth and Lt. Aqua Vinyl
JL .... Lt. Silver Cloth and Lt. Silver Vinyl
JY .... Lt. Nugget Gold Cloth and Lt. Nugget Gold Vinyl
KA .... Black Leather
KB .... Dk. Blue Leather
KG .... Dk. Ivy Gold Leather
KL .... Lt. Silver Leather
KU .... Pastel Parchment Leather
RA .... Black Leather
RB .... Dk. Blue Leather
RG .... Dk. Ivy Gold Leather
RL .... Lt. Silver Leather
RU .... Pastel Parchment Leather
SB .... Lt. Blue Leather
SG .... Lt. Ivy Gold Leather

DATE CODES

The code letters for the month are preceded by a numeral to show the day of the month when the car was completed. The second year code letters are to be used if the model production exceeds 12 months.

Month	1 st Yr.	2nd Yr.
January	A	N
February	B	P
March	C	Q
April	D	R
May	E	S
June	F	T
July	G	U
August	H	V
September	J	W
October	K	X
November	L	Y
December	M	Z

DISTRICT CODES (DSO)

Domestic Special Orders, Foreign Special Orders, Limited Production Option, and Pre-Approved Special Orders have the complete order number recorded in this space. Also to appear in this space is the two-digit code number of the District which ordered the unit. If the unit is regular production, only the District code number appears.

District	Code
Boston	11
Philadelphia	16
New York	15
Washington	17
Atlanta	21
Dallas	22
Jacksonville	23
Memphis	26
Buffalo	31
Cincinnati	32
Cleveland	33
Detroit	34
Chicago	41
St. Louis	42
Twin Cities	46
Denver	51
Los Angeles	52
Oakland	53
Seattle	54
Home Office Reserve	84
Export	90-99

REAR AXLE RATIO CODES

"A number designates a convention axle, while a letter designates a locking differential."

Ratio	Code
2.75:1	1
2.79:1	2
2.83:1	4
3.00:1	5
3.20:1	6
3.25:1	7
3.50:1	8
3.10:1	9
2.75:1	A
2.80:1	C
2.80:1	3
3.00:1	E
3.20:1	F
3.25:1	G
3.50:1	H

TRANSMISSION CODES

Type	Code
3-Speed Manual	1
4-Speed Manual	5
C4 Automatic (XP3)	W
C6 Automatic (XPL)	U
C6 Automatic (XPL Special)	Z

ENGINE IDENTIFICATION AND APPLICATION

Engine CID	Warranty Plate Code	Cougar	Montego	Compression Ratio	Brake HP
428 V-8 4-V CJ	Q	X	X	10.6:1	335
200 Six 1-V	T		X	8.8:1	115
302 V-8 2-V	F	X	X	9.0:1	210
302 V-8 4-V	J	X	X	10.0:1	230
390 V-8 2-V	Y		X	9.5:1	265
390 V-8 2-V	X	X		10.5:1	280
390 V-8 4-V	S	X	X	10.5:1	325
427 V-8 4-V	W	X	X	10.9:1	390

MERCURY

Engine CID	Warranty Plate Code	Compression Ratio	Brake Horsepower
390 V-8 (2-V)	Y	9.5:1	265 @ 4400
390 V-8 (2-V)	X	10.5:1	280 @ 4400
390 V-8 (4-V)	Z	10.5:1	315 @ 4600
428 V-8 (4-V)	Q	10.5:1	340 @ 460
428 V-8 (4-V)		10.5:1	360 @ 5400

LINCOLN

Engine CID	Warranty Plate Code	Compression Ratio	Brake Horsepower
462 (4-V)	A	10.25:1	340
460 (4-v)	A	10-5:1	265

VEHICLE IDENTIFICATION NUMBER

VEHICLE WARANTY NUMBER

| 9 H 8 2 A 8 0 0 5 5 1 |

LINCOLN-VIN Stamped on Metal Tab Aluminum Riveted to Instrument Panel on Left Hand Side. VIN Visible through Windshield.

MERCURY-VIN Stamped on Metal Tab Aluminum Riveted to Instrument Panel on Left Hand Side. VIN Visible through Windshield.

1967 Model Year 9
Assembly Plant Code ....H
Body Series Code 82
Engine Code ....A
Consecutive Unit No. 800551

ASSEMBLY PLANT CODES

Assembly Plant	Code Letter
Atlanta	A
Oakville (Canada)	B
Ontario Truck	C
Dallas	D
Mahwah	E
Dearborn	F
Chicago	G
Lorain	H
Los Angeles	J
Kansas City	K
Michigan Truck	L
Norfolk	N
Twin Cities	P
San Jose	R
Allen Park	S
Metuchen	T
Louisville	U
Wayne	W
St. Thomas	X
Wixom	Y
St. Louis	Z

SERIAL NUMBER
8H64Z 500551

BODY	COLOR	TRIM	DATE	DIST	AXLE		TRANS
53A	A	3A	11G	32	4		U

VEHICLE WARRANTY NUMBER

The vehicle warranty number is the first line of numbers and letters appearing on the Warranty Plates . The Warranty Plate is riveted to the left front door lock face panel. The first number indicates the model year. The letter following the model year number indicates the manufacturing assembly plant. The next two numbers designate the Body Serial Code followed by a letter expressing the Engine Code. The group of six digits remaining on the firsit line indicate the Consecutive Unit Number.

BODY SERIAL AND STYLE CODES

The two-digit numeral which follows the assembly plant code identifies the body series. This two-digit number is used in conjunction with the Body Style Code, in the Vehicle Data, which consists of a two-digit number with a letter suffix. The following chart lists the Body Serial Codes, Body Style Codes and the model.

LINCOLN CONTINENTAL

Body Type	Serial Code	Style Code
4-Door Sedan	82	53A
2-Door Hardtop	80	65A
CONTINENTAL MARK II		
2-Door Hardtop	89	65A
COUGAR - STANDARD		
2-Door Hardtop (1)	91	65C
2-Door Hardtop(3)	91	65A
Convertible (3)	92	76A
COUGAR - XR-7 Luxury		
2-Door Hardtop (3)	93	65B
Convertible (3)	94	76B
(1) Bench Seat		
(2) Split Bench		
(3) Bucket Seats		
MERCURY		
MONTEREY		
4-Door Sedan (1)	44	54A
2-Door Hardtop-Formal (1)	46	65A
4-Door Hardtop (1)	48	57A
Convertible (1)	45	76A
MARQUIS (CANADA ONLY)		
4-Door Hardtop Sedan (1)	40	53M
2-Door Hardtop Formal (1)	41	65M
4-Door Hardtop (1)	42	57M
MONTEREY-CUSTOM		
4-Door Sedan (1)	54	54C
2-Door Hardtop Formal (1)	56	65B
4-Door Hardtop (1)	58	57B
MARQU9S (U.S.) - BROUGHAM (CANADA)		
4-Door Hardtop sedan (1) (2)	63	53F
2-Door Hardtop Formal (1) (2)	66	65F
4-Door Hardtop (1) (2)	68	57F
Convertible (1) (2)	65	76F
Brougham (Option)		
4-Door Hardtop sedan (2)	63	53C
2-Door Hardtop Formal(2)	66	65C
4-Door Hardotp (2)	68	57C

STYLE NUMBER

Body Style Code	53A
Exterior Paint and Tone Code(lower, upper)	A
Trim Code	3A
Day and Month of YearBuilt Code	116
District Code	32
Axle Code	4
Transmission Code	U

VEHICLE DATA

The vehicle data appears on the second or lower line on the Warranty Plate. The first two numbers and a letter identify the Body Style. A letter or a number appears next indicating the Exterior Paint Color followed by a number-letter combination designating the Interior Trim. To the right of this code appears the Date Code indicating the date the car was manufactured. A two digit number next designates the district in which the car was ordered and may appear in conjunction with a Domestic Special Order or Foreign Special Order number when applicable. The final two spaces indicate the Rear Axle Ratio (numbers for regular axles, letters for locking-types) and the Transmission type (numbers for manual, letters for automatic).

MERCURY - Cont.

MARAUDER

Serial Code Style Code	Body Type
2-Door Hardtop (1) (3)	60	63G
2-Door Hardtop (1) (2) (3)	61	63H

MONTEREY WAGON

| 4-Door 2 Seat (1) | 72 | 71B |
| 4-Door 3 Seat (Side Facing) (1) | 72 | 71C |

MONEREY CUSTOM WAGON

| 4-Door 2 Seat (1) | 74 | 71F |
| 4-Door 3- Seat (Side Facing) (1) | 74 | 71G |

MARQUIS COLONY PARK

| 4-Door 2-Seat (1) (2) | 76 | 71E |
| 4-Door 3 Seat (Siden Facing) (1) (2) | 76 | 71A |

(1) Bench Seat
(2) Split Bench
(3) Bucket Seats

MONTEGO
COMET

| 2-Door Hardtop (1) | 1 | 65A |
| 4-Door Sedan (1) | 2 | 54A |

MONTEGO

| 4-Door Sedan (1) | 6 | 54B |
| 2-Door Hardtop (1) | 7 | 65B |

MONTEGO MX

4-Door Sedan (1)	10	54D
2-Doro Hardtop (1)	11	65D
Convertible (1)	12	76D

MONTEGO MX

| 2-Door Hardtop (3) | 11 | 65E |
| Convertible (3) | 12 | 76B |

MONMTEGO MX BROUGHAM

| 4-Door Sedan | 10 | 54C |
| 2-Door Hardtop | 11 | 65C |

CYCLONE/CYCLONE CJ

2-Door Hardtop (1)	15	63A
2-Door Hardtop (3)	15	63C
2-Door Hardtop GT (3)	16	63H

STATION WAGONS

Montego (1)	3	71B
Montego MX (1)	8	71C
Montego MX (1)	8	71A

(1) Bench Seat
(2) Split Bench
(3) Bucket Seats

ENGINE CODES

Code	Type
L	6 Cyl. 250 Cu. In. (1V)
3	6 Cyl. (1) 250 Cu. In. (1V)
F	8 Cyl. 302 Cu. In. (2V)
6	8 Cyl. (1) 302 Cu. In. (2V)
H	8 Cyl. 351 Cu. IN. (2V)
M	8 Cyl. 351 Cu. In. (4V)
Y	8 Cyl. 390 Cu. In. (2V)
X	8 Cyl. (2) 390 Cu. In. (2V)
S	8 Cyl. (3) 390 Cu. In. (4V)
Q	8 Cyl. 428 Cu. In. (4V) CJ
R	8 Cyl. (5) 428 Cu. In. (4V) CJ
P	8 Cyl. (2) 428 Cu. In. (4V) Police
K	8 Cyl. 429 Cu. In. (2V)
N	8 Cyl. 429 Cu. In. (4V)
A	8 Cyl. 460 Cu. In. (4V)

(1) Low Compression
(2) Premium Fuel
(3) Improved Performance
(4) High Performance
(5) Ram Air Induction

CONSECUTIVE UNIT NUMBER

Starting Serial Numbers - 1969 Passenger Cars 500,001 - Mercury, Montego, Cougar 848,001 - Lincoln Continental & Mark III

EXTERIOR PAINT COLOR CODES

Code	Color
A	Black
B	Maroon
C	Dk. Ivy Green Met
D	Pastel Gray
E	Lt. Aqua
F	Dk. Aqua Met
G	Med. Orchid Met
H	Lt. Green
I	Med. Lime Met
J	Dk. Aqua Met
K	Dk. Orchid Met
L	Lt. Gray Met
M	White
N	Platinum
P	Med. Blue Met
Q	Med. Blue Met
R	Lt. Gold
S	Med. Gold Met
T	Red
U	Med. Aqua Met
V	Lt. Aurora Copper Met
W	Yellow
X	Dk. Blue Met
Y	Burnt Orange Met
Z	Dk. Grey Met
2	Lt. Ivy Yellow
3	Calpyso Coral
4	Med. Emerald Met
6	Med. Blue Met
7	Lt. Emerald Green Met
8	Lt. Blue

NTERIOR TRIM CODES

Code	Trim
1A	Black Vinyl (Cougar, Falcon)
1A	Black Cloth & Vinyl
1B	Med./Lt. Blue Vinyl
1B	Dk. Blue Cloth & Vinyl (Lincoln, T-Bird, Mark III, Mercury)
1B	Lt. Blue Cloth & Vinyl (Ford, Montego, Meteor)
1D	Dk. Red Cloth and/or Dk. Red Vinyl
1F	Med. Saddle Vinyl (Cougar)
1G	Dk. Ivy Gold Cloth & Vinyl
1G	Lt. Ivy Gold Vinyl (Cougar)
1K	Lt. Aqua Cloth and/or Lt. Aqua Vinyl
1D	Med. Grey Cloth & Vinyl (Mark III)
1Y	Lt. Nugget Gold Vinyl (Cougar-Falcon)
1Y	Lt. Nugget Gold Cloth & Vinyl
2A	Black Vinyl
2A	Black Leather & Vinyl (Lincoln)
2A	Black Leather (Mark III)
2B	Dk. & Lt. Blue Vinyl
2B	Dk. Blue Leather & Vinyl (Lincoln)
2B	Dk. Blue Leather (Mark III)
2D	Dk. Red Vinyl
2D	Dk. Red Leather & Vinyl (Lincoln)
2D	Dk. Red Leather (Mark III)
2F	Med. Saddle Vinyl
2F	Med. Saddle Leather & Vinyl (Lincoln)
2G	Dk. Ivy Gold Vinyl
2G	Dk. Ivy Gold Leather & Vinyl (Lincoln)
2K	Lt. Aqua Vinyl
2K	Lt. Aqua Leather & Vinyl (Lincoln)
2K	Lt. Aqua Leather (Mark III)
2P	Me.d Grey Leather & Vinyl (Lincoln)
2P	Pastel Parchment Leather (Mark III)
2U	Pastel Parchment Leather (Mark III)
2W	White Vinyl
2W	White Leather & Vinyl (Lincoln)
2W	White Leather (Mark III)
2Y	Lt. Nugget Gold Vinyl
2Y	Lt. Nugget Gold Leather & Vinyl (Lincoln)
2Y	Lt. Nugget Gold Leather (Mark III)
3A	Black Vinyl (Mustang, MOntego)
3A	Black Cloth & Vinyl
3A	Black Leather & Vinyl (Lincoln)
3B	Lt/Dk. Blue Vinyl
3B	Lt. Blue Cloth & Vinyl (Falcon, Fairlane, Ford, Montego, Meteor)
3B	Dk. Blue Cloth & Vinyl (T-Bird, Mercury)
3B	Dk. Blue Leather & Vinyl (Lincoln)
3D	Dk. Red Vinyl
3G	Dk. Ivy Gold Cloth & Vinyl
3G	Dk. Ivy Gold Leather & Vinyl (Lincoln)
3K	Lt. Aqua Cloth & Lt. Aqua Vinyl
3W	White Vinyl
3W	White Leather & Vinyl (Lincoln)
3Y	Lt. Nugget Gold Cloth & Viny
3Y	Lt. Nugget Gold Vinyl (T-Bird)
4A	Black Vinyl
4B	Dk./Lt. Blue Vinyl
4D	Dk. Red Vinyl
4G	Dk. Ivy Gold Vinyl
4W	White Vinyl
4Y	Lt. Nugget Gold Vinyl
5A	Black Cloth and/or Black Vinyl
5A	Black Leather & Vinyl (Lincoln)
5B	Lt. Blue Cloth & Vinyl (Montego, Meteor, Ford)
5B	Dk. Blue Leather & Vinyl (Lincoln)
5B	Dk. & Lt. Blue Vinyl
5B	Dk. Blue Cloth & Vinyl (Mercury)
5D	Dk. Red Cloth & Vinyl (Montego)
5D	Dk. Red Vinyl

INTERIOR TRIM CODES - Cont.

5D .... Dk. Red Leather & Vinyl (Lincoln)
5F .... Med. Saddle Leather & Vinyl (Lincoln)
5G .... Dk. Ivy Gold Vinyl
5G .... Dk. Ivy Gold Cloth & Vinyl
5G .... Dk. Ivy Gold Leather & Vinyl (Lincoln)
5K .... Lt. Aqua Cloth & Vinyl (Montego)
5K .... Dk. & Lt. Aqua Vinyl
5K .... Lt. Aqua Leather & Vinyl (Lincoln)
5W .... White Vinyl
5W .... White Leather & Vinyl (Lincoln)
5Y .... Lt. Nugget Gold Cloth & Vinyl
5Y .... Lt. Nugget Gold Vinyl (Mustang, Fairlane)
5Y .... Lt. Nugget Gold Leather & Vinyl (Lincoln)
6A .... Black Vinyl
6A .... Black Cloth & Vinyl (Lincoln)
6A .... Black Leather & Vinyl (Cougar)
6B .... Dk. & Lt. Blue Vinyl
6B .... Dk. Blue Leather & Vinyl (Cougar)
6D .... Dk. Red Vinyl
6D .... Dk. Red Leather & Vinyl (Cougar)
6F .... Med. SAddle Leather & Vinyl
6G .... Dk. Ivy Gold Vinyl
6G .... Dk. Ivy Gold Cloth & Vinyl
6G .... Dk. Ivy Gold Leather & Vinyl (Cougar)
6K .... Lt. Aqua Vinyl
6K .... Lt. Aqua Leather & Vinyl (Cougar)
6W .... White Vinyl
6Y .... Lt. Nugget Gold Vinyl
6Y .... Lt. Nugget Gold Leather & Vinyl (Cougar)
7A .... Black Vinyl
7A .... Black Cloth & Vinyl (Fairlane)
7A .... Black Leather & Vinyl (Lincoln)
7B .... Lt. Blue Vinyl (Cougar, Montego)
7B .... Dk. Blue Cloth & Vinyl (Ford)
7B .... Dk. Blue Leather & Vinyl (Lincoln)
7D .... Dk. Red Cloth & Vinyl
7D .... Dk. Ivy Gld Vinyl
7G .... Dk. Ivy Gold Leather & Vinyl (Lincoln)
7K .... Lt. Aqua Cloth & Vinyl
7W .... White Vinyl
7W .... White Leather & Vinyl (Lincoln)
7Y .... Lt. Nugget Gold Cloth & Vinyl
7Y .... Lt. Nugget Gold Vinyl (Ford, Meteor, Mustang)
8A .... Black Vinyl
8A .... Black Leather & Vinyl (T-Bird)
8B .... Dk./Lt. Blue Vinyl
8D .... Dk. Red Vinyl
8F .... Med. Saddle Vinyl

8G .... Dk. Ivy Gold Vinyl
8W .... White Vinyl
8W .... White Leather & Vinyl (T-Bird)
9A .... Black Vinyl
9A .... Black Cloth & Vinyl (Ford, Meteor)
9B .... Lt. Blue Vinyl
9B .... Lt. Blue Cloth & Vinyl (Ford, Meteor)
9D .... Dk. Red Vinyl
9D .... Dk. Red Cloth & Vinyl (Ford, Meteor)
9G .... Dk. Ivy Gold Cloth & Vinyl
9K .... Lt. Aqua Cloth & Vinyl
9Y .... Lt. Nugget Gold Cloth & Vinyl
AA .... White Vinyl with Black
AB .... White Vinyl with Blue
AD .... White Vinyl with Red
AG .... Whtie Vinyl with Ivy Gold
AK .... White Vinyl with Aqua
AY .... White Vinyl with Nugget Gold
BA .... White Vinyl with Black (Cougar)
BA .... Black Vinyl (Fairlane)
BB .... White Vinyl with Blue (Cougar)
BB .... Lt. Blue Vinyl (Fairlane)
BD .... White Vinyl with Red (Cougar)
BG .... White Vinyl with Ivy Gold (Cougar)
BK .... White Vinyl with Aqua (Cougar)
BY .... White Vinyl with Lt. Nugget Gold (Cougar)
BY .... Lt. Nugget Gold Vinyl (Fairlane)
CA .... Black Cloth & Vinyl
CA .... Black Vinyl (Montego)
CB .... Dk. Blue Cloth & Vinyl
CB .... Lt. Blue Vinyl (Montego)
CG .... Dk. Ivy Gold Cloth & Vinyl
CK .... Lt. Aqua Cloth & Vinyl
CY .... Lt. Nugget Gold Cloth & Vinyl
CY .... Lt. Nugget Gold Vinyl (Montego)
DA .... Black Cloth & Vinyl
DA .... White Vinyl with Black (Cougar)
DA .... Black Vinyl (Montego, Mercury)
DB .... Dk. Blue Vinyl (Mercury)
DB .... White Vinyl with Blue (Cougar)
DB .... Lt. Blue Vinyl (Montego)
DD .... White Vinyl with Red (Cougar)
DD .... Dk. Red Cloth & Vinyl
DG .... Dk. Ivy Gold Cloth & Vinyl
DK .... Lt. Aqua Cloth & Vinyl
DY .... Lt. Nugget Gold Vinyl (Mercury)
DY .... Lt. Nugget Gold Vinyl (Mercury)
EA .... Black Cloth & Vinyl
EB .... Dk. Blue Cloth & Vinyl
ED .... Dk. Red Cloth & Vinyl
EG .... Dk. Ivy Gold Cloth & Vinyl
EK .... Lt. Aqua Cloth & Vinyl
EY .... Lt. Nugget Gold Cloth

FA .... Black Vinyl
FA .... White Vinyl with Black (Cougar)
FB .... Lt./Dk. Blue Vinyl
FB .... White Vinyl with Blue (Cougar)
FD .... Dk. Red Vinyl
FD .... White Vinyl with Red (Cougar)
FG .... Dk. Ivy Gold Vinyl
FG .... White Vinyl with Dk. Ivy Gold (Cougar)
FK .... Lt. Aqua Vinyl
FK .... White Vinyl with Lt. Aqua (Cougar)
FW .... White Vinyl
FY .... Lt. Nugget Gold Vinyl
FY .... White Vinyl with nugget Gold (Cougar)
GB .... Lt. Blue Vinyl
GD .... Dk. Red Vinyl
GG .... Dk. Ivy Gold Vinyl
GY .... Lt. Nugget Gold Vinyl
HA .... Black Vinyl
HA .... White Vinyl with Black (Cougar)
HA .... Black Leather & Vinyl (Mercury)
HB .... Lt. Blue Vinyl
HB .... White Vinyl with Blue (Cougar)
HD .... Dk. Red Vinyl
HD .... Dk. Red Leather & Vinyl (Mercury)
HD .... White Vinyl with Dk. Red (Cougar)
HG .... Dk. Ivy Gold Vinyl
HG .... White Vinyl with Ivy Gold (Cougar)
HK .... Lt. Aqua Vinyl
HK .... White Vinyl with Lt. Aqua (Cougar)
HW .... White Leather & Vinyl (Mercury)
HW .... White Vinyl (Fairlane)
HY .... White Vinyl wiht Nugget Gold (Cougar)
HY .... Lt. Nugget Gold Vinyl
JA .... Black Vinyl
JB .... Lt. Blue Vinyl & Vinyl (Lincoln)
JG .... Lt. Ivy Gold Cloth & Vinyl
JW .... White Vinyl
JY .... Lt. Nugget Gold Vinyl
JY .... Lt. Nugget Gold Cloth & Vinyl (Lincoln)
KA .... Black Vinyl
KA .... Black Cloth & Vinyl (Ford, Mercury, Meteor)
KA .... Black Leather & Vinyl (Lincoln)
KB .... Dk. Blue Cloth & Vinyl
KB .... Med. Blue CLoth & Vinyl (Ford, Montego)
KB .... Dk. Blue Leather & Vinyl (Lincoln)
KD .... Dk. Ivy Gold Leather & Vinyl (Lincoln)
KG .... Dk. Ivy Gold Leather & Vinyl (Lincoln)
KG .... Dk. Ivy Gold Cloth & Vinyl
KL .... Lt. Silver Leather & Vinyl (Lincoln)

KW .... White Vinyl
KW .... White Leather
KY .... Lt. Nugget Gold Vinyl
LA .... Black Vinyl
LA .... Black Leather & Vinyl (Lincoln)
LB .... Lt. Blue Vinyl
LB .... Dk. Blue Leather & Vinyl (Lincoln)
LD .... Dk. Red Vinyl
LE .... Lt. & Med. Beige Vinyl
LW .... White Vinyl
LW .... White Leather & Vinyl (Lincoln)
LY .... Lt. Nugget Gold Vinyl
MA .... Black Vinyl
MB .... Dk. & Lt. Blue Vinyl
MD .... Dk. Red Vinyl
MW .... White Vinyl
NA .... Black Vinyl
NB .... Lt. Blue Vinyl
NY .... Lt. Nugget Gold Vinyl
PA .... Black Vinyl
PB .... Lt. Blue Vinyl
PY .... Lt. Nugget Gold Vinyl
QA .... Black Vinyl
QB .... Dk. & Lt. Blue Vinyl
QW .... White Vinyl
QY .... Lt. Nugget Gold Vinyl
RA .... Black Vinyl
RB .... Lt. Blue Vinyl
RD .... Dk. Red Vinyl
RW .... White Vinyl
RY .... Lt. Nugget Gold Vinyl
SB .... Lt. Blue Leather & Vinyl (Lincoln)
SG .... Lt. Ivy Gold Leather & Vinyl (Lincoln)
TG .... Lt. Ivy Gold Leather & Vinyl (Lincoln)
VA .... Black Vinyl
VB .... Dk. Blue Vinyl
VG .... Dk. Ivy Gold Vinyl
VW .... White Vinyl
VY .... Lt. Nugget Gold Vinyl
WA .... Black Vinyl

WW .... White Vinyl
WY .... Lt. Nugget Gold Vinyl
YA .... Black Cloth & Vinyl
YB .... Dk. Blue Cloth & Vinyl
YD .... Dk. Red Cloth & Vinyl
YG .... Dk. Ivy Gold Cloth & Vinyl
YK .... Lt. Aqua Cloth & Vinyl
YY .... Lt. Nugget Gold Cloth & Vinyl
ZA .... Black Cloth & Vinyl
ZB .... Dk. Blue Cloth & Vinyl
ZG .... Dk. Ivy Gold Cloth & Vinyl

DATE CODES

The code letters for the month are preceded by a numeral to show the day of the month when the car was completed. The second year code letters are to be used if the model production exceeds 12 months.

Month	1 st Yr.	2 nd Yr.
January	A	N
February	B	P
March	C	Q
April	D	R
May	E	S
June	F	T
July	G	U
August	H	V
September	J	W
October	K	X
November	L	Y
December	M	Z

DISTRICT CODES (DSO)

Units built on a Domestic Special Order, Foreign Special Order, or other special orders will have the complete order numer in this space. Also to appear in this space is the two-digit code number of the District which ordered the unit. If the unit is a regular production unit, only the Districtcode number will appear.

LINCOLN, MERCURY

Code	District
11	Boston
15	New York
16	Philadelphia
17	Washington
21	Atlanta
22	Dallas
23	Jacksonville
26	Memphis
31	Buffalo
32	Cincinnati
33	Cleveland
34	Detroit
41	Chicago
42	St. Louis
46	Twin Cities
51	Denver
52	Los Angeles
53	Oakland
54	Seattle
84	Home Office Reserve
90	Export

REAR AXLE RATIO CODES

Conventional	Limited-Slip	Ratio
2	K	2.75:1
3	L	2.79:1
4	M	2.80:1
6	O	3.00:1
7	P	3.10:1
9	R	3.25:1
A	S	3.50:1
C	U	3.08:1
D	V	3.91:1
E	W	4.30:1

TRANSMISSION CODES

Code	Type
1	3-Speed Manual
5	4-Speed Manual - Wide Ratio
6	4-Speed Manual - Close Ratio
W	Automatic (C4)
U	Automatic (C6)
X	Automatic (FMX)
Z	Automatic (C6 Special)

ENGINE IDENTIFICATION AND APPLICATION

Engine CID	Warranty Plate Code	Cougar	Montego	Compression Ratio	Brake HP
302 V-8 2-V	F	X	X	9.5:1	220
389 V-8 4-V	S	X	X	10.5:1	320
460 (4-V)				10:.5:1	355
250 6-CYL	L	X	X	9.5:1	250
351 V-8 4-V CJ	M	X	X	10.7:1	290
428 V-8 4-V CJ	Q & R	X	X	10.6:1	335

MERCURY

Engine CID	Warranty Plate Code	Compression Ratio	Brake Horsepower
390 V-8 (2-V)	Y	9.5:1	265 @ 4400
390 V-8 (2-V)	X	10.5:1	280 @ 4400
428 V-8 (4-V)	P	10.5:1	360 @ 5400
429 V-8 (2-V)	K	10.5:1	320
429 V-8 (4-V)	N	10.5:1	360

VEHICLE IDENTIFICATION NUMBER

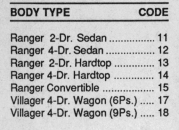

OU13W700001

The VIN is stamped into the Top of the right side of the frame side-rail in front of the firewall.

First Digit - Year 1960

Second Digit - Assembly Plant
Louisville .... U

BODY TYPE	CODE
Ranger 2-Dr. Sedan	11
Ranger 4-Dr. Sedan	12
Ranger 2-Dr. Hardtop	13
Ranger 4-Dr. Hardtop	14
Ranger Convertible	15
Villager 4-Dr. Wagon (6Ps.)	17
Villager 4-Dr. Wagon (9Ps.)	18

Fifth Digit - Engine Code

ENGINE	CODE
223 CID 6Cyl.	V
292 CID 2-BBL	W
292 CID Export	T
352 CID 4-BBL	Y
352 CID Export	G

PATENT PLATE

The patent plate, whichg includes the serial number, body style, body color, trim code, date of assembly, transmission code, and axle ratio cod, is riveted to the left front fody pillar between the front door hinges.

SERIAL NUMBER: The serial number is a repeat of the VIN.

DAY AND MONTH OF YEAR CODE: The number indicates the day of the month the vehicle was built and the letter indicates the month. Following is the month of the year code chart:

MONTH	CODE
January	A
February	B
March	C
April	D
May	E
June	F
July	G
August	H

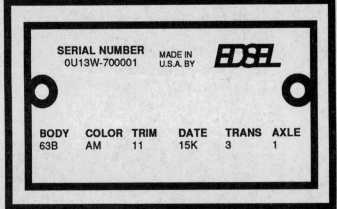

SERIAL NUMBER 0U13W-700001	MADE IN U.S.A. BY	EDSEL			
BODY 63B	**COLOR** AM	**TRIM** 11	**DATE** 15K	**TRANS** 3	**AXLE** 1

September	J
October	K
November	L
December	M

TRANSMISSION CODE: The transmission code number indicates the type of transmission installed in the vehicle.

TRANSMISSION	CODE
STANDARD	1
Mile-O-Matic (2 speed)	3
Dual Power (3 speed)	4

THE BODY CODE:

BODY	CODE
Ranger 2-Dr. Sedan	64A
Ranger 4-Dr. Sedan	58A
	58B
Ranger 2-Dr. Hardtop	63A
	63B
Ranger 4-Dr. Hardtop	57A
	57B
Ranger 2-Dr. Convertible	76B
Villager 4-Dr. Wagon, 6-Ps.	71F
Villager 4-Dr. Wagon, 9-Ps.	71E

REAR AXLE RATION CODE: The rear axle ratio code indicates the ratio of the axle installed in the vehicle.

STD	EQUA-LOCK	AXLE RATIO
1	A	3:56
2	B	3:89
3	C	3:10
8		2:91

THE COLOR CODE: A single letter designates a solid body color and two letters denote a two-tone; the first letter the lower color and the second letter the upper color.

CODE	COLOR	CODE
A	Black Velvet	AA1
C	Turquois	CC1
E	Cadet Blue Met.	EE1
F	Hawaiian Blue	FF1
H	Alasfan Gold Met.	HH1
J	Regal Red	JJ1
K	Turquoise Met.	KK1
M	Polar White	MM1
N	Sahara Beige	NN1
Q	Lilac Met.	QQ1
R	Buttercup Yellow	RR1
U	Sherwood Green Met	UU1
W	Sea Foam Green	WW1
Z	Cloud Silver Met.	ZZ1

THE TRIM CODE: A two digit number indicates the color and type of trim.

RANGER STANDARD INTERIOR TRIM CODES (Sedans and Hardtops)

BOLSTER	INSERT	CODE
Silver Moroccan Vinyl	Black Pebblecloth	20
Blue Moroccan Vinyl	Black Pebblecloth	22
Green Moroccan Vinyl	Brown Pebblecloth	23
Med. Gold Moroccan Vinyl	Brown Pebblecloth	24
Red Moroccan Vinyl	Black Pebblecloth	25

RANGER INTERIOR TRIM CODES

BOLSTER	INSERT	CODE
Med. Gold Moroccan Vinyl	Light Gold Moroccan Vinyl	54
Red Moroccan vionyl	Silver Moroccan Vinyl	55
Black Moroccan Vinyl	Black Moroccan Vinyl	56
Light Turquoise	Med. Turquoise	57
Moroccan Vinyl	Moroccan Vinyl	

RANGER DELUXE INTERIOR TRIM CODES

BOLSTER	INSERT	CODE
Silver Moroccan vinyl	Gray Champagne Cloth	11
Red Moroccan vinyl	Gray Champagne Cloth	15
Light Turquoise Turquoise	Champagne Cloth	17
Moroccan Vinyl		

ENGINE SPECIFICATIONS

CID	Comp. Ratio	Fuel Req.
223	8.4:1	Regular
292	8.8:1	Regular
352	10.0:1	Premium

ENGINE NUMBER

Stamped on a boss behind the water pump. The number provides the code to identify the series, block, displacement, and month/day production date.

EXAMPLE

R	36	2	24
YEAR	361	FEBRUARY	DAY

Engine #	Engine Name	CID	Comp Ratio	HP	Transmission
R-22-2-24	6 CYL. - In Line	223	8.4: 1	145	S-475-500
R-29-2-24	8 Cyl. - 90 "V" O.H.V.	292	8.8: 1	185	S-500-525
R-35-2-24	8 Cyl. - 90 "V" O.H.V.	352	9.6: 1	300	S-500-525

VEHICLE IDENTIFICATION NUMBER

8203100551

The vehicle number (serial number) is stamped and embossed on a stainless steel plate attached to the left front door hinge pillar. It consists of car make symbol, series code, model year code, assembly plant symbol & a sequential production number.

1st Digit Car make
Chrysler 8
Imperial 9

2nd Digit Series
Windsor, Imperial Custom 1
Saratoga, Imperial Crown 2
New Yorker, Imperial LeBaron 3
300F 4
Windsor, Suburban 5
Taxi 6
Crown Limousine 9

3rd Digit Year...........................1960

4th Digit Assembly plant
Jefferson Plant - Detroit 3
Imperial Plant - Detroit 4
Los Angeles - Calif. 5
Newark Plant - Del. 6
St. Louis Plant - Mo. 7
5th through 10th digit are production sequence code.

BODY CODE PLATE

Stamped and embossed on a stainless steel plate under the hood. It is attached to: right or left fender, cowl, or radiator cross member depending on the model and assembly plant. This plate will indicate; schedule date, body production number, body series, trim, paint, and accessory code.

THE SHIPPING ORDER NUMBER is assigned prior to production. It consists of a 4 digit planned delivery month/day date code, 0224 (February 24th). Then a plant production sequence number follows (0555)

BODY NUMBER is a 3 digit number which indicates the model and body style.

```
1 2 3 4 5 6 7 8 9 0
A B C D E F G H J X L M N P Q R S T V W X Y Z

SO        NUMBER      BDY      TRM      PNT
0224        0555        812      101      BB1
```

WINDSOR   CODE
6-Ps. 2-Dr. Hardtop 812
6-Ps. 4-Dr. Sedan 813
6-Ps. 4-Dr. Hardtop 814
6-Ps. 2-Dr. Convertable............. 815
6-Ps. 2-Seat T&C Wag.............. 858
9-Ps. 3-Seat T&C Wag............. 859

SARATOGA   CODE
6-Ps. 2-Dr. Hardtop......... 822
6-Ps. 4-Dr. Sedan 823
6-Ps. 4-Dr. Hardtop 824

NEW YORKER   CODE
6-Ps. 2-Dr. Hardtop 832
6-Ps. 4-Dr. Sedan 833
6-Ps. 4-Dr. Hardtop 834
6-Ps. 2-Dr. Convertable .. 835

6-Ps. 2-Seat T&C Wag. 878
9-Ps. 3-Seat T&C Wag. 879

300F   CODE
4-Ps. 2-Dr. Hardtop 842
4-Ps. 4-Dr. Convertable 845

IMPERIAL CUSTOM   CODE
6-Ps. 2-Dr. Southhampton ... 912
6-Ps. 4-Dr. Sedan 913
6-Ps. 4-Dr. Southhampton ... 914

IMPERIAL CROWN   CODE
6-Ps. 2-Dr. Southhampton ... 922
6-Ps. 4-Dr. Sedan 923
6-Ps. 4-Dr. Southhampton ... 924
6-Ps. 2-Dr. Convertable 925

IMPERIAL LE BARON   CODE
6-Ps. 4-Dr. Sedan 933
6-Ps. 4-Dr. Southhampton ... 934

CROWN IMPERIAL   CODE
8-Ps. 4-Dr. Limousine 993

THE PAINT CODE furnishes the key to the paint used on the car. A two digit code indicates the top and bottom colors respectively. A number follows which designates two-tone, sports-tone, convertible top, etc.

CODE	COLOR	CODE
A	Sunburst	AA1
B	Formal Black	BB1
C	Starlight Blue	CC1
D	Polar Blue	DD1
F	Surf Green	FF1
G	Ivy Green	GG1
H	Silverpine	HH1
J	Seaspray	JJ1
K	Bluegrass	KK1
L	Sheffield Silver	LL1
N	Executive Gray	NN1
P	Toreador Red	PP1
R	Lilac	RR1
S	Iris	SS1
T	Daytona Sand	TT1
U	Autumn Haze	UU1
W	Alaskan White	WW1
Y	Petal Pink	YY1
Z	Terra Cotta	ZZ1

TRIM CODE: Furnishes the key to the interior color and material.

Note: **H - Hardtop**   **S - Sedan**   **T&C - Town & Country Wagon**   **C - Convertible**

CODE	SERIES/MODEL	COLOR
101	Windsor/ S, H	Blue
103	Windsor/ S, H	Tan
104	Windsor/ S, H	Silver
105	Windsor/ S, H	Turquoise
106	Windsor/ S, H	Mauve
107	Windsor/ S, H	Terra Cotta
113	Windsor/ T & C	Tan
114	Windsor/ T & C	Black
134	Windsor/ C, H	Black
118	Windsor/ T & C	Red
138	Windsor/ C, H	Red
119	Windsor/ T & C	White
139	Windsor/ C, H	White
131	Windsor/ C	Blue
141	Windsor/ S-Optional	Blue
143	Windsor/ S-Optional	Black, Tan
144	Windsor/ S-Optional	Black, Silver
221	Saratoga/ S	Blue
201	Saratoga/ H	Blue
223	Saratoga/ S	Tan
203	Saratoga/ H	Tan
224	Saratoga/ S	Silver
204	Saratoga/ H	Silver
225	Saratoga/ S	Turquoise
205	Saratoga/ H	Turquoise
226	Saratoga/ S	Mauve
206	Saratoga/ H	Mauve
227	Saratoga/ S	Terra Cotta
207	Saratoga/ H	Terra Cotta
234	Saratoga/ H-Optional	Black
238	Saratoga/ H-Optional	Red
239	Saratoga/ H-Optional	White
241	Saratoga/ S-Optional	Blue
243	Saratoga/ S-Optional	Tan, Black
244	Saratoga/ S-Optional	Silver, Black

361	New Yorker/ S	Blue
363	New Yorker/ S	Tan
364	New Yorker/ S	Silver
367	New Yorker/ S	Terra Cotta
321	New Yorker/ S	Blue
323	New Yorker/ S	Tan
324	New Yorker/ S	Black
325	New Yorker/ S	Turquoise
326	New Yorker/ S	Mauve
327	New Yorker/ S	Terra Cotta
301	New Yorker/ T&C, H	Blue
303	New Yorker/ T&C, H	Tan
304	New Yorker/ H	Silver, Black
305	New Yorker/ T&C, H	Turquoise
306	New Yorker/ H, C	Mauve
307	New Yorker/ T&C, H, C	Terra Cotta
313	New Yorker/ T&C	Tan
314	New Yorker/ T&C	Black
318	New Yorker/ T&C	Red
319	New Yorker/ T&C	White
331	New Yorker/ C	Blue
334	New Yorker/ C, H	Black
338	New Yorker/ C, H	Red
339	New Yorker/ C, H	White
341	New Yorker/ S-Optional	Blue
343	New Yorker/ S-Optional	Tan, Black
344	New Yorker/ S-Optional	Silver, Black

CONVERTIBLE TOPS

Black
White
Blue
Terra Cotta

ENGINE NUMBER

Stamped on a boss behind the water pump. The number provides the code to identify the series, block, displacement, and month/day production date.

EXAMPLE

P	**38**	**2**	**24**
YEAR	383	FEBRUARY	24th DAY

Engine#s	Engine Name	CID	Comp Ratio	Carb Type	HP	Transmission
P-38-2-24	Golden Lion	383	10.1	2B1	305	S-Torqueflite
P-38-2-24	Golden Lion	383	10.1	4Bl	325	S-Torqueflite
P-41-2-24	300F	413	10.1	2/4Bl Ram	375	S-Torqueflite
P-41-2-24	300F	413	10.1	2/4BBL RAM	400	O-Manual
Y-41-2-24	Imperial V8	413	10.1	4Bl	350	S-Torqueflite

NOTE - Last two digits are month and day engine was built.

VEHICLE IDENTIFICATION NUMBER

8214100551

The vehicle number (serial number) is stamped and embossed on a stainless steel plate attached to the left front door hinge pillar. It consists of car make symbol, series code, model year code, assembly plant symbol & a sequential production number.

1st Digit - Car make
Chrysler 8
Imperial 9

2nd Digit - Series
Windsor, Imperial Custom 1
Saratoga, Imperial Crown 2
New Yorker, Imperial LeBaron .. 3
300G 4
Windsor 5
New Yorker 7
Taxi 8
Police 9
Crown Limousine 10

3rd Digit - Year 1961

4th Digit - Assembly plant
Jefferson Plant - Detroit 3
Imperial Plant - Detroit 4
Los Angeles - Calif. 5
Newark Plant - Del. 6
St. Louis Plant - Mo. 7

5th through 10th digit are production sequence code.

BODY CODE PLATE

Stamped and embossed on a stainless steel plate under the hood. It is attached to: right or left fender, cowl, or radiator cross member depending on the model and assembly plant. This plate will indicate; schedule date, body production number, body series, trim, paint, and accessory code.

THE SHIPPING ORDER NUMBER is assigned prior to production. It consists of a 4 digit planned delivery month/day date code, 0224 (February 24th). Then a plant production sequence number follows (0555)

BODY NUMBER is a 3 digit number which indicates the model and body style.

```
1234567890
A B C D E F G H J X L M N P Q R S T V W X Y Z

SO        NUMBER      BDY      TRM      PNT
0224      0555        812      701      BB1
```

NEWPORT   **CODE**
6-Ps. 2-Dr. Hardtop 812
6-Ps. 4-Dr. Sedan 813
6-Ps. 4-Dr. Hardtop 814
6-Ps. 2-Dr. Convertible 815
6-Ps. 2-Seat T&C Wag 858
9-Ps. 3-Seat T&C Wag 859

WINDSOR   **CODE**
6-Ps. 2-Dr. Hardtop 822
6-Ps. 4-Dr. Sedan 823

6-Ps. 4-Dr. Hardtop 824

NEW YORKER   **CODE**
6-Ps. 2-Dr. Hardtop 832
6-Ps. 4-Dr. Sedan 833
6-Ps. 4-Dr. Hardtop 834
6-Ps. 2-Dr. Convertible 835
6-Ps. 2-Seat T&C Wag. 878
9-Ps. 3-Seat T&C Wag. 879

300G   **CODE**
4-Ps. 2-Dr. Hardtop 842
4-Ps. 2-Dr. Convertible 845

IMPERIAL CUSTOM   **CODE**
6-Ps. 2-Dr. Southhampton ... 912
6-Ps. 4-Dr. Southhampton ... 914

IMPERIAL CROWN   **CODE**
6-Ps. 2-Dr. Southhampton ... 922
6-Ps. 4-Dr. Southhampton ... 924
6-Ps. 2-Dr. Convertible 925

IMPERIAL LE BARON   **CODE**
6-Ps. 4-Dr. Southhampton ... 934

THE PAINT CODE furnishes the key to the paint used on the car. A three digit code indicates the top and bottom colors respectively. A number follows which designates two-tone, sports-tone, convertible top, etc.

CODE	COLOR	CODE
B	Formal Black	BB1
C	Parisian Blue	CC1
D	Capri Blue	DD1
G	Pinehurst Green	GG1
J	Tahitian Turquoise	JJ1
L	Sheffield Silver	LL1
O	Dubonnet	OO1
P	Mardi Gras Red	PP1
R	Cinnamon	RR1
W	All Colors	WW1
Y	Tuscan Bronze	YY1
Z	Alaskan White	ZZ1

TRIM CODE: Furnishes the key to the interior color and material.

Material						Color					
	Blue	Topaz	Gray	Russet	Black	Red	White	Green	Brown	Cersise	Tan
Cloth & Leather	921	971	974	978				922			
		971	923	924	928						
Cloth	721		724		966	965	967	752		759	753
	931				754						
Leather	951		958		956	955	957				833
Cloth & Vinyl	731	903	904	908	704			732	703	709	733
	711		906		734			902			
	901				714						
	701										
Vinyl	821				826	825	807				843
	801				806	805	827				803
						845					

Convertible Top

Black
White

ENGINE NUMBER

Stamped on a boss behind the water pump. The number provides the code to identify the series, block, displacement, and month/day production date.

EXAMPLE

R	38	2	24
YEAR	383	FEBRUARY	24th DAY

Engine#s	Engine Name	CID	Comp Ratio	Carb Type	HP	Transmission
R-38-2-24	Golden Lion	361	9.0	2B1	305	S-A745 Heavy-duty 3-speed Manual O-A466 Torqueflite 3-speed Automatic
R-38-2-24	Golden Lion	383	10.1	4Bl	305	Same
R-41-2-24	Golden Lion	413	10.1	4Bl	350	S-A-466
R-41-2-24	300G	413	10.1	4Bl	375	S-A-466 O-A-745
	300G Power Pack	413	10.1	2/4Bl	400	S-A-745
	Imperial V8	413	10.1	4Bl	350	S-A-466
	Golden Lion Power Pack	413	10.1	4Bl	350	S-A-745

NOTE - Last two digits are month and day engine was built.

VEHICLE IDENTIFICATION NUMBER

8323100551

The vehicle number (serial number) is stamped and embossed on a stainless steel plate attached to the left front door hinge pillar. It consists of car make symbol, series code, model year code, assembly plant symbol & a sequential production number.

1st Digit - Car make

Chrysler 8
Imperial 9

2nd Digit - Series

Windsor, Imperial Custom 1
Saratoga, Imperial Crown 2
New Yorker, Imperial LeBaron .. 3
Windsor 5
New Yorker 7
Taxi 8
Police 9
Commercial.............................. 10

3rd Digit - Year..................1962

4th Digit - Assembly plant

Jefferson Plant - Detroit 3
Los Angeles - Calif. 5
Newark Plant - Del. 6
St. Louis Plant - Mo. 7

5th through 10th digit are production sequence code.

BODY CODE PLATE

Stamped and embossed on a stainless steel plate under the hood. It is attached to: right or left fender, cowl, or radiator cross member depending on the model and assembly plant. This plate will indicate; schedule date, body production number, body series, trim, paint, and accessory code.

THE SHIPPING ORDER NUMBER is assigned prior to production. It consists of a 4 digit planned delivery month/day date code, 0224 (February 24th). Then a plant production sequence number follows (0555)

BODY NUMBER is a 3 digit number which indicates the model and body style.

```
1234567890
A B C D E F G H J X L M N P Q R S T V W X Y Z

SO          NUMBER      BDY      TRM      PNT
0224        0555        812      301      BB1
```

NEWPORT	CODE
6-Ps. 2-Dr. Hardtop	812
6-Ps. 4-Dr. Sedan	813
6-Ps. 4-Dr. Hardtop	814
6-Ps. 2-Dr. Convertable	815
6-Ps. Suburban	858
9-Ps. Suburban	859

NEWPORT (300)	CODE
6-Ps. 2-Dr. Hardtop	822
6-Ps. 4-Dr. Hardtop	824

6-Ps. Convertible	825

NEW YORKER	CODE
6-Ps. 4-Dr. Sedan	833
6-Ps. 4-Dr. Hardtop	834
6-Ps. Suburbang.	878
9-Ps. Suburban.	879

NEW YORKER (300-H)	CODE
6-PS. 2-Dr. Hardtop	842

6-Ps. Convertible	845

IMPERIAL	CODE
6-Ps. 2-Dr. Hardtop	912
6-Ps. 4-Dr. Hardtop	914

CROWN IMPERIAL	CODE
6-Ps. 2-Dr. Hardtop	922
6-Ps. 4-Dr. Hardtop	924
6-Ps. 2-Dr. Convertable	925

LE BARON	CODE
6-Ps. 4-Dr. Hardtop	934

THE PAINT CODE furnishes the key to the paint used on the car. A thre digit code indicates the top and bottom colors respectively. A number follows which designates two-tone, sports-tone, convertible top, etc.

CODE	COLOR	CODE
B	Formal Black	BB1
C	Dawn Blue	CC1
D	Sapphire Blue	DD1
E	Moonlight Blue	EE1
G	Willow Green	GG1
H	Sage Green	HH1
J	Bermuda Turquoise	JJ1
L	Dove Gray	LL1
O	Alabaster	OO1
P	Festival Red	PP1
Q	Embassy Red	QQ1
R	Silver Lilac	RR1
S	Coral Gray	SS1
T	Cordovan	TT1
U	Caramel	UU1
Y	Rosewood	YY1
Z	Oyster White	ZZ1

504	*	*	-	Gray
511	*	-	*	Blue
512	*	-	*	Green
513	*	-	*	Cocoa
514	*	-	*	Gray
515	*	-	*	Red
516	*	-	*	Black
553	-	-	*	Tan
555	-	-	*	Red
556	-	-	*	Black
557	-	-	*	Off White
521	*	-	-	Black
522	*	-	*	Green
523	*	-	*	Cocoa
524	*	-	*	Gray
534	*	-	-	Gray

Conertible Top

Black
White

TRIM CODE: Furnishes the key to the interior color and material.

CODE	CLOTH	VINYL	LEATHER	COLOR
301	*	*	-	Blue
303	*	*	-	Cocoa
304	*	*	-	Gray and Black
305	*	*	-	Red
313	*	*	-	Tan
314	*	*	-	Gray and Black
315	*	*	-	Red
321	*	-	-	Blue
323	*	-	-	Cocoa
324	*	-	-	Gray
331	*	*	-	Blue
333	*	*	-	Cocoa
334	*	*	-	Gray
335	*	*	-	Red
401	-	*	-	Blue
404	-	*	-	Black
405	-	*	-	Red
413	-	*	-	Gold
414	-	*	-	Black
415	-	*	-	Red
423	-	*	-	Cocoa
424	-	*	-	Black
425	-	*	-	Red
444	-	*	-	Gray
453	-	-	*	Gold
454	-	-	*	Black
455	-	-	*	Red
463	-	-	*	Tan
464	-	*	-	Black
465	-	*	-	Red
501	*	*	-	Blue
502	*	*	-	Green
503	*	*	-	Cocoa
534	*	-	-	Gray

ENGINE NUMBER

Stamped on a boss behind the water pump. The number provides the code to identify the series, block, displacement, and month/day production date.

EXAMPLE

S	38	2	24
YEAR	383	FEBRUARY	24th DAY

Engine #s	Engine Name	CID	Comp Ratio	Carb Type	Horse Power	Transmission
S-36-6-1	Firebolt	361	9.0	1, 2Bl	265	S- A-745 3-Speed manual O- A-727 Torqueflite
S-38-6-1	Firepower 305	383	10.0	1, 2Bl	305	Same
S-41-6-1	Firepower 340	413	10.1	1, 4Bl	340	S- A-745 O- A-727
	Firepower 380	413	10.1	2, 4Bl	380 Runner	S- A-727
	High Performance	413	11.0 10.1	1-4Bl 2-4Bl	365 380 Runner	S- A-745 S- A-745 O- A-727
	Options		11.0	2-4Bl	405 Ram	S- A-745 O- A-727
	Imperial V8	413	10.1	1-4Bl	340	S- A-727
No Info.	High performance	426	11.0 12.0 11.0	1-4Bl 1-4Bl 2-4Bl Ram	373 385 413	S- A-745 S- A-745 S- A-745 O- A-727
			12.0	2-4Bl Ram	421	S- A-745 O- A-727

NOTE - Last two digits are month and day engine was built.

VEHICLE IDENTIFICATION NUMBER

8533100551

The vehicle number (serial number) is stamped and embossed on a stainless steel plate attached to the left front door hinge pillar. It consists of car make symbol, series code, model year code, assembly plant symbol & a sequential production number.

1st Digit - Car make
Chrysler 8
Imperial 9

2nd Digit - Series
Windsor, Imperial Custom 1
Saratoga, Imperial Crown 2
New Yorker, Imperial LeBaron .. 3
Chrysler 300J 4
Windsor 5
New Yorker 7
Taxi 8
Police 9
Commercial............................... 10

3rd Digit - Year...................1963

4th Digit - Assembly plant
Jefferson Plant - Detroit 3
Los Angeles - Calif. 5
Newark Plant - Del. 6
St. Louis Plant - Mo. 7

5th through 10th digit are production sequence code.

BODY CODE PLATE

Stamped and embossed on a stainless steel plate under the hood. It is attached to: right or left fender, cowl, or radiator cross member depending on the model and assembly plant. This plate will indicate; schedule date, body production number, body series, trim, paint, and accessory code.

THE SHIPPING ORDER NUMBER is assigned prior to production. It consists of a 4 digit planned delivery month/day date code, 0224 (February 24th). Then a plant production sequence number follows (0555)

BODY NUMBER is a 3 digit number which indicates the model and body style.

1 2 3 4 5 6 7 8 9 0				
A B C D E F G H J X L M N P Q R S T V W X Y Z				
SO	NUMBER	BDY	TRM	PNT
0224	0555	812	301	BB1

NEWPORT	CODE
6-Ps. 2-Dr. Hardtop 812
6-Ps. 4-Dr. Sedan 813
6-Ps. 4-Dr. Hardtop 814
6-Ps. 2-Dr. Convertable 815
6-Ps. Suburban......................858
9-Ps. Suburban 859
$-Dr. (Police) Sedan 893
6-Ps. (police) Suburban 898

NEW YORKER	CODE
6-Ps. 4-Dr. Sedan 833
6-Ps. 4-Dr. Hardtop 834
6-Ps. Suburbang. 878
9-Ps. Suburban. 879
6-Ps. 4-Dr. Limousine 884

NEW YORKER (300-J)	CODE
6-PS. 2-Dr. Hardtop................842

IMPERIAL	CODE
6-Ps. 2-Dr. Hardtop 912
6-Ps. 4-Dr. Hardtop...............914

CROWN IMPERIAL	CODE
6-Ps. 2-Dr. Hardtop 922
6-Ps. 4-Dr. Hardtop 924
6-Ps. 2-Dr. Convertable 925

IMPERIAL LE BARON	CODE
6-Ps. 4-Dr. Hardtop 934

THE PAINT CODE furnishes the key to the paint used on the car. A three digit code indicates the top and bottom colors respectively. A number follows which designates two-tone, sports-tone, convertible top, etc.

CODE	COLOR	CODE
B	Formal Black	BB1
C	Glacier Blue	CC1
D	Cord Blue	DD1
E	Navy Blue	EE1
G	Surf Green	GG1
H	Forest Green	HH1
J	Holiday Turquoise	JJ1
K	Teal	KK1
N	Madison Gray	NN1
O	Dubonnet	OO1
P	Festival	PP1
Q	Claret	QQ1
T	Fawn	TT1
U	Cypress Tan	UU1
W	Alabaster	WW1
Y	Embassy Gold	YY1
Z	Oyster White	ZZ1

TRIM CODE: Furnishes the key to the interior color and material.

CODE	CLOTH	VINYL	LEATHER	COLOR
301	*	*	-	Blue
303	*	*	-	Cocoa
304	*	*	-	Gray and Black
305	*	*	-	Red
313	*	*	-	Tan
314	*	*	-	Gray and Black
315	*	*	-	Red
321	*	-	-	Blue
323	*	-	-	Cocoa
324	*	-	-	Gray
331	*	*	-	Blue
333	*	*	-	Cocoa
334	*	*	-	Gray
335	*	*	-	Red
401	-	*	-	Blue
404	-	*	-	Black
405	-	*	-	Red
413	-	*	-	Gold
414	-	*	-	Black
415	-	*	-	Red
423	-	*	-	Cocoa
424	-	*	-	Black
425	-	*	-	Red
444	-	*	-	Gray
453	-	-	*	Gold
454	-	-	*	Black
455	-	-	*	Red
463	-	-	*	Tan
464	-	*	-	Black
465	-	*	-	Red
501	*	*	-	Blue
502	*	*	-	Green
503	*	*	-	Cocoa
534	*	-	-	Gray
504	*	*	-	Gray
511	*	-	*	Blue
512	*	-	*	Green
513	*	-	*	Cocoa
514	*	-	*	Gray
515	*	-	*	Red
516	*	-	*	Black
553	-	-	*	Tan
555	-	-	*	Red
556	-	-	*	Black
557	-	-	*	Off White
521	*	-	-	Black
522	*	-	-	Green
523	*	-	-	Cocoa
524	*	-	*	Gray
534	*	-	-	Gray

ENGINE NUMBER

Stamped on a boss behind the water pump. The number provides the code to identify the series, block, displacement, and month/day production date.

EXAMPLE

T	38	2	24
YEAR	383	FEBRUARY	24th DAY

Engine #s	Engine Name	CID	Comp Ratio	Carb Type	Horse Power	Transmission
T-36-2-24	Firebolt	361	9.0	1- 2Bl	265	S- A-745 O- A-727
T-38-2-24	Firepower 305	383	10.1	1-2Bl	305	S- A-745 O- A-727
T-41-2-24	Firepower 340	413	10.1	1-4Bl	340	S- A-745 O- A-727
	Firepower 360	413	10.1	1-4Bl	365	S- A-727
	Imperial V8	413	10.1	1-4Bl	340	S- A-727
C 300J-2-24	300J	413	9.6	2-4Bl	390	S- A-727
				Ram		O- A-745

NOTE - Last two digits are month and day engine was built.

VEHICLE IDENTIFICATION NUMBER

8445100551

The vehicle number (serial number) is stamped and embossed on a stainless steel plate attached to the left front door hinge pillar. It consists of car make symbol, series code, model year code, assembly plant symbol & a sequential production number.

1st Digit - Car make
Chrysler 8
Imperial 9

2nd Digit - Series
Windsor, Imperial Custom 1
Saratoga, Imperial Crown 2
New Yorker, Imperial LeBaron .. 3
Chrysler 300J 4
Windsor 5
New Yorker 7
Taxi 8
Police 9
Commercial................................ 10

3rd Digit - Year...................1964

4th Digit - Assembly plant
Jefferson Plant - Detroit 3
ILos Angeles - Calif. 5
Newarc Plant - Del. 6
St. Louis Plant - Mo. 7

5th through 10th digit are production sequence code.

BODY CODE PLATE

Stamped and embossed on a stainless steel plate under the hood. It is attached to: right or left fender, cowl, or radiator cross member depending on the model and assembly plant. This plate will indicate; schedule date, body production number, body series, trim, paint, and accessory code.

THE SHIPPING ORDER NUMBER is assigned prior to production. It consists of a 4 digit planned delivery month/day date code, 0224 (February 24th). Then a plant production sequence number follows (0555)

BODY NUMBER is a 3 digit number which indicates the model and body style.

```
1 2 3 4 5 6 7 8 9 0
A B C D E F G H J X L M N P Q R S T V W X Y Z

SO        NUMBER     BDY      TRM      PNT
0224      0555       812      L1B      BB1
```

NEWPORT   CODE
6-Ps. 2-Dr. Hardtop 812
6-Ps. 4-Dr. Sedan 813
6-Ps. 4-Dr. Hardtop 814
6-Ps. 2-Dr. Convertable 815
6-Ps. Suburban 858
9-Ps. Suburban 859

CHRYSLER 300   CODE
6-Ps. 2-Dr. Hardtop............. 822

6-Ps. 4-Dr. Hardtop 824
6-Ps. 2-Dr. Convertible 825

300K   CODE
6-Ps. 2-Dr. Hardtop 842
6-Ps. 2-Dr. Convertible............ 845

NEW YORKER   CODE
6-Ps. 4-Dr. Sedan 833
6-Ps. 4-Dr. Hardtop 834

6-Ps. T&C Wagon. 878
9-Ps. T&C Wagon. 879

NEW YORKER SALON   CODE
6-Ps. 4-Dr. Hardtop 884

CROWN IMPERIAL   CODE
6-Ps. 2-Dr. Hardtop 922
6-Ps. 4-Dr. Hardtop 924
6-Ps. 2-Dr. Convertable 925

LE BARON   CODE
6-Ps. 4-Dr. Hardtop 934

THE PAINT CODE furnishes the key to the paint used on the car. A three digit code indicates the top and bottom colors respectively. A number follows which designates two-tone, sports-tone, convertible top, etc.

CODE	COLOR	CODE
B	Formal Black	BB1
C	Wegewood	CC1
D	Chrysler/Nassau Blue	DD1
E	Monarch Blue	EE1
F	Pine Mist	FF1
G	Sequoia Green	GG1
K	Silver Turquoise	KK1
L	Royal Turquoise	LL1
M	Madison Gray	MM1
N	Charcoal Gray	NN1
O	Rosewood	OO1
P	Royal Ruby	PP1
R	Royal Ruby	RR1
S	Ivory	SS1
T	Roman Red	TT1
W	Persian White	WW1
X	Dune Beige	XX1
Y	Sable Tan	YY1

CODE				COLOR
"M3R, M9R"	-	*	*	Red
"M3T, M9T"	-	*	*	Yellow Tan
"M3W, M9W"	-	*	*	White
"M3X, M9X"	-	*	*	Black
"M3F, M9F"	-	*	*	Green
"M3V, M9V, M9W"	-	*	*	Red & White
"M7H, M8H"	*	*	*	Green & Tan
"M7M, M8M"	*	*	*	Mauve or Maroon
"M7N, M8N"	*	*	*	Black & White
"M7Q, M8Q"	*	*	*	Turquoise
M7P	*	*	*	Black & Gray
"H3B, H7B"	*	*	*	Blue
H3C	*	*	*	Blue & White
H3R	-	*	*	Red
H3W	-	*	*	White
H3X	-	*	*	Black
H3F	-	*	*	Green
H3V	-	*	*	Red & White
H7H	*	*	*	Green & Tan
H7M	*	*	*	Mauve or Maroon
H7T	*	*	*	Yellow Tan
H7P	*	*	*	Black & Gray

TRIM CODE: Furnishes the key to the interior color and material.

CODE	CLOTH	VINYL	LEATHER	COLOR
"L1B, L2B, L4B"	*	*	-	Blue
"L1F, L2F"	*	*	-	Yellow Green
"L1M, L2M"	*	*	-	Mauve or Maroon
"L1N, L4N"	*	*	-	Black & White
"L1Q, L2Q, L4Q"	*	*	-	Turquoise
"L1T, L2T, L4T"	*	*	-	Yellow Tan
L4R	-	*	-	Red
"K1B, K4B"	*	*	-	Blue
K1F	*	*	-	Yellow Green
K1M	*	*	-	Mauve or Maroon
"K1N, K4N"	*	*	-	Black & White
"K1T, K4T"	*	*	-	Yellow Tan
K4	-	*	-	Red
"K5A, K8A"	*	*	-	Gray
"M1B, M4B"	*	*	-	Blue
M1M	*	*	-	Mauve or Maroon
M1N	*	*	-	Black & White
"M1T, M4T"	*	*	-	Yellow Tan
"M4X, M8X"	-	*	-	Black
"M4W, M8W"	-	*	-	White
M4	-	*	-	Red
"H1B, H4B"	*	*	-	Blue
"H3B, H7B"	*	-	*	Blue
H1F	*	*	-	Yellow Green
"H3L, H7L"	*	-	*	Yellow Gold
H1M	*	*	-	Mauve or Maroon
"H1N, H2N"	*	*	-	Black & White
"H1Q, H4Q"	*	*	-	Turquoise
H4R	-	*	-	Red
"H1T, H4T"	*	*	-	Yellow Tan
H4W	-	*	-	White
"M3B, M9B"	-	*	*	Blue
"M7B, M8B"	*	*	*	Blue
M9C	-	*	*	Blue & White

ENGINE NUMBER

Stamped on a boss behind the water pump. The number provides the code to identify the series, block, displacement, and month/day production date.

EXAMPLE

V	38	2	24
YEAR	383	FEBRUARY	24th DAY

Engine#s	Engine	CID	Comp Ratio	Carb Type	Horse power	Transmission
V-36-2-24	Firebolt 265	361	9.0	2Bl	265	S- A-745 O- A-727
T-38-2-24	Firepower 305	383	10.0	2, 4Bl	305	S- A-745 O- A-833 O- A-727
T-41-2-24 C300K-2-24	Firepower 360	413	10.1	1, 4Bl	360	S- A-745 O- A-843 O- A-833 O- A-727
	Firepower 390	413	9.6	2-4Bl Ram	390	S- A-727
	Firepower 340	413	10.1	1-4Bl	340	S- A-727
	Imperial V8	413	10.1	1-4Bl	340	S- A-727

NOTE - Last two digits are month and day engine was built.

VEHICLE IDENTIFICATION NUMBER

C453100003

The vehicle number (serial number) is stamped and embossed on a stainless steel plate attached to the left front door hinge pillar. It consists of car make symbol, series code, model year code, assembly plant symbol & a sequential production number.

1st Digit - Car make
Chrysler C
Imperial .... Y

2nd Digit - Series
Newport 1
300 Crown 2
New Yorker, LeBaron 3
300L 4
Newport Station Wagon........... 5
New Yorker Station Wagon 7
Police 9

3rd Digit - Year.................1965

4th Digit - Assembly plant
Jefferson Plant - Detroit 3
Los Angeles - Calif. 5
Newark Plant - Del. 6
St. Louis Plant - Mo. 7

5th through 10th digit are production sequence code.

BODY CODE PLATE

Stamped and embossed on a stainless steel plate under the hood. It is attached to: right or left fender, cowl, or radiator cross member depending on the model and assembly plant. This plate will indicate; schedule date, body production number, body series, trim, paint, and accessory code.

THE SHIPPING ORDER NUMBER is assigned prior to production. It consists of a 4 digit planned delivery month/day date code, 0224 (February 24th). Then a plant production sequence number follows (0555)

BODY NUMBER is a 3 digit number which indicates the model and body style.

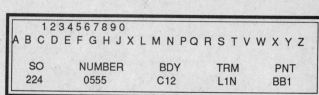

```
1234567890
ABCDEFGHJXLMNPQRSTVWXYZ

SO        NUMBER     BDY      TRM      PNT
224       0555       C12      L1N      BB1
```

NEWPORT	CODE
6-Ps. 2-Dr. Hardtop	C12
6-Ps. 4-Dr. Sedan	C13
6-Ps. 4-Dr. Hardtop	C14
6-Ps. 2-Dr. Convertable	C15
6-Ps. 4-Dr Town Sedan	C18
6-Ps. 4-Dr. T&C Wagon	C56
9-Ps. 4-Dr. T&C Wagon	C57

CHRYSLER 300	CODE
6-Ps. 2-Dr. Hardtop	C22
6-Ps. 4-Dr. Hardtop	C24
6-Ps. 2-Dr. Convertible	C25
6-Ps. 4-Dr. Town Sedan	C28

300L	CODE
6-Ps. 2-Dr. Hardtop	C42
6-Ps. 2-Dr. Convertible	C45

NEW YORKER	CODE
6-Ps. 2-Dr. Hardtop	C33
6-Ps. 4-Dr. Hardtop	C34
6-Ps. 4-Dr. Sedan	C38
6-Ps. T&C Wagon	C76
9-Ps. T&C Wagon	C77

CROWN IMPERIAL	CODE
6-Ps. 2-Dr. Hardtop	922
6-Ps. 4-Dr. Hardtop	924
6-Ps. 2-Dr. Convertable	925

LE BARON	CODE
6-Ps. 4-Dr. Hardtop	934

THE PAINT CODE furnishes the key to the paint used on the car. A thre digit code indicates the top and bottom colors respectively. A number follows which designates two-tone, sports-tone, convertible top, etc.

CODE	COLOR	CODE
A	Royal Gold Metallic	AA1
B	Formal Black	BB1
C	Ice Blue	CC1
D	Nassau Blue Metallic	DD1
E	Navy Blue Metallic	EE1
F	Mist Blue Metallic	FF1
G	Sequoia Green Metallic	GG1
4	Moss Gold Metallic	441
2	Sage Green Metallic	221
K	Peacock Turquoise Metallic	KK1
L	Royal Turquoise Metallic	LL1
N	Silver Mist Metallic	NN1
M	Granite Gray Metallic	MM1
3	Pink Silver Metallic	331
S	French Ivory	SS1
T	Spanish Red Metallic	TT1
V	Cordovan Metallic	VV1
W	Persian White	WW1
X	Sand Dune Beige	XX1
Y	Sable Tan Metallic	YY1
Z	Frost Turquoise Metallic	ZZ1

CODE	CLOTH	VINYL	LEATHER	COLOR
M3B, M7B, M8B,	*	-	*	Blue
M9B, M3C, M9C	-	-	*	Blue 7 White
M7G, M8G	*	-	*	Green & Gold
M3K, M9K	-	-	*	Purple
M7N, M8N	*	-	*	Black & White
M7P	*	-	*	Gray & Black
M7Q	*	-	*	Turquoise
M3R, M5R, M7R, M9R	*	-	*	Red
M3T, M7T, M9T	*	-	*	Tan

TRIM CODE: Furnishes the key to the interior color and material.

CODE	CLOTH	VINYL	LEATHER	COLOR
L1B, L2B, L4B, L5B, L8B, L9B	*	*	-	Blue
L2L, L4L	*	*	-	Gold & Black
L1N, L2N, L4N	*	*	-	Black & White
L1Q, L2Q, L8Q	*	*	-	Turquoise
L1R, L2R, L4R, L5R, L8R, L9R	*	*	-	Red
L1T, L2T, L4T, L5T, L8T	*	-	-	Tan
L4X, L9X	-	*	-	Black
M4B	*	*	-	Blue
M4L	*	-	-	Gold & Black
M3R, M4R	-	-	*	Red
M4T	*	-	-	Tan
M4W	-	*	-	White
M3X, M4X	-	*	*	Black
H1B, H4B	*	*	-	Blue
H1L, H4L	*	*	-	Gold & Black
H1N	*	*	-	Black & White
H1Q	*	*	-	Turquoise
H1R, H4R	*	*	-	Red
H1T, H4T	*	*	-	Tan
H4X	-	*	-	Black
P4B	-	*	-	Blue
P4L	-	*	-	Gold & Black
P3R, P4R	-	*	-	Red
P4T	-	*	-	Tan
P4W	-	*	-	White
P3X, P4X	-	*	*	Black
M3V, M9V	-	-	*	Red & White
M3W, M5W, M9W	-	-	*	White
M3X, M5X, M9X	-	-	*	Black

ENGINE NUMBER

Stamped on a boss behind the water pump. The number provides the code to identify the series, block, displacement, and month/day production date.

EXAMPLE

V	38	2	24
YEAR	383	FEBRUARY	24th DAY

Engine #s	Engine Name	CID	Comp Ratio	Carb Type	Horse power	Transmission
A-383-2-24	Firebolt	383	9.2	2-Bl	270	S- A-745
						O- A-727
	Firepower 315	383	10.0	4-Bl	315	S- A-727
						O- A-745
						O- A-833
A-413-2-24	Firepower 340	413	10.1	4-Bl	340	S- A-727
	Firepower 360	413	10.1	4-Bl	360	S- A-727
						O- A-833
	Imperial V8	413	10.1	4-Bl	340	S- A-727

NOTE - Last two digits are month and day engine was built.

VEHICLE IDENTIFICATION NUMBER

CH42G63100551

The vehicle number (serial number) is stamped and embossed on a stainless steel plate attached to the left front door hinge pillar. It consists of car make symbol, series code, model year code, assembly plant symbol & a sequential production number.

1st Digit - Car make
Chrysler C
Imperial .... Y

2nd Digit - Class
Ecconomy .... E
Low L
High .... H
Medium .... M
Premium .... P
Police .... K
Taxi .... T
VIP V

3rd Digit & 4th Digit - Body style
2-Dr. Sedan 21
2-Dr. Hardtop 23
Convertible 27
2-Dr. Sports Hardtop 29
4-Dr. Sedan 41
4-Dr. Hardtop 43
6-Ps. Station Wagon 45
9-Ps. Station Wagon 46

Fifth Digit - CID
440 Cu. In. .... J
Special Order 8 Cyl. .... K

Sixth Digit - Year 1966

Seventh Digit - Assembly plant
Jefferson Plant - Detroit 3
Belvedere Plant - ILL................. 4
Los Angeles - Calif. 5
Newark Plant - Del. 6
St. Louis Plant - Mo. 7
Windsor Plant - Onterio 9

Last six digits is the production sequence code.

BODY CODE PLATE

Stamped and embossed on a plate which is attavhed on the engine side of the cowl just above the master cylinder on imperial models. On Chrysler models the plate is located above the top hinge of the driver's side door. The plate shows the body type, trim code, schedual date, paint code, and some accessory codes.

THE SHIPPING ORDER NUMBER consists of a tree digit month and day schedualed production date, and a five digit production order number.

```
 1234567890
ABCDEFGHJXLMNPQRSTVWXYZ

SO       NUMBER    BDY     TRM     PNT
224      0555      CH42    L1R     BB1
```

MONTH	CODE
JAN	1
FEB	2
MAR	3
APR	4
MAY	5
JUN	6
JULY	7
AUG	8
SEPT	9

OCT .... A
NOV .... B
DEC C
(O1 THROUGH 31 DAYS)

BODY NUMBER is a 4 digit number which indicates the car line, price class, and body style. Same first four digits of the vin.

NEWPORT	CODE
6-Ps. 2-Dr. Hardtop..............CL23	
6-Ps. 4-Dr. Sedan CL41	
6-Ps. 4-Dr. Hardtop.............CL48	
6-Ps. 2-Dr. Convertable CL27	
6-Ps. 4-Dr Town Sedan CL42	
6-Ps. 4-Dr. T&C Wagon.......CL45	
9-Ps. 4-Dr. T&C Wagon CL46	

CHRYSLER 300	CODE
6-Ps. 2-Dr. Hardtop..........CM23	
6-Ps. 4-Dr. Hardtop CM43	
6-Ps. 2-Dr. Convertible CM27	

NEW YORKER	CODE
6-Ps. 2-Dr. Hardtop CH23	
6-Ps. 4-Dr. Hardtop CH43	
6-Ps. 4-Dr. Town Seda.......CH42	

CROWN IMPERIAL	CODE
6-Ps. 2-Dr. Hardtop YM23	
6-Ps. 4-Dr. Hardtop YM43	
6-Ps. 2-Dr. Convertable YM27	

IMPERIAL LE BARON	CODE
6-Ps. 4-Dr. Hardtop YH43	

THE PAINT CODE furnishes the key to the paint used on the car. A thre digit code indicates the top and bottom colors respectively. A number follows which designates two-tone, sports-tone, convertible top, etc.

CODE	COLOR	CODE
A	Silver Mist Metallic	AA1
B	Black	BB1
C	Blue (Powder)	CC1
D	Crystal Blue Metallic	DD1
E	Roayl Blue Metallic	EE1
F	Haze Green Metallic	FF1
G	Sequoia Green Metallic	GG1
K	Frost Turquoise Metallic	KK1
L	Royal Turquoise Metallic	LL1
P	Scorch Red	PP1
Q	Spanish Red Metallic	QQ1
7	Ruby Metallic	771
R	Daffodil Yellow	RR1
S	Ivory	SS1
W	Persian White	WW1
X	Desert Beige	XX1
Y	Saddle Bronze	YY1
Z	Spice Gold Metallic	ZZ1
4	Moss Gold Metallic	441
6	Lilac	661

TRIM CODE: Furnishes the key to the interior color and material.

CHRYSLER TRIM

MATERIAL	RED	GREEN	BLUE	TAN	TURQUOISE	BLACK	WHITE & BLACK	SILVER	WHITE
CLOTH &	L1R	L1F	L1D	L1T	L1J	L6X	M1N		
VINYL	L2R	L2F	L2D	L2T	L–J		H8N		
	L8R	L8F	L8D	L8T	L8J				
	H1R	H1F	M1D	H1T	H1J				
			H1D						
			H8D						
VINYL	L5R		L5D	L7T		L5X	M1N	M4A	M4W
	L7R		L7D	M4T		L7X	H8N		H4W
	L9R		L9D			L9X			
	M4R		L0D			L6X			
	H4R		M1D			L0X			
			M4D			M4X			
						H4X			
						M3X			
LEATHER	M3R					M3X			

IMPERIAL TRIM

MATERIAL	BLUE	DUSTY GOLD	RED	WHITE & BLACK	TURQUOISE	GREEN & GOLD	BLACK & SILVER
LEATHER &	M70	M7L	M7M	M7N	M7Q	M7G	M7P
CLOTH	H79	H7L		M8W	M8Q	H7G	H7P
	M8B					M8G	

MATERIAL	BLACK & GOLD	WHITE	BLACK	BLUE	GOLD	RED	GREEN	SILVER
LEATHER	M3E	M3W	M3X	M3B	M3L	M3M	M3F	M9A
	H3E	M3C	M9X	M9B	M9L	M9M	M9F	
		M9W	H3X	H3B	H3L	H3M	H3F	
		M9C						
		H3W						
		H3C						
CLOTH								H6A

ENGINE NUMBER

Stamped on a boss behind the water pump. The number provides the code to identify the series, block, displacement, and month/day production date.

EXAMPLE

B	38	2	24
YEAR	383	FEBRUARY	24th DAY

Engine #s	Engine Name	CID	Comp Ratio	Carb Type	Horse power	Transmission
B-383-2-24	Firepower 383	383	9.2	1, 2Bl	270	S- A-727 or A-745 O- A-727
	Firepower 383XP	383	10.0	1-4Bl	325	S- A-727 or A-745 O- A-727
B-440-2-24	Firepower 440	440	10.1	1-4Bl	350	S-A-727
	Firepower TNT 440	440	10.1	1, 4Bl	365	S- A-727
	440 V8 (Imperial)	440	10.1	1-4Bl	350	S- A-727

VEHICLE IDENTIFICATION NUMBER

CH41K73100551

The vehicle number (serial number) is stamped and embossed on a stainless steel plate attached to the left front door hinge pillar. It consists of car make symbol, series code, model year code, assembly plant symbol & a sequential production number.

1st Digit - Car make
Chrysler C
Imperial ....Y

2nd Digit - Class
Ecconomy .... E
Low L
High ....H
Medium ....M
Premium ....P
Police ....K
Taxi ....T
SPECIAL...........................S

3rd Digit & 4th Digit - Body style
2-Dr. Sedan 21
2-Dr. Hardtop 23
Convertible 27
2-Dr. Sports Hardtop 29
4-Dr. Sedan 41
4-Dr. Hardtop 43
6-Ps. Station Wagon 45
9-Ps. Station Wagon 46

Fifth Digit - CID
440 CID .... K
440 High Performsance CID..... L
Special Order 8 Cyl. .... M

Sixth Digit - Year 1967

Seventh Digit - Assembly plant
Jefferson Plant - Detroit 3
Belvidere Plant - ILL. 4
ILos Angeles - Calif. 5
Newarc Plant - Del. 6
St. Louis Plant - Mo. 7
Windsor Plant - Onterio 9

Last digits - production sequence code.

BODY CODE PLATE

Stamped and embossed on a stainless steel plate attached to the fender shield under the hood. The plate indicates the code for: Body type, Engine, Transmission,

abcdefghjkmnpqrtuwy				
A B C D E F G H J X L M	N P Q R	S T V	W X Y Z	
1 2 3 4 5 6 7 8	AX	TRM	PNT	UBS
	4	H1T	BB1	S
CH41	815	635	224	055551

Schedual date, Paint, Trim and some Option codes. The plate is read left to right, bottom to top. Starting with the bottom row of numbers.

THE BODY NUMBER is a four digit number which indicates the Car line, Price class, and Body style. Same first four digits of the VIN.

The two digit ENGINE CID CODE identifies the engine.

ENGINE CID	CODE
383 1-BBL 8 Cyl.	61
383 1-4BBL 8 Cyl.	62

TRANSMISSION	CODE
3-Speed Automatic	5
3-Speed Automatic HD	6
Special Order Transmission	9

The three digit code which indicates tire size and type, this option code is not included.

The last right digit of the bottom row is the SHIPPING ORDER NUMBER which consists of a three digit month and day scheduled production date, and a five digit production order number.

The next row up there will be one digit AXLE CODE found directly under the AX column.

NEWPORT	CODE
6-Ps. 4-Dr. Sedan	CE41
6-Ps. 4-Dr. Hardtop	CE43
6-Ps. 2-Dr. Coupe	CE23
6-Ps. 2-Dr. Convertable	CE27
6-Ps. 4-Dr. T&C Wagon	CE45
9-Ps. 4-Dr. T&C Wagon	CE46

NEWPORT CUSTOM	CODE
6-PS. 4-Dr. Sedan	CL41
6-Ps. 2-Dr. Hardtop	CL43
6-Ps. 4-Dr. Hardtop	CL23

CHRYSLER 300	CODE
6-Ps. 2-Dr. Hardtop	CM23
6-Ps. 4-Dr. Hardtop	CM43
6-Ps. Convertible	CM27

NEW YORKER	CODE
6-Ps. 4-Dr. Sedan	CH41
6-Ps. 2-Dr. Hardtop	CH23
6-Ps. 4-Dr. Hardtop	CH43

CROWN IMPERIAL	CODE
6-Ps. 4-Dr. Sedan	YM41
6-Ps. 2-Dr. Hardtop	YM23
6-Ps. 4-Dr. Hardtop	YM43
6-Ps. 2-Dr. Convertible	YM27

LEBARON	CODE
6-Ps. 4-Dr. Hardtop	YH43

THE UBS CODE identifies the upper door frame color, and the accent stripe color.

THE PAINT CODE furnishes the key to the paint used on the car. A thre digit code indicates the top and bottom colors respectively. A number follows which designates two-tone, sports-tone, convertible top, etc.

CODE	COLOR	CODE
A	Silver Mist Metallic	AA1
B	Black	BB1
C	Blue (Powder)	CC1
D	Crystal Blue Metallic	DD1
E	Roayl Blue Metallic	EE1
F	Haze Green Metallic	FF1
G	Sequoia Green Metallic	GG1
K	Frost Turquoise Metallic	KK1
L	Royal Turquoise Metallic	LL1
P	Scorch Red	PP1
Q	Spanish Red Metallic	QQ1
7	Ruby Metallic	771
R	Daffodil Yellow	RR1
S	Ivory	SS1
W	Persian White	WW1
X	Desert Beige	XX1
Y	Saddle Bronze	YY1
Z	Spice Gold Metallic	ZZ1
4	Moss Gold Metallic	441
6	Lilac	661

1967 CHRYSLER / IMPERIAL

TRIM CODE: Furnishes the key to the interior color and material.

CODE	CLOTH	VINYL	LEATHER	COLOR
E1B	*	*	-	Blue
E1Q	*	*	-	Turquoise
E1R	*	*	-	Red
E1T	*	*	-	Tan
E5B	-	*	-	Blue
E5R	-	*	-	Red
E5T	-	*	-	Tan
E5X	-	*	-	Black
E5Y	-	*	-	Gold
E6B	-	*	-	Turquoise
E6R	-	*	-	Red
E6W	-	*	-	Black
E6X	-	*	-	Gold
E8X	*	*	-	Blue
E9B	-	*	-	Red
E9T	-	*	-	Black
L2B	*	*	-	Blue
M2Q	*	*	-	Turquoise
M2R	*	*	-	Red
M2X	*	*	-	Black
M2Y	*	*	-	Gold
M3R	-	-	*	Red
M3X	-	-	*	Black
M6B	-	*	-	Blue
M6R	-	*	-	Red
M6W	-	*	-	White
M6X	-	*	-	Black
H1B	*	*	-	Blue
H1Q	*	*	-	Turquoise
H1R	*	*	-	Red
H1T	*	*	-	Tan
H1Y	*	*	-	Gold
H2B	*	*	-	Blue
H2Q	*	*	-	Turquoise
H2T	*	*	-	Tan
H2Y	*	*	-	Gold
H3R	-	-	*	Red
H3X	-	-	*	Black
H6B	*	-	-	Blue
H6R	*	-	-	Red
H6X	*	-	-	Black
H6Y	*	-	-	Gold
H8B	*	-	-	Blue
H8X	*	*	-	Black
H8Y	*	*	-	Gold

CODE	CLOTH	VINYL	LEATHER	COLOR
H9R	-	*	-	Red
H9X	-	*	-	Black
M1D	*	*	-	Dark Blue
M1G	*	*	-	Lt. & Dk. Green
M1N	*	*	-	Black & White
M1Q	*	*	-	Turquoise
M1R	*	*	-	Dark Red
M1T	*	*	-	Tan & Chestnut
M3A	-	-	*	Silver & Black
M3B	-	-	*	Lt. & Md. Blue
M3E	-	-	*	Gold & Black
M3G	-	-	*	Green
M3R	-	-	*	Dark Red
M3W	-	-	*	White & Black
M3X	-	-	*	Black
M3Y	-	-	*	Gold
M7B	*	-	*	Lt. & Md. Blue
M7N	*	-	*	Black & White
M7G	*	-	*	Lt. & Dk. Green
M8D	*	-	*	Dark Blue
M8G	*	-	*	Lt. & Dk. Green
M8N	*	-	*	Black & White
M8Q	*	-	*	Turquoise
M8R	*	-	*	Dark Red
M8T	*	-	*	Tan & Chestnut
M9B	-	-	*	Lt. & Md. Blue
M9E	-	-	*	Gold & Black
M9D	-	-	*	Dark Blue
M9G	-	-	*	Green
M9Q	-	-	*	Turquoise
M9R	-	-	*	Dark Red
M9W	-	-	*	White & Black
M9X	-	-	*	Black
M9Y	-	-	*	Gold
H8D	*	-	*	Dark Blue
H8Q	*	-	*	Turquoise
H8T	*	-	*	Tan & Chestnut
H8X	*	-	*	Black
H0A	*	*	-	Gray & Black
H9A	-	-	*	Silver & Black
H9B	-	-	*	Lt. & Md. Blue
H9D	-	-	*	Dark Blue
H9E	-	-	*	Gold & Black
H9G	-	-	*	Green
H9R	-	-	*	Dark Red
H9W	-	-	*	White & Black
H9X	-	-	*	Black
H9Y	-	-	*	Gold

ENGINE NUMBER

Stamped on a boss behind the water pump. The number provides the code to identify the series, block, displacement, and month/day production date.

EXAMPLE

C	38	2	24
YEAR	383	FEBRUARY	24th DAY

Engine Number	CID	Comp. ratio	Carb Type	HP Power	Transmission
C-383-2-24	383	9.2	2Bl	270	A-745 A-727 Torqueflite
Optional	383	10.0	4Bl	325	Same
Optional	440	10.0	4Bl	350	Same
C-440-2-24	440	10.0	4Bl	350	A-745 A-727 Torqueflite

VEHICLE IDENTIFICATION NUMBER

CH41K8F100551

The vehicle number (serial number) is stamped and embossed on a stainless steel plate attached to the left front door hinge pillar. It consists of car make symbol, series code, model year code, assembly plant symbol & a sequential production number.

1st Digit - Car make
Chrysler C
Imperial .... Y

2nd Digit - Class
Economy ....E
Low L
High ....H
Medium ....M
Premium ....P
Police ....K
Taxi ....T
SPECIAL............................S

3rd Digit & 4th Digit - Body style
2-Dr. Hardtop 23
Convertible 27
4-Dr. Sedan 41
4-Dr. Hardtop 43
6-Ps. Station Wagon 45
9-Ps. Station Wagon 46

Fifth Digit - CID
383 CID .... G
383 High Performsance CID..... H
440 CID .... K
440 High Performsance CID..... L
Special Order 8 Cyl. .... M

Sixth Digit - Year 1966

Seventh Digit - Assembly plant
Jefferson Plant - Detroit C
Belvedere Plant - ILL................ D
Los Angeles - Calif. ....E
Newark Plant - Del. ....F
St. Louis Plant - Mo. .... G
Windsor Plant - Onterio .... R

Last six digits: production sequence code.

BODY CODE PLATE

Stamped and embossed on a stainless steel plate attached to the fender shield under the hood. The plate indicates the code for: Body type, Engine, Transmission,

```
  abcdefghjkmnpqrtuwy
A B C D E F G H J X L M N P Q R S T V W X Y Z
 1 2 3 4 5 6 7 8      AX     TRM    PNT    UBS
                       4     H1T    BB1     W
    CH41              815     63    224   005551
```

Schedual date, Paint, Trim and some Option codes. The plate is read left to right, bottom to top. Starting with the bottom row of numbers.

THE BODY NUMBER is a four digit number which indicates the Car line, Price class, and Body style. Same first four digits of the VIN.

The two digit ENGINE CID CODE identifies the engine.

ENGINE CID	CODE
383 1-BBL 8 Cyl.	61
383 1-4BBL 8 Cyl.	62

TRANSMISSION	CODE
3-Speed Automatic	5
3-Speed Automatic HD	6
Special Order Transmission	9

The three digit code which indicates tire size and type, this option code is not included.

The last right digit of the bottom row is the SHIPPING ORDER NUMBER which consists of a three digit month and day scheduled production date, and a five digit production order number.

The next row up there will be one digit AXLE CODE found directly under the AX column.

NEWPORT   **CODE**
-Ps. 2-Dr. Hardtop CE23
-Ps. 4-Dr. Sedan CE41
-Ps. 4-Dr. Hardtop CE43
-Ps. 2-Dr. Convertable CE27
-Ps. 4-Dr. T&C Wagon...... CE45
-Ps. 4-Dr. T&C Wagon CE46

NEWPORT CUSTOM   **CODE**
-Ps. 4-Dr. Sedan CL41
-Ps. 2-Dr. Hardtop CL43
-Ps. 4-Dr. Hardtop CL23

CHRYSLER 300   **CODE**
-Ps. 2-Dr. Hardtop.......... CM23
-Ps. 4-Dr. Hardtop CM43
-Ps. Convertible CM27

NEW YORKER   **CODE**
-Ps. 4-Dr. Sedan CH41
-Ps. 2-Dr. Hardtop CH23
-Ps. 4-Dr. Hardtop CH43

CROWN IMPERIAL   **CODE**
-Ps. 4-Dr. Sedan YM41
6-Ps. 2-Dr. Hardtop YM23
6-Ps. 4-Dr. Hardtop YM43
6-Ps. 2-Dr. Convertable YM27

LEBARON   **CODE**
6-Ps. 4-Dr. Hardtop YH43

THE UBS CODE identifies the upper door frame color, and the accent stripe color.

THE PAINT CODE furnishes the key to the paint used on the car. A thre digit code indicates the top and bottom colors respectively. A number follows which designates two-tone, sports-tone, convertible top, etc.

CODE	COLOR	CODE
A	Silver Haze Metallic	AA1
B	Formal Black	BB1
C	Consort Blue Metallic	CC1
D	Sky Blue Metallic	DD1
E	Military Blue Metallic	EE1
F	Frost Green Metallic	FF1
G	Forest Green Metallic	GG1
H	Antique Ivory	HH1
J	Sovereign Gold Metallic	JJ1
K	Mist Turquoise Metallic	KK1
M	Turbine Bronze Metallic	MM1
R	Burgundy Metallic	RR1
T	Meadow Green Metallic	TT1
W	Polar White	WW1
X	Sandalwood	XX1
Y	Beige Mist Metallic	YY1

TRIM CODE: Furnishes the key to the interior color and material.

TRIM CODE	MATERIAL	COLOR
E1B	F&V	Md.Blue
E1F	F&V	Md. Green
E1Q	F&V	Md. Turquoise
E1T	F&V	Md. Tan
E1X	F&V	Black
E5B	V&V	Md. Blue
E5R	V&V	Md. Red
E5T	V&V	Md. Tan
E5X	V&V	Black
E5Y	V&V	Lt. Gold
E6B	V&V	Md. Blue
E6F	V&V	Dk. Green
E6R	V&V	Md. Red
E6W	V&V	White
E6X	V&V	Black
E8X	F&V	Black
E9B	V&V	Md. Blue
E9T	V&V	Md. Tan
L2B	F&V	Md. Blue
L2F	F&V	Md. Green
L2Q	F&V	Lt. Turquoise
L2X	F&V	Black
L2Y	F&V	Light Gold
L6B	V&V	Md. Blue
L6F	V&V	Dk. Green
L6R	V&V	Md. Red
L6X	V&V	Black
L9B	V&V	Md. Blue
L9X	V&V	Black

M2B	F&V	Md. Blue
M2F	F&V	Dk. Green
M2X	F&V	Black
M2Y	F&V	Lt. Gold
M3X	L&L	Black
M5B	V&V	Md. Blue
M5X	V&V	Black
M5Y	V&V	Lt. Gold
M6B	V&V	Md. Blue
M6F	V&V	Dk. Green
M6R	V&V	Md. Red
M6W	V&V	White
M6X	V&V	Black
M7X	F&V	Black
H1B	F&V	Dk. Blue
H1F	F&V	Md. Green
H1Q	F&V	Lt. Turquoise
H1T	F&V	Md. tan
H1X	F&V	Black
H2B	F&V	Dk. Blue
H2Q	F&V	Lt. Turquoise
H2T	F&V	Md. Tan
H2X	F&V	Black
H3X	L&L	Black
H6B	V&V	Dk. Blue
H6F	V&V	Dk. Green
H6R	V&V	Md. Red
H6W	V&V	White
H6X	F&V	Black
H8B	F&V	Dk. Blue
H8T	F&V	Lt. Tan
H8X	F&V	Black
H9R	V&V	Md. Red
H9X	V&V	Black
H9Y	V&V	Lt. Gold

"F=Fabric, V=Vinyl, L=Leather"

ENGINE NUMBER

Stamped on a boss behind the water pump. The number provides the code to identify the series, block displacement, and month/day production date.

EXAMPLE

PM	**383**	**2187**	**2401**	
PLANT	CID	JULIAN	DAILY	ENGINE PLANTS
CODE		DATE	SEQUENTIAL	PM-Mound Rd.
				PT-Trenton

Engine Number	CID	Comp. ratio	Carb Type	HP Power	Transmission
PM383xxxx2401	383	9.2	2-Bl	270	A-745 A-727 Torqueflite
Optional	383	10.0	4-Bl	325	Same
Optional	440	10.0	4-Bl	350	Same
PM440xxxx2401	440	10.0	4-Bl	350	A-745 A-727 Torqueflite

VEHICLE IDENTIFICATION NUMBER

CH41K9F100551

The vehicle number (serial number) is stamped and embossed on a stainless steel plate attached to the left front door hinge pillar. It consists of car make symbol, series code, model year code, assembly plant symbol & a sequential production number.

1st Digit - Car make
Chrysler C
Imperial ....Y

2nd Digit - Class
Ecconomy ....E
Low L
High ....H
Medium ....M
Premium ....P
Police ....K
Taxi ....T
SPECIAL.....................................S

3rd Digit & 4th Digit - Body style
2-Dr. Hardtop 23
Convertible 27
4-Dr. Sedan 41
4-Dr. Hardtop 43
6-Ps. Station Wagon 45
9-Ps. Station Wagon 46

Fifth Digit - CID
383 CID ....G
383 High Performsance CID..... H
440 CID ....K
440 High Performsance CID..... L
Special Order 8 Cyl. ....M

Sixth Digit - Year 1969

Seventh Digit - Assembly plant
Jefferson Plant - Detroit C
Belvedere Plant - ILL................D
Los Angeles - Calif.. ....E
Newark Plant - Del. ....F
St. Louis Plant - Mo. ....G
Windsor Plant - Onterio ....R

Last six digits - production sequence code.

BODY CODE PLATE

THE BODY CODE PLATE is read left to right, bottom to top. For 1969 Chrysler Corp. started a new system on their BODY CODE PLATES. Each body code

```
abcdefghjkmnpqrtuwy
A B C D E F G H J X L M N P Q R S T V W X Y Z
 1 2 3 4 5 6 7 8      AX      TRM      PNT      UBS
          X9      X9      HX3      BB1      W
   CH41         E83      D32      K9F      100555
```

plate contains all the code numbers for every option on the car. If one plate didn't hold all the information, a second tag was used. Listed here will be the codes found (usually) on the bottom two rows.

First a four digit BODY MODEL and STYLE CODE, a three digit ENGINE CODE and a three digit TRANSMISSION CODE, and the last nine digits of the VIN NUMBER. The next row up is a four digit PLANT CODE number, a three digit TRIM CODE number followed by special TRIM, STRIPPING AND DOOR FRAME COLOR CODES if any.

THE BODY NUMBER is a four digit number which indicates the Car line, Price class, and Body style. Same first four digits of the VIN.

The three digit ENGINE CID CODE identifies the engine.

ENGIINE CID CODE
383 1-2BBL 8 Cyl. .... E 61
383 1-4BBL 8 Cyl. .... E 62
440 1-4BBl 8 Cyl. .... E 85
440 1-BBl 8 Cyl. HP .... E 86

TRANSMISSION

	CODE
3-Speed Automatic	D31
3-Speed Automatic HD	D32
Special Order Transmission	D35

The three digit code which indicates tire size and type, this option code is not included.

The last digits of the bottom row are a repeat of the last nine digits of the VIN plate.

ENGINE NUMBERS: All engine serial numbers contain fourteen characters and digits. The first two designate the engine plant, the next three are the cubic inch displacement, the next one designates low compression, the next four are based on a Julian calander and the production sequence number of engines built that day. All 383 and 440 cubic inch engines have the serial number stanped on the cylinder block.

NEWPORT

	CODE
6-Ps. 2-Dr. Hardtop	CE23
6-Ps. 4-Dr. Sedan	CE41
6-Ps. 4-Dr. Hardtop	CE43
6-Ps. 2-Dr. Convertable	CE27
6-Ps. 4-Dr. T&C Wagon	CE45
9-Ps. 4-Dr. T&C Wagon	CE46

NEWPORT CUSTOM

	CODE
6-PS. 4-Dr. Sedan	CL41
6-Ps. 2-Dr. Hardtop	CL43
6-Ps. 4-Dr. Hardtop	CL23

CHRYSLER 300

	CODE
6-Ps. 2-Dr. Hardtop	CM23
6-Ps. 4-Dr. Hardtop	CM43
6-Ps. Convertible	CM27

NEW YORKER

	CODE
6-Ps. 4-Dr. Sedan	CH41
6-Ps. 2-Dr. Hardtop	CH23
6-Ps. 4-Dr. Hardtop	CH43

CROWN IMPERIAL

	CODE
6-Ps. 4-Dr. Sedan	YM41
6-Ps. 2-Dr. Hardtop	YM23
6-Ps. 4-Dr. Hardtop	YM43
6-Ps. 2-Dr. Convertable	YM27

LEBARON

	CODE
6-Ps. 4-Dr. Hardtop	YH43

THE UBS CODE identifies the upper door frame color, and the accent stripe color.

THE PAINT CODE furnishes the key to the paint used on the car. A thre digit code indicates the top and bottom colors respectively. A number follows which designates two-tone, sports-tone, convertible top, etc.

CODE	COLOR
Bahama Blue Metallic	B3
Jubilee Blue Metallic	B7
Dk. Briar Metallic	E7
Surf Green Metalli	F3
Avacado Metallic	F5
Jade Green Metallic	F8
Sandalwood	L1
Aquamarine Metallic	Q4
Bronze Mist MEtallic	T3
Burnished Bronze Metallic	T5
Tuscan Bronze Metallic	T7
Formal Black	X9
Antique Ivory	Y3
Classic Gold Metallic	Y4
Platinum Metallic	A4
Crimson	R6
Spinnaker White	W1

TRIM CODE: Furnishes the key to the interior color and material.

TRIM CODE	MATERIAL	COLOR
E1D, L3D, H1D, H3D, H7D	C&V	Dk. Blue
E2D, E4D, L4D, M4D, M6D, H6D	V&V	Dk. Blue
L7E, H7E	C&V	Dk. Red
E4E, L4E, M4E	V&V	Dk. Red
E1G	C&V	Lt. Green
L3G, M3G, H1G, H3G	C&V	Dk. Green
E4G, E8G, M6G	V&V	Dk. Green
E1L, E7L, L7L, M5L, H7L	C&V	Lt. Gray
H8L	V&V	Lt. Gray
E1Q, H1Q, H3Q	C&V	Lt. Turquoise
L3Q	C&V	Md. Turquoise
E2T, E4T, E6T, M6T, H6T	V&V	Md. Tan
HST	L&V	Md. Tan
E6W, M6W, H6W	V&V	White
E1X, L3X, M3X, H1X, H3X	C&V	Black
E2X, E4X, E6X, E8X, L4X, L8X, M4X, M6X, H6X, H8X	V&V	Black
L3Y, M3Y, H1Y, H3Y	C&V	Md. Gold
E2Y	V&V	Md. Gold
MBG, MDG	C&L	Dk. Green
MBK, MDK	C&L	Lt. Tan
MBM, MDM	C&L	Dk. Burgundy
MBQ, MDQ	C&L	Lt. Turquoise
MBX, MDX	C&L	Black
MID	C&V	Dk. Blue
MIG	C&V	Lt. Green
MIK	C&V	Lt. Tan
MIM	C&V	Dk. Burgundy
MIQ	C&V	Lt. Turquoise
MIX	C&V	Black
MSB, MRB	L&V	Lt. Blue
MSD	L&V	Dl. Blue
MSN	L&V	Black/Gold
MSG, MRG	L&V	Dk. Green
MRS	L&V	Md. Red
MST, MRT	L&V	Dk. Tan
MSW, MRW	L&V	White
MSX, MRX	L&V	Black
MSY	L&V	Gold
MBD, MDD	C&L	Dk. Blue

C=Cloth, V=Vinyl, L=Leather

ENGINE NUMBER

Stamped on a boss behind the water pump. The number provides the code to identify the series, block displacement, and month/day production date.

EXAMPLE

PM PLANT CODE	383 CID	2187 JULIAN DATE	2401 DAILY SEQUENTIAL NUMBER	ENGINE PLANT PM-Mound Rd. PT-Trenton

Engine Number	CID	Comp. ratio	Carb Type	HP Power	Transmission
PM383xxxx2401	383	9.2	2Bl	270	A-745 A-727 Torqueflite
Optional	383	10.0	4Bl	325	Same
Optional	440	10.0	4Bl	350	Same
PM440xxxx2401	440	10.0	4Bl	350	A-745 A-727 Torqueflite

VEHICLE IDENTIFICATION NUMBER

6105100553

The vehicle number (serial number) is stamped and embossed on a stainless steel plate attached to the left front door hinge pillar. It consists of car make symbol, series code, model year code, assembly plant symbol & a sequential production number.

1st Digit Car make
Dodge Dart (6 Cyl.) 4
Dodge Dart (8 Cyl.) 5
Dodge (8 Cyl.) 6

2nd Digit Series
Seneca Matador 1
Pioneer 2
Phoenix, Polara 3
Seneca Matador Wagon 5
Pioneer Wagon 6
Polara Wagon 7
Taxi 8
Special, Police 9

3rd Digit Year..........................1960

4th Digit Assembly plant
Detroit 2-3
Los Angeles. 5
Newark 6
St. Louis Plant 7
Fifth through tenth digits indicate the production sequence number.

BODY CODE PLATE

Stamped and embossed on a stainless steel plate under the hood. It is attached to: right or left fender, cowl, or radiator cross member depending on the model and assembly plant. This plate will indicate; schedule date, body production number, body series, trim, paint, and accessory code.

THE SHIPPING ORDER NUMBER is assigned prior to production. It consists of a 4 digit planned delivery month/day date code, 0224 (February 24th). Then a plant production sequence number follows (0555)

BODY NUMBER is a 3 digit number which indicates the model and body style.

```
1 2 3 4 5 6 7 8 9 0
A B C D E F G H J X L M N P Q R S T V W X Y Z

  SO          NUMBER        BDY      TRM      PNT
 0224          0555          643               BB1
```

DART SENECA

	CODE	
	6 cyl	**8 cyl**
4-Dr. Sedan	411	511
4-Dr. Sedan.................	413	513
4-Dr. Wagon............	456	556

DAART PIONEER

	CODE	
	6 cyl	**8 cyl**
2-Dr. Sedan..........	421	521
4-Dr. Sedan	423	523
4-Dr. Wagon.......	466	566
4-Dr. Wagon.......	467	567
2-Dr. Hardtop.......	422	522

DART PHOENIX

	CODE	
	6 cyl	**8 cyl**
4-Dr. Sedan	433	533
4-Dr. Hardtop	434	534
2-Dr. Hardtop.............	432	532
Convertible	435	535

MATADOR

	CODE
4-Dr. Sedan	643
2-Dr. Hardtop	642
4-Dr. Hardtop	644
4-Dr. Wagon	678
4-Dr. Wagon	679

POLARA

	CODE
4-Dr. Sedan	543
2-Dr. Hardtop	542
4-Dr. Hardtop	544
Convertible	545
4-Dr. Wagon	578
4-Dr. Wagon	579

THE PAINT CODE furnishes the key to the paint used on the car. A two digit code indicates the top and bottom colors respectively. A number follows whick designates two-tone, sports-tone, convertible top, etc."

TRIM CODE:

As of print date no trim codes were available for 1960 Dodge.

CODE	COLOR	CODE
B	Raven	BB1
C	Azure	CC1
D	Mediterranean	DD1
F	Spray	FF1
G	Spruce	GG1
H	Cactus	HH1
J	Frost Turquoise	JJ1
K	Teal	KK1
L	Cloud	LL1
M	Charcoal	MM1
P	Vermilion	PP1
R	Deep Bugundy	RR1
S	Raw Sienna	SS1
T	Fawn	TT1
W	Satin	WW1
X	Pewter	XX1
Y	Cocoa	YY1

ENGINE NUMBER

Stamped on a boss behind the water pump. The number provides the code to identify the series, block displacement, and month/day production date.

EXAMPLE

P	38	2	24
YEAR	383	FEBRUARY	24th DAY

Engine #s	Engine Name	CID	Comp Ratio	Carb Type	HP	Transmission
P-22-2-24	Economy Slant 6	225	8.5	1Bl	145	S — manual O — Torqueflite Six
P-31-2-24	Red Ram V8 Red Ram V8	318 318	9 9	2Bl 4Bl	230 255	S — manual Same
P-36-2-24	D-500 Ram induction	361	10	2-4Bl Ram	310	S — Torqueflite
P-38-2-24	D-500 Ram induction	383	10	2-4 Bl Ram	330	Same
P-36-2-24	Super Red Ram V8	361	10	2Bl	295	S — manual O — Torqueflite O — Powerflite
P-38-2-24	Ramfire V8	383	10	4Bl	325	S — T-85 manual O — Torqueflite
P-38-2-24	Maximum Performance Police Packages	383 383 383	10 10 10	4Bl 2-4Bl Runner 2-4Bl Ram	325 330 330	Same Same Same

VEHICLE IDENTIFICATION NUMBER

5212100553

The vehicle number (serial number) is stamped and embossed on a stainless steel plate attached to the left front door hinge pillar. It consists of car make symbol, series code, model year code, assembly plant symbol & a sequential production number.

1st Digit Car make
Dodge Dart (6 Cyl.) 4
Dodge (8 Cyl.) 5
Lancer 7

2nd Digit Series
Seneca, Lancer "170" 1
Pioneer 2
Phoenix, Polar 3
Polara 4
Seneca "170" Wagon 5
Pioneer Wagon 6
"770" Polara Wagon 7
Taxi 8
Special, Police 9

3rd Digit Year.........................1961

4th Digit Assembly plant
Detroit 2-3
Los Angeles. 5
Newark 6
St. Louis Plant 7
Fifth through tenth digits indicate the production sequence number.

BODY CODE PLATE

Stamped and embossed on a stainless steel plate under the hood. It is attached to: right or left fender, cowl, or radiator cross member depending on the model and assembly plant. This plate will indicate; schedule date, body production number, body series, trim, paint, and accessory code.

THE SHIPPING ORDER NUMBER is assigned prior to production. It consists of a 4 digit planned delivery month/day date code, 0224 (February 24th). Then a plant production sequence number follows (0555)

BODY NUMBER is a 3 digit number which indicates the model and body style.

1 2 3 4 5 6 7 8 9 0				
A B C D E F G H J X L M N P Q R S T V W X Y Z				
SO	NUMBER	BDY	TRM	PNT
0224	0555	523	201	BB1

LANCER	170	CODE 770
2-Dr. Sedan..............	711	---
4-Dr. Sedan..............	713	733
2-Dr. Hardtop	---	732

	CODE	
2-Dr. Sports .... --- 731		
Coupe		
4-Dr. Wagon..... 756 776		

DART SENECA	CODE	
	6 cyl	8 cyl
4-Dr. Sedan............	411	511
4-Dr. Sedan............	413	513
4-Dr. Wagon............	456	556

DART PIONEER	CODE	
	6 cyl	8 cyl
2-Dr. Sedan...............	421	521
4-Dr. Sedan...............	423	523
4-Dr. Wagon............	466	566
4-Dr. Wagon............	467	567
2-Dr. Hardtop.............	422	522

DART PHOENIX	CODE	
	6 cyl	8 cyl
4-Dr. Sedan	433	533
4-Dr. Hardtop	434	534
2-Dr. Hardtop..........	432	532
Convertible	435	535

POLARA	CODE
4-Dr. Sedan	543
2-Dr. Hardtop	542
4-Dr. Hardtop	544
Convertible	545
4-Dr. Wagon	578
4-Dr. Wagon	579

THE PAINT CODE furnishes the key to the paint used on the car. A two digit code indicates the top and bottOm colors respectively. A number follows whicH designates two-tone, sports-tone, convertible op, etc."

CODE	COLOR	CODE
A	Bamboo	AA1
B	Midnight	BB1
C	Glacier Blue	CC1
D	Marlin Blue	DD1
F	Sping Green	FF1
G	Frosted Mint	GG1
H	Cactus	HH1
J	Turquoise	JJ1
K	Nassau Green	KK1
L	Silver Grey	LL1
P	Vermillion	PP1
S	Rose Mist	SS1
U	Aztec Gold	UU1
W	Snow	WW1
Y	Buckskin	YY1
Z	Roman Bronze	ZZ1

TRIM CODE: Furnishes the key to the interior color and material.

CODE	COLOR	MATERIAL
201	Gray	Cloth & Vinyl
202	Gray	Cloth & Vinyl
203	Gray	Cloth & Vinyl
204	Gray	Cloth & Vinyl
205	Gray	Cloth & Vinyl
231	Blue	Cloth & Vinyl
234	Black	Cloth & Vinyl
235	Red	Cloth & Vinyl
311	Blue	Cloth & Vinyl
312	Green	Cloth & Vinyl
313	Brown	Cloth & Vinyl
314	Gray	Cloth & Vinyl
321	Blue	Cloth & Vinyl
322	Green	Cloth & Vinyl

CODE	COLOR	MATERIAL
331	Blue	Cloth & Vinyl
332	Green	Cloth & Vinyl
333	Brown	Cloth & Vinyl
334	Gray	Cloth & Vinyl
335	Red	Cloth & Vinyl
431	Blue	Vinyl
432	Green	Vinyl
433	Tan	Vinyl
434	Gray	Vinyl
435	Red	Vinyl
411	Blue	Vinyl
421	Blue	Vinyl
413	Brown	Vinyl
423	Brown	Vinyl
414	Silver	Vinyl
424	Silver	Vinyl
425	Red	Vinyl
401	Blue	Vinyl
404	Brown	Vinyl
404	Black	Vinyl
301	Blue	Cloth & Vinyl
303	Brown	Cloth & Vinyl
304	Gray	Cloth & Vinyl
251	Gray	Vinyl
252	Gray	Vinyl
254	Gray	Vinyl
255	Gray	Vinyl

ENGINE NUMBER

Stamped on a boss behind the water pump. The number provides the code to identify the series, block displacement, and month/day production date.

EXAMPLE			
R	38	2	24
YEAR	383	FEBRUARY	24th DAY

Engine #s	Engine Name	CID	Comp Ratio	Carb Type	HP	Transmission
R-17-2-24	Lancer 6	170	8.2:1	1Bl	101	S — A903G 3SM, O — A904 TF6
R-22-2-24	Economy Slant 6	225	8.2:1	1Bl	145	Same
R-31-2-24	Dart V8	318	9.0:1	2Bl	230	S — A903G 3SM, O — A466 TF O — A323 PF
	Dart V8 with Power Pack	318	9.0:1	4Bl	260	S — A466 TF
R-36-2-24	Dart D500	361	9.0:1	4Bl	305	S — A745 HDM, O — A466 TF
	Polara V8	361	9.0:1	2Bl	265	Same
R-38-2-24	Polara D500	383	10.0:1	4Bl	325	A745 HDM, A466 TF
	Ram Induction	383	10.0:1	2-4Bl Long Ram	330	Same
R-38-2-24 or	Maximum Special	383	10.0:1	2-4Bl Short Ram	340	Same
R-41-2-24	Police	413		4Bl	325	Same
	Package			2-4Bl Runner	330	Same

TF = Torqueflite   HDM = Heavy Duty 3 speed manual   3SM = 3 speed manual   TF6 = Torqueflite 6 PF = Powerflite

1962 DODGE

VEHICLE IDENTIFICATION NUMBER

4222100553

The vehicle number (serial number) is stamped and embossed on a stainless steel plate attached to the left front door hinge pillar. It consists of car make symbol, series code, model year code, assembly plant symbol & a sequential production number.

1st Digit Car make
Dart (6 Cyl.) 4
Dart (8 Cyl.), Polar 500 5
Lancer 170, 770, GT 7

2nd Digit Series
Lancer 170, Dart 1
Dart 330 2
Lancer 770, Dart 440 3
Lancer GT, Polara 500 4
Lancer 170, Dart Custom Wagon .. 5
Dart 330 Wagon 6
Lancer 770, Dart 440 Wagon 7
Taxi 8
Special 9
Fleet 10

3rd Digit Year......................... 1962

4th Digit Assembly plant
Detroit 2-3
Los Angeles. 5
Newark 6
St. Louis Plant 7
Fifth through tenth digits indicate the production sequence number.

BODY CODE PLATE

Stamped and embossed on a stainless steel plate under the hood. It is attached to: right or left fender, cowl, or radiator cross member depending on the model and assembly plant. This plate will indicate; schedule date, body production number, body series, trim, paint, and accessory code.

THE SHIPPING ORDER NUMBER is assigned prior to production. It consists of a 4 digit planned delivery month/day date code, 0224 (February 24th). Then a plant production sequence number follows (0555)

BODY NUMBER is a 3 digit number which indicates the model and body style.

```
    1234567890
A B C D E F G H J X L M N P Q R S T V W X Y Z

   SO        NUMBER      BDY      TRM      PNT
  0224        0555       413      704      EB1
```

LANCER 170	CODE
4-Dr. Sedan	713
2-Dr. Sedan	711
4-Dr. Wagon	756

LANCER 770	CODE
2-Dr. Sedan	731
4-Dr. Sedan	733
4-Dr. Wagon	776

LANCER GT	CODE
2-Dr. Hardtop Coupe	742

DART	6 cyl	8 cyl
	CODE	
2-Dr. Sedan	411	511
2-Dr. Sedan	413	513
4-Dr. Wagon	456	556

DART 330	6 cyl	8 cyl
	CODE	
2-Dr. Sedan	421	521
4-Dr. Sedan	423	523
2-Dr. Hardtop	422	522
4-Dr. Wagon	466	566

4-Dr. Wagon	---		567

DART 330	6 cyl	8 cyl
		CODE
4-Dr. Sedan	433	533
2-Dr. Hardtop	421	521
4-Dr. Hardtop	---	522
Convertible	---	535
4-Dr. Wagon	---	576
4-Dr. Wagon	---	577

FLEET	6 cyl	8 cyl
		CODE
2-Dr. Sedan	401	501
4-Dr. Sedan	403	503

CUSTOM 880

	CODE
4-Dr. Sedan	613
2-Dr. Hardtop	612
4-Dr. Hardtop	614
Convertible	615
4-Dr. Wagon	658

	CODE
4-Dr. Wagon	659

POLARA

	CODE
2-Dr. Hardtop	542
4-Dr. Hardtop	544
Convertible	545

THE PAINT CODE furnishes the key to the paint used on the car. A two digit code indicates the top and bottom colors respectively. A number follows which designates two-tone, sports-tone, convertible top, etc."

CODE	COLOR	CODE
A	Flax	AA1
B	Onyx	BB1
C	Powder Blue	CC1
D	Medium Blue	DD1
E	Cobalt Blue	EE1
F	Light Green	FF1
G	Glade Green	GG1
H	Metallic Emerald	HH1
M	Pearl Gray	MM1
P	Vermilion	PP1
R	Dusty Rose	RR1
S	Deep Cordovan	SS1
T	Buff	TT1
U	Shell Beige	UU1
W	Polar	WW1
Y	Nutmeg Brown	YY1

TRIM CODE: Furnishes the key to the interior color and material.
Note: V - VINYL   C - CLOTH

CODE	Cloth	Vinyl	Leather	COLOR
611	*	*	-	Black & Gray w/Blue
614	*	*	-	Black & Gray
615	*	*	-	Black & Gray w/Red
641	-	*	-	Black & Gray w/Blue
644	-	*	-	Black & Gray
645	-	*	-	Black & Gray w/Red
631	*	*	-	Blue
632	*	*	-	Green
633	*	*	-	Cocoa
635	*	*	-	Red
651	-	*	-	Blue
652	-	*	-	Green
653	-	*	-	Cocoa
655	-	*	-	Red
671	-	*	-	Blue
675	-	*	-	Red
694	-	*	-	Gray
701	*	*	-	Blue
703	*	*	-	Cocoa
704	*	*	-	Gray
711	*	*	-	Blue
712	*	*	-	Green
713	*	*	-	Cocoa
714	*	*	-	Gray
715	*	*	-	Red
721	*	*	-	Blue
722	*	*	-	Green
723	*	*	-	Cocoa
724	*	*	-	Gray
725	*	*	-	Red
801	-	*	-	Blue
803	-	*	-	Cocoa
804	-	*	-	Gray
811	-	*	-	Blue
812	-	*	-	Green
813	-	*	-	Cocoa
814	-	*	-	Gray
815	-	*	-	Red
821	-	*	-	Blue
824	-	*	-	Gray
831	-	*	-	Blue
834	-	*	-	Gray
841	-	*	-	Blue
844	-	*	-	Gray
851	-	*	-	Blue & Beige
852	-	*	-	Green & Beige
853	-	*	-	Cocoa & Beige
855	-	*	-	Red & Beige

ENGINE NUMBER

Stamped on a boss behind the water pump. The number provides the code to identify the series, block displacement, and month/day production date.

EXAMPLE

R	38	2	24
YEAR	383	FEBRUARY	24th DAY

Engine #	Engine Name	CID	Comp. ratio	Carb	HP	Transmission
S-17-8-3	70 Slant 6	170	8.2:1	1, 1Bl	101	Stand — A-903 G, 3SM Opt — A-904 G, TF6
S-22-8-3	225 Slant 6	225	8.2:1	1, 1Bl	145	Stand — A-903 G, 3SM Opt — A-904 RG, TF6
S-31-8-3	318 V8 318 V8 with power package	318	9.0:1	1, 2Bl/1, 4Bl	230/260	Stand — A-745 3SM/A-727 TF8 Opt — A-727, TF8
S-36-8-3	361 V8/High performance option	361	9.0:1	1, 4Bl/2, 4Bl Runner	305/310	Stand — A-745, 3SM Opt — A-727, TF8
S-38-8-3	High performance option	383	10.0:1	1, 4Bl/2, 4Bl Runner	330/335	Stand — A-745, 3SM Opt — A-727, TF8
S-41-8-3	High performance option	413	11.0:1	1, 4Bl/2, 4Bl Runner 410 2, 4Bl Ram	365/385	Stand — A-745, 3SM Opt — A-727, TF8

3SM=Three speed Automatic   TF6/TF8 = Torqueflite 6/8

VEHICLE IDENTIFICATION NUMBER

7432100553

The vehicle number (serial number) is stamped and embossed on a stainless steel plate attached to the left front door hinge pillar. It consists of car make symbol, series code, model year code, assembly plant symbol & a sequential production number.

1st Digit Car make
Dodge (6 Cyl.) 4
Dodge (8 Cyl.), Polar 500 5
Dart 170, 270, GT 7

2nd Digit Series
170, 330, Custom 880 1
440 2
270 Polar 3
Dart GT, Polar 500 4
170, 330, 880 Custom Wagon 5
Dart 330 Wagon 6
440 Wagon 7
Taxi 8
Special 9
880 10

3rd Digit Year........................1963

4th Digit Assembly plant
Detroit 2-3
Los Angeles. 5
Newark 6
St. Louis Plant 7
Fifth through tenth digits indicate the production sequence number.

BODY CODE PLATE

Stamped and embossed on a stainless steel plate under the hood. It is attached to: right or left fender, cowl, or radiator cross member depending on the model and assembly plant. This plate will indicate; schedule date, body production number, body series, trim, paint, and accessory code.

THE SHIPPING ORDER NUMBER is assigned prior to production. It consists of a 4 digit planned delivery month/day date code, 0224 (February 24th). Then a plant production sequence number follows (0555)

BODY NUMBER is a 3 digit number which indicates the model and body style.

1 2 3 4 5 6 7 8 9 0				
A B C D E F G H J X L M N P Q R S T V W X Y Z				
SO	NUMBER	BDY	TRM	PNT
0224	0551	742	655	BB1

880	CODE
4-Dr. Sedan 503	
4-Dr. Wagon 556	
4-Dr. Wagon 557	

CUSTOM 880	CODE
4-Dr. Sedan..................... 513	
2-Dr. Hardtop................... 512	
4-Dr. Hardtop 514	
Convertible 515	
4-Dr. Wagon 558	
4-Dr. Wagon 559	

DART 170	CODE
2-Dr. Sedan...................... 711	
2-Dr. Sedan...................... 713	
4-Dr. Wagon.................... 756	

DART 270	CODE
2-Dr. Sedan 731	
Convertible................................ 735	
4-Dr. Sedan.............................. 733	
4-Dr. Wagon............................. 776	

DART GT	CODE
2-Dr. Hardtop.......................... 742	
Convertible................................ 745	

440	CODE	
	6 cyl	8 cyl
2-Dr. Sedan............ 421 621		
2-Dr. Hardtop......... 422 622		
4-Dr. Sedan............ 423 623		
4-Dr. Wagon .... --- 656		
4-Dr. Wagon ...--- 657		

330	CODE	
	6 cyl	8 cyl
2-Dr. Sedan............ 411 611		
4-Dr. Sedan............ 413 613		
4-Dr. Wagon 456 656		
4-Dr. Wagon 457 657		

FLEET	CODE	
	6 cyl	8 cyl
2-Dr. Sedan............ 401 601		
4-Dr. Sedan............ 403 603		

880	CODE
4-Dr. Sedan	503
4-Dr. Wagon	556
4-Dr. Wagon	557

CUSTOM 880	CODE
4-Dr. Sedan	513
2-Dr. Hardtop	512
4-Dr. Hardtop	514
Convertible	515
4-Dr. Wagon	558
4-Dr. Wagon	559

POLARA	CODE	
	6 cyl	8 cyl
2-Dr. Hardtop	432	632
4-Dr. Sedan	433	633
Convertible		635
4-Dr. Hardtop		634

POLARA 500	CODE
2-Dr. Hardtop	642
Convertible	645

TRIM CODE: Furnishes the key to the interior color and material.

CODE	Cloth	Vinyl	Leather	COLOR
801	*	*	-	Blue
803	*	*	-	Tan
805	*	*	-	Red
808	*	*	-	Turquoise
851	-	*	-	Blue
853	-	*	-	Tan
855	-	*	-	Red
858	-	*	-	Turquoisse
871	-	*	-	Blue
873	-	*	-	Tan
875	-	*	-	Red
894	-	*	-	Grey
831	*	*	-	Blue
833	*	*	-	Tan
835	*	*	-	Red
838	*	*	-	Turquoise
878	-	*	-	Turquoise
891	-	*	-	Blue
893	-	*	-	Tan
895	-	*	-	Red
898	-	*	-	Turquoise
501	*	*	-	Blue

CODE	Cloth	Vinyl	Leather	COLOR
503	*	*	-	Tan
505	*	*	-	Red
508	*	*	-	Turquoise
601	-	*	-	Blue
603	-	*	-	Tan
605	-	*	-	Red
608	-	*	-	Turquoise
611	-	*	-	Blue
613	-	*	-	Tan
694	-	*	-	Gray
521	*	*	-	Blue
523	*	*	-	Tan
525	*	*	-	Red
526	*	*	-	Alabaster & Black
528	*	*	-	Turquoise
621	-	*	-	Blue
623	-	*	-	Tan
625	-	*	-	Red
626	-	*	-	Alabaster & Black
628	-	*	-	Turquoise
541	*	*	-	Blue
543	*	*	-	Tan
545	*	*	-	Red
546	*	*	-	Alabaster & Black
548	*	*	-	Turquoise
641	-	*	-	Blue
643	-	*	-	Tan
645	-	*	-	Red
646	-	*	-	Alabaster & Black
648	-	*	-	Turquoise
651	-	*	-	Blue
653	-	*	-	Tan
655	-	*	-	Red
656	-	*	-	Alabaster & Black
658	-	*	-	Turquoise
571	*	*	-	Blue
572	*	*	-	Green
573	*	*	-	Tan
575	*	*	-	Red
578	*	*	-	Turquoise
584	*	*	-	Gray
671	-	*	-	Blue
672	-	*	-	Green
673	-	*	-	Tan
675	-	*	-	Red
678	-	*	-	Turquoise
684	-	*	-	Gray

THE PAINT CODE furnishes the key to the paint used on the car. A two digit code indicates the top and bottom colors respectively. A number follows which designates two-tone, sports-tone, convertible top, etc."

CODE	COLOR	CODE
A	Ivory	AA1
B	Onyx	BB1
C	Light Blue	CC1
D	Medium Blue	DD1
E	Dark Blue	EE1
F	Light Green	FF1
G	Forest Green	GG1
H	Slate Green	HH1
J	Aqua	JJ1
K	Turquoise	KK1
L	Dark Turquoise	LL1
N	Steel Gray	NN1
P	Vermilion	PP1
S	Cordovan	SS1
U	Beige	UU1
W	Polar	WW1
Y	Sandalwood	YY1

ENGINE NUMBER

Stamped on a boss behind the water pump. The number provides the code to identify the series, block displacement, and month/day production date.

EXAMPLE

R	38	2	24
YEAR	383	FEBRUARY	24th DAY

Engine #	Engine Name	CID	Comp.ratio	Carb Type	HP	Transmission
T-17-8-3	170 Slant 6	170	8.2	1, 1Bl	101	Stand — A-903 G, Opt — A-904 G
T-22-8-3 RG	225 Slant 6	225	8.2	1, 1Bl	145	Stand — A-903 RG, Opt — A-904
T-31-8-3	318 V8	318	9	1, 2Bl	230	Stand — A-745, Opt — BWT-10 Opt — A-727
T-36-8-3	Commando 361	361	9.0	1, 2Bl	265	Stand - A-745 Opt- BWT-10 Opt - A-727
T-38-8-3	383 V8 383 power Pack V8 High performance options	383	10.0/10.0 11	1, 2Bl/1, 4Bl 2, 4Bl Runner	305/330 320	Stand — A-745, Opt — BWT-10 Opt — A-727
T-42-8-3	High performance options	426	1.0/13.5 11.0/13.5	1, 4Bl/2 1, 4Bl/2 4Bl Runner 1, 4Bl 2, 4Bl Ram	370/375 415/425	Stand — BWT-85 Opt — A-727

1964 DODGE

VEHICLE IDENTIFICATION NUMBER

7442100559

The vehicle number (serial number) is stamped and embossed on a stainless steel plate attached to the left front door hinge pillar. It consists of car make symbol, series code, model year code, assembly plant symbol & a sequential production number.

1st Digit Car make
Dodge (6 Cyl.) 4
880 5
Dodge (8 Cyl.) 6
Dart 7

2nd Digit Series
170, 330, 880 1
440, Custom 880 2
270, Polara 3
Dart GT, Polara 4
170, 330, 880 Wagon 5
440, Custom 880 Wagon 6
Dart 270 Wagon 7
Taxi 8
Special 9

3rd Digit Year........................1964

4th Digit Assembly plant
Detroit 2-3
Los Angeles. 5
Newark 6
St. Louis Plant 7
Fifth through tenth digits indicate the production sequence number.

BODY CODE PLATE

Stamped and embossed on a stainless steel plate under the hood. It is attached to: right or left fender, cowl, or radiator cross member depending on the model and assembly plant. This plate will indicate; schedule date, body production number, body series, trim, paint, and accessory code.

THE SHIPPING ORDER NUMBER is assigned prior to production. It consists of a 4 digit planned delivery month/day date code, 0224 (February 24th). Then a plant production sequence number follows (0555)

BODY NUMBER is a 3 digit number which indicates the model and body style.

```
1234567890
A B C D E F G H J X L M N P Q R S T V W X Y Z

SO          NUMBER       BDY        TRM        PNT
0224        0551         742        H4R        BB1
```

DART 170   CODE
2-Dr. Sedan............................711
2-Dr. Sedan............................713
4-Dr. Wagon.........................756

DART 270   CODE
2-Dr. Sedan 731
4-Dr. Sedan 733
Convertible..................... 735
4-Dr. Wagon................... 776

DART GT   CODE
2-Dr. Hardtop....................742
Convertible......................745

330   CODE

	6 cyl	8 cyl
2-Dr. Sedan........ ....411.	 611
4-Dr. Sedan........ ....413.	.613
4-Dr. Wagon	..456..... 656
4-Dr. Wagon .. ..457....... 657

440   CODE

	6 cyl	8 cyl
2-Dr. Sedan............... 421	621
2-Dr. Hardtop... ....422..... 622
4-Dr. Sedan ....423..... 623

4-Dr. Wagon .... --- .... 66•
'4-Dr. Wagon ....--- .... 66'

POLARA   CODE

	6 cyl	8 cyl
2-Dr. Hardtop.......... 432	63:
4-Dr. Sedan 433	63
4-Dr. Hardtop........ --- 63
Convertible............. --- 63

880   CODE
4-Dr. Sedan.............................. 51
4-Dr. Wagon............................ 55
4-Dr. Wagon............................ 55

CUSTOM 880   CODE
2-Dr. Hardtop 522
Convertible 52
4-Dr. Sedan........................52
4-Dr. Hardtop....................52•
4-Dr. Wagon........................568
4-Dr. Wagon........................569

THE PAINT CODE furnishes the key to the paint used on the car. A two digit code indicates the top and bottom colors respectively. A number follows which designates two-tone, sports-tone, convertible top, etc."

CODE	COLOR	CODE
B	Black	BB1
C	Light Blue	CC1
D	Medium Blue	DD1
E	Dark Blue	EE1
J	Light Turquoise/Aqua	JJ1
K	Medium Turquoise Metallic	KK1
L	Dk. Green/Dk. Turquoise Metallic	LL1
P	Red	PP1
S	Ivory	SS1
W	White	WW1
X	Beige/Light Tan	XX1
Y	Tan/Medium/Tan Metallic	YY1
Z	Anniversary Gold/Med. Gold Metallic	ZZ1

TRIM CODE: Furnishes the key to the interior color and material.

CODE	Cloth	Vinyl	Leather	COLOR
L1B, L4B	*	*	-	Blue
L1Q	*	*	-	Turquoise
L1R, L4R	*	*	-	Red
"L1T, L4T	*	*	-	Yellow Tan
L5B	-	*	-	Blue
L5Q	-	*	-	Turquoise
L5R	-	*	-	Red
L5T	-	*	-	Yellow Tan
H1B, H4B	*	*	-	Blue
H1Q	*	*	-	Turquoise
H1R, H4R	*	*	-	Red
H1T, H4T	*	*	-	Yellow Tan
H4B	-	*	-	Blue
H4Q	-	*	-	Turquoise
H4R	-	*	-	Red
H4T	-	*	-	Yellow Tan
P4B	-	*	-	Blue
P4R	-	*	-	Red
P4T	-	*	-	Yellow Tan
P4Y	-	*	-	Gold
P4X	-	*	-	Black
L1B, K1B	*	*	-	Blue
L1Q, K1Q	*	*	-	Turquoise
L1R, K1R	*	*	-	Red
L1T, K1T	*	*	-	Yellow tan"L4B,
L4B, K4B	-	*	-	Blue

CODE	Cloth	Vinyl	Leather	COLOR
L4Q, K4Q	-	*	-	Turquoise
L4R, K4R	-	*	-	Red
L4T, K4T	-	*	-	Yellow tan
L5B	-	*	-	Blue
L5R	-	*	-	Red
L5T	-	*	-	Yellow tan
L2A, K2A, L8A, K8A, T8A	*	*	-	Gray
X1P	*	*	-	Black and Gray
M1B, M5B	*	*	-	Blue
M1Q	*	*	-	Turquoise
M1R, M5R	*	*	-	Red
M1T, M5T	*	*	-	Yellow tan
M1Y	*	*	-	Gold
M4B	-	*	-	Blue
M4Q	-	*	-	Turquoise
M4R	-	*	-	Red
M4T	-	*	-	Yellow tan
M4Y	-	*	-	Gold
M8A	-	*	-	Gray
H1B	*	*	-	Blue
H1Q	*	*	-	Turquoise
H1R	*	*	-	Red
H1T	*	*	-	Yellow tan
H1Y	*	*	-	Gold
H4B	-	*	-	Blue
H4Q	-	*	-	Turquoise
H4R	-	*	-	Red
H4T	-	*	-	Yellow tan
H4Y	-	*	-	Gold
P4B	-	*	-	Blue
P4Q	-	*	-	Turquoise
P4R	-	*	-	Red
P4T	-	*	-	Yellow tan
P4Y	-	*	-	Gold
E1B, K1B	*	*	-	Blue
E1Q, K1Q	*	*	-	Turquoise
E1T, K1T	*	*	-	Yellow tan
E1Y, K1Y	*	*	-	Gold
K2A, K4A	-	*	-	Gray
L1B	-	*	-	Blue
L1Q	-	*	-	Turquoise
L1R	-	*	-	Red
L1T	-	*	-	Yellow tan
L1Y	-	*	-	Gold
L4B	-	*	-	Blue
L4Q	-	*	-	Turquoise
L4R	-	*	-	Red
L4T	-	*	-	Yellow tan
L4Y	-	*	-	Gold

ENGINE NUMBER

Stamped on a boss behind the water pump. The number provides the code to identify the series, block displacement, and month/day production date.

EXAMPLE

V	38	2	24
YEAR	383	FEBRUARY	24th DAY

Engine#	Engine Name	CID	Comp.ratio	Carb	HP	Transmission
V-17-2-24	170 Slant 6	170	8.5	1, 1Bl	101	Stand — A-903 G, Opt — A-833, Opt — A-904 G
V-22-2-24	225 Charger	225	8.4	1, 1Bl	145	Stand — A-903 RG, Opt — A-833, Opt — A-904 RG
V-273-2-24	273 Charger V8	273	8.8	1, 2Bl	180	Stand — A-745, Opt — A-833, Opt — A-904 A
V-318-2-24	318 V8	318	9	1, 2Bl	230	Stand — A-745, Opt — A-727
V-36-2-24	361 V8	361	9	1, 2Bl	265	Stand — A-745, Opt — A-727
V-38-2-24	383 V8	383	10	1, 2Bl/1, 4Bl	305/330	Stand — A-745, Opt — A-833, Opt — A-727
TMP-426-2-24	426 Ram Charger	426	11	2, 4Bl Ram	415	Stand — BWT-85, Opt — A-833, Opt — A-727
V-426-2-24	426 V8	426	10.3	1, 4Bl Ram	365	Stand — A-833, Opt — A-727
TMB-HC-2-24-426	426 Ram Charger	426	12.5	2, 4Bl Ram	425	Stand — S-BWT, Opt — A-833, Opt — A-727

VEHICLE IDENTIFICATION NUMBER

W352100553

The vehicle number (serial number) is stamped and embossed on a stainless steel plate attached to the left front door hinge pillar. It consists of car make symbol, series code, model year code, assembly plant symbol & a sequential production number.

1st Digit Car make
Dart (6 Cyl.) 2
Dart (8 Cyl.) L
Coronet (6 Cyl.) 4
Coronet (8 Cyl.) .... W

2nd Digit Series
170, Deluxe Polara 1
Coronet 2
270, Coronet 440, Custom 880 3
Dart GT, Coronet 440, Monaco 4
170, Deluxe Polara, Wagons 5
270, Coronet 440, ... 7
Custom 880 Wagons
Special 9

3rd Digit Year 1965

4th Digit Assembly plant
Detroit 2-3
Los Angeles. 5
Newark 6
St. Louis Plant 7
Fifth through tenth digits indicate the production sequence number.

BODY CODE PLATE

Stamped and embossed on a stainless steel plate under the hood. It is attached to: right or left fender, cowl, or radiator cross member depending on the model and assembly plant. This plate will indicate; schedule date, body production number, body series, trim, paint, and accessory code.

THE SHIPPING ORDER NUMBER is assigned prior to production. It consists of a 4 digit planned delivery month/day date code, 0224 (February 24th). Then a plant production sequence number follows (0555)

BODY NUMBER is a 3 digit number which indicates the model and body style.

1 2 3 4 5 6 7 8 9 0				
A B C D E F G H J X L M N P Q R S T V W X Y Z				
SO	NUMBER	BDY	TRM	PNT
224	00553	W32	H4R	BB1

DART 170

	CODE	
	6 cyl	8 cyl
2-Dr. Sedan	211	L11
2-Dr. Sedan	213	L13
4-Dr. Wagon	256	L56

DART 270

	CODE	
	6 cyl	8 cyl
2-Dr. Sedan	231	L31
4-Dr. Sedan	233	L33
2-Dr. Hardtop	232	L32
Convertible	235	L35
4-Dr. Wagon	276	L76

DART GT

	CODE	
	6 cyl	8 cyl
2-Dr. Hardtop	242	L42
Convertible	245	L45

CORONET

	CODE	
	6 cyl	8 cyl
2-Dr. Sedan	421	W21
4-Dr. Sedan	423	W23

CORONET DELUXE

	CODE	
	6 cyl	8 cyl
2-Dr. Sedan	411	W11
4-Dr. Sedan	413	W13
4-Dr. Wagon	456	W56

CORONET 440

	CODE	
	6 cyl	8 cyl
2-Dr. Sedan	432	W32
2-Dr. Hardtop	433	W33
Convertible	435	W35
4-Dr. Wagon	476	W76
4-Dr. Wagon	477	W77

CORONET HEMI-CHARGER

	CODE
2-Dr. Hardtop	W01

CORONET 500

	CODE
2-Dr. Hardtop	W42
Convertible	W42

POLARA	CODE
-Dr. Sedan	D13
-Dr. Sedan	D23
-Dr. Hardtop	D12
-Dr. Hardtop	D14
Convertible	D15
-Dr. Wagon	D56
-Dr. Wagon	D57

CUSTOM 880	CODE
4-Dr. Sedan	D38
2-Dr. Hardtop	D32
4-Dr. Hardtop	D34
Convertible	D35
4-Dr. Wagon	D76
4-Dr. Wagon	D77

MONACO	CODE
2-Dr. Hardtop	D42

THE PAINT CODE furnishes the key to the paint used on the car. A two digit code indicates the top and bottom colors respectively. A number follows which designates two-tone, sports-tone, convertible top, etc."

CODE	COLOR	CODE
A	Gold Metallic	AA1
B	Black	BB1
C	Light Blue	CC1
D	Medium Blue Metallic	DD1
E	Dark Blue Metallic	EE1
F	Pale Blue Metallic	FF1
G	Dark Green Metallic	GG1
J	Light Turquoise	JJ1
K	Medium Turquoise Metallic	KK1
L	Dark Turquoise Metallic	LL1
N	Pale Silver Metallic	NN1
P	Bright Red	PP1
R	Beige	RR1
S	Ivory	SS1
T	Ruby Red	TT1
V	Cordovan Metallic	VV1
W	White	WW1
X	Light Tan	XX1
Y	Medium Tan Metallic	YY1
Z	Pale Turquoise Metallic	ZZ1
2	Medium Green Metallic	221
3	Pink Gold Metallic	331
8	Yellow	881

TRIM CODE: Furnishes the key to the interior color and material.

CODE	Cloth	Vinyl	Leather	COLOR
L1B, K1B	*	*	-	Blue
L1Q, K1Q	*	*	-	Turquoise
L1R, K1R"	*	*	-	Red
L1T, K1T, L2T, K2T	*	*	-	Tan
L4B, K4B	-	*	-	Blue
L4Q, K4Q	-	*	-	Turquoise
L4R, K4R	-	*	-	Red
L4T, K4T	-	*	-	Tan
L8T, K8T, T8T	-	*	-	Tan
L5B	-	*	-	Blue
L5R	-	*	-	Red
L5T	-	*	-	Tan
P1B	-	*	-	Blue
P1Q	-	*	-	Turquoise
P4R	-	*	-	Red
P4T	-	*	-	Tan
P4U	-	*	-	Cordovan
P4X	-	*	-	Black
P4W	-	*	-	White
L1B, K1B	*	*	-	Blue
L1Q, K1Q	*	*	-	Turquoise
L1R, K1R	*	*	-	Red
L1T, K1T	*	*	-	Tan
L1Y, K1Y	*	*	-	Gold
L2T, K2T	*	*	-	Tan
L4B	-	*	-	Blue
L4Q	-	*	-	Turquoise
L4R	-	*	-	Red
L4T	-	*	-	Tan
L4Y	-	*	-	Gold
L5B	-	*	-	Blue
L5R	-	*	-	Red
L5T	-	*	-	Tan
L8T, K8T	-	*	-	Tan
L9B	-	*	-	Blue
L9R	-	*	-	Red
L9X	-	*	-	Black
H1B	-	*	-	Blue
H1Q	-	*	-	Turquoise

CODE	Cloth	Vinyl	Leather	COLOR
H1R	-	*	-	Red
H1T	-	*	-	Tan
H1Y	-	-	-	Gold
H4B	-	*	-	Blue
H4Q	-	*	-	Turquoise
H4X	-	*	-	Black
H4R	-	*	-	Red
H4T	-	*	-	Tan
H4Y	-	*	-	Gold
H1B	*	*	-	Blue
H1Q	*	*	-	Turquoise
H1R	*	*	-	Red
H1T	*	*	-	Tan
H4B	-	*	-	Blue
H4Q	-	*	-	Turquoise
H4R	-	*	-	Red
H4T	-	*	-	Tan
H5B	-	*	-	Blue
H5R	-	*	-	Red
H5T	-	*	-	Tan
P4B	-	*	-	Blue
P4Q	-	*	-	Turquoise
P4R	-	*	-	Red
P4T	-	*	-	Tan
P4X	-	*	-	Black
P4Y	-	*	-	Gold
L1B, L4B, L5B	*	*	-	Blue
L1R, L4R, L5R	*	*	-	Red
L1T, L4T, L5T	*	*	-	Tan
P4R	-	*	-	Red
P4T	-	*	-	Tan
L1Q, L4Q	*	*	-	Turquoise
H1B, H4B, H5B	*	*	-	Blue
H1R, H4R, H5R	*	*	-	Red
H1T, H4T, H5T	*	*	-	Tan
H1Q, H4Q	*	*	-	Turquoise
P4B	-	*	-	Blue
P4X	-	*	-	Black
P4Y	-	*	-	Gold

ENGINE NUMBER

Stamped on a boss behind the water pump. The number provides the code to identify the series, block displacement, and month/day production date

EXAMPLE

A YEAR	38 383	2 FEBRUARY	24 24th DAY

Engine #	Engine Name	CID	Comp. ratio	Carb type	HP	Transmission
A-170-2-24	70 CID-6	170	8.5	1, 1Bl	101	Stand — A-903 G Opt — A-904 G
A-22-2-24	225 CID-6	225	8.4	1, 1Bl	145	Stand — A-903 RG Opt — A-833 Opt — A-904 RG
A-31-2-24	318 V8	318	9	1, 2Bl	230	Stand — A-745 Opt — A-727
A-38-2-24	383 V8/393 V8 High Performance Option	383	10.0/9.2 11	1,4Bl 1, 2Bl/1, 4B	315/270 330	Stand — A-745 Opt — A-833 Opt — A-727
T-42-2-24	Hemi Charger 426 426 V8	426	12.5/10.3	1, 4Bl /1, 4Bl 2, 4Bl Ram	400/425 365	Stand — A-745, A-833 Opt — A-727
A-273-2-24	273 V8	273	8.8/10.5	1, 2Bl/1, 4Bl	180/235	Stand — A-745 Opt — A-833 Opt — A-904 A
A-361-2-24	361 V8	361	9	1, 2Bl	265	Stand — A-745 Opt — A-833 Opt — A-727

VEHICLE IDENTIFICATION NUMBER

PM21B65100551

The vehicle number (serial number) is stamped and embossed on a stainless steel plate attached to the left front door hinge pillar. It consists of car make symbol, series code, model year code, assembly plant symbol & a sequential production number.

1st Digit - Car make
Charger	X
Dart	L
Coronet	W
Polara, Monaco	D

2nd Digit - Class
Ecconomy	E
Low	L
High	H
Premium	P
Police	K
Taxi	T
VIP	S

3rd Digit & 4th Digit -Body style
2-Dr. Sedan	21
2-Dr. Hardtop	23
Convertible	27
2-Dr. Sports Hardtop	29
4-Dr. Sedan	41
4-Dr. Hardtop	43
6-Ps. Station Wagon	45
9-Ps. Station Wagon	46

Fifth Digit - Engines
170	A
225	B
Special Order 6 Cyl.	C
237	D
318	E
361	F
383	G
426 Hemi	H
440	J
Special Order 8 Cyl.	K

Sixth Digit - Year 1966

Seventh Digit - Assembly plant
Lynch Rd	1
Hamtramck	2
Jefferson	3
Belvedere Plant	4
Los Angeles	5
Newark Plant	6
St. Louis Plant	7
Windsor Plant	9

5th through 10th digit are production sequence code.

```
1 2 3 4 5 6 7 8 9 0
A B C D E F G H J X L M N P Q R S T V W X Y Z

SO        NUMBER      BDY      TRM      PNT
224       0555        LL21     L6R      BB1
```

BODY CODE PLATE

Stamped and embossed on a plate which is attached on the engine side of the cowl just above the master cylinder onhe driver's side door. The plate shows the body type, trim code, schedual date, paint code, and some accessory codes.

THE SHIPPING ORDER NUMBER consists of a tree digit month and day scheadualed Based on 01 through 31 days production date, and a five digit production order number.

MONTH	CODE
JAN	1
FEB	2
MAR	3
APR	4
MAY	5
JUN	6
JULY	7
AUG	8
SEPT	9
OCT	A
NOV	B
DEC	C

BODY NUMBER is a 4 digit number which indicates the car line, price class, and body style. Same first four digits of the vin.

DART	CODE
2-Dr. Sedan	LL21
4-Dr. Sedan	LL41
4-Dr. Wagon	LL45

DART 270	CODE
2-Dr. Sedan	LH21
4-Dr. Sedan	LH41
2-Dr. Hardtop	LH23
Convertible	LH27
4-Dr. Wagon	LH45

DART GT	CODE
2-Dr. Hardtop	LP23
Convertible	LP27

CORONET	CODE
2-Dr. Sedan	WE21
4-Dr. Sedan	WE41

CORONET DELUXE	CODE
2-Dr. Sedan	WL21
4-Dr. Sedan	WL41
4-Dr. Wagon (2 seat)	WL45

CORONET 440	CODE
4-Dr. Sedan	WH41
2-Dr. Hardtop Sedan	WH23
Convertible	WH27
4-Dr. Wagon	WH45
4-Dr. Wagon	*WH46

CORONET 500	CODE
2-Dr. Hardtop	WP23
4-Dr. Sedan	WP41
Convertible	WP27

DODGE CHARGER	CODE
2-Dr. Hardtop	XP29*

POLARA 318	CODE
4-Dr. Sedan	DE41*

POLARA	CODE
4-Dr. Sedan	DL41*
2-Dr. Hardtop	DL23*
4-Dr. Hardtop	DL43*
Convertible	DL27*
4-Dr. Wagon	DL45*
4-Dr. Wagon	DL46*

MONACO	CODE
2-Dr. Hardtop	DH23*
4-Dr. Sedan	DH41*
4-Dr. Hardtop	DH43*
4-Dr. Wagon (2 seat)	DH45*
4-Dr. Wagon (3 seat)	DH46*

MONACO 500	CODE
2-Dr. Hardtop	DP23*

*Indicates 8 cylinder only in these models.

THE PAINT CODE furnishes the key to the paint used on the car. A three digit code indicates the top and bottom colors respectively. A number follows which designates two-tone, sports-tone, convertible top, etc.

CODE	COLOR	CODE
A	Silver Metallic	AA1
B	Black	BB1
C	Light Blue	CC1
D	Medium Blue Metallic	DD1
E	Dark Blue Metallic	EE1
F	Light Green Metallic	FF1
G	Dark Green Metallic	GG1
K	Medium Turquoise Metallic	KK1
P	Bright Red	PP1
Q	Red Metallic	QQ1
R	Yellow	RR1
S	Cream	SS1
W	White	WW1
X	Beige	XX1
Y	Bronze Metallic	YY1
Z	Gold Metallic	ZZ1
4	Sandstone Metallic	441
6	Mauve Metallic	661
7	Maroon Metallic	771

TRIM CODE: Furnishes the key to the interior color and material.

CODE	CLOTH	VINYL	LEATHER	COLOR
L1B	*	*	-	Blue
L1Q	*	*	-	Turquoise
L1T	*	*	-	Tan
L6R	*	*	-	Red
L1X	*	*	-	Black
L5W	-	*	-	White
L6B	*	*	-	Blue
L6Q	*	*	-	Turqoise
L6T	*	*	-	Tan
L1R	*	*	-	Red
L4B	-	*	-	Blue
L4Q	-	*	-	Turqoise
L4T	-	*	-	Tan
L5R	-	*	-	Red
L5X	-	*	-	Black
L4W	-	*	-	White
L5B	-	*	-	Blue
L4R	-	*	-	Red
L4X	-	*	-	Black
P1D	*	*	-	Blue
P1Q	*	*	-	Turquoise
P1T	*	*	-	Tan
P4H	-	*	-	Red
P1X	*	*	-	Black
P4W	-	*	-	Whitw

CODE	CLOTH	VINYL	LEATHER	COLOR
P4U	-	*	-	Cordovan
P4Y	-	*	-	Gold
P4B	*	*	-	Blue
P4T	-	*	-	Tan
P4R	-	*	-	Red
P4X	-	*	-	Black
P4B	*	*	-	Blue
P4D	-	*	-	Blue
H1B	*	*	-	Blue
H1Q	*	*	-	Turquoise
H1T	*	*	-	Tan
H1H	*	*	-	Red
H1X	*	*	-	Black
H4W	-	*	-	White
H4B	-	*	-	Blue
H4J	-	*	-	Turquoise
H4T	-	*	-	Tan
H1R	*	*	-	Red
H4X	-	*	-	Black
H4D	-	*	-	Blue
H4H	-	*	-	Red
H4Y	-	*	-	Gold
H4R	-	*	-	Red
E1B	*	*	-	Blue
E1Q	*	*	-	Turqouise
E1T	*	*	-	Tan

ENGINE NUMBER

Stamped on a boss behind the water pump. The number provides the code to identify the series, block displacement, and month/day production date.

EXAMPLE

B	38	2	24
YEAR	383	FEBRUARY	24th DAY

Engine #	Engine Name	CID	Comp. ratio	Carb type	HP	Transmission
B-170-2-24	170 Six	170	8.5	1, 1Bl	101	Stand — A-903 G Opt — A-904 G
B-225-8-2-24	225 Six	225	8.4	1, 1Bl	145	Stand — A-903 G A-904 RG/A-745 Opt — A-904 RG Opt — A-727
B-273-2-24	273 V8	273	8.8/10.5	1, 2Bl/1, 4Bl	180/235	Stand — A-833/A-745 Opt — A-904-A
B-318-2-24	318 V8	318	9	1, 2Bl	230	Stand — A-745 Opt — A-727
B-361-2-24	361 V8	361	9	1, 2Bl	265	Stand — A-727 Opt — A-833
B-383-2-24	383 V8	383	9.2/10.0	1, 2Bl/1, 4Bl	270/325	Stand — A-745 Opt — A-833 Opt — A-727
B-426-B-2-24	426 Hemi	426	10.25	2, 4Bl	425	Stand — A-833 Opt — A-727
B-440-8-2-24	440 V8	440	10.1	1, 4Bl	350	Stand — A-727 Opt — A-833

VEHICLE IDENTIFICATION NUMBER

DP23K74100553

The vehicle number (serial number) is stamped and embossed on a stainless steel plate attached to the left front door hinge pillar. It consists of car make symbol, series code, model year code, assembly plant symbol & a sequential production number.

1st Digit - Car make

Charger	X
Dart	L
Coronet	W
Polara, Monaco	D

2nd Digit - Class

Economy	E
Low	L
High	H
Medium	M
Premium	P
Police	K
Taxi	T
VIP	S

3rd Digit & 4th Digit -Body style

2-Dr. Sedan	21
2-Dr. Hardtop	23
Convertible	27
2-Dr. Sports Hardtop	29
4-Dr. Sedan	41
4-Dr. Hardtop	43
6-Ps. Station Wagon	45
9-Ps. Station Wagon	46

Fifth Digit - Engines

170	A
225	B
Special Order 6 Cyl.	C
273	D
273 HP	E
318	F
383	G
383 HP	H
426 Hemi	J
440	K
440 HP	L
Special Order 8 Cyl.	M

Sixth Digit - Year 1967

Seventh Digit - Assembly plant

Lynch Rd	1
Hamtramck	2
Jefferson	3
Belvidere Plant	4
ILos Angeles	5
Newarc Plant	6
St. Louis Plant	7
Windsor Plant	9

BODY CODE PLATE

```
1 2 3 4 5 6 7 8 9 0
A B C D E F G H J X L M N P Q R S T V W X Y Z
1 2 3 4 5 6 7 8        AX      TRM    PNT    UBS
                   4           H4R    BB1      S
DP23          81   5           635    224    00551
```

Stamped and embossed on a stainless steel plate attached to the fender shield under the hood. The plate indicates the code for: Body type, Engine, Transmission, Schedual date, Paint, Trim and some Option codes. The plate is read left to right, bottom to top.Starting with the bottom row of numbers.

THE BODY NUMBER is a four digit number which indicates the Car line, Price class, and Body style. Same first four digits of the VIN.

The two digit ENGINE CID CODE identifies the engine.

ENGIINE CID   **CODE**

170 1BBL.	11
225 1BBL.	21
273 2BBL	31
273 4BBI HP	32
318 2BBL	41
383 2BBL	61
383 4BBL	62
426 24BBI Hemi HP	73
440 4BBL	81
440 4BBL HP	83

TRANSMISSION	CODE
3-Speed Manual	1
3-Speed Manual HD	2
4-Speed Manual	3
3-Speed Automatic	5
3-Speed Automatic HD	6
Special Order Transmission	9

The three digit code which indicates tire size and type, this option code is not included.

The last right digit of the bottom row is the SHIPPING ORDER NUMBER which consists of a three digit month and day scheduled production date, and a five digit production order number.

The next row up there will be one digit AXLE CODE found directly under the AX column.

DART	CODE
2-Dr. Sedan	LL21
4-Dr. Sedan	LL41

DART 270	CODE
4-Dr. Sedan	LH41
2-Dr. Hardtop	LH23

DART GT	CODE
2-Dr. Hardtop	LP23
Convertible	LP27

CORONET	CODE
4-Dr. Wagon	WE45

CORONET DELUXE	CODE
2-Dr. Sedan	WL21
4-Dr. Sedan	WL41
4-Dr. Wagon (2 seat)	WL45

CORONET 440	CODE
2-Dr. Hardtop	WH23
4-Dr. Sedan	WH41
Convertible	WH27
4-Dr. Wagon	WH45

CORONET 500	CODE
2-Dr. Hardtop	WP23
4-Dr. Sedan	WP41
Convertible	WP27

CORONET R/T	CODE
2-Dr. Hardtop	WS23
Convertible	WS27

DODGE CHARGER	CODE
2-Dr. Hardtop	XP29*

POLARA 318	CODE
4-Dr. Sedan	DE41*

POLARA	CODE
4-Dr. Sedan	DL41*
2-Dr. Hardtop	DL23*
4-Dr. Hardtop	DL43*
Convertible	DL27*
4-Dr. Wagon	DL45*
4-Dr. Wagon	DL46*

POLARA 500	CODE
2-Dr. Hardtop	DM43*
Convertible	DM27*

MONACO	CODE
2-Dr. Hardtop	DH23*
4-Dr. Sedan	DH41*
4-Dr. Hardtop	DH43*
4-Dr. Wagon (2 seat)	DH45*
4-Dr. Wagon (3 seat)	DH46*

MONACO 500	CODE
2-Dr. Hardtop	DP23*

* Indicates 8 cylinder only in these models.

ENGINE NUMBER

Stamped on a boss behind the water pump. The number provides the code to identify the series, block displacement, and month/day production date.

EXAMPLE

C	38	2	24
YEAR	383	FEBRUARY	24th DAY

THE UBS CODE identifies the upper door frame color, and the accent stripe color.

THE PAINT CODE furnishes the key to the paint used on the car. A three digit code indicates the top and bottom colors respectively. A number follows which designates two-tone, sports-tone, convertible top, etc.

CODE	COLOR	CODE
A	Silver Metallic	AA1
B	Black	BB1
C	Medium Blue Metallic	CC1
D	Light Blue Metallic	DD1
E	Dark Blue Metallic	EE1
F	Light Green Metallic	FF1
G	Dark Green Metallic	GG1
H	Dark Copper Metallic	HH1
J	Chestnut Metallic	JJ1
K	Medium Turquoise Metallic	KK1
L	Dark Turquoise Metallic	LL1
M	Bronze Metallic	MM1
P	Bright Red	PP1
Q	Dark Red Metallic	QQ1
R	Yellow	RR1
S	Cream	SS1
T	Medium Copper Metallic	TT1
W	White	WW1
X	Light Tan	XX1
Y	Medium Tan Metallic	YY1
Z	Gold Metallic	ZZ1
6	Mauve Metallic	661
8	Bright Blue Metallic	881

Engine #	Engine Name	CID	Comp. Ratio	Carb Type	HP	Transmission
C-170-2-24	170 Six	170	8.5	1, 1Bl	101	Stand -A-903 G, Opt -A-904 G
C-225-8-2-24	225 Six	225	8.4	1, 1Bl	145	Stand A-903 G, A-904 RG/A-745 Opt A-904 RG, Opt A-727
C-273-2-24	273 V8	273	8.8/10.5	1, 2Bl/1, 4Bl	180/235	Stand -A-833/A-745, Opt -A-904-A
C-318-8-2-24	318 V8	318	9	1, 2Bl	230	Stand - A-745, Opt -A-727
C-361-8-2-24	361 V8	361	9	1, 2Bl	265	Stand -A-727, Opt -A-833
C-383-8-2-24	383 V8	383	9.2/10.0	1, 2Bl/1, 4Bl	270/325	Stand -A-745, Opt -A-833 Opt -A-727
C-426-B-2-24	426 Hemi	426	10.25	2, 4Bl	425	Stand -A-833, Opt -A-727
C-440-8-2-24	440 V8	440	10.1	1, 4Bl	350	Stand -A-727, Opt -A-833

1967 DODGE

THE TRIM CODE : furnishes the key to the interior color and material

CODE	Cloth	Vinyl	Leather	COLOR	CODE	Cloth	Vinyl	Leather	COLOR
E1B	*	*	-	Blue	M6R	-	*	-	Red
E1R	*	*	-	Red	M6W	-	*	-	White and Black
E1T	*	*	-	Tan	M6X	-	*	-	Black
E4B	-	*	-	Blue	H1B	*	*	-	Blue
E4R	-	*	-	Red	H1Q	*	*	-	Turquoise
E4T	-	*	-	Tan	H1T	*	*	-	Tan
K1T	*	*	-	Tan	H1X	-	*	-	Black
K4T	-	*	-	Tan	H1Y	*	*	-	Gold
T4T	-	*	-	Tan	H5B	-	*	-	Blue
L1B	*	*	-	Blue	H5Q	-	*	-	Turquoise
L1R	*	*	-	Red	H5R	-	*	-	Red
L1T	*	*	-	Tan	H5T	-	*	-	Tan
L4B	-	*	-	Blue	H5X	-	*	-	Black
L4R	-	*	-	Red	H6B	-	*	-	Blue
L4T	-	*	-	Tan	H6T	-	*	-	Tan
H1B	*	*	-	Blue	H6X	-	*	-	Black
H1Q	*	*	-	Turquoise	P6B	-	*	-	Blue
H1T	*	*	-	Tan	P6K	-	*	-	Copper
H1X	*	*	-	Black	P6Q	-	*	-	Turquoise
H4B	-	*	-	Blue	P6R	-	*	-	Red
H4K	-	*	-	Copper	P6W	-	*	-	White and Black
H4R	-	*	-	Red	P6X	-	*	-	Black
H4T	-	*	-	Tan	P6Y	-	*	-	Gold
H4W	-	*	-	White and Black	P7X	*	*	-	Black
H4X	-	*	-	Black	L4B	-	*	-	Blue
P1B	-	*	-	Blue	L4R	-	*	-	Red
P1E	-	*	-	Black and Gold	L4T	-	*	-	Tan
P1Q	-	*	-	Turquoise	X1B	*	*	-	Blue
P1X	-	*	-	Black	X1R	*	*	-	Red
P6B	-	*	-	Blue	X1T	*	*	-	Tan
P6E	-	*	-	Black and Gold	X5Q	-	*	-	Turquoise
P6K	-	*	-	Copper	X5X	-	*	-	Black
P6R	-	*	-	Red	H1B	*	*	-	Blue
P6W	-	*	-	White and Black	H1Q	*	*	-	Turquoise
P6X	-	*	-	Black	H1R	*	*	-	Red
S6B	-	*	-	Blue	H1T	*	*	-	Tan
S6E	-	*	-	Black and Gold	H4B	-	*	-	Blue
S6K	-	*	-	Copper	H4R	-	*	-	Red
S6R	-	*	-	Red	H4T	-	*	-	Tan
S6W	-	*	-	White and Black	H4W	-	*	-	White and Black
S6X	-	*	-	Black	H4X	-	*	-	Black
E1B	*	*	-	Blue	H4C	-	*	-	White and Blue
E1Q	*	*	-	Turquoise	H4V	-	*	-	White and Red
E1T	*	*	-	Tan	H6B	-	*	-	Blue
E1X	*	*	-	Black	H6R	-	*	-	Red
K1A	*	*	-	Gray	H6X	-	*	-	Black
K4A	-	*	-	Gray	P4B	-	*	-	Blue
T4A	-	*	-	Gray	P4K	-	*	-	Copper
L1B	*	*	-	Blue	P4R	-	*	-	Red
L1Q	*	*	-	Turquoise	P4W	-	*	-	White and Black
L1R	*	*	-	Red	P4X	-	*	-	Black
L1T	*	*	-	Tan	P4C	-	*	-	White and Blue
L1X	*	*	-	Black	P4V	-	*	-	White and Red
L4B	-	*	-	Blue	P6B	-	*	-	Blue
L4R	-	*	-	Red	P6R	-	*	-	Red
L4T	-	*	-	Tan	P6W	-	*	-	White and Black
L4W	-	*	-	White and Black	P6X	-	*	-	Black
L4X	-	*	-	Black	P6C	-	*	-	White and Blue
M6B	-	*	-	Blue	P6V	-	*	-	White and Red
					P6K	-	*	-	Copper

VEHICLE IDENTIFICATION NUMBER

WH23G8E100551

The vehicle number (serial number) is stamped and embossed on a stainless steel plate attached to the left front door hinge pillar. It consists of car make symbol, series code, model year code, assembly plant symbol & a sequential production number.

1st Digit - Car make

Charger	X
Dart	L
Coronet	W
Polara, Monaco	D

2nd Digit - Class

Economy	E
Low	L
High	H
Medium	M
Premium	P
Police	K
Taxi	T
VIP	S
Super Stock	O
Sports Top	X

3rd Digit & 4th Digit -Body style

2-Dr. Sedan	21
2-Dr. Hardtop	23
Convertible	27
2-Dr. Sports Hardtop	29
4-Dr. Sedan	41
4-Dr. Hardtop	43
6-Ps. Station Wagon	45
9-Ps. Station Wagon	46

Fifth Digit - Engines

170	A
225	B
Special Order 6 Cyl.	C
273	D
318	F
383	G
383 HP	H
426 Hemi	J
440	K
440 HP	L
Special Order 8 Cyl.	M
340	P

Sixth Digit - Year 1968

Seventh Digit - Assembly plant

Lynch Rd	A
Hamtramck	B
Jefferson	C
Belvedere Plant	D
Los Angeles	E
Newark Plant	F
St. Louis Plant	G
Windsor Plant	R

BODY CODE PLATE

```
  1234567890
ABCDEFGHJXLMNPQRSTVWXYZ
 12345678      AX    TRM   PNT    UBS
               4     H4R   BB1     S
  WH23      61  5     50   224   00551
```

Stamped and embossed on a stainless steel plate attached to the fender shield under the hood. The plate indicates the code for: Body type, Engine, Transmission, Schedual date, Paint, Trim and some Option codes. The plate is read left to right, bottom to top Starting with the bottom row of numbers.

THE BODY NUMBER is a four digit number which indicates the Car line, Price class, and Body style. Same first four digits of the VIN. The two digit ENGINE CID CODE identifies the engine.

ENGINE CID	CODE
170 1BBL.	11
225 1BBL.	21
273 2BBL.	31
318 2BBL.	41
340 4BBL.	52
383 2BBL.	61
383 4BBL.	62
426 24BBl Hemi HP	73
440 4BBL.	81
440 4BBL HP	83

TRANSMISSION	CODE
3-Speed Manual	1
3-Speed Manual HD	2
4-Speed Manual	3
3-Speed Automatic	5
3-Speed Automatic HD	6
Special Order Transmission	9

The three digit code which indicates tire size and type, this option code is not included.

The last right digit of the bottom row is the SHIPPING ORDER NUMBER which consists of a three digit month and day scheduled production date, and a five digit production order number.

The next row up there will be one digit AXLE CODE found directly under the AX column.

DART	CODE
2-Dr. Sedan	LL21
4-Dr. Sedan	LL41

DART 270	CODE
4-Dr. Sedan	LH41
2-Dr. Hardtop	LH23

DART GT	CODE
2-Dr. Hardtop	LP23
Convertible	LP27

DART GTS	CODE
2-Dr. Hardtop	LS23
Convertible	LS27

CORONET SUPER BEE	CODE
2-Dr. Coupe	WM21

CORONET DELUXE	CODE
2-Dr. Coupe	WL21
4-Dr. Sedan	WL41
4-Dr. Wagon (2 seat)	WL45

CORONET 440	CODE
2-Dr. Coupe	WH21
2-Dr. Hardtop	WH23

4-Dr. Sedan	WH41
4-Dr. Wagon	WH45
4-Dr. Wagon	WH46

CORONET 500	CODE
2-Dr. Hardtop	WP23
4-Dr. Sedan	WP41
Convertible	WP27
4-Dr. Wagon	WP45
4-Dr. Wagon	WP46

CORONET R/T	CODE
2-Dr. Hardtop	WS23
Convertible	WS27

DODGE CHARGER	CODE
2-Dr. Hardtop	XP29

DODGE CHARGER RT *	CODE
2-Dr. Hardtop	XS29

POLARA *	CODE
4-Dr. Sedan	DL41
2-Dr. Hardtop	DL23
4-Dr. Hardtop	DL43
4-Dr. Wagon	DL45
4-Dr. Wagon	DL46
Convertible	DL27

POLARA 500 *	CODE
2-Dr. Hardtop	DM23
Convertible	DM27

MONACO *	CODE
4-Dr. Sedan	DH41
2-Dr. Hardtop	DH23
4-Dr. Hardtop	DH43
4-Dr. Wagon	DH45
4-Dr. Wagon	DH46

MONACO 500 *	CODE
2-Dr. Hardtop	DP23

* Indicsates 8 cylinder only in these models.

THE UBS CODE identifies the upper door frame color, and the accent stripe color.

THE PAINT CODE furnishes the key to the paint used on the car. A three digit code indicates the top and bottom colors respectively. A number follows which designates two-tone, sports-tone, convertible top, etc.

CODE	COLOR	CODE
A	Silver Metallic	AA1
B	Black	BB1
C	Medium Blue Metallic	CC1
D	Pale Blue Metallic	DD1
E	Dark Blue Metallic	EE1
F	Light Green Metallic	FF1
G	Racing Green Metallic	GG1
H	Light Gold	HH1
J	Medium Gold Metallic	JJ1
K	Light Turquoise Metallic	KK1
L	Medium Dark Turquoise Metallic	LL1
M	Bronze Metallic	MM1
P	Red	PP1
Q	Bright Blue Metallic	QQ1
R	Burgundy Metallic	RR1
S	Yellow	SS1
T	Medium Green Metallic	TT1
U	Light Blue Metallic	UU1
W	White	WW1
X	Beige	XX1
Y	Medium tan Metallic	YY1

ENGINE NUMBER

Stamped on a boss behind the water pump. The number provides the code to identify the series, block displacement, and month/day production date.

EXAMPLE

PM	**383**	**2187**	**2401**	
PLANT CODE	CID	JULIAN DATE	DAILY SEQUENTIAL NUMBER	ENGINE PLANTS PM-Mound Rd. PT-Trenton

Engine #	Engine Name	CID	Comp. Ratio	Carb Type	HP	Transmission
PM170xxxx0001	170 Six	170	8.5	1, 1Bl	101	Stand -A-903 G, Opt -A-904 G
PM225xxxx0001	225 Six	225	8.4	1, 1Bl	145	Stand A-903 G, A-904 RG/A-745 Opt A-904 RG, Opt A-727
PM273xxxx0001	273 V8	273	8.8/10.5	1, 2Bl/1, 4Bl	180/235	Stand -A-833/A-745, Opt -A-904-A
PM318xxxx0001	318 V8	318	9	1, 2Bl	230	Stand - A-745, Opt -A-727
PM361xxxx0001	361 V8	361	9	1, 2Bl	265	Stand -A-727, Opt -A-833
PM383xxxx0001	383 V8	383	9.2/10.0	1, 2Bl/1, 4Bl	270/325	Stand -A-745, Opt -A-83 Opt -A-727
PM426xxxx0001	426 Hemi	426	10.25	2, 4Bl	425	Stand -A-833, Opt -A-727
PM440xxxx0001	440 V8	440	10.1	1, 4Bl	350	Stand -A-727, Opt -A-833

THE TRIM CODE : furnishes the key to the interior color and material

CODE	Cloth	Vinyl	Leather	COLOR	CODE	Cloth	Vinyl	Leather	COLOR
E1B	*	*	-	Blue	M6R	-	*	-	Red
E1R	*	*	-	Red	M6W	-	*	-	White & Black
E1T	*	*	-	Tan	M6X	-	*	-	Black
E4B	-	*	-	Blue	H1B	*	*	-	Blue
E4R	-	*	-	Red	H1Q	*	*	-	Turquoise
E4T	-	*	-	Tan	H1T	*	*	-	Tan
K1T	*	*	-	Tan	H1X	*	*	-	Black
K4T	-	*	-	Tan	H1Y	*	*	-	Gold
T4T	-	*	-	Tan	H5B	-	*	-	Blue
L1B	*	*	-	Blue	H5Q	-	*	-	Turquoise
L1R	*	*	-	Red	H5R	-	*	-	Red
L1T	*	*	-	Tan	H5T	-	*	-	Tan
L4B	-	*	-	Blue	H5X	-	*	-	Black
L4R	-	*	-	Red	H6B	-	*	-	Blue
L4T	-	*	-	Tan	H6T	-	*	-	Tan
H1B	*	*	-	Blue	H6X	-	*	-	Black
H1Q	*	*	-	Turquoise	P6B	-	*	-	Blue
H1T	*	*	-	Tan	P6K	-	*	-	Copper
H1X	*	*	-	Black	P6Q	-	*	-	Turquoise
H4B	-	*	-	Blue	P6R	-	*	-	Red
H4K	-	*	-	Copper	P6W	-	*	-	White & Black
H4R	-	*	-	Red	P6X	-	*	-	Black
H4T	-	*	-	Tan	P6Y	-	*	-	Gold
H4W	-	*	-	White & Black	P7X	*	*	-	Black
H4X	-	*	-	Black	L4B	-	*	-	Blue
P1B	-	*	-	Blue	L4R	-	*	-	Red
P1E	-	*	-	Black & Gold	L4T	-	*	-	Tan
P1Q	-	*	-	Turquoise	X1B	*	*	-	Blue
P1X	-	*	-	Black	X1R	*	*	-	Red
P6B	-	*	-	Blue	X1T	*	*	-	Tan
P6E	-	*	-	Black & Gold	X5Q	-	*	-	Turquoise
P6K	-	*	-	Copper	X5X	-	-	-	Black
P6R	-	*	-	Red	H1B	*	*	-	Blue
P6W	-	*	-	White & Black	H1Q	*	*	-	Turquoise
P6X	-	*	-	Black	H1R	*	*	-	Red
S6B	-	*	-	Blue	H1T	*	*	-	Tan
S6E	-	*	-	Black & Gold	H4B	-	*	-	Blue
S6K	-	*	-	Copper	H4R	-	*	-	Red
S6R	-	*	-	Red	H4T	-	*	-	Tan
S6W	-	*	-	White & Black	H4W	-	*	-	White & Black
S6X	-	*	-	Black	H4X	-	*	-	Black
E1B	*	*	-	Blue	H4C	-	*	-	White & Blue
E1Q	*	*	-	Turquoise	H4V	-	*	-	White & Red
E1T	*	*	-	Tan	H6B	-	*	-	Blue
E1X	*	*	-	Black	H6R	-	*	-	Red
K1A	*	*	-	Gray	H6X	-	*	-	Black
K4A	-	*	-	Gray	P4B	-	*	-	Blue
T4A	-	*	-	Gray	P4K	-	*	-	Copper
L1B	*	*	-	Blue	P6C	-	*	-	White & Blue
L1Q	*	*	-	Turquoise	P6V	-	*	-	White & Red
L1R	*	*	-	Red	P4R	-	*	-	Red
L1T	*	*	-	Tan	P4W	-	*	-	White & Black
LIX	*	*	-	Black	P4X	-	*	-	Black
L4B	-	*	-	Blue	P4C	-	*	-	White & Blue
L4R	-	*	-	Red	P4V	-	*	-	White & Red
L4T	-	*	-	Tan	P6B	-	*	-	Blue
L4W	-	*	-	White & Black	P6K	-	*	-	Copper
L4X	-	*	-	Black	P6R	-	*	-	Red
M6B	-	*	-	Blue	P6W	-	*	-	White & Black
					P6X	-	*	-	Black

VEHICLE IDENTIFICATION NUMBER

WH23F9F100551

The vehicle number (serial number) is stamped and embossed on a stainless steel plate attached to the left front door hinge pillar. It consists of car make symbol, series code, model year code, assembly plant symbol & a sequential production number.

1st Digit - Car make
Charger	X
Dart	L
Coronet	W
Polara, Monaco	D

2nd Digit - Class
Economy	E
Low	L
High	H
Medium	M
Premium	P
Police	K
Taxi	T
VIP	S
Super Stock	O
Sports Top	X

3rd Digit & 4th Digit -Body style
2-Dr. Sedan	21
2-Dr. Hardtop	23
Convertible	27
2-Dr. Sports Hardtop	29
4-Dr. Sedan	41
4-Dr. Hardtop	43
6-Ps. Station Wagon	45
9-Ps. Station Wagon	46

Fifth Digit - Engines
170	A
225	B
Special Order 6 Cyl.	C
273	D
318	F
383	G
383 HP	H
426 Hemi	J
440	K
440 HP	L
Special Order 8 Cyl.	M
340 HP	P

Sixth Digit - Year 1969

Seventh Digit - Assembly plant
Lynch Rd	A
Hamtramck	B
Jefferson	C
Belvidere Plant	D
ILos Angeles	E
Newark Plant	F
St. Louis Plant	G
Windsor Plant	R

```
   abcdefghjkmnpqrtuwy
A B C D E F G H J X L M N P Q R S T V W X Y Z
  1 2 3 4 5 6 7 8      AX      TRM    PNT     UBS
            X9       X9      HX3    BB1     W
    WH23            E44      D31    F9F     100551
```

BODY CODE PLATE

Stamped and embossed on a stainless steel plate attached to the fender shield under the hood. The plate indicates the code for: Body type, Engine, Transmission, Schedule date, Paint, Trim and some Option codes. The plate is read left to right, bottom to top.starting with the bottom row of numbers.

THE BODY NUMBER is a four digit number which indicates the Car line, Price class, and Body style. Same first four digits of the VIN. The two digit ENGINE CID CODE identifies the engine.

ENGIINE CID   **CODE**

Special 6 Cyl.	E06
Special 8 Cyl.	E08
170 1BBL.	E11
225 1BBL.	E24
225 1BBL.	E25
273 2BBL.	E31
318 2BBL.	E44
340 4BBL.	E 55
383 2BBL.	E 61
383 4BBL.	E62
426 24BBl Hemi HP	E74
440 4BBL.	E85
440 4BBL HP	E86

TRANSMISSION	CODE
3-Speed Manual	D11
3-Speed Manual	D12
3-Speed Manual HD	D13
4-Speed Manual	D21
3-Speed Automatic	D31
3-Speed Automatic	D32
3-Speed Automatic HD	D34
Clutch HD	D41
Special Order Transmission	D49

The three digit code which indicates tire size and type, this option code is not included.

The last digits of the bottom row are a repeat of the last nine digits of the VIN plate.

ENGINE NUMBERS: All engine serial numbers contain fourteen characters and digits. The first two designate the engine plant, the next three are the cubic inch displacement, the next one designates low compression, the next four are based on a Julian calander and the production sequence number of engines built that day. All 383 and 440 cubic inch engines have the serial number stanped on the cylinder block.

DART SWINGER	CODE
2-Dr. Hardtop	LL23

DART	CODE
4-Dr. Sedan	LL41

DART CUSTOM	CODE
4-Dr. Sedan	LH41
2-Dr. Hardtop	LH23

CORONET SUPER BEE *	CODE
2-Dr. Coupe	WM21
2-Dr. Hardtop	WM23

DART GT	CODE
2-Dr. Hardtop	LP23
Convertible	LP27

DART SWINGER 340 *	CODE
2-Dr. Hardtop	LM23

DART GTS °	CODE
2-Dr. Hardtop	LS23
Convertible	LS27

CORONET DELUXE	CODE
2-Dr. Coupe	WL21
4-Dr. Sedan	WL41
4-Dr. Wagon (2 seat)	WL45

CORONET 440	CODE
2-Dr. Coupe	WH21
2-Dr. Hardtop	WH23
4-Dr. Sedan	WH41
4-Dr. Wagon	WH45
4-Dr. Wagon	WH46

CORONET 500	CODE
2-Dr. Hardtop	WP23
4-Dr. Sedan	WP41
Convertible	WP27
4-Dr. Wagon	WP45
4-Dr. Wagon	WP46

CORONET R/T *	CODE
2-Dr. Hardtop	WS23
Convertible	WS27

DODGE CHARGER	CODE
2-Dr. Hardtop	XP29

DODGE CHARGER RT *	CODE
2-Dr. Hardtop	XS29

DODGE CHARGER 500 *	CODE
2-Dr. Hardtop	XX29

POLARA *	CODE
4-Dr. Sedan	DL41
2-Dr. Hardtop	DL23
4-Dr. Hardtop	DL43
Convertible	DL27
4-Dr. Wagon	DL45
4-Dr. Wagon	DL46

POLARA 500 *	CODE
2-Dr. Hardtop	DM23
Convertible	DM27

MONACO *	CODE
4-Dr. Sedan	DH41
2-Dr. Hardtop	DH23
4-Dr. Hardtop	DH43
4-Dr. Wagon	DH45
4-Dr. Wagon	DH46

* Indicsates 8 cylinder only in these models.

THE UBS CODE identifies the upper door frame color, and the accent stripe color.

THE PAINT CODE furnishes the key to the paint used on the car. A threE digit code indicates the top and bottOm colors respectively. A number follOws which designates two-tone, sports-tone, convertible top, etc.

CODE	COLOR	CODE
	Medium Blue Metallic	B7
	Bright Blue Metallic	B5
	Light Blue Metallic	B3
	Dark Green Metallic	F8
	Medium Green Metallic	F5
	Light Green Metallic	F3
	Bright Turquoise metallic	Q5
	Cream	Y3
	Gold Metallic	Y4
	Yellow	Y2
	Dark Bronze Metallic	T7
	Copper Metallic	T5
	Light Bronze Metallic	T3
	Beige	L1
	Red	R6
	Silver Metallic	A4
	white	W1
	Black	X9

ENGINE NUMBER

Stamped on a boss behind the water pump. The number provides the code to identify the series, block displacement, and month/day production date.

EXAMPLE

PM	383	2187	2401		ENGINE PLANT
PLANT CODE	CID	JULIAN DATE	DAILY SEQUENTIAL		PM-Mound Rd. PT-Trenton

Engine #	Engine Name	CID	Comp.	Carb	HP	Transmission
PM170xxxx0001	170 Six	170	8.5	1, 1Bl	101	Stand -A-903 G, Opt -A-904 G
PM225xxxx0001	225 Six	225	8.4	1, 1Bl	145	Stand A-903 G, A-904 RG/A-745 Opt A-904 RG, Opt A-727
PM273xxxx0001	273 V8	273	8.8/10.5	1, 2Bl/1, 4Bl	180/235	Stand -A-833/A-745, Opt -A-904-A
PM318xxxx0001	318 V8	318	9	1, 2Bl	230	Stand - A-745, Opt -A-727
PM361xxxx0001	361 V8	361	9	1, 2Bl	265	Stand -A-727, Opt -A-833
PM383xxxx0001	383 V8	383	9.2/10.0	1, 2Bl/1, 4Bl	270/325	Stand -A-745, Opt -A-833 Opt -A-727
PM426xxxx0001	426 Hemi	426	10.25	2, 4Bl	425	Stand -A-833, Opt -A-727
PM440xxxx0001	440 V8	440	10.1	1, 4Bl	350	Stand -A-727, Opt -A-833

THE TRIM CODE : furnishes the key to the interior color and material

CODE	Cloth	Vinyl	Leather	COLOR	CODE	Cloth	Vinyl	Leather	COLOR
P6Y	-	*	-	Gold	L2W	-	*	-	Black (White Int.)
P6B	-	*	-	Blue	C6X	-	*	-	Black
P6G	-	*	-	Green	C6D	-	*	-	Blue
P6R	-	*	-	Red	C6G	-	*	-	Green
P6X	-	*	-	Black	C6R	-	*	-	Red
P6C	-	*	-	Blue (White Int.)	C6T	-	*	-	Tan
P6F	-	*	-	Green (White Int.)	C5X	*	*	-	Black
P6W	-	*	-	Black (White Int.)	C6W	-	*	-	Black (White Int.)
P6E	-	*	-	Gold (White Int.)	CRD	-	*	*	Blue
P2X	-	*	-	Black	CRG	-	*	*	Green
P2B	-	*	-	Blue	CRT	-	*	*	Tan
P2R	-	*	-	Red	CRX	-	*	*	Black
P2W	-	*	-	Black (White Int.)	P6D	-	*	-	Blue
H2B	-	*	-	Blue	P6X	-	*	-	Black
H2G	-	*	-	Green	P6R	-	*	-	Red
H2T	-	*	-	Tan	P6G	-	*	-	Green
H2X	-	*	-	Black	P6T	-	*	-	Tan
H2R	-	*	-	Red	P6C	-	*	-	Blue (White Int.)
H2C	-	*	-	Blue (White Int.)	P6F	-	*	-	Green (White Int.)
H2W	-	*	-	Black (White Int.)	P6V	-	*	-	Red (White Int.)
H1G	*	*	-	Green	P6W	-	*	-	Black (White Int.)
H1B	*	*	-	Blue	M6R	-	*	-	Red
H1X	*	*	-	Black	M6B	-	*	-	Blue
H1L	*	*	-	Black (Champagne Int.)	M6G	-	*	-	Green
L2B	-	*	-	Black	M6T	-	*	-	Tan
L2T	-	*	-	Black (Tan Int.)	M6X	-	*	-	Black
L2X	-	*	-	Black	M6C	-	*	-	Blue (White Int.)
D2B	-	*	-	Black (Blue Int.)	M6F	-	*	-	Green (White Int.)
D2T	-	*	-	Black (Tan Int.)	M6W	-	*	-	Black (White Int.)
D2X	-	*	-	Black	P3G	-	*	-	Green
H4D	-	*	-	Blue	P3D	-	*	-	Blue
H4G	-	*	-	Green	P3X	-	*	-	Black
H4T	-	*	-	Tan	P3Y	-	*	-	Gold
H4X	-	*	-	Black	P2D	-	*	-	Blue
H4H	-	*	-	Tan (White Int.)	P2G	-	*	-	Green
H1L	*	*	-	Gold (Champagne Int.)	P2X	-	*	-	Black
H1B	*	*	-	Blue	P2T	-	*	-	Tan
H1G	*	*	-	Green	P2W	-	*	-	Black (White Int.)
H1X	*	*	-	Black	D2T	-	*	-	Tan
H1Y	*	*	-	Gold	D2D	-	*	-	Blue
H6G	-	*	-	Green	D2G	-	*	-	Green
H6X	-	*	-	Black	D2X	-	*	-	Black
H6Y	*	*	-	Gold	H2T	-	*	-	Tan
H6W	-	*	-	Black (White Int.)	H2B	-	*	-	Blue
H7B	*	*	-	Blue	H2X	-	*	-	Black
H7G	*	*	-	Green	H2G	-	*	-	Green
H7X	*	*	-	Black	L1L	*	*	-	Black
H8X	*	*	-	Black	L2X	-	*	-	Black
H8T	*	*	-	Tan	L2B	-	*	-	Blue
M6G	-	*	-	Green	L2T	-	*	-	Black
M6B	-	*	-	Blue	M2T	-	*	-	Tan
M6X	-	*	-	Black	M2B	-	*	-	Blue
M6T	-	*	-	Tan	M2X	-	*	-	Black
M6X	-	*	-	Black (White Int.)	H2R	-	*	-	Red
L1Y	*	*	-	Gold	H2C	-	*	-	Blue (White Int.)
L1B	*	*	-	Blue	H2F	-	*	-	Green (White Int.)
L1G	*	*	-	Green	H2W	-	*	-	Black (White Int.)
L1X	*	*	-	Black	H1G	*	*	-	Green
L2B	-	*	-	Blue	H1B	*	*	-	Blue
L2G	-	*	-	Green	H1Y	*	*	-	Gold
L2X	-	*	-	Black	H1X	*	*	-	Black
L2T	-	*	-	Tan	L1B	*	*	-	Blue

VEHICLE IDENTIFICATION NUMBER

3303100551

The vehicle number (serial number) is stamped and embossed on a stainless steel plate attached to the left front door hinge pillar. It consists of car make symbol, series code, model year code, assembly plant symbol & a sequential production number.

1st Digit Car make

Valiant	1
Plymouth (6 Cyl.)	2
Plymouth (8 Cyl.)	3

2nd Digit Series

V-100 Savoy	1
Belvedere	2
V-200 Fury	3
V 100 S.W., Savoy S.W	5
Belvedere S.W.	6
V 200 S.W., Fury S.W.	7
Taxi	9
Fleet	0

3rd Digit Year 1960

4th Digit Assembly plant

Detroit	3
Los Angeles.	5
Newark	6
St. Louis Plant .	7

Last six digits indicate the production sequence number.

BODY CODE PLATE

Stamped and embossed on a stainless steel plate under the hood. It is attached to: right or left fender, cowl, or radiator cross member depending on the model and assembly plant. This plate will indicate; schedule date, body production number, body series, trim, paint, and accessory code.

THE SHIPPING ORDER NUMBER is assigned prior to production. It consists of a 4 digit planned delivery month/day date code, 0224 (February 24th). Then a plant production sequence number follows (0555)

BODY NUMBER is a 3 digit number which indicates the model and body style.

```
1 2 3 4 5 6 7 8 9 0
A B C D E F G H J X L M N P Q R S T V W X Y Z

  SO       NUMBER      BDY      TRM      PNT
 0224       0555       321      751      BB1
```

VALIANT V 100	CODE
4-Dr. Sedan	113
4-Dr. 2-Seat Wagon	156
4-Dr. 3-Seat Wagon	157

VALIANT V 200	CODE
4-Dr. Sedan	133
4-Dr. 2-Seat Wagon	176
4-Dr. 3-Seat Wagon	177

FLEET | CODE |
---|---|---
| 6 cyl | 8 cyl
2-Dr. Sedan | 201 | 301
4-Dr. Sedan | 203 | 303

SAVOY | CODE |
---|---|---
| 6 cyl | 8 cyl
2-Dr. Sedan | 211 | 321
4-Dr. Sedan | 213 | 313
2-Dr. Wagon | 255 | 355
4-Dr. Wagon | 256 | 356

BELVEDERE | CODE |
---|---|---
| 6 cyl | 8 cyl
2-Dr. Sedan | 221 | 311
2-Dr. HT Coupe | 222 | 322
4-Dr. Sedan | 223 | 323
4-Dr. Wagon | 266 | 366
4-Dr. Wagon | --- | 367

FURY | CODE |
---|---|---
| 6 cyl | 8 cyl
2-Dr. HT Coupe | 232 | 332
4-Dr. Sedan | 233 | 333
4-Dr. HT Sedan | 234 | 334
Convertible | --- | 335
4-Dr. Wagon | --- | 376
4-Dr. Wagon | --- | 377

THE PAINT CODE furnishes the key to the paint used on the car. A two digit code indicates the top and bottom colors respectively. A number follows whick designates two-tone, sports-tone, convertible top, etc.

TRIM CODE: Furnishes the key to the interior color and material.

Note: **V - VINYL   C - CLOTH**

CODE	COLOR	CODE
A	Buttercup Yellow	AA1
B	Jet Black	BB1
C	Sky Blue	CC1
D	Twilight Blue Metallic	DD1
F	Spring Green	FF1
G	Chrome Green Metallic	GG1
J	Aqua Mist	JJ1
K	Turquois Metallic	KK1
L	Platinum Metallic	LL1
P	Plum Red Metallic	PP1
T	Desert Beige	TT1
W	Oyster White	WW1
Y	Caramel Metallic	YY1

CODE	SERIES/MODEL	COLOR
—	V 100/ V, C Silver	Silver
—	V 100 Wagon/ V ,C	Silver/Black
751	V 200/ V, C	Blue, White, Silver, Black
751	V 200 Wagon/ V, C	Blue, White, Silver, Black
752	V 200/ V, C	Green, White, Silver, Black
752	V 200 Wagon/ V, C	Green, White, Silver, Black
753	V 200/ V, C	Red, White, Silver, Black
753	V 200 Wagon/ V, C	Red, White, Silver, Black
121	Fury/ V,C	Blue
121	Sport Suburban/ V,C	Blue
122	Fury/ V,C	Green
122	Sport Suburban/ V,C	Green
123	Fury/ V,C	Caramel
123	Sport Suburban/ V,C	Caramel
124	Fury/ V,C	Red
124	Sport Suburban/ V,C	Red
125	Fury/ V,C	Turquoise
125	Sport Suburban/ V,C	Turquoise
341	Custom Suburban/ V,C	Blue
342	Custom Suburban/ V,C	Green
343	Custom Suburban/ V,C	Beige/Black
345	Custom Suburban/ V,C	Turquoise
347	Custom Suburban/ V,C	Red
111	Belvedere/ V,C	Blue
112	Belvedere/ V,C	Green
113	Belvedere/ V,C	Beige/Black
114	Belvedere/ V,C	Red
115	Belvedere/ V,C	Turquoise
101	Savoy/ V,C	Blue
102	Savoy/ V,C	Green
103	Savoy/ V,C.	Beige/Black
331	Deluxe Suburban/ V,C	Blue
332	Deluxe Suburban/ V,C	Green
333	Deluxe Suburban/ V,C	Beige/Black
244	Saratoga/ S-Optional	Silver, Black

CONVERTIBLE TOPS

Black 331
White 332
Blue 334

ENGINE NUMBER

Stamped on a boss behind the water pump. The number provides the code to identify the series, block displacement, and month/day production date.

EXAMPLE

P	38	2	24
YEAR	383	FEBRUARY	24th DAY

Engine #	Engine Name	CID	Comp ratio	Carb. type	HP	Transmission
P-17-2-24	Valiant Six/Hyperpack	170	8.5/10.5	1Bl/4Bl	101/148	Stand — Manual Opt — Auto 3 speed
P-22-2-24	30-D Economy	225	8.5	1Bl	145	Stand — Manual Opt — Torqueflite Six
P-31-2-24	Fury V-800 power pack	318	9.0	2Bl/4Bl	230/260	Stand — Manual/ Powerflite Opt — Powerflite Opt — Torqueflite
P-36-2-24	Golden Commando 395 Sonoramic Commando 435	361	10.0	4Bl/2, 4Bl Ram	330/330	Stand — Manual T85/Torqueflite Opt — Torqueflite
PR-38-2-24	Golden Commando 435 Golden Commando 425 Sonoramic Commando 460	383	10.0	4Bl/2, 4Bl Ram 4Bl Runner/2	325/330 330	Stand — Manual T85 Opt — Torqueflite

VEHICLE IDENTIFICATION NUMBER

3313100001

The vehicle number (serial number) is stamped and embossed on a stainless steel plate attached to the left front door hinge pillar. It consists of car make symbol, series code, model year code, assembly plant symbol & a sequential production number.

1st Digit Car make
Valiant (6 Cyl.) 1
Plymouth (6 Cyl.) 2
Plymouth (8 Cyl.) 3

2nd Digit Series
V-100 Savoy 1
Belvedere 2
V-200 Fury 3
V 100 S.W., Savoy S.W 5
Belvedere S.W. 6
V 200 S.W., Fury S.W. 7
Taxi 8
Special/Police 9
Fleet 0

3rd Digit Year..........................1960

4th Digit Assembly plant
Detroit 3
Los Angeles. 5
Newark 6
St. Louis Plant 7
Last six digits indicate the production sequence number.

BODY CODE PLATE

Stamped and embossed on a stainless steel plate under the hood. It is attached to: right or left fender, cowl, or radiator cross member depending on the model and assembly plant. This plate will indicate; schedule date, body production number, body series, trim, paint, and accessory code.

THE SHIPPING ORDER NUMBER is assigned prior to production. It consists of a 4 digit planned delivery month/day date code, 0224 (February 24th). Then a plant production sequence number follows (0555)

BODY NUMBER is a 3 digit number which indicates the model and body style.

1 2 3 4 5 6 7 8 9 0				
A B C D E F G H J X L M N P Q R S T V W X Y Z				
SO	NUMBER	BDY	TRM	PNT
0224	0555	311	501	BB1

VALIANT V 100 CODE
4-Dr. Sedan 113
4-Dr. 2-Seat Wagon...................156
2-Dr. Sedan................................111

VALIANT V 200 CODE
4-Dr. Sedan 133
4-Dr. 2-Seat Wagon.........176
2-Dr. Hardtop Coupe........132

FLEET	CODE	
	6 cyl	8 cyl
2-Dr. Sedan	201	301
4-Dr. Sedan	203	303

SAVOY	CODE	
	6 cyl	8 cyl
2-Dr. Sedan	211	311
4-Dr. Sedan	213	313
2-Dr. Wagon	255	355
4-Dr. Wagon	256	356

BELVEDERE	CODE	
	6 cyl	8 cyl
2-Dr. Sedan	221	311
2-Dr. HT Coupe	222	322
4-Dr. Sedan	223	323
4-Dr. Wagon	266	366
$-Dr. Wagon	---	367

FURY	CODE	
	6 cyl	8 cyl
2-Dr. HT Coupe	232	332
4-Dr. Sedan	233	333
4-Dr. HT Sedan	234	334
Convertible	---	335
4-Dr. Wagon	---	376
4-Dr. Wagon	---	377

THE PAINT CODE furnishes the key to the paint used on the car. A two digit code indicates the top and bottom colors respectively. A number follows which designates two-tone, sports-tone, convertible top, etc.

CODE	COLOR	CODE
A	Maize	AA1
B	Jet Black	BB1
C	Robbins Egg Blue	CC1
D	Air Force Blue Metallic	DD1
F	Mint Green	FF1
G	Emerald Green Metallic	GG1
K	Twilight Turquois	KK1
L	Silver Gray Metallic	LL1
R	Cardinal Red Metallic	RR1
S	Lavender Metallic	SS1
W	Alpine White	WW1
Y	Fawn Beige	YY1
Z	Bronze Metallic	ZZ1

TRIM CODE: Furnishes the key to the interior color and material.
Note: V - VINYL   C - CLOTH

CODE	SERIES/MODEL	COLOR
103	V 100 Sedan/ V, C	Silver
113	V 100 Wagon/ V, C	Black
101	V 100 Sedan/ V, C	Lt. Blue
101	V 100 Sedan/ V, C	Metallic Blue
111	V 100 Wagon/ V, C	Lt. Blue
111	V 100 Wagon/ V, C	Metallic Blue
102	V 100 Sedan/ V, C	Lt. Green
102	V 100 Sedan/ V, C	Metallic Green
112	V 100 Wagon/ V, C	Lt. Green
112	V 100 Wagon/ V, C	Metallic Green
103	V 100 Sedan/ V, C	Metallic Silver
113	V 100 Wagon/ V, C	Metallic Silver
103	V 100 Sedan/ V, C	White
113	V 100 Wagon/ V, C	White
103	V 100 Sedan/ V, C	Red
113	V 100 Wagon/ V, C	Red
151	V 200 All Models/ V, C	Black
151	V 200 All Models/ V, C	Lt. Blue
151	V 200 All Models/ V, C	Metallic Blue
152	V 200 All Models/ V, C	Lt. Green
152	V 200 All Models/ V, C	Metallic Green
155	V 200 All Models/ V, C	Metallic Silver
153	V 200 All Models/ V, C	Red
153	V 200 All Models/ V, C	White
504	Savoy/ V,C	Maize
501	Savoy/ V,C	Jet Black
501	Savoy/ V,C	Robbins Egg Blue
501	Savoy/ V,C	Air Force Blue
502	Savoy/ V,C	Mint Green
502	Savoy/ V,C	Metallic Emerald Green
504	Savoy/ V,C	Metallic TwilightTurquoise
501	Savoy/ V,C	Metallic Silver
504	Savoy/ V,C	Carnival Red
504	Savoy/ V,C	Coral
504	Savoy/ V,C	Metallic Lavender
501	Savoy/ V,C	Alpine White
604	Delux Suburban/ V,C	Maize
601	Delux Suburban/ V,C	Jet Black
601	Delux Suburban/ V,C	Robbins Egg Blue
601	Delux Suburban/ V,C	Air Force Blue
602	Delux Suburban/ V,C	Mint Green
602	Delux Suburban/ V,C	Metallic Emerald Green
604	Delux Suburban/ V,C	Metallic Twilight Turquoise
601	Delux Suburban/ V,C	Metallic Silver
604	Delux Suburban/ V,C	Carnival Red
604	Delux Suburban/ V,C	Coral
604	Delux Suburban/ V,C	Metallic Lavender
601	Delux Suburban/ V,C	Alpine White
514	Belvedere/V, C	Maize
511	Belvedere/V, C	Jet Black
511	Belvedere/V, C	Robins Egg Blue
511	Belvedere/V, C	Air Force Blue
512	Belvedere/V, C	Mint Green
512	Belvedere/V, C	Metallic Emerald
514	Belvedere/V, C	Metallic Twilight Turquoise
511	Belvedere/V, C	Metallic Silver
514	Belvedere/V, C	Carnival Red
514	Belvedere/V, C	Coral
514	Belvedere/V, C	Metallic Lavender
511	Belvedere/V, C	Alpine White
513	Belvedere/V, C"	Fawn Beige
513	Belvedere/V, C"	Metallic Bronze
614	Custom Suburban/V, C	Maize
611	Custom Suburban/V, C	Jet Black
611	Custom Suburban/V, C	Robins Egg Blue
611	Custom Suburban/V, C	Air Force Blue
612	Custom Suburban/V, C	Mint Green
612	Custom Suburban/V, C	Metallic Emerald Green
614	Custom Suburban/V, C	Metallic Twilight Turquoise
611	Custom Suburban/V, C	Metallic Silver
614	Custom Suburban/V, C	Carnival Red
614	Custom Suburban/V, C	Coral
614	Custom Suburban/V, C	Metallic Lavender
611	Custom Suburban/V, C	Alpine White
613	Custom Suburban/V, C	Fawn Beige
613	Custom Suburban/V, C	Metallic Bronze
524	Fury & Sports Suburban	Maize
521	Fury & Sports Suburban	Jet Black
521	Fury & Sports Suburban	Robins Egg Blue
521	Fury & Sports Suburban	Air Force Blue
522	Fury & Sports Suburban	Mint Green
522	Fury & Sports Suburban	Metallic Emerald Green
524	Fury & Sports Suburban	Metallic Twilight Turquoise
521	Fury & Sports Suburban	Metallic Silver
524	Fury & Sports Suburban	Carnival Red
524	Fury & Sports Suburban	Coral
524	Fury & Sports Suburban	Metallic Lavender
521	Fury & Sports Suburban	Alpine White
523	Fury & Sports Suburban	Fawn Beige
523	Fury & Sports Suburban	Metallic Bronze
654*	Fury & Sports Suburban/V	Maize
651	Fury & Sports Suburban/V	Jet Black
651	Fury & Sports Suburban/V	Robins Egg Blue
651	Fury & Sports Suburban/V	Air Force Blue
652*	Fury & Sports Suburban/V	Mint Green
652*	Fury & Sports Suburban/V	Metallic Emerald Green
654*	Fury & Sports Suburban/V	Metallic Twilight Turquoise
651	Fury & Sports Suburban/V	Metallic Silver
655	Fury & Sports Suburban/V	Carnival Red
654*	Fury & Sports Suburban/V	Coral
654*	Fury & Sports Suburban/V	Metallic Lavender
651	Fury & Sports Suburban/V	Alpine White
653	Fury & Sports Suburban/V	Fawn Beige
653	Fury & Sports Suburban/V	Metallic Bronze

CONVERTIBLE TOPS

Black 331
White 332
Blue 334

ENGINE NUMBER

Stamped on a boss behind the water pump. The number provides the code to identify the series, block displacement, and month/day production date.

EXAMPLE

R	38	2	24
YEAR	383	FEBRUARY	24th DAY

Engine #	Engine Name	CID	Comp ratio	Carb. type	HP	Transmission
R-17-2-24	Valiant Six/ Hyperpack	170	8.2	1Bl/4Bl	101/148	Stand - A-903G,35M Opt - A-904, Torqueflite HD
R-22-2-24	30-D Economy Six	225	8.2	1Bl	145	Stand - A-903G,35M Opt - A-904, Torqueflite Six
R-31-2-24	Fury V-800 Super Fury V-800	318	9.0	2Bl/4Bl	230/260	Stand - A-903A,35M A-466 Torqueflite Opt - A-373 Powerflite Opt - A-466 Torqueflite
R-36-2-24	Golden Commando	361	9.0	4Bl	305	Stand - A-745 HD Opt - A-466 Torqueflite
R-38-2-24	Sonoramic Commando	383	10.0	4Bl/2,4Bl 330 LongRam		Stand - A-745 HD Opt - A-466 Torqueflite
R-38-2-24	Maximum Performance	383/413	10.0	4Bl Runner Short Ram	330	Stand - A-745 HD
R-41-2-24	Special Police			4Bl/2,4Bl Runner	325 330	Opt - A-466 Torqueflite

VEHICLE IDENTIFICATION NUMBER

3323100551

The vehicle number (serial number) is stamped and embossed on a stainless steel plate attached to the left front door hinge pillar. It consists of car make symbol, series code, model year code, assembly plant symbol & a sequential production number.

1st Digit Car make
Valiant (6 Cyl.) 1
Plymouth (6 Cyl.) 2
Plymouth (8 Cyl.) 3

2nd Digit Series
V-100 Savoy 1
Belvedere 2
V-200 Fury 3
Valiant Signeyt, Sport Fury 4
V 100 S.W., Savoy S.W 5
Belvedere S.W. 6
V 200 S.W., Fury S.W. 7
Taxi 8
Police 9
Fleet 0

3rd Digit Year..........................1960

4th Digit Assembly plant
Detroit 3
Los Angeles. 5
Newark 6
St. Louis Plant 7
Last six digits indicate the production sequence number.

BODY CODE PLATE

Stamped and embossed on a stainless steel plate under the hood. It is attached to: right or left fender, cowl, or radiator cross member depending on the model and assembly plant. This plate will indicate; schedule date, body production number, body series, trim, paint, and accessory code.

THE SHIPPING ORDER NUMBER is assigned prior to production. It consists of a 4 digit planned delivery month/day date code, 0224 (February 24th). Then a plant production sequence number follows (0555)

BODY NUMBER is a 3 digit number which indicates the model and body style.

1 2 3 4 5 6 7 8 9 0				
A B C D E F G H J X L M N P Q R S T V W X Y Z				
SO	NUMBER	BDY	TRM	PNT
0224	0555	131	501	BB1

VALIANT V 100	CODE
2-Dr. Sedan....................	111
4-Dr. Sedan	113
4-Dr. 3-Seat Wagon....................	156

VALIANT V 200	CODE
2-Dr. Sedan	131
4-Dr. Sedan	133
4-Dr. 2-Seat Wagon........	176

VALIANT SIGNET	CODE
2-Dr. HT Sedan	142

FLEET SPECIAL	CODE	
	6 cyl	8 cyl
2-Dr. Sedan.......	201	301
4-Dr. Sedan	203	303

SAVOY	CODE	
	6 cyl	8 cyl
2-Dr. Sedan	211	311
4-Dr. Sedan	213	313
4-Dr. Wagon	256	356

BELVEDERE	CODE	
	6 cyl	8 cyl
2-Dr. Sedan	221	321
2-Dr. HT Coupe	222	322
4-Dr. Sedan	223	323
4-Dr. Wagon	266	36
4-Dr. Wagon	---	36

FURY	COD	
	6 cyl	8 cy
2-Dr. HT Coupe	232	33
4-Dr. Sedan	233	33
4-Dr. HT Sedan	234	33
Convertible	---	33
4-Dr. Wagon	---	37
4-Dr. Wagon	---	37
Convertible	---	33

SPORT FURY	COD
2-Dr. HT Sedan	34
Convertible	34

THE PAINT CODE furnishes the key to the paint used on the car. A two digit code indicates the top and bottom colors respectively. A number follows which designates two-tone, sports-tone, convertible top, etc.

CODE	COLOR	CODE
A	Sun-Glo	AA1
B	Silhouette Black	BB1
C	Pale Blue	CC1
D	Luminous Blue	DD1
F	Pale Jade Green	FF1
G	Luminous Green	GG1
K	Luminous Turquoise	KK1
M	Pale Gray	MM1
P	Cherry Red	PP1
S	Luminous Cordovan	SS1
T	Sandstone	TT1
W	Ermine White	WW1
Y	Luminous Brown	YY1

TRIM CODE: Furnishes the key to the interior color and material.
Note: V - VINYL   C - CLOTH

CODE	Cloth	Vinyl	Leather	COLOR	CODE	Cloth	Vinyl	Leather	COLOR
501	*	*	-	Gray and Blue	122	*	*	-	Green
504	*	*	-	Gray	123	*	*	-	Cocoa
505	*	*	-	Gray and Red	124	*	*	-	Black and Gray
521	*	*	-	Blue	125	*	*	-	Red
522	*	*	-	Green	131	*	*	-	Blue
525	*	*	-	Red	132	*	*	-	Green
551	*	*	-	Gray and Blue	133	*	*	-	Cocoa
554	*	*	-	Gray	134	*	*	-	Gray
555	*	*	-	Gray and Red	201	-	*	-	Blue
564	-	*	-	Gray	203	-	*	-	Cocoa
571	-	*	-	Blue	204	-	*	-	Gray
573	-	*	-	Red	211	-	*	-	Blue
575	-	*	-	Red	214	-	*	-	Gray
594	-	*	-	Gray	231	-	*	-	Blue
101	*	*	-	Blue	234	-	*	-	Gray
103	*	*	-	Cocoa	241	-	*	-	Blue
104	*	*	-	Gray	244	-	*	-	Gray
111	*	*	-	Blue	245	-	*	-	Red
112	*	*	-	Green	251	-	*	-	Red
113	*	*	-	Cocoa	253	-	*	-	Blue
114	*	*	-	Gray	254	-	*	-	Black
121	*	*	-	Blue	294	-	*	-	Gray

ENGINE NUMBER

Stamped on a boss behind the water pump. The number provides the code to identify the series, block displacement, and month/day production date.

EXAMPLE

R	38	2	24
YEAR	383	FEBRUARY	24th DAY

Engine#	Engine Name	CID	Comp.ratio	Carb	HP	Transmission
S-17-8-3	Valiant Six	170	8.2	1Bl	101	Stand- A-903 6,3SM Opt-A 904 6,TF6
S-22-8-3	Super 225	225	1Bl	1Bl	145	Stand -A-903 G,3SM
	30-D Economy Six					Opt - A 904 R6,TF6
S-31-8-3	Fury V-800	318	9.0	1, 2Bl/1	230/260	Stand - A-745,3S MA-727TF8
	Superfury V-800			4Bl		Opt-A-727TF8
S-36-8-3	Golden Commando	361	9.0	1, 4Bl	305/310	Stand — A-745 3SM
	High-performance option			2,4Bl Runner		Opt — A-727 TF8
S-38-8-3	High-performance Option	383	10.0	1, 4Bl	330/335	Stand — A-745 3SM
				2, 4Bl runner		Opt — A-727 TF8
S-41-8-3	High-performance Option	413	11.0	1, 4Bl	365/385	Stand — A-745 3SM
				2, 4Bl Runner	410	Opt — A-727 TF8
				2, 4Bl Ram		Opt - A-466 Torqueflight

Note: 3SM = 3-speed manual TF8 = Torqueflite 8TF6 = Torqueflite 6

VEHICLE IDENTIFICATION NUMBER

3331100001

The vehicle number (serial number) is stamped and embossed on a stainless steel plate attached to the left front door hinge pillar. It consists of car make symbol, series code, model year code, assembly plant symbol & a sequential production number.

1st Digit Car make
Valiant (6 Cyl.)	1
Plymouth (6 Cyl.)	2
Plymouth (8 Cyl.)	3

2nd Digit Series
V-100 Savoy	1
Belvedere	2
V-200 Fury	3
Valiant Signet, Sport Fury	4
V 100 S.W., Savoy S.W	5
Belvedere S.W.	6
V 200 S.W., Fury S.W.	7
Taxi	8
Police	9
Fleet	0

3rd Digit Year 1960

4th Digit Assembly plant
Detroit	1-2
Los Angeles.	5
Newark	6
St. Louis Plant .	7

Last six digits indicate the production sequence number.

BODY CODE PLATE

Stamped and embossed on a stainless steel plate under the hood. It is attached to: right or left fender, cowl, or radiator cross member depending on the model and assembly plant. This plate will indicate; schedule date, body production number, body series, trim, paint, and accessory code.

THE SHIPPING ORDER NUMBER is assigned prior to production. It consists of a 4 digit planned delivery month/day date code, 0224 (February 24th). Then a plant production sequence number follows (0555)

BODY NUMBER is a 3 digit number which indicates the model and body style.

```
1 2 3 4 5 6 7 8 9 0
A B C D E F G H J X L M N P Q R S T V W X Y Z

SO        NUMBER      BDY     TRM     PNT
0224      0555        211     325     BB1
```

VALIANT V 100
	CODE
2-Dr. Sedan	111
4-Dr. Sedan	113
4-Dr. Suburban	156

VALIANT V 200
	CODE
2-Dr. Sedan	131
4-Dr. Sedan	133
Convertible	135
4-Dr. Suburban	176

VALIANT SIGNET
	CODE
2-Dr. HT Sedan	142
Convertible	145

SAVOY
	CODE 6 cyl	8 cyl
2-Dr. Sedan(Fleet)	201	301
4-Dr. Sedan (Fleet)	203	303
2-Dr. Sedan	211	311
4-Dr. Sedan	213	313
4-Dr. Wagon	256	356
4-Dr. Wagon	257	357
4-Dr. Sedan (Taxi)	283	383
4-Dr. Sedan (Police)	293	393
4-Dr. Wagon (Police)	296	396

BELVEDERE
	CODE 6 cyl	8 cyl
2-Dr. Sedan	221	311
2-Dr. HT Coupe	222	322
4-Dr. Sedan	223	323
4-Dr. Wagon	---	366
$-Dr. Wagon	---	367

FURY
	CODE 6 cyl	8 cyl
2-Dr. HT Coupe	232	332
4-Dr. Sedan	233	333
4-Dr. HT Sedan	-----	334
Convertible	---	335
4-Dr. Wagon	---	376
4-Dr. Wagon	---	377

SPORT FURY
	CODE
2-Dr. HT Sedan	342
Convertible	345

THE PAINT CODE furnishes the key to the paint used on the car. A two digit code indicates the top and bottom colors respectively. A number follows which designates two-tone, sports-tone, convertible top, etc.

CODE	COLOR	CODE
B	Ebony	BB1
C	Lt. Blue	CC1
D	Med. Metallic Blue	DD1
E	Dk. Metallic Blue	EE1
F	Lt. Green	FF1
G	Metallic Green	GG1
M	Lt. Beige	MM1
P	Ruby	PP1
R	Coppertone	RR1
X	Ermine White	XX1
W	Med. Beige	WW1
Y	Metallic Brown	YY1

TRIM CODE: Furnishes the key to the interior color and material.

Note: V - VINYL   C - CLOTH

CODE	Cloth	Vinyl	Leather	COLOR
501	*	*	-	Gray and Blue
301	*	*	-	Blue
303	*	*	-	Tan
306	*	*	-	Alabaster & Black
394	*	*	-	Gray
401	-	*	-	Blue
403	-	*	-	Tan
406	-	*	-	Alabaster & Black
411	-	*	-	Blue
413	-	*	-	Tan
494	-	*	-	Gray
421	*	*	-	Blue
422	*	*	-	Green
423	*	*	-	Tan

CODE	Cloth	Vinyl	Leather	COLOR
325	*	*	-	Alabaster & Black
326	*	*	-	Red
346	*	*	-	Alabaster & Black
441	-	*	-	Blue
442	-	*	-	Green
445	-	*	-	Red
446	-	*	-	Alabaster & Black
447	-	*	-	Alabaster & Black
443	-	H	-	Tan
451	-	*	-	Blue
455	-	*	-	Red
459	-	*	-	Copper & Black
701	*	*	-	Blue
702	*	*	-	Green
704	*	*	-	Gray
751	-	*	-	Blue
752	-	*	-	Green
754	-	*	-	Gray
761	-	*	-	Blue
721	-	*	-	Blue
722	-	*	-	Green
725	-	*	-	Red
771	-	*	-	Blue
773	-	*	-	Tan
775	-	*	-	Red
791	-	*	-	Blue
793	-	*	-	Tan
795	-	*	-	Red
421	-	*	-	Blue
423	-	*	-	Alabaster & Black
425	-	*	-	Red
426	-	*	-	Alabaster & Black
431	-	*	-	Blue
433	-	*	-	Tan
341	*	*	-	Blue
342	*	*	-	Green
343	-	*	-	Tan
345	*	-	-	Red

ENGINE NUMBER

Stamped on a boss behind the water pump. The number provides the code to identify the series, block displacement, and month/day production date.

EXAMPLE

T	38	2	24
YEAR	383	FEBRUARY	24th DAY

Engine Number	Engine Name	CID ratio	Comp.	Carb	HP	Transmission
17-8-3	Standard 170	170	8.2	1, 1Bl	101	Stand - A-903 G Opt - A 904 G
22-8-3	Super 225 30-D Economy Six	225	8.2	1, 1Bl	145	Stand- A-903 G Opt - A- 904 RG
31-8-3	Fury V-800	318	9.0	1, 2Bl		Stand - A-745 Opt - BWT-10 Opt - A-727
36-8-3	Commando 361	361	9.0	1, 2Bl	265	Stand - A-745 Opt- BWT-10 Opt - A-727
38-8-3	Golden Commando High performance Option	383	10.0/11.0	1, 4Bl/1, 4Bl 2, 4Bl Runner	330/320 325	Stand - A-745 Opt - A-727 Opt - BWT-10
42-8-3	High performance Option	426	11.0/13.5 11.0/13.5	4Bl/1, 4Bl 2, 4Bl Ram 2, 4Bl Ram	370/37 415/425	Stand - BWT-85 Opt - BWT-10 Opt - A-727

1964 PLYMOUTH / VALIANT

VEHICLE IDENTIFICATION NUMBER

2347100551

The vehicle number (serial number) is stamped and embossed on a stainless steel plate attached to the left front door hinge pillar. It consists of car make symbol, series code, model year code, assembly plant symbol & a sequential production number.

1st Digit Car make
Valiant (8 Cyl.)..................V
Valiant (6 Cyl.) 1
Plymouth (6 Cyl.) 2
Plymouth (8 Cyl.) 3

2nd Digit Series
V-100 Savoy 1
Belvedere 2
V-200 Fury 3
Valiant Signeyt, Sport Fury 4
V 100 S.W., Savoy S.W 5
Belvedere S.W. 6
V 200 S.W., Fury S.W. 7
Taxi 8
Police 9
Fleet 0

3rd Digit Year..................1964

4th Digit Assembly plant
Detroit 1-3
Los Angeles. 5
Newark 6
St. Louis Plant 7
Last six digits indicate the production sequence number.

BODY CODE PLATE

Stamped and embossed on a stainless steel plate under the hood. It is attached to: right or left fender, cowl, or radiator cross member depending on the model and assembly plant. This plate will indicate; schedule date, body production number, body series, trim, paint, and accessory code.

THE SHIPPING ORDER NUMBER is assigned prior to production. It consists of a 4 digit planned delivery month/day date code, 0224 (February 24th). Then a plant production sequence number follows (0555)

BODY NUMBER is a 3 digit number which indicates the model and body style.

| 1 2 3 4 5 6 7 8 9 0 |
| A B C D E F G H J X L M N P Q R S T V W X Y Z |

SO	NUMBER	BDY	TRM	PNT
0224	5555	223	LIR	BB1

VALIANT V 100   CODE
2-Dr. Sedan..................111
4-Dr. Sedan 113
4-Dr. Sedan..................156

VALIANT V 200   CODE
2-Dr. Sedan 131
4-Dr. Sedan 133
Convertible 135
4-Dr. Wagon..................176

VALIANT SIGNET   CODE

	6 cyl	8 cy
2-Dr. HT Sedan	142	V42
Convertible	145	V45
Barracuda	149	V49

SAVOY   CODE

	6 cyl	8 cyl
2-Dr. Sedan	211	311
4-Dr. Sedan	213	313
4-Dr. Wagon	256	356
4-Dr. Wagon	257	357

BELVEDERE   CODE

	6 cyl	8 cyl
2-Dr. Sedan	221	321
2-Dr. HT Coupe	222	322
4-Dr. Sedan	223	323
4-Dr. Wagon	---	36
4-Dr. Wagon	---	36

FURY   COD

	6 cyl	8 c
2-Dr. HT Coupe	232	33
4-Dr. Sedan	233	33
Convertible	---	33
4-Dr. Wagon	---	37
4-Dr. Wagon	---	37

SPORT FURY   COD
2-Dr. HT Sedan..................34
Convertible 34

THE PAINT CODE furnishes the key to the paint used on the car. A two digit code indicates the top and bottom colors respectively. A number follows which designates two-tone, sports-tone, convertible top, etc.

CODE	COLOR	CODE
B	Ebony	BB1
C	Light Blue	CC1
D	Medium Blue Metallic	DD1
E	Dark Blue Metallic	EE1
H	Sandalwood Metallic	HH1
J	Light Turquoise	JJ1
K	Medium Turquoise Metallic	KK1
L	Dark Turquoise Metallic	LL1
M	Medium Gray Metallic	MM1
P	Ruby	PP1
T	Signet Royal Red	TT1
V	Chestnut Metallic	VV1
W	White	WW1
X	Light Tan	XX1
Y	Medium Tan Metallic	YY1

TRIM CODE: Furnishes the key to the interior color and material.
Note: V - VINYL   C - CLOTH

CODE	CLOTH	VINYL	LEATHER	COLOR
L1B, L2B, L4B	*	*	-	Blue
L1F, L2F	*	*	-	Yellow Green
L1M, L2M	*	*	-	Mauve / Maroon
L1N, L4N	*	*	-	Black & White

CODE	Cloth	Vinyl	Leather	COLOR
L1Q, L2Q, L4Q	*	*	-	Turquoise
L1T, L2T, L4T *	*	-		Yellow Tan
L4R	-	*	-	Red
K1B, K4B	*	*	-	Blue
K1F	*		-	Yellow Green
K1M	*	*	-	Mauve / Maroon
K1N, K4N	*	*	-	Black & White
K1T, K4T	*	*	-	Yellow Tan
K4	-	*	-	Red
K5A, K8A	*		-	Gray
M1B, M4B	*	*	-	Blue
M1M	*	*	-	Mauve / Maroon
M1N	*	*	-	Black & White
M1T, M4T	*	*	-	Yellow Tan
M4X, M8X	*		-	Black
M4W, M8W	-		*	White
M4	-	*	-	Red
H1B, H4B	*	*	-	Blue
H3B, H7B	*	-	*	Blue
H1F	*		-	Yellow Green
H3L, H7L	*	-	*	Yellow Gold
H1M	*	*	-	Mauve / Maroon
H1N, H2N	*	*	-	Black & White
H1Q, H4Q	*	*	-	Turquoise
H4R	-	*	-	Red
H1T, H4T	*	*	-	Yellow Tan
H4W	-	*	-	White
M3B, M9B	*	-	*	Blue
M7B, M8B	*	*	*	Blue
M9C	-	*	*	Blue & White

ENGINE NUMBER

Stamped on a boss behind the water pump. The number provides the code to identify the series, block, displacement, and month/day production date.

EXAMPLE

V	38	2	24
YEAR	383	FEBRUARY	24th DAY

Engine #	Engine Name	CID	Comp. ratio	Carb	HP	Transmission
-17-8-3	170	170	8.5	1, 1Bl	101	Stand - A-903 G Opt - A-833
22-8-3	Super 225 30-D Economy Six	225	8.4	1, 1Bl		Opt - A 904 G Stand - A-903 G
273 11-20	Standard 273 V8	273	8.8	1, 2Bl	180	Opt - A 904 RG Stand - A-745
318-1001	Fury V-800	318	9	1, 2Bl	230	Opt - A-833 Opt - A-904-A Stand - A-745 Opt - A-727
36-8-1	Commmando 361	261	9	1, 2Bl	265	Stand - A-745
38-8-1	Commando 383	383	10	1, 4Bl	330	Opt - A-833 Opt - A-727 Stand - A-745
MP-426-2-8-1 MP HC-426-2-8-1	Super Stock 426-111	426	11.0/12.5	2, 4Bl Ram	415/425	Opt - A-833 Opt - A-727 Stand — BWT-85 Opt — A-833
426-8-1	Commando 426	426	10.3	1, 4Bl	365	Stand — A-833 Opt — A-727

1965 PLYMOUTH / VALIANT

VEHICLE IDENTIFICATION NUMBER

5157100551

The vehicle number (serial number) is stamped and embossed on a stainless steel plate attached to the left front door hinge pillar. It consists of car make symbol, series code, model year code, assembly plant symbol & a sequential production number.

1st Digit Car Line
Barracuda (8 Cyl.)	1
Belvedere (6 Cyl.)	3
Fury (6 Cyl.)	5
Fury (8 Cyl.)	P
Belvedere (8 Cyl.)	R
Barracuda (8 Cyl.)	V

2nd Digit Series
V-100, Belvedere I , Fury I	1
Fury II	2
V-200, Belvedere II, Fury III	3
Signet, Satellite, Sport Fury	4
V 100 S.W., Belvedere I S.W., Fury I S.W.	5
Fury II S.W.	6
V 200 S.W., Belvedere II Fury III S.W.	7
Barracuda	8
Police	9

3rd Digit Year 1965

4th Digit Assembly plant
Detroit	1-2
Los Angeles.	5
Newark	6
St. Louis Plant .	7

Last six digits indicate the production sequence number.

BODY CODE PLATE

Stamped and embossed on a stainless steel plate under the hood. It is attached to: right or left fender, cowl, or radiator cross member depending on the model and assembly plant. This plate will indicate; schedule date, body production number, body series, trim, paint, and accessory code.

THE SHIPPING ORDER NUMBER is assigned prior to production. It consists of a 4 digit planned delivery month/day date code, 0224 (February 24th). Then a plant production sequence number follows (0555)

BODY NUMBER is a 3 digit number which indicates the model and body style.

1 2 3 4 5 6 7 8 9 0
A B C D E F G H J X L M N P Q R S T V W X Y Z

SO	NUMBER	BDY	TRM	PNT
0224	00551	R11	L1R	BB1

VALIANT V 100	CODE	
	6 cyl	8 cyl
2-Dr. Sedan	111	V11
4-Dr. Sedan	113	V13
4-Dr. Wagon	156	V56

VALIANT V 200	CODE	
	6 cyl	8 cyl
2-Dr. Sedan	131	V31
4-Dr. Sedan	133	V33
Convertible	135	V35
4-Dr. Wagon	176	V76

VALIANT SIGNET	CODE	
	6 cyl	8 cyl
2-Dr. HT Sedan	142	V42
Convertible	145	V45

BARRACUDA	CODE	
	6 cyl	8 cyl
2-Dr. Sport HT	189	V89

BELVEDERE I	CODE	
	6 cyl	8 cyl
2-Dr. Sedan	311	R11

4-Dr. Sedan	313	R13
4-Dr. Wagon	356	R56
2-Dr. Sedan (Police)	---	R91
4-Dr. Sedan (Police)	---	R93
$-Dr. Wagon (p0live)	---	R96

BELVEDERE II		CODE
	6 cyl	8 cyl
2-Dr. Hardtop	332	R32
Convertible	335	R35
4-Dr. Sedan	333	R33
4-Dr. Wagon	376	R76
$-Dr. Wagon	377	R7.

SATELLITE		CODE
2-Dr. Hardtop		R4.
Convertible		R4.

FURY I

	CODE	
	6 cyl	8 cyl
2-Dr. Sedan	511	P11
4-Dr. Sedan	513	P13
4-Dr. Wagon	556	P56
4-Dr. Sedan (Taxi)	583	P83
2-Dr. Sedan (Police)	---	P91
4-Dr. Sedan (Police)	---	P93
$-Dr. Wagon (polive)	---	P96

FURY II

	CODE	
	6 cyl	8 cyl
2-Dr. Sedan	521	P21
4-Dr. Sedan	523	P23
4-Dr. Wagon	566	P66

TRIM CODE: Furnishes the key to the interior color and material.

Note: **V - VINYL   C - CLOTH**

	CODE
4-Dr. Wagon	567 .... P67

FURY III

	CODE	
	6 cyl	8 cyl
2-Dr. Hardtop	532	P32
Convertible		P35
4-Dr. Sedan	533	P33
4-Dr. Hardtop		P34
4-Dr. Wagon		P76
4-Dr. Wagon		P77

SPORT FURY

	CODE	
	6 cyl	8 cyl
2-Dr. HT Sedan	---	P42
Convertible	---	P45

THE PAINT CODE furnishes the key to the paint used on the car. A two digit code indicates the top and bottom colors respectively. A number follows which designates two-tone, sports-tone, convertible top, etc.

CODE	COLOR	CODE
A	Gold Poly	AA1
B	Black	BB1
C	Light Blue	CC1
D	Medium Blue Poly	DD1
E	Dark Blue Poly	EE1
H	Copper Poly	HH1
J	Light Turquoise	JJ1
K	Medium Turquoise Poly	KK1
L	Dark Turquoise Poly	LL1
N	Barracuda Silver Poly	NN1
P	Ruby	PP1
S	Ivory	SS1
T	Medium Red Poly	TT1
W	White	WW1
X	Light Tan	XX1
Y	Medium Tan Poly	YY1

CODE	Cloth	Vinyl	Leather	COLOR
L1B, K1B"	*	*	-	Blue
L1R, K1R"	*	*	-	Red
L1T, K1T, L2T, K2T	*	*	-	Tan
L4B, K4B"	-	*	-	Blue
L4R, K4R"	-	*	-	Red
L4T, K4T"	-	*	-	Tan
L8T, K8T, T8T"	-	*	-	Tan
5B	-	*	-	Blue
5R	-	*	-	Red
5T	-	*	-	Tan
H1B, H4B"	-	*	-	Blue
H1Q, H4Q"	-	*	-	Turquoise
H1R, H4R"	-	*	-	Red
H1T, H4T"	-	*	-	Tan
4X	-	*	-	Black
1Y	-	*	-	Gold
4B	-	*	-	Blue
4Q	-	*	-	Turquoise
4R	-	*	-	Red
4T	-	*	-	Tan
4Y	-	*	-	Gold
4B	-	*	-	Blue
4Q	-	*	-	Turquoise
4R	-	*	-	Red
4X	-	*	-	Black
4Y	-	*	-	Gold
1B, K1B"	*	*	-	Blue
1R, K1R"	*	*	-	Red
1T, K1T"	*	*	-	Tan
2T, K2T"	*	*	-	Tan
4B, K4B"	-	*	-	Blue
4R, K4R"	-	*	-	Red
4T, K4T"	-	*	-	Tan
B	-	*	-	Blue
R	-	*	-	Red
T	-	*	-	Tan
8T, K8T, T8T	-	*	-	Tan
B	*	*	-	Blue
Q	*	*	-	Turquoise
R	*	*	-	Red
T	*	*	-	Tan
B	*	*	-	Blue
Q	*	*	-	Turquoise
R	*	*	-	Red
T	*	*	-	Tan
B	-	*	-	Blue
R	-	*	-	Red
T	-	*	-	Tan
B	*	*	-	Blue
Q	*	*	-	Turquoise

CODE	Cloth	Vinyl	Leather	COLOR
H1R	*	*	-	Red
H1T	*	*	-	Tan
H1Y	*	*	-	Gold
H1B	*	*	-	Blue
H1Q	*	*	-	Turquoise
H1R	*	*	-	Red
H1T	*	*	-	Tan
H1Y	*	*	-	Gold
H2B	*	*	-	Blue
H2Q	*	*	-	Turquoise
H2R	*	*	-	Red
H2T	*	*	-	Tan
H2Y	*	*	-	Gold
H5B	-	*	-	Blue
H5Q	-	*	-	Turquoise
H5R	-	*	-	Red
H5X	-	*	-	Black
H5Y	-	*	-	Gold
H5B	-	*	-	Blue
H5Q	-	*	-	Turquoise
H5R	-	*	-	Red
H5X	-	*	-	Black
H5Y	-	*	-	Gold
H4B	-	*	-	Blue
H4Q	-	*	-	Turquoise
H4R	-	*	-	Red
H4T	-	*	-	Tan
H4Y	-	*	-	Gold
P4B	-	*	-	Blue
P4Q	-	*	-	Turquoise
P4R	-	*	-	Red
P4U	-	*	-	Black and Copper
P4X	-	*	-	Black
P4Y	-	*	-	Gold
L4B	-	*	-	Blue
L4R	-	*	-	Red
L4T	-	*	-	Tan
L4B	-	*	-	Blue
L4R	-	*	-	Red
L4T	-	*	-	Tan
"H1B, H4B"	*	*	-	Blue
"H1R, H4R"	*	*	-	Red
"H1T, H4T"	*	*	-	Tan
"H1Q, H4Q"	*	*	-	Turquoise
P4B	-	*	-	Blue
P4X	-	*	-	Black
P4Y	-	*	-	Gold
P4R	-	*	-	Red

ENGINE NUMBER

Stamped on a boss behind the water pump. The number provides the code to identify the series, block displacement, and month/day production date.

```
EXAMPLE
 A        38        2          24
 YEAR     383    FEBRUARY    24th DAY
```

Engine #	Engine Name	CID	Comp. Ratio	Carb Type	HP	Transmission
A-170-8-1	Standard 170	170	8.5	1, 1Bl	101	Stand — A-903 G Opt — A-904 G Opt — A 904 G
A-225-8-1	Super 225 Economy Six	225	8.4	1, 1Bl	145	Stand — A-903 RG Opt — A-833 Opt — A-904 RG
A-273-8-1	Plymouth 273 Commando 273	273	8.8/10.5	1, 2Bl/1, 4Bl	180/ 235	Stand — A-745 Opt — A-833 Opt — A-904-A
A-318-8-1	Fury 318	318	9	1, 2Bl	230	Stand — A-745 Opt — A-727
A-361-8-1-2	Commando 361	261	9	1, 2Bl	265	Stand — A-745 Opt — A-833 Opt — A-727
A-383-8-1-2	Commando 383	383	9.2/10.0	1, 2Bl/1, 4Bl	270/ 330	Stand — A-745 Opt — A-833 Opt — A-727
A-426-8-1-2	Commando 426 Super Commando	426	10.3/12.5	1, 4Bl /1, 4Bl 2, 4Bl Ram	365/ 400 425	Stand — A-745 Opt — A-833 Opt — A-727

VEHICLE IDENTIFICATION NUMBER

PM21B65100551

The vehicle number (serial number) is stamped and embossed on a stainless steel plate attached to the left front door hinge pillar. It consists of car make symbol, series code, model year code, assembly plant symbol & a sequential production number.

1st Digit - Car make
Valiant	Y
Belvedere / Satellite	R
Fury	P
Barracuda	B

2nd Digit - Class
Ecconomy	E
Low	L
High	H
Medium	M
Premium	P
Police	K
Taxi	T
VIP	S

3rd Digit & 4th Digit -Body style
2-Dr. Sedan	21
2-Dr. Hardtop	23
Convertible	27
2-Dr. Sports Hardtop	29
4-Dr. Sedan	41
4-Dr. Hardtop	43
6-Ps. Station Wagon	45
9-Ps. Station Wagon	46

Fifth Digit - Engine
170	A
225	B
Special Order 6 Cyl.	C
237	D
318	E
361	F
383	G
426\	H
440	J
Special Order 8 Cyl.	K

Sixth Digit - Year 1966

Seventh Digit - Assembly plant
Lynch Rd	1
Hamtramck	2
Belvedere Plant	4
Los Angeles	5
Newark Plant	6
St. Louis Plant	7
Windsor Plant	9

```
1 2 3 4 5 6 7 8 9 0
A B C D E F G H J X L M N P Q R S T V W X Y Z

SO      NUMBER    BDY      TRM      PNT
224     05551     VL21     L4B      BB1
```

5th through 10th digit are production sequence code.

BODY CODE PLATE

Stamped and embossed on a plate which is attavhed on the engine side of the cowl just above the master cylinder. On Valiant models the plate is located above the top hinge of the driver's side door. The plate shows the body type, trim code, schedual date, paint code, and some accessory codes.

THE SHIPPING ORDER NUMBER consists of a three digit month and day scheduled based on 01 through 31 days production date, and a five digit production order number.

MONTH	COD
JAN	
FEB	
MAR	
APR	
MAY	
JUN	
JULY	
AUG	
SEPT	
OCT	
NOV	
DEC	

BODY NUMBER is a 4 digit number which indicates the c line, price class, and body styl Same first four digits of the vin.

VALIANT 100	CODE
2-Dr. Sedan	VL21
4-Dr. Sedan	VL41
4-Dr. Wagon	VL45

VALIANT 200	CODE
4-Dr. Sedan	VH41
4-Dr. Wagon	VH45

SIGNET	CODE
2-Dr. Hardtop	VH23
Convertible	VH27

BARRACUDA	CODE
2-Dr. Hardtop	BP29

FURY I	CODE
2-Dr. Sedan	PL21
4-Dr. Sedan	PL41
4-Dr. Wagon	PL45

FURY II	CODE
2-Dr. Sedan	PM21
4-Dr. Sedan	PM41
4-Dr. Wagon (2 seat)	PM45*

FURY III	CODE
2-Dr. Hardtop	PH23
4-Dr. Sedan	PH41
4-Dr. Hardtop	PH43*
Convertible	PH27*
4-Dr. Wagon (2 seat)	PH45*
4-Dr. Wagon (3 seat)	PH46*

SPORT FURY	CODE
2-Dr. Hardtop	PP23*
Convertible	PP27*

VIP	CODE
4-Dr. Hardtop	PS43

BELVEDERE I	CODE
2-Dr. Sedan	RL21
4-Dr. Sedan	RL41
4-Dr. Wagon	RL45

BELVEDERE II	CODE
2-Dr. Hardtop	RH23
4-Dr. Sedan	RH41
Convertible	RH27
4-Dr. Wagon (2 seat)	RH45
4-Dr. Wagon (3 seat)	RH46

* Indicates 8 cylinder only in these models.

THE PAINT CODE furnishes the key to the paint used on the car. A thre digit code indicates the top and bottom colors respectively. A number follows which designates two-tone, sports-tone, convertible top, etc.

CODE	COLOR	CODE
A	Silver Metallic	AA1
B	Black	BB1
C	Light Blue	CC1
D	Light Blue Metallic	DD1
E	Dark Blue Metallic	EE1
G	Dark Green Metallic	GG1
K	Light Turquoise Metallic	KK1
L	Dark Turquoise Metallic	LL1
O	Bright Red	PP1
Q	Dark Red Metallic	QQ1
R	Yellow	RR1
S	Soft Yellow	SS1
W	White	WW1
X	Beige	XX1
Y	Bronze Metallic	YY1
Z	Citron Gold Metallic	ZZ1
6	Light Mauve Metallic	661

TRIM CODE: Furnishes the key to the interior color and material.

	Blue	Black	Citron	Red	Tan & White	Tan	Turquoise
Vinyl	P4B	P4X	P4Y	P4H	P4V	L4T	H4Q
	L4B	H4X	H4Y	L4H		H4T	M4Q
	H4B	H5X		H4H		H5T	H5Q
	H5B			H5H		M4T	
	M4B			L4R			
				H4R			
				P4R			
				M4R			
Cloth and Vinyl	L1B		H1Y	L1R		L1T	M1Q
	M1B		H2Y	M1R		M1T	H1Q
	H1B			H1R		H1T	H2Q
	H2B			H2R		H2T	
				H1H			
Cloth	H8B	H8X		H8R			

ENGINE NUMBER

Stamped on a boss behind the water pump. The number provides the code to identify the series, block displacement, and month/day production date.

EXAMPLE

B	38	2	24
YEAR	383	FEBRUARY	24th DAY

Engine #	Engine Name	CID	Comp. Ratio	Carb Type	HP	Transmission
B-170-8-1	170	70	8.5	1, 1Bl	101	Stand — A-903 G Opt — A-904 G
B-225-8-1	Standard 225/225	225	8.4	1, 1Bl	145	Stand — A-903 RG Opt — A-833 Opt — A-904 RG
B-273-8-1	Commando 273 Commando 273 V8	273	8.8/10.5	1, 2Bl/1, 4Bl	180/ 235	Stand — A-745 Opt — A-833 Opt — A-904-A
B-318-8-1	Opt. 318	318	9	1, 2Bl	230	Stand — A-745 Opt — A-727
B-361-8-1-2	Commando 361 V8	261	9	1, 2Bl	265	Stand — A-745 Opt — A-833 Opt — A-727
B-383-8-1-2	Commando 383	383	9.2/10.0	1, 2Bl/1, 4Bl	270/ 330	Stand — A-745 Opt — A-833 Opt — A-727
B-H-426-B-8-1	Hemi 426	426	10.25	2, 4Bl	425	Stand — A-833 Opt — A-727
B-440-B-8-1-2	Commando 440	440	10.1	1, 4Bl	365	Stand — A-833 Opt — A-727

VEHICLE IDENTIFICATION NUMBER

PM23F75100551

The vehicle number (serial number) is stamped and embossed on a stainless steel plate attached to the left front door hinge pillar. It consists of car make symbol, series code, model year code, assembly plant symbol & a sequential production number.

1st Digit - Car make

Valiant	Y
Belvedere / Satellite	R
Fury	P
Barracuda	B

2nd Digit - Class

Ecconomy	E
Low	L
High	H
Medium	M
Premium	P
Police	K
Taxi	T
VIP	S

3rd Digit & 4th Digit -Body style

2-Dr. Sedan	21
2-Dr. Hardtop	23
Convertible	27
2-Dr. Sports Hardtop	29
4-Dr. Sedan	41
4-Dr. Hardtop	43
6-Ps. Station Wagon	45
9-Ps. Station Wagon	46

Fifth Digit - Engine

170	A
225	B
Special Order 6 Cyk.	C
237	D
273 (4-BBI) HP	E
318	F
383	G
383 (4-BBI) HP	H
426 HP Hemi	J
440	K
440 HP	L
Special Order 8	M

Sixth Digit - Year 1967

Seventh Digit - Assembly plant

Lynch Rd	1
Hamtramck	2
Belvedere Plant	4
Los Angeles	5
Newark Plant	6
St. Louis Plant	7
Windsor Plant	9

Final Digits: Production sequence number.

```
1234567890
ABCDEFGHJXLMNPQRSTVWXYZ
12345678        AX    TRM   PNT   UBS
                 4    L4R   BB1    S
PM41      62     5    635   224   00551
```

BODY CODE PLATE

Stamped and embossed on a stainless steel plate attached to the fender shield under the hood. The plate indicates the code for: Body type, Engine, Transmission, Schedual date, Paint, Trim and some Option codes. The plate is read left to right, bottom to top. Starting with the bottom row of numbers.

THE BODY NUMBER is a four digit number which indicates the Car line, Price class, and Body style. Same first four digits of the VIN.

The two digit ENGINE CID CODE identifies the engine.

ENGINE CID	CODE
170 6 Cyl.	11
225 6 Cyl.	21
273 8 Cyl.	31
273 4-BBI HP 8 Cyl.	32
318 8 Cyl.	41
383 1-BBL 8 Cyl.	61
383 1-4BBL 8 Cyl.	62
426 2-4BBI HP 8 Cyl.	73
440 8 Cyl.	81
440 HP 8 Cyl.	83

TRANSMISSION	CODE
3-Speed Manual Collumn Shift	1
3-Speed Manual Collumn Shift HD	2
4-Speed Manual Floor Shift	3
3-Speed Automatic	5
3-Speed Automatic HD	6
Special Order Transmission	9

The three digit code which indicates tire size and type, this option code is not included.

The last right digit of the bottom row is the SHIPPING ORDER NUMBER which consists of a three digit month and day schedualed production date, and a five digit production order number.
The next row up there will be one digit AXLE CODE found directly under the AX column.

VALIANT	CODE
2-Dr. Sedan	VL21
4-Dr. Sedan	VL41

SIGNET	CODE
2-Dr. Sedan	VH21
4-Dr. Sedan	VH41

BARRACUDA	CODE
2-Dr. Hardtop	BH23
2-Dr. Special Hardtop	BH29
Convertible	BH27

BELVEDERE	CODE
4-Dr. Wagon (2 seat)	RE45
4-DR. Wagon (3 seat)	RK45

BELVEDERE I	CODE
2-Dr. Sedan	RL21
2-Dr. Sedan	RL41
4-Dr. Wagon	RL45

BELVEDERE II	CODE
2-Dr. Hardtop	RH23
4-Dr. Sedan	RH41

Convertible	RH27
4-Dr. Wagon (2 seat)	RH45
4-Dr. Wagon (3 seat)	RH46

GTX	CODE
2-Dr. Hardtop	RS23
Convertible	RS27

FURY I	CODE
2-Dr. Sedan	PE21
4-Dr. Sedan	PE41
4-Dr. Wagon	PE45
4-Dr. Sedan	PT41
2-Dr. Sedan	PK21
4-Dr. Sedan	PK41
4-Dr. Wagon	PK45

FURY II	CODE
2-Dr. Sedan	PL21
4-Dr. Sedan	PL41
4-Dr. Wagon (2 seat)	PL45
4-Dr. Wagon (3 seat)	PL46

FURY III	CODE
2-Dr. Hardtop	PM23
4-Dr. Sedan	PM41
4-Dr. Hardtop	PM43
Convertible	PM27
4-Dr. Wagon (2 seat)	PM45
4-Dr. Wagon (3 seat)	PM46

SPORT FURY	CODE
2-Dr. Hardtop	PH23
Convertible	PH27
2-Dr. Fast Top	PS23

VIP	CODE
4-Dr. Hardtop	PP43
Convertible	PP27

SATELLITE	CODE
2-Dr. Hardtop	RP23
Convertible	RP27

THE UBS CODE identifies the upper door frame color, and the accent stripe color.

THE PAINT CODE furnishes the key to the paint used on the car. A thre digit code indicates the top and bottom colors respectively. A number follows which designates two-tone, sports-tone, convertible top, etc.

CODE	COLOR	CODE
A	Buffed Silver Metallic	AA1
B	Black	BB1
C	Medium Blue Metallic	CC1
D	Light Blue Metallic	DD1
E	Dark Blue Metallic	EE1
8	Bright Blue Metallic	881
F	Light Green Metallic	FF1
G	Dark Green Metallic	GG1
H	Dark Copper Metallic	HH1
K	Light Turquoise Metallic	KK1
L	Dark Turquoise Metallic	LL1
M	Turbine Bronze Metallic	MM1
P	Bright Red Metallic	PP1
Q	Dark Red Metallic	QQ1
6	Mauve Metallic	661
R	Yellow	RR1
S	Soft Yellow	SS1
T	Copper Metallic	TT1
W	White	WW1
X	Beige	XX1
Y	Light Tan Metallic	YY1
Z	Gold Metallic	ZZ1

ENGINE NUMBER
Stamped on a boss behind the water pump. The number provides the code to identify the series, block displacement, and month/day production date.

EXAMPLE

B	38	2	24
YEAR	383	FEBRUARY	24th DAY

Engine #	Engine Name	CID	Comp. Ratio	Carb Type	HP	Transmission
3-170-8-1	170	70	8.5	1, 1Bl	101	Stand — A-903 G, Opt — A-904 G
3-225-8-1	Standard 225/225	225	8.4	1, 1Bl	145	Stand — A-903 RG, Opt — A-833 Opt — A-904 RG
3-273-8-1	Commando 273 Commando 273 V8	273	8.8/10.5	1, 2Bl/1, 4Bl	180/ 235	Stand — A-745, Opt — A-833 Opt — A-904-A
3-318-8-1	Opt. 318	318	9	1, 2Bl	230	Stand — A-745, Opt — A-727
3-361-8-1-2	Commmando 361 V8	261	9	1, 2Bl	265	Stand — A-745, Opt — A-833 Opt — A-727
3-383-8-1-2	Commando 383	383	9.2/10.0	1, 2Bl/1, 4Bl	270/ 330	Stand — A-745, Opt — A-833 Opt — A-727
H-426-B-8-1	Hemi 426	426	10.25	2, 4Bl	425	Stand — A-833, Opt — A-727
440-B-8-1-2	Commando 440	440	10.1	1, 4Bl	365	Stand — A-833 Opt — A-727

THE TRIM CODE : furnishes the key to the interior color and material

CODE	Cloth	Vinyl	Leather	COLOR	CODE	Cloth	Vinyl	Leather	COLOR
E4B	-	*	-	Blue	M4B	-	*	-	Blue
E4R	-	*	-	Red	M4K	-	*	-	Copper
E4T	-	*	-	Tan	M4Q	-	*	-	Turquoise
L1B	*	*	-	Blue	M4R	-	*	-	Red
L1R	*	*	-	Red	M4T	-	*	-	Tan
L1T	*	*	-	Tan	M4X	-	*	-	Black
L4B	-	*	-	Blue	H6B	-	*	-	Blue
L4R	-	*	-	Red	H6K	-	*	-	Copper
L4T	-	*	-	Tan	H6R	-	*	-	Red
K1T	*	*	-	Tan	H6W	-	*	-	White
K4T	-	*	-	Tan	H6X	-	*	-	Black
T4T	-	*	-	Tan	P1B	*	*	-	Blue
H1B	*	*	-	Blue	P1K	*	*	-	Copper
H1K	*	*	-	Copper	P1Q	*	*	-	Turquoise
H1Q	*	*	-	Turquoise	P1X	*	*	-	Black
H1T	*	*	-	Tan	P9T	-	-	*	Tan
H1X	*	*	-	Black	L1B	*	*	-	Blue
H4B	-	*	-	Blue	L1Q	*	*	-	Turquoise
H4K	-	*	-	Copper	L1R	*	*	-	Red
H4R	-	*	-	Red	L1T	*	*	-	Tan
H4T	-	*	-	Tan	L4B	-	*	-	Blue
H4W	-	*	-	White & Black	L4R	-	*	-	Red
H4X	-	*	-	Black	L4T	-	*	-	Tan
H4P	-	*	-	White & Turquoise	X1B	*	*	-	Blue
					X1R	*	*	-	Red
H4M	-	*	-	Copper & Black	X1T	*	*	-	Tan
P6B	-	*	-	Blue	X4X	-	*	-	Black
P6K	-	*	-	Copper	X5X	-	*	-	Black
P6R	-	*	-	Red	H1B	*	*	-	Blue
P6V	-	*	-	White & Red	H1Q	*	*	-	Turquoise
P6W	-	*	-	White & Black	H1R	*	*	-	Red
P6X	*	-	-	Black	H1T	*	*	-	Tan
E1B	*	*	-	Blue	H1X	*	*	-	Black
E1Q	*	*	-	Turquoise	H4B	-	*	-	Blue
E1T	*	*	-	Tan	H4R	-	*	-	Red
E4B	-	*	-	Blue	H4T	-	*	-	Tan
E4Q	-	*	-	Turquoise	H4X	-	*	-	Black
E4T	-	*	-	Tan	H6B	-	*	—	Blue
K1T	*	*	-	Tan	H6R	-	*	—	Red
K4T	-	*	-	Tan	H6T	-	*	-	Tan
T4T	-	*	-	Tan	H6X	-	*	-	Black
X4B	-	*	-	Blue	H5B	-	*	-	Blue
X4Q	-	*	-	Turquoise	H5C	-	*	-	White / Blue
X4T	-	*	-	Tan	H5K	-	*	-	Copper
L1B	-	*	-	Blue	H5R	-	*	-	Red
L1Q	-	*	-	Turquoise	H5T	-	*	-	Tan
L1R	*	*	-	Red	H5V	-	*	-	White & Red
L1T	*	*	-	Tan	H5W	-	*	-	White & Black
L4B	-	*	-	Blue	H5X	-	*	-	Black
L4Q	-	*	-	Turquoise	H6B	-	*	-	Blue
L4R	-	*	-	Red	H6C	-	*	-	White / Blue
L4T	-	*	-	Tan	H6K	-	*	-	Copper
M1B	*	*	-	Blue	H6R	-	*	-	Red
M1K	*	*	-	Copper	H6T	-	*	-	Tan
M1Q	*	*	-	Turquoise	H6V	-	*	-	White & Red
M1R	*	*	-	Red	H6W	-	*	-	White & Black
M1T	*	*	-	Tan					

VEHICLE IDENTIFICATION NUMBER

PM41G8A100001

The vehicle number (serial number) is stamped and embossed on a stainless steel plate attached to the left front door hinge pillar. It consists of car make symbol, series code, model year code, assembly plant symbol & a sequential production number.

1st Digit - Car make
Valiant	Y
Belvedere	R
Fury	P
Barracuda	B

2nd Digit - Class
Ecconomy	E
Low	L
High	H
Medium	M
Premium	P
Police	K
Taxi	T
Special	S
Superstock	O

3rd Digit & 4th Digit -Body style
2-Dr. Sedan	21
2-Dr. Hardtop	23
Convertible	27
2-Dr. Sports Hardtop	29
4-Dr. Sedan	41
4-Dr. Hardtop	43
6-Ps. Station Wagon	45
9-Ps. Station Wagon	46

Fifth Digit - CID
170	A
225	B
Special Order 6 Cyk.	C
237	D
273 H/Perf	E
318	F
383	G
383 H/perf	H
426 HP Hemi	J
440	K
440 H/Perf.	L
Special Order 8	M
340	N
340 H/Perf.	P

Sixth Digit - Year 1968

Seventh Digit - Assembly plant
Lynch Rd	A
Hamtramck	B
Jefferson	C
Belvedere Plant	D

Final Digits: Production sequence numbers.

Los Angeles	E
Newarc Plant	F
St. Louis Plant	G
Windsor Plant	R

BODY CODE PLATE

Stamped and embossed on a stainless steel plate attached to the fender shield under the hood. The plate indicates the code for:

```
1234567890
ABCDEFGHJXLMN PQRS TVW XYZ
12345678      AX    TRM PNT UBS
              4     L4R BB1 S
PM41     62   5     635 224 00551
```

Body type, Engine,Transmission, Schedual date, Paint, Trim and some Option codes. The plate is read left to right, bottom to top.starting with the bottom row of numbers.

THE BODY NUMBER is a four digit number which indicates the Car line, Price class, and Body style. Same first four digits of the VIN.

The two digit ENGINE CID CODE identifies the engine.

ENGIINE CID	CODE
170 6 Cyl.	11
225 6 Cyl.	21
273 8 Cyl.	31
273 4-BBI HP 8 Cyl.	32
318 8 Cyl.	41
383 1-BBL 8 Cyl.	61
383 1-4BBL 8 Cyl.	62
426 2-4BBI HP 8 Cyl.	73
440 8 Cyl.	81
440 HP 8 Cyl.	83

TRANSMISSION	CODE
3-Speed Manual Collumn Shift	1
3-Speed Manual Collumn Shift HD	2

4-Speed Manual Floor Shift 3
3-Speed Automatic 5
3-Speed Automatic HD............. 6
Special Transmission 9
The three digit code which indicates tire size and type, this option code is not included.

The last right digit of the bottom row is the SHIPPING ORDER NUMBER which consists of a three digit month and day schedualed production date, and a five digit production order number.
The next row up there will be one digit AXLE CODE found directly under the AX column.

VALIANT	CODE
2-Dr. Sedan	VL21
4-Dr. Sedan	VL41

SIGNET	CODE
2-Dr. Sedan	VH21
4-Dr. Sedan	VH41

BARRACUDA	CODE
2-Dr. Hardtop	BH23
2-Dr. Special Hardtop	BH29
Convertible	BH27

BELVEDERE	CODE
2-Dr. Sedan	RL21
4-Dr. Sedan	RL41
4-Dr. Wagon	RL45

SPORT SATELLITE	CODE
2-Dr. Hardtop	RP23

Convertible RP27

SATELLITE	CODE
2-Dr. Hardtop	RH23
4-Dr. Sedan	RH41
Convertible	RH27
4-Dr. Wagon (2 seat)	RH45
4-Dr. Wagon (3 seat)	RH46

GTX	CODE
2-Dr. Hardtop	RS23
Convertible	RS27

FURY I	CODE
2-Dr. Sedan	PE21
4-Dr. Sedan	PE41
4-Dr. Wagon	PE45

FURY II	CODE
2-Dr. Sedan	PL21
4-Dr. Sedan	PL41
4-Dr. Wagon (2 seat)	PL45
4-Dr. Wagon (3 seat)	PL46

FURY III	CODE
2-Dr. Hardtop	PM23
4-Dr. Sedan	PM41
4-Dr. Hardtop	PM43
Convertible	PM27
4-Dr. Wagon (2 seat)	PM45
4-Dr. Wagon (3 seat)	PM46
2-DR. Fast Top	PX23

SPORT FURY	CODE
2-Dr. Hardtop	PH23
Convertible	PH27
2-Dr. Fast Top	PS23

VIP	CODE
4-Dr. Hardtop	PP43
Convertible	PP27
4-Dr. Wagon (2 seat)	PM45
4-Dr. Wagon (3 seat)	PM46

THE UBS CODE identifies the upper door frame color, and the accent stripe color.

THE PAINT CODE furnishes the key to the paint used on the car. A thre digit code indicates the top and bottom colors respectively. A number follows which designates two-tone, sports-tone, convertible top, etc.

CODE	COLOR	CODE
A	Buffed Silver Metallic	AA1
B	Black Velvet	BB1
D	Mist Blue Metallic	DD1
F	Mist Green Metallic	FF1
G	Forest Green Metallic	GG1
H	Yellow Mist	HH1
J	Ember Gold Metallic	JJ1
K	Mist Turquoise Metallic	KK1
L	Surf Turquoise Metallic	LL1
M	Turbine Bronze Metallic	MM1
P	Matador Red	PP1
Q	Electric Blue Metallic	QQ1
R	Burgundy Metallic	RR1
S	Sunfire Yellow	SS1
T	Avocado Green Metallic	TT1
U	Frost Blue Metallic	UU1
W	Sable White	WW1
X	Satin Beige	XX1
Y	Sierra Tan Metallic	YY1

CODE	CLOTH	VINYL	LEATHER	COLOR
H6W	-	*	-	White/Black
H5B/H6B	-	*	-	Frost Blue
H6F (Bucket)	-	*	-	Forest Green
H6R (Bucket)	-	*	-	Burgundy
H5X/H6X	-	*	-	Black
H5C/H6C	-	*	-	White/Frost Blue
H5D/H6D	-	*	-	White/Forest Green
H5V/H6V	-	*	-	White/BurgundyZ
H5W/H6W	-	*	-	White/Black
D6B	-	*	-	Frost Blue
D6F	-	*	-	Forest Green
D6R	-	*	-	Burgundy
D6X	-	*	-	Black
D6Y	-	*	-	Ember Gold
D6C	-	*	-	White/Frost Blue
D6D	-	*	-	White/Forest Green
D6E	-	*	-	White/Ember Gold
D6V	-	*	-	White/Burgundy
D6W	-	*	-	White/Black
L1B	*	-	-	Blue
L1T	*	-	-	Tan
B4X	-	*	-	Black
L4B	-	*	-	Blue
L4T	-	*	-	Tan
D4B	-	*	-	Blue
D4L	-	*	-	Parchment/Tan
D4S	-	*	-	Silver/Black
H1B	*	*	-	Blue
H1F	*	*	-	Green
H1N	*	*	-	Gold/Black
H1T	*	*	-	Tan
H1X	*	*	-	Black
H4B	-	*	-	Blue
H1N	*	*	-	Gold/Black
H4B	-	*	-	Blue
H4F	-	*	-	Green
H4X	-	*	-	Black

* Indicsates 8 cylinder only in these models.

THE TRIM CODE : furnishes the key to the interior color and material

CODE	CLOTH	VINYL	LEATHER	COLOR
L4B	-	*	-	Frost Blue
L4T	-	*	-	Sierra Tan
L4X	-	*	-	Black
H1B	*	*	-	Frost Blue
H1F	*	*	-	Forest Green
H1X	*	*	-	Black
H4B	-	*	-	Frost Blue
H4R	-	*	-	Burgundy
H4X	-	*	-	Black
H4Y	-	*	-	Ember Gold
M5R	-	*	-	Red
M5T	-	*	-	Tan
M5X	-	*	-	Black
H6X	-	*	-	Black
H6C	-	*	-	White/Blue
H6D	-	*	-	White/Green
H6E	-	*	-	White/Gold
H6V	-	*	-	White/Burgundy

CODE	CLOTH	VINYL	LEATHER	COLOR	CODE	CLOTH	VINYL	LEATHER	COLOR
H4N	-	*	-	Gold/Black	S6R	-	*	-	Red
H4R	-	*	-	Red	S6X	-	*	-	Black
H4T	-	*	-	Tan	S6Y	-	*	-	Gold
H4C	-	*	-	White/Blue	P1B/P2B	*	*	-	Blue
H4D	-	*	-	White/Green	P1F/P2F	*	*	-	Green
H4H	-	*	-	White/Tan	P1X/P2X	*	*	-	Black
H4V	-	*	-	White/Red	P4R/P5R	-	*	-	Red
P6B/S6B	-	*	-	Blue	P4Y/P5Y	-	*	-	Gold
P6F/S6F	-	*	-	Green	P4W/P5W	-	*	-	White/Black
P6N/S6N	-	*	-	Gold/Black	P9X/P0X	*	*	-	Black
P6R/S6R	-	*	-	Red	P7X/P8X	*	*	-	Black
P6X/S6X	-	*	-	Black	E4B	-	*	-	Blue
P6C/S6C	-	*	-	White/Blue	E4R	-	*	-	Red
P6D/S6D	-	*	-	White/Green	L4B	-	*	-	Blue
P6V/S6V	-	*	-	White/Red	L4F	-	*	-	Green
E1B	*	*	-	Blue	L4R	-	*	-	Red
E1R	*	*	-	Red	L4T	-	*	-	Tan
E1T	*	*	-	Tan	L4X	-	*	-	Black
L1B	*	*	-	Blue	M5B	-	*	-	Blue
L1T	*	*	-	Tan	M5F	-	*	-	Green
L1X	*	*	-	Black	M1G	*	-	-	Dark Green
L4B	-	*	-	Blue	M5B	-	*	-	Blue
L4F	-	*	-	Green	M5R	-	*	-	Red
L4R	-	*	-	Red	M5X	-	*	-	Black
L4T	-	*	-	Tan	M5F	-	*	-	Light Green
M1B	*	*	-	Blue	M5G	-	*	-	Dark Green
M1R	*	*	-	Red	M5T	-	*	-	Tan
M1X	*	*	-	Black	M5Y	-	*	-	Gold
M1Y	*	*	-	Gold	M5W	-	*	-	White/Black
M1F	*	*	-	Light Green	H6B	-	*	-	Blue
H6Y	-	*	-	Gold	H6F	-	*	-	Dark Green
S6B	-	*	-	Blue	H6R	-	*	-	Red
S6F	-	*	-	Dark Green	H6X	-	*	-	Black

ENGINE NUMBER: Stamped on a boss behind the water pump. The number provides the code to identify the series, block displacement, and month/day production date.

EXAMPLE

PM	383	2187	2401	
PLANT	CID	JULIAN	DAILY	ENGINE PLANTS
CODE		DATE	SEQUENTIAL	PM-Mound Rd.
			NUMBER	PT-Trenton

Engine #	Engine Name	CID	Comp. Ratio	Carb Type	HP	Transmission
PM170xxxx0001	170	70	8.5	1, 1Bl	101	Stand — A-903 G, Opt — A-904 G
PM225xxxx0001	Standard 225/225	225	8.4	1, 1Bl	145	Stand — A-903 RG, Opt — A-833 Opt — A-904 RG
PM273xxxx0001	Commando 273 Commando 273 V8	273	8.8/10.5	1, 2Bl/1, 4Bl	180/ 235	Stand — A-745, Opt — A-833 Opt — A-904-A
PM318xxxx0001	Opt. 318	318	9	1, 2Bl	230	Stand — A-745, Opt — A-727
PM361xxxx0001	Commmando 361 V8	261	9	1, 2Bl	265	Stand — A-745, Opt — A-833 Opt — A-727
PM383xxxx0001	Commando 383	383	9.2/10.0	1, 2Bl/1, 4Bl	270/ 330	Stand — A-745, Opt — A-833 Opt — A-727
PM426xxxx0001	Hemi 426	426	10.25	2, 4Bl	425	Stand — A-833, Opt — A-727
PM440xxxx0001	Commando 440	440	10.1	1, 4Bl	365	Stand — A-833, Opt — A-727

VEHICLE IDENTIFICATION NUMBER

BH29K9F100551

The vehicle number (serial number) is stamped and embossed on a stainless steel plate attached to the left front door hinge pillar. It consists of car make symbol, series code, model year code, assembly plant symbol & a sequential production number.

1st Digit - Car make
Valiant	Y
Belvedere	R
Fury	P
Barracuda	B

2nd Digit - Class
Ecconomy	E
Low	L
High	H
Medium	M
Premium	P
Police	K
Taxi	T
Special	S
Superstock	O
Fast Top	X

3rd Digit & 4th Digit - Body style
2-Dr. Sedan	21
2-Dr. Hardtop	23
Convertible	27
2-Dr. Sports Hardtop	29
4-Dr. Sedan	.41
4-Dr. Hardtop	43
6-Ps. Station Wagon	45
9-Ps. Station Wagon	46

Fifth Digit - CID
170	A
225	B
Special Order 6 Cyk.	C
237	D
318	F
383	G
383 H/perf	H
426	J
440	K
440 H/Perf.	L
Special Order 8	M
340	P

Sixth Digit - Year 1969

Seventh Digit - Assembly plant
Lynch Rd	A
Hamtramck	B
Jefferson	C
Belvidere Plant	D

Last Digits: Production sequence number.

BODY CODE PLATE

```
    abcdefghjkmnpqrtuwy
A B C D E F G H J X L M N P Q R S T V W X Y Z
  1 2 3 4 5 6 7 8      AX    TRM     PNT    UBS
               A9      A9    HX3     BB1     W
  BH29               E55     D21     P9A   100551
```

THE BODY CODE PLATE is read left to right, bottom to top. For 1969 Chrysler Corp. started a new system on their BODY CODE PLATES. Each body code plate contains all the code numbers for every option on the car. If one plate didn't hold all the information, a second tag was used. Listed here will be the codes found (usually) on the bottom two rows.

First a four digit BODY MODEL and STYLE CODE, a three digit ENGINE CODE and a three digit TRANSMISSION CODE, and the last nine digits of the VIN NUMBER. The next row up is a four digit PLANT CODE number, a three digit TRIM CODE number followed by special TRIM, STRIPPING AND DOOR FRAME COLOR CODES if any.

THE BODY NUMBER is a four digit number which indicates the Car line, Price class, and Bodystyle. Same first four digits of the VIN.

The three digit ENGINE CID CODE identifies the engine.

ENGIINE CID
ENGIINE CID	CODE
Special Order 6 cyl.	E06
Special Order 8 cyl.	E08
170 6 cyl.	E11
225 6 cyl.	E24

225 Special 6 cyl. E25
273 8 Cyl. E31
318 8 Cyl. E44
340 4BBL 8 Cyl. E55
383 1-2BBL 8 Cyl. .... E 61
383 1-4BBL 8 Cyl. .... E 62
440 1-4BBl 8 Cyl. .... E 85
440 1-BBl 8 Cyl. HP .... E 86

TRANSMISSION	CODE
3-Speed Manual	D11
3-Speed Manual	D12
3-Speed Manual	D14
4-Speed Manual	D21
3-Speed Automatic	D31
3-Speed Automatic	D32
3-Speed Automatic	D34

The three digit code which indicates tire size and type, this option code is not included.

The last digits of the bottom row are a repeat of the last nine digits of the VIN plate.

ENGINE NUMBERS: All engine serial numbers contain fourteen characters and digits. The first two designate the engine plant, the next three are the cubic inch displacement, the next one designates low compression, the next four are based on a Julian calander and the production sequence number of engines built that day. All 383 and 440 cubic inch engines have the serial number stanped on the cylinder block.

VALIANT	CODE
2-Dr. Sedan	VL21
4-Dr. Sedan	VL41

SIGNET	CODE
2-Dr. Sedan	VH21
4-Dr. Sedan	VH41

BARRACUDA	CODE
2-Dr. Hardtop	BH23
2-Dr. Sport Coupe	BH29
Convertible	BH27

BELVEDERE	CODE
2-Dr. Coupe	RL 21
4-Dr. Sedan	RL 41
4-Dr. Wagon (2 seat)	RL45

SATELLITE	CODE
2-Dr. Hardtop	RH23
Convertible	RH27
4-Dr. Sedan	RH41
4-Dr. Wagon (2 seat)	RH45
4-Dr. Wagon (3 seat)	RH46

SPORT SATELLITE	CODE
2-Dr. Hardtop	RP23
Convertible	RP27
4-Dr. Sedan	RP41
4-Dr. Wagon (2 seat)	RP45
4-Dr. Wagon (3 seat)	RP46

BELVEDERE (POLICE)	CODE
2-Dr. Coupe	RK21
4-Dr. Sedan	RK41
4-Dr. Wagon	RK45

BELVEDERE (TAXI)	CODE
4-Dr. Sedan	RT41

FURY I	CODE
2-Dr. Sedan	PE21
4-Dr. Sedan	PE41
4-Dr. Wagon	PE45

FURY II	CODE
2-Dr. Sedan	PL21
4-Dr. Sedan	PL41
4-Dr. Wagon (2 seat)	PL45
4-Dr. Wagon (3 seat)	PL46

FURY III	CODE
2-Dr. Hardtop	PM23
4-Dr. Sedan	PM41
4-Dr. Hardtop	PM43
Convertible	PM27
4-Dr. Wagon (2 seat)	PM45
4-Dr. Wagon (3 seat)	PM46
2-Dr. Hardtop Formal	PM29

SPORT FURY	CODE
2-Dr. Hardtop	PH23
Convertible	PH27
2-Dr. Hardtop Formal	PH29

FURY I (POLICE)	CODE
2-Dr. Sedan	PK21
4-Dr. Sedan	PK41
4-Dr. Wagon (2 seat)	PK45

FURY (TAXI)	CODE
4-Dr. Sedan	PT41

VIP	CODE
4-Dr. Hardtop	PP23
4-Dr. Hardtop	PP43
2-Dr. Hardtop Formal	PP29

ROADRUNNER	CODE
2-Dr. Coupe	RM21
2-Dr. Hardtop	RM23
Convertible	RM27

GTX	CODE
2-Dr. Hardtop	RS23
Convertible	RS27

THE UBS CODE identifies the upper door frame color, and the accent stripe color.

THE PAINT CODE furnishes the key to the paint used on the car. A thre digit code indicates the top and bottom colors respectively. A number follows which designates two-tone, sports-tone, convertible top, etc.

CODE	COLOR
Charcoal Metallic..	A9
Silver Metallic...	A4
Blue Fire Metallic..	B5
Ice Blue Metallic...	B3
Frost Green Metallic..	F3
Jamaica Blue Metallic..	B7
Ivy Green Metallic...	F8
Limelight Metallic...	F5
Seafoam Turquoise Metallic....................................	Q5
Sandpebble Beige — N/A Barracuda.........................	L1
Honey Bronze Metallic..	T3
Scorch Red...	R6
Bronze Fire Metallic...	T5
Saddle Bronze Metallic...	T7
Black Velvet...	X9
Alpine White...	W1
Yellow Gold..	Y3
Sunfire Yellow — N/A/ Fury, Valiant	Y2
Spanish Gold Metallic...	Y4

TRIM CODE: Furnishes the key to the interior color and material.

Color	Trim Code	Material
Blue	H4B, H2B	V
	H1B	C&V
Gold	H4Y, H2Y	V
Green	H1G	C&V
Red	H4R, H2R	V
Black	H6X, H4X, H2X	V
	H1X	C&V
White/Black	H6W	V
White/Blue	H6C	V
White/Gold	H6E	V
White/Green	H6F	V
White/Red	H6V	V
Blue	D4B, D2B	V
	D1B	C&V
	L2B	V
Red	D4R, D2R	V
Tan	L2T	V
Black	D4X, D2X, L2X	V
	D1X	C&V
Blue	P3D, M1D, L1B, E1B	C&V
	H6D, M4D, E2B	V
Green	P3G, M1G, L1G	C&V
	H6G, M4G	V
Champagne	M1L, L1L, E1L	C&V
	E2L	V
Red	H6R, M4R, L2R, E2R	V
	M1R	C&V
Platinum	H6S, M4S	V

Color	Trim Code	Material
Tan	P4T, H6T, M4T	V
White	P4W, H6W, M4W, L2W	V
Black	PPX	L&V
	P8X, P6X, H6X, M8X, M4X	V
	P3X, M1X	C&V
Blue	D6B, H6B	V
Green	D6G	V
Red	D6R	V
Tan	D6T	V
Black	D6X, H6X, H4X	V
Yellow/Black	D6P	V
White/Black	H4W	V
White/Blue	H4C	V
White/Green	H4F	V
White/Red	H4V	V
Tan/Green	D6J	V
Tan/Black	D6U	V

Color	Trim Code	Material
Blue	P3B	C&V
	P2B, M6B, P6D, F2Q	V
Green	P2G, H2G, P6G, M6G	V
Pewter/Black	P6S, P2S, M2S, M6S, H2S	V
Red	P6R	V
Tan	P6T, P2T, H2T, M6T	V
	H1T, P3T	C&V
Black	P6X, P2X, H2X, M6X	V
	P3X	C&V
White/Blue	P6C, P2C, H2C, M6C	V
White/Green	P6F, P2F, H2F, M6F	V
White/Red	P6V	V
White/Tan	P6H, P2H, H2H, M6H	V
White/Black	P6W, H2W, M6W	V
Blue	M2B	V
	L1B	C&V
Tan	M2T, L2T	V
	L1T	C&V
Black	M2X	V

C=Cloth, V=Vinyl, L=Leather

ENGINE NUMBER

Stamped on a boss behind the water pump. The number provides the code to identify the series, block displacement, and month/day production date.

EXAMPLE

PM	383	2187	2401		ENGINE PLANT
PLANT	CID	JULIAN	DAILY		PM-Mound Rd.
CODE		DATE	SEQUENTIAL		PT-Trenton
			NUMBER		

Engine #	Engine Name	CID	Comp. Ratio	Carb Type	HP	Transmission
PM170xxxx0001	170	70	8.5	1, 1Bl	101	Stand — A-903 G Opt — A-904 G
PM225xxxx0001	Standard 225	225	8.4	1, 1Bl	145	Stand — A-903 RG Opt — A-833 Opt — A-904 RG
PM273xxxx0001	Commando 273 Commando 273 V8	273	8.8/10.5	1, 2Bl/1, 4Bl	180/ 235	Stand — A-745 Opt — A-833 Opt — A-904-A
PM318xxxx0001	Opt. 318	318	9	1, 2Bl	230	Stand — A-745 Opt — A-727
PM361xxxx0001	Commando 361 V8 261		9	1, 2Bl	265	Stand — A-745 Opt — A-833 Opt — A-727
PM383xxxx0001	Commando 383	383	9.2/10.0	1, 2Bl/1, 4Bl	270/ 330	Stand — A-745 Opt — A-833 Opt — A-727
PM426xxxx0001	Hemi 426	426	10.25	2, 4Bl	425	Stand — A-833 Opt — A-727
PM440xxxx0001	Commando 440	440	10.1	1, 4Bl	365	Stand — A-833 Opt — A-727

VEHICLE IDENTIFICATION NUMBER

7103100551

The vehicle number (serial number) is stamped and embossed on a stainless steel plate attached to the left front door hinge pillar. It consists of car make symbol, series code, model year code, assembly plant symbol & a sequential production number.

1st Digit Car make
De Soto 7

2nd Digit Series
Fireflight 1
Adventurer 2

3rd Digit Year 1960

4th Digit Assembly plant
Detroit 3
5th through 10th digit are production sequence code.

BODY CODE PLATE

Stamped and embossed on a stainless steel plate under the hood. It is attached to: right or left fender, cowl, or radiator cross member depending on the model and assembly plant. This plate will indicate; schedule date, body production number, body series, trim, paint, and accessory code.

THE SHIPPING ORDER NUMBER is assigned prior to production. It consists of a 4 digit planned delivery month/day date code, 0224 (February 24th). Then a plant production sequence number follows (0555)

BODY NUMBER is a 3 digit number which indicates the model and body style.

FIREFLIGHT	CODE
2-Dr. Hardtop	612
4-Dr. Sedan	613
4-Dr. Hardtop	614

ADVENTURER	CODE
2-Dr. Hardtop	712
4-Dr. Sedan	713
4-Dr. Hardtop	714

```
1 2 3 4 5 6 7 8 9 0
A B C D E F G H J X L M N P Q R S T V W X Y Z

SO        NUMBER      BDY      TRM      PNT
0224      0551        612      811      BB1
```

THE PAINT CODE furnishes the key to the paint used on the car. A two digit code indicates the top and bottom colors respectively. A number follows which designates two-tone, sports-tone, convertible top, etc.

COLOR	CODE
Yuma Yellow	A
Black	B
Jamaica Blue	C
Arctic Blue	D
Willow Green	F
Cypress Green	G
Marine Aqua	J
Marine Turquoise	K
Silverglow	L
Smoke Pearl	N
Winterberry Red	P
Calcutta Ivory	T
Gabardine	U
Shell White	W
Adobe Rust	Y
Russett Red	Z

TRIM CODE: Furnishes the key to the interior color and material.

CODE	BODY CLOTH MATERIAL	COLOR
811	"Samoa" / Cloth	Blue
812		Green
814		Gray
816		Red / Gray
818		Tan
801	"Saluda" / Cloth	Dark Blue
802		Dark Green
804		Black & Silver
806		Black & Red
808		Tan

ENGINE NUMBER

Stamped on a boss behind the water pump. The number provides the code to identify the series, block, displacement, and month/day production date.

EXAMPLE

P	36	2	24
YEAR	361	FEBRUARY	DAY

Engine #	Engine Name	CID	Comp Ratio	Carb Type	HP	Transmission
P-36-2-24	Turbo Flash	361	10.0: 1	2-BBl	295	S - 3 Speed Manual O - Torqueflight
P-38-2-24	Adventurer	383	10.0: 1	2-BBl	305	Torqueflight
	Adventurer Mark I	383	10.0: 1	4-BBl	325	Torqueflight
	DeSoto Ram	383	10.0: 1	2/4-BBl	330	Torqueflight

VEHICLE IDENTIFICATION NUMBER

6113100551

The vehicle number (serial number) is stamped and embossed on a stainless steel plate attached to the left front door hinge pillar. It consists of car make symbol, series code, model year code, assembly plant symbol & a sequential production number.

1st Digit Car make
De Soto 6

2nd Digit Series
De Soto 1

3rd Digit Year..........................1961

4th Digit Assembly plant
Detroit 3

5th through 10th digit are production sequence code.

BODY CODE PLATE

Stamped and embossed on a stainless steel plate under the hood. It is attached to: right or left fender, cowl, or radiator cross member depending on the model and assembly plant. This plate will indicate; schedule date, body production number, body series, trim, paint, and accessory code.

THE SHIPPING ORDER NUMBER is assigned prior to production. It consists of a 4 digit planned delivery month/day date code, 0224 (February 24th). Then a plant production sequence number follows (0555)

BODY NUMBER is a 3 digit number which indicates the model and body style.

DeSOTO	CODE
2-Dr. Coupe	612
4-Dr. Hardtop	614

```
1 2 3 4 5 6 7 8 9 0
A B C D E F G H J X L M N P Q R S T V W X Y Z

   SO        NUMBER      BDY      TRM      PNT
  0224        0551        612      101      BB1
```

THE PAINT CODE furnishes the key to the paint used on the car. A two digit code indicates the top and bottom colors respectively. A number follows which designates two-tone, sports-tone, convertible top, etc.

CODE	COLOR	CODE
A	Goldenrod Yellow	AA1
B	Black	BB1
C	Morning Blue	CC1
D	Mediterranean Blue	DD1
F	Spring Green	FF1
G	Jade Green	GG1
J	Tangier Aqua	JJ1
K	Surf Turquoise	KK1
L	Platinum Gray	LL1
P	Regal Red	PP1
W	Glacier White	WW1
Y	Tahiti Tan	YY1
Z	Bahama Bronze	ZZ1

THE TRIM CODE: Furnishes the key to the interior color and material.

CODE	BODY CLOTH MATERIAL	COLOR
101	Nylon Jaquard	Blue
104	Nylon Jaquard	Gray
105	Nylon Jaquard	Red
101	Ribbed Nylon	Blue
104	Ribbed Nylon	Gray
105	Ribbed Nylon	Red
101	Saddle Grain Vinyl	Blue
104	Saddle Grain Vinyl	Gray
105	Saddle Grain Vinyl	Red
101	Stipple, Perforated Vinyl	Blue
104	Stipple, Perforated Vinyl	Gray
105	Stipple, Perforated Vinyl	Red
101	Painted	Blue
104	Painted	Gray
105	Painted	Red
101	Carpet	Blue
104	Carpet	Gray
105	Carpet	Red

ENGINE NUMBER

Stamped on a boss behind the water pump. The number provides the code to identify the series, block, displacement, and month/day production date.

EXAMPLE

R	36	2	24
YEAR	361	FEBRUARY	DAY

Engine #	Engine Name	CID	Comp Ratio	Carb Type	HP	Transmission
R-36-2-24		361	10.0: 1	2-BBl	265	S - 3 Speed Manual O - Powerflight

VEHICLE IDENTIFICATION NUMBER

```
STUDEBAKER-PACKARD
   CORPORATION
    SERIAL NO.
    60S10551
```

The serial number is stamped on a plate welded to the left front door pillar.

Example

60S	10551
Engine Year	Production Number

FIRST AND SECOND DIGIT: Represents the model year 1960.

THIRD DIGIT: Identifies the engine.

ENGINE

	Code
170CID - 6 cyl.	S
259CID - 8 cyl.	V

* A letter "C" following the engine code indicates assembled in Canada.

LAST DIGIT: Indicates the production sequence number.

BODY TAG

```
60S - W6
  671
```

The BODY TAG indicates the year, engine, body style, and trim is stamped on a tag riveted to the cowl under the hood.

FIRST, SECOND AND THIRD DIGITS: are a repeat of the VIN plate. It identifies the YEAR AND ENGINE.

FOURTH AND FIFTH DIGITS: a two digit BODY STYLE identifies the series and body style.

LARK DELUXE

	Code
Sedan 4-Dr, 6 Pass.	W4
Sedan 2-Dr, 6-Pass.	F4
Station Wagon 4-Dr, 6-Pass	P4
Station Wagon 2-Dr, 6-Pass	D4

LARK REGAL

	Code
Sedan 4-Dr, 6 Pass.	W6
Hardtop 2-Dr, 6 Pass.	J6
Coupe, Convertible, 6 Pass.	L6
Station Wagon 4-Dr, 6 Pass.	P6

TAXI CAB

	Code
4-Dr	Y1

HAWK

	Code
Coupe Sport, 6 Pass.	C6

The TRIM CODE furnishes the key to trim color and material code dictates the availability of exterior paint color.

Key to Upholstery Symbols:

RB=Red & Black Cloth	RDV=Red Vinyl	BLV=Blue Vinyl
GR=Green Cloth	BRV=Brown Vinyl	TNV=Tan Vinyl
BL=Blue Cloth	GRV=Green Vinyl	BKV=Black Vinyl
BR=Brown Cloth		

60S-F4 and 60V-F4

Color	Code	Std. Cloth	Opt. Cloth	Opt. Vinyl
Velvet Black	6010	472 RB	422 BL	552 RDV
			432 GR	522 BLV
			442 BR	532 GRV
				542 BRV
White Sand	6011	442 BR	422 BL	542 BRV
			432 GR	522 BLV
			472 RB	532 GRV
				552 RDV
Gulfstream Blue	6012	422 BL	None	522 BLV
				552 RDV
Oasis Green	6013	432 GR	None	532 GRV
Williamsburg Green	6014	432 GR	None	532 GRV
Sandalwood Beige	6015	442 BR	None	542 BRV
				552 RDV
Colonial Red	6016	472 RB	None	552 RDV

60S-W4 and 60V-W4

Color	Code	Std. Cloth	Opt. Cloth	Opt. Vinyl
Velvet Black	6010	471 RB	421 BL	551 RDV
			431 GR	521 BLV
			441 BR	531 GRV
				541 BRV
White Sand	6011	441 BR	421 BL	541 BRV
			431 GR	521 BLV
			471 RB	531 GRV
				551 RDV
Gulfstream Blue	6012	421 BL	None	521 BLV
				551 RDV
Oasis Green	6013	431 GR	None	531 GRV
Williamsburg Green	6014	431 GR	None	531 GRV
Sandalwood Beige	6015	441 BR	None	541 BRV
				551 RDV
Colonial Red	6016	471 RB	None	551 RDV

60S-D4 and 60V-D4

Color	Code	Std. Cloth	Opt. Cloth	Opt. Vinyl
Velvet Black	6010	556 RDV	526 BLV	None
			536 GRV	
			546 BRV	
White Sand	6011	546 BRV	526 BLV	None
			536 GRV	
			556 RDV	
Gulfstream Blue	6012	526 BLV	556 RDV	None
Oasis Green	6013	536 GRV	None	None
Williamsburg Green	6014	536 GRV	None	None
Sandalwood Beige	6015	546 BRV	556 RDV	None
Colonial Red	6016	556 RDV	None	None

60S-P4 and 60V-P4

Color	Code	Std. Cloth	Opt. Cloth	Opt. Vinyl
Velvet Black	6010	557 RDV	527 BLV	None
			537 GRV	
			547 BRV	
White Sand	6011	547 BRV	527 BLV	None
			537 GRV	
			557 RDV	
Gulfstream Blue	6012	527 BLV	557 RDV	None
Oasis Green	6013	537 GRV	None	None
Williamsburg Green	6014	537 GRV	None	None
Sandalwood Beige	6015	547 BRV	557 RDV	None
Colonial Red	6016	557 RDV	None	None

60S-W6 and 60V-W6

Color	Code	Std. Cloth	Opt. Cloth	Opt. Vinyl
Velvet Black	6010	671 RB	621 BL	751 RDV
			631 GR	721 BLV
			641 BR	731 GRV

(continued)

Color	Code	Std. Cloth	Opt. Cloth	Opt. Vinyl
(continued)				741 BRV 761 TNV 711 BKV
White Sand	6011	641 BR	621 BL 631 GR 671 RB	741 BRV 721 BLV 731 GRV 751 RDV 761 TNV 711 BKV
Gulfstream Blue	6012	621 BL	None	721 BLV 761 TNV 711 BKV 751 RDV
Oasis Green	6013	631 GR	None	731 GRV 761 TNV 711 BKV
Williamsburg Green	6014	631 GR	None	731 GRV 761 TNV 711 BKV
Sandalwood Beige	6015	641 BR	None	741 BRV 761 TNV 711 BKV 751 RDV
Colonial Red	6016	671 RB	None	751 RDV 761 TNV 711 BKV

60S-J6 and 60V-J6

Color	Code	Std. Vinyl	Opt. Vinyl	Opt. Vinyl
Velvet Black	6010	679 RB	629 BL 639 GR 649 BR	759 RDV 729 BLV 739 GRV 749 BRV 769 TNV 719 BKV
White Sand	6011	649 BR	629 BL 639 GR 679 RB	749 BRV 729 BLV 739 GRV 759 RDV 769 TNV 719 BKV
Gulfstream Blue	6012	629 BL	None	729 BLV 769 TNV 719 BKV 759 RDV
Oasis Green	6013	639 GR	None	739 GRV 769 TNV 719 BKV
Williamsburg Green	6014	639 GR	None	739 GRV 769 TNV 719 BKV
Sandalwood Beige	6015	649 BR	None	749 BRV 769 TNV 719 BKV 759 RDV
Colonial Red	6016	679 RB	None	759 RDV 769 TNV 719 BKV

60S-L6 and 60V-L6

Color	Code	Std. Vinyl	Opt. Vinyl	Opt. Cloth	Std. Top	Opt. Top
Velvet Black	6010	758 RDV	728 BLV 738 GRV 748 BRV 768 TNV 718 BKV	None	Light (Tan)	Dark (Tan)
White Sand	6011	748 BRV	728 BLV 738 GRV 758 RDV 768 TNV 718 BKV	None	Dark (Black)	Light (Tan)
Gulfstream Blue	6012	728 BLV	768 TNV 718 BKV	None	Light (Tan)	Dark (Black)
Oasis Green	6013	738 GRV	768 TNV 718 BKV	None	Dark (Black)	Light (Tan)
Williamsburg Green	6014	738 GRV	768 TNV 718 BKV	None	Light (Tan)	Dark (Black)
Sandalwood Beige	6015	748 BRV	768 TNV 718 BKV 758 RDV	None	Dark (Black)	Light (Tan)
Colonial Red	6016	758 RDV	768 TNV 718 BKV	None	Dark (Black)	Light (Tan)
Jonquil Yellow	6017	748 BRV	768 TNV 718 BKV 758 RDV	None	Dark (Black)	Light (Tan)

60S-P6 and 60V-P6

Color	Code	Std. Vinyl	Opt. Vinyl	Opt. Cloth
Velvet Black	6010	757 RDV	727 BLV 737 GRV 747 BRV 767 TNV 717 BKV	None
White Sand	6011	747 BRV	727 BLV 737 GRV 757 RDV 767 TNV 717 BKV	None
Gulfstream Blue	6012	727 BLV	767 TNV 717 BKV 757 RDV	None
Oasis Green	6013	737 GRV	767 TNV 717 BKV	None
Williamsburg Green	6014	737 GRV	767 TNV 717 BKV	None
Sandalwood Beige	6015	747 BRV	767 TNV 717 BKV 757 RDV	None
Colonial Red	6016	757 RDV	767 TNV 717 BKV	None

60V-C6

Color	Code	Std. Cloth	Opt. Cloth	Opt. Vinyl
Velvet Black	6010	673 RB	623 BL 633 GR 643 BR	753 RDV 723 BLV 733 GRV 743 BRV 763 TNV 713 BKV
White Sand	6011	643 BR	623 BL 633 GR 673 RB	743 BRV 723 BLV 733 GRV 753 RDV 763 TNV 713 BKV
Gulfstream Blue	6012	623 BL	None	723 BLV 763 TNV 713 BKV 753 RDV
Oasis Green	6013	633 GR	None	733 GRV 763 TNV 713 BKV
Williamsburg Green	6014	633 GR	None	733 GRV 763 TNV 713 BKV
Sandalwood Beige	6015	643 BR	None	743 BRV 763 TNV 713 BKV 753 RDV
Colonial Red	6016	673 RB	None	753 RDV 763 TNV 713 BKV

The PAINT CODE can be found on a piece of paper attached to the bottom of the glove box.

COLOR	Code
Black Velvet	6010
White Sand	6011
Gulfstream Blue	6012
Oasis Green (Light Green)	6013
Williamsburg Green (Dark Green)	6014
Sandalwood Beige	6015
Colonial Red	6016
Jonquil Yellow	6017

ENGINE NUMBER

Engines are stamped with a prefix code denoting the cubic inch displacement, plus a numeric production number.

6-cylinder engine numbers are located on a pad at the upper left front of the cylinder block.

V-8 engine numbers are located on a pad at the upper left front of the cylinder block.

ENGINE	Code
170 Cid. 6-cyl.	S
259 Cid. V-8	V
289 Cid. V-8	P

* Note: If a letter "C" follows the engine code, it designates Canadian manufacture.

No. of Cylinders	Engine Code Prefix	Cid	Std. Comp. Ratio	Opt. Comp. Ratio	Carburetor	H.P.
6	S	170	8.3:1	7.0:1	Carter 1-bb1	90
8	V	259	8.5:1	7.5:1	Stromberg 2-bb1*	180**
8	P	289	8.5:1	7.5:1	Stromberg 2-bb1*	210***

* Optional: Carter WCFB - 4-bb1 available on all models except Taxi.

** 195 H.P. with 4-bb1 carburetor.

***225 H.P. with 4-bb1 carburetor.

VEHICLE IDENTIFICATION NUMBER

STUDEBAKER-PACKARD
CORPORATION
SERIAL NO.
61S10551

The serial number is stamped on a plate welded to the left front door pillar.

Example

61S	10551
Engine Year	Production Number

FIRST AND SECOND DIGIT: Represents the model year 1961.

THIRD DIGIT: Identifies the engine.

ENGINE	Code
6-cyl., 170 Cid.	S
8-cyl., 259 Cid.	V
8-cyl., 289 Cid.	P

* A letter "C" following the engine code indicates assembled in Canada.

LAST DIGITS: Is the production sequence number.

BODY TAG

61S - P4
557

The BODY TAG indicates the year, engine, body style, and trim is stamped on a tag riveted to the cowl under the hood.

FIRST, SECOND AND THIRD DIGITS: are a repeat of the VIN plate. It identifies the YEAR AND ENGINE.

FOURTH AND FIFTH DIGITS: a two digit BODY STYLE identifies the series and body style.

LARK DELUXE	Code
Sedan 4-Dr, 6 Pass.	W4
Sedan 2-Dr, 6-Pass.	F4
Station Wagon 4-Dr, 6-Pass	P4
Station Wagon 2-Dr, 6-Pass	D4

LARK REGAL	Code
Sedan 4-Dr, 6 Pass.	W6
Hardtop Coupe 2-Dr, 6 Pass.	J6
Convertible 2-Dr, 6 Pass.	L6
Station Wagon 4-Dr, 6 Pass.	P6

LARK	Code
Cruiser, 4-Dr	Y6
Taxicab	Y1

HAWK	Code
Coupe Sport, 6 Pass.	C6

The TRIM CODE furnishes the key to the trim color and material. The trim code dictates the availability of exterior paint colors.

Key to Upholstery Symbols:

RB=Red & Black Cloth	RDV=Red Vinyl	BLV=Blue Vinyl
GR=Green Cloth	BRV=Brown Vinyl	TNV=Tan Vinyl
BL=Blue Cloth	GRV=Green Vinyl	BKV=Black Vinyl
BR=Brown Cloth		

61S-F4 and 61V-F4

Color	Code	Std. Cloth	Opt. Cloth	Opt. Vinyl
Velvet Black	6110	472 RB	422 BL	552 RDV
			432 GR	522 BLV
			442 BR	532 GRV
				542 BRV
Ermine	6111	472 RB	422 BL	542 BRV
			432 GR	522 BLV
			442 BR	532 GRV
				552 RDV
Riviera Blue	6112	422 BL	None	522 BLV
				552 RDV
Green Jade	6113	432 GR	None	532 GRV
Desert Sand	6114	442 BR	None	542 GRV
				552 RDV
Blaze	6116	472 RB	442 BR	542 BRV
				552 RDV
Suntone	6117	432 GR	442 BR	532 GRV
			472 RB	542 BRV
				552 RDV
Autumn Haze	6118	442 BR	472 RB	542 BRV
				552 RDV

61S-W4 and 61V-W4

Color	Code	Std. Cloth	Opt. Cloth	Opt. Vinyl
Velvet Black	6110	471 RB	421 BL	551 RDV
			431 GR	521 BLV
			441 BR	531 GRV
				541 BRV
Ermine	6111	471 RB	421 BL	541 BRV
			431 GR	521 BLV
			441 RB	531 GRV
				551 RDV
Riviera Blue	6112	421 BL	None	521 BLV
				551 RDV
Green Jade	6113	431 GR	None	531 GRV
Desert Sane	6115	441 BR	None	541 BRV
				551 RDV
Blaze	6116	471 RB	None	551 RDV
				541 BRV
Suntone	6117	431 GR	441 BR	531 GRV
			471 RB	541 BRV
				551 RDV
Autumn Haze	6118	441 BR	471 RB	541 BRV
				551 RDV

61S-D4 and 61V-D4

Color	Code	Std. Cloth	Opt. Cloth	Opt. Vinyl
Velvet Black	6110	556 RDV	526 BLV	None
			536 GRV	
			546 BRV	
Ermine	6111	556 RDV	526 BLV	None
			536 GRV	
			546 BRV	
Riviera Blue	6112	526 BLV	556 RDV	None
Green Jade	6113	536 GRV	None	None
Desert Sand	6115	546 BRV	556 RDV	None
Blaze	6116	556 RDV	546 BRV	None
Suntone	6117	536 GRV	546 BRV	None
			556 RDV	
Autumn Haze	6118	546 BRV	55 RDV	None

61S-P4 and 61V-P4

Color	Code	Std. Cloth	Opt. Cloth	Opt. Vinyl
Velvet Black	6110	557 RDV	527 BLV	None
			537 GRV	
			547 BRV	

Color	Code	Std.	Opt.	Opt. Cloth
Ermine	6111	557 RDV	527 BLV / 537 GRV / 547 BRV	None
Riviera Blue	6112	527 BLV	557 RDV	None
Green Jade	6113	537 GRV	None	None
Desert Sand	6115	547 BRV	557 RDV	None
Blaze	6116	557 RDV	547 BRV	None
Suntone	6117	537 GRV	547 BRV / 557 RDV	None
Autumn Haze	6118	547 BRV	557 RDV	None

Color	Code	Std.	Opt.	Opt.	Opt. Top
Suntone	6117	639 GR	649 BR / 679 RB	719 BKV / 739 GRV / 749 BRV / 759 RDV / 769 TNV	
Autumn Haze	6118	649 BR	679 RB	719 BKV / 749 BRV / 759 RDV / 769 TNV	

61S-W6 and 61V-W6 (with Regal Kit)

Color	Code	Std.	Opt.	Opt. Cloth
Velvet Black	6110	671 RB	621 BL / 631 GR / 641 BR	751 RDV / 721 BLV / 731 GRV / 741 BRV / 761 TNV / 711 BKV
Ermine	6111	671 RB	621 BL / 631 GR / 641 BR	741 BRV / 721 BLV / 731 GRV / 751 RDV / 761 TNV / 711 BKV
Riviera Blue	6112	621 BL	None	721 BLV / 761 TNV / 711 BKV / 751 RDV
Green Jade	6113	631 GR	None	731 GRV / 761 TNV / 711 BKV
Desert Sand	6115	641 BR	None	741 BRV / 761 TNV / 711 BKV / 751 RDV
Blaze	6116	671 RB	641 BR	751 RDV / 761 TNV / 711 BKV / 741 BRV
Suntone	6117	631 GR	641 BR / 671 RB	711 BKV / 731 GRV / 741 BRV / 751 RDV / 761 TNV

61S-L6 and 61V-L6

Color	Code	Std. Vinyl	Opt. Vinyl	Opt. Cloth	Std. Top	Opt. Top
Velvet Black	6110	758 RDV	728 BLV / 738 GRV / 748 BRV / 768 TNV / 718 BKV	None	White	Black
Ermine	6111	758 RDV	728 BLV / 738 GRV / 748 BRV / 768 TNV / 718 BKV	None	White	Black
Riviera Blue	6112	728 BLV	768 TNV / 758 RDV / 718 BKV	None	White	Black
Green Jade	6113	738 GRV	768 TNV / 718 BKV	None	White	Black
Flamingo	6114	748 BRV	718 BKV / 768 TNV	None	White	Black
Desert Sand	6115	748 BRV	768 TNV / 718 BKV / 758 RDV	None	White	Black
Blaze	6116	758 RDV	768 TNV / 718 BKV / 748 BRV	None	White	Black
Suntone	6117	738 GRV	768 TNV / 718 BKV / 758 RDV / 748 BRV	None	White	Black
Autumn Haze	6118	748 BRV	718 BKV / 758 RDV / 768 TNV	None	White	Black

61S-J6 and 61V-J6

Color	Code	Std.	Opt.	Opt. Cloth
Velvet Black	6110	679 RB	629 BL / 639 GR / 649 BR	759 RDV / 729 BLV / 739 GRV / 749 BRV / 769 TNV / 719 BKV
Ermine	6111	679 RB	629 BL / 639 GR / 649 BR	749 BRV / 729 BLV / 739 GRV / 759 RDV / 769 TNV / 719 BKV
Riviera Blue	6112	629 BL	None	729 BLV / 769 TNV / 719 BKV / 759 RDV
Green Jade	6113	639 GR	None	739 GRV / 769 TNV / 719 BKV / 759 RDV
Desert Sand	6115	649 BR	None	749 BRV / 769 TNV / 719 BKV / 759 RDV
Blaze	6116	679 RB	None	759 RDV / 769 TNV / 719 BKV / 749 BRV

61S-P6 and 61V-P6 (with Regal Kit)

Color	Code	Std. Vinyl	Opt. Vinyl	Opt. Cloth
Velvet Black	6110	757 RDV	727 BLV / 737 GRV / 747 BRV / 767 TNV / 717 BKV	None
Ermine	6111	757 RDV	727 BLV / 737 GRV / 747 BRV / 767 TNV / 717 BKV	None
Riviera Blue	6112	727 BLV	767 TNV / 717 BKV / 757 RDV	None
Green Jade	6113	737 GRV	767 TNV / 717 BKV / 757 RDV	None
Desert Sand	6115	747 BRV	767 TNV / 717 BKV / 757 RDV	None
Blaze	6116	757 RDV	767 TNV / 717 BKV / 747 BRV	None
Suntone	6117	737 GRV	717 BKV / 747 BRV / 757 RDV / 767 TNV	None
Autumn Haze	6118	747 BRV	717 BKV / 757 RDV / 767 TNV	None

61V-Y6

Color	Code	Std. Cloth	Opt. Cloth	Opt. Vinyl
Velvet Black	6110	675 RB	625 BL, 635 GR, 645 BR	755 RDV, 725 BLV, 735 GRV, 745 BRV, 765 TNV, 715 BKV
Ermine	6111	675 RB	625 BL, 635 GR, 645 BR	745 BRV, 725 BLV, 735 GRV, 755 RDV, 765 TNV, 715 BKV
Riviera Blue	6112	625 BL	None	725 BLV, 765 TNV, 715 BKV
Green Jade	6113	635 GR	None	755 RDV, 735 GRV, 765 TNV, 715 BKV
Desert Sand	6115	645 BR	None	745 BRV, 765 TNV, 715 BKV
Blaze	6116	675 RB	645 BR	755 RDV, 755 RDV, 765 TNV, 715 BKV
Suntone	6117	635 GR	645 BR, 675 RB	745 BRV, 715 BKV, 735 GRV, 745 BRV, 755 RDV, 765 TNV
Autumn Haze	6118	645 BR	675 RB	715 BKV, 745 BRV, 755 RDV, 765 TNV

61V-C6

Color	Code	Std. Cloth	Opt. Cloth	Opt. Vinyl
Velvet Black	6110	673 RB	623 BL, 633 GR, 643 BR	753 RDV, 723 BLV, 733 GRV, 743 BRV, 763 TNV, 713 BKV
Ermine	6111	673 RB	623 BL, 633 GR, 643 BR	743 BRV, 723 BLV, 733 GRV, 753 RDV, 763 TNV, 713 BKV
Riviera Blue	6112	623 BL	None	723 BLV, 763 TNV, 713 BKV, 753 RDV
Green Jade	6113	633 GR	None	733 GRV, 763 TNV, 713 BKV
Flamingo	6114	643 BR	None	713 BKV, 743 BRV, 763 TNV
Desert Sand	6115	643 BR	None	743 BRV, 763 TNV, 713 BKV, 753 RDV
Blaze	6116	673 RB	643 BR	753 RDV, 763 TNV, 713 BKV, 743 BRV
Suntone	6117	633 GR	643 BR, 673 RB	713 BKV, 733 GRV, 743 BRV, 753 RDV
Autumn Haze	6118	643 BR	673 RB	713 BKV, 743 BRV, 753 RDV, 763 TNV

61S-Y1 AND 61V-Y1

Color	Code	Std. Cloth	Opt. Cloth	Opt. Vinyl
ALL Paint Except Flamingo		145 BRV	155 RDV	None

ENGINE NUMBER

Engines are stamped with a prefix code denoting the cubic inch displacement, plus a numeric production number.

6-cylinder engine numbers are located on a pad at the upper left front of the cylinder block.

V-8 engine numbers are located on a pad at the upper left front of the cylinder block.

ENGINE	Code
170 Cid. 6-cyl.	S
259 Cid. 8-cyl.	V
289 Cid. 8-cyl.	P

* Note: If a letter "C" follows the engine code, it designates Canadian manufacture.

The PAINT CODE can be found on a piece of paper attached to the bottom of the glove box.

COLOR	Code
Black Velvet	6110
Ermine	6111
Riviera Blue	6112
Green Jade	6113
Flamingo	6114
Desert Sand	6115
Blaze	6116
Suntone	6117
Autumn Haze	6118

FLAMINGO PAINT is optional on Convertibles and Hawks only.

NOTE: All wheels painted silver. No other color available.

No. of Cylinders	Engine Code Prefix	Cid	Std. Comp. Ratio	Opt. Comp. Ratio	Carburetor	H.P.
6	S	170	8.5:1	7.0:1	Carter 1-bbl	112
8	V	259	8.8:1	7.5:1	Stromberg 2-bbl*	180**
8	P	289	8.8:1	7.5:1	Stromberg 2-bbl*	210***

* Optional: Carter WCFB - 4-bbl available on all models except Taxi.
** 195 H.P. with 4-bbl carburetor.
***225 H.P. with 4-bbl carburetor.

VEHICLE IDENTIFICATION NUMBER

```
┌─────────────────────────────┐
│   STUDEBAKER-PACKARD         │
│      CORPORATION             │
│      SERIAL NO.              │
│       62S10551               │
└─────────────────────────────┘
```

The serial number is stamped on a plate welded to the left front door pillar.

Example

62S	10551
Engine	Production
Year	Number

FIRST AND SECOND DIGIT: Represents the model year 1962.

THIRD DIGIT: Identifies the engine.

ENGINE	Code
6-cyl., 170 Cid.	S
8-cyl., 259 Cid.	V
8-cyl., 289 Cid.	P

* A letter "C" following the engine code indicates assembled in Canada.

LAST DIGITS: Is the production sequence number.

BODY TAG

```
┌─────────────────┐
│    62S - Y4     │
│      445        │
└─────────────────┘
```

The BODY TAG indicates the year, engine, body style, and trim is stamped on a tag riveted to the cowl under the hood.

FIRST, SECOND AND THIRD DIGITS: are a repeat of the VIN plate. It identifies the YEAR AND ENGINE.

FOURTH AND FIFTH DIGITS: a two digit BODY STYLE identifies the series and body style.

LARK DELUXE	Code
Sedan 4-Dr, 6 Pass.	Y4
Sedan 2-Dr, 6-Pass.	F4

LARK REGAL	Code
Sedan 4-Dr, 6 Pass.	Y6
Hardtop Coupe 2-Dr, 6 Pass.	J6
Convertible 2-Dr, 6 Pass.	L6

LARK DAYTONA	Code
Hardtop Coupe 2-Dr	J8

Convertible 2-Dr	L8

LARK STATION WAGONS	Code
Station Wagon 4-Dr (Dlx)	P4
Station Wagon 4-Dr (Regal)	P6

LARK CRUISER	Code
Sedan 4-Dr	Y8

TAXICAB	Code
Sedan 4-Dr	Y1

POLICE	Code
Sedan 2-Dr	F3
Sedan 4-Dr	Y3
Station Wagon 4-Dr	P3

GRAND TURISMO HAWK	Code
Hardtop Coupe	K6

The TRIM CODE furnishes the key to the trim color and material. The trim code dictates the availability of exterior paint colors.

Key to Upholstery Symbols:

BL=Blue Cloth	BKV=Black Vinyl	BLV=Blue Vinyl
GR=Green Cloth	GRV=Green Vinyl	TAV=Taupe Vinyl
TA=Taupe Cloth	RDV=Red Vinyl	STV=Saddle Tan Vinyl

62S-F4 and 62V-F4 (Deluxe 2 Dr. Sedan)

Color	Code	Std. Cloth	Opt. Cloth	Opt. Vinyl
Velvet Black	6210	442 TA	422 BL	552 RDV
			432 GR	522 BLV
				532 GRV
				542 TAV
Ermine White	6211	422 BL	432 GR	522 BLV
			442 TA	532 BLV
				542 GRV
				552 RDV
Riviera Blue	6212	422 BL	442 TA	522 BLV
				552 RDV
				542 TAV
Metallic Green	6213	432 GR	442 TA	532 GRV
				542 TAV
Metallic Silver	6214	442 TA	422 BL	522 BLV
			432 GR	532 GRV
				542 TAV
				552 RDV
Desert Tan	6215	442 TA	432 GR	532 GRV
				542 TAV
				552 RDV
Blaze Red	6216	442 TA	None	542 TAV
				552 RDV
Metallic Brown	6217	442 TA	None	542 TAV
				552 RDV

62S-P4 and 62V-P4 (Deluxe 4 Dr. Station Wagon)

Color	Code	Std. Vinyl	Opt. Vinyl	Opt. Cloth
Velvet Black	6210	557 RDV	527 BLV	None
			537 GRV	
			547 TAV	
Ermine White	6211	557 RDV	527 BLV	None
			537 GR	
			547 TAV	
Riviera Blue	6212	527 BLV	547 TAV	None
			557 RDV	
Metallic Green	6213	537 GRV	547 TAV	None
Metallic Silver	6214	547 TAV	527BLV	None
			537 GRV	
			557 RDV	
Desert Tan	6215	547 TAV	537 GRV	None
			557 RDV	
Blaze Red	6216	547 TAV	557 RDV	None
Metallic Brown	6217	547 TAV	557 RDV	None

62S-Y4 and 62V-Y4 (Deluxe 2 Dr. Sedan)

Color	Code	Std. Cloth	Opt. Cloth	Opt. Vinyl
Velvet Black	6210	445 TA	425 BL	555 RDV
			435 GR	525 BLV
				535 GRV
				545 TAV
Ermine White	6211	425 BL	435 GR	525 BLV
			445 TA	535 GRV
				545 TAV
				555 RDV
Riviera Blue	6212	425 BL	445 TA	525 BLV
				555 RDV
				545 TAV
Metallic Green	6213	435 GR	445 TA	535 GRV
				545 TAV
Metallic Silver	6214	445 TA	425 BL	525 BLV
			435 GR	535 GRV
				545 TAV
				555 RDV

Color	Code	Std. Cloth	Opt. Cloth	Opt. Vinyl	Opt. Vinyl Matching Inserts
Desert Tan	6215	445 TA	435 GR	535 GRV	
				545 TAV	
				555 RDV	
Blaze Red	6216	445 TA	None	545 TAV	
				555 RDV	
Metallic Brown	6217	445 TA	None	545 TAV	
				555 RDV	

62S-J6 and 62V-J6 (Regal 4 Dr. Sedan)

Color	Code	Std. Cloth	Opt. Cloth	Opt. Vinyl	Opt. Vinyl Matching Inserts
Velvet Black	6210	645 TA	625 BL	715 BKV	7151 BKV
			635 GR	725 BLV	7251 BLV
				735 GRV	7351 GRV
				745 TAV	7451 TAV
				755 RDV	7551 RDV
				765 STV	7651 STV
Ermine White	6211	625 BL	635 GR	715 BKV	7151 BKV
			645 TA	725 BLV	7251 BLV
				735 GRV	7351 GRV
				745 TAV	7451 TAV
				755 RDV	7551 RDV
				765 STV	7651 STV
Riviera Blue	6212	625 BL	645 TA	715 BKV	7151 BKV
				725 BLV	7251 BLV
				745 TAV	7451 TAV
				755 RDV	7551 RDV
				765 STV	7651 STV
Metallic Green	6213	635 GR	645 TA	715 BKV	7151 BKV
				735 GRV	7351 GRV
				745 TAV	7451 TAV
				765 STV	7651 STV
Metallic Silver	6214	645 TA	625 BL	715 BKV	7151 BKV
			635 GR	725 BLV	7251 BLV
				735 GRV	7351 GRV
				745 TAV	7451 TAV
				755 RDV	7551 RDV
				765 STV	7651 STV
Desert Tan	6215	645 TA	635 GR	715 BKV	7151 BKV
				735 GRV	7351 GRV
				745 TAV	7451 TAV
				755 RDV	7551 RDV
				765 STV	7651 STV
Blaze Red	6216	645 TA	None	715 BKV	7151 BKV
				745 TAV	7451 TAV
				755 RDV	7551 RDV
				765 STV	7651 STV
Metallic Brown	6217	645 TA	None	715 BKV	7151 BKV
				745 TAV	7451 TAV
				755 RDV	7551 RDV
				765 STV	7651 STV

62S-J6 and 62V-J6 (Regal 2 Dr. Hardtop)

Color	Code	Std. Cloth	Opt. Cloth	Opt. Vinyl	Opt. Vinyl Matching Inserts
Velvet Black	6210	649 TA	629 BL	719 BKV	7191 BKV
			639 GR	729 BLV	7291 BLV
				739 GRV	7391 GRV
				749 TAV	7491 TAV
				759 RDV	7591 RDV
				769 STV	7691 STV
Ermine White	6211	629 BL	639 GR	719 BKV	7191 BKV
			649 TA	729 BLV	7291 BLV
				739 GRV	7391 GRV
				749 TAV	7491 TAV
				759 RDV	7591 RDV
				769 STV	7691 STV
Riviera Blue	6212	629 BL	649 TA	719 BKV	7191 BKV
				729 BLV	7291 BLV
				749 TAV	7491 TAV
				759 RDV	7591 RDV
				769 STV	7691 STV
Metallic Green	6213	639 GR	649 TA	719 BKV	7191 BKV
				739 GRV	7391 GRV

(continued from preceding section)

Color	Code	Std. Cloth	Opt. Cloth	Opt. Vinyl	Opt. Vinyl Matching Inserts
				749 TAV	7491 TAV
				769 STV	7691 STV
Metallic Silver	6214	649 TA	629 BL	719 BKV	7191 BKV
			639 GR	729 BLV	7291 BLV
				739 GRV	7391 GRV
				749 TAV	7491 TAV
				759 RDV	7591 RDV
				769 STV	7691 STV
Desert Tan	6215	649 TA	639 GR	719 BKV	7191 BKV
				739 GRV	7391 GRV
				749 TAV	7491 TAV
				759 RDV	7591 RDV
				769 STV	7691 STV
Blaze Red	6216	649 TA	None	719 BKV	7191 BKV
				749 TAV	7491 TAV
				759 RDV	7591 RDV
				769 STV	7691 STV
Metallic Brown	6217	649 TA	None	719 BKV	7191 BKV
				749 TAV	7491 TAV
				759 RDV	7591 RDV
				769 STV	7691 STV

62S-J8 and 62V-J8 (Daytona 2 Dr. Hardtop)

Color	Code	Std. Cloth	Opt. Cloth	Opt. Vinyl	Opt. Vinyl Matching Inserts
Velvet Black	6210	849 TA	829 BL	919 BKV	9191 BKV
			839 GR	929 BLV	9291 BLV
				939 GRV	9391 GRV
				949 TAV	9491 TAV
				959 RDV	9591 RDV
				969 STV	9691 STV
Ermine White	6211	829 BL	839 GR	919 BKV	9191 BKV
			849 TA	929 BLV	9291 BLV
				939 GRV	9391 GRV
				949 TAV	9491 TAV
				959 RDV	9591 RDV
				969 STV	9691 STV
Riviera Blue	6212	829 BL	849 TA	919 BKV	9191 BKV
				929 BLV	9291 BLV
				949 TAV	9491 TAV
				959 RDV	9591 RDV
				969 STV	9691 STV
Metallic Green	6213	839 GR	849 TA	919 BKV	9191 BKV
				939 GRV	9391 GRV
				949 TAV	9491 TAV
				969 STV	9691 STV
Metallic Silver	6214	849 TA	829 BL	919 BKV	9191 BKV
			839 GR	929 BLV	9291 BLV
				939 GRV	9391 GRV
				949 TAV	9491 TAV
				959 RDV	9591 RDV
				969 STV	9691 STV
Desert Tan	6215	849 TA	839 GR	919 BKV	9191 BKV
				939 GRV	9391 GRV
				949 TAV	9491 TAV
				959 RDV	9591 RDV
				969 STV	9691 STV
Blaze Red	6216	849 TA	None	919 BKV	9191 BKV
				949 TAV	9491 TAV
				959 RDV	9591 RDV
				969 STV	9691 STV
Metallic Brown	6217	849 TA	None	919 BKV	9191 BKV
				949 TAV	9491 TAV
				959 RDV	9591 RDV
				969 STV	9691 STV

62S-L6 and 62V-L6 (Regal 2 Dr. Convertible)

Color	Code	Std. Vinyl	Opt. Vinyl	Opt. Vinyl Matching Inserts	Opt. Cloth	Std. Top	Opt. Top
Velvet Black	6210	758RDV	718 BKV	7181 BKV	None	White	Black
			728 BLV	7281 BLV			
			738 GRV	7381 GRV			
			748 TAV	7481 TAV			
			768 STV	7581 RDV			
				7681 STV			
Ermine White	6211	758 RDV	718 BKV	7181 BKV	None	Black	White
			728 BLV	7281 BLV			
			738 GRV	7381 GRV			
			748 TAV	7481 TAV			
			768 STV	7581 RDV			
				7681 STV			
Riviera Blue	6212	728 BLV	718 BKV	7181 BKV	None	White	Black
			748 TAV	7481 TAV			
			758 RDV	7581 RDV			
			768 STV	7681 STV			
				7281 BLV			
Metallic Green	6213	738 GRV	718 BKV	7181 BKV	None	White	Black
			748 TAV	7381 GRV			
			768 STV	7481 TAV			
				7681 STV			
Metallic Silver	6214	758 RDV	718 BKV	7181 BKV	None	Black	White
			728 BLV	7281 BLV			
			738 GRV	7381 GRV			
			748 TAV	7481 TAV			
			768 STV	7581 RDV			
				7681 STV			
Desert Tan	6215	768 STV	718 BKV	7181 BKV	None	White	Black
			738 GRV	7381 GRV			
			748 TAV	7481 TAV			
			768 STV	7581 RDV			
				7681 STV			
Blaze Red	6216	718 BKV	748 TAV	7181 BKV	None	White	Black
			758 RDV	7481 TAV			
			768 STV	7581 RDV			
				7681 STV			
Metallic Brown	6217	748 TAV	718 BKV	7181 BKV	None	White	Black
			758 RDV	7481 TAV			
			768 STV	7581 RDV			
				7681 STV			

62S-L6 and 62V-L6 (Daytona 2 Dr. Convertible)

Color	Code	Std. Vinyl	Opt. Vinyl	Opt. Vinyl Matching Inserts	Opt. Cloth	Std. Top	Opt. Top
Velvet Black	6210	958RDV	918 BKV	9181 BKV	None	White	Black
			928 BLV	9281 BLV			
			938 GRV	9381 GRV			
			948 TAV	9481 TAV			
			968 STV	9581 RDV			
				9681 STV			
Ermine White	6211	958 RDV	918 BKV	9181 BKV	None	Black	White
			928 BLV	9281 BLV			
			938 GRV	9381 GRV			
			948 TAV	9481 TAV			
			968 STV	9581 RDV			
				9681 STV			
Riviera Blue	6212	928 BLV	918 BKV	9181 BKV	None	White	Black
			948 TAV	9481 TAV			
			958 RDV	9581 RDV			
			968 STV	9681 STV			
				9281 BLV			
Metallic Green	6213	938 GRV	918 BKV	9181 BKV	None	White	Black
			948 TAV	9381 GRV			
			968 STV	9481 TAV			
				9681 STV			
Metallic Silver	6214	958 RDV	918 BKV	9181 BKV	None	Black	White
			928 BLV	9281 BLV			
			938 GRV	9381 GRV			
			948 TAV	9481 TAV			
			968 STV	9581 RDV			
				9681 STV			
Desert Tan	6215	968 STV	918 BKV	9181 BKV	None	White	Black
			938 GRV	9381 GRV			
			948 TAV	9481 TAV			
			968 STV	9581 RDV			
				9681 STV			
Blaze Red	6216	918 BKV	948 TAV	9181 BKV	None	White	Black
			958 RDV	9481 TAV			
			968 STV	9581 RDV			
				9681 STV			
Metallic Brown	6217	948 TAV	918 BKV	9181 BKV	None	White	Black
			958 RDV	9481 TAV			
			968 STV	9581 RDV			
				9681 STV			

62S-P6 and 62V-P6 (Regal 4 Dr. Station Wagon)

Color	Code	Std. Vinyl	Opt. Vinyl	Opt. Vinyl Matching Inserts	Opt. Cloth
Velvet Black	6210	757RDV	717 BKV	7171 BKV	None
			727 BLV	7271 BLV	
			737 GRV	7371 GRV	
			747 TAV	7471 TAV	
			767 STV	7571 RDV	
				7671 STV	
Ermine White	6211	757 RDV	717 BKV	7171 BKV	None
			727 BLV	7271 BLV	
			737 GRV	7371 GRV	
			747 TAV	7471 TAV	
			767 STV	7571 RDV	
				7671 STV	
Riviera Blue	6212	727 BLV	717 BKV	7171 BKV	None
			747 TAV	7471 TAV	
			757 RDV	7571 RDV	
			767 STV	7671 STV	
				7271 BLV	
Metallic Green	6213	737 GRV	717 BKV	7171 BKV	None
			747 TAV	7371 GRV	
			767 STV	7471 TAV	
				7671 STV	
Metallic Silver	6214	747 TAV	717 BKV	7171 BKV	None
			727 BLV	7271 BLV	
			737 GRV	7371 GRV	
			747 TAV	7471 TAV	
			768 STV	7571 RDV	
				7671 STV	
Desert Tan	6215	767 STV	718 BKV	7171 BKV	None
			738 GRV	7371 GRV	
			747 TAV	7471 TAV	
			757 RDV	7571 RDV	
				7671 STV	
Blaze Red	6216	717 BKV	747 TAV	7171 BKV	None
			757 RDV	7471 TAV	
			767 STV	7571 RDV	
				7671 STV	
Metallic Brown	6217	747 TAV	717 BKV	7171 BKV	None
			757 RDV	7471 TAV	
			767 STV	7571 RDV	
				7671 STV	

62V-Y8 (Regal 4 Dr. Sedan Cruiser)

Color	Code	Std. Cloth	Opt. Cloth	Opt. Vinyl	Opt. Vinyl Matching Inserts
Velvet Black	6210	845 TA	825 BL	915 BKV	9151BKV
			835 GR	925 BLV	9251 BLV
				935 GRV	9351 GRV
				945 TAV	9451 TAV
				955 RDV	9551 RDV
				965 STV	9651 STV
Ermine White	6211	825 BL	835 GR	915 BKV	9151BKV
			845 TA	925 BLV	9251 BLV
				935 GRV	9351 GRV
				945 TAV	9451 TAV

Color	Code	Std. Cloth	Opt. Cloth	Opt. Vinyl With White Inserts	Opt. Vinyl Matching Inserts
Riviera Blue	6212	825 BL	845 TA		955 RDV 9551 RDV 965 STV 9651 STV 915 BKV 9151BKV 925 BLV 9251 BLV 945 TAV 9451 TAV 955 RDV 9551 RDV 965 STV 9651 STV
Metallic Green	6213	835 GR	845 TA		915 BKV 9151BKV 925 BLV 9251 BLV 945 TAV 9451 TAV 955 RDV 9551 RDV 965 STV 9651 STV
Metallic Silver	6214	845 TA	825 BL 835 GR		915 BKV 9151BKV 925 BLV 9251 BLV 935 GRV 9351 GRV 945 TAV 9451 TAV 955 RDV 9551 RDV 965 STV 9651 STV
Desert Tan	6215	845 TA	835 GR		915 BKV 9151BKV 935 GRV 9351 GRV 945 TAV 9451 TAV 955 RDV 9551 RDV 965 STV 9651 STV
Blaze Red	6216	845 TA	None		915 BKV 9151BKV 945 TAV 9451 TAV 955 RDV 9551 RDV 965 STV 9651 STV
Metallic Brown	6217	845 TA	None		965 STV 9651 STV 915 BKV 9151BKV 945 TAV 9451 TAV 955 RDV 9551 RDV

62V-K6 (Gran Turismo Hawk)

Color	Code	Std. Cloth	Opt. Cloth	Opt. Vinyl With White Inserts	Opt. Vinyl Matching Inserts
Velvet Black	6210	644 TA	624 BL 634 GR	714 BKV	7141BKV 724 BLV 734 GRV 744 TAV 754 RDV 764 STV
Ermine White	6211	624 BL	634 GR 644 TA	714BLV	7141 BLV 724 BLV 734 GRV 744 TAV 754 RDV 764 STV
Riviera Blue	6212	624 BL	644 TA	714 BKV	7141 BKV 724 BLV 744 TAV 754 RDV 764 STV
Metallic Green	6213	634 GR	644 TA	714 BKV	7141 BKV 734 GRV 744 TAV 764 STV
Metallic Silver	6214	644 TA	624 BL 634 GR	714 BKV	7141BKV 724 BLV 734 GRV 744 TAV 754 RDV 764 STV
Desert Tan	6215	644 TA	634 GR	714 BKV	7141BKV 734 GRV 744 TAV 754 RDV 764 STV
Blaze Red	6216	644 TA	None	714 BKV	7141BKV 744 TAV 754 RDV 764 STV
Metallic Brown	6217	644 TA	None	714 BKV	7141 BKV 744 TAV 754 RDV 764 STV

62S-F3 and 62V-F3 (2 Dr. Sedan)

Color	Code	Std. Cloth	Opt. Cloth	Opt. Heavy Duty Vinyl (Plain Style)
Velvet Black	6210	442TA	422 BL 432 GR	122 BLV 132 GRV 142 TAV 152 RDV
Ermine White	6211	422 BL	432 GR 442 TA	122 BLV 132 GRV 142 TAV 152 RDV
Riviera Blue	6212	422 BL	442 TA	122 BLV 142 TAV 152 RDV
Metallic Green	6213	432 GR	442 TA	132 GRV 142 TAV
Metallic Silver	6214	442 TA	422 BL 432 GR	122 BLV 132 GRV 142 TAV 152 RDV
Desert Tan	6215	442 TA	432 GR	132 GRV 142 TAV 152 RDV
Blaze Red	6216	442 TA	None	142 TAV 152 RDV
Metallic Brown	6217	442 TA	None	142 TAV 152 RDV

62S-Y3 and 62V-Y3 (4 Dr. Sedan)

Color	Code	Std. Cloth	Opt. Cloth	Opt. Heavy Duty Vinyl (Plain Style)
Velvet Black	6210	445TA	425 BL 435 GR	125 BLV 135 GRV 145 TAV 155 RDV
Ermine White	6211	425 BL	435 GR 445 TA	125 BLV 135 GRV 145 TAV 155 RDV
Riviera Blue	6212	425 BL	445 TA	125 BLV 145 TAV 155 RDV
Metallic Green	6213	435 GR	442 TA	135 GRV 145 TAV
Metallic Silver	6214	445 TA	425 BL 435 GR	125 BLV 135 GRV 145 TAV 155 RDV
Desert Tan	6215	445 TA	435 GR	135 GRV 145 TAV 155 RDV
Blaze Red	6216	445 TA	None	145 TAV 155 RDV
Metallic Brown	6217	445 TA	None	145 TAV 155 RDV

62S-P3 and 62V-P3 (4 Dr. Station Wagon)

Color	Code	Std. Vinyl	Opt. Vinyl	Opt. Heavy Duty Vinyl (Plain Style)	Opt. Cloth
Velvet Black	6210	557 RDV	527 BLV 537 GRV 547 TAV	127 BLV 137 GRV 147 TAV 157 RDV	None
Ermine White	6211	557 RDV	527 BLV 537 GRV 547 TAV	127 BLV 137 GRV 147 TAV 157 RDV	None
Riviera Blue	6212	527 BLV	547 TAV 557 RDV	127 BLV 147 TAV 157 RDV	None
Metallic Green	6213	537 GRV	547 TAV	137 GRV 147 TAV	None
Metallic Silver	6214	547 TAV	527 BLV 537 GRV 557 RDV	127 BLV 137 GRV 147 TAV 157 RDV	None
Desert Tan	6215	547 TAV	537 GRV 557 RDV	137 GRV 147 TAV 157 RDV	None
Blaze Red	6216	547 TAV	557 RDV	147 TAV 157 RDV	None
Metallic Brown	6217	547 TAV	557 RDV	147 TAV 157 RDV	None

62S-Y1 and 62V-Y1 (4 Dr. Taxicab)

Color	Std. Heavy Duty Vinyl (Plain Style)	Opt. Heavy Duty Vinyl (Plain Style)	Opt. Cloth
All Paint	245 TAV	225 BLV 235 GRV 255 RDV	None

The PAINT CODE can be found on a piece of paper attached to the bottom of the glove box.

COLOR	Code
Black Velvet	6210
Ermine White	6211
Riviera Blue	6212
Metallic Green	6213
Metallic Silver	6214
Desert Tan	6215
Blaze Red	6216
Metallic Brown	6217

ENGINE NUMBER

Engines are stamped with a prefix code denoting the cubic inch displacement, plus a numeric production number.

6-cylinder engine numbers are located on a pad at the upper left front of the cylinder block.

V-8 engine numbers are located on a pad at the upper left front of the cylinder block.

ENGINE	Code
170 Cid. 6-cyl.	S
259 Cid. 8-cyl.	V
289 Cid. 8-cyl.	P

* Note: If a letter "C" follows the engine code, it designates Canadian manufacture.

No. of Cylinders	Engine Code Prefix	Cid	Std. Comp. Ratio	Opt. Comp. Ratio	Carburetor	H.P.
6	S	170	8.0:1	8.5:1	Carter 1-bbl	112
8	V	259	8.25:1	8.5:1	Stromberg 2-bbl*	180**
8	P	289	8.25:1	8.5:1	Stromberg 2-bbl*	210***

* Optional: Carter WCFB - 4-bbl available on all models except Taxi.
** 195 H.P. with 4-bbl carburetor.
***225 H.P. with 4-bbl carburetor.

VEHICLE IDENTIFICATION NUMBER

```
STUDEBAKER-PACKARD
    CORPORATION
     SERIAL NO.
      63S10551
```

The serial number is stamped on a plate welded to the left front door pillar. On the Avanti the plate is located under the hood on the top right frame rail.

Example

63S	10551
Engine Year	Production Number

FIRST AND SECOND DIGIT: Represents the model year 1963.

THIRD DIGIT: Identifies the engine.

ENGINE	Code
6-cyl., 170 Cid.	S
8-cyl., 259 Cid.	V
8-cyl., 289 Cid.	P
Avanti	R

* A letter "C" following the engine code indicates assembled in Canada.

LAST DIGITS: Is the production sequence number.

Note: Near the end of the 1963 production year, Avanti dropped the year designation from the VIN. Example: R-4835.

BODY TAG

```
63S - F4
  442
```

The BODY TAG indicates the year, engine, body style, and trim is stamped on a tag riveted to the cowl under the hood.

FIRST, SECOND AND THIRD DIGITS: are a repeat of the VIN plate. It identifies the YEAR AND ENGINE.

FOURTH AND FIFTH DIGITS: a two digit BODY STYLE identifies the series and body style.

STANDARD	Code
Sedan 4-Dr, 6 Pass.	Y2
Sedan 2-Dr, 6-Pass.	F2
Station Wagon 4-Dr, 6-Pass.	P2

LARK REGAL	Code
Sedan 4-Dr	Y4
Sedan 2-Dr	F4

LARK CUSTOM	Code
Sedan 4-Dr	Y6
Sedan 2-Dr	F6

LARK DAYTONA	Code
Hardtop 2-Dr	J8
Convertible 2-Dr	L8

LARK STATION WAGONS	Code
Regal 4-Dr	P4
Daytona 4-Dr	P8

LARK CRUISER	Code
Sedan 4-Dr	Y8

GRAN TURISMO HAWK	Code
Hardtop 2-Dr	VK6

AVANTI	Code
Sport Coupe	RQ

TAXICAB	Code
Sedan 4-Dr	Y1

POLICE	Code
Sedan 2-Dr	F3
Sedan 4-Dr	Y3
Station Wagon 4-Dr	P3

The TRIM CODE furnishes the key to the trim color and material. The trim code dictates the availability of exterior paint colors.

Key to Upholstery Symbols:
BC=Blue Cloth **RC**=Red Cloth **GC**=Green Cloth **CC**=Chestnut Cloth
BV=Blue Vinyl **RV**=Red Vinyl **GV**=Green Vinyl **CV**=Chestnut Vinyl
BKV=Black Vinyl

63S-F4 and 63V-F4 (Regal 2 Dr. Sedan)

Color	Code	Std. Cloth	Opt. Cloth
Velvet Black	P6310	442 CC	422 BC
			432 GC
			452 RC
Ermine White	P6311	422 BC	432 GC
			442 CC
			452 RC
Blue Mist	P6312	422 BC	442 CC
			452 RC
Green Mist	P6313	432 GC	442 CC
Silver Mist	P6314	452 RC	422 BC
			432 GC
			442 CC
Champagne Gold	P6315	452 RC	422 BC
			432 GC
			442 CC
Regal Red	P6316	452 RC	422 BC
			442 CC
Rose Mist	P6317	442 CC	432 GC
			452 RC

63S-F3 and 63V-F3 (Heavy Duty 2 Dr. Sedan)

Color	Code	Std. Cloth	Opt. Cloth
Velvet Black	P6310	442 CC	422 BC
			432 GC
			452 RC
Ermine White	P6311	422 BC	432 GC
			442 CC
			452 RC
Blue Mist	P6312	422 BC	442 CC
			452 RC
Green Mist	P6313	432 GC	442 CC
Silver Mist	P6314	452 RC	422 BC
			432 GC
			442 CC
Champagne Gold	P6315	452 RC	422 BC
			432 GC
			442 CC
Regal Red	P6316	452 RC	422 BC
			442 CC
Rose Mist	P6317	442 CC	432 GC
			452 RC

63S-Y4 and 63V-Y4 (Regal 4 Dr. Sedan)

Color	Code	Std. Cloth	Opt. Cloth
Velvet Black	P6310	445 CC	425 BC
			435 GC
			455 RC
Ermine White	P6311	425 BC	435 GC
			445 CC
			455 RC
Blue Mist	P6312	425 BC	445 CC
			455 RC
Green Mist	P6313	435 GC	445 CC
Silver Mist	P6314	455 RC	425 BC
			435 GC
			445 CC
Champagne Gold	P6315	455 RC	425 BC
			435 GC
			445 CC
Regal Red	P6316	455 RC	425 BC
			445 CC
Rose Mist	P6317	445 CC	435GC
			455 RC

63S-Y3 and 63V-Y3 (Heavy Duty 4 Dr. Sedan)

Color	Code		
Velvet Black	P6310	445CC	425 BC
			435GC
			455 RC
Ermine White	P6311	425 BC	435 GC
			445 CC
			455 RC
Blue Mist	P6312	425 BC	445 GC
			445 CC
			455 RC
Green Mist	P6313	435 GC	445 CC
Silver Mist	P6314	455 RC	425 BC
			435 GC
			445 CC
Champagne Gold	P6315	455 RC	425 BC
			435 GC
			445 CC
Regal Red	P6316	455 RC	425 BC
			445 CC
Rose Mist	P6317	445 CC	435 GC
			455 RC

63S-P4 and 63V-P4 (Regal 4 Dr. Station Wagon)

Color	Code	Std. Vinyl	Opt. Vinyl
Velvet Black	P6310	557 RV	527 BV
			537 GV
			547 CV
Ermine White	P6311	527 BV	537 GV
			547 CV
			557 RV
Blue Mist	P6312	527 BV	547 CV
			557 RV
Green Mist	P6313	537 GV	547 CV
Silver Mist	P6314	557 RV	527 BV
			537 GV
			547 CV
Champagne Gold	P6315	557 RV	527 BV
			537 GV
			547 CV
Regal Red	P6316	557 RV	527 BC
			547 CV
Rose Mist	P6317	547 CV	537 GV
			557 RV

63S-P3 and 63V-P3 (Heavy Duty 4 Dr. Station Wagon)

Color	Code	Std. Vinyl	Opt. Vinyl
Velvet Black	P6310	557 RV	527 BV
			537 GV
			547 CV
Ermine White	P6311	527 BV	537 GV
			547 CV
			557 RV
Blue Mist	P6312	527 BV	547 CV
			557 RV
Green Mist	6213	537 GV	547 CV
Silver Mist	6214	557 RV	527 BV
			537 GV
			547 CV
Champagne Gold	6215	557 RV	527 BV
			537 GV
			547 CV
Regal Red	6216	557 RV	527 BV
			547 CV
Rose Mist	6217	547 CV	537 GV
			557 RV

63S-F4 and 63V-F4 (Regal 2 Dr. Sedan)

Color	Code	Opt. Vinyl
Velvet Black	P6310	522 BV
		532 GV
		542 CV
		552 RV
Ermine White	P6311	522 BV
		532 GV
		542 CV
		552 RV
Blue Mist	P6312	522 BV
		542 CV
		552 RV
Green Mist	P6313	532 GV
		542 CV
Silver Mist	P6314	522 BV
		532 GV
		542 CV
		552 RV
Champagne Gold	P6315	522 BV
		532 GV
		542 CV
		552 RV
Regal Red	P6316	522 BV
		542 CV
		552 RV
Rose Mist	P6317	532 GV
		542 CV
		552 RV

63S-Y4 and 63V-Y4 (Regal 4 Dr. Sedan)

Color	Code	Opt. Vinyl
Velvet Black	P6310	525 BV
		535 GV
		545 CV
		555 RV
Ermine White	P6311	525 BV
		535 GV
		545 CV
		555 RV
Blue Mist	P6312	525 BV
		545 CV
		555 RV
Green Mist	P6313	535 GV
		545 CV
Silver Mist	P6314	525 BV
		535 GV
		545 CV
		555 RV
Champagne Gold	P6315	525 BV
		535 GV
		545 CV
		555 RV
Regal Red	P6316	525 BV
		545 CV
		555 RV
Rose Mist	P6317	535 GV
		545 CV
		555 RV

62S-L6 and 62V-L6 (Regal 2 Dr. Convertible)

Color	Code	Opt. Vinyl with White Inserts	Opt. Vinyl with Matching Inserts
Velvet Black	P6310	919 BKV	9191 BKV
		929 BV	9291 BV
		939 GV	9391 GV
		949 CV	9491 CV
		959 RV	9591 RV
		969 TV	9691 TV
Ermine White	P6311	919 BKV	9191 BKV
		929 BV	9291 BV
		939 GV	9391 GV
		949 CV	9491 CV
		959 RV	9591 RV
		969 TV	9691 TV
Blue Mist	P6312	919 BKV	9191 BKV
		929 BV	9291 BV
		949 CV	9491 CV
		959 RV	9591 RV
		969 TV	9691 TV

Color	Code				
Green Mist	P6313	919 BKV	9191 BKV		
		939 GV	9391 GV		
		949 CV	9491 CV		
		969 TV	9691 TV		
Silver Mist	P6314	919 BKV	9191 BKV		
		929 BV	9291 BV		
		939 GV	9391 GV		
		949 CV	9491 CV		
		959 RV	9591 RV		
		969 TV	9691 TV		
Champagne Gold	P6315	919 BKV	9191 BKV		
		929 BV	9291 BV		
		939 GV	9391 GV		
		949 CV	9491 CV		
		959 RV	9591 RV		
		969 TV	9691 TV		
Regal Red	P6316	919 BKV	9191 BKV		
		929 BV	9291 BV		
		949 CV	9491 CV		
		959 RV	9591 RV		
		969 TV	9691 TV		
Rose Mist	P6317	919 BKV	9191 BKV		
		939 GV	9391 GV		
		949 CV	9491 CV		
		959 RV	9591 RV		
		969 TV	9691 TV		

63V-K6 (Gran Turismo Hawk)

Color	Code		
Velvet Black	P6310	714 BKV	7141 BKV
		724 BV	7241 BV
		734 GV	7341 GV
		744 CV	7441 CV
		754 RV	7541 RV
		764 TV	7641 TV
Ermine White	P6311	714 BKV	7141 BKV
		724 BV	7241 BV
		734 GV	7341 GV
		744 CV	7441 CV
		754 RV	7541 RV
		764 TV	7641 TV
Blue Mist	P6312	714 BKV	7141 BKV
		724 BV	7241 BV
		744 CV	7441 CV
		754 RV	7541 RV
		764 TV	7641 TV
Green Mist	P6313	714 BKV	7141 BKV
		734 GV	7341 GV
		744 CV	7441 CV
		764 TV	7641 TV
Silver Mist	P6314	714 BKV	7141 BKV
		724 BV	7241 BV
		734 GV	7341 GV
		744 CV	7441 CV
		754 RV	7541 RV
		764 TV	7641 TV
Champagne Gold	P6315	714 BKV	7141 BKV
		724 BV	7241 BV
		734 GV	7341 GV
		744 CV	7441 CV
		754 RV	7541 RV
		764 TV	7641 TV
Regal Red	P6316	714 BKV	7141 BKV
		724 BV	7241 BV
		744 CV	7441 CV
		754 RV	7541 RV
		764 TV	7641 TV
Rose Mist	P6317	714 BKV	7141 BKV
		734 GV	7341 GV
		744 CV	7441 CV
		754 RV	7541 RV
		764 TV	7641 TV

63V-Y8 (4 Dr. Sedan Cruiser)

Color	Code		
Velvet Black	P6310	915 BKV	9151 BKV
		925 BV	9251 BV
		935 GV	9351 GV
		945 CV	9451 CV
		955 RV	9551 RV
		965 TV	9651 TV
Ermine White	P6311	915 BKV	9151 BKV
		925 BV	9251 BV
		935 GV	9351 GV
		945 CV	9451 CV
		955 RV	9551 RV
		965 TV	9651 TV
Blue Mist	P6312	915 BKV	9151 BKV
		925 BV	9251 BV
		945 CV	9451 CV
		955 RV	9551 RV
		965 TV	9651 TV
Green Mist	P6313	915 BKV	9151 BKV
		935 GV	9351 GV
		945 CV	9451 CV
		965 TV	9651 TV
Silver Mist	P6214	915 BKV	9151 BKV
		925 BV	9251 BV
		935 GV	9351 GV
		945 CV	9451 CV
		955 RV	9551 RV
		965 TV	9651 TV
Champagne Mist	P6315	915 BKV	9151 BKV
		925 BV	9251 BV
		935 GV	9351 GV
		945 CV	9451 CV
		955 RV	9551 RV
		965 TV	9651 TV
Regal Red	P6316	915 BKV	9151 BKV
		925 BV	9251 BV
		945 CV	9451 CV
		955 RV	9551 RV
		965 TV	9651 TV
Rose Mist	P6317	915 BKV	9151 BKV
		935 GV	9351 GV
		945 CV	9451 CV
		955 RV	9551 RV
		965 TV	9651 TV

63S-P8 and 63V-P8 (Daytona 4 Dr. Station Wagon)

Color	Code	Std. Vinyl with White Inserts	Opt. Vinyl with White Inserts	Opt. Vinyl with Matching Inserts
Velvet Black	P6310	957 RV	917 BKV	9171 BKV
			927 BV	9271 BV
			937 GV	9371 GV
			947 CV	9471 CV
			967 TV	9571 RV
				9671 TV
Ermine White	P6311	927 BV	917 BKV	9171 BKV
			937 GV	9271 BV
			947 CV	9371 GV
			957 RV	9471 CV
			967 TV	9571 RV
				9671 TV
Blue Mist	P6312	927 BV	917 BKV	9171 BKV
			947 CV	9271 BV
			957 RV	9471 CV
			967 TV	9571 RV
				9671 TV
Green Mist	P6313	937 GV	917 BKV	9171 BKV
			947 CV	9371 GV
			967 TV	9471 CV
				9671 TV

Color	Code			
Silver Mist	P6314	957 RV	917 BKV	9171 BKV
			927 BV	9271 BV
			937 GV	9371 GV
			947 CV	9471 CV
			967 TV	9571 RV
				9671 TV
Champagne Gold	P6315	957 RV	917 BKV	9171 BKV
			927 BV	9271 BV
			937 GV	9371 GV
			947 CV	9471 CV
			967 TV	9571 RV
				9671 TV
Regal Red	P6316	957 RV	917 BKV	9171 BKV
			927 BV	9271 BV
			947 CV	9471 CV
			967 TV	9571 RV
				9671 TV
Rose Mist	P6317	947 CV	917 BKV	9171 BKV
			937 GV	9371 GV
			957 RV	9471 CV
			967 TV	9571 RV
				9671 TV

63S-F3 and 63-F3 (Heavy Duty 2 Dr. Sedan)

Color	Code	Opt. Heavy Duty Vinyl (Plain Style)
Velvet Black	P6310	122 BV
		132 GV
		142 CV
		152 RV
Ermine White	P6311	122 BV
		132 GV
		142 CV
		152 RV
Blue Mist	P6312	122 BV
		142 CV
		152 RV
Green Mist	P6213	132 GV
		142 CV
Silver Mist	P6314	122 BV
		132 GV
		142 CV
		152 RV
Champagne Gold	P6315	122 BV
		132 GV
		142 CV
		152 RV
Regal Red	P6316	122 BV
		142 CV
		152 RV
Rose Mist	P6317	132 GV
		142 CV
		152 RV

63S-Y3 and 63V-Y3 (Heavy Duty 4 Dr. Sedan)

Color	Code	
Velvet Black	P6310	125 BV
		135 GV
		145 CV
		155 RV
Ermine White	P6311	125 BV
		135 GV
		145 CV
		155 RV
Blue Mist	P6312	125 BV
		145 CV
		155 RV
Green Mist	P6213	135 GV
		145 CV
		155 RV
Silver Mist	P6314	125 BV
		135 GV
		145 CV
		155 RV
Champagne Gold	P6315	125 BV
		135 GV
		145 CV
		155 RV
Regal Red	P6316	125 BV
		145 CV
		155 RV
Rose Mist	P6317	135 GV
		145 CV
		155 RV

63S-P3 and 63V-P3 (Heavy Duty 4 Dr. Station Wagon)

Color	Code	
Velvet Black	P6310	127 BV
		137 GV
		147 CV
		157 RV
Ermine White	P6311	127 BV
		137 GV
		147 CV
		157 RV
Blue Mist	P6312	127 BV
		147 CV
		157 RV
Green Mist	P6213	137 GV
		147 CV
		157 RV
Silver Mist	P6314	127 BV
		137 GV
		147 CV
		157 RV
Champagne Gold	P6315	127 BV
		137 GV
		147 CV
		157 RV
Regal Red	P6316	127 BV
		147 CV
		157 RV
Rose Mist	P6317	137 GV
		147 CV
		157 RV

63S-Y1 and 63V-Y1 (4 Dr. Taxicab)

All Paint	245 CV	225 BV
		235 GV
		255 RV

63S-L8 and 63V-L8 (Daytona 2 Dr. Convertible)

Color	Code	Std. Top	Opt. Top
Velvet Black	P6310	White	Black
Ermine White	P6311	Black	White
Blue Mist	P6312	White	Black
Green Mist	P6313	White	Black
Silver Mist	P6314	Black	White
Champagne Gold	P6315	White	Black
Regal Red	P6316	White	Black
Rose Mist	P6317	White	Black

63V-Y8 (4 Dr. Sedan Cruiser)

Color	Code	Opt. Broadcloth
Velvet Black	P6310	875 BBC
		885 GBC
		895 CBC
		805 RBC
Ermine White	P6311	875 BBC
		885 GBC
		895 CBC
		805 RBC
Blue Mist	P6312	875 BBC
		895 CBC
		805 RBC
Green Mist	P6313	885 GBC
		895 CBC

Silver Mist	P6314	875 BBC
		885 GBC
		895 CBC
		805 RBC
Champagne Gold	P6315	875 BBC
		885 GBC
		895 CBC
		805 RBC
Regal Red	P6316	875 BBC
		895 CBC
		805 RBC
Rose Mist	P6317	885 GBC
		895 CBC
		805 RBC

63V-Y8 (4 Dr. Sedan Cruiser)

Color	Code	Std. Cloth	Opt. Cloth
Velvet Black	P6310	845CC	825 BC
			835 GC
			855 RC
Ermine White	P6311	825 BC	835 GC
			845 CC
			855 RC
Blue Mist	P6312	825 BC	845 CC
			855 RC
Green Mist	P6313	835 GC	845 CC
Silver Mist	P6314	855 RC	825 BC
			835 GC
			845 CC
Champagne Mist	P6315	855 RC	825 BC
			835 GC
			845 CC
Regal Red	P6316	855 RC	825 BC
			845 CC
Rose Mist	P6317	845 CC	835 GC
			855 RC

63V-K6 (Gran Turismo Hawk)

Velvet Black	P6310	644 CC	624 BC
			634 GC
			654 RC
Ermine White	P6311	624 BC	634 GC
			644 CC
			654 RC
Blue Mist	P6312	624 BC	644 CC
			654 RC
Green Mist	P6313	634 GC	644 CC
Silver Mist	P6314	654 RC	624 BC
			634 GC
			644 CC
Champagne Gold	P6315	654 RC	624 BC
			634 GC
			644 CC
Regal Red	P6316	654 RC	624 BC
			634 GC
			644 CC
Rose Mist	P6317	644 CC	634 GC
			654 RC

63S-J8 and 63V-J8 (Daytona 2 Dr. Hardtop)

Velvet Black	P6310	849 CC	829 BC
			839 GC
			859 RC
Ermine White	P6311	829 BC	839 GC
			849 CC
			859 RC
Blue Mist	P6312	829 BC	849 CC
			859RC
Green Mist	P6313	839 GC	849 CC
Silver Mist	P6314	859 RC	829 BC
			839 GC
			849 CC

Champagne Gold	P6315	859 RC	829 BC
			839 GC
			849 CC
Regal Red	P6316	859 RC	829 BC
			849 CC
Rose Mist	P6317	849 CC	839 GC
			859 RC

63S-L8 and 63V-L8 (Daytona 2 Dr. Convertible)

Velvet Black	P6310	958 RV	918 BKV	9181 BKV
			928 BV	9281 BV
			938 GV	9381 GV
			948 CV	9481 CV
			968 TV	9581 RV
				9681 TV
Ermine White	P6311	958 RV	918 BKV	9181 BKV
			928 BV	9281 BV
			938 GV	9381 GV
			948 CV	9481 CV
			968 TV	9581 RV
				9681 TV
Blue Mist	P6312	928 BV	918 BKV	9181 BKV
			948 CV	9281 BV
			958 RV	9481 CV
			968 TV	9581 RV
				9681 TV
Green Mist	P6313	938 GV	918 BKV	9181 BKV
			948 CV	9381 GV
			968 TV	9481 CV
				9681 TV
Silver Mist	P6314	958 RV	918 BKV	9181 BKV
			928 BV	9281 BV
			938 GV	9381 GV
			948 CV	9481 CV
			968 TV	9581 RV
				9681 TV
Champagne Gold	P6315	958 RV	918 BKV	9181 BKV
			928 BV	9281 BV
			938 GV	9381 GV
			948 CV	9481 CV
			968 TV	9581 RV
				9681 TV
Regal Red	P6316	918 BKV	948 CV	9181 BKV
			958 RV	9481 CV
			968 TV	9581 RV
				9681 TV
Rose Mist	P6317	948 CV	918 BKV	9181 BKV
			958 RV	9481 CV
			968 TV	9581 RV
				9681 TV

63S-F6 and 63V-F6 (Custom 2 Dr. Sedan)

Color	Code	Opt. Vinyl with White Inserts	Opt. Vinyl with Matching Inserts
Velvet Black	P6310	712 BKV	7121 BKV
		722 BV	7221 BV
		732 GV	7321 GV
		742 CV	7421 CV
		752 RV	7521 RV
		762 TV	7621 TV
Ermine White	P6311	712 BKV	7121 BKV
		722 BV	7221 BV
		732 GV	7321 GV
		742 CV	7421 CV
		752 RV	7521 RV
		762 TV	7621 TV
Blue Mist	P6312	712 BKV	7121 BKV
		722 BV	7221 BV
		742 CV	7421 CV
		752 RV	7521 RV
		762 TV	7621 TV

Color	Code		
Green Mist	P6313	712 BKV	7121 BKV
		732 GV	7321 GV
		742 CV	7421 CV
		762 TV	7621 TV
Silver Mist	P6314	712 BKV	7121 BKV
		722 BV	7221 BV
		732 GV	7321 GV
		742 CV	7421 CV
		752 RV	7521 RV
		762 TV	7621 TV
Champagne Mist	P6315	712 BKV	7121 BKV
		722 BV	7221 BV
		732 GV	7321 GV
		742 CV	7421 CV
		752 RV	7521 RV
		762 TV	7621 TV
Regal Red	P6316	712 BKV	7121 BKV
		722 BV	7221 BV
		742 CV	7421 CV
		752 RV	7521 RV
		762 TV	7621 TV
Rose Mist	P6317	712 BKV	7121 BKV
		732 GV	7321 GV
		742 CV	7421 CV
		752 RV	7521 RV
		762 TV	7621 TV

63S-Y6 and 63V-Y6 (Custom 4 Dr. Sedan)

Color	Code		
Velvet Black	P6310	715 BKV	7151 BKV
		725 BV	7251 BV
		735 GV	7351 GV
		745 CV	7451 CV
		755 RV	7551 RV
		765 TV	7651 TV
Ermine White	P6311	715 BKV	7151 BKV
		725 BV	7251 BV
		735 GV	7351 GV
		745 CV	7451 CV
		755 RV	7551 RV
		765 TV	7651 TV
Blue Mist	P6312	715 BKV	7151 BKV
		725 BV	7251 BV
		745 CV	7451 CV
		755 RV	7551 RV
		765 TV	7651 TV
Green Mist	P6313	715 BKV	7151 BKV
		725 GV	7351 GV
		745 CV	7451 CV
		765 TV	7651 TV
Silver Mist	P6314	715 BKV	7151 BKV
		725 BV	7251 BV
		735 GV	7351 GV
		745 CV	7451 CV
		755 RV	7551 RV
		765 TV	7651 TV
Champagne Mist	P6315	715 BKV	7151 BKV
		725 BV	7251 BV
		735 GV	7351 GV
		745 CV	7451 CV
		755 RV	7551 RV
		765 TV	7651 TV
Regal Red	P6316	715 BKV	7151 BKV
		725 BV	7251 BV
		745 CV	7451 CV
		755 RV	7551 RV
		765 TV	7651 TV
Rose Mist	P6317	715 BKV	7151 BKV
		735 GV	7351 GV
		745 CV	7451 CV
		755 RV	7551 RV
		765 TV	7651 TV

63S-Y6 and 63V-Y6 (Custom 4 Dr. Sedan)

Color	Code		
Velvet Black	P6310	645 CC	625 BC
			635 GC
			655 RC
Ermine White	P6311	625 BC	635 GC
			645 CC
			655 RC
Blue Mist	P6312	635 BC	645 CC
			655 RC
Green Mist	P6313	635 GC	645 CC
Silver Mist	P6314	655 RC	625 BC
			635 GC
			645 CC
Champagne Gold	P6315	655 RC	625 BC
			635 GC
			645 CC
Regal Red	P6316	655 RC	625 BC
			645 CC
Rose Mist	P6317	645 CC	635 GC
			655 RC

63S-F6 and 63V-F6 (Custom 2 Dr. Sedan)

Color	Code		
Velvet Black	P6310	642 CC	622 BC
			632 GC
			652 RC
Ermine White	P6311	622 BC	632 GC
			642 CC
			652 RC
Blue Mist	P6312	632 BC	642 CC
			652 RC
Green Mist	P6313	632 GC	642 CC
Silver Mist	P6314	652 RC	622 BC
			632 GC
			642 CC
Champagne Gold	P6315	652 RC	622 BC
			632 GC
			642 CC
Regal Red	P6316	652 RC	622 BC
			642 CC
Rose Mist	P6317	642 CC	632 GC
			652 RC

Avanti

Color	Code	Trim Vinyl
Avanti Black	P6330	813 Black
		823 Turquoise
		833 Claret
		843 Smoked Elk
		853 Metallic Red
Avanti White	P6331	813 Black
		823 Turquoise
		833 Claret
		843 Smoked Elk
		853 Metallic Red
Avanti Turquoise	P6332	813 Black
		823 Turquoise
Avanti Gold	P6333	813 Black
		833 Claret
		843 Smoked Elk
Avanti Red	P6334	813 Black
		843 Smoked Elk
		853 Metallic Red
Avanti Gray	P6335	813 Black
		833 Claret
		853 Metallic Red
Avanti Maroon	P6336	813 Black
		833 Claret

The PAINT CODE can be found on a piece of paper attached to the bottom of the glove box.

COLOR	Code
Black Velvet	P6310
Ermine White	P6311
Blue Mist	P6312
Green Mist	P6313
Silver Mist	P6314
Champagne Gold	P6315
Regal Red	P6316
Rose Mist	P6317
Avanti Black	P6330
Avanti White	P6331
Avanti Turquoise	P6332
Avanti Gold	P6333
Avanti Red	P6334
Avanti Gray	P6335
Avanti Maroon	P6336

ENGINE NUMBER

Engines are stamped with a prefix code denoting the cubic inch displacement, plus a numeric production number.

6-cylinder engine numbers are located on a pad at the upper left front of the cylinder block.

V-8 engine numbers are located on a pad at the upper left front of the cylinder block.

ENGINE	Code
170 Cid. 6-cyl.	S
259 Cid. 8-cyl.	V
289 Cid. 8-cyl.	P
R1 289 Cid.	R
R2 289 Cid. Supercharged	RS
R3S 304.5 Supercharged	R3S

* Note: If a letter "C" follows the engine code, it designates Canadian manufacture.

No. of Cylinders	Engine Code Prefix	Cid	Std. Comp. Ratio	Opt. Comp. Ratio	Carburetor	H.P.
6	S	170	8.00:1	7.0:1	Carter 1-bbl	112
8	V	259	8.25:1	7.5:1	Stromberg 2-bbl*	180**
8	P	289	8.25:1	7.5:1	Stromberg 2-bbl*	210***
Avanti						
8	R	289	10.25:1			240
8	RS	289	9.00:1			289
8	R3S	304.5	9.75:1			335

* Optional: Carter WCFB - 4-bbl available on all models except Taxi.
** 195 H.P. with 4-bbl carburetor.
***225 H.P. with 4-bbl carburetor.

VEHICLE IDENTIFICATION NUMBER

```
STUDEBAKER-PACKARD
    CORPORATION
    SERIAL NO.
     64S10551
```

The serial number is stamped on a plate welded to the left front door pillar. On the Avanti the plate is located under the hood on the top right frame rail.

Example

64S	10551
Engine	Production
Year	Number

FIRST AND SECOND DIGIT: Represents the model year 1964.

THIRD DIGIT: Identifies the engine.

ENGINE	Code
6-cyl., 170 Cid.	S
8-cyl., 259 Cid.	V
8-cyl., 289 Cid.	P
Avanti	R

* A letter "C" following the engine code indicates assembled in Canada.

LAST DIGITS: Is the production sequence number.

Note: Near the end of the 1964 production year, Avanti droped the year desination from the VIN. Example: R-4835.

BODY TAG

```
 64 - F4
   442
```

The BODY TAG indicates the year, engine, body style, and trim is stamped on a tag riveted to the cowl under the hood.

FIRST, SECOND AND THIRD DIGITS: are a repeat of the VIN plate. It identifies the YEAR AND ENGINE.

FOURTH AND FIFTH DIGITS: a two digit BODY STYLE identifies the series and body style.

CHALLENGER	Code
2 Dr. Sedan	F2
4 Dr. Sedan	Y2
4 Dr. Station Wagon	P2

COMMANDER	Code
2 Dr. Sedan	F4
4 Dr. Sedan	Y4
4 Dr. Station Wagon	P4

DAYTONA	Code
4 Dr. Sedan	Y8
2 Dr. Hardtop	J8
2 Dr. Convertible	L8
4 Dr. Station Wagon	P8

CRUISER	Code
4 Dr. Sedan	Y9

TAXICAB	Code
4 Dr. Sedan	Y1

POLICE	Code
2 Dr. Sedan	F3
4 Dr. Sedan	Y3
4 Dr. Station Wagon	P3

HAWK	Code
2 Dr. Hardtop	K6

The TRIM CODE furnishes the key to the trim color and material. The trim code dictates the availability of exterior paint colors.

Key to Upholstery Symbols:

BC=Blue Cloth	BB=Blue Broadcloth	BV=Blue Vinyl
RC=Red Cloth	RB=Red Broadcloth	RV=Red Vinyl
GC=Green Cloth	GB=Green Broadcloth	GV=Green Vinyl
BRC=Brown Cloth	BRB=Brown Broadcloth	BRV=Brown Vinyl
	BKV=Black Vinyl	

Color	Code	Std. Cloth	Opt. Cloth	Opt. Vinyl
64S-F2 and 64V-F2 (Challenger 2 Dr. Sedan)				
Midnight Black	P6410	522 BV	552 RV	422 BC
				452 RC
Astra White	P6411	522 BV	532 GV	422 BC
			552 RV	432 GC
				452 RC
Laguna Blue	P6412	522 BV	542 BRV	422 BC
				442 BRC
Strato Blue	P6413	522 BV	542 BRV	422 BC
				442 BRC
Horizon Green	P6414	532 GV	542 BRV	432 GC
				442 BRC
Jet Green	P6415	532 GV	542 BRV	432 GC
				442 BRC
Moonlight Silver	P6416	552 RV	532 GV	432 GC
				452 RC
Golden Sand	P6417	542 BRV	532 GV	432 GC
				442 BRC
				452 RC
Bordeaux Red	P6418	552 RV	542 BRV	442 BRC
				452 RC
Bermuda Brown	P6419	542 BRV	532 GV	432 GC
				442 BRC
64S-F3 and 64V-F3 (Heavy Duty 2 Dr. Sedan)				
Midnight Black	P6410	622 BC	652 RC	122 BV
				152 RV
Astra White	P6411	622 BC	632 GC	122 BV
			652 RC	132 GV
				152 RV
Laguna Blue	P6412	622 BC	642 BRC	122 BV
				142 BRV
Strato Blue	P6413	622 BC	642 BRC	122 BV
				142 BRV
Horizon Green	P6414	632 GC	642 BRC	132 GV
				142 BRV
Jet Green	P6415	632 GC	642 BRC	132 GV
				142 BRV
Moonlight Silver	P6416	652 RC	632 GC	132 GV
				152 RV
Golden Sand	P6417	642 BRC	632 GC	132 GV
				142 BRV
				152 RV
Bordeaux Red	P6418	652 RC	642 BRC	142 BRV
				152 RV
Bermuda Brown	P6419	642 BRC	632 GC	132 GV
				142 BRV

Color	Code	Std. Cloth	Opt. Cloth	Opt. Vinyl

64S-F4 and 64V-F4 (Commander 2 Dr. Sedan)

Color	Code	Std. Cloth	Opt. Cloth	Opt. Vinyl
Midnight Black	P6410	622 BC	652 RC	722 BV / 752 RV
Astra White	P6411	622 BC	632 GC / 652 RC	722 BV / 732 GV / 752 RV
Laguna Blue	P6412	622 BC	642 BRC	722 BV / 742BRV
Strato Blue	P6413	622 BC	642 BRC	722 BC / 742 BRV
Horizon Green	P6414	632 GC	642 BRC	732 GV / 742 BRV
Jet Green	P6415	632 GC	642 BRC	732 GV / 742 BRV
Moonlight Silver	P6416	652 RC	632 GC	732 GV / 752 RV
Golden Sand	P6417	642 BRC	632 GC / 652 RC	732 GV / 742 BRV / 752 RV
Bordeaux Red	P6418	652 RC	642 BRC	742 BRV / 752 RV
Bermuda Brown	P6419	642 BRC	632 GC	732 GV / 742 BRV

64S-Y2 and 64V-Y2 (Challenger 4 Dr. Sedan)

Color	Code	Std. Cloth	Opt. Cloth	Opt. Vinyl
Midnight Black	P6410	521 BV	551 RV	421 BC / 451 RC
Astra White	P6411	521 BV	531 GV / 551 RV	421 BC / 431 GC / 451 RC
Laguna Blue	P6412	521 BV	541 BRV	421 BC / 441 BRC
Strato Blue	P6413	521 BV	541 BRV	421 BC / 441 BRC
Horizon Green	P6414	531 GV	541 BRV	431 GC / 441 BRC
Jet Green	P6415	531 GV	541 BRV	431 GC / 441 BRC
Moonlight Silver	P6416	551 RV	531 GV	431 GC / 451 RC
Golden Sand	P6417	541 BRV	531 GV / 551 RV	431 GC / 441 BRC / 451 RC
Bordeaux Red	P6418	551 RV	541 BRV	441 BRC / 451 RC
Bermuda Brown	P6419	541 BRV	531 GV	431 GC / 441 BRC

64S-Y3 and 64V-Y3 (Heavy Duty 4 Dr. Sedan)

Color	Code	Std. Cloth	Opt. Cloth	Opt. Vinyl
Midnight Black	P6410	621 BC	651 RC	121 BV / 151 RV
Astra White	P6411	621 BC	631 GC / 651 RC	121 BV / 131 GV / 151 RV
Laguna Blue	P6412	621 BC	641 BRC	121 BV / 141 BRV
Strato Blue	P6413	621 BC	641 BRC	121 BC / 141 BRV
Horizon Green	P6414	631 GC	641 BRC	131 GV / 141 BRV
Jet Green	P6415	631 GC	641 BRC	131 GV / 141 BRV
Moonlight Silver	P6416	651 RC	631 GC	131 GV / 151 RV

Color	Code	Std. Cloth	Opt. Cloth	Opt. Vinyl
Golden Sand	P6417	641 BRC	631 GC / 651 RC	131 GV / 141 BRV / 151 RV
Bordeaux Red	P6418	651 RC	641 BRC	141 BRV / 151 RV
Bermuda Brown	P6419	641 BRC	631 GC	131 GV / 141 BRV

64S-Y4 and 64V-Y4 (Commander 4 Dr. Sedan)

Color	Code	Std. Cloth	Opt. Cloth	Opt. Vinyl
Midnight Black	P6410	621 BC	651 RC	721 BV / 751 RV
Astra White	P6411	621 BC	631 GC / 651 RC	721 BV / 731 GV / 751 RV
Laguna Blue	P6412	621 BC	641 BRC	721 BV / 741 BRV
Strato Blue	P6413	621 BC	641 BRC	721 BV / 741 BRV
Horizon Green	P6414	631 GC	641 BRC	731 GV / 741 BRV
Jet Green	P6415	631 GC	641 BRC	731 GV / 741 BRV
Moonlight Silver	P6416	651 RC	631 GC	731 GV / 751 RV
Golden Sand	P6417	641 BRC	631 GC / 651 RC	731 GV / 741 BRV / 751 RV
Bordeaux Red	P6418	651 RC	641 BRC	741 BRV / 751 RV
Bermuda Brown	P6419	641 BRC	631 GC	731 GV / 741 BRV

64S-P2 and 64V-P2 (Challenger 4 Dr. Wagonaire)

Color	Code	Std. Cloth	Opt. Cloth	Opt. Vinyl
Midnight Black	P6410	527 BV	557 RV	None
Astra White	P6411	527 BV	537 GV / 557 RV	None
Laguna Blue	P6412	527 BV	547 BRV	None
Strato Blue	P6413	527 BV	547 BRV	None
Horizon Green	P6414	537 GV	547 BRV	None
Jet Green	P6415	537 GV	547 BRV	None
Moonlight Silver	P6416	557 RV	537 GV	None
Golden Sand	P6417	547 BRV	537 GV / 557 RV	None
Bordeaux Red	P6418	557 RV	557 BRV	None
Bermuda Brown	P6419	547 BRV	537 GV	None

64S-P3 and 64V-P3 (Heavy Duty 4 Dr. Wagonaire)

Color	Code	Std. Cloth	Opt. Cloth	Opt. Vinyl
Midnight Black	P6410	727 BV	757 RV	127 BV / 157 RV
Astra White	P6411	727 BV	737 GV / 757 RV	127 BV / 137 GV / 157 RV
Laguna Blue	P6412	727 BV	747 BRV	127 BV / 147 BRV
Strato Blue	P6413	727 BV	747 BRV	127 BV / 147 BRV
Horizon Green	P6414	737 GV	747 BRV	137 GV / 147 BRV
Jet Green	P6415	737 GV	747 BRV	137 GV / 147 BRV
Moonlight Silver	P6416	757 RV	737 GV	137 GV / 157 RV
Golden Sand	P6417	747 BRV	737 GV / 757 RV	137 GV / 147 BRV / 157 RV

Color	Code	Std. Cloth	Opt. Cloth	Opt. Vinyl
Bordeaux Red	P6418	757 RV	757 BRV	147 BRV / 157 RV
Bermuda Brown	P6419	747 BRV	737 GV	137 GV / 147 BRV

64S-P4 and 64V-P4 (Commander 4 Dr. Wagonaire)

Color	Code	Std. Cloth	Opt. Cloth	Opt. Vinyl
Midnight Black	P6410	727 BV	757 RV	None
Astra White	P6411	727 BV	737 GV / 757 RV	None
Laguna Blue	P6412	727 BV	747 BRV	None
Strato Blue	P6413	727 BV	747 BRV	None
Horizon Green	P6414	737 GV	747 BRV	None
Jet Green	P6415	737 GV	747 BRV	None
Moonlight Silver	P6416	757 RV	737 GV	None
Golden Sand	P6417	747 BRV	737 GV / 757 RV	None
Bordeaux Red	P6418	757 RV	747 BRV	None
Bermuda Brown	P6419	747 BRV	737 GV	None

64V-Y8 (Daytona 4 Dr. Sedan)

Color	Code	Std. Cloth	Opt. Cloth	Opt. Vinyl
Midnight Black	P6410	821 BC	851 RC	911 BKV / 921 BV / 951 RV
Astra White	P6411	821 BC	831 GC / 851 RC	911 BKV / 921 BV / 931 GV / 951 RV
Laguna Blue	P6412	821 BC	841 BRC	911 BKV / 921 BV / 941 BRV
Strato Blue	P6413	821 BC	841 BRC	921 BV / 941 BRV
Horizon Green	P6414	831 GC	841 BRC	911 BKV / 931 GV / 941 BRV
Jet Green	P6415	831 GC	841 BRC	931 GV / 941 BRV
Moonlight Silver	P6416	851 RC	831 GC	911 BKV / 931 GV / 951 RV
Golden Sand	P6417	841 BRC	831 GC / 851 RC	911 BKV / 931 GV / 941 BRV / 951 RV
Bordeaux Red	P6418	851 RC	841 BRC	911 BKV / 941 BRV / 951 RV
Bermuda Brown	P6419	841 BRC	831 GC	931 GV / 941 BRV

64V-J8 (Daytona 2 Dr. Hardtop)

Color	Code	Std. Cloth	Opt. Cloth	Opt. Vinyl
Midnight Black	P6410	829 BC	859 RC	919 BKV / 929 BV / 959 RV
Astra White	P6411	829 BC	839 GC / 859 RC	919 BKV / 929 BV / 939 GV / 959 RV
Laguna Blue	P6412	829 BC	849 BRC	919 BKV / 929 BV / 949 BRV
Strato Blue	P6413	829 BC	849 BRC	929 BV / 949 BRV
Horizon Green	P6414	839 GC	849 BRC	919 BKV / 939 GV / 949 BRV
Jet Green	P6415	839 GC	849 BRC	939 GV / 949 BRV
Moonlight Silver	P6416	859 RC	839 GC	919 BKV / 939 GV / 959 RV
Golden Sand	P6417	849 BRC	839 GC / 859 RC	919 BKV / 939 GV / 949 BRV / 959 RV
Bordeaux Red	P6418	859 RC	849 BRC	919 BKV / 949 BRV / 959 RV
Bermuda Brown	P6419	849 BRC	839 GC	939 GV / 949 BRV

Avanti

Color	Code	Trim	Vinyl
Avanti Black	P6430	813	Black
		823	Turquoise
		833	Claret
		843	Smoked Elk
		853	Metallic Red
Avanti White	P6431	813	Black
		823	Turquoise
		833	Claret
		843	Smoked Elk
		853	Metallic Red
Avanti Turquoise	P6432	813	Black
		823	Turquoise
Avanti Gold	P6433	813	Black
		833	Claret
		843	Smoked Elk
Avanti Red	P6434	813	Black
		843	Smoked Elk
		853	Metallic Red
Avanti Gray	P6435	813	Black
		833	Claret
		853	Metallic Red
Avanti Maroon	P6436	813	Black
		833	Claret

The PAINT CODE can be found on a piece of paper attached to the bottom of the glove box.

COLOR	Code
Midnight Black	P6410
Astra White	P6411
Laguna Blue	P6412
Strato Blue	P6413
Horizon Green	P6414
Jet Green	P6415
Moonlight Silver	P6416
Golden Sand	P6417
Bordeaux Red	P6418

ENGINE NUMBER

Engines are stamped with a prefix code denoting the cubic inch displacement, plus a numeric production number.

6-cylinder engine numbers are located on a pad at the upper left front of the cylinder block.

V-8 engine numbers are located on a pad at the upper left front of the cylinder block.

ENGINE	Code
170 Cid. 6-cyl.	S
259 Cid. 8-cyl.	V
289 Cid. 8-cyl.	P
R1 289 Cid.	R
R2 289 Cid. Supercharged	RS
R3S 304.5 Supercharged	R3S

* Note: If a letter "C" follows the engine code, it designates Canadian manufacture.

No. of Cylinders	Engine Code Prefix	Cid	Std. Comp. Ratio	Opt. Comp. Ratio	Carburetor	H.P.
6	S	170	8.25:1	7.0:1	Carter 1-bb1	112
8	V	259	8.5:1	7.5:1	Carter AFB	195
8	P	289	8.5:1	7.5:1	Cater AFB	225
Avanti						
8	R1	289	10.25:1			240
8	R2	289	9.00:1			289
8	R3	304.5	9.75:1			335

Studebaker operations ceased at South Bend, Indiana Plant in 1965. All 1965 and 1966 Studebaker Vehicles were produced in Canada. Studebaker designated as 1965 and 1966 models differed very little from the 1964 models. Minor trim changes and reduction in the number of vehicles built in the individual model lines can be noted, cars exported to the United States were powered by General Motors engines as no Studebaker engine plant remained in production. Aproximately 11, 000 Studebakers were exported to the U. S. in 1965 and only 8, 000 total units were produced in 1966 - the last year of production.